C000130942

The Routledge International Handbook of Creative Learning

Contemporary education systems are now concerned to make the experience of school more relevant, challenging and innovative; and to equip young people who need to be able to contribute to today's increasingly creative economy when they leave education. In order to help achieve this aim they have become increasingly interested in creativity, and in creative approaches to learning. This collection addresses this concern. It brings together an impressive range of international authors to address the values, philosophies, practices and strategies that realise the engagement, participation, rigour and challenge offered through creative learning.

The *International Handbook of Creative Learning* is the first single text to draw together the many dimensions and disciplines of creative learning into one comprehensive volume. It features new research and new ideas from experts within the field of creative teaching and learning; not only from the UK but also from countries around the world, including France, Norway, Canada, Australia, Japan and the United States. The book addresses a range of topics which include:

- a comprehensive guide to the varied field of creative learning, a resource that enables teachers to become different kinds of instructors;
- evaluative case studies of educational reform showing the impact it has on children worldwide;
- arts learning traditions, including sub-sections on discrete art forms such as drama and visual art;
- policy change and reform ranging from individual schools to national curriculum;
- the introduction of a more authentic assessment process.

This book strongly communicates the importance of bringing more thoughtful and vibrant challenges into the classroom and will be an invaluable mine of information for education students and teachers, research academics and policy specialists.

Julian Sefton-Green is an independent consultant and researcher working in education and the cultural and creative industries. He is Special Professor of Education at the University of Nottingham, UK.

Pat Thomson is Professor of Education at the University of Nottingham, UK, an Adjunct Professor at the University of South Australia and a Visiting Professor at Deakin University, Australia.

Ken Jones is Professor of Education at Goldsmiths, University of London, UK.

Liora Bresler is a Professor at the University of Illinois, Champaign, USA.

The Routledge International Handbook Series

The Routledge International Handbook of English, Language and Literacy Teaching
Edited by Dominic Wyse, Richard Andrews and James Hoffman

The Routledge International Handbook of the Sociology of Education
Edited by Michael W. Apple, Stephen J. Ball and Luis Armand Gandin

The Routledge International Handbook of Higher Education
Edited by Malcolm Tight, Ka Ho Mok, Jeroen Huisman and Christopher C. Morpew

The Routledge International Companion to Multicultural Education
Edited by James A. Banks

The Routledge International Handbook of Critical Education
Edited by Michael W. Apple, Wayne Au, and Luis Armando Gandin

The Routledge International Handbook of Lifelong Learning
Edited by Peter Jarvis

The Routledge International Handbook of Early Childhood Education
Edited by Tony Bertram, John Bennett, Philip Gammage and Christine Pascal

The Routledge International Handbook of Creative Learning
Edited by Julian Sefton-Green, Pat Thomson, Ken Jones and Liora Bresler

The Routledge International Handbook of Creative Learning

Edited by Julian Sefton-Green, Pat Thomson,
Ken Jones and Liora Bresler

Routledge
Taylor & Francis Group

LONDON AND NEW YORK

First published 2011
by Routledge
2 Park Square, Milton Park, Abingdon, Oxon, OX14 4RN

Simultaneously published in the USA and Canada
by Routledge
711 Third Avenue, New York, NY 10017

Routledge is an imprint of the Taylor & Francis Group, an informa business

© 2011 Julian Sefton-Green, Pat Thomson, Liora Bresler and Ken Jones for selection and editorial material. Individual chapters, the contributors.

The right of the editor to be identified as the author of the editorial material, and of the authors for their individual chapters, has been asserted in accordance with sections 77 and 78 of the Copyright, Designs and Patents Act 1988.

All rights reserved. No part of this book may be reprinted or reproduced or utilised in any form or by any electronic, mechanical, or other means, now known or hereafter invented, including photocopying and recording, or in any information storage or retrieval system, without permission in writing from the publishers.

Trademark notice: Product or corporate names may be trademarks or registered trademarks, and are used only for identification and explanation without intent to infringe.

British Library Cataloguing in Publication Data
A catalogue record for this book is available from the British Library

Library of Congress Cataloging-in-Publication Data
The Routledge international handbook of creative learning / Julian Sefton-Green... [et al.].
    p. cm. – (Routledge international handbooks of education)
    1. Creative thinking–Handbooks, manuals, etc. 2. Creative ability–Handbooks, manuals, etc. I. Sefton-Green, Julian.
    LB1062.R66 2011
    370.15'2–dc22   2010053787

ISBN13: 978-0-415-54889-2 (hbk)
ISBN13: 978-0-203-81756-8 (ebk)

Typeset in Bembo by
Taylor & Francis Books

MIX
Paper from
responsible sources

FSC   FSC® C004839
www.fsc.org

Printed and bound in Great Britain by
CPI Antony Rowe, Chippenham, Wiltshire

Contents

Contents

Contents

Illustrations

Figures

Tables

Acknowledgements

We need to thank our Publisher, Philip Mudd, who was not only enthusiastic about the idea of the handbook and generous in support, but also forgiving of our delays. The Routledge editorial and production team were efficient, informative and helpful, as always. We want to put on record our regard for the English arts initiative Creative Partnerships (CP), without which we would not have had the impetus and context for the book, and for the support from Creativity, Culture and Education for Julian to work on this project. We think English schools have been the better for the singular emphasis CP has placed on creative learning. Finally we need to acknowledge that we have worked as a productive team – despite distance, changing jobs (Ken) and frenetic work practices – and this has been made possible by the fact that we share not only a strong commitment to the imaginative pedagogies that are featured in this text, but also the lucky coincidence of work patterns – when one of us was overwhelmingly busy, another found time to pick up the threads.

We want to extend our thanks to the authors in the book, who generally dealt with our naggings and requests for changes promptly and generously. A few of the chapters in this collection are based on articles or chapters published elsewhere. We would like to thank the copyright holders for permission to publish from the following. 'A' is for Aesthetics by Peter Abbs, London: Falmer Press (1989); 'English for an Era of Instability: Aesthetics, ethics, creativity and design' by Gunter Kress, English in Australia/AATE, 44(3) (2002); 'Reconciliation pedagogy, identity and community funds of knowledge: borderwork in South African classrooms' by Ana Ferreira and Hilary Janks, The English Academy Review, 24(2) 71–84 (2007); Curriculum Integration and the Disciplines of Knowledge, by James Beane, Phi Delta Kappan Journal, 78(8), pp. 616–22 (1995); 'Miners, diggers, ferals and show-men: school-community projects that affirm and unsettle identities and place' by Pat Thomson, British Journal of Sociology of Education, 27(1), 81–96 (2006); 'Spatial literacies, design texts and emergent pedagogies in purposeful literacy curriculum' by Barbara Comber and Helen Nixon in Pedagogies: An International Journal 3(4), 221–40 (2008); Adams, J., 'Room 13 and the Contemporary Practice of Artist-Learners', Studies in Art Education, 47(1), 23–33 (2005); Lieberman, A., Journal of Educational Change 3(3–4), 315–37 (2002); 'Learning in the Gallery: context, process, outcomes' by Emily Pringle, London: Arts Council England and engage (2006).

Notes on contributors

Peter Abbs was born and grew up on the North Norfolk coast in England. He has written and lectured widely on the nature of creativity and the poetics of culture. This work is most fully developed in *Against the Flow: Education, the Arts and Postmodern Culture* (RoutledgeFalmer, 2003). In 2004 he was Writer-in-Residence at Lyon College, Arkansas. He is the Poetry Editor of *Resurgence* and editor of *Earth Songs,* the first Anglo-American anthology of contemporary eco-verse. He has published ten volumes of poetry, including, most recently, *The Flowering of Flint* and *Voyaging Out.* He is currently Research Professor of Creative Writing at the University of Sussex.

Jeff Adams is Professor of Education at the University of Chester, and Principal Editor of the *International Journal of Art and Design Education.* He was leader of the MA Artist Teachers and Contemporary Practices programme at Goldsmiths College. Jeff has taught art, education and art history at Edge Hill University, Liverpool John Moores University and the Open University. His books include *Documentary Graphic Novels and Social Realism* (Peter Lang, 2008); *Teaching Through Contemporary Art* (with Worwood, Atkinson, Dash, Herne and Page, Tate, 2008); *The Application of Theory to Education Research* (with Cochrane and Dunne (eds), Wiley-Blackwell, 2011).

Arnold Aprill is Founding and Creative Director of Chicago Arts Partnerships in Education (CAPE), a network of artists and schools dedicated to school improvement through arts education partnerships. He comes from a background in professional theatre as an award-winning director, producer and playwright. He is a co-author of *Renaissance in the Classroom: Arts Integration and Meaningful Learning* (Lawrence Erlbaum, 2001). He consults nationally and internationally on the role of the arts in effective school improvement. He has been recognised for exceptional leadership by the Chicago Community Trust and by the Ford Foundation's Leadership for a Changing World initiative.

Shakuntala Banaji, PhD, is a Lecturer in Media and Communications at the London School of Economics and Political Science. From 2006 to 2009 she was the UK Researcher on the EU project *CIVICWEB*, at the Centre for the Study of Children, Youth and Media. She lectures in Film Theory, World Cinema, Media, Communication and Development and has published widely on Cinema, Audiences, Youth, Gender, Ethnicity and Politics, Creativity and Online Civic Participation. Recent books include *South Asian Media Cultures* (Anthem Press, 2010) and *The Civic Web: Young People, Civic Participation and the Internet in Europe* (co-authored with David Buckingham, MIT Press, 2011).

James A. Beane is a former classroom teacher who currently divides his time between his position as a professor at National-Louis University and as a school reform coach at Sherman Middle School in Madison, Wisconsin. He is the author of *Curriculum Integration* (Teachers College Press, 1997), *A Middle School Curriculum* (National Middle School Association, 1993) and *Affect in the Curriculum* (Teachers College Press, 1990). He is also co-author of *Democratic Schools* (ASCD, 1995), *The Middle School and Beyond* (ASCD, 1992), *When the Kids Come First* (National Middle School Association, 1987), *Self-Concept, Self-Esteem, and the Curriculum* (Allyn & Bacon, 1986) and *Curriculum Planning and Development* (Allyn & Bacon, 1986). Additionally, he was co-editor, *ONE WORD of Democratic Schools*; and edited the 1995 *ASCD Yearbook Toward a Coherent Curriculum*. Beane has spoken at numerous conferences, has consulted for international educational projects, and served in leadership capacities for several education professional associations.

Eleonora Belfiore is Associate Professor in Cultural Policy at the Centre for Cultural Policy Studies at the University of Warwick, UK. Her research interests revolve around the notion of the 'social impacts' of the arts, and the effect that the transformational rhetoric of impact has had on British cultural policy. Most recently, Eleonora's research interests have developed around the often unacknowledged role of deeply held beliefs and cultural values in the process of policy-making, especially in the context of the professed reliance on empirically acquired 'evidence' as a basis for decision-making in the policy sphere.

Jorunn Spord Borgen is Research Professor at NIFU (Nordic Institute for Studies of Innovation, Research and Education) and Professor at Vestfold University College. Borgen has more than thirty years of experience in the educational field and as a researcher. She began her career as an art teacher in lower and upper secondary education, and held a four-year R&D leadership position at Oslo University College, Faculty of Education. Her expertise is studies in arts and cultural education and policies, and R&D in the arts. Borgen holds a master's degree in education and a doctoral degree in art history from Bergen University, Norway.

Liora Bresler is a Professor at the University of Illinois, Champaign, USA. Her research and teaching focus on Arts and Aesthetic Education, Qualitative Research Methodology and Educational/Artistic. She is the co-founder and co-editor of the *International Journal of Education and the Arts*. Bresler has published 100+ papers, book chapters and books on the arts in education, including the *International Handbook of Research in Arts Education* (2007), and *Knowing Bodies, Moving Minds* (2004). Her work has been translated into German, French, Portuguese, Spanish, Hebrew and Chinese. Bresler has given keynote speeches, invited talks, seminars and short courses in some thirty countries in Europe, Asia, Australia, Africa and the Americas.

Catherine Burke is a Senior Lecturer in Education at the Faculty of Education, University of Cambridge, where she teaches the history of education and childhood. Her research and publications over the past decade have become focused on the relationship between the material environment of school and the view of the child. This focus was initially inspired by the rich and inspirational views offered by school children who were invited to describe the 'school I'd like' in 2001 for a research project in collaboration with the *Guardian* newspaper. She is currently writing a biography of the architect Mary Medd (née Crowley).

Gail E. Burnaford is Professor in Curriculum, Culture and Educational Inquiry at Florida Atlantic University in Boca Raton, Florida. She is co-author of *Renaissance in the Classroom: Arts*

Integration and Meaningful Learning (Lawrence Erlbaum, 2001) and *Teachers Doing Research: The Power of Action Through Inquiry* (Lawrence Erlbaum, 2003), and author of *Images of Schoolteachers in America* (Lawrence Erlbaum, 2003) and *Arts Integration Frameworks, Research and Practice* (Arts Education Partnership, 2007). Gail has conducted programme evaluations for organisations including Chicago Arts Partnerships in Education (CAPE), Hubbard Street Dance Chicago and Arts for Learning Miami. She presented at the UNESCO World Arts Education Conference.

Pamela Burnard, BMus, MMus, MEd, PhD, is a Senior Lecturer at the University of Cambridge, UK, where she manages Higher Degree courses in Arts, Culture and Education and in Educational Research. She is co-editor of the *British Journal of Music Education*, Associate Editor of *Psychology of Music* and serves on numerous editorial boards. She is section editor of the 'Creativity Section' in the *International Handbook of Research in Arts Education* (Springer, 2007) and the section 'Musical Creativity as Practice' of *The Oxford Handbook of Music Education* (Oxford University Press, 2011). She is co-convenor of *British Education Research Association*, Creativity in Education SIG.

Pat Cochrane is founding CEO of CapeUK, a research and development organisation focusing on creativity and learning. Pat comes from a background of teaching, education leadership, teacher training, community development and the arts. Pat is co-author of *Building a Creative School: A Dynamic Approach to School Development* (Trentham Books, 2007), as well as many other articles on pedagogy and creativity. She has acted as government advisor on creativity in education and presents regularly at conferences and seminars in England and Europe – most recently at the North of England education conference. She is a consultant to the Creative Partnerships Schools of Creativity programme.

Barbara Comber is a Research Professor in the Faculty of Education at the Queensland University of Technology. Her interests include literacy education and social justice, teachers' work and identities, place and space, and practitioner inquiry. She has recently co-edited two books: *The Hawke Legacy: Towards a Sustainable Society* (with Bloustien and McKinnon, Wakefield Press, 2009) and *Literacies in Place: Teaching Environmental Communication* (with Nixon and Reid, Primary English Teaching Association, 2007). She is currently conducting two research projects, one focusing on mandated literacy assessment and the other on new literacy demands in the middle years of schooling.

James Conroy is Dean of the Faculty of Education, University of Glasgow. He was previously Head of Graduate School and Head of Department of Religious Education at the university and has taught in higher education, schools and adult education. He is President of the Association of Moral Education and visiting Professor in the Department of Educational Leadership at Fordham University, New York. Professor Conroy has written widely on the politics of Catholic education, sectarianism, liberal democracy in education and religious education. He currently holds a £413,000 research grant from the AHRC/ESRC to examine the effectiveness of Religious Education across Britain.

Tracie E. Costantino is an Associate Professor of Art Education at the University of Georgia. Her PhD is in aesthetic education from the Department of Curriculum and Instruction at the University of Illinois at Urbana-Champaign, and her MA in art history from Brown University. Her research focuses on the nature of artistic cognition, creativity and the transformative potential of aesthetic experience as an educative event. In addition to numerous published articles and book chapters, recent work in this area was published in the book she co-edited with Boyd White, *Essays on Aesthetic Education for the 21st Century* (Sense Publishers, 2010).

Anna Craft is Professor of Education at the University of Exeter, and at the Open University. Her twin research interests are creativity in education and learning futures. With a background in primary teaching her development and research work now span early years, primary, secondary and post-compulsory education. She has acted as government advisor in England and abroad. Anna directs several studies, including Dance Partners for Creativity (AHRC), Possibility Thinking and Aspire. She is founding co-editor of *Thinking Skills and Creativity* and Co-Convenor BERA SIG, *Creativity in Education*. She is the author of *Creativity and Education Futures* (Trentham Books, 2011).

Bernard Darras is Professor of semiotics and of research methodologies at the University Paris 1 Panthéon-Sorbonne. He is currently Director of the Research Centre Images, Culture and Cognition, of the Master of Interactive Multimedia, and the Masters of Cultural Studies and Arts and Culture Management at the University Paris 1. His research focuses primarily on pragmatic semiotic constructivism and systemic interactionism in the fields of visual and material cultures, particularly in arts and design. He has published or edited thirteen books and eleven journal issues, and about 180 academic articles.

Michael Dezuanni lectures in media education in the Faculty of Education at Queensland University of Technology. He was a secondary school Media teacher for thirteen years and continues to contribute to the development of curriculum in Queensland. He is the Media Arts contributor to the Australian National Curriculum for the Arts.

Kirsten Drotner is professor of media studies at the University of Southern Denmark and founding director of DREAM: Danish Research Centre on Education and Advanced Media Materials. She has extensive experience in researching children, media and learning in and out of school, with particular focus on ethnographic studies of aesthetic practices. Her most recent books in English are *The International Handbook of Children, Media and Culture* (Sage, 2008, co-editor Sonia Livingstone), *Informal Learning and Digital Media* (Cambridge Scholars Publishing, 2008, co-editors Kim Schrøder and Hans Jensen) and *Digital Content Creation: Creativity, Competence, Critique* (Peter Lang, 2010, co-editor Kim Schrøder).

Ana Ferreira lectures in the English department at the School of Education of the University of the Witwatersrand in Johannesburg, South Africa. Her teaching interests include critical literacy; film, media and popular culture; sociolinguistics and language in education; and language methodologies. She has published on multiliteracies, reconciliation pedagogies, language and identity, and on engaging difference productively in educational contexts. She is also the editor of *Teaching Language* (Macmillan, 2009), designed for teachers in South African language classrooms. Her current research uses a teaching intervention in the English classroom to investigate subjectivity and positioning in classroom discourse.

Mike Fleming is Professor of Education at Durham University, where at various times he has acted as Director of Initial Teacher Training and as Director, Research and Postgraduate Studies. He has had extensive experience teaching in schools and in teacher education. His research interests are in the areas of teaching English and drama, the arts in education and interculturalism. He has published a number of books, edited collections and papers in these areas.

He is currently a member of a steering group working on a Council of Europe project, 'Languages in and for Education', promoting values of plurilingualism and interculturalism.

Max Fuchs studied mathematics and economics (MA Math) as well as educational sciences and sociology (MA, Dr Phil). He is Director of the Remscheid Academy for Cultural Education, President of the German Cultural Council and Honorary Chairman of BKJ, the German Federation for Arts Education and Cultural Learning. Professor Fuchs teaches programmes concerning cultural work at the universities of Duisburg-Essen and Basel.

Michael G. Gunzenhauser is an associate professor of Administrative and Policy Studies at the University of Pittsburgh, where he studies issues of equity and social justice in education. He focuses on ethics, philosophy of education and qualitative research methodology. Currently he is working on a book about professional ethics for educators working under the pressure for external accountability. He is president-elect of the Ohio Valley Philosophy of Education Society and co-edits the journal *Philosophical Studies in Education*. He is a former co-principal investigator of the research and evaluation of the Oklahoma A+ Schools and currently consults for that organisation.

Andy Hargreaves is the Thomas More Brennan Chair in Education at the Lynch School of Education at Boston College. His teaching and research at Boston College concentrate on educational change, performing beyond expectations, sustainable leadership and the emotions of teaching. He taught in primary schools and lectured in a number of English universities. In 1987 he moved to the Ontario Institute for Studies in Education in Canada, where he co-founded and directed the International Center for Educational Change. He has authored or edited more than twenty-five books, which have been translated into a dozen languages.

Richard Hatcher is professor of education at Birmingham City University. His principal research interest is in the field of policy sociology, and in particular the analysis of government education policy, its impact on the school system at local, institutional and individual levels, and the responses it generates.

Akiko Hayashi is a PhD student in early childhood education at Arizona State University. She is interested in teachers' beliefs and practices, social emotional development in young children, and comparative education, within the context of early childhood education, with a focus on Japan and US–Japan comparisons. Her research is ethnographic and interpretive. Her publications include 'Lessons from China and Japan for preschool practice in the United States', *Educational Perspectives* 40(1) (2007): 7–12; and 'The Japanese preschool's pedagogy of feeling: cultural strategies for supporting young children's emotional development', *Ethos* 37(1) (2009): 32–49.

Debra Hayes is an Associate Professor in the Faculty of Education and Social Work at the University of Sydney. Her research is located in contexts in which there are high levels of poverty and difference. She draws upon systems of thinking that focus on the effects of disadvantage to examine how these are constituted by schooling discourses and teaching practices.

Lois Hetland, EdD, Professor of Art Education at the Massachusetts College of Art and Design and Research Associate at Harvard Project Zero, taught in K-8 general classrooms for seventeen years, was founding Education Chair of Project Zero's annual summer institute 1996–2005, and led US DOE funded research in Alameda County, CA, from 2003 to 2010, based on *Studio Thinking: The Real Benefits of Visual Arts Education* (Teachers College Press, 2007). She was Co-

Principal Investigator on *The Qualities of Quality: Understanding Excellence in Arts Education*, and is currently Co-Principal Investigator on a National Science Foundation study testing the relationship between visual arts and geometry learning.

David Holland is a management consultant with particular interests in the economic and social aspects of culture, his work spanning public, private and non-profit sectors. Formerly a senior manager with NESTA, an innovation and technology funder, and Arts & Business, an organisation that supports private investment in the arts, David went on to set up his own private consultancy practice, advising clients in the arts, media and film and mental health fields. He also served as a Trustee of Arts Community Exchange, an arts education charity. He has written publications for the British Council, Arts Council England, and Culture, Creativity and Education. While a consultant with BOP Consulting, he worked extensively on their creative education portfolio.

Moira Hulme is Lecturer in Educational Research and Co-Director of the Chartered Teacher programme at the University of Glasgow. She has conducted numerous studies on teacher education, teacher enquiry and professional development for, among others, the Scottish government, the General Teaching Council for Scotland and Learning and Teaching Scotland. She is involved in undergraduate and postgraduate teacher education programmes and was Project Coordinator of Research to Support Schools of Ambition (2006–10). She is Co-Convenor of Network 3 of the European Educational Research Association: Curriculum Innovation by Schools and Teachers.

Hilary Janks is a professor in the School of Education at the University of the Witwatersrand, Johannesburg, South Africa. She is the editor and an author of the *Critical Language Awareness Series* of workbooks and the author of *Literacy and Power* (Routledge, 2009). Her teaching and research are in the areas of language education in multilingual classrooms, language policy and critical literacy. Her work is committed to a search for equity and social justice in contexts of poverty.

Anita Jetnikoff lectures in English Curriculum and Literature Studies in the Faculty of Education at Queensland University of Technology. She was a secondary school English teacher for thirteen years and networks actively with teachers in media literacy. She is a Queensland State Review panel member and Syllabus writer for senior English.

Ken Jones is Professor of Education at Goldsmiths, University of London. His research focuses on two areas: the first is policy, and its contestation ('Schooling in Western Europe: The New Order and Its Adversaries', 2008); the second is the (re)emergence and development of 'creativity' as a theme in educational and cultural policy. Sometimes, these areas overlap. Recent work includes the literature review 'Culture and Creative Learning' (Arts Council England, 2009); with Pat Thomson and Christine Hall, he worked on the Creative Partnerships funded research project 'Creative School Change' (2006–9).

Alain Kerlan is a philosopher and a professor in educational sciences at University Lyon 2. He is the Director of the Institute for Sciences and Education and Training Practices (ISPEF). He works at the junction between arts and education and between philosophy and pedagogy. As a member of the mixed research unit 'Éducation & Politiques', he focuses on artistic and cultural practices and more largely on the aesthetic dimension. He is the author of several books concerning philosophy and education for the arts.

Gunther Kress is Professor of Semiotics and Education at the Institute of Education, University of London. His interests are in meaning-making and communication in contemporary environments; with an interest in developing a social semiotic theory of multimodal communication. Some relevant books are *Social Semiotics* (Cornell University Press, 1988, with R. Hodge); *Before Writing: Rethinking the Paths to Literacy* (Routledge, 1996); *Reading Images: The Grammar of Graphic Design* (Routledge, 1996/2006); *Multimodal Discourse: The Modes and Media of Contemporary Communication* (Hodder Arnold, 2002), both with T. van Leeuwen; *Multimodal Learning and Teaching: The Rhetorics of the Science Classroom* (Continuum, 2001); *Literacy in the New Media Age* (Routledge, 2003); *Multimodality: A Social Semiotic Approach to Contemporary Communication* (Routledge, 2010).

Samuel Leong is Professor and Associate Dean (QA) of the Faculty of Arts and Sciences and Head of the Cultural and Creative Arts Department at the Hong Kong Institute of Education. His areas of professional and research interests include creativity and arts assessment, cross-cultural learning, metacognition, and e-learning, and his interdisciplinary work over thirty-five years has spanned four continents. A recipient of competitive grants from the Australian Research Council, Hong Kong Research Grants Council and Arts Development Council of Hong Kong, he has seventeen years of experience supervising and examining master's and doctoral research projects.

Ann Lieberman is an emeritus professor from Teachers College, Columbia University, and was a Senior Scholar at the Carnegie Foundation for the Advancement of Teaching for ten years. She is now a senior scholar at Stanford University.

Julian McDougall is Reader in Media and Education and Head of Creative Arts at Newman University College, Birmingham, and a Principal Examiner for A Level Media Studies. He is co-editor of *Media Education Research Journal* and author of a range of textbooks, including *The Media Teacher's Book* (Hodder, 2010), *Studying Videogames* (Auteur, 2008) and *After the Media: Culture and Identity in the 21st Century* (Routledge, 2011). His published research in recent years has concerned gaming and media literacy and audience reception in the era of convergence.

Koji Matsunobu is a postdoctoral research fellow at the University of Queensland. Originally from Japan, he holds PhDs in music and arts education. Former Fulbright Graduate Scholar in the United States, he explored possibilities of incorporating non-Western ideas into Western contexts of education. His research interests include arts integration, indigenous knowledge production, spirituality in arts education, world music pedagogy and creativity. Recent work, documented in his dissertation (submitted to the University of Illinois), focuses on the interface among spirituality, ecology and aesthetics in the context of *shakuhachi* practice. His postdoctoral project involves exploring values, structures and processes of place-based education.

Ian Menter is Professor of Teacher Education in the Faculty of Education at the University of Glasgow, UK. He was deputy Dean for Research in the Faculty from 2005 to 2009. He has published on teacher education, education policy and the development of research capacity in education. He was President of the Scottish Educational Research Association from 2005 to 2007, is an editor of the *British Educational Research Journal* and an Academician of the Academy of Social Science

Jonothon Neelands is a National Teaching Fellow, Chair of Drama and Theatre Education and Academic Director of the RSC/Warwick International Centre for Teaching Shakespeare.

He is an experienced trainer and workshop leader with a national and international reputation for delivering high quality professional training and development opportunities. He has advised government on the identification and training of talented young performers and is Research Consultant for the National Council of Drama Training and a member of the RSC Education Advisory Group. Research interests include: participatory theatre and democracy; cultural and creative learning; the politics of cultural and education policy-making; teaching in urban settings; the sociology of educational disadvantage and the articulation of a pro-social pedagogy of arts education.

Helen Nixon is Associate Professor of Education at the Queensland University of Technology, Australia. Her research focuses on literacy and social justice, literacy and new media, and literacy and place. She has co-edited books for English and literacy educators, published widely in the fields of English and literacy education and cultural studies, and is an editorial board member of several academic journals in the fields of literacy studies and literacy and new media.

George W. Noblit is the Joseph R. Neikirk Distinguished Professor of Sociology of Education in the School of Education at the University of North Carolina at Chapel Hill. He was the co-author of *Creating and Sustaining Arts-Based School Reform* (Routledge, 2009). Currently he is co-editing a book on arts, education and social justice, *A Way Out of No Way*, and is the co-editor of *The Urban Review*.

Nick Owen, PhD, is Director of the Aspire Trust, the Merseyside-based Arts Education company which works in formal and informal educational settings across the UK and increasingly across the world. Heading up a range of services from research, evaluation, professional development for artists and teachers, he led the reseach for the National Association of Writers in Education *Class Writing* research project as well as *Closing Schools for the Future*: a research programme which examines what is lost from a school community in the final stages of a programme of school closure.

Alexander R. Pagnani is currently a doctoral candidate in Educational Psychology – Gifted and Creative Education – at the University of Georgia. His research interests include creativity, gender, underachievement, the acceleration of highly able and creative students, and early-entrance-to-college programmes. He currently lives in Athens, GA, where he is teaching and completing an ethnographic dissertation on the experiences of students who matriculated to college two or more years earlier than the norm.

David Parker is Creativity Culture and Education's strategic lead on research and evaluation, and has managed a series of externally led, objective research and evaluation programmes. Previously, David was Head of Research at the British Film Institute, where he took a particular interest in the uses of moving image media in the teaching and learning of literacy. Before this he was a Research Fellow at King's College London. He completed his PhD in Film and Literature in 1998 and since then has published several papers and book chapters on the links between print and moving image media. He has undertaken evaluations for a number of arts and cultural programmes both in the UK and abroad.

Rob Pope is Professor of English at Oxford Brookes University and a UK National Teaching Fellow. He has taught at universities in Wales, Russia and New Zealand, and run curriculum and staff development programmes in America, Australia, Europe and Japan. He is interested in experiments combining creative and critical activity, and particularly in forms of rewriting:

parody, adaptation, translation, imitation and intervention. His publications include *Textual Intervention: Creative and Critical Strategies for Literary Studies* (Routledge, 1995), *Creativity: Theory, History, Practice* (Routledge, 2005) and *Creativity, Language, Literature: the State of the Art* (co-edited with Joan Swann and Ronald Carter, Palgrave, 2011).

Emily Pringle, PhD, originally trained as a painter and went on work as an artist and educator in a variety of arts and education contexts. From 1995 to 1998 she was the Education Co-ordinator for the Chisenhale Gallery in London. For the last fifteen years she has programmed, researched and written on arts education practice, working closely with organisations including the National Gallery, the Serpentine Gallery, Arts Council England, Creative Partnerships and Tate. Currently she is the Head of Learning Practice, Research and Policy at Tate Gallery in London.

Mark A. Runco joined the University of Georgia at Athens in 2008. He is the Torrance Professor of Creative Studies and the Director of the Torrance Creativity Center. His has been Senior Editor of the *Creativity Research Journal* since its founding in 1989 and is currently co-editing the second edition of the *Encyclopedia of Creativity* (Academic Press). His textbook on creativity, also published by Academic Press, appeared in 2007. He has received the Lifetime Achievement Award from the National Association for Gifted Children and is a Fellow in the American Psychological Association. His empirical research focuses on divergent thinking and creative ideation. He resides in Athens, Georgia.

Naranee Ruthra-Rajan is the Research Manager for Creativity Culture Education (CCE), a national organisation which aims to transform the lives of children and families by harnessing the potential of creative learning and cultural opportunity to enhance their aspirations, achievements and skills. She has worked on the monitoring, evaluation and research of the Creative Partnerships initiative and the CCE Literature Review Series since 2004. She has experience of working within a variety of cultural and research organisations, including the British Film Institute, Arts Council England and BOP Consulting.

Julian Sefton-Green is an independent researcher working in Education and the Cultural and Creative Industries. He is a special Professor of Education at the University of Nottingham, UK, an adjunct Associate Research Professor at the University of South Australia and a research associate at the University of Oslo. He has worked in an out-of-school centre for informal education and as a Media Studies teacher in an inner city comprehensive as well as in teacher training. He has researched and written widely on many aspects of media education, new technologies and informal learning. Recent Publications include *Researching Creative Learning: Methods and Issues* (with Pat Thomson, Routledge, 2010).

Pat Thomson, PSM PhD, is Professor of Education, School of Education, at the University of Nottingham and Director of the Centre for Research in Schools and Communities. She is an Adjunct Professor at the University of South Australia and a Visiting Professor at Deakin University. Her current research focuses primarily on the arts and creativity and school and community change; details of projects can be found at www.artsandcreativityresearch.org.uk. Her most recent publications include *Researching Creative Learning: Methods and Issues* (with Julian Sefton-Green, Routledge, 2010), *The Routledge Doctoral Student's Companion* and *The Routledge Doctoral Supervisor's Companion* (with Melanie Walker, 2010), *School Leadership: Heads on the Block?* (Routledge, 2009) and *Doing Visual Research with Children and Young People* (Routledge, 2008).

Joseph Tobin is a Professor in the School of Social Transformation at Arizona State University. His research interests include cross-cultural studies of early childhood education, immigration and education, children and the media, and qualitative research methods. Among his publications are *Preschool in Three Cultures Revisited, Good Guys Don't Wear Hats: Children's Talk about the Media* and *Pikachu's Global Adventure: The Rise and Fall of Pokemon*. He directed the Children Crossing Borders project, a five-country study of preschool services for children of recent immigrants. His newest project is a study of Deaf kindergartens in Japan, France and the US.

Dave Trotman is principal lecturer in Education and Professional Studies at Newman University College, Birmingham. His research interests include creativity and imagination, management of change processes and collaborative professional learning cultures. A former teacher in secondary and primary schools, he teaches on undergraduate, master's and doctoral programmes in Education Studies, and works extensively with practitioners on school-based teacher-research projects. His doctoral research examined teacher interpretations of pupil imaginative experiences in primary phase education and he has contributed to a range of international work in the field of imaginative education.

Grant Wiggins is the President of Authentic Education in Hopewell, New Jersey, USA. He earned his EdD from Harvard University and his BA from St John's College in Annapolis. Grant consults with schools, districts, state and national education departments on a variety of reform matters. Grant is the co-author, with Jay McTighe, of *Understanding by Design (UbD)* (ASCD, 1998). He is the author of *Educative Assessment* (1998) and *Assessing Student Performance* (1999), both published by Jossey-Bass. He works with Pearson Publishing on more than a dozen textbook programs in which UbD is infused.

Ellen Winner is Professor of Psychology, Boston College, and Senior Research Associate, Harvard Project Zero. She completed her PhD at Harvard University in 1978. Her writings include *Invented Worlds: The Psychology of the Arts* (Harvard University Press, 1982); *The Point of Words: Children's Understanding of Metaphor and Irony* (Harvard University Press, 1988); *Gifted Children: Myths and Realities* (Basic Books, 1997); and *Studio Thinking: The Real Benefits of Visual Arts Education* (Teachers College Press, 2007, co-authored with Lois Hetland, Shirley Veenema and Kimberly Sheridan). She received the Rudolf Arnheim Award for Outstanding Research by a Senior Scholar in Psychology and the Arts from the American Psychological Association.

Rolf Witte studied social work at the Freiburg University for Applied Sciences. From 1990 to 1995 he was the director of the Bayreuth International Cultural Youth Centre and the French–German Forum of Young Artists. Since 1996 he has been the International Relations Officer of BKJ, the German Federation for Arts Education and Cultural Learning. Since 2008 he has been a member of the Executive Committee of Culture Action Europe, the European Forum for the Arts and Heritage. Rolf is a member of the German Council for the European Youth in Action Programme and of the Council for European Cultural Politics of the German Cultural Council.

Diane R. Wood worked as a secondary English teacher and administrator. Her doctorate is from Teachers College, Columbia University. She is passionate about development of professional cultures in schools that foster teacher dialogue, agency, inquiry and knowledge, as well as the adoption of a critical multicultural perspective on teaching and learning. Her most recent book, co-edited with Betty Lou Whitford, is *Teachers Learning in Community: Realities and Possibilities*, published by SUNY Press in 2010. Currently at George Mason University, Diane teaches practising teachers in the Masters for New Professional Studies programme in the College of Education and Human Development.

Jie Zhang is on the faculty of the Department of Early Childhood Education at East China Normal University, where she received her doctoral degree. During the course of her graduate training, she spent a year studying and doing research at Arizona State University. Her research interests are focused on the field of early childhood education, including cross-cultural studies, preschool curriculum and teacher professional development. She is currently working on an international social-emotional curriculum for young children. Her publications include journal articles and book chapters on research and teaching in early childhood education.

1

Introduction

Julian Sefton-Green, Pat Thomson, Ken Jones and Liora Bresler

As teachers, governments and employers around the world discuss how to change education and schooling, they often arrive at the idea of making young people more creative. But being creative in an educational context can mean many things. It can mean turning classrooms into more exciting experiences or curriculum into more thoughtful challenges; or developing teachers to become different kinds of instructors or making assessment more authentic. It can also mean putting young people's voice at the heart of learning. These aspirations are motivated by two key concerns: to make schooling more exciting, relevant, challenging and dynamic; and to ensure that young people leave education able to contribute to the creative economy, or, more broadly, to the 'knowledge society' which will underpin growth in the twenty-first century.

Transforming these common aspirations into informed practice is not easy. Yet there are programmes, projects and initiatives which have consistently attempted to offer change and transformation to generate just such creative learning. At present there is no single text bringing together the significant literature exploring the dimensions of creative learning, despite the development of a cadre of creative teaching and learning specialists and (especially) artists who work in schools. This present volume aims to perform such a function. It brings together major theorists and current research comprising key readings about creative education.

Yet, despite shared values – and often shared practices – key ideas about what 'creative learning' might mean, and how it could be defined and enacted, are frequently contradictory and confused. This introduction aims to trace these uncertainties and map some of the concerns to which they give rise. In so doing, it will explain the thinking behind our organisation of this emerging field represented in the four parts which follow – although we will also introduce and narrate key ideas within each of these parts.

Why 'creative learning'?

In the considerable literature describing creativity and education, ranging from treatises on child development, to government reports, policy manifestos and research from classrooms, we can identify two distinct but overlapping foci. The first of these has been described as 'teaching for creativity'; that is, where the aims of interventions, principles and practices have as their object making children and young people more creative (however defined). In some instances work within this focus isn't so much concerned with individuals and their capabilities but more broadly with the idea of increasing creativity in general. The second focus is on 'teaching creatively'; that is, attention falls on the structure and organisation of schools and classrooms, on the production of teaching materials and on interactions between teachers and students in order to change curriculum, pedagogy and assessment. These two foci are interdependent and both foci may use different or complementary dimensions of teaching, learning *and* creativity.

In England,[1] at least, the term creative learning has been used as an amalgam of both of these ambitions and to an extent we use it here in the volume's title as a kind of shorthand to sum up a fusion or synthesis of a very wide range of interests. Whilst maybe not exact – creative doesn't perhaps quite 'work' as an adjective to describe learning – the phrase has come to represent a set of values and ambitions. We will see below how these coalesce around an attention to a quality of personal 'challenge' for young learners, and to the making of certain kinds of subjectivity. Beyond this emphasis, 'creative' is used to describe ways of framing a new place for authority and knowledge within learning, and an active, production – rather than consumption – based curriculum.

At its most basic, the idea of creative learning stands in opposition to a steady diet of teacher-directed, atomised and reductive worksheets, quizzes, exercises and tests, many of which render the teacher a mere delivery agent for a syllabus developed elsewhere. In this context, creative learning is an experimental, destabilising force; it questions the starting-points and opens up the outcomes of curriculum. It makes the school permeable to other ways of thinking, knowing, being and doing. As such, it creates uncertainty and instability, and it thus takes a confident and knowledgeable teacher and staff to take up the idea to its full extent. It is this open-endedness, which does not frame creative learning only as a process or as a means to predetermined ends, that leads to change.

As the essays collected here testify, unpinning the idea of both teaching for creativity and teaching creatively is a desire for change – at times expressed in utopian terms as nothing less than 'world-changing or self-changing' transformation. Whilst many essays in this book are of course cautious and careful, it is this spirit of change at individual, classroom and even at whole institution or system level that is captured well by the idea of creative learning. As we shall see, the phrase has come to stand for the analysis of forms of teaching *and* modes of learning, as well as acting both implicitly and explicitly as an irritant to, and critique of, what are assumed to be the norms of educational activities.

Here, then, the complex idea of being creative is less an absolute state than a comparative one. It is a question of creative learning offering a 'more than' or 'different than' kind of approach – albeit across a series of discrete domains associated with creativity. But this of course begs the question of what we might mean by creativity in the first place.

What is creativity?

The first substantive section, Part I, deals with this question from historical and theoretical perspectives. This part maps out the factors associated with contrasting definitions as well as introducing some of the key issues that have come to be associated with 'creativity', such as the relations between individuals and their social worlds, disciplinary knowledge and individual identity. Here, we need to map out some of the very general, almost meta-level, categories from that discussion as we continue defining the place of creative learning within this matrix of ideas.

The first point to note is that despite the significant traditional overlap between domains the concept of creativity is not coterminous with the Arts. At an abstract level, this idea is not very difficult to comprehend and indeed is quite established as a kind of common sense. We are quite happy talking about creativity in the sciences as well in relation to innovation and economic growth. However, within the conventional arrangement of subject disciplines within schools and at university level, as well as in the common discourse of many people associated with education, there is a tendency to lump together creative activities with arts education. In an effort to disentangle this knot of ideas, Part II explores the intersection between creativity, the Arts and schools, examining a set of practices in subjects like Drama and Art as well as ways in which attitudes towards children, teachers and schools have attempted to situate artistic creativity within forms of curriculum and assessment. As a number of writers discuss in both parts, there are continuities as well as differences between the notions of creativity inherited from the tropes or myths of the Arts and broader notions of creative learning in schools.

Yet, in general, there is consensus that studies of the making processes in the Arts do influence how we conceptualise creativity (and of course there are simply more academic studies of artists and the field of cultural production in relation to creativity than of other domains). But this also gives rise to a challenge for educators in that studies of artistic creativity tend to focus on the extra-ordinary. A key point made by a number of contributors is that, because in educational discourse the idea of creativity is more democratic and accessible than that often ascribed to great artists, we need to think of creativity as common to all of us rather than the gift of a privileged few.

The general orientation in the literature towards studies of exceptional people or unique experiences biases some of the ways we think about creativity. However, more general extrapolations of creative processes as applied to learning also include developed notions of the social. These derive from studies of fields of endeavour (often defined in terms of disciplinary activity, e.g. sculpture) and ideas about the regulation of disciplinary domains. Quite diverse scholars from sociology and psychology (Bourdieu, 1993; Csikszentmihalyi, 1996) offer models of creativity which locate individuals within complex networks of social activity. And as we shall see, such analyses offer ideas for educational intervention.

Indeed, studies of the social construction of creativity have also identified an important theme for creative learning – namely how it may be possible to describe creativity in terms of 'behaviours'. This approach is in interesting contrast to more traditional studies which have emphasised issues of cognition and the purely 'mental' or thought based sets of processes which may be presumed to underpin what creativity means (see Part I). Again, like the tension between social and individual approaches, it is helpful to approach our understanding of the concept of creativity on a continuum where questions about behaviour cannot be divorced from their relation to thinking and being.

Finally, studies of the tension between common and special notions of creativity also raise questions of definition. Can we conceptualise creativity as a question of degree rather than solely as an issue of kind? Is it creative when we do something even if it's not new or original in the history of the world? Can we talk about creative moments, of being more creative than 'usual'? Or of learning to become creative? Or do we need to hold on to an idea of *ab nihilo* – making something out of nothing, of being original in an absolutist sense – as our benchmark?

We have collected studies of creativity which have approached the problem of definition from a series of historically conflicting dimensions; in relationship to and distinct from the Arts; as social processes; as individual behaviours; as common to all or special to a few; and in degrees as well as in kind. This plurality of approaches also suggests a final perspective, namely considering the idea of creativity as a form of discourse – as a way of legitimating some sets of values and practices above others.

What is creative learning?

If Parts I and II explore the meaning of creativity, the following sections, Part III and Part IV aim to work outwards through the 'levels' of the education system, as it were, exploring creative learning in practice. Part III aims to collect together discussion exploring what we think of as a meso level of analysis, looking at innovative classrooms, curriculum and pedagogy, whilst Part IV expands the frame further, looking at even larger 'macro' studies of creative learning taking into account whole school change, the broader educational ecology and larger reform interventions at system level. Although we don't imagine that readers will use this book in strict linear fashion, our aim is to work in widening concentric circles offering analyses and examples of creative teaching and learning. Each part will introduce and discuss key concepts in more detail, but by way of a general introduction we want to outline the cornerstones of the debate.

New learners for new times

In some respects the essays in Parts I and II target different constituencies. Some contributions are aimed at critiquing the web of intersecting policy aspirations, which they argue have reached unprecedented interest in this field in recent years. On the other hand, some are more oriented towards developing theories or telling histories which offer models of action for teaching and learning. A key issue from the former set of debates – those aimed at policy critique – is important here in that they discuss how the idea of creative learning is heavily bound up with aspirations towards changing education for 'New Times', the economies of the future and, especially, for the alleged shift to a knowledge economy.

In this scenario – or sets of possible futures – creative learning sits squarely at the heart of deep rooted change. The kinds of workers and the kinds of skills and aptitudes presumed to carry this project forward are, it is frequently argued, not the outcomes of the current sets of educational arrangements – as manifest in schools, testing and so forth. Creative learning is a way of describing the knowledge work of the post-Fordist economy. A meta-review by Lucas and Claxton, (2009) uses the phrase 'wider skills' to encompass a very wide series of interventions over the last 10 years in curriculum and research analyses. These focused on the sets of behaviours and skills deemed to be valuable but which, it is broadly agreed (although this is of course disputed), are not (satisfactory) outcomes produced by conventional educational arrangements. 'Soft outcomes', 'life-skills for the twenty-first century', as well as creative learning fall into these catch-all ideas. These are well described in a recent book by the OECD looking at new learners for new times and advocating a model of education which:

> encourages students to become "self-regulated learners". This means developing the "meta-cognitive skills" for learners to monitor, evaluate and optimise their acquisition and use of knowledge. It also means to be able to regulate one's emotions and motivations during the learning process.
>
> *(Dumont et al., 2010: 14)*

The kinds of behaviour derived from studies of creativity and creative practices especially (but not, as already noted, exclusively) based on the Arts, and those understandings of the social relationships that constitute creative capabilities, have thus been introduced into this matrix of 'change' discourses. We shall see in Parts III and IV, later in this book, how they underpin a range of initiatives to change teaching and learning.

Some scholars in this collection are sceptical of some of the claims made for this sea-change. They suggest that the turn to the creative and an attention to previously unschooled competencies represent no more than a kind of 'liberationist' discourse, arguing that perfectly valid but culturally located processes of making and learning embedded in a long tradition of arts education have been recuperated into a divisive educational project which seeks to fetishise the individual and the individualistic (see contributions to Part I). Whilst acknowledging that creative learning may offer a useful banner, it is suggested that the term has been used as a stalking horse for some processes of school reform (see Part IV). Such reform is sometimes imagined to be under local control, but in most circumstances it is located within the current national policy regimes of school improvement or school effectiveness. Those of an historical bent argue that creative learning is the latest protean shape taken by a longstanding search pursued within education, from Dewey onwards, for an authentic, personal and meaningful learning experience in contrast to a presumed norm of stifling exclusion and failure.

Teaching and learning

Because the local and national circumstances of analysis will inevitably differ, debates about the value of the term 'creative learning' will continue to be contested – especially whilst the purpose and nature of public education systems continues to be such a volatile subject for political claim and counter-claim. One way of circumventing this argument has been to look for more disinterested and objective understanding of the learning processes as part of attempts to formulate a 'new science of learning' (Kalantzis and Cope, 2008). Here the idea of 'creative learning' is at the forefront of attempts to theorise learning in different and, where possible, new and subtle ways. For example, attention has focused on the micro processes of classroom interactions, exploring in particular the effects that a reconfigured role of the teacher-as-artist and of the artist-as-teacher may have on ways of working and ways of knowing.

In general, the paradigm combines distinct elements. Significant attention has been paid to: the role of the teacher as a different locus of authority; an interest in active, production based kinds of learning activities; an emphasis on developing habits of curiosity, collaboration and co-operation in group work; an insistence on the value of performances and the development of audiences within the school and in the wider community. This approach especially values the products of making (not just artefacts but performances). It focuses analysis on wider meaning-making process, such as those located 'in' the learner's body through performance. A further piece of this jigsaw has been attempts to build explicitly on those forms of play and playful thinking which, as a range of studies from different disciplinary background suggest, are integral to creativity. These include developing forms of structured and semi-structured play within the curriculum and the inculcation of the long-term habits of playfulness which are often presumed to lie at the heart of creative learning.

Positive values

Raymond Williams observed that 'no word in English carries a more consistently positive reference than "creative"' and that 'we should be glad of this when we think of the values it seeks to express and the activities it offers to describe' (Williams, 1961, in Neelands and Choe, 2010: 90). The unremitting rhetorical glow that transfers to any use of the term may discourage critical evaluation. Equally, attempts to programmatise and normalise creative learning can lead to the very banality and orthodoxy of practice that so many claim to be seeking to remedy.

From this point of view we aren't necessarily promoting creative learning as a simple 'solution' and, equally, as our qualifications in this text have suggested, we don't necessarily subscribe to any single monolithic view of schooling in the first place. The current state of schooling is of course as varied in quality as are forms of creative learning, when introduced either as a kind of corrective or as an addition to the current state of affairs.

At its best, however, and as developed and explored in contributions throughout this volume, creative learning denotes an ensemble of diverse practices working across a range of 'levels' within the education system, intertwining policies, curriculum, partnerships, a different notion of the subjectivity of learners and a series of values about relationships between learners and teachers, and between authority and knowledge. We are not offering a collection of simple prescriptions here because, as Part IV in particular shows, developing forms of creative learning requires a careful attention to the processes of change and a local and particular understanding of how to knit together this ensemble of practices for best effect.

An international approach

Three of the four of us are based in England, and in differing capacities have been involved with a national initiative, Creative Partnerships (CP). To date, CP is one of the most elaborate investments in the field of creative teaching and learning. Established as a joint project of the Department of Culture Media and Sport and the then Department for Education and Skills in 2002, its stated mission was to develop the skills of young people across England, raising their aspirations and achievements, and opening up more opportunities for their futures. It has now worked with over 2,400 schools across the age range in areas of deprivation across England, operating originally in 36 areas in England, including intensive work with around 1,100 schools. It has delivered projects to young people or continuing professional development (CPD) to teachers in a further 1,500 schools and disseminated best practice to a further 7,000, so that already over one-third of schools in England have had some contact with the programme. It has worked with 550,000 young people and 50,000 teachers, provided training to over 32,000 teachers and creative practitioners, and has employed over 4,500 creative practitioners and cultural organisations. It has probably received around £160 million (2002–10), making it one of the largest State investments in creative learning around the world.[2]

This kind of infrastructure is rare and has encouraged a more systematic appraisal and interest in creative learning than is usually possible, which may explain the pattern of contributions to this collection. This English context may be unique but itself has emerged out of more long-standing traditions and progressive (and progressivist, according to Jones (2003)) approaches to learning and education. Whilst the phrase 'creative learning' is not that prevalent outside the UK, there is no shortage of documentation about the values and change initiatives we have identified above. Scholarship and interest from other countries in the creative learning field are, of course, to an extent reliant on local contexts. Perhaps the key determinants affecting the flavour of different national approaches have been the nature of pre-existing arts learning, cultural assumptions about the nature of creativity and the extent to which different countries have been interested in modernising in response to the perceived global challenge of the knowledge economy/society.

We haven't set out to offer a systematic or comprehensive world-wide appraisal of creative learning, but we have collected diverse and stimulating accounts from interesting scholars and practitioners from around the world. A comparative understanding of what different national cultures mean by creativity is useful in weighting the import of the social and cognitive, the aesthetic and the practical and the individual and the collective. Perhaps more important are pre-existing approaches to arts education; here tensions between models of the Arts as a form of cultural maintenance, as disciplinary skills and knowledge or as general aesthetics and experiential learning are important – notwithstanding how influential the Arts have been in determining funding priorities within local education budgets. Paradoxically perhaps, it seems that where the Arts are well established within education systems there has been less of an interest in exploring more instrumentalist uses of the Arts and generalising about wider types of learning.

In countries with well-resourced progressive education agendas where there has been a clear interest in creative capabilities there has been a very explicit attention to researching and even measuring creativity as a more formal output of learning (McWilliam and Haukka, 2008). In meta-reviews of more student centred, non-traditional outcomes of learning (Lucas and Claxton, 2009; Facer and Pykett, 2007) creative behaviours and habits emerge as desirable outcomes and as the object of scholarly and policy interest framing a shift in the subjectivities of learners within the knowledge economy.

Visions and values

In some respects creative learning mirrors very deep questions about the purpose and nature of public education systems, and reveals a concern for the quality of relationships and for individual lives. Many studies of creative learning in practice in Parts III and IV explore questions about purposes, school practices and interpersonal relationships between young people and between teachers and taught. They explore deep issues of how we think, feel and work. Here we can see how this field deals implicitly with contemporary paradigms of childhood and youth. Questions about identity, authority and the agency of young people as social actors are clearly key to what creative learning might mean, and many studies of schools and system change show how competing paradigms of young people are at work within conflicting visions of educational transactions.

Whilst some contributors to Part I locate the origins of these ideas in humanist notions of 'being', one of the distinguishing features of some interpretations of creative learning is its attempt to marry theses ideas with more economistic notions of human capital – with an emphasis on contemporary forms of subjectivity. This makes it a peculiarly contemporary educational 'ideology' and one which is likely to be key to the ways we frame education over the next 10–20 years. The idea of creative learning additionally often focuses on the individual and the individualistic, supporting personal growth, with an emphasis on developing everybody's potential. Yet when applied at a curriculum or policy level it is also capable of addressing whole system and collective values in studies of change and school reform. This too is key to debates about public education in many countries around the world.

This book is offered to contextualise further research and study. We are especially pleased with the breadth of its coverage and the fact that we have collected together a wide range of accounts. We are also keen to establish deep foundations in the field, given that there is a tendency for scholars within these disciplines to start from an ahistorical perspective and, as can be seen in Part IV especially, from a naïve 'tradition' within many 'new' initiatives of ignoring what amounts to a substantial and important body of research, study and experience. We hope this handbook will offer a solid marker amidst this shifting rhetoric and help knit together an incomplete or amnesiac research corpus by setting out clear frameworks for study and by offering well-founded benchmarks of thought and grounded research.

Notes

1 The four 'nations' of the United Kingdom are all subject to different governance and policy regimes. See contributions to this volume, Part II.
2 http://www.creativitycultureeducation.org/.

References

Bourdieu, P. (1993) *The Field of Cultural Production: Essays on Art and Literature* (trans. R. Johnson), Cambridge: Polity Press.

Csikszentmihalyi, M. (1996) *Creativity: Flow and the Psychology of Discovery and Invention* (1st ed.), New York: HarperCollins Publishers.

Dumont, H., Istance, D. and Benavides, F. (eds) (2010) *The Nature of Learning: Using Research to Inspire Practice*, Paris: OECD.

Facer, K. and Pykett, J. (2007) *Developing and Accrediting Personal Skills and Competencies: Report and Ways Forward*, Bristol: Futurelab.

Jones, K. (2003) *Education in Britain: 1944 to the Present*, Cambridge: Polity Press.

Kalantzis, M. and Cope, B. (2008) *New Learning: Elements of a Science of Education*, Cambridge: Cambridge University Press.

Lucas, B. and Claxton, G. (2009) *Wider Skills for Learning: What Are They, How They Can Be Cultivated, How They Could Be Measured and Why They Are Important for Innovation?*, NESTA Research Report. London: NESTA.

McWilliam, E. and Haukka, S. (2008) Educating the creative workforce: new directions for twenty-first century schooling, *British Educational Research Journal* 34(5): 651–66.

Neelands, J. and Choe, B. (2010) The English model of creativity: cultural politics of an idea, *International Journal of Cultural Policy* 16(3): 287–304.

Williams, R. (1961) *The Long Revolution*, London: Chatto & Windus.

Part I
Theories and histories
Creative learning and its contexts

Julian Sefton-Green and Liora Bresler

This section consists of a collection of writings exploring definitions of creativity and creative learning. This introduction will locate these contributions in a broader discussion of key themes and tensions which criss-cross individual chapters. These include questions about:

- the relationship of creativity to originality (are all creative acts original and if so for whom?);
- the role of discipline-specific fields of knowledge and skillsets in theories of generic creativities (is there such a thing as a non-discipline-specific mode of creativity or is creativity always rooted in specific practices, be they art or science?);
- tensions in creativity theory between the social and individual (is creativity something that only occurs within individuals or is it a property of broader social groups and practices?);
- the relationship of the politics of creativity to discourses of modernity (how much is creativity a Modern Western concept not found in other outlooks around the world?);
- ways of approaching questions of definition (is creativity a question of mental or embodied characteristics? Is it measurable or transferable?);
- and a consideration of the banality of creativity in current incarnations (how much is the tem over-used in contemporary political discourse?).

Approaching the field

The authors in this section were invited to explore the contexts for 'creative learning'. As several contributors note, this means investigating the question 'What is creativity?' as well as the question 'What is learning?' Much of the section is concerned with a history of ideas as contributors (Abbs (Chapter 11), Belfiore (Chapter 3), Darras (Chapter 10) and Jones (Chapters 2 and 9)) explore some of the philosophical and theoretical paradigms underpinning notions of creativity. This is because most authors argue that such intellectual formations are present today, albeit in unacknowledged or fossilised forms, and that they continue to act as benchmarks and norms in discussion about the field. Excavating these norms is even more imperative today as some claims about the desirability of creative learning – about which there is little controversy – benefit from being tempered by an understanding of expectations which come from this wider appreciation.

Perhaps as a consequence of this, the contributors to this section tend to operate with two senses of time. On the one hand, a number of authors (like Drotner (Chapter 8) or Darras) pay attention to the policy here and now: they explore how contemporary governments are trying to fit education to the specific challenges of a changing economic order. Yet, they are also interested in how deep-seated assumptions about creativity, its traditions, processes and meanings derive from older intellectual ideas extending back, in Belfiore's case, to fifth century Athens or, as Jones (Chapter 2) shows, rooted in the Enlightenment and taking flight in visions of Modernity. Of course scholars enjoy nothing more than pointing out that there is nothing new under the sun and that politicians are always making up new dawns – that there is always a tension between the claims of policy and the lessons of history. Banaji (Chapter 4) and Pope (Chapter 12) turn this problem on its head by framing a history of creativity studies as a series of discourses each rooted in a distinctive set of power relations. Abbs attempts to find ways of bringing older structures of understanding creativity into a contemporary focus.

Criticism of the contemporary resurgence of interest in creativity is all the more strange when we consider how on one level there is no dispute about the *value* of creative learning or creativity in general. It seems to be a universal good. Indeed the only writing about creativity which might address negative features concerns the personal psychological burden of being creative and the cost that has exacted on creative people and their relationships – a common feature in many biographical studies of artists (Miller, 2000) – and traced by Runco and Pagnani here (Chapter 7). Yet this 'optimistic' assumption itself about the value of creativity may be fundamentally misplaced. The contemporary fascination with creativity and its role in the economy as a generator of wealth creation as described by Drotner, for example in conjunction with idealistic and almost problematic aspirations for personal self-fulfilment, have led to an almost impossible set of expectations, as Darras argues later in this section (Chapter 10).

Elite/democratic: individual/social

One common thread across many chapters has been how ideas about creativity have moved away from the study of elites and exceptions towards the normal and the everyday: see the arguments pursued in Boden (1994) and exemplified by the examples in Abbs here (Chapter 11). Elsewhere this has been characterised as big and little 'C' creativity (Craft, 2005; and see also Runco and Pagnani, Chapter 7). This is a change in academic focus about both what creativity is and also what its significance might be for learning. For if mass education is to take up the challenge of creativity it has to be premised on wider and more accessible notions than the more old-fashioned belief in the qualities of special individuals. Whist there are many disinterested reasons why academic research may have changed its focus, and much interest in the topic from an education perspective is of course elitist in character, it is also true that State education policy finds it hard to accommodate concerns that cannot be justified on equity grounds. Jones (Chapter 9) refers to the democratisation of creativity, introducing a more popular concept of 'common culture' into the debate and opening up theorists who have explored everyday creativity (Willis, 1990). A broader acceptance of more general and widely distributed creativity helps change an agenda which, in the past, may have been overly concerned with special individuals or 'genius'.

The idea that creativity may be more broadly distributed and more common than is often assumed can now be found across a wide range of different academic disciplines. Indeed it is a feature of change in disparate studies from Psychology to Sociology, Aesthetics and Cultural Studies that creativity resides as much in the wider social context as it does within individual psyches. Thus Abbs (from Aesthetics) talks about vertical and horizontal axes, where the individual intersects with traditions, conventions and artistic form, and Csikszentmihalyi (from

Psychology) argues that creativity needs to be acknowledged as such by the wider society before any creations or acts can be defined as creative in the first place (Csikszentmihalyi, 1996). Sociologists of cultural production like Bourdieu (1986, 1993) have developed notions of fields and practice to explain the interplay of the individual, their formation and their actions.

All of these models or theories may derive from different conceptions of the human subject and even rest upon differing notions of the relationship of human agency to social structure but they all try to address the same conundrum: how to account for change, newness or difference. Different interpretative traditions give different weight to the determining influence of form (how the new creation is expressed) and how the reception of the newness is regulated and accepted. It is here that Kuhn's well-known ideas about 'paradigm shifts' and the work of Bruno Latour, with his anthropological studies of the work of scientists, come into play, as we strive for theories to explain how new ideas are imagined, conceived, implemented and received (Latour, 1986). What unifies all of these diverse disciplines is the idea of a complex social process, in some theories involving more of an attention to intra-personal cognitive processes and in other models to inter-personal and social negotiations and how they play out in specific domains.

Clearly there is a connection between studies of field/domain and the more democratic accounts of creativity because the weight attributed to the individual is, as it were more, distributed in these field/domain accounts. Even in studies of creative persons, more attention is now paid to groups and collaboration (Miell and Littleton, 2004).

Art, the Arts and originality

A second common interest in this section is the origins of studies about creativity within broader discussion of the Arts. This theme is more directly addressed in Part II but it is also discussed here. Not only are the Arts usually taken as the paradigmatic site for creation but aesthetic studies actually contain some of the most developed analysis of how creativity might work in practice: the effects of form, the role of tools and the place of reception. Some scholars, like Abbs, move across Science and Arts domains extrapolating principles about creativity from a focus on common 'new' or 'original' works (be they painting or theories about cell structure).

There are two key themes across contributions to this section. The first relates to the question of originality. Leong (Chapter 6) and Matsunobu (Chapter 5) outline how the question of originality in Art is a very particular historical cultural construct and indeed antithetical to traditions of Art across various parts of the world. Western obsession with originality relates strongly to the demands of the market and the incorporation of Art in capitalism (see subsection below or Becker, 1984), and have no place in the ritualistic, folk, religious and other originality narratives about Art in society. There are of course whole swathes of art forms and traditions that are ideologically opposed to change, and whether or in what ways they are conceptualised as creative (as distinct from being new) is a generative enquiry.

Whether Art can offer itself as a paradigmatic case for creativity is also a moot point. First of all, whether it is productive to sustain what C. P. Snow called two cultures, describing a dualistic split between arts and sciences, is even more tendentious in an era of technological flux. Nevertheless, the yoking of creativity and the Arts is a kind of common sense – despite the analyses provided in many of these chapters – and certainly it is where many education initiatives begin in practice across the school systems of the developed world. This theme is pursed in more detail in Part II of this volume.

Despite any or all of these qualifications, the Arts occupy a privileged place in our conceptualisations of creativity. Whether they can be mined instrumentally, as Belfiore (Chapter 3) or Banaji (Chapter 4) enquire, to provide templates for other kinds of creative production is open to question, but they offer the values and processes most amenable for use in many kinds of learning. In education this also has something to do with the position that the Arts occupy in the overall discursive field of schooling as the privileged site of cultural values and with a special role in the formation of individual growth; this is pursued by Jones (Chapter 9), Drotner, Darras and Pope. Part II develops and explores this theme in more detail.

Progress, identity and transformation

Drotner, Darras, Jones (Chapter 2) and Pope also engage with the question 'Why creativity now?' Why is the current era seemingly so intrigued by a quality which, irrespective of any definition, is assumed to have existed in equal quantity in previous generations. An important theme here is the alleged shift to a different and new kind of economy, one underpinned by knowledge and network structures (Castells, 2000). Creativity, especially that contributing to innovation, has driven an interest in developing creative people, most explicitly expressed, as Darras argues, in the idea of a creative class (Florida, 2003). The imperative for creativity is allied to the neo-liberal restructuring of capital in terms of both the need for new products for new markets to ensure continuous growth through the turnover of novelties and shifts to a knowledge economy where especially the exploitation of intellectual property is another engine for wealth creation.

The set of socio-economic circumstances behind current interests in creativity may of course change as a result of the 2008 world recession but they have clearly created an orientation towards creative learning. Whilst many of the contributors in this section are more than cautious about embracing this outlook – as much as from an historical concern that creativity embeds a host of assumptions as from the question of the democratisation of creativity – it has fed into a distinctive interest in the creative self or creative person, which is of course is where the interest in creative learning comes in, as we shall see especially in Parts II and III of this volume.

There are three dimensions to a focus on the creative self. The first is psychological, and Runco and Pagnani's chapter (Chapter 7) and previous work (Runco, 2007) outline a significant history of scholarship which attempts to describe and measure abstract cognitive processes. A second aspect of this approach is the attention to creative behaviour and the construction of a creative self or creative identities, as Drotner also explores (Chapter 8). Rather than exploring a psychological state, this analytical frame looks at social interactions and is frequently found in studies of industrial production, especially those with an interest in innovation. There is also a critical sociology of creative workers and creative work (Ross, 2003; Banks, 2007) examining how the growth of the Creative and Cultural industries – a feature of the new knowledge based economy – has also played its part in constituting a particular kind of self-exploiting labour demonstrating all the traits of the creative self (Oakley, 2009).

A third dimension of this attention to the creative self is the work attributed to creativity in ideas about actualising and fulfilling the self. Obviously part of the psychological dimension, and key to progressivist theories of education (Thomson and Sefton-Green, 2010) where being creative is germane to realising individual potential (see Darras, Chapter 10, too), this aspect feeds into a deeper set of values about the role of creativity in everyday life. In some respects, studies in the rest of this volume pursue this theme in more detail as they explore how creative learning plays out in curriculum, pedagogy and whole school and system level change. Here, as Pope and Drotner imply, we need to move beyond notions of individual fulfilment to consider rhetorics, as Banaji would put it, about our wider beliefs in social change. This quest is at the heart of Jones' chapter on Capitalism, creativity and learning (Chapter 2). In quasi-religious terms many authors frequently reify ideas of creativity to stand for utopian aspirations underpinning beliefs in progress and improvement. Here we come full circle as aspirations for economic growth meet notions of personal growth and transformation in deep-seated narratives of hope and change.

The banality of creativity

Against these more idealistic positions we have to set the aphorism that creativity is 1 per cent inspiration and 99 per cent perspiration. This kind of common sense deliberately invokes the everyday and practical; but this too creates its own problems as it is often used to suggest a simplistic universality. Indeed, we have to account for the ways in which creativity is now used in a range of policy rhetorics as a simple platitude aiming to remediate difficult social change, deprivation and poverty – at least in the UK, US and Australia. Whilst the weight of scholarship may now have moved away from special cases toward the more common, this has also led to a diminution of creativity's specialness to the point of no return. The challenge is almost to escape how creativity is now used so routinely that it appears banal. Whilst Pope tries to steer us away from a kind of creativity fatigue, we also need a certain self-discipline to avoid an accusation of banality.

If creativity tends to be over-used as a catch-all to express contemporary individualistic values, to sum up a quality of learning for the modern era it runs the risk of shooting itself in the foot. As has been noted on a number of occasions, an education perspective leads us into a conundrum in respect of creativity. When all young people do things for the first time, it doesn't necessarily mean that they are new. In other words, for the learner there will always be an element of novelty and change in learning, however conventional or trite such achievements are to the teacher or adult. All progress associated with young people is bound to contain a creative dimension but we need to keep the significance of this in a sensible perspective.

The question then becomes: what does creativity add to our understanding of learning, its organisation and its processes; and how does our understanding of learning determine our understanding of creativity? And whilst these questions are more directly explored in the rest of this volume, here, authors tease out the contexts for these arguments. The historical and cultural focus of their contributions points to how this topic embeds deep assumptions about human nature and what it means to be an individual. We hope that unpicking and reflecting on these in a rigorous and sustained fashion will help readers navigate their research, their classrooms, their schools and school systems with greater authority and confidence.

References

Banks, M. (2007) *The Politics of Cultural Work*, London: Palgrave Macmillan.

Becker, H. S. (1984) *Art Worlds*, Berkeley: University of California Press.

Boden, M. A. (ed.) (1994) *Dimensions of Creativity*, Cambridge, MA: MIT Press.

Bourdieu, P. (1986) *Distinction: A Social Critique of the Judgement of Taste*, London: Routledge.

—— (1993) *The Field of Cultural Production: Essays on Art and Literature* (trans. R. Johnson). Cambridge: Polity Press.

Castells, M. (2000) *The Rise of the Network Society: Economy, Society and Culture*, vol.1: *The Information Age*, Oxford: WileyBlackwell.

Craft, A. (2005) *Creativity in Schools: Tensions and Dilemmas*, London: Routledge.

Csikszentmihalyi, M. (1996) *Creativity: Flow and the Psychology of Discovery and Invention* (1st ed.), New York: HarperCollins.

Florida, R. (2003) *The Rise of the Creative Class: And How It's Transforming Work, Leisure, Community and Everyday Life*, New York: Basic Books.

Latour, B. (1986) *Science in Action*, Milton Keynes: Open University Press.

Miell, D. and Littleton, K. (eds) (2004) *Collaborative Creativity: Contemporary Perspectives*, London: Free Association Press.

Miller, A. I. (2000) *Insights of Genius: Imagery and Creativity in Science and Art*, Cambridge, MA: MIT Press.

Oakley, K. (2009) *'Art Works' – Cultural Labour Markets: A Literature Review*, London: Creativity, Culture and Education; available at http://www.creativitycultureeducation.org/data/files/cce-lit-review-8-a5-web-130.pdf (accessed April 2010).

Ross, A. (2003) *No-Collar*, New York: Basic Books.

Runco, M. A. (2007) *Creativity: Theories and Themes: Research, Development, and Practice*, Burlington, MA: Elsevier Academic Press.

Thomson, P. and Sefton-Green, J. (2010) Introduction, in P. Thomson and J. Sefton-Green (eds) *Researching Creative Learning: Methods and Approaches*, London: Routledge.

Willis, P. E. (1990) *Common Culture: Symbolic Work at Play in the Everyday Cultures of the Young*, Milton Keynes: Open University Press.

2

Capitalism, creativity and learning

Some chapters in a relationship

Ken Jones

Introduction

Long ago, in the 1960s, the radical Catholics of the Slant group wrote that for much of its existence their Church had danced a slow jive with capitalism (Cunningham *et al.*, 1966). Anachronistic though it is, the metaphor is an attractive one; it suggests a partnership-in-movement whose terms are always changing, yet in which the partners share a kind of responsive relationship, that patterns, reciprocally, their movements. Jiving is a promiscuous kind of metaphor that can work just as well if the Catholic Church is replaced as partner by some other entity or practice, such as the nation state or warfare. It also works, up to a point, to illuminate the history of a discourse, such as the subject of this collection, creativity, whose birth and rapid development coincide with capitalism's, and which learned to dance, as it were, in the spaces opened up by its more powerful partner.

But here the metaphor reaches its limits. The Church as an institution possesses a relative unity, across time and space; the discourse of creativity is much less of an integral thing. Discourses, according to Voloshinov, are multi-accentual rather than monolithic; they are the outcome of myriad encounters between social groups, registering a continuous clashing of social interests (Voloshinov, 1986). 'Creativity' is more multi-accentual a discourse than most (see Banaji, Chapter 4), a territory over which many intersecting lines of thought have passed. If we want to hold on to the idea that creativity has been shaped by its relationship to an economic and political order, we need also a sense of the different modalities of this relationship – its antagonistic as well as its pliant forms. Some such understanding, of the plentiful and contradictory repertoire supplied by the wider territory of creativity to our immediate field of educational practice, should enrich contemporary debates about creative learning.

This chapter aims to offer a perspective on creativity that identifies its historical co-ordinates, in particular those provided by social theories that are themselves responses to shifts in politics, culture and economic life. Such an effort involves simplification, of course; but so long as such simplification retains some sense of Voloshinov's dialogism, it can be heuristically useful. In particular, it can elucidate the connections and the tensions between different elements in the central cluster of meanings that 'creativity' has assumed in learning contexts – elements whose common matrix was formed in the Enlightenment.

A radical Enlightenment tradition

At certain points in the twentieth century, social and cultural theorists rediscovered a strand of Enlightenment thought in which questions of language, creativity, freedom and social organisation were intertwined. In the 1960s, Noam Chomsky drew lines of connection between his work and that of the German theorist of language Wilhelm von Humboldt (1767–1835). Humboldt had suggested that learning, in particular the learning of language, was a form of creative action. 'Man' did not understand language behaviouristically, 'as an animal understands a command or the sound of the whip', but rather as an 'instrument for discovering previously unrecognized truths', and as an 'inner need of mankind … necessary for the development of its spiritual energies' (Humboldt, 1963: 239, 246). Children, when they learned a language, 'created far more than they memorised', and entered language 'actively, as it were, instead of just receptively' (ibid.: 243). Chomsky derived from these principles a link between language and other kinds of human capacity and desire: freedom in language had its analogue in the characteristic political impulses of the Enlightenment: 'people should be free; they shouldn't be under the control of authoritarian institutions' (Chomsky, 1992, quoted in Barsky, 1998: 112). He thus discovered in Humboldt's work a libertarian social and political orientation, that connected language, creativity and social action and grounded them in a sense that 'the fundamental human capacity is the capacity and need for creative self-expression, for free control of all aspects of one's life and thought' (Chomsky, 1969: 31). This capacity was on a collision course with the authority of the church and the absolutist state – and, at a later point, with the wage slavery of capitalist society.

In *All That is Solid Melts into Air* (1981) Marshall Berman traces a similar, though more sinuous, path, to delineate a German philosophical tradition, culminating in Karl Marx, that focused on 'self-development' as a fundamental value. For this tradition, Berman says, self-development is 'the form of the good life': 'if Marx is fetishistic about anything, it is not workers and production, but rather the far more complex and comprehensive ideal of development' (1981: 127), with communism being seen as 'the absolute working out of man's creative potentialities' (Marx, 1858/1973: 487). Shifting from philosophical explication to intellectual and cultural history, Berman suggests a link between this tradition and the social conditions of capitalist modernity addressed in the *Communist Manifesto* – in which text the paradoxes of self-development begin to emerge. 'The 'humanistic ideal of self-development', Berman writes, grows out of the 'emerging reality of bourgeois economic development' (1981: 96); a mobile 'melting' society offers opportunities for self-transformation for individuals, and they in turn transform social conditions. Capitalism opens up 'roads and vistas', establishes 'new images and paradigms' of the good life as a life of action (ibid.). But in Marx's dialectical vision, capitalism's offer has a darker side. It 'forces self-development for everybody, but people can develop only in restricted and distorted ways'. 'Liberation of human capacity' and the 'drive for self-development' are connected to and shaped by the pressures of competition (ibid.). Modern men and women must learn, as a condition for survival as autonomous beings, 'to yearn for change' – but the terms of that change are deeply ambivalent.

It could be argued that on the basis of this two-sidedness, which from Marx and from Berman's point of view is integral to human development in conditions of capitalism, different branches of thinking about modernity and the realisation of creative potential have grown up. The first branch begins with Enlightenment aesthetics. The lineage of argument here has been traced by Peter Burger (1992). Kant, in the *Critique of Judgement* (1790/2008), sought to establish the sphere of aesthetics as separate from the totality of social activities and 'practical life contexts'. Schiller (1794/1954) introduced into this separation a relationship of critique: the development of civilisation had destroyed the unity of the senses and of reason: 'we see not merely individuals but whole classes of human beings developing only part of their capacities while the rest of them, like a stunted plant, show only a feeble vestige of their nature' (ibid.: 38). It was in this context that art took on a particular importance. For Schiller, its function was to put back together the halves of man that had been torn asunder – to make possible the development of the totality of human potentialities that the individual might develop in his sphere of activity (Burger, 1984: 45). It is on the very basis of its autonomy, its not being tied to immediate ends, that art can fulfil a task that cannot be fulfilled in any other way – the furtherance of human development.

Radical aesthetics

Schiller understood 'art' from two perspectives. From one, it was a specialised practice, concerned with self-conscious symbolic crafting, and the making of Form. From the second, it belonged in a spectrum of free and creative activity which also included 'play'. Art and play are universal qualities, but are at the same time distinct from and in tension with the contexts of practical life; a universalist claim about human creativity exists alongside a counterposition of innate creative impulses against constraining social structures. This distinction is meant by Schiller to be functional: because art is removed from practical contexts it can develop the totality of human potentialities. But the space of 'removal', and the distance thus opened up between art and the social, also left its theorists open to critique. Lukacs points to the contradictions inherent in Schiller's belief that only a small class of men 'active without working … can preserve the beautiful unity of human nature' (1968: 135); Eagleton notes the impossibility of a philosophy that maintains culture as both an 'active social remaking and a ethereal realm of being' (1990: 117); reviewing the post-Schiller tradition, Marcuse summarises its beliefs in caustic terms:

> Art is not (or not supposed to be) a use value to be consumed in the course of the daily performance of men; its utility is of a transcendent kind, utility for the soul or mind which does not enter the normal behaviour of men and does not really change it – except for precisely that short period of elevation, the cultured holiday: in church, in the museum, the concert hall, the theatre, before monuments and ruins of the great past. After the break, real life continues: business as usual.
>
> *(Marcuse, 1972: 53)*

Marcuse goes on to sketch the history of artistic movements – avant-gardes – that have rejected the idea of art as restorative intermission, rebelled against the 'anaesthetising' effects of Form, that inhibit a recognition of the brutality of the real, and sought to produce 'desublimated' projects – Conceptualism, for instance – that stripped art of its separate status and integrated it with life. Marcuse was sceptical about such projects: 'anti-Art' could not escape the problem of Form, and in attempting to do so, produced degraded work. For him, the essence of Marxist aesthetics was the recognition that only in a future, 'qualitatively different society', in which there developed 'a new type of men and women, no longer the subject or object of exploitation', could art and life, the beautiful and the true, play and reality, be reconciled and everyday life become the site of creativity and self-realisation (Marcuse, 1972: 57). Until then, 'authentic' art could only be negative and distanced from the real, could only be that which was capable of 'confronting man with the dreams he betrays and the crimes he forgets'. Beckett and Schoenberg, Picasso and Stockhausen, were its exemplars.

The European avant-garde movements at which Marcuse took aim had a different orientation. From Dada and Constructivism onwards, they conceived projects that were critical of 'bourgeois society', but rather than develop a negative aesthetic of disengagement, they sought to annihilate the divisions between 'art' and 'life' that underpinned the social order. In doing so, they subsumed 'art' into a larger category, that of 'creativity'. In 1950s Paris, complaining that 'functionalism is attempting to entirely eliminate play', the cultural activists who later became the Situationist International (SI) aimed to 'overcome our discordance with the world' (Debord, 1958a/2006) by converting social situations into art events – events in which the boundaries between art form and social practice would become blurred. The early debates of the (proto-) situationists are organised around proposals for interventions in everyday life – cultural shocks – that challenge and transfigure its routines:

> Train stations should be left as they are. Their rather poignant ugliness contributes to the feeling of transience that makes these buildings mildly attractive. Gil J Wolman proposed removing or scrambling all information regarding departures (destinations, timetables, etc.) in order to facilitate *dérives*.[1] After a lively debate, those opposing this motion retracted their objections and it was wholeheartedly approved. It was also agreed that background noise in the stations should be intensified by broadcasting recordings from many other stations, as well as from certain harbours.
>
> *(Lettrist International, 1955)*

From an initial disgust at the combination of hyper-planning and cultural conservatism that they thought blighted the post-war city, the SI's critique rapidly evolved, to become as much political and social as artistic and cultural. 'First of all', wrote Guy Debord, 'we think the world must be changed. We want the most liberating change of society and life' (Debord, 1957/2006). From this followed the situationists' immersion in the events of May 1968, whose rhetorics their work had both anticipated and shaped: the imagination had taken power, the doors to a qualitatively different society had been thrown open, and creativity, so it seemed, had become a principle of everyday life (Horn, 2007).[2] This was both an ephemeral state of affairs and a future landmark. As Horn suggests, 1968, and the situationist contribution to it, continue to provide the maxims of a politicised avant-garde: the gap between art and 'ordinary' culture should be a narrow one; creativity, in both kinds of space, is incompatible with the established order.

From this vantage point, subaltern and previously unrecognised cultures also come more easily into focus, as instances of symbolic creativity every bit as powerful as that of canonical forms of art, and as valued resources for a culture of critique and dissidence. Marcuse had postponed the reconciliation of art and social life until some post-capitalist time; the radical cultural movements of the late twentieth century saw things differently: creativity was an already-existing property of social groups. It existed in the here and now, in forms which academic and high art traditions had failed to recognise: it was ordinary, it was 'crucial to the sustenance of individual and group identities' (Willis *et al.*, 1990: 2) and – implicitly at least – at odds with dominant cultural values. 'What are works of art', wrote Raoul Vaneigem, 'beside the creative energy displayed by everyone a thousand times a day?' (Vaneigem, 1967/1983: 147). A number of currents of thought converged on such a position: ethnographic work, which enriched understandings of the values and meanings produced by subordinate social groups; artistic interest in the popular, whether in folk or modern forms; political commitments – including a commitment to construct the genealogy of cultural forms outside the mainstream culture. In this last respect, the work of Paul Gilroy is particularly significant, charting alternative histories in all their cultural and intellectual richness (Gilroy, 1993a, 2007), so that it is no longer possible to discuss the culture of British or American society without acknowledging the ways in which it has been shaped by subaltern cultures. It is from this viewpoint that in *Small Acts* (1993), Gilroy discusses black musical cultures, 'artistic forms' that have 'produced and sustained an interpretive community outside the orbit of formal politics in a long sequence of struggle that has been [both] cultural and political'. In its rebel creativity, this community, with its 'powerful sense of locality and rootedness in tradition' has decisively shaped urban cultures, so that 'the white working class has danced for forty years to its syncopated rhythms' (Gilroy, 1993b: 34–5). In this sense of the constructive social power of creative practice, writers like Gilroy surpass the limits imagined by Marcuse.

Creative capitalism/anti-capitalism

Much thinking about art, and creativity more generally, thus took its bearings, post-1968, from a generic anti-capitalism; in doing so, it was accentuating positions inherent in post-Enlightenment thinking. The influence these viewpoints exert on interpretations of 'creativity' remains strong. But they are not the only points of reference. There is a second branch of thinking about modernity, self-development and the realisation of creative potential that is intertwined with but different from the Schillerian tradition, and claims a common lineage with some aspects of Marxism. It locates a major source of creativity in economic production and enterprise. Even before the industrial take-off of the eighteenth century, it was customary to praise the spirit and inventiveness of artisanal production – de Certeau quotes the early *philosophe* Fontenelle to this effect (1980: 26). Later, Adam Smith saw 'improvements in machinery' as products of the 'ingenuity' of 'philosophers or men of speculation', who are 'often capable of combining together the powers of the most distant and dissimilar objects' (1776/1904: 9). As Berman shows, this poeticising of enterprise and invention was taken to promethean heights by Marx and Engels, for whom the creative powers of the capitalist class had expanded the capabilities of humanity, and demonstrated its world-changing potential:

> It has been the first to show what man's activity can bring about. It has accomplished wonders far surpassing Egyptian pyramids, Roman aqueducts, and Gothic cathedrals; it has conducted expeditions that put in the shade all former Exoduses of nations and crusades.
>
> *(Marx and Engels, 1848/1968: 38)*

Of course, among Marxists, this celebration was combined with other, quite different emphases. Marx insisted that the achievements of the bourgeoisie rested upon an unequal transaction, in which the worker surrendered the 'creative power' of his labouring capacity in return for the 'mess of pottage' represented by the weekly wage (1858/1973: 307). William Morris evoked the damage that capitalism inflicted on creativity: over-production led to crises in which the creative fire was burned out: 'the thing is overdone, and the market is glutted, and all that fury of manufacture has to sink into cold ashes': 'labour ... skill ... cunning ... life' are all laid waste (1888/1962: 163). This way of interpreting industrial capitalism extended beyond Marxism, to a much wider cultural formation – one whose English branch was delineated by Raymond Williams in *Culture and Society* (1958).

In these accounts, the promise of creativity is brief; it soon collapses in on itself. Other paradigms of business creativity, however, drew away attention away from the wastelands of industrialism in order to celebrate the energies of the business class. Particularly important here were the figures of the entrepreneur and the manager. In the mid-twentieth century, Joseph Schumpeter saw the 'entrepreneurial type' as an agent of 'creative destruction', who 'acted beyond the range of familiar beacons', to 'reform or revolutionise the pattern of production' (1942/1975: 132); management theorists from Drucker onwards have contrasted the creativity of innovative management with the routinism to which firms tend, after a period, to succumb (Drucker, 1970). With the rise of neo-liberalism and the eclipse of systematic opposition to the capitalist order, this discourse has become more powerful (Frank, 2001). The entrepreneur, the venture-capitalist and the risk-taking manager have become embodiments of creativity; their 'experiments' are viewed as 'adventures' in which they participate with a 'heightened consciousness and passion' (Gilder, 1993: 35). Beyond these typologies of individualism, the capitalist collective – the firm – is presented as the locus of creativity. In a business world characterised by its unpredictability, the practices and discourses of business have changed; survival depends upon rapid adaptation; multi-skilling and flexibility are at a premium (Thrift, 1999). In these circumstances, according to Boltanski and Chiapello, economic discourse makes an audacious raid upon what they call the 'artistic critique' of capitalism, seizing its key themes and claiming them as its own. The rhetoric of 1968 is re-presented, to describe the working principles of the late twentieth century enterprise: 'autonomy, spontaneity ... conviviality, openness to others ... creativity, visionary intuition, sensitivity to difference' are claimed to capture the working practices of the knowledge economy (Boltanski and Chiapello, 2005: 97). From this point of view, creativity, whatever its antecedents, now lives under the sign of capital, and this is a norm that applies as much to commercialised sub-cultures (Willis *et al.*, 1990) as it does to the workplace.

For some, this is a sign that the artistic critique has been recuperated, chained to neo-liberalism's triumphal chariot, alongside all its other defeated prisoners (trade unionism, social democratic parties and so on). For others, the interchange is more complex. In Italy, a tradition of autonomist social thought diverges from Boltanski and Chiapello, to emphasise less the hegemonic power of capitalism than the mass creativity of the working population, paid and unpaid. Writers like Paolo Virno (1996) and Hardt and Negri (2001) seek to resume a line of thinking established in the *Grundrisse*: creativity is not simply a differential trait of the human species. In a knowledge society characterised by the ubiquitous presence of immaterial labour, it is a resource integral to economic life; it is the raw material of capitalist organisation, that sustains capital, and is exploited by it. Moreover, though capitalist social relations have expanded to the point where all kinds of labour, including creative labour, are subsumed within their ambit, the mass, creative population has the capacity to transform the social relations of production that presently constrain it, in order that production, in its broadest sense, is organised so as to serve creativity, and not the other way around.

Creativity and learning

How does thinking about creativity and learning map on to these more general patterns of argument? In one sense, there is a clear connection between the artistic critique of capitalism (and of modernity more generally) and major strands of educational thinking about creativity. The progressive, or child-centred, tradition revolves around the idea that there is a tension between the possibilities of self-development and the constraining forces of the social; it thus performs in its own field the same scission between the expressive/aesthetic domain and the contexts of 'practical life' that was enacted by Kant and Schiller. Froebel's *Autobiography* is an early, classic rendering of this disjuncture, in which the educator's 'outward life and profession', first as a soldier in the war against Napoleon, then as assistant in the mineralogical museum in Berlin, is radically separate from the creative life within. In a moment of epiphany, 'one lovely bright spring morning' where 'the Main unites herself with the Rhine', Froebel realises that education is the means of freeing life from contradiction, and of 'restoring man to himself' (1889: 104–5). Herbert Read, one hundred years later, founds his argument on a similar counterposition: 'we are all born artists … and become insensitive citizens in bourgeois society' (1945: 8). Education, working against the grain of insensitivity, can perhaps – Read is very doubtful – return the individual to his childhood condition, so as to 'preserve within us some trace of the penetration and the delight of the innocent eye'; in the 'child's creative activities' could be fused 'the sensibility and the intellect' (Read, 1945: 111; 1943: 187).

Froebel and Read can stand for the different ends of a line of thought in which creativity is attached to conditions understood as virtually pre-social – nature in Froebel's case, childhood in Read's. In other intellectual traditions concerned with education, the relationship between creativity and the social is more positively presented. The significant link here – established in the work of Humboldt and continued in the twentieth century by Vygotsky and Cassirer – is between the ideal of self-development and the human capacity for symbolisation (Hardcastle, 2007). For this tradition, any human development beyond the stage of elementary mental functioning is dependent on sign-making; it occurs through the individual's interiorisation of social signs. This process is a species characteristic, of which creativity forms an integral part, present 'whenever a person imagines, combines, alters, and creates something new' (Vygotsky, 1930/2004: 10). In other words, creativity is present whenever symbolisation occurs, and Marx's stress on human creative powers is given a linguistic inflection. Specific individual actions coalesce into a general, collective creativity, which is a defining and sustaining property of humanity:

> When we consider the phenomenon of collective creativity, which combines all these drops of individual creativity that frequently are insignificant in themselves, we readily understand what an enormous percentage of what has been created by humanity is a product of the anonymous collective creative work of unknown inventors. The overwhelming majority of inventions were produced by unknown individuals … A scientific understanding of this phenomenon thus compels us to consider creativity as the rule rather than the exception. Of course, the highest expressions of creativity remain accessible only to a select few human geniuses; however, in the everyday life that surrounds us, creativity is an essential condition for existence and all that goes beyond the rut of routine and involves innovation, albeit only a tiny amount, owes its existence to the human creative process.
>
> *(Vygotsky, 1930/2004: 10–11)*

Symbolisation, like Schiller's 'art', is thus a term that embraces both the self-conscious creation of works of art, and everyday, spontaneous forms of meaning-making (see Kerlan, Chapter 13). Through symbolisation, humans make new meanings and in the process develop both themselves and 'the commonality of meanings on which collective life depends' (Hardcastle, 2007: 467). This creative faculty, essential to cognitive development and social life, originates in early childhood. Knowledge begins in childhood play, embedded in playful encounter with the world that is immediately at hand. Sensory experience provides a concrete support for conceptualisation and symbolisation (Vygotsky, 1931/1994). In one happy formulation, 'the very idea of grasping reality has its beginnings in the infant's outstretched hand' (Gooding, 2009). Much of the learning theory developed in the late twentieth century was an elaboration of this insight. Play is understood as an 'essential element of the human being', through which children 'confront reality and escape from a reality that is often too oppressive' (Rinaldi, 2001: 117–18)

Yet from another point of view, work in the Vygotskian tradition explores those social conditions that enable humans to move beyond their childhood state – 'development' has this strong meaning, and creativity is less the recovery of a childhood condition or a natural state than a capability sustained, as Rinaldi's account of practice in early years settings in Reggio Emilia puts it, 'relationally' through a mutual process of listening and communication between teacher and learner (ibid.).

For this tradition, then, creativity is both a universal capacity and one which is socially developed. But this does not mean that it flourishes in all conditions: the distance between creativity and economic life that we have seen registered in the critique of capitalism made by Marx and others was replicated in Vygotsky's work on education. 'Questions of education', he wrote in 1921, 'will be fully solved only when questions of social order have been fully solved' (1921/1997: 236); between the work of education and the promise of a fuller realisation of human capacity fell the shadows of social underdevelopment. It could be argued that for the past hundred years creative educators have lived among these shadows. The American progressive John Dewey, though writing in a different theoretical idiom, arrived at a similar conclusion. Dewey distinguished between 'aesthetic' and 'artistic' domains. The former consisted of the 'inner play of sentiments and fancies', in which 'feelings and ideas were turned in on themselves', morbid and 'effeminate' symptoms of a social order in which work occupied the time but not the intellectual energies of those involved in it. The latter was a 'mode of action' that modified experience and brought about 'changes in the world … specific transformations of things, making them more significant for mind'. Artistic activity was thus an instance of a more general human quality, the capacity to respond imaginatively to problems, in a way that reconstructed initial experience and satisfied complex human needs. Despite exclusion from a workplace dominated by immediately instrumental concerns, the artistic capability, offering a training in dealing with 'things and facts in active occupations having a purpose (in play or work)', could allow a path to be steered between 'an academic and aloof knowledge' and a 'hard, narrow and merely "practical" practice' (Dewey, 1916/1947: 205). Albeit in a less transcendental mode than Schiller, Dewey thus arrived at comparable conclusions. Art, or at least an educational practice informed by artistic principles, could repair civilisation's self-inflicted damage, and 'aid individuals to share in the arts of living' (Dewey, 1934: 336).

Creativity and education

Dewey's philosophy had no space for Schiller-like paradoxes about the essential impracticality of this essential domain, and his view of education's function was that it should be more 'constructive' than 'critical' (Donald, 1992: 141). Not one to shirk the strategic implications of his analyses, he asked continually how feasible was the project of an educational practice that could incorporate these insights. The answers he gave were various. In *Democracy and Education* (1916), Dewey was cautiously optimistic. The school could not 'immediately escape from the ideals set by prior social conditions' but it could 'contribute through the type of intellectual and emotional disposition which it forms to the improvement of those conditions'. At other times, he took a bleaker view: the 'great part played by personal competition and the desire for private profit' made it unlikely that 'the ideals of educational reformers [could] be carried into operation' (Dewey, 1929/1964: 88).

This sense of an antagonism between the artistic and the social was one of Dewey's legacies. In 2002, giving the John Dewey lecture at Stanford, Elliot Eisner charted the rise of a 'technised, cognitive culture', and took his distance from 'the array of values and assumptions' that attended its most recent incarnation in the school effectiveness movement. In attempting to construct a 'more generous conception of the practice of schooling', the principle that it ought to be conceived as 'the preparation of artists' and the development of 'artistically rooted qualitative forms of intelligence' was vital for American education, something that was needed 'now more than ever' to 'frame imaginative solutions to the problems we face' (Eisner, 2002). On this basis a 'culture of schooling' could be created 'in which more importance is placed on exploration than on discovery, more value is assigned to surprise than to control, more attention is devoted to what is distinctive than to what is standard, more interest is related to what is metaphorical than to what is literal'. In such a culture there would be 'a greater focus on becoming than on being, more value [placed] on the imaginative than on the factual'. In all of this, Eisner is eloquently representative of an enduring educational spirit, that includes others such as Maxine Greene (1995) – but eloquence cannot help him, or those who share his aspirations, navigate the strategic difficulties of the creative project: it seems to require change on a vast scale, but the means of attaining such change are scant; Eisner's rhetoric becomes profusely metaphorical, registering the gulf between earthly conditions – treacherous seas, unfriendly winds – and the heavenly possibilities held out by 'stars worth stretching for', and the strain in the language suggests much about the historic problems of creativity as a discourse.

Other kinds of educational response to the tensions between creativity and the social order are less strategic than pedagogic. This is not to say that in the pedagogic mode the tensions are treated as any less significant, rather that they are worked through in an immediate context of practice, where the momentariness and fragility, as well as the promise, of creative education are equally apparent. This is a mode of exploration that is scarcely recognised as such, though it is one of the main forms in which the problems that attend creativity have been registered (e.g. Ashton-Warner, 1963/1986), and shapes such major work as Steedman's *The Tidy House* (1982). Steedman writes about a short period of 'extraordinary creativity' in the lives of three eight-year-old working-class girls in an English primary school, as they write a story together about 'romantic love, marriage and sexual relations, the desire of mothers for children and their resentment of them, and the means by which those children are brought up in a social world' (1982: 1). The text and contexts of the story are Steedman's subject matter, and are intricately treated, in ways that parallel other accounts of the hard-won insights of unrecognised creativities, such as Rancière's *Nights of Labor* (1981/1989). Not the least illuminating insight is that the creativity of the girls is an anomalous moment in a process of 'quiet, genteel and sentimental oppression' inflicted via the school (Steedman, 1982: 3). Steedman's conclusion, that the girls' story is a small piece of evidence of how 'people can, without the benefit of theory or the expectations of others, critically confront the way things are, and dimly imagine, out of those very circumstances, how things might be', (1982: 157) takes on all the more force in the context of this judgement about institutional effects, and continues to pose issues of compelling interest for the creative project in education.

These are some of the educational legacies of the artistic critique of capitalism. What of the effects on educational discourse of the second intellectual lineage reviewed earlier, that located a major source of creativity in economic production and enterprise? Educationalists have tended to be ambivalent about such a claim. Dewey may have assumed that 'occupational roles in capitalist society are best filled by individuals who have achieved the highest possible levels of personal development', and implied thus a positive evaluation of the economic order (Bowles and Gintis, 1976: 22); but at the same time, and with greater emphasis, he was prone to criticise the 'soul-less monotony of machine industry' (Dewey, 1916/2008: 140). In the post-Dewey period, however, with the development of a knowledge economy, a space has opened for a discourse in which the compatibility of 'creativity' with economic life becomes a given, and creativity in the process changes its meanings. This reconfiguration has had powerful educational effects.

The distinctive rhetorical move of new discourses of creativity is to invert the terms of the education–economy relationship. The radical moment of 1968 had counterposed the '*cadences infernales*' of the massified workplace to the liberated spaces of an education-based insurgency. Thirty years later, creativist reformers represented things differently. Seltzer and Bentley argued that whereas the 'underlying economic structures of society were undergoing a dramatic transformation' – the Fordist factory had gone – 'educational structures' were 'lagging behind' the pace of change. They taught skills and knowledge appropriate only to an earlier time (1999: vii). The economy, like personal well being, depended on a new education system capable of unlocking creative abilities, defined as 'the application of knowledge and skills in new ways to achieve a valued goal' (ibid.: viii); a shift in the direction of this principle required that the school learned from the workplace, with a consequent re-inflection of 'creativity'. Severed from notions of critique and autonomous self-development, creativity was understood as a mode of being, a set of dispositions involving qualities such as initiative, innovativeness, commitment, patience and concentration, whose stimulus and justification lay primarily in economic life. *All Our Futures*, the report written for the Departments of Culture and of Education in England in 1999, accentuated the point (NACCCE, 1999). It was not that creativity was defined exclusively in economic terms, nor that arts-based forms of creativity were set aside – that was far from the case. It was rather that the pattern of discursive association developed in policy texts like this was such as to suggest that creativity would find its most productive spaces in a new relationship to the business world, while other kinds of connection, of the sort elaborated in much of the work discussed above, became weaker.

There can be no doubt, then, about which accentuations of 'creativity' presently structure education debate and policy-making. Prominent for two centuries, conceptions of creativity that rest on some concept of social antagonism and critique have been quite rapidly marginalised and recuperated by other understandings, in a process that has been one of neo-liberalism's most interesting achievements. The duration and degree of totality of this eclipse are uncertain, however. The period of austerity promised by governments in the wake of the financial crisis of 2008 is likely to widen rather than stitch together discourses of economy and creativity, and it is doubtful that the range of aspirations and needs which post-Schillerian notions of creativity have elaborated can for long be bypassed by a discourse in which immediate economic justifications are paramount. In education, as more generally, the territory of creativity will remain contested ground.

Notes

1 Dérive: 'a technique of rapid passage through varied ambiences'. See Debord (1958b/2006).
2 Horn writes that 'The chronicler of the Situationist spirit, Laurent Chollet, claims that the majority of the imaginative graffiti gracing the walls of the Sorbonne, the Odéon National Theatre and other high temples of the student revolt – for example 'All Power to the Imagination' and 'Under the Cobblestones lies the Beach' – were the product of a little known Situationist activist by the name of Christian Sébastiani. ... This assertion should best be interpreted as ... another example of characteristic Situationist hyperbole' (2007, 15).

References

Ashton-Warner, S. (1963/1986) *Teacher*, London: Touchstone Books.
Barsky, R. (1998) *Noam Chomsky: A Life of Dissent*, Cambridge, MA: MIT Press.
Berman, M. (1981) *All that Is Solid Melts into Air*, London: New Left Books.
Boltanski, L. and Chiapello, E. (2005) *The New Spirit of Capitalism* (trans. G. Elliott), London: Verso.
Bowles, S. and Gintis, H. (1976) *Schooling in Capitalist America*, London: Routledge and Kegan Paul.

Burger, P. (1984) *Theory of the Avant-Garde* (trans. M. Shaw), Manchester: Manchester University Press.

—— (1992) On the problem of the autonomy of art in bourgeois society, in F. Frascina and J. Harris (eds) *Art in Modern Culture: An Anthology of Critical Texts*, London: Phaidon Press in association with the Open University.

Certeau, M. de (1980) On the oppositional practices of everyday life, *Social Text* 3 (Fall): 3–43.

Chomsky, N. (1969) Interview: linguistics and politics, *New Left Review* I(57): 21–34.

—— (1992) Speech at Conference on 'Creation and Culture', Barcelona.

Cunningham, A., Eagleton, T., Wicker, B., Redfern, M. and Bright, L. (1966) *Slant Manifesto: Catholics and the Left*, London: Sheed & Ward.

Debord, G. (1957/2006) *Report on the Construction of Situations and on the International Situationist Tendency's Conditions of Organization and Action* (trans. K. Knabb), published online by Bureau of Public Secrets, www.bopsecrets.org (accessed 3 August 2010).

—— (1958a/2006) *Theses on Cultural Revolution* (trans. K. Knabb), published online by Bureau of Public Secrets, www.bopsecrets.org (accessed 3 August 2010).

—— (1958b/2006) *Theory of the Derive* (trans. K. Knabb), published online by Bureau of Public Secrets, www.bopsecrets.org (accessed 3 August 2010).

Dewey, J. (1916/1947) *Democracy in Education*, Section 10: Interest and Discipline, available at http://en.wikisource.org/wiki/Democracy_and_Education/Section_10 (accessed 3 August 2010).

—— (1916/2008) The need for an industrial education in an industrial democracy, in J. A. Boydston (ed.) *John Dewey: The Middle Works 1899–1924*, vol. 10: *1916–17*, Carbondale: Southern Illinois University Press.

—— (1929/1964) *John Dewey's Impressions of Soviet Russia and the Revolutionary World: Mexico–China–Turkey*, New York: Columbia University Press.

—— (1934) *Art as Experience*, New York: Minton, Balch & Co.

Donald, J. (1992) *Sentimental Education*, London: Verso.

Drucker, P. (1970) *The Age of Discontinuity: Guidelines to Our Changing Society*, New York: Harper and Row.

Eagleton, T. (1990) *The Ideology of the Aesthetic*, Oxford: Blackwell.

Eisner, E. W. (2002) *What Can Education Learn from the Arts about the Practice of Education*, John Dewey Lecture, Stanford University, *The Encyclopedia of Informal Education*; available at http://www.infed.org/biblio/eisner_arts_and_the_practice_of_education.htm (accessed 3 August 2010).

Froebel, F. (1889) Letter to Krause, 24th March 1828 (trans. E. Michaelis and H. Moore), reprinted in *Autobiography of Friedrich Froebel*, Syracuse, NY: Bardeen; available at www.gutenborg.org (accessed 3 August 2010).

Frank, J. (2001) *One Market under God*, London: Secker & Warburg.

Gilder, G. (1993) *Wealth and Poverty*, San Francisco: ICS Press.

Gilroy, P. (1993a) *The Black Atlantic: Modernity and Double Consciousness*, Cambridge, MA: Harvard University Press.

—— (1993b) *Small Acts: Thoughts on the Politics of Black Cultures*, London: Serpent's Tail.

—— (2007) *Black Britain: A Photographic History*, London: Saqi.

Gooding, M. (2009) *Let's Play*, in J. Rothenstein (ed.) *A Russian Diary: Russian Children's Books 1920–1935*, London: Redstone Press.

Greene, M. (1995) *Releasing the Imagination: Essay; on Education, the Arts, and Social Change*, San Francisco: Jossey-Bass Publishers.

Hardcastle, J. (2007) Explaining the actions of men and gods: elements of English pedagogy, *Pedagogy* 7(3): 453–80.

Hardt, M. and Negri, T. (2001) *Empire*, Cambridge, MA: Harvard University Press.

Horn, G.-R. (2007) *The Spirit of '68: Rebellion in Western Europe and North America 1956–76*, Oxford: Oxford University Press.

Humboldt, W. von (1963) *Humanist without Portfolio: An Anthology of the Writings of Wilhelm von Humboldt* (trans. M. Cowan), Detroit, MI: Wayne University Press.

Kant, I. (1790/2008) *Critique of Judgement* (ed. N. Walker, trans. J. Meredith), Oxford: Oxford University Press.

Lettrist International (1955) Proposals for rationally improving the city of Paris' (trans. K. Knabb), published online by Bureau of Public Secrets, www.bopsecrets.org (accessed 3 August 2010).

Lukacs, G. (1968) *Goethe and His Age* (trans. R. Anchor), London: Merlin.

Marcuse, H. (1972) Art as form of reality, *New Left Review* I(74): 51–8.

Marx, K. (1858/1973) *Grundrisse: Foundations of the Critique of Political Economy* (ed. and trans. M. Nicolaus), Harmondsworth: Penguin.

Marx, K. and Engels, F. (1848/1968) *Manifesto of the Communist Party*, Selected Works, Moscow: Foreign Publishing House.

Morris, W. (1962) How we live and how we might live, *Selected Writings and Designs* (ed. A. Briggs), Harmondsworth: Penguin.

National Advisory Committee on Creative and Cultural Education (NACCCE) (1999) *All Our Futures*, London DCMS/DfES.

Rancière, J. (1981/1989) *The Nights of Labor: The Workers' Dream in Nineteenth-century France* (trans. J. Drury), Philadelphia, PN: Temple University Press.

Read, H. (1943) *Education through Art*, London: Faber.

—— (1945) *Art and Society*, London: Faber.

Rinaldi, C. (2001) *In Dialogue with Reggio Emilia: Listening, Researching and Learning*, London: Routledge.

Schiller, F. (1794/1954) *On the Aesthetic Education of Man in a Series of Letters* (ed. and trans. R. Snell), Yale, CT: Yale University Press.

Schumpeter, J. (1942/1975) *Capitalism, Socialism and Democracy*, New York: Harper Books.

Seltzer, K. and Bentley, T. (1999) *The Creative Age: Knowledge and Skills for the New Economy*, London: Demos.

Situationist International (1958/2006) *Preliminary Problems in Constructing a Situation* (trans. K. Knabb), published online by Bureau of Public Secrets, www.bopsecrets.org (accessed 3 August 2010).

Smith, A. (1776/1904) *An Inquiry into the Nature and Causes of the Wealth of Nations*, vol. I (ed. Edwin Cannan, 1904, 5th ed.), London: Methuen and Co., Ltd.

Steedman, C. (1982) *The Tidy House*, London: Virago.

Thrift, N. (1999) Capitalism's cultural turn, in L. Ray and A. Sayer (eds) *Culture and Economy after the Cultural Turn*, London: Sage.

Vaneigem, R. (1967/1983) *The Revolution of Everyday Life* (trans. D. Nicholson-Smith), London: Left Bank Books and Rebel Press.

Virno, P. (1996) Do you remember counter-revolution?, in M. Hardt and P. Virno (eds) *Radical Political Thought in Italy: A Potential Politics*, Minneapolis: University of Minnesota Press.

Vygotsky, L. S. (1921/1997) *Educational Psychology* (trans. R. Silverman), Boca Raton, FL: St Lucie Press.

—— (1930/1967) Imagination and creativity in childhood (trans. M. E. Sharpe), *Journal of Russian and East European Psychology* 42(1): 7–97.

—— (1931/1994) Imagination and creativity of the adolescent, in R. van der Veer and J. Valsiner (eds) *The Vygotsky Reader*, Oxford: Blackwell.

Voloshinov, V. N. (1986) *Marxism and the Philosophy of Language* (trans. L. Matejka and I. R. Titunik), Cambridge, MA: Harvard University Press.

Williams, R. (1958) *Culture and Society 1780–1950*, London: Chatto & Windus.

Willis, P., Jones, S., Canaan, J. and Hurd, G. (1990) *Common Culture*, Buckingham: Open University Press.

3

The 'transformative power' of the arts

History of an idea

Eleonora Belfiore

An official 'rhetoric of positive transformation' seems to dominate contemporary debates around the effects of artistic engagement and creative activities in the cultural policy and educational fields. In the West, over the past thirty years, this rhetoric has been explicitly called upon to underpin and justify several policy initiatives aiming at tackling social exclusion, criminal offending, educational underachievement and health-related problems through the encouragement of artistic participation (whether as audiences or creators) among targeted groups. For example, in 2003 (at the zeitgeist moment of the rhetoric of personal and social transformation through the arts in Britain), the Arts Council England's (ACE) manifesto *Ambitions for the Arts 2003–2006* explicitly put the 'transformative powers' of the arts at the heart of both its 'vision' and advocacy agenda:

> We will argue that being involved with the arts can have a lasting and transforming effect on many aspects of people's lives. This is true not just for individuals, but also for neighbourhoods, communities, regions and entire generations, whose sense of identity and purpose can be changed through art.
>
> *(ACE, 2003: 3)*

In his New Statesman Arts Lecture, delivered in July 2006, ACE's then Chief Executive Peter Hewitt (2006: 3) claimed: 'The arts need to be recognised both for the inherent personal value they deliver for citizens and for their contribution to other public agendas, such as education, health, home affairs, foreign policy and the economy'. Despite the acknowledged lack of evidence that the arts and creativity can achieve any of these aims,[1] and the concerns over the perceived excessive 'instrumentalisation' of the arts and culture that have been voiced by many cultural professionals, media pundits and researchers, equally grandiose claims have been consistently and persistently made by the Department of Culture, Media and Sport – the government department with responsibilities for the cultural sector.

Similar assumptions and beliefs in the potential of engagement with the arts to bring about deep personal change underpin the ideology of 'creative learning', and animate the professionals who are charged with delivering that creative learning. Large scale arts-in-education programmes, such as 'Creative Partnerships' in Britain, define their aim as 'raising aspirations and achievement through the transformative power of creative learning partnerships'.[2] Indeed, in their Eleventh Report on Education and Skills, prepared in 2007, the relevant Select Committee in the British Parliament acknowledged having received 'a vast amount of anecdotal evidence from teachers, heads and creative practitioners on the effects of being involved in creative partnerships projects, and it is clear that many feel strongly about the potential transformative power of a creative approach to teaching and learning'. Yet, the report also acknowledges that research conducted into the educational impact of the programme does not fully support the broad range of claims for profound impact made by those involved in designing and delivering 'creative learning' initiatives.[3]

An 'argumentation model' of policy-making and the importance of ideas

The resilience of the faith in the positive transformative powers of the arts in the face of the lack of evidence points us towards the fact that official statements regarding the place of evidence in the policy formation process need to be taken with a pinch of salt. In reality, the primary driver behind the policy-making process is not always the available evidence, but rather *values* and *beliefs* (not always explicitly acknowledged) about what is valuable and the reasons why. So, the continued emphasis on the powers of the arts to change lives, regenerate localities and communities and promote creative learning is based on very longstanding beliefs about what the arts can do to both individuals and society as a whole rather than on actual evidence of impact (Belfiore, 2009).

The key ideas around the 'transformative powers' of the arts have been in circulation among Western intellectuals, politicians and artists for as long Western civilisation itself has existed. These ideas have consistently fed into thinking on the role of the arts in society and how politicians can best harness their powers for the good of the polity (or, as the case might be, themselves) from the times of Plato in the fifth century BC. Looking at this longstanding tradition of thinking and writing on the effects of creative endeavours on both creators and audiences might throw light on contemporary policy developments and bring to light the powerful beliefs in the powers of the arts to affect people deeply (whether for the better or the worse), to shape behaviour and even change the world that underscore the workings of Western cultural institutions, the educational system and the mechanisms for public support of the creative arts.

As Banaji and Burn (with Buckingham, 2006: 5) point out, a 'rhetoric' is a discursive form which is constructed so as to generate consensus and even affect specific concrete policy measures; rhetoric is also key in the production of 'discursive frameworks' which provide the terms and the concepts in which issues come to be discussed in the public domain. Given the discursive nature of the policy-making process, rhetoric has the power to shape public opinion, political debates and ultimately the policy process itself. In order to understand the current state of contemporary cultural and educational policies, and the centrality of the imagery of transformation through artistic engagement in the policy rhetoric in this area, we need to identify what ideas about the arts and their effect on people have become dominant in policy discourse and why.

To this end, it might be helpful to refer to an 'argumentation model' of the policy process, which puts the stress on the element of public deliberation and argumentation that characterises the political process in a democracy. Giandomenico Majone (1989: 1), one of the most prominent proponents of this understanding of the policy process, explains that, '[w]hether in written or oral form, argument is central in all stages of the policy process'. The logical consequence of this mode of looking at the political process is that 'facts and values are so intertwined in policy-making that factual arguments unaided by persuasion seldom play a significant role in public debate' (ibid.: 8).

As Greenhalgh and Russell (2006: 36) point out, '[p]olicy making is not a series of decision nodes into which evidence, however robust, can be 'fed', but the messy unfolding of collective action, achieved mostly through dialogue, argument, influence and conflict and retrospectively made sense of through the telling of stories'. In this perspective, looking more closely at the origins of the prevalent ideas about the arts within the Western intellectual tradition which have fed into official policy discourses can be a useful exercise: identifying the themes that seem to predominate and those which appear neglected or silenced can tell us a lot about the priorities and central agendas of the government in power.

Negative vs positive transformation: a fundamental ambivalence in Western thought

Looking historically at the question of what artistic experiences might 'do' to people, we can identify, within Western culture, three main strands of thought about the 'impacts' of the arts (using the term loosely): a positive tradition, a negative one, and a more recent intellectual tradition centred around the rejection of the very notion that the effects that the arts may or may not have on individuals' ethics, knowledge and behaviour should represent a legitimate grounds for the assessment of the arts' worth or place in society.

As we have seen, ideas derived from what we have referred to as the 'positive tradition', and the perception of the beneficial transformation that the arts can supposedly bring about, account for most of the arguments officially endorsed in public debates around the funding and promotion of the arts and the need to encourage young people's engagement in creative and artistic pursuits. Yet, historically, views of the effects and nature of the arts and creativity have actually been significantly more conflicting. Already in fifth century BC Athens, Plato's dialogues (which represent the first instances of recorded aesthetic thought in the West) showed a definite ambivalence towards the arts and their potential effects. As a matter of fact, both the 'positive' and the 'negative' traditions can be seen to originate in his thought (Belfiore, 2006b).

In his *Republic*, Plato presented one of the most forceful and influential condemnations of the arts in Western civilisation. His argument was that the mimetic arts[4] constitute a corrupting influence because of the hold they have on the emotional, irrational – and therefore especially susceptible – part of the soul over the more rational and, therefore, sensible part. Nevertheless, and precisely because they can affect people and behaviour so powerfully, Plato also thought that, when properly censored and selected on the basis of their edifying content, those very mimetic arts can also have a profound educational effect. By provoking correct and morally desirable emotional reactions, then, the arts (when properly administered) might prove a very useful tool for the Philosopher Kings in the education of the citizenry and the promotion of the values and forms of behaviour which are conducive to the good polity.

Plato's writings are peppered with what are, ostensibly, similarly ambivalent comments about the nature of creativity and artistic inspiration, so that modern critics are divided between those who argue that Plato, in line with his condemnation of the moral and cognitive fallacies of poetry in the *Republic*, saw artistic inspiration as a form of insanity and those who (basing their conclusion on the *Ion* especially) maintain that Plato saw the poet as a divinely inspired creator of beauty, whose insight is only slightly inferior to that of the philosopher (Partee, 1971).

Plato's opinion on the power of the arts to provide knowledge and insight was also mixed. On the one hand, the *Republic* denies a cognitive function for the arts on the grounds that they are merely an imperfect copy of the world, which is itself a copy of the 'forms' or 'ideas', the only true reality. As such, artistic representations are twice removed from reality and, consequently, can hardly be relied upon for the transmission of true knowledge. Yet, whilst not 'true' *per se*, artistic representations have a hold on people and, therefore, can lend themselves to being skillfully manipulated by the ruling philosophers so as to play an important educational role in the ideal state (Belfiore, 2006b).

Plato's influential elaborations on the nature and the psychological and cognitive effects of the arts effectively present us, *in nuce*, with the main arguments that eventually developed into both the positive and negative traditions. There is no space here to describe the evolution over time of these two fundamental understandings of how the arts may affect those who enjoy them, so what follows will only attempt to identify crucial nodal points in the intellectual history of these ideas about the transformative powers of the arts.[5]

On the 'negative' front, Platonic concerns over the powers of the arts to corrupt and instigate socially and morally undesirable behaviours were later shared by the Fathers of the Church – the group of Christian philosophers who, between the first and sixth century AD developed the fundamental tenets of Christian theology and philosophy. The most prominent representative of this group of thinkers is arguably St Augustine (fourth century), who raised concerns about the desensitising and distancing effect of theatre on its audience, who – especially where tragic theatre was concerned – are encouraged to enjoy witnessing pain, humiliation and suffering on stage, a pastime that he saw as hardly compatible with the Christian virtue of compassion.

The endorsement of Platonic negative perceptions of the impact of the arts by the ideologues of the Church was important, in that it guaranteed their survival and continued influence throughout the Middle Ages and early modernity. The example of the venomous moral polemic launched by the Elizabethan anti-theatrical pamphleteers is indeed representative of the ways in which Platonic themes survived and were adapted to fit the cultural battles of later times. Interestingly, those very same arguments against the theatre (which centred around the claim that theatre encouraged emulation of the actions portrayed on the scene, and therefore promoted lust, violence, immoral and unlawful behaviour) have survived in our contemporary times, and are behind the very modern preoccupation with what sociologists refer to as 'media effects' (Barker and Petley, 2001). The mass media, particularly television, and other forms of popular entertainment such as computer games, are often criticised for allegedly promoting dangerous copycat behaviour. Because of the perceived risk of 'social contagion', these cultural forms are seen as a negative influence from which the young and psychologically vulnerable ought to be protected. The existence of bodies dedicated to film and videogames classification throughout the West is the result of precisely such concerns over the possibility that some cultural experiences might prove harmful for younger audiences.

Another crucial moment in the historical evolution of the negative tradition is represented by Jean-Jacques Rousseau (1712–78), who ensured the survival of Platonic preoccupations into the modern, and increasingly secular, era. Rousseau indeed had studied Plato's dialogues in preparation for his essay *Lettre à M. d'Alembert sur les spectacles* (1758), which argued against the notion that the theatre can have a beneficial moralising (or a cognitive and educational) effect on its audience. Rousseau maintained that theatre is in fact mere entertainment, and potentially dangerous entertainment at that, since it is a waste of man's time, which ought to be devoted to the nobler pursuits of work and family.

Another aspect of Rousseau's position which echoes contemporary concerns was the conviction that theatre might have an undesirable 'distancing' effect, whereby audiences who could respond intensely and be deeply moved by the hero's vicissitudes on stage might well find themselves indifferent to the plight of real people in everyday life. Modern aesthetic theory refers to this phenomenon as 'psychic distance'. This is seen as problematic, in that it might well result in the kind of aesthetic contemplation which supplants direct political and moral action. In this perspective, then, rather than encouraging positive social and cultural transformation, the arts are seen as, in fact, potentially constraining change, by diverting attention and action away from reality and towards the world of the imagination.

If we move from the negative to the positive tradition, Plato, as we have seen, remains an important reference point for those theorists who posit that the arts and creative endeavours, when carefully overseen, can play a positive formative and educational role in the life of young and malleable minds. However, it is with Plato's most illustrious disciple, Aristotle (fourth century BC) that the idea that the mimetic arts can have beneficial impacts enters Western thought – deprived of the negative undertones and the ambivalence that it had in Plato's dialogues. In his *Poetics*, Aristotle argued that the experience of 'pity and fear' afforded by the theatre can have a cathartic effect on audiences. No further details or clarification are offered in what we have left of the *Poetics*, which has arrived to us most probably in an incomplete form. Scholars agree that Aristotle's intention was to offer a counterbalance to the Platonic indictment of mimetic art (and especially theatre) in the *Republic*, but no consensus exists on what Aristotle actually meant when he wrote of the 'cathartic' powers of theatre. It is therefore unsurprising that, over time, a number of different interpretations have emerged, which eventually developed into full blown theories about the beneficial transformative powers of the arts and make up what we have termed the 'positive tradition' of thinking and writing about the impacts of the arts.

The most influential interpretations of Aristotelian catharsis can be grouped into three main categories, depending on whether catharsis is seen mainly as an emotional, intellectual or ethical process. The psychological interpretation of catharsis as a process of emotional release sees the aesthetic experience as an effective 'purgation' of undesirable or noxious feelings. This view has a long and illustrious pedigree, and is at the root of the belief in the contribution that the arts may make to healing both the body and the mind. Contemporary arts in health policies and arts-based psychotherapies – such as, for instance the psychotherapeutic theatre movement championed by Jacob L. Moreno (1975) – represent the present-day developments of the fundamental Aristotelian notion that through an aesthetic experience people can be helped to deal with and free themselves from the grip of traumatic experiences and troubling emotions.

An alternative interpretation of the catharsis that can be achieved through aesthetic experiences sees it as a cognitive process. Here intellectual confusion is purged, to be replaced by insight, clearer understanding and deeper knowledge. This view of the formative and knowledge-building effects of the arts has enjoyed a remarkable longevity within Western culture and a number of personalities were pivotal in ensuring its survival and diffusion. One of these is the Latin poet Horace (65–68 BC), who was the first to explicitly state that the very best poet is the one who can, with his verses, both delight and improve. The notion of the arts as a 'useful delight' is indeed at the very heart of both the idea of the transformative powers of artistic endeavours and the perception of the arts as a force for the good, and therefore worthy of support and promotion. The argument that the 'usefulness' of the pleasure which artistic engagement provides has specifically to do with learning, cognitive development and the process of self-improvement was a point elaborated by the Italian humanists of the Renaissance and, later, by the German philosophers of *Bildung* in the eighteenth and nineteenth centuries. The latter, and particularly thinkers and poets such as Herder, Humboldt, Goethe and Schiller, played a crucial role in elaborating one of the most influential notions of education and the formative role of aesthetic experiences in the West. These still resonate in contemporary educational theories and scholastic curricula.

The third interpretation of aesthetic catharsis is indebted to this notion of the arts as a tool for self-development, but places the emphasis on the moral, rather than cognitive dimension of the process. I refer here to the strand of thinking that posits that the catharsis or 'purification' in question is of an ethical nature, so that the encounter with the arts has a humanising, moralising and ultimately civilising effect. The notions that familiarity with the arts makes us better people and that a society that promotes the arts and culture is, for that very reason, a higher form of civilisation are deeply embedded in Western culture. They are indeed one of the principal justifications for state involvement in cultural matters (Bennett, 1995). The key difference between notions of the arts as a vehicle for *Bildung* and the theories belonging to this last group is the shift in emphasis from the personal to the societal. The arts are conceived of as a means to educate and improve the whole of humankind. It is with the French thinkers of the eighteenth century that this change of perspective takes root. Diderot, Alembert, Voltaire and the other Enlightenment *philosophes* endeavoured to highlight the social value of the aesthetic sphere, and advocated the production of the type of art that could instil civic values, thus contributing to the progress of humankind. They promoted a new hierarchy of cultural production, in which artistic work that had moral and civic utility was considered superior to work that aimed merely to delight or help pass the time. This ethical regard for the role of the arts in society and the attribution of a crucial moral function of guidance to artists reached its apogee with the Romantic movement. Shelley's confident declaration that 'poets are the unacknowledged legislators of the world' and that 'poetry redeems from decay the visitations of the divinity in man' represent a compelling and illustrious example of this position, which through its later incarnations in personalities such as Matthew Arnold, F. R. Leavis, and more recently, Roger Scruton and Brian McMaster has had, and still has, great influence over British cultural policy-making.

Looking at the history of the belief in the powers of the arts to moralise and civilise is helpful as it reveals the less savoury and routinely ignored aspects of the 'impact rhetoric'. For instance, the civilising effects of the arts were consistently referred to in order to defend and justify the colonial enterprise in nineteenth century Imperial Europe. The myth of the civilised European regaling the savage colonies with the gift of culture was indeed a recurring image in the writings of this period. Rudyard Kipling's poem on the 'white man's burden' to bring civilisation to the 'half-devil and half-child' folk in the colonies is a case in point.

The two broad intellectual traditions that we have looked at so far both centre around the effects of the arts on audiences and their resulting function in society. Whether they are seen as a social and moral panacea or a source of corruption and distraction from worthier preoccupations, in both the positive and negative traditions, cultural value is attributed or denied on the basis of the arts' perceived impact. A third body of thinking developed in Europe around in the mid-eighteenth century, and denied absolutely the legitimacy of any link between the value of the arts and their supposed utility or perniciousness. This strand of thinking originally developed in response to the perceived subordination of aesthetic concerns to ethical, religious, political or social considerations in the discussion of the value and role of the arts in society; the incipient growth of the arts market and mass produced cultural products (and the contingent emphasis on their market value as opposed to a 'pure' aesthetic value); and to the rejection of the notion that any art that did not move to good and socially accepted behaviour ought to be condemned on moral grounds. Noël Carroll explains that, in this perspective, 'art and ethics are autonomous realms of value and, thus, criteria from the ethical realm should not be imported to evaluate the aesthetic realm' (in Belfiore and Bennett, 2008: 176). The writers in this tradition indeed suggested − as French novelist Gautier put it − that 'nothing is really beautiful unless it is useless' and that ethical considerations ought to be inherently extraneous to any aesthetic judgement: the value of art resides in the aesthetic sphere alone.

Interestingly, the origin of this strand of thought can be attributed to one of the great misunderstandings in history. The German idealist philosopher Kant was considered by his contemporaries as the originator of this theoretical position arguing for a complete autonomy of the aesthetic sphere from all others. In his *Critique of Judgement* (1790) Kant did write that art is 'purposiveness without a purpose' and that 'neither does perfection gain by beauty, nor beauty by perfection'. He was indeed attempting to move away from classical views of art as the handmaiden of theology, or – in increasingly more secular times – politics and social reform. However, Kant remained convinced of the deeply moral nature and function of art and art appreciation, and would probably have been puzzled by the way in which nuggets of his philosophical system travelled abroad and eventually developed into the much more radical positions of the Aesthetic movement of the late nineteenth/early twentieth century, epitomised by writers such as Oscar Wilde in England, Théophile Gautier in France and the pre-Raphaelite artists.

The rejection of the notion of public utility and the positive impacts of the arts as a proxy for their value has survived in contemporary cultural policy discourses, where this position is often referred to as advocating 'art for art's sake'. Declarations condemning the instrumental attitudes of politicians and policy-makers (who are felt to appreciate the arts purely for the contribution they can make to the political agendas of the day) abound in public debates around the arts and culture. They are often accompanied by a great deal of nostalgia for the allegedly less overtly instrumental policies of the past, even though there is in fact no evidence that 'art for art's sake' ever was a guiding rationale for cultural policies.

Conclusions

Arguably, the most striking and distinguishing feature of public debates around the public value of the arts and cultural policy in the West today is the growing difficulty in elaborating a convincing argument in support of state funding of the arts by politicians, arts administrators, artists and tax payers alike. The reasons behind the arts community's increasing struggle to 'make a case' for funding are hardly mysterious but, in fact, well documented. First, these difficulties arise from the supposed crisis of the welfare state, brought about by an alleged globalisation-induced 'retreat of the state'; second, they relate to the growing difficulties of convincingly explaining why certain forms of artistic expression should find institutional validation and support through public funding while others are left to fend for themselves in the free market.

The result of the postmodern onslaught on traditional cultural values and the institutions that represented them has inevitably complicated the formulation of any cultural policy, predicated as they always are on value judgements as the basis for funding allocation and decisions about what artistic practices to support. In this context, the cultural sector's response to the increasingly challenging cultural and political environment has been a strategy of 'policy attachment' (Gray, 2002). Here the arts, although a policy area commanding small budgets and little political clout, have progressively attached themselves to economic and social agendas, thus benefiting from the larger budgets and the greater political influence of those areas of public policy. At the root of the rhetorical prominence of the ideas about the effects of artistic engagement produced within what we have called the 'positive tradition' is therefore their consonance with the political priorities of the government of the time.

In Britain, the arts and creativity were made key elements in the delivery of New Labour's social policy agenda, and the arguments that have been referred to in order to build the case for the positive impacts of the arts were carefully chosen from an available pool of ideas so as to make the case more compelling. In this process, the ideas and interpretations elaborated within both the 'negative' and 'autonomy' traditions found themselves in a rhetorically weaker position. As a result, they have been relatively neglected and absent from public debates around the social impacts of the arts, which have been articulated as reliably positive, predictable and generalisable across a wide population. Whilst the power of the belief in the transformative powers of the arts has been especially significant in shaping cultural policies, as Sefton-Green (2008: 22) points out, 'the prospect of deep change' is also at the root of the more recent fascination with the notion of 'creative learning', which, he argues, 'taps into folk-theories around the idea of developing creative thinking'. Creative learning, indeed, 'embodies a series of values and deep beliefs about human nature and personal development, which although at odds with some social scientific models, again derive their legitimacy from their popularity and broad principles' (ibid.: 24). Therefore, a belief in the positive impacts of arts engagement represents another crucial 'frame' that contributes to the popularity of creative learning among both education professionals and policy-makers.

However, this chapter has attempted to show that the official rhetoric of cultural organisations, government and public discourses around education often tells a very partial story, and that discourses of the arts' impact and creative learning are in fact imbued with a number of value-laden beliefs about the arts' positive transformative powers, rather than emerging from any research-based evidence. As such, it is important that this transformational rhetoric should be subjected to close intellectual scrutiny, in order to reveal its underlying values, and the alternative views that are obscured in the processes of policy formation.

Notes

1 See Belfiore, 2006a; Selwood, 2002.
2 http://www.creative-partnerships.com/area-delivery-organisations/hull/creative-partnerships-hull-humber-north-yorkshire,18,ADO.html.
3 http://www.parliament.the-stationery-office.co.uk/pa/cm200607/cmselect/cmeduski/1034/103402.htm.
4 That is, those arts based on the imitation of reality.
5 The three intellectual traditions are discussed in much greater detail in Belfiore and Bennett (2008), on which this section of the chapter is based.

References

ACE (2003) *Ambitions for the Arts 2003–2006*, London: Arts Council England.
Banaji, S. and Burn, A. with Buckingham, D. (2006) *The Rhetorics of Creativity: A Review of the Literature*, London: Creative Partnerships, Arts Council England.
Barker, M. and Petley, J. (eds) (2001) *Ill Effects: The Media Violence Debate*, London: Routledge.
Belfiore, E. (2006a) The social impact of the arts: myth or reality?, in M. Mirza (ed.) *Culture Vultures: Is UK Arts Policy Damaging the Arts?* London: Policy Exchange.
—— (2006b) The unacknowledged legacy: Plato, the *Republic* and cultural policy, *International Journal of Cultural Policy: Special Issue – Intellectuals and Cultural Policy, Part 1*, 12(1): 229–44.
—— (2009) Bullshit in cultural policy practice and research: notes from the British case, *International Journal of Cultural Policy* 15(3): 343–59.
Belfiore, E. and Bennett, O. (2008) *The Social Impact of the Arts: An Intellectual History*, Basingstoke: Palgrave.
Bennett, O. (1995) Cultural policy in the United Kingdom: collapsing rationales and the end of a tradition, *International Journal of Cultural Policy* 1(2): 199–216.
Gray, C. (2002) Local government and the arts, *Local Government Studies* 28(1): 77–90.
Greenhalgh, T. and Russell, J. (2006) Reframing evidence synthesis as rhetorical action in the policy making drama, *Healthcare Policy* 1(2): 34–42.
Hewitt, P. (2006) *Arts in the Core Script – Writing Ourselves In. The New Statesman Arts Lecture*, London: New Statesman.

Majone, G. (1989) *Evidence, Argument, & Persuasion in the Policy Process*, New Haven, CT: Yale University Press.

Moreno, J. L. (1975) *Psychodrama: Foundations of Psychotherapy*, New York: Beacon House.

Partee, M. H. (1971) Inspiration in the aesthetics of Plato, *Journal of Aesthetics and Art Criticism* 30(1): 87–95.

Selwood, S. (2002) The politics of data collection: gathering, analysing and using data about the subsidised cultural sector in England, *Cultural Trends* 12(47): 14–84.

Sefton-Green, J. (2008) What is creative learning?, in J. Sefton-Green (ed.) *Creative Learning*, London: ACE.

4

Mapping the rhetorics of creativity

Shakuntala Banaji

Introduction: the rhetorics of creativity[1]

This chapter explores understandings of creativity via an analysis of the rhetorical or discursive traditions that have contributed to the subjects' study: where these understandings come from in terms of their theoretical heritage, what functions they serve, how they are used, and in whose interest. The focus, as in previous work (Banaji and Burn, 2007b; Banaji, 2008), is on discourses about creativity circulating in the public domains of academia, practice and policy. The aim of this approach is not to investigate creativity itself, but rather what is written and said about it. Creativity is thus presented here as something *constructed through discourse*, and the ensuing discussion aims to envision more clearly how such constructions work, what claims are being made, and how we as researchers, practitioners, project evaluators and/or policy-makers might choose to locate ourselves in relation to these claims. Saliently, this approach aims to clarify understandings of and strengthen judgements about claims made in relation to creativity. In the critical review of literature from which this chapter originates (Banaji and Burn, 2007a), the rhetorics of creativity are given names which broadly correspond to the main theoretical underpinnings or the ideological beliefs of those who deploy them. Thus: Creative Genius; Democratic Creativity and Cultural Re/Production; Ubiquitous Creativity; Creativity for Social Good; Creativity as Economic Imperative; Play and Creativity; Creativity and Cognition; the Creative Affordances of Technology; the Creative Classroom; and Creative Arts and Political Challenge. As other chapters in this collection testify, the rhetorics identified have complex histories, particularly in traditions of philosophical thought about creativity since the European Enlightenment and in parallel forms of artistic practice, and in pedagogic traditions related to creativity over the same period.

In delineating the rhetorics outlined, the chapter asks whose interests some of these conceptualisations serve: and the conclusion will evaluate critically some of the claims made about the benefits of creativity within specific rhetorics.

It is worth prefacing the discussion of individual rhetorics with a series of questions that cut across and connect several rhetorics to each other. For instance, two questions running through the rhetorics of *Genius* and *Democratic* and *Ubiquitous creativity* are: does creativity reside in everyday aspects of human life or is it something special? And what are the differences between Cultural Learning and Creative Learning? Similarly the issue of whether there is, in fact, any difference between 'good' pedagogy and 'creative' pedagogy is the focus of attention in a number of the rhetorics. Is there creative learning that does not deliver effective educational outcomes? Meanwhile, the questions of how significant play and individual socialisation are as components of creativity implicitly link rhetorics as diverse as those concerned with *Technology* and the *Economy* to *Cognitive* and *Play* theories.

Creativity: unique or democratic?

A rhetoric which has the oldest provenance and has remained resilient within educational pedagogies in the twentieth and twenty-first centuries is *Creative Genius*. This is a Romantic and post-Romantic rhetoric that dismisses modernity and popular culture as vulgar, and argues for creativity as a special quality of a few highly educated and disciplined individuals (who possess genius) and of a few cultural products. Culture in this rhetoric is defined by a particular discourse about aesthetic judgement and value, manners, civilisation and the attempt to establish literary, artistic and musical canons. It can be traced back to aspects of European Enlightenment thought. Perhaps the most influential Enlightenment definition of genius is in Kant's *Critique of Judgement* (1790), which presents genius as the 'mental aptitude' necessary for the production of fine art, a capacity characterised by originality, and opposed to imitation.

Some contemporary commentators remain implicitly attached to the idea of genius (Simonton, 1999; Scruton, 2000). This view is interestingly at odds with a common definition of creativity as needing to involve novelty. While the language used by writers in this tradition contrasts the ordinary with the exceptional, there is a sense in which 'novelty' is viewed as a negative, almost dangerous, attribute when proposed by those who do not possess the requisite skill and inspiration to maintain links with 'the best' from the past. Scruton is not alone in his concerns about the debasement of 'real' Art, the rejection of 'training', 'rules', 'traditions' and so on. Websites such as the Illinois Loop pride themselves on taking issue with 'creative' aspects of the modern arts curriculum:

> When your 6th grader comes home and proudly shows you the "art project" he made in school from shoeboxes, duct tape, and spray paint, a valid question is, "Is my child learning anything about art?" … *Yes, it's fun. And some of the projects are indeed delightful. And no one doubts that kids should have time to be kids and let their creativity thrive.* But what is missing?
>
> *(Illinois Loop, 2007, emphasis in original)*

The view of art as being about self-expression is derided as a mere loss of skill. Significantly for the rhetorics *Play and Creativity* and *The Creative Classroom*, such discussions caricature the supposed 'opposition' and mobilise parental concern around a constructed binary opposition between 'pointless playing around' (creativity) and 'real learning' (academic progression within a sanctioned tradition). Many scholars, educators and parents still operate within frameworks such as the one outlined here and this proves deeply problematic for children's overall learning (see Cremin *et al.*, 2007; Maisuria, 2005).

Attempting to sidestep the divide between democratic and elitist conceptions, some commentators write as if there are two different 'categories' of creativity – 'high' and 'common' (Cropley, 2001) or 'Historical' and 'Psychological' (Boden, 1990) or 'special' and 'everyday'. The former comprises the work and powers of those who are considered 'geniuses' in the rhetoric just examined, and is pursued via studies of the work and lives of 'great' creative individuals (Csikszentmihalyi, 1997; Simonton, 1999) and is seen as being 'absolute', while the latter is far less well defined but can be fostered, increased and measured (Craft, 2000) in ordinary individuals.

Providing an explicitly anti-elitist conceptualisation of creativity as inherent in the everyday cultural and symbolic practices of all human beings is a rhetoric relating to *Democratic Creativity* and *Cultural Re/Production*. This rhetoric, most familiar in the academic discipline of Cultural Studies, sees everyday cultural practices in relation to the cultural politics of identity construction. It focuses particularly on the meanings made from and with popular cultural products. This rhetoric provides a theory derived from the Gramscian perspective on youth subcultures developed by the Birmingham Centre for Contemporary Cultural Studies. It constitutes practices of cultural consumption (especially of films, magazines, fashion and popular music) as forms of production through activities such as music sampling, subcultural clothing and fan activity (Cunningham, 1998); and thus belongs to an influential strand of cultural studies which attributes considerable creative agency to those social groups traditionally perceived as audiences and consumers or even as excluded from creative work by virtue of their social status (Willis, 1990).

Similarly egalitarian, but without the basis in cultural politics, is the rhetoric of *Ubiquitous Creativity*. Here, creativity is not just about consumption and production of artistic products but involves a skill in terms of responding to the demands of everyday life. To be more creative, in this discourse, involves having the flexibility to respond to problems and changes in the modern world and one's personal life (Craft, 2000, 2003). While much of the writing in this rhetoric is targeted at early years education with the aim of giving young children the ability to deal reflexively and ethically with problems encountered during learning and family life, examples used to illustrate 'everyday creativity' include attempts by working-class individuals or immigrants to find jobs against the odds without becoming discouraged. This too is a highly resilient strand in commentaries on this subject and has a strong appeal for educators (Jeffrey, 2005; Cohen, 2000) who wish to emphasise the significance of ethical, life-based education that does not simply rely on the transmission of particular traditionally judged types of knowledge and skills.

Clearly for those even nominally in favour of retaining a *particular* link between creativity and the arts and culture, who see creativity as something 'special' (or indeed who see it as being about challenge and critique rather than conformity to rules), this approach raises a number of key questions. Is this view of creativity as an ability to be *flexible in meeting the demands of life* incompatible with the notion of creativity as something that adds a *special quality* to life? What accounts for the rarity of references in such discussions to the work of revolutionary or anti-authoritarian philosophers whose creativity is applied to altering thought about social relationships, which impinge on both the special and the everyday?

While maintaining an emphasis on the links between creative moments and everyday existence, Negus and Pickering develop a strong critique of little 'c' creativity. They argue that 'we cannot collapse creativity into everyday life, as if they are indistinguishable. … Only certain of our everyday experiences involve creativity; only some of our everyday actions are creative' (Negus and Pickering, 2004: 44–5). While this view goes some way towards reconciling the problematic of collapsing creativity into the everyday by de-linking it from mundane activities, it leaves in place the tensions between activities, ideas and creations that are socially accepted as 'creative' in particular social contexts or historical moments and those that are rejected for fear of their playful, disruptive or anarchic potential. It is, in fact, this tension that can be found as an undercurrent in debates around the supposedly pro-social, benevolent effects of creativity and the significance of play, fantasy, social transformation and critique.

Creativity for 'successful' societies

The rhetoric of *Creativity for Social Good* sees individual creativity as linked to social structures. This rhetoric is characterised by its emphasis on the importance for educational policy of the arts as tools for personal empowerment and ultimately for social regeneration (the NACCCE report: Robinson and NACCCE, 1999). It stresses the integration of communities and individuals who have become 'socially excluded' (for example by virtue of race, location or poverty) and generally invokes educational and, tangentially, economic concerns as the basis for generating policy interest in creativity. This rhetoric emerges largely from contemporary social democratic discourses of inclusion and multiculturalism. In this view, a further rationale for encouraging creativity in education focuses on the social and personal development of young people in communities and other social settings. This encompasses a bow to multiculturalism (Robinson and NACCCE, 1999: 22–3) and anti-racism, as well as an avowed desire to combat growing drug use, teenage alcoholism and other social problems. In this view, 'creative and cultural programmes' are seen to be two-fold mechanisms of social cohesion, 'powerful ways of revitalising the sense of community in a school and engaging the whole school with the wider community' (ibid.: 26).

Robinson's team favours a 'democratic' definition of creativity over an 'elite' one: 'Imaginative activity fashioned so as to produce outcomes that are both original and of value' (ibid.: 29). For them imaginative activity entails a process of generating or producing something original. This sets it apart from rhetorics which encourage a view of creative and imaginative activity as play or fantasy. The NACCCE report is implicitly suggesting that the preparatory and exploratory time in art, media, technology and drama classrooms and projects is only *valuable* insofar as it contributes to the final product or to the reinsertion of 'excluded youth' into the official school system. 'Culture' and 'other cultures' are things to be 'dealt with' and 'understood'. While this reductive view has been implicitly critiqued on various occasions (Marshall, 2001; Buckingham and Jones, 2001), it has a broad appeal amongst those who see creativity as a tool in the project of engineering a harmonious national society.

In an allied rhetoric, *Creativity as Economic Imperative*, the future of a competitive national economy is seen to depend on the knowledge, flexibility, personal responsibility and problem solving skills of workers and their managers (cf. Scholtz and Livingstone, 2007). These are, apparently, fostered and encouraged by creative methods in business, education and industry (Seltzer and Bentley, 1999). There is a particular focus here on the contribution of the 'creative industries', broadly defined, although the argument is often applied to the commercial world more generally. Again, but far more explicitly than in the more diverse and pedagogically orientated NACCCE report, this rhetoric annexes the concept of creativity in the service of a neo-liberal economic programme and discourse (Landry, 2000). Indeed, although they claim to be interested in a diversity of contexts, flexibility of learning, self-evaluation and student empowerment, much of Seltzer's and Bentley's emphasis is directed towards getting more IT literacy and knowledge of computers into the curriculum and getting young people into industrial/business placements. Instead of being about imagination or the motivation to learn and create, the imperative here is the requirement to assist the modern national capitalist economy in its quest for global expansion (or, currently, in a quest to prevent the implosion of capitalist institutions).

Training courses in 'creativity', promising anything from personal fulfilment and office bonding to higher profits and guaranteed jobs, abound both on- and off-line. But, realistically, we must ask questions about the variety of arenas and domains in which those who buy into this 'new' vision of creativity would be allowed to function. Would time for playful testing of ideas be built into the working days of 'knowledge workers'? Or would they have to accommodate such peripheral business in their own personal time by giving up leisure (as is increasingly the case with the penetration of work-related ICT in the home)? And would the mere acquisition of *skills* be enough as a contribution to a greater collective or corporate endeavour? Clearly, while the newly flexible workforce described by Seltzer and Bentley (1999) might be encouraged to manage themselves and their departments or sections, their control over the overall structures and practices of their organisations remains as limited as ever, Rob Pope (2005: 28) poignantly describes.

The role of play

The rhetoric of *Creativity and Cognition* can be seen as incorporating two quite different traditions. One includes theories of multiple intelligences (Gardner, 1993) and the testing of mental creativity 'levels', and explorations of the potential of artificial intelligence to demonstrate the links made during and conditions for creative thought and production (Boden, 1990). Its emphasis is on the internal production of creativity by the mind, rather than on external contexts and cultures. The other consists of more intra-cognitive and culturally situated notions of creative learning expounded by Vygotsky, who asserts that 'If a person "cannot do something that is not directly motivated by an actual situation" then they are neither free nor using imagination or creativity' (Vygotsky, 1994: 267). Vygotsky's suggestion that creativity requires patience and an appreciation of the playful, and perhaps the fanciful and insubstantial, does not lend itself to arbitrary testing and assessment criteria, and has hence been ignored by many modern policymakers.

A persistent strand in writing about creativity, the rhetoric of *Play and Creativity*, turns on the notion that childhood-play models, and perhaps scaffolds, adult problem solving and creative thought. It explores the functions of play in relation to both creative production and cultural consumption. Some cognitivist approaches to play do share the emphasis of the *Creative Classroom* rhetoric on the importance of divergent thinking. Sandra Russ, for instance, argues that '[p]lay has been found to facilitate insight ability and divergent thinking' (Russ, 2003: 291), and that 'theoretically play fosters the development of cognitive and affective processes that are important in the creative act' (ibid.: 291). Challenging a mainstay of the economistic conceptualisation of creativity, she sees children as being excluded by definitions of creative products as effective, novel and valuable. She argues that the ways in which children use language, toys, role-plays and objects to represent different things in play are habitual ways of practising divergent thinking skills. Accounts such as these raise questions for those interested in creativity, pedagogy and learning.

A digital 'creativity pill'?

The rhetoric constructed around *The Creative Affordances of Technology* covers a range of positions from those who applaud all technology as inherently improving to those who welcome it cautiously and see creativity as residing in an as yet under-theorised relationship between users and applications. But is the use of technology itself inherently creative?

For Loveless (2003) a complex set of features of ICT – provisionality, interactivity, capacity, range, speed and automatic function, – mean that digital technologies open up new and authentic ways of being creative. Loveless notes that during a school digital arts project, in addition to the generation of great enthusiasm and enjoyment during the use of visual packages on the computer, the question of evaluation was not forgotten by the children, who 'had a sense of ownership of their images and lively ideas on how they might adapt or improve them in the future' (Loveless, 1999: 38). Teachers, however, were concerned about their own levels of understanding and skill in relation to the software. Given this context, for technologies to be used in innovative pedagogic ways, teachers need to be given time and training which is broader than specific software packages.

Supporting a socially situated view of the *potentially* creative uses of digital technologies and cautioning against those who champion digital technologies as *inherently* creative, Scanlon *et al.* (2005) and Seiter (2005) note that many computer programmes designed to increase children's knowledge and skills are not in the least bit creative, relying on rote learning, repetition and drill exercises. Thus they argue that digital technology can, but does not necessarily, support the expression and development of creativity. In a society where technology is not equally available to all, children may well be enthusiastic and confident users of digital technologies when offered the opportunities for playful production, but they are still divided by inequalities of access outside school and across the school system (Sefton-Green, 1999: 153). Ultimately the social contexts of digital technology's use help or hinder its creative potential.

Creative teaching and learning

The Creative Classroom rhetoric focuses on pedagogy, investigating questions about the connections between knowledge, skills, literacy, teaching and learning, and the place of creativity in an increasingly regulated and monitored curriculum (cf. Beetlestone, 1998; Starko, 2005; Jeffrey, 2005). This rhetoric locates itself in pragmatic accounts of 'the craft of the classroom', rather than in academic theories of mind or culture. Creative learning is *interactive*, incorporating discussion, social context, sensitivity to others, the acquisition and improvement of literacy skills; it is *contextual*, and has a sense of *purpose* and thus cannot be based around small units of testable knowledge; however, it can also be thematic and highly specific.

In this view, in terms of the content of creative lessons, it is vital that concepts are not taught as being immutable entities but as contextually and culturally anchored; subject divisions too need to be seen as frequently arbitrary and socially constructed rather than as rigid and binding; for it is in crossing such divisions – between art and mathematics, physical activity, numeracy, languages and music, geography and science, philosophy and poetry that children (and adults) stand the greatest chance of being independently creative. All this is unquestionably sound advice. Indeed, this rhetoric is consistent in identifying holistic teaching and learning – which link playful and affective processes to different types and domains of knowledge and methods of communication – as more conducive to creative thought and production than the splintered, decontextualised, top-down and monitored content and skills which are favoured as being academically 'effective'. There is, however, a tension in this work between a wish to view creativity as something that enhances the human soul and helps young people to blossom, and the need to give practical advice to trainee teachers, thus fitting them for the fairly chaotic but restricted milieu into which they will soon be going. At points this tension is practical, in the sense that it prevents the educational perspective on creativity from sidestepping issues such as assessment and time management. However, at times the tension also appears to lead to contradiction: risk-taking is to be encouraged but it is also to be kept within easily controllable bounds; time is required for playful engagement with ideas and materials, but this time has stringent external parameters in terms of the school day.

Jackson *et al.*'s interviews with university staff and students uncover patterns that fit the rhetorics outlined: a liking for creative or inspirational teachers/lecturers and a sense that being around enthusiastic, critical and engaged individuals enhances creativity; a dislike of dogmatic teaching, deadlines, narrow theoretical parameters, subject hierarchies which devalue drama and the arts in relation to mathematics and science; depression at the lack of reward for critical or divergent work and about forced targets; as well as anxieties around performing creativity 'on demand' and being shown as uncreative in front of other students were frequently expressed. However, highlighting institutional barriers to individual and group creativity, 'in many students' comments there was a sense of frustration at a perceived conflict between being creative and being "academic"' (Jackson *et al.*, 2006: 54).

In response to such institutional realities, and setting a challenge to aspects of foregoing rhetorics, *Creative Arts and Political Challenge* sees participation in creative education as politically challenging, and potentially transformative of the consciousness of those who engage in it. It describes the processes of institutional pressure that militate against positive and challenging experiences of creativity by young people, regardless of the efforts of teachers and practitioners (Thomson *et al.*, 2006). In previous work on this topic (Banaji and Burn, 2007a; Banaji and Burn, 2007b), this rhetoric is pursued further, with an emphasis on questions it raises about creative partnerships, social contexts and political or philosophical presuppositions. Do we, indeed, wish to retain the idea of cultural creativity as having an oppositional rather than a merely socialising force? How do these broader inflections of discourses of creativity relate to the micro-politics of particular social settings? This is of particular relevance in relation to the setting of the classroom. The very fluidity and confusion in talk about creativity can mean that the term is used as window dressing to appease educators who are interested in child-centred learning without actually being incorporated into the substantive work of the classroom.

Conclusion

In exploring questions about the nature and significance of creativity via engagement with symptomatic texts that use one or more of the different rhetorics, this chapter has attempted to show that the public discourse about creativity is characterised by a lack of clarity that allows participants to gain the benefits of aligning themselves with conflicting or mutually incompatible ideas and views without being seen to do so. In an educational context, the emphasis on creativity is part of an effort to draw back from the perceived excesses of a highly regulated, performance-based audit culture and to recover something that existed before, whether this be called 'enjoyment', 'good teaching' or 'creativity', without, however, losing apparent 'excellence' and 'standards'. Unfortunately, given that currently 'excellence' and 'standards' are criteria that are set by the very 'audit culture' from which *The Creative Classroom* hopes to depart, there are very real limits on the freedom of teachers and students to incorporate and interpret creativity in practical situations.

Another strong strand identified in this chapter is a relatively bland discourse of pro-social intervention: creative projects and strategies that encourage tolerance, co-operation and social harmony. A sharper version of that argument posits creativity as being about social inclusion and cultural diversity. In the name of creativity, this rhetoric uses broad aspirational terms such as 'empowerment' and 'democratisation', although the precise nature of the goals that are sought often remains unclear. But how do we assess whether any of the grand or even the more modest political ambitions of particular rhetorics and creative projects have been achieved? How do we understand and respond to the relationship between the *cultural politics* of talk about creativity or play and a *wider politics*? While there is evidence from numerous studies (Balshaw, 2004; Starko, 2005) that creative ways of teaching and learning offer a wider range of learners a more enjoyable, sustainable and independent experience of education than some traditional methods, there is no evidence that simply giving young people or workers brief opportunities for creative play or work substantially alters social inequalities, exclusions and injustices. Creativity is not a substitute for social justice. It is all the more important, then, that the complex and not always transparent *cultural politics* behind many rhetorics of creativity should be clearly and precisely understood. Gaining clarity about the different discourses and traditions in the delineation of the subject is, as this chapter has suggested, a first step towards understanding and assessing the claims being made on its behalf.

Notes

1 I am grateful for the contributions and critiques of Andrew Burn, David Buckingham and Julian-Sefton Green, and for funding from Creative Partnerships which facilitated the initial research.

References

Banaji, S. (2008) Creativity: exploring the rhetorics and the realities, in R. Willett, M. Robinson and J. Marsh (eds) *Play Creativity and Digital Cultures*, London and New York: Routledge.

Banaji, S. and Burn, A. (2007a) *The Rhetorics of Creativity: A Review of the Literature*, London: Arts Council of England.

—— (2007b) Creativity through rhetorical lens: implications for schooling, literacy and media education, *Literacies* 41(2): 62–70.

Balshaw, M. (2004) Risking creativity: building the creative context, *Support for Learning* 19(2): 71–6.

Beetlestone, F. (1998) *Creative Children, Imaginative Teaching*, Buckingham: Open University Press.

Boden, M. (1990) *The Creative Mind: Myths and Mechanisms*, London: Weidenfeld and Nicolson.

Brennan, C. (2005) Supporting play, supporting quality, conference proceedings *Questions of Quality*, 23–25 September 2004, Centre for Early Childhood Development and Education, Dublin Castle.

Buckingham, D. and Jones, K. (2001) New Labour's cultural turn: some tensions in contemporary educational and cultural policy, *Journal of Educational Policy* 16(1): 1–14.

Cohen, G. (2000) *The Creative Age: Awakening Human Potential in the Second Half of Life*, New York: HarperCollins.

Craft, A. (2000) *Creativity Across the Primary Curriculum: Framing and Developing Practice*, London: Routledge.

—— (2003) Creative thinking in the early years of education, *Early Years* 23(2): 147–58.

Cremin, T., Comber, B. and Wolf, S. (eds) (2007) *Creativity and Literacy*, Literacies, Special Issue 41(2) (July).

Cropley, A. J. (2001) *Creativity in Education and Learning: A Guide for Teachers and Educators*, London: Kogan Page.

Csikszentmihalyi, M. (1997) *Creativity: Flow and the Psychology of Discovery and Invention*, New York: Harper Perennial.

Cunningham, H. (1998) Digital culture: the view from the dance floor, in J. Sefton-Green (ed.) *Digital Diversions: Youth Culture in the Age of Multimedia*. London and Bristol, PN: UCL Press.

Gardner, H. (1993) *Frames of Mind: The Theory of Multiple Intelligences*, London: Fontana Press.

Illinois Loop (2007) Arts and the curriculum pages; available at http://www.illinoisloop.org/artmusic.html (accessed 28 March 2009).

Jeffrey, G. (ed.) (2005) *The Creative College: Building a Successful Learning Culture in the Arts*, Stoke on Trent, UK, and Sterling, VA: Trentham Books.

Kant, I. (1790 [2000]) *The Critique of Judgement*, New York: Prometheus Books.

Landry, C. (2000) *The Creative City: A Toolkit for Urban Innovators*, London and Sterling, VA: Commedia, Earthscan Publications.

Loveless, A. M. (1999) A digital big breakfast: the Glebe School Project, in J. Sefton-Green (ed.) *Young People, Creativity and New Technologies: The Challenge of Digital Arts*, London and New York: Routledge.

—— (2003) Creating spaces in the primary curriculum: ICT in creative subjects, *Curriculum Journal* 14(1): 5–21.

Marshall, B. (2001) Creating danger: the place of the arts in education policy, in A. Craft (ed.) *Creativity in Education*, London: Continuum.

Maisuria, A. (2005) The turbulent times of creativity in the National Curriculum, *Policy Futures in Education* 3(2): 141–52.

Negus, K. and Pickering, M. (2004) *Creativity, Communication and Cultural Value*, London, Thousand Oaks, CA, and New Delhi: Sage.

Jackson, N., Oliver, M., Shaw, M. and Wisdom, J. (eds) *Developing Creativity in Higher Education: An Imaginative Curriculum*, London: RoutledgeFalmer.

Pope, R. (2005) *Creativity: Theory, History, Practice*, London and New York: Routledge.

Robinson, K. and National Advisory Committee on Creative and Cultural Education (NACCCE) (1999) *All Our Futures: Creativity, Culture and Education*, Sudbury, Suffolk: DfEE Publications.

Russ, S. (2003) Play and creativity: developmental issues, *Scandinavian Journal of Educational Research* 47(3): 291–303.

Scanlon, M., Buckingham, D. and Burn, A. (2005) Motivating maths: digital games and mathematical learning, *Technology, Pedagogy and Education* 14(1): 127–39.

Scholtz, A. and Livingstone, D. W. (2007) 'Knowledge workers' and the 'new economy': a critical assessment', in J. Curtis and L. Tepperman (eds) *Sociology in Canada*, Toronto: Oxford University Press.

Scruton, R. (2000) After Modernism, *City Journal* 10(2).

Sefton-Green, J. (1999) A framework for digital arts and the curriculum, in J. Sefton-Green (ed.) *Young People, Creativity and New Technologies: The Challenge of Digital Arts*, London and New York: Routledge.

Seiter, E. (2005) *The Internet Playground: Children's Access, Entertainment and Mis-Education*, New York: Peter Lang.

Seltzer, K. and Bentley, T. (1999) *The Creative Age: Knowledge and Skills for the New Economy*, London: Demos.

Simonton, D. K. (1999) *Genius, Creativity, and Leadership: Historiometric Inquiries*, Cambridge, MA: Harvard University Press.

Starko, A. J. (2005) *Creativity in the Classroom: Schools of Curious Delight*, London: Lawrence Erlbaum Associates Publishers.

Sternberg, R. (ed.) (1999) *The Handbook of Creativity*, Cambridge: Cambridge University Press.

Thomson, P., Hall, C. and Russell, L. (2006) An arts project failed, censored or … ? A critical incident approach to artist-school partnerships, *Changing English* 13(1): 29–44.

Vygotsky, L. S. (1994 [1931]) Imagination and creativity in the adolescent, in R. Van Der Veer and J. Valsinger (eds) *The Vygotsky Reader*, Oxford and Cambridge, MA: Blackwell.

Willis, P. (1990) *Common Culture*, Milton Keynes: Open University Press.

5

Creativity of formulaic learning

Pedagogy of imitation and repetition

Koji Matsunobu

Each culture defines what aspects of creative endeavor are (and are not) preferable in a given context (Lubart, 1999; Weiner, 2000). Culture also determines which domains of human activity are perceived as expressions of creativity. What are legitimate creative acts in some cultures may be considered unacceptable and even ethically inappropriate in other cultures. For example, in societies where freshness and originality hold no special value, the artist (e.g. mask maker) may enjoy repetitive work and reproduce the same object with no substantial innovations or changes in interpretation and representation (Ludwig, 1992). Examples of such societies are abundant. In the East Asian context, Rudowicz (2004) observes that the Chinese put less emphasis on external performance than inner experience and peace brought by familiar experiences (also see Ng, 2001; and Leong, Chapter 6). Similarly, Lubart argues that the Eastern concept of creativity is "less focused on innovative products. Instead, creativity involves a state of personal fulfillment, a connection to a primordial realm, or the expression of an inner essence or ultimate reality" (Lubart, 1999: 340). For this reason, East Asians normally underline mastering and perfecting skills through rigid training while often shrugging off new products or ideas.

This chapter is concerned with understanding how creativity relates to a larger system of culture that determines its cultural pedagogy. The subsequent discussions provide an explanation of creativity from the viewpoint of Japanese artists within the traditional realm. Particular attention is given to the creativity of embodied learning and imitation of form. These two aspects are normally perceived as irrelevant, and even an impediment, to creative learning in societies where creativity refers to "product" creativity (Weiner, 2000). Central to my discussion is the Japanese notion of *kata*, or somatic form, as a method of embodied learning. While *kata*-based learning has been viewed and criticized as formulaic from the perspective of product-oriented creativity (Rohlen and Le Tendre, 1996/1998), significant aspects of *kata*-based learning, such as the importance of breaking the *kata* (called *katayaburi*), have been ignored. To be sure, only gifted artists are historically allowed to change the form of tradition and establish a new style in Japan. However, this does not mean that creative impulse is not part of *kata*-based learning. The second half of the chapter is concerned with providing a cultural explanation of what Rudowicz (2004) views as the characteristics of Eastern approaches to creativity—an attitude that puts a premium on the richness of inner experience rather than the uniqueness of external performance—by drawing on the notion of self-cultivation (Yuasa, 1987).

Creativity of imitation

To some extent, learning art involves mastery of a basic form that underpins the elements of its artistic expression. This holds true for any art domain. Whether the artist's intention is to follow, modify, or break the form, some sort of reference to what has been refined and accumulated as a form is evident in his or her expression of art. In other words, art is no less an expression of the individual artist's mind than that of a set of cultural, social, and historical artifacts available to the artist. Therefore, the significant aspect of creative learning in the arts involves an imitation of form. This is especially so in the early stages of learning in performing arts.

In Japan, imitation of a model has traditionally been the core of the transmission of artistry in every field of arts domains, from martial arts to performing and fine arts (Malm, 1959/2000; Hahn, 2007; Trimillos, 1989). From an American cultural perspective, Rohlen and LeTendre observe that imitation is the "highest form of praise" in the logic of Japanese culture. They observe:

> Whereas Americans relegate imitation to a position inferior to creativity, Japanese culture elevates imitation as a powerful road to mastery. … The term "mastery" has meanings far different from our Western sense of domination and rule. Mastery is a process of adapting oneself to the material rather than of controlling or subordinating the material to oneself.
>
> *(Rohlen and LeTendre, 1996/1998: 371)*

Similarly, upon observing differences of belief system between Japanese and American teachers of the Suzuki violin method, Peak states:

> Japanese teachers … do not consider imitation in such a negative light. They believe that in the effort to approximate an ideal model, students will gain the superior qualities of a great performer, rather than lose that which is distinctive about themselves. … "Creative" or merely different interpretations are not valued solely for their distinctive quality if they lack a concomitant excellence of artistic taste and a high level of technical skills. Students are believed to gain such technical control through tireless attempts to approximate a worthy model, and to develop taste by becoming so imbued with the style of an excellent performer that it becomes their second nature.
>
> *(Peak, 1998: 358–9)*

These scholars highlight the core of the Japanese artistry transmission system that relies on imitation. Central to this cultural logic is the notion of mastery that celebrates the embodiment of a model to the extent that the learner reconstructs and reforms his or her corporeal sense through the model. As Rohlen and LeTendre write, "The learner must first accept his or her subordination to the material, task, or form" (1996/1998: 371). It is for this reason that art objects or forms are often considered sacred, and engage the practitioner in self-development. Rohlen and LeTendre introduce an advanced potter who said that "he has learned from the clay" (ibid.: 371). Similarly, bamboo flute players in Matsunobu's (2009) work are engaged in self-cultivation by adjusting and accommodating themselves to the character of each material. For these artists, learning *about* the clay (bamboo) coincides with learning *from* the clay (bamboo).

Creativity in the Japanese context is believed to be achieved only through imitation and repeated practice of a given form. Music composition is reserved only for the greatest performers who have mastered the form after decades of training. The following remark by Jin Nyodo

(1891–1966), one of the legendary *shakuhachi* bamboo flute players of the twentieth century, testifies how he approached the act of creating a new song as a natural result of the imitation and mastery of existing music rather than his enduring effort to compose an individual work:

> Creating great music is not a result of an individual's intention and effort. The movement of the universe manifests itself through humans and becomes music. Thus, music is not to be composed but "born." This is how I see it. … I have never intended to compose music by myself. But I have had this hope in mind; that is, someday a piece of music naturally develops out of my life spirit. Interestingly enough, this dream came true when I was traveling in China. This piece of music, I would say, is not my "composition" [*sakkyoku*] but "naturally born" [*shokyoku*].[1]

Composition as "naturally born," as opposed to "intentionally crafted," is a culturally constructed view of creativity that values the mastery of a bodily form of artistry through years of practice and imitation of the model. The embodiment of the model eventually allows the practitioner to be skillful and imaginative enough to represent the model in a personalized way; it can then become a new piece (Matsunobu, 2009).

When explaining great players' personalization of music, the word *interpretation* may not be appropriate, as interpretation often refers to analysis and mind-centered reflection rather than "naturally born" operation of the body. In fact, interpretation often involves devising ways to construct one's own individual, unique expression and digging out hidden meanings inherent in written music, as often understood and practiced in musicology. The notion of interpretation as an individual rendition of otherwise formulaic performance runs counter to the idea of "naturally born" musical expression through the trained body. The latter type of music making is gained through embodied learning in which the student goes through repeated practice of a form and imitation of a model. In this system, individuality develops from an embodied apprehension of the form rather than from analytical interpretation.

Scholars have pointed out that in traditional East Asian societies, invention is often imitation, and creativity is achieved only by imitation. Rudowicz argues that, from a Chinese cultural perspective, people tend to be "more willing to rearrange the pattern or make a modest alteration to existing knowledge or practices than to start a radical change or reconceptualization" (Rudowicz, 2004: 62). Whereas "elements of invention and novelty, celebration of individual accomplishment, and concentration on the future are almost inherent to the Western conception of creativity," these aspects are "foreign to the traditional Chinese ideals of respect for the past, and maintaining harmony with the forces of the nature [sic]" (Rudowicz, 2004: 59). Thus, creativity in the East takes the form of modification, adaptation, renovation, or reinterpretation. Similarly, the view of creativity as "modification of the old"—originating in the Confucian idea of "gaining new insights through reviewing old materials"—is identified in Japanese cultural logic. Traditionally, great players and composers added a few notes and phrases to already existing pieces, instead of composing new pieces from scratch, to make their own music (Matsunobu, 2009). Ownership of music was also loosely defined.

Pedagogy of *kata*: a method of embodying the form

In the context of Japanese knowledge transmission, the primacy of bodily form is evident (Tsujimoto, 1999). *Kata* is the philosophical principle that underpins the bodily form of artistry transmission (e.g. Hahn, 2007; Matsunobu, 2007b, 2009; Powell, 2003; Yuasa, 1987). Traditionally, Japanese arts have been preserved and transmitted through *kata*, literally "form" or "mold," through which students learn structures of art, patterns of artistic and social behaviors, and moral and ethical values, all in accordance with prescribed formulae. *Kata* is a set of bodily movements that have been developed and preserved by precedent artists. The most efficient and authentic way to master the artistry, it is believed, is to follow the model defined as *kata*.

Central to this pedagogy is the repeated practice and imitation of the model through the body. The acquisition of *kata* is thus a "discipline for shaping one's body into a form" (Yuasa, 1987: 105). Trimillos' observation of a Japanese teacher epitomizes the characteristics of *kata* learning: "The teacher seldom identifies the error, but waits until the phrase is played correctly and then expresses approval" (repetition of practice), and the "goal is to perform the piece exactly as the teacher has presented it" (Trimillos, 1989: 39). Yano (2002) observes that the Western dualism between form and content, each of which traditionally corresponds to the false and the true, dissolves as continuous and interpenetrating parts in the theory of *kata*. *Kata* is content attendant upon form. The creative goal of *kata*-training is "to fuse the individual to the form so that the individual becomes the form and the form becomes the individual" (Yano, 2002: 26). *Kata* is also a social practice in that it involves the body directly in a social setting. Through the correct imitation of formal patterns that define not only ideal artistic expressions but also ideal moral behaviors, students participate in the social embodiment of values. The difference between *kata* and what we are familiar with as "form" (called *katachi* in Japanese) is that the former is a content-attendant, embodied, habitual, contextualized, and value-laden form, whereas the latter is an abstract and empty form. *Kata* historicizes, socializes, and spiritualizes the individual, but *katachi* formulates, abstracts, and standardizes one's imagination and thought.

In the context of noh performance, the distinction between *kata* and *katachi* is explained through the concept of *tai* ("embodied form") and *yū* ("expressiveness" or "taste"). If someone expresses a piece only with *yū* (that is, without *tai*), the performance is not considered a representation of the piece. The founder of noh, Zeami Motokiyo (1364–1443), elaborates it in this way:

> One must know *tai-yū* in Noh. *Tai* is like a flower and *yū* is like its scent. Or *tai* is like the moon and *yū* like the moon-light. If one has a thorough comprehension of *tai*, one should naturally possess *yū*. … No one should copy the *yū*, the outer appearance of the performance. Those who know enough see another actor's performance with heart and soul and so copy the work of *tai*. When the *tai* is closely copied, the actor's performance will naturally have *yū* with it.
>
> *(Sekine, 1985: 117–8)*

The core of a piece of work derives from *tai* (or *kata*) not *yū* (or *katachi*). If someone has copied only the latter, but not the former, then his or her expression becomes superficial and lacks spirit.

Another distinction is made between *kata* and *kuse*. While *kata* is an embodied form, *kuse* is an idiosyncratic "habit" acquired through the course of individual learning. Often, the student habituates the body to the task in a way that feels most comfortable to him or her. In *kata*-based learning, personalization is not recommended—however demanding the task is—because the purpose of learning is to embrace an external form as an embodied form. Therefore, any kind of personalization before the form becomes one's natural habit is not considered genuine learning. Naturally acquired individual expressions emanating from the complete mastery of *kata* are recommended.

Because *kata* signifies an embodied lineage of artistry, the continuity of performing style (represented in *kata*) is essential. This is realized, for example, when the teacher shows a significant degree of individual habit compared to his or her own teacher. The student then needs to question the lineage of artistry transmitted through the teacher. This may not happen within a cultural system in which individual creativity is highly valued. In the Japanese cultural system, *kuse* is not thought of as one's individual, unique disposition: It only implies his or her failure of mastering and embodying the *kata*. The authentic bearer of the tradition needs to represent *kata*, not *kuse*.

Kata as a historical depository of living artistry is what the student must master and eventually overcome in order to create a new form of artistry. Minamoto (1992) sheds light on this system of Japanese artistry mastery that consists of three steps: *Shu, ha*, and *ri*. The first stage of *shu* (or "hold," "keep," "preserve") is to follow the traditional method of learning through the established *kata*. At this stage, the dominant task of learning is blind imitation of the form. The stage of *ha* (or "break") involves breaking the traditional form of *kata*. It is in this stage that the personalization of the form is gradually recognized. Once the form is fully embodied by the learner, he or she is allowed to experiment, such as incorporating other styles of playing. Finally, establishing a new form or style of performance is achieved by "abandoning the form" or "distancing the tradition" in the stage of *ri* (the meaning of *ri*, or a different reading of the same word *hanareru*, includes "abandoning," "distancing," and "exceeding"). A level of artistry, often described as *hanare-waza* ("exceeding artistry," or feat), is believed to be achieved by someone who has mastered the basic form of *kata*, studied the maximum possibilities of artistic expression, and established a new form of expression.

A related aesthetic concept is *shin-gyo-so*, often used in calligraphy, architecture, garden design, tea ceremony, flower arrangement, and noh drama performance as an expression to describe different degrees of formality and personalization. The terms *shin, gyo*, and *so* correspond, respectively, to formal, semi-formal, and informal styles of drawing, designing, or performing. Rigid drawing in calligraphy is *shin*, whereas more natural flowing brushstrokes represent *gyo* and *so* qualities. Nakamura (1983) argues that *shin-gyo-so* is an aesthetic concept originating in calligraphy discourses from medieval times that distinguished degrees of formality. It then developed into a learning theory of performing arts comprised of three stages, similar to *shu-ha-ri*. Zeami (1984) explains in the case of noh performance: *Shin* is the stage in which the student learns the basic repertoire (two songs) and the basic form (three set roles). Having mastered the basics, the student in the *gyo* stage is ready to study advanced styles of acting. By the time the student has reached the stage of *so*, he is able to perform the roles without thinking. Zeami placed a premium on imitation-based practice of performance so as to establish a new genre of performance dedicated to the art of imitating the models (called *mononame*).

One aspect of *kata*-based learning is that it inevitably involves a "non-step-by-step" process of learning (Matsunobu, 2007b; Murao, 2003). Ikuta (1987) argues that the transmission of artistry through *kata* contradicts the school curriculum, in which content is organized in a sequential manner, from the easy to the difficult. In *kata*, students experience the whole from the beginning, not bit by bit or piece by piece, utilizing their entire bodies. The first piece students learn may be as difficult as the last piece in terms of technical demands, though the emphasis on the spiritual value of those pieces may vary. The first piece may serve many practitioners as a basic form of music, a sort of *kata*, as they practice this piece on a daily basis. Throughout the process, verbal instruction and conceptual understanding are intentionally avoided as they may distract a whole-body grasp of artistry (Hare, 1998). Keister relates that "with training based on *kata*, there is no artistic content for the performer to 'grasp' cognitively, but instead a surface aesthetic that 'grasps' or transforms the performer, shaping the artist into the form of the art itself" (Keister, 2004: 103).

The *kata*-based learning system highlights our understanding of the role of tradition. A Western student of Japanese music once expressed his understanding of tradition: "Tradition is like a canoe. You need it until you cross the river. But once you have reached the other shore and walked on the soil, you don't have to carry it."[2] This student was unaware of the fact that Japanese teachers believe crossing the river is a lifetime endeavor and that tradition carries much more value than individuality within the context of Japanese artistry transmission. Kikkawa observes that, "For the Japanese, *kata* is not a shell that they have yet to break but the ideal form of expression that has already been achieved and formed by striving for the best" (Kikkawa, 1979: 154). From this logic emerges a respect for the achievement of their predecessors and a cultivation of spirit by subordination to the art form.

Creation of inner richness: renewing the engagement with the world

From a systems view of creativity that values novelty of external product and progress, the Japanese system of *kata*-based learning may look formulaic and repressive. It seems as if no individuality is accepted and only a talented few are allowed to experience the joy of creation in the final stage of learning. The early stage of learning appears to be full of rote work, deprived of discovery and creative learning. From the internal perspective, however, this view does not always hold true. Put simply, creative impulse in the course of Japanese arts learning is geared more toward cultivating the inner richness—that is, cultivating the relationship with the tools, instruments, teachers, colleagues, and practitioner's own minds—than toward creating new objects. The emphasis of such practices is more on the art of impression over the art of expression (Matsunobu, 2007a). The fact that "the body and the inner experience of the performer are the focal points of Japanese performing arts," states Keister, is "the main reason why Japanese dance, music, and theater are so often misunderstood, even by Japanese people themselves" (Keister, 2007: 503).

In fact, the traditional learning style of Japanese arts is process-oriented, as typically represented by the spirit of tea ceremony: "The art of the ceremony is not in the tea, but rather in the careful preparation of the tea, the deft handling of utensils, the graceful manner of movement, and the elegance of conversation" (Keister, 2005: 40). Tea masters do not try to create new objects but seek to create artful minds, bodies, and spirits through heightened perceptions that bring about holistic, intuitive views of the objects (Yanagi, 1989). In so doing, they discover the beauty of objects through the interactions with their utensils. The goal of such practices is not the perfection of an art object as an end in itself, but the development of the self as a never-ending, lifelong process (Keister, 2004).

Traditionally, Japanese martial arts and fine arts are considered a lifelong path of self-cultivation (called "*do*," as in *aiki-do, ju-do, ken-do*) and are practiced in ways to enhance one's personality through achieving mind–body oneness (Yuasa, 1987). Another example of such a practice, besides tea ceremony, is *ensō* drawing (Matsunobu, in press). *Ensō* is a calligraphy painting of a circle and is a frequent theme of Japanese Zen calligraphy. *Ensō* in Japanese means "shape of a circle," literally; "shape of the mind," figuratively. The circle is a symbol of one's own boundary. It can be depicted in countless ways, just as the boundary of human mind can be extended, blurred, and ultimately erased. In the act of drawing a simple circle, one's mental state is fully exposed in the painted circle. Practitioners of *ensō* drawing paint the circle every day, as a sort of spiritual diary, just as tea masters make tea each day as part of their spiritual training.

Matsunobu (2009) argues that in the case of the spiritual practice of Japanese music creativity and technique bear different meanings; together, they signify the capacity to reduce the hindrance to more direct experience of the world rather than the ability to create new objects or new ways of expression. In his ethnographic study, practitioners of spiritual music, like those of *ensō* drawing, played certain pieces over and over again every day to confront the mental and physical conditions of their day. By intentionally limiting the scope of outward expression, they tried to maximize the possibility of experiencing the inner richness of music. Rather than playing so many pieces and so many notes, they played a limited number of pieces and notes to engage in the self-cultivation process.

In sum, within the system of Japanese artistic training, creative force is given to mastering the form, *kata*, through which the practitioner explores his or her inner experience, participates in the community of practice, and develops spiritual maturity. As previously discussed, the Japanese sense of self-cultivation is achieved by adapting oneself to the art form, to the extent that one "dissolves" or "discards" the self. Using an art form as a mirror, the artist faces his or her internal condition and engages in self-development. This process is recursive and involves a series of self-reflection of the artist, as portrayed in the following poem:

> Seeing a mountain as the mountain
> The mountain was not the mountain
> Seeing the mountain as a mountain

This type of realization is achieved by critically engaging in self-reflection. Nakagawa argues that art is a form of self-cultivation in the sense that it is an exploration of the self. He observes that "the way of art has nothing to do with creativity in problem-solving. It pays little attention to each problem. On the contrary, it solves the problem of the 'self'" (Nakagawa, 2000: 204). The creativity inherent in this value system involves endless attempts at self-development and renewal of engagement with the world.

Implications

The negative image of *kata*-based learning emerged from its blind application in the democratic context of youth education. The difference between the traditional and modern (or Western) pedagogies has not been compromised theoretically, even though these two seem to have incorporated each other. For example, the pedagogy of *kata* is identified in Western music teaching models originated in Japan. Peak (1998) illustrates the influence of traditional Japanese pedagogy on the formation of the Suzuki violin method, highlighting the importance of repeated practice, imitation of the model, and socially enhanced motivation of the students. Murao (2003) examines how the *kata* of violin technique is formulated in *Twinkle, Twinkle, Little Star*, the first song of the repertoire in the Suzuki method, and learned through repeated practices of certain variations on the theme that demand little expressive artifice.

Yet, these indications of compatibility are not powerful enough to promote research on the creativity of embodied learning and imitation. Most studies on creative learning in Japan do not seem to pay enough attention to the possibilities of traditional pedagogy applied in the modern context of education: They rather promote a dualistic view that the traditional and the creative are two different matters. This situation is understandable, as the kind of creativity promoted in Japanese education is product creativity: For example, the idea of "creative music making" (CMM)—originating in England and imported to Japan in the 1980s (Adachi and Chino, 2004)—has become the method of music composition practiced in Japanese schools, resulting in many workshops for teachers and publications in relation to CMM. Further efforts are necessary to suggest that consideration of tradition can be a significant part of educational attempts to create a culturally responsive pedagogy of the arts.

Finally, while research on creativity generally tends to focus on children's development and capacity, the Eastern perspective urges us to look at human development as maturing further during adulthood. In fact, the majority of students in the Japanese arts are adult students. Because Japanese arts traditionally developed as a form of self-cultivation, it is assumed that the purpose of artistic training is to engage in life and make art part of everyday experience toward spiritual maturity. In contrast, most developmental theories and intelligence theories in the West support children's early start of learning in the arts. Given this cultural difference, creativity research needs to incorporate a perspective that asks: What does it mean to study the arts as adult learners? What is the view of creativity that is applicable to and useful for adult learners? Perhaps, creativity in some cultures needs to be discussed along with other issues such as well-being, spirituality, and aging.

Notes

1 Jin Nyodo's Shakuhachi: Compiling classical honkyoku pieces [Jin Nyodo no shakuhachi: Koten honkyoku no shutaiseisha], Teichiku Records, Tokyo, 1998.
2 Taken from: http://shakuhachiforum.com/ (accessed March 10, 2010).

References

Adachi, M. and Chino, Y. (2004) Inspiring creativity through music, in S. Lau, A. H. H. Hui, and G. Y. C. Ng (eds.) *Creativity: When East Meets West*, River Edge, NJ: World Scientific Publishing.

Feld, S. (1982) *Sound and Sentiment: Birds, Weeping, Poetics, and Song in Kaluli Expression*, Philadelphia: University of Pennsylvania Press.

Hahn, T. (2007) *Sensational Knowledge: Embodying Culture through Japanese Dance*, Middletown, CT: Wesleyan University Press.

Hare, T. (1998) Try, try again: Training in noh drama, in T. P. Rohlen and G. K. LeTendre (eds.) *Teaching and Learning in Japan*, New York: Cambridge University Press.

Ikuta, K. (1987) *Waza kara shiru* [Knowing through waza artistry], Tokyo: Tokyo Daigaku Shuppankai.

Keister, J. (2004) The shakuhachi as spiritual tool: a Japanese Buddhist instrument in the West, *Asian Music* 35(2): 99–131.

—— (2005) Seeking authentic experience: spirituality in the Western appropriation of Asian music, *The World of Music* 47(3): 35–53.

—— (2007) Review of the book *Sensational Knowledge: Embodying Culture through Japanese Dance*, *Journal of the American Musicological Society* 62(2): 497–503.

Kikkawa, E. (1979) *Nihon ongaku no seikaku* [Characteristics of Japanese music], Tokyo: Ongaku no Tomosha.

Lubart, T. I. (1999) Creativity across culture, in R. J. Sternberg (ed.) *Handbook of Creativity*, Cambridge: Cambridge University Press.

Ludwig, A. M. (1992) Culture and creativity, *American Journal of Psychotheraphy* 46(3): 454–69.

Malm, W. P. (1959/2000) *Traditional Japanese Music and Musical Instruments*, Tokyo: Kodansha International.

Matsunobu, K. (2007a) Japanese spirituality and music practice: art as self-cultivation, in L. Bresler (ed.) *The International Handbook of Research in Arts Education*, New York: Springer.

—— (2007b) Japanese perspectives and research on the body, in L. Bresler (ed.) *The International Handbook of Research in Arts Education*, New York: Springer.

—— (2009) Artful encounters with nature: ecological and spiritual dimensions of music learning, unpublished doctoral dissertation submitted to the University of Illinois at Urbana-Champaign.

—— (in press) Art of simplicity: teaching Japanese spiritual arts, in S. K. Chung (ed.) *Teaching Asian Art: Content, Context, and Pedagogy*, Reston, VA: National Art Education Association.

Minamoto, R. (1992) *Kata to nihon bunka* [Kata and the Japanese culture], Tokyo: Sobunsha.

Moriya, T. (1994) The lesson culture (trans. M. Eguchi), in A. Ueda (ed.) *The Electric Geisha: Exploring Japanese Popular Culture*, New York: Kodansha International.

Murao, T. (2003) Suzuki mesoddo "kira kira boshi hensokyoku" ni miru "kata kara no gakushu" ni tsuite [Learning through kata in *Twinkle, Twinkle, Little Star Variations* in the Suzuki violin method], *Gendai no esupuri* 428: 165–75.

Nakamura, Y. (1983) *Nihon geinoshi: Chusei*, vol. 3 [The history of Japanese arts: medieval times], Tokyo: Hosei Daigaku Shuppankyoku.

—— (2000) *Education for Awakening: An Eastern Approach to Holistic Education*, Brandon, VT: Foundation for Educational Renewal.

Ng, A. (2001) *Why Asians Are Less Creative than Westerners*, Singapore: Prentice Hall.

Peak, L. (1998) The Suzuki method of music instruction, in T. Rohlen and G. LeTendre (eds.) *Teaching and Learning in Japan*, Cambridge: Cambridge University Press.

Powell, K. A. (2003) Learning together: practice, pleasure and identity in a taiko drumming world, unpublished doctoral dissertation, Stanford University, Stanford, CA.

Rohlen, T. P. and LeTendre, G. K. (1996/1998) Conclusion: themes in the Japanese culture of learning, in T. P. Rohlen and G. K. LeTendre (eds.) *Teaching and Learning in Japan*, New York: Cambridge University Press.

Rudowicz, E. (2004) Creativity among Chinese people: beyond western perspective, in S. Lau, A. H. H. Hui, and G. Y. C. Ng (eds.) *Creativity: When East Meets West*, River Edge, NJ: World Scientific Publishing.

Sekine, M. (1985) *Ze-ami and His Theories of Noh Drama*, Gerrards Cross, UK: Colin Smythe.

Trimillos, R. D. (1989) Halau, Hochschule, Maystro, and Ryu: cultural approaches to music learning and teaching, *International Journal of Music Education* 14: 32–43.

Tsujimoto, M. (1999) *Manabi no fukken: Moho to shujuku* [Revival of learning: imitation and mastery], Tokyo: Kadokawa shtoen.

Weiner, R. P. (2000) *Creativity and Beyond: Cultures, Values, and Change*, New York: State University of New York Press.

Yanagi, S. (1989) *The Unknown Craftsman*, Tokyo: Kodansha International.

Yano, C. R. (2002) *Tears of Longing: Nostalgia and the Nation in Japanese Popular Song*, Cambridge, MA: Harvard University Asia Center.

Yuasa, Y. (1987) *The Body: Toward an Eastern Mind–Body Theory*, Albany: State University of New York Press.

Zeami (1984) *On the Art of the No Drama: The Major Treatises of Zeami* (trans. T. Rimer and M. Yamazaki), Princeton, NJ: Princeton University Press.

6

Creativity and the arts in Chinese societies

Samuel Leong

Introduction

The role played by culture in creativity has become increasingly recognised around the world (European Commission, 2009). However, traditional Confucian thinking continues to exert a strong influence on the culture, ethics, politics, religion and philosophy of many East and South-East Asia countries (Ee and Tan, 2008), including their businesses and organisations (Wang *et al.*, 2005). These countries have scored low on the Individualism Index: Hong Kong (25); Singapore, China and Vietnam (20); Korea (18); and Taiwan (17) (Nguyen *et al.*, 2006: 9). This chapter examines some of the misconceptions about Chinese creativity against the backdrop of Confucian thinking and related cultural traditions.

Chinese education and the confucian legacy

In Chinese societies, social harmony and stability are central to how people interact and communicate amongst themselves and with others (Beamer and Varner, 2008). Because traditional Confucian-based socialisation practices emphasise obedience, duty, cooperation, compromise and sacrifice, it is generally accepted that people in Chinese societies tend to be less expressive of their personal opinions, feelings and desires, being more concerned about social harmony and conforming to in-group *mores*. A person's success in life is judged by several factors: contributions to the welfare of society or country, the degree to which his or her achievements are passed on to the next generation, being an exemplar of moral living and founding a school of thought. The behaviour of individuals is governed by respect for age and authority, collective/group orientation, importance of family relationships, tight social relationships (*guan xi*; 关系), 'face/image' (*mian zi*; 面子), 'human feelings' (*ren qing*; 人情) and 'reciprocity/repayment' (*bao*; 报). The norms of reciprocity are heavily embedded within hierarchical networks of social relationships (*guan xi*; 关系), strengthened by the public nature of obligations that are expected to be repaid (*bao*; 报), even over a long period of time, and by a self-conscious manipulation of image/face (*mian zi*; 面子).

The educability and perfectibility of humanity are central to Confucian thinking, which places a high value on self-cultivation and education (Lee, 1996). The revered master teacher (*fu zi*; 夫子) of China Confucius (551–479 BC) proposed that education should be for all, and ultimately develops learners in five areas: (1) benevolence and morality; (2) intelligence and knowledge; (3) courage and constitution; (4) aesthetics and music; and (5) talent and faculty (Guo, 2002). Apart from teaching his students morality, proper speech and government, Confucius also emphasised the 'Six Arts' – rites, music, archery, charioteering, calligraphy and mathematics/computing (Shusterman, 2009). The study of ancient texts was important to Confucius, who was said to have studied and partially edited the 'Five Classics' (*wu jing*; 五经). The value of venerating the classical canons was inculcated by the 'Five Classics' and 'Four Books of Confucius', constituting the official core curriculum of the highly centralised Imperial Examination (*ke ju*; 科举) during the Ming (1368–1644) and Qing (1644–1911/12) dynasties.

Consequently, Confucian thinking became entrenched in the Chinese way of life as all prospective government officials must undertake in-depth studies of Confucian literature and values (see Confucianism, 2009). This system of meritocracy and education meant that the arduous selection process based on formal examinations determined the future of the elite and powerful. It also determined the content of the examinations and the criteria by which individuals were judged to be capable or talented. Those who demonstrated their competence and talents through open competition and according to established criteria were rewarded with position, social status and wealth in the civil service, where they were expected to be loyal to the legitimate feudal government and be obedient to upright authority. Candidates were also tested on their skills in writing essays on moral issues and current affairs, composing poems in a variety of formal styles, and calligraphy.

While the meritocratic examination system's open competitive system rewarded effort and hard work, it reinforced the high regard accorded to teachers, who were the models of knowledge and virtue for society, wielding huge influence over the future careers of their students. Their status is reflected by the salutary Chinese terms given to them: *shi fu* (literally, 'teacher-father'; 师父) and *lao shi* ('old teacher'; 老师). Students study under the tutelage of masters, considered society's sources of wisdom and knowledge, and were responsible for passing on to future generations what they learned. Guided by masters, students depended on their self-cultivating efforts to memorise and recall the classical materials and enhance their writing skills. The goals of learning and teaching were pragmatic: to be successful in the high-stakes written examinations, to prepare potential officials for competent conduct in the civil service, and to contribute to the prosperity and harmony of society as moral leaders. The content of the curriculum was determined by the requirements of the examinations. Pedagogy was not a matter of concern in a system that demanded the acquisition of established knowledge rather than the discovery or generation of new knowledge. With the written word of elders enshrined in power and authority and oral discourse not being an examination requirement, the traditional Chinese education system did not develop the creative and critical faculties of individuals in the modern Western sense.

Misconceptions of creativity in Chinese education

The education systems in Chinese societies have been criticised for being didactic, controlling and paternalistic, emphasising conformity and rote learning at the expense of creative and critical thinking. Criticisms related to the lack of creativity have been attributed to the values underlying Confucian thinking. Recent studies indicate that traditional Chinese values such as *guanxi* persist as a fundamental aspect of interpersonal relationships and social orientations in contemporary Chinese societies (Gilbert and Tsao, 2000). They remain operative despite Confucian core values being reduced in strength over generations (Ho, 1994). There is a 'Confucian Renaissance'

(Crowell, 2005), with a resurgence of Confucian values in Mainland China (Shi, 2009) and outside China, which is considered relevant to modern Singapore (White Paper on Shared Values, 1991) and Hong Kong (Cheng, 2008).

Some studies have challenged earlier conclusions about the ineffective learning styles of Chinese students, shedding light on the 'paradox' of Chinese learners (Watkins and Biggs, 2001). For years, the repetitive learning style of Chinese students has been misinterpreted as mindless rote learning (Biggs, 1994). In reality, they prefer deep learning strategies and consider it so (Ho *et al.*, 1999). For them, repetition facilitates the accurate recall of important factual information, enables them to attach meaning to the material they are learning, and helps them to be better prepared for examinations by having the key facts and points memorised. The two terms for 'practice' – *xue xi* ('learning practice'; 学习) and *lian xi* ('training practice'; 练习) – indicate that repetition is necessary in the training and learning process until the desired habits (*xi guan*; 习惯) are formed. For years, too, people in Western countries have been believed to possess creative intelligence superior to people in Asian countries. In reality, Western students have not performed as well as their East Asian peers in standardised achievements tests, especially in mathematics and science (Watkins and Biggs, 2001). Asians have been found to possess slightly higher mean IQs than Europeans (Lynn and Vanhanen, 2002), with their visualisation IQ much higher than their verbal IQ (Lynn, 2006). The success of the Chinese people in spatial tasks such as mathematics has been attributed to the nature of the Chinese language, which requires learners to think visually/spatially rather than verbally (Bond, 1992).

Many criticisms raised against so-called Confucian educational practices are based on incomplete understanding of Chinese traditions and their underlying beliefs. The two most common Chinese terms for 'knowledge' – *xue wen* (literally, 'learn and ask'; 学问) and *zhi shi* ('know and understand'; 知识) – indicate that questioning and understanding are integral to the learning process. Confucius' pedagogical approach was said to involve posing questions, citing passages from the classics, using apt analogies and waiting for his students to arrive at the correct answers: 'I only instruct the eager and enlighten the fervent. If I hold up one corner and a student cannot come back to me with the other three, I do not go on with the lesson' (Lunyu, 7.8). His students were expected to undertake long and careful study with some reflective learning: 'He who learns but does not think is lost. He who thinks but does not learn is in great danger' (Analects, 2.15); 'Knowing through silent reflection, learning without satiety, and teaching others without becoming weary – these are merits which I can claim' (Analects, 7.2). There are those who act without knowing why. But I am not like that. To hear much and then to select the good and follow it; to see much and then to ponder it – this comes next to true knowledge' (Analects, 7.27). Confucius also believed that prior knowledge is intrinsically connected to new knowledge, which cannot be derived without the mastery of prior knowledge. Moreover, critical reflection is possible when learning is repeated, and a learner is able to instruct others only after acquiring the new knowledge based on prior knowledge. Repetition does not hinder reflection but enhances it: 'To be able to acquire new knowledge while reviewing the old qualifies one as an instructor of men' (Confucius, quoted in Chai and Chai, 1965: 45).

The significance of the self within Chinese education has also been misunderstood (Li and Yue, 2004). Lifelong learning is central to the Confucian concept of *ren* (仁), which encourages individuals to become the most moral person (i.e. genuine, sincere and humane) one can be (Tu, 1979). This process of self-perfection includes both academic pursuit and individual moral development. It is noteworthy that every person has a right to seek self-perfection and each individual has control of this process. This 'need to perfect oneself' has been found still to exist today in Chinese college students (Li, 2002), who, unlike their Western counterparts, see knowledge as 'something that they must have' (Li, 2003: 265). In contrast to Western educational approaches that are more technical and rational, traditional Chinese education has aimed for more holistic outcomes. Chinese teachers see their educational role extending beyond the classroom into the moral and affective aspects of life. The goals of learning go beyond grasping the common and general knowledge to help learners form their own conviction, values and ideals (Lu and Chi, 2007: 28).

The arts and creativity in Chinese societies

While Confucius focused on moral behaviour and the classics, practical and scientific knowledge were completely ignored. Despite this, the Chinese have been credited with the invention of the compass, gunpowder, papermaking, movable type printing and the abacus. China's emergence as a world financial player is compelling, declaring to the world that she has what it takes to transform her third-world factory economy into a force in creativity to be reckoned with (Sinha, 2008).

Culture and the arts are intricately integrated in Chinese societies. Confucius repeatedly emphasised the importance of music (*yue*; 乐) and ritual (*li*; 礼), believing that aesthetic judgement and the arts are vital to the self-cultivation of benevolence in the moral person: 'Let a man be stimulated by poetry, established by the rules of propriety, and perfected by music' (Analects, 8:9). He accorded the Book of Songs (poems) an important place in his curriculum, frequently quoting and explaining them, teaching that '[c]eremonies and music in their nature resemble Heaven and Earth, penetrate the virtues of the spiritual intelligences, bring down spirits from above and lift the souls that are abased' (Li Ki, Bk xvii., sect. iii., v. 2.). A record from the Tang period provides a glimpse of how the arts played an integral role in the lives of the emperor and his scholar-officials: 'Whenever the emperor was moved by something, he would write a poem, and all the Scholars would follow suit using the same rhyme. This indeed was what men of that age took delight in and yearned after' (from 'The Records of Occasions in T'ang Poetry', cited in Owen, 1977: 256). The rigorously trained scholar-artists were skilled in the arts and held official positions as powerful politicians. This elevated the level of artistic accomplishment in court life, and the arts played a central functional role in all official ceremonies and banquets.

An artist belonging to this elite breed was called *wen ren* (文人) or 'the person with the ultimate knowledge of the arts' (有文德之人). He was 'simultaneously a scholar or scientist, a statesman, as well as an artist accomplished in a variety of artistic media' (Chou, 2002: 19). The *wen ren* were also described as 'men of culture' (Shin, 2006), who were typically accomplished artists in the four literary arts of music, poetry, calligraphy and painting (琴, 诗, 书, 画). The *wen ren* spirit was both Chinese and universal: Chinese in that it was responsible for the cultural and social life of the Chinese civilisation for more than 2,000 years; universal in its 'commitment to true quality and deep sincerity, to independence, honesty and courage' (Chou, 2002: 24). The former director of research for the Shanghai Art Museum, Li Xu, provides an insight into the *wen ren* from a twenty-first-century perspective:

> the 'wen ren', the polymathic scholar artist, is at the root of Chinese visual culture … Throughout history, Western society has laid emphasis on the specialised division of labour, so no social system for cultivating broad and comprehensive talent was ever fostered,' he says. 'Differing from the Western concept of an intellectual, Chinese wen ren were not only erudite scholars; many were also talented artists and designers.' Li gives as an example the highly sophisticated tradition of teapot design by wen ren scholars. Sometimes exuberantly formal, they were also often inscribed with poetry written by the wen ren. Creating a teapot was one of the best ways to disseminate a poem among other members

of the cultural elite, an alternative form of publication. Li says: 'The creation of a teapot saw the convergence of a variety of disciplines, including modelling, mud colouring, inscription, poetry, calligraphy, painting, sculpture and seal cutting.'

(Long, 2006: 1)

Heritage forms the foundation of creativity by which the *wen ren* was nurtured within the scholastic traditions of the Imperial Examinations. Over time, such a legacy is revitalised through a process that involves 'assimilation and introspection' and a person's own responses to 'stimuli from beyond as well as within the heritage' (Chou, 2002: 19).

Chinese ideals of creativity are rooted in respect for the past and the search for harmony with the forces of nature. Creativity was seen as 'an inspired imitation of the forces of nature' within the Taoist and Buddhist traditions. Both Eastern and Western conceptions of individual creativity have developed from a theistic or cosmic tradition of either divinely inspired or natural creativity (Niu and Sternberg, 2006). Western divine creativity and Chinese natural creativity (*dao*; 道) share three common characteristics of representing the ultimate origin of everything, in which there are 'endless producing and renovating changes' and the creating of 'all goodness'. The significant difference between the two conceptions lies in the definition of the production (Western) and non-production (Eastern) of something 'new'. Continual transformation is inherent in Chinese natural creativity, which is perceived to be 'ever-renovating' and 'producing' or 'as unexpectedly developing into various genuine entities' (Niu and Sternberg, 2006: 29). This is in tune with Eastern 'polychronic' conceptions of time, human action and progress, viewing creative acts as reiterative and rediscovery processes (LeBaron and Pillay, 2006) or 'successive reconfigurations' (Lubart, 1999: 341). This requires adaptability (*hua*; 化) in order to find a balance between continual change (*bian*; 变) through time and space and the social goal of harmony. As water flows and adapts to avoid obstacles in its way, Chinese creativity demands a unique type of creative flexibility to adapt to specific situations and conditions (Ee *et al.*, 2007). Whereas the East sees creativity as a re-interpretation of ideas, the West sees creativity as a break from tradition (Kristeller, 1983).

Western creativity ideals that include the 'elements of invention and novelty, a willingness to reject tradition, orientation on self-actualization, celebration of individual accomplishment, and concentration on the future' are foreign to Chinese traditional ideals (Lau *et al.*, 2004: 59). The West tends to be more deductive (Pattberg, 2009) and values novelty more than the East, which tends to be more inductive and values the authentic expression of an art work, i.e. effective in representing the creator's personal values and beliefs (Averill *et al.*, 2001). The emphasis on products is an idiosyncratic trait of the West, which adopts novelty and appropriateness as criteria and indicators of creativity (Raina *et al.*, 2001). The Western view of creativity is progressive in outlook, emphasising method and the most appropriate way to solve problems, leans towards the logical and demands that everything fits together in accordance with existing laws (Rudowicz, 2003).

In contrast, the East puts more attention on 'mastering and perfecting skills' (ibid.: 62), the inner 'experience of personal fulfillment' and the creative process (Raina *et al.*, 2001: 148). The arts are found to feature more prominently in Western perceptions of creativity than in the East (Rudowicz and Yue, 2000), with Westerners believing that exploration should precede skill development whereas Chinese educators believe skills should be developed first (requiring repetitive learning), so as to provide a foundation for creative expression (Wang and King, 2008). Several recent studies (Rudowicz, 2003) have found overlaps between Eastern and Western implicit concepts regarding creativity and the characteristics of a creative person. But Chinese people seem to care more about the creator's social influence, status, fame, charisma and contribution to society than his or her contribution to culture. They also associated creative achievement with financial and political accomplishments rather than with aesthetic or artistic ones, rarely nominating artists, musicians and business people as examples of creative people (Yue, 2003; Yue and Rudowicz, 2002) (see Table 6.1).

A specific illustration of the differences between East and West can be found in painting (Lau et al., 2004). Eastern painters do not need concrete models in their creative work as the production of realistic representations is not their goal. They paint according to their imagination of the desired object or scene, which is limited in range as restricted by tradition. The aesthetic categories governing their art works relate to the forces of 'contrasts' and 'contradictions' such as solid–empty and light–dark. Calmness and spontaneous energy are simultaneous aims in their paintings. Chinese painters are given the traditional freedom to represent 'imagined' objects and scenes, generate their own expressive aesthetic categories and distinctive styles, and individualise their brush techniques (Li and Gardner, 1993: 97–8). Table 6.2 summarises these differences between Eastern and Western painting.

Table 6.1 Comparison of Eastern and Western views on creativity

Eastern	Western
Seeks to be authentic to creator's own values and beliefs	Seeks novelty
Introverted	Extroverted
Encourages cooperation, compromise and conformity; adaptive	Encourages deliberation and divergence; innovative
More constrained and consistent with works of the past; reuse and reinterpretation of traditions and ideas; successive reconfigurations of old	Innovation; break from tradition; changing and modifying pre-existing structures
Inductive; intuitive	Deductive; logical; having a finite beginning and end
Focus on personal fulfilment and the understanding of an inner sense of ultimate reality	Focus on person's ability to generate creative products
Value the characteristics of 'goodness', 'moral goodness' and 'contribution to society'	Concerned with analytical abilities and focus on the characteristics of unconventionality, inquisitiveness, imagination and freedom
Less focus on the artistic and humorous	More focus on the artistic and humorous
Respect for creator's contribution to society	Respect for creator's contribution to culture
Prefers financial and political accomplishments	Prefers aesthetic or artistic accomplishments

Table 6.2 Differences between Eastern and Western painting

Eastern	Western
Limited range of objects depicted, e.g. mountains, rivers, flowers, trees, birds, few body parts	Virtually no limitations on choice of objects
Models not needed as realistic representation not the goal	Models needed for creative work
Aesthetic categories relate to 'contradictions', e.g. solid–empty, light–dark, fast–slow	Aesthetic categories include contour, shape, light, shadow, colour, space, perspective, proportion, geometric principles
Calm and spontaneous energy desired	Liberal energy desired

Source: adapted from Li and Gardner, 1993; and Lau et al., 2004

The perspectives of five contemporary Chinese musicians (Kang, 2009; Jing, 2005; Zhang, 2005; Zhong, 2005; Jia, 1998) indicate that innovation is a breakthrough of inherited traditions, which forms the basis of progress. Three sources of inspiration for the musical imagination are a person's external experiences, internal experiences and arts experiences. By assimilating different musical cultures and selectively absorbing the essence of contemporary Western music, internationally acceptable music pieces are created for their time, allowing the world to feel the unique charms of Chinese music. An outstanding performing artist must attain unity between the instrument and the self, expressing the inner emotions and thoughts in artistic ways. Craftsmanship is important to enable the 'hand' and the 'mind' to connect during the creative process. The zenith of the arts is attained when the artist skilfully creates what is in the mind. A peaceful and stable emotional state provides the conditions that are conducive for inspiration to be captured. Related basic knowledge and professional field knowledge are prerequisites for cultivating creativity. Without them, creative endeavours become meaningless 'random thinking' and 'unconstrained thinking', which cannot be transformed into real creativity. The ability to master and apply musical skills forms a major part in developing creative talent.

The perspectives on creativity from Chinese artists and musicians suggest that creativity and innovation are important to the Chinese people, whose artistic and pedagogic practices by and large continue along traditional lines.

Conclusions

This chapter has examined the way Chinese cultural traditions influenced the development of creativity in Chinese societies. Strongly influenced by Confucian thinking, key aspects of Chinese culture have been misinterpreted as uncreative by those who have applied Western criteria in their judgement. Chinese artists and musicians have demonstrated creativity in different and sometimes subtle ways, and there are distinct cultural differences between the East and West. These provide valuable perspectives by which people can understand one other.

Comparisons of differences between East and West are becoming increasingly challenging in a globalised world, where there are more intercultural exchanges taking place, more multicultural communities living together, and where nationality may not constitute cultural membership (Craft et al., 2008). In any case, 'cultures differ [and] cannot and should not be directly compared' (Runco, 2001: x). China and other Chinese societies today are living with the confluences of Eastern and Western cultures (Lee, 2003), where the more conformist traditional values intersect with those of capitalism and internationalisation. This might result in more people from these societies becoming 'bi-cultural', better able to cross between differing social constraints and social interests in relating to each other (Nisbett, 2003). If creativity in learning is about fostering 'flexibility, openness for the new, the ability to adapt or to see new ways of doings things and the courage to face the unexpected' (Cropley, 2001: 136), arts educators should make reference to the different cultural manifestations to facilitate staff and students thinking in new ways, and making connections with the unfamiliar. Educational extensions beyond the culturally convenient, comfortable and familiar could do wonders to expand the creative imagination and horizons of those involved.

References

Averill, J. R., Chon, K. K. and Hahn, D. W. (2001) Emotions and creativity, East and West, *Asian Journal of Social Psychology* 4: 165–83.

Beamer, L. and Varner, I. (2008) *Intercultural Communication in the Global Workplace* (4th ed.), New York: McGraw-Hill.

Biggs, J. B. (1994) Asian learners through Western eyes, *Australian and New Zealand Journal of Vocational Educational Research* 2(2): 40–63.

Bond, M. H. (1992). *Beyond the Chinese Face*, Oxford: Oxford University Press.

Chai, C. and Chai, W. (1965) *The Sacred Books of Confucius and Other Confucian Classics*, New York: University Books.

Cheng, J. Y. S. (2008) Confucian values and democratic governance in Hong Kong, *International Journal of the Humanities* 6(1): 25–32.

Chou, W. C. (2002) Wen Ren and culture, in K. S. Tong and S. W. Chan (eds.) *Culture and Humanity in the New Millennium*, Hong Kong: The Chinese University Press.

Confucianism (2009) *Encyclopædia Britannica Online*; available at http://www.britannica.com/EBchecked/topic/132104/Confucianism (accessed 25 September 2009).

Craft, A., Gardner, H., Claxton, G. *et al.* (eds) (2008) *Creativity, Wisdom and Trusteeship*, Thousand Oaks, CA: Corwin Press.

Cropley, A. (2001) *Creativity in Education and Learning*, London: Routledge.

Crowell, T. (2005) The Confucian renaissance, *Asian Times Online*, 16 November.

Ee, J. and Tan, O. S. (2008) Cultural influences of the East & West, *KEDI Journal of Educational Policy* 5(1): 49–62.

Ee, J., Tan, O. S. and Ng, A. K. (2007) Styles of creativity, *Asia Pacific Education Review* 8(3): 364–73.

European Commission (2009) *The Impact of Culture on Creativity*, Brussels: KEA European Affairs.

Gilbert, D. and Tsao, J. (2000) Exploring Chinese cultural influences and hospitality marketing relationships, *International Journal of Contemporary Hospitality Management* 12(1): 45–53.

Guo, Q. (2002) Essentials of traditional Chinese education thoughts and contemporary competency education, *Journal of Southern Yangtze University Humanities & Social Sciences Edition* 1(1): 80–6.

Ho, D. Y. F. (1994) Filial piety, authoritarian moralism and cognitive conservatism, *Genetic, Social and General Psychology Monographs* 120: 347–65.

Ho, I. T., Salili, F., Biggs, J. B. and Hau, K. T. (1999) The relationship among causal attributions, learning strategies and level of achievement: a Hong Kong Chinese study, *Asia-Pacific Journal of Education* 19(1): 44–58.

Kristeller, P. O. (1983) 'Creativity' and 'tradition', *Journal of the History of Ideas* 44: 105–13.

Lau, S., Hui, A. N. N. and Ng, G. Y. C. (2004) *Creativity: When East Meets West*, Singapore: World Scientific.

LeBaron, M. and Pillay, V. (2006) *Conflict across Cultures*, Boston, MA: Intercultural Press.

Lee, C. Y. (2003) Do traditional values still exist in modern Chinese societies?, *Asia Europe Journal* 1: 43–59.

Lee, W. O. (1996) The cultural context for Chinese learners, in D. Watkins and J. B. Biggs (eds.) *The Chinese Learner*, Melbourne and Hong Kong: Australian Council for Educational Research and the Comparative Education Research Centre, University of Hong Kong.

Li, J. (2002) A cultural model of learning, *Journal of Cross-Cultural Psychology* 33(3): 248–69.

—— (2003) U.S. and Chinese cultural beliefs about learning, *Journal of Educational Psychology* 95(2): 258–67.

Li, J. and Gardner, H. (1993) How domains constrain creativity, *American Behavioral Scientist* 37(1): 94–101.

Li, J. and Yue, X. D. (2004) Self in learning among Chinese children, *New Directions for Child and Adolescent Development* 104: 27–43.

Long, K. (2006) Design art in Shanghai, *IconEye* 42 (December); available at http://www.iconeye.com/index.php?option=com_content&view=article&id=2440:design-art-in-shanghai-icon-042–december-2006 (accessed 25 August 2009).

Lu, Y. Q. and Chi, Y. J. (2007) Educational philosophy in China, *Frontiers of Education in China* 2(1): 13–29.

Lubart, T. I. (1999) Creativity across cultures, in R. J. Sternberg (ed.) *Handbook of Creativity*, New York: Cambridge University Press.

Lynn, R. (2006) *Race Differences in Intelligence*, Augusta: Washington Summit Publishers.

Lynn, R. and Vanhanen, T. (2002) *IQ and the Wealth of Nations*, Westport, CT: Praeger.

Nakagawa, Y. (2000) *Education for Awakening: An Eastern Approach to Holistic Education*. Volume Two of the Foundations of Holistic Education Series. Brandon, VT: Foundation for Educational Renewal.

Nguyen, P.-M., Terlouw, C. and Pilot, A. (2006) Culturally appropriate pedagogy, *Intercultural Education* 17(1): 1–19.

Nisbett, R. E. (2003) *The Geography of Thought*, New York: The Free Press.

Niu, W. and Sternberg, R. J. (2006) The philosophical roots of Western and Eastern conceptions of creativity, *Journal of Theoretical and Philosophical Psychology* 26: 18–38.

Owen, S. (1977) *The Poetry of the Early T'ang*, New Haven, CT: Yale University Press.

Pattberg, T. (2009) *The East–West Dichotomy*, New York: Thorsten Pattberg.

Raina, M. K., Srivasta, A. K. and Misra, G. (2001) Explorations in literary creativity, *Psychological Studies* 46: 148–60.

Runco, M. A. (2001) Foreword, in A. K. Ng, *Why Asians Are Less Creative than Westerners*, Singapore: Prentice-Hall.

Rudowicz, E. (2003) Creativity and culture: two way interaction, *Scandinavian Journal of Educational Research* 47: 273–90.

Rudowicz, E. and Yue, X. (2000) Concepts of creativity, *Journal of Creative Behavior* 34: 175–92.

Shi, J.-Y. (2009) Return of the sage, *South China Morning Post*, 23 September.

Shin, L. K. (2006) *The Making of the Chinese State*, Cambridge and New York: Cambridge University Press.

Shusterman, R. (2009) Pragmatist aesthetics and Confucianism, *Journal of Aesthetic Education* 43(1): 18–29.

Sinha, K. (2008) *China's Creative Imperative*, Singapore: John Wiley & Sons (Asia) Pte. Ltd.

Tu, W. M. (1979) *Humanity and Self-Cultivation*, Berkeley, CA: Asian Humanities Press.

Wang, J., Wang, G. G., Ruona, W. E. A. and Rojewski, J. W. (2005) Confucian values and the implications for international HRD, *Human Resource Development International* 8(3): 311–26.

Wang, V. C. X. and King, K. P. (2008) Transformative learning and ancient Asian educational perspectives, *Journal of Transformative Education* 6:136–50.

Watkins, A. and Biggs, J. B. (eds) (2001) *Teaching the Chinese Learner*, Hong Kong: Comparative Education Research Centre.

White Paper on Shared Values (1991) Singapore: Ministry of Information, Communication, and the Arts.

Yang, B. (1958) *Lunyu yizhu*, Beijing: Zhonghua Shuju.

Yue, X. D. (2003) Meritorious evaluation bias, *Journal of Creative Behavior* 37: 88–104.

Yue, X. D. and Rudowicz, E. (2002) Perception of the most creative Chinese by undergraduates in Beijing, Guangzhou, Hong Kong and Taipei, *Journal of Creative Behavior* 36: 155–77.

References in Chinese (retrieved from China Journals Full-Text Database)

Jia, Q. Y. (1998) A warning about contemporary lyrics writing, *Chinese TV* 08: 62–3 (accessed 18 August 2009).

Jing, Z. (2005) Liberating the sentiment and soul, *ShuoFang* 12: 69–70 (accessed 18 August 2009).

Kang, X. H. (2009) Discussing the 'facility' of performing artists, *Playwright* 1: 123 (accessed 18 August 2009).

Zhang, D. F. (1998) Diligence is the mother of success, *Arts Exploration* 02: 19–22 (accessed 18 August 2009).

Zhang, K. X. (2005) Discussing the facilitation effects of music education to enhance the creative ability of university students, *The World of Music* 9: 7–9 (accessed 18 August 2009).

Zhong, J. C. (2005) The conceptual renewal of contemporary music creation, *Arts Exploration, Journal of Guanxi Arts College* 19(5): 105–6 (accessed 18 August 2009).

7

Psychological research on creativity

Mark A. Runco and Alexander R. Pagnani

Good ideas endure. They are tested and applied. They are also questioned and stimulate debate; but that too is a valuable thing. One way or another, good ideas have impact (Runco, 1995). According to Csikszentmihalyi (1990), good ideas begin with an individual, and if they are truly creative, they eventually have an impact on others working in the same field. They may change the assumptions and basic premises of a domain, and if they do so, they will eventually change the material provided to other individuals as they move into the field.

Creative studies has had its share of this kind of good idea. It is, for instance, easy to see the value of Wallas' (1926) theory of the creative process, which is still widely used (e.g. Norlander and Gustafson, 1998; Runco, 1997). It is also easy to see the value of Guilford's (1950, 1968) structure of intellect model, Torrance's (1962, 1995) ideas about assessing creative potential, and Rhodes' (1961) framework for organizing the various perspectives on creativity. The last of these is nearly always used when the intent is to review the field of creativity studies. Rhodes proposed a "Four P" framework that recognizes four distinct components, which he called strands: personality (and persons), press, products, and processes. "Press" was taken from the concept of pressure, the idea being that environments exert pressures which influence creative behavior.

Rhodes' (1961) model was extended when Simonton (1995) added *persuasion*, the idea being that creative people and things change the way others think. Clearly, this fits well with what was said above about impact. Runco (2007) then argued for adding *potential* to the list as well. He created a hierarchy, with creative performance and creative potential as the two overarching categories for research and theory (see Table 7.1).

This chapter presents a brief overview of the academic research concerning creativity. More detailed overviews were presented not long ago (Runco, 2004, 2007). Here we use Rhodes' (1961) model and Runco's (2007) framework for structure. Within this framework, we seek to explore many of the key questions that guide and shape this investigative field. We address the following questions:

- What do we know about highly creative people?
- How are creative products evaluated?
- What mental processes are associated with creative thought?
- How can environment support or suppress creativity?

Table 7.1 Hierarchical framework for the study of creativity

Creative Potential	Creative Performance
Person Personality traits and characteristics	**Products** Ideas Patents, inventions, and publications
Process Cognition	**Persuasion** Historical reputation
Press Distal • Evolution • Culture and zeitgiest Immediate • Places, settings, environment	Systems • Individual-field-domain Social attributions
	Interactions State × trait Person × environment

The creative person

Most people, if asked to identify a "creative" individual, will quickly offer the names of eminent artists and scientists. Most will first think of artists, or perhaps only think of artists. This "*art bias*" reflects the assumption that creative talent is always expressed in the arts. Even when other domains are recognized, there is a tendency to think only of eminent persons. These great thinkers and creators, such as da Vinci, Picasso, or Edison, have certainly earned distinction through their dedication, ingenuity, and originality. Yet the tendency to focus on major creative accomplishments can obscure the fact that we all have creativity in our own more daily lives. We all have the potential that is at the top of Table 7.1.

Eminent creativity is sometime labeled "Big C" creativity. This designates the monumental and socially lauded accomplishments of eminent individuals. "Small c" creativity is used to describe more routine creative endeavors that are not often not praised by an audience. Consider the preparation of a dinner party. One might develop a menu and select recipes, prepare and decorate the home, mix and match from one's wardrobe for just the "right" look, and perhaps even design a floral arrangement for the table's centerpiece. Each of these tasks requires some measure of creativity, yet none is likely to earn heaps of recognition from society at large. When discussing creative persons, it is vital that we recognize that creativity can be found both in the people whose paintings are displayed in museums and also in our family members, friends, neighbors, and in our own lives.

Decades of empirical research have shown that certain personality traits correlate at moderate and sometimes high levels with independent, original, creative thought (Barron and Harrington, 1981; Feist, 1999; Runco, 2004). Understanding these traits may allow the prediction of creative action. Note, however, that the presence of the traits which have been correlated with creativity in the research is only indicative of creative potential. If someone has those key traits, they have potential but may not use it! This is why the hierarchy in Table 7.1 separates potential from actual performance. It also implies that if potential is supported by the environment, creative behavior is almost certain to manifest itself.

The key or *core characteristics* associated with creativity include originality, independence, willingness to take risks, intrinsic motivation, curiosity, humor, attraction to complexity, open-mindedness, and wide interests (Farley, 1986; Feist, 1999; Torrance, 1962). A few seemingly negative personality traits have been found to correlate with creative behaviors as well, including hyperactivity, rebelliousness, egocentricity, cynicism, sarcasm, absentmindedness, disobedience, and argumentativeness (Torrance, 1962; Davis, 2003). No wonder creative behaviors are not always valued in the classroom. Highly creative children are sometimes seen by their teachers as the least cooperative and agreeable students in the class (Westby and Dawson, 1995). Importantly, many of the core characteristics of creativity have been identified psychometrically with personality tests (Barron, 1995; Helson, 1996), but some triangulation is offered by case studies which often uncover the same traits (Davis *et al.*, in press).

Core characteristics often have *domain specificity*. Most of the research on this issue has focused on differences between artistic creativity and scientific creativity (Feist, 1999; Runco and Bahleda, 1987). Creative artists seem to be more emotionally sensitive and behaviorally impulsive than scientists, while creative scientists less frequently reject societal norms and are more organized than their artistic peers (Feist, 1999). There are also domain differences in the likelihood of psychopathology (Ludwig, 1998). Still, the two groups share much of their personality profile, reinforcing the notion that creativity and creative accomplishment are closely linked to a stable and predictable profile of behavioral traits. Both creative artists and scientists have been found to possess openness to new experiences and imagination (Domino, 1974), impulsivity (Dudek *et al.*, 1991), emotional sensitivity (Feist, 1991), nonconformity (Hall and MacKinnon, 1969), hostility (Drevdahl and Cattell, 1958), and introversion (Storr, 1988).

The creative process

Research on the creative process complements research on creative persons. That is because there may be processes used by creative individuals that are not used as frequently by less creative individuals. Theories of the creative process are, like findings about creative personality, mostly useful for understanding creative potential (see Table 7.1). A person may have the capacity for creative ideation but not use it. It is an open question whether or not there is a process that guarantees creative performance.

Ideation is one of the more commonly studied processes (Guilford, 1968; Runco, 1991; Torrance, 1995). Much of this relies on tests of divergent thinking to elicit ideation. According to Plucker and Renzulli (1999: 39), "divergent thinking tests require individuals to produce several responses to a specific prompt, in sharp contrast to most standardized tests." Although divergent thinking is not synonymous with creativity, it is clearly related to original thinking, and originality is a prerequisite for creativity. Runco (1991) put it this way: divergent thinking tests provide useful estimates of the potential for creative problem solving. The key terms are *estimates* (since no test is perfectly reliable and valid) and *potential* (since there is no guarantee that skills will in fact be used in the natural environment). The *problem solving* in that conclusion is also important, given that creativity may sometimes require more original problem *finding* than problem *solving* (Getzels, 1975; Runco, 1994).

In tests of divergent thinking, examinees are asked to generate numerous responses to a specific question or task, with performance quantified in terms of the number of responses (fluency), the statistical infrequency of those responses (originality), the level of detail (elaboration), and the diversity of concepts suggested by the ideas (flexibility). While these tasks do not encompass all aspects of the creative process, the better tests do produce highly valid and reliable estimates of creative potential.

Not all creativity tests target creative processes. There are also tests of interests, prior experiences, personality, and preference inventories (Davis, 2003). Many of these assume that the best predictor of future creative behavior is past creative behavior (Okuda *et al.*, 1991; Plucker, 1999; Torrance, 1962). Other tests focus on motivation (Renzulli and Reis, 1997) or childhood hobbies, imaginary playmates, and theater experience. According to Davis (2003: 312), "Adults who had an imaginary playmate or have a background in theatre—they often admit to both—will always show creative personality traits, creative abilities, and a history of creative involvement," making these two questions alone anecdotal yet positive indicators of creative potential. Taylor (in press), Runco and Pina (in press), and Root-Bernstein and Root-Bernstein (2006) provided additional support for the relevance of imaginary worlds.

Two other process theories should be mentioned. First is the often-cited theory of Wallas (1926). He described the creative process with four stages: preparation, incubation, illumination, and verification. This theory is still widely used (e.g. Norlander and Gustafson, 1998), though *recursion* (recycling through the process) is often added, and the stages are sometimes given different labels. Preparation is often described as problem finding, for example, and verification is often called evaluative thinking (Runco, 1994).

Chand and Runco (1992) outlined a two tiered process model, with three components on the primary tier (i.e. problem finding, ideation, evaluation) and two on the secondary tier (i.e. motivation, knowledge). The secondary tier contains influences on the primary tier. Motivation may be intrinsic or extrinsic. Knowledge is factual information or procedural. The latter is especially important because it applies to the know-how and tactics that are provided by enhancement efforts (Runco, 1999).

Other process, stage, and componential models exist (e.g. Amabile, 1990; Baughman and Mumford, 1995). In every case the assumption is that if the process is followed, creative products or behavior will result. But what exactly is a creative product?

The creative product

Many theories of creativity assume that there must be a product (e.g. Rogers, 1959). That is unfortunate because it relegates personal creativity (Runco, 1995), everyday creativity (Runco and Richards, 1998), and most of the creativity of children (Runco, 1996). Children often paint and use clay but the results of their efforts are rarely in museums, and frequently their creativity is manifested without a tangible product, as in their play (Russ *et al.*, 1999). It is useful to study creative products as long as one's definition of creativity does not require a socially recognized product. Not all creative efforts result in a product.

Creative products do have an advantage in that they can be studied in a highly objective fashion. Table 7.1 mentions patents, inventions, and paintings, but creative products take many forms. There is a large literature on publications, probably because they are a matter of record and can be counted (Albert, 1975; Simonton, 1990). In fact, the quality of a publication is estimated from citations. Higher quality publications are defined as those that are frequently cited by others. (That is another way of phrasing Simonton's (1995) idea of creativity as persuasion.) One result from studies of publications (as products) is that the distribution shows that a small number of authors produce the majority of the works. This is known as *Lotka's Law*. It may apply very broadly, to paintings, inventions, and all kinds of products. Huber (1998) described research specifically on inventions, and for obvious reasons much recent research is looking to design and technological products (e.g. Howe, 1992). O'Quin and Besemer (1989) presented a detailed but broadly applicable framework for the assessment of products.

The creative press

Perhaps the broadest category of creativity research is that of environmental "press," a term first coined by Murray (1938) to describe pressures (hence "press") that influence creative people or the creative process. Press factors are not all-important: Creative efforts depend not only on the person or environment but rather on meaningful interaction between the two (Csikszentmihalyi, 1988; Hemlin *et al.*, 2008). This view was implied by Rhodes (1961) when he described press as "the relationship of human beings and their environment," and was later underscored by Bronfenbrenner (1979), in his ecological theory of child development, and by Simonton (1990) and Csikszentmihalyi (1999), in their theories of social, cultural, economic, and political influences.

At least six levels of socialization have been suggested as press factors: physical surroundings, family upbringing, schooling experiences, workplace environments, cultural traditions, and the historical milieu in which we happen to have been born. At each point in our lives, both our past and present influences from each of these levels are subtly guiding our creative processes and production.

The most basic environmental press on creativity is that of the immediate, physical surroundings. The materials, lighting, organization, and layout of certain locations can contribute to a sense of ease or discomfort, benefiting or stifling our creative potential. Consider, for example, the differing senses of comfort that one feels when in an art-house coffee shop versus a whitewall, cinder-block meeting room. McCoy and Evans (2002) explored the effects of such locations, demonstrating not only that people tend to judge some physical spaces as being more creatively conducive than others but that these locations actually possess the perceived effects on creative production as well. Vithayathawornwong, Danko, and Tolbert (2003) discovered that the most creative organizations were those whose layouts promoted both a sense of dynamism and freedom among the employees. In order to craft such an environment, institutions must set clear circulation paths, move workspaces closer together, install numerous windows and telephones, allow employees opportunities for privacy and personalization of their spaces, and include physical areas for relaxation and freeform uses. Immediate environmental factors are not solely physical. There are clear interpersonal effects, including perceived support of supervisors and leaders in the workplace. Not surprisingly, there is a positive correlation between subordinates' perceived leader support and their peer-rated creativity (Amabile *et al.*, 2004). Leaders' attitudes are also pertinent.

In a parallel fashion parental attitudes are potential influences on children's creativity. According to Sheldon (1995), creative people perceived their parents to be more autonomy supportive. Siegelman (1973) also examined the parent–child relationship and children's creativity. Fathers' rejecting and neglecting relations correlated with male subjects' creativity; loving, neglecting, and protecting relations correlated with female subjects' creativity. Mothers' loving, rejecting, and neglecting relations correlated with male subjects' creativity; and loving and neglecting relations with female subjects' creativity.

Authoritative parenting, which creates a loving and accepting environment for children, with rules that are reasonable and fair, has been found to nurture creativity in children most effectively (Jensen and Kingston, 1986; Michel and Dudek, 1991). Yeh (2004) pointed to the need for parents to provide good models of the creative process and an open and flexible home environment. Structurally, larger families with less autonomy tend to de-emphasize creativity, perhaps due to limited resources and the parenting style needed for large families (Albert and Runco, 1989). Sulloway (1996) found that rebelliousness is most commonly found in middle children, with clear implications for their creative potential (Runco, 2004).

Dudek, Strobel, and Runco (1993) demonstrated that school atmospheres can support or undermine creative potential. Physical location and layout, student empowerment and decision making, opportunities for risk-taking and leadership, student encouragement, interdisciplinary approaches to content, and open and accepting teaching styles have all been found to exert a positive influence (Fleith, 2000; Yeh, 2004). Although creative performances differ from domain to domain, interdisciplinary education may very well offer huge benefits for creativity (Root-Bernstein, 1989). This is especially important in higher education and professional academia, where interdisciplinary discovery and integration may lead to creative leaps in knowledge and understanding for both fields.

The institutional workplace atmosphere has been investigated most often (see Williams and Yang, 1999, for a review). Of special interest is the tensions between the traditional foci on narrow specialization and production-line structures vs. the desires of managers that their employees think broadly and search for opportunities to innovate.

Then there is the macrosystem of general culture and temporal influence that continuously works to shape identities, beliefs, assumptions, and creative cognition. These are obvious in traditional views of creativity in Western culture, with the emphasis on novelty and usefulness, in contrast to the Eastern focus on beauty and the perfection of delineated practice. Indian Hindi culture views creativity as probing the depths of the soul in search of self-actualization. The Kaluli tribe of Papua New Guinea values different elements within creative music depending on the gender of the performer (Lubart, 1999). The Kaluli are not alone in holding different creative standards for men and women; significant work has demonstrated the sweeping effects of culture upon gendered creative performance, in terms of both historical resource denial to females and the continuing perceptions of "appropriate" gendered avenues for creative expression, such as increased support for female ballerinas but lessened support for female architects (Pagnani, in press).

The effects of culture upon creativity vary in response to three variables: the level of resources available; the degree of modernization found in the culture; and the specific zeitgeist of that moment of time. (Cultures are dynamic systems that change and evolve as time marches on.) Studies have typically focused on populations which have been denied resources. Dhillon and Mehra (1987), for example, examined the creative production of females from both wealthy and impoverished classes in India. Modernization, with its cultural focus on gender equality, has also been found to positively impact creative production, with Mar'i and Karayanni (1983) confirming that the creative production of females in Arab nations correlates strongly with assessments of modernization in those countries. The effects of temporal fluctuations in cultural support have also been examined at length. Simonton (1992), for instance, explored cultural and religious changes over 1,400 years of Japanese history. He detailed the ebbs and flows of creative production by Japanese females over the centuries, as correlated with cycles of power and influence between rigid Confucian gender ideals and comparatively permissive Buddhist philosophies.

Conclusions

Clearly the research on creativity is diverse. Just as clearly, much of it is quite practical. This may be most obvious in the case of press and environmental research, especially on the level of immediate environments. Note the parallels between supportive work environments and supportive educational or home environments (e.g. autonomy is valued). There is a great deal of research specifically on settings and environments, probably because it is so practical. It suggests many things for the fulfillment of potential. Finally, note that the research on environments and press confirms that the person, process, product, and press research overlaps in important ways. In the case of environments, there is an interaction with personality such that what the individual perceives about the setting is more important than any objective indicator of that same setting.

Several concepts cut across the various categories of research. One involved domain differences. There may be differences among domains, but also commonalities. One recent suggestion for a commonality is the "original interpretation of experience" that is involved in all creative thinking, regardless of domains (Runco, 1996). At least as useful is the concept of everyday and eminent creativity. That relates to Big C and little c creativity, though care must be taken since it is too easy to assume that Big C is entirely unrelated to little c. Someone having an impact on society (Big C) may also be creative in a very personal but not socially impressive (little c) manner. Eminent creativity requires the talents involved in everyday creativity but has unique features as well (e.g. determination and energy; Gruber, 1988).

The four Ps and the hierarchy in Table 7.1 cover most of creativity studies, but there are theories and investigations that defy categorization. There is, for example, tentative genetic research suggesting that dopamine reception may be associated with divergent thinking, or at least with ideational fluency (Reuter et al., 2005; Runco et al., in press). The fact that the association is just with fluency and not originality suggests that dopamine (i.e. DRD2 and DRD4 alleles) contributes to productivity with ideas but not with the quality of ideas. Creativity requires quality, as is implied by definitions of creativity that emphasize originality and effectiveness (Runco, 2007). Where does research on genetics of creativity fit into Table 7.1? Perhaps "potential," yet there is no need to force all research into a category. After all, creativity studies tell us that it is good to be flexible and to consider new ideas and directions of thought.

References

Albert, R. S. (1975) Toward a behavioral definition of genius, *American Psychologist* 30: 140–51.

Albert, R. S. and Runco, M. A. (1989) Independence and cognitive ability in gifted and exceptionally gifted boys, *Journal of Youth and Adolescence* 18: 221–30.

Amabile, T. M. (1990) Within you, without you: the social psychology of creativity, and beyond, in M. A. Runco and R. S. Albert (eds.) *Theories of Creativity*, Newbury Park, CA: Sage.

Amabile, T. M., Schatzel, E. A., Moneta, G. B., and Kramer, S. J. (2004) Leader behaviors and the work environment for creativity, *Leadership Quarterly* 15: 5–33.

Barron, F. (1995) *No Rootless Flower: An Ecology of Creativity*, Cresskill, NJ: Hampton Press.

Barron, F. and Harrington, D. (1981) Creativity, intelligence, and personality, *Annual Review of Psychology* 32: 439–76.

Baughman, W. A. and Mumford, M. D. (1995) Process analytic models of creative capacities: operations involved in the combination and reorganization process, *Creativity Research Journal* 8: 37–62.

Bronfenbrenner, U. (1979) *The Ecology of Human Development*, Cambridge, MA: Harvard.

Chand, I. and Runco, M. A. (1992) Problem finding skills as components in the creative process, *Personality and Individual Differences* 14: 155–62.

Csikszentmihalyi, M. (1988) Society, culture, and person: a systems view of creativity, in R. J. Sternberg (ed.) *The Nature of Creativity*, New York: Cambridge University Press.

—— (1990) The domain of creativity, in M. A. Runco and R. S. Albert (eds.) *Theories of Creativity*, Newbury Park, CA: Sage.

—— (1999) Implications of a systems perspective for the study of creativity, in R. J. Sternberg (ed.) *Handbook of Creativity*, New York: Cambridge University Press.

Davis, G. A. (2003) Identifying creative students, teaching for creative growth, in N. Colangelo and G. A. Davis (eds.) *Handbook of Gifted Education* (3rd ed.), Boston: Allyn & Bacon.

Davis, S., Keegan, R., and Gruber, H. E. (in press) Creativity as purposeful work: the evolving systems view, in M. A. Runco (ed.) *Creativity Research Handbook*, vol. 2, Cresskill, NJ: Hampton.

Dhillon, P. K. and Mehra, D. (1987) The influence of social class and gender on primary school children's creative thinking, *Asian Journal of Psychology and Education* 19: 1–10.

Domino, G. (1974) Assessment of cinematographic creativity, *Journal of Personality and Social Psychology* 30: 150–4.

Drevdahl, J. E. and Cattell, R. B. (1958) Personality and creativity in artists and writers, *Journal of Clinical Psychology* 14: 107–11.

Dudek, S. Z., Bernèche, R., Bérubé, H., and Royer, S. (1991) Personality determinants of the commitment to the profession of art, *Creativity Research Journal* 4: 367–89.

Dudek, S. Z., Strobel, M. G., and Runco, M. A. (1993) Cumulative and proximal influences on the social environment and children's creative potential, *Journal of Genetic Psychology* 154: 487–99.

Farley, F. H. (1986) The big T in personality, *Psychology Today* (May): 47–52.

Feist, G. J. (1991) Synthetic and analytic thought: similarities and differences among art and science students, *Creativity Research Journal* 4: 145–55.

—— (1999) The influence of personality on artistic and scientific creativity, in R. J. Sternberg (ed.) *Handbook of Creativity*, New York: Cambridge University Press.

Fleith, D. S. (2000) Teacher and student perceptions of creativity in the classroom environment, *Roeper Review* 22(3): 148–53.

Getzels, J. W. (1975) Problem finding and the inventiveness of solutions, *Journal of Creative Behavior* 9: 12–18.

Gruber, H. (1988) The evolving systems approach to creative work, *Creativity Research Journal* 1: 27–51.

Guilford, J. P. (1950) Creativity, *American Psychologist* 5; 444–54.

—— (1968) *Creativity, Intelligence, and Their Educational Implications*, San Diego: EDITS/Knapp.

Hall, W. B. and MacKinnon, D. W. (1969) Personality inventory correlates of creativity among architects, *Journal of Applied Psychology* 53: 322–6.

Helson, R. (1996) In search of the creative personality, *Creativity Research Journal* 9: 295–306.

Hemlin, S., Allwood, C. M., and Martin, B. R. (2008) Creative knowledge environments, *Creativity Research Journal* 20: 196–210.

Howe, R. (1992) Uncovering the creative dimensions of computer based graphic design products, *Creativity Research Journal* 5: 233–43.

Huber, J. C. (1998) Invention and inventivity is a random, Poisson process: a potential guide to analysis of general creativity, *Creativity Research Journal* 11: 231–41.

Jensen, L. C. and Kingston, M. (1986) *Parenting*, Orlando: Holt Rinehart Winston.

Lubart, T. I. (1999) Creativity across cultures, in R. J. Sternberg (ed.) *Handbook of Creativity*, New York: Cambridge University Press.

Ludwig, A. (1998) Method and madness in the arts and sciences, *Creativity Research Journal* 11: 93–101.

McCoy, J. M. and Evans, G. W. (2002) The potential role of the physical environment in fostering creativity, *Creativity Research Journal* 14: 409–26.

Mar'i, S. K. and Karayanni, M. (1983) Creativity in Arab culture: two decades of research, *Journal of Creative Behavior* 16: 227–38.

Michel, M. and Dudek, S. Z. (1991) Mother–child relationship and creativity, *Creativity Research Journal* 4: 281–6.

Murray, H. A. (1938) *Explorations in Personality*, New York: Oxford University Press.

Norlander, T. and Gustafson, R. (1998) Effects of alcohol on a divergent figural fluency test during the illumination phase of the creative process, *Creativity Research Journal* 11: 265–74.

O'Quin, K. and Besemer, S. (1989) The development, reliability, and validity of the revised creative product semantic scale, *Creativity Research Journal* 2: 268–78.

Okuda, S. M., Runco, M. A., and Berger, D. E. (1991) Creativity and the finding and solving of real-world problems, *Journal of Psychoeducational Assessment* 9: 45–53.

Pagnani, A. R. (in press) Gender differences, in M. A. Runco and S. Pritzker (eds.) *Encyclopedia of Creativity* (2nd ed.), Oxford: Elsevier.

Pirola-Merlo, A. and Mann, L. (2004) The relationship between individual creativity and team creativity: aggregating across people and time, *Journal of Organizational Behavior* 25: 235–57.

Plucker, J. A. (1999) Reanalysis of student responses to creativity checklists: evidence of content generality, *Journal of Creative Behavior* 33: 126–37.

Plucker, J. A. and Renzulli, J. S. (1999) Psychometric approaches to the study of human creativity, in R. J. Sternberg (ed.) *Handbook of Creativity*, New York: Cambridge University Press.

Renzulli, J. S. and Reis, S. M. (1997) *Schoolwide Enrichment Model*, Mansfield Center, CT: Creative Learning Press.

Reuter, M., Panksepp, J., Schnabel, N., Kellerhoff, N., Kempel, P., and Hennig, J. (2005) Personality and biological markers of creativity, *European Journal of Personality* 19(2): 83–95.

Rhodes, M. (1961) An analysis of creativity, *Phi Delta Kappan* 42: 305–10.

Rogers, C. R. (1959) Toward a theory of creativity, in H. H. Anderson (ed.) *Creativity and Its Cultivation*, New York: Harper & Row.

Root-Bernstein, M. and Root-Bernstein, R. S. (2006) Imaginary worldplay in childhood and maturity and its impact on adult creativity, *Creativity Research Journal* 18(4): 405–25.

Root-Bernstein, R. (1989) *Discovering*, Cambridge, MA: Harvard University Press.

Runco, M. A. (1991) *Divergent Thinking*, Norwood, NJ: Ablex.

—— (1994) *Problem Finding, Problem Solving, and Creativity*, Norwood, NJ: Ablex.

—— (1995) Insight for creativity, expression for impact, *Creativity Research Journal* 8: 377–90.

—— (1996) Creativity and development: recommendations, *New Directions for Child Development* 72: 87–90.

—— (ed.) (1997) *Critical Creative Processes*, Cresskill, NJ: Hampton Press.

—— (1999) Tactics and strategies for creativity, in M. A. Runco and S. R. Pritzker (eds.) *Encyclopedia of Creativity*, San Diego: Academic Press.

—— (2004) Creativity, *Annual Review of Psychology* 55: 657–87.

—— (2007) A hierarchical framework for the study of creativity, *New Horizons in Education* 55(3): 1–9.

Runco, M. A. and Bahleda, M. D. (1987) Implicit theories of artistic, scientific, and everyday creativity, *Journal of Creative Behavior* 20: 93–8.

Runco, M. A. and Pina, J. (in press) Imagination and creativity, in M. Taylor (ed.) *Handbook of Imagination*, New York: Cambridge University Press.

Runco, M. A. and Richards, R. (eds.) (1998) *Eminent Creativity, Everyday Creativity, and Health*, Stamford, CT: Ablex.

Runco, M. A., Noble, E., Reiter-Palmon, R., Acar, S., Ritchie, T., and Yurkovich, J. (in press) The genetic basis of creativity and ideational fluency.

Russ, S., Robins, D., and Christiano, B. (1999) Pretend play: longitudinal prediction of creativity and affect in fantasy in children, *Creativity Research Journal*, 12: 129–39.

Sheldon, K. M. (1995) Creativity and self-determination in personality, *Creativity Research Journal* 8: 25–36.

Siegelman, M. (1973) Parent behavior correlates of personality traits related to creativity in sons and daughters, *Journal of Consulting Clinical Psychology* 40: 43–47.

Simonton, D. K. (1990) History, psychology, chemistry, and genius, in M. A. Runco and R. S. Albert (eds.) *Theories of Creativity*, Newbury Park, CA: Sage.

—— (1992) Gender and genius in Japan: feminine eminence in masculine culture, *Sex Roles* 27: 101–19.

—— (1995) Exceptional personal influence, *Creativity Research Journal* 8: 371–6.

Storr, A. (1988) *Solitude: A Return to the Self*, New York: Free Press.

Sulloway, F. (1996) *Born to Rebel*, New York: Pantheon.

Taylor, M. (in press) *Handbook of Imagination*, New York: Cambridge University Press.

Torrance, E. P. (1962) *Guiding Creative Talent*, Englewood Cliffs, NJ: Prentice-Hall.

—— (1995) *Why Fly?*, Cresskill, NJ: Hampton.

Vithayathawornwong, S., Danko, S., and Tolbert, P. (2003) The role of the physical environment in supporting organizational creativity, *Journal of Interior Design* 29: 1–16.

Wallach, M. A. and Kogan, N. (1965) *Modes of Thinking in Young Children*, New York: Holt.

Wallas, G. (1926) *The Art of Thought*, New York: Harcourt Brace World.

Westby, E. L. and Dawson, V. L. (1995) Creativity: asset or burden in the classroom? *Creativity Research Journal* 8: 1–10.

Williams, W. M. and Yang, L. T. (1999) Organizational creativity, in R. J. Sternberg (ed.) *Handbook of Creativity*, New York: Cambridge University Press.

Yeh, Y.-C. (2004) The interactive influences of three ecological systems on R& D employees' technological creativity, *Creativity Research Journal* 16; 11–25.

8

The cult of creativity

Opposition, incorporation, transformation

Kirsten Drotner

Within the European Union, 2009 marked the Year of Creativity and Innovation. The tradition of defining annual themes as focal points of joint policy efforts may be seen as ways in which the European Commission seeks to facilitate processes of coordination and cooperation across member states, political domains and organisational boundaries. On a grander canvas, these annual themes serve as important indicators of wider discourses to do with Europe's position in the global economy and political landscape.

This chapter begins with an outline of the EU initiative in 2009, its key actors, documents and forms of organisation, as a way of mapping current themes in the discourses on creativity and its ramifications. It then goes on to review the conceptual development of creativity as it relates to learning, drawing on two empirical studies on young people's media productions which I undertook in the late 1980s and mid-2000s, respectively. I will pay particular attention to the ways in which children's and young people's creative learning figures in recent debates, because these groups in the global North have been seen as harbingers of the future since the nineteenth century, thus illuminating with particular clarity more general notions of social values and their inflections of power. Also, the review will explore European debates beyond Britain in an attempt to identify traditions of thought still resonating within, at least European, policy-making today. In the final part of the chapter, I reflect on current dilemmas in studying creativity and learning, and I argue for more attention to be paid in future to digital forms of creativity with a view to their implications for lifelong learning.

'Imagine, create, innovate'

The official website of the European Year of Creativity and Innovation states that the objectives of the initiative are 'to raise awareness of the importance of creativity and innovation for personal, social and economic development; to disseminate good practices; to stimulate education and research, and to promote policy debate on related issues' (http://create2009.europa.eu/). These objectives state the main areas of action, namely to raise awareness, disseminate good practice, stimulate education and research and promote policy debates. But they also illuminate the possible dilemmas inherent in fulfilling these objectives. First, they link the concepts of creativity and innovation; second, they assume a connection between these two concepts *and* personal, social and economic development; third, they make no reference to ways in which these types of development may be prioritised or balanced through the advancement of creativity and innovation. Naturally, no brief mission statement can include nuanced arguments or logical deliberations. Still, the opening statement merits some reflection since it offers a condensed version of the rationale for launching the initiative as it emerges from its organisation, background papers and policy statements.

The main actors responsible for the year's actions are a mixture of public and private players. At EU level, the responsible bodies are the European Commission's Directorate-General for Education and Culture in association with the Directorate-General for Enterprise and Industry. In addition, partners contributing to the year range from pan-European think tanks such as the European Policy Centre and the Lisbon Council, through major corporate stakeholders like EuroChambers, a trade association representing over 19 million enterprises, and the European Interest Group on Creativity and Innovation to private foundations and non-profit organisations such as the International Yehudi Menuhin Foundation and the European Federation for Intercultural Learning.

The organisational distribution of stakeholder groups – corporations, government agencies and NGOs – and the thematic mixture of culture, the arts, education and commerce also figure in the composition of projects. The project portfolio indicates that creativity and innovation are particularly to do with popular culture and media arts, and that children and especially young people are key participants in promoting these processes. In tandem with the overall objectives of raising awareness of economic as well as social and personal benefits to be gained from creativity and innovation, the diversity of projects also illuminates how the European Commission seems at pains to harness these processes as means of community building and cultural citizenship as well as means of more immediate corporate ends.

The slogan of the year, 'imagine, create, innovate', is clearly flagged on the main website. Again, the assumption seems to be not only a logical connection between the three aspects, but equally a temporal connection. Imagination is seen as the catalyst for creating new products and services that, in turn, may spur innovation, a term that is routinely associated with commercial competitiveness and gain. In addition to this neat logic, the slogan indicates a sequential link between individual capabilities and joint outcomes of wider societal and economic significance.

Taken together, the organisation and the substance of the EU initiative 2009 demonstrate two interlocking sets of relations. One is the link made between creativity, innovation and learning for the rising generation, a link that indicates not only that creativity is the precursor of innovation, but, perhaps more important, that creativity is a means to an end, namely competence formation that the individual as well as society may profit from. The other assumed relationship is the one set up between creativity, innovation and particular forms of production to do with culture and the arts. Introducing innovation into the equation makes a clear connection to an economic rationale, a connection that refashions traditional notions of creativity.

The overarching logic, binding together the two sets of relations, is as simple as it is well rehearsed in current policy-making. Europe is part of a global knowledge economy dependent upon the shaping and sharing of intangible forms of production such as information, entertainment, services and knowledge. In order to survive and thrive within this competition, it is argued, Europe needs populations endowed with competences that may facilitate innovation within these areas. Cultural industries and cultural creativities figure prominently here, because intangible forms of production fundamentally involve the generation, modification and exchange of signs – images, text, sound and numbers. Such semiotic processes are meaning-making cultural practices in the sense defined by Stuart Hall: 'meaning … is constructed through signifying – i.e. meaning-producing – practices' (Hall, 1997: 28). Viewed through the policy prism of the European Commission, there is a close fit between competitive knowledge economies, social coherence and cultural production and exchange.

This logic is evident in the background reports and EU policy statements that have fed into the Year of Creativity and Innovation. For example, in 2007 the European Commission issued a communication on the central importance of culture in Europe in order to promote three key objectives: cultural diversity and intercultural dialogue; culture as a catalyst for creativity in the framework of the Lisbon Strategy for growth and jobs; and culture as a vital element in the Union's international relations (European Commission, 2007: 8). This harnessing of cultural creativities for knowledge societies is spelled out in a report by the Brussels-based consultancy KEA aiming to explore the educational importance of what is termed 'culture-based creativity ... that finds its source in art and culture' (KEA, 2009: 31). This broad-based remit is arguably an objective for all member states, because in an 'increasingly complex world, creativity and the ability to continue to learn and to innovate will count as much as, if not more than, specific areas of knowledge liable to become obsolete' (European Commission, 2008: 3).

The European Union's initiative the Year of Creativity and Innovation sums up key economic, social and policy moves since the early 1990s to position culture and creativity at the heart, not only of individual and social life, but of the economy at large (Sales and Fournier, 2007). It equally offers a prism through which key dilemmas deriving from this foregrounding may be viewed: is creativity a lever of economic advancement or of socio-cultural development? Are creative learning processes specific to the arts and the cultural sectors? Or can, and should, such processes be mainstreamed at all educational levels and in all disciplines? The central positioning of creativity in socio-economic discourse, I would argue, marks a decisive shift in thinking about the relationship between creativity and learning. Creativity is now becoming widely accepted as a key social demand, not a unique, individual gift or a general human capacity that one may choose to nurture; nor, even, a social capacity to cope imaginatively with everyday challenges (Craft, 2000). In order to situate the current situation, and substantiate my argument, I shall revisit recent developments in forging a conceptual nexus between creativity and learning, developments that have impacted on young people's creative practices – and my own possibilities of studying these.

Creativity as a means of social inclusion

In the late 1980s, I conducted a one-year study of 14–18-year-old Danes making video in their leisure time. The group met at a youth club that had recently begun to offer courses in video production along with more traditional courses in, for example, photography, dance, metalwork and dressmaking. The course was extremely popular and attracted a mixture of very engaged young women and men, few of whom had any previous experience with visual practices. I made participant observations during the entire production process, conducted two rounds of individual in-depth interviews with the participants and analysed their final products, which were proudly presented at a public event at the end of the club season. In retrospect, the study was an early example of media ethnography (Lull, 1978; Bryce, 1980; overview in Schrøder et al., 2003), although this term was unknown to me at the time.

What was clear, though, already during my long spells of observation, was the participants' creative use of existing narrative and formal repertoires of which they had an intimate knowledge from film, television, magazines, popular music and, to a lesser extent, the arts. In my resulting study, I sought to identify the contexts conducive to these creative practices and to spell out the characteristics of the participants' modes of production and interaction (Drotner,

1989; 1991/1995). These characteristics included aspects well known from theories of creativity: learning and training in the conventions of the medium were interspersed by attempts to explore their boundaries; phases of intense and self-forgetting involvement were followed by spells of disengagement, disagreement and frustration; individual ideas were picked up, discussed and sometimes discarded within a community of practice (Lave and Wenger, 1991) that operated as both production and evaluation team. Sudden insights resulted from wrestling with the semiotic resources at hand, and these articulations fed into iterative processes of joint exploration and reflection.

My access to the club was easy and my study met with immediate interest from the city council and local head teachers as well as from social workers at the club. This interest was undoubtedly spurred by recent domestic moves in cultural and social policies. The minister of culture, Ole Vig Jensen, exercised his political visions according to the credo of his liberal party, which in highly publicised newspaper adverts of the late 1980s claimed that 'the best social policy is an effective cultural policy'. When Jensen later became minister of education, he slightly modified the slogan into 'good educational policies are the prime social policies'. Culture was not seen as an end in itself defined in terms of high art and according to normative criteria of taste. Rather, culture was thought to be a means of democratic participation and social inclusion, both of which might be facilitated through education. The diversity of course topics at Danish youth clubs, which at the time attracted about two-thirds of those in the age-band 14–18, testifies to one of the ways in which these ideas were put into practice.

A range of policy initiatives to explore the connections between culture, social inclusion and education were set in motion in the late 1980s and early 1990s in Denmark and other Scandinavian countries. Several of these focused on creative processes in general, and aesthetic experiences in particular. For example, a Danish report feeding into a revision of primary and lower-secondary education defined 'aesthetic competences' as one of five key competences with the argument that 'it is increasingly understood that aesthetic values may play an increasingly important role in the next century' (Lund et al., 1988: 44). A major grant scheme was launched to transform Danish primary and lower-secondary schools into cultural resource centres for local communities; and soon after, reforms of upper-secondary schools increased students' options for choosing subjects such as design, film, visual communication and advertising. Interestingly, these options were taken up primarily by students in vocational streams, while students in the academic streams focused on core subjects such as maths and languages. Conversely, the academically inclined groups were more active in out-of-school practices involving music-making, singing, design and video production. My own study confirmed that middle-class students, envisioning an academic career, downplayed the importance of creative leisure pursuits while at the same time being the most active in engaging with these activities.

Conceptual trajectories: from Scandinavia to Germany and back

The initiatives launched in Scandinavia in the late 1980s and early 1990s may be seen as the epitome of a long and conflicted development in relating creativity, learning and education. Emblematic of early efforts is the work of the Swedish author and philanthropist Ellen Key, whose *The Century of the Child* saw timely publication in 1900. Two of her main arguments in the bestselling book were to have a lasting impact on cultural and educational discourses in Sweden and abroad. As is indicated by the title, she made strong claims to defining children as independent beings to be understood and respected on their own terms, not measured by adult standards. Also, she considered an attention to aesthetic simplicity as a means to enhance the quality of everyday life and advocated that children be actively involved from an early age in, for example, exploration of natural phenomena, woodwork and drawing in order to nurture their imagination and creative capabilities.

Key's ideas were picked up by the so-called child-study movement and by progressive education, particularly as these trends evolved in Germany at the time (Röhrs, 1991). Here, creativity is understood as an individual capacity that can be developed. Children and young people are therefore regarded as key agents in training these capacities. Moreover, creative practices are seen to encompass areas beyond the arts, following a romantic notion that manual skills and use of tools are more natural to the uninitiated. Particularly in Germany, the promotion of creativity and aesthetic practices is seen as a necessary antidote to the perceived negative effects of industrialisation and urbanisation. These perceptions serve to underpin arguments for educational reforms based on the German idea of *Bildung*, to denote a rounded character formation involving emotional, rational as well as practical aspects.

Through much of the twentieth century, cultural and educational reforms in Scandinavia and elsewhere play out these ideas. Importantly, proponents of the reforms see their efforts as part of a wider social critique. Notably after the Second World War, education and culture become pillars of the Scandinavian welfare states. Through the 1960s and 1970s there is a clear policy development from a democratisation of Culture on to cultural democratisation, playing out two very different notions of culture that in the United Kingdom are epitomised by Matthew Arnold and Raymond Williams, respectively. In a Scandinavian context, Arnold's normative view of culture as 'the best which has been thought and said in the world' (Arnold, 1869: viii) and Williams' more anthropological understanding of culture as 'a whole way of life' (Williams, 1958/1975: 18) are intimately bound up with different ideals of societal, and indeed human, development in modernity. While the normative view sees culture as a civilising force and a lever of personal betterment, the anthropological view largely disbands normative assessments in favour of embracing human diversity.

These opposing views on culture also serve to position education very differently. If culture is defined as a source of social and personal advancement, it is open to elaboration and refinement through training, which is a less evident perspective if culture is defined in inclusive terms as a dimension of life. Danish educational objectives speak to these oppositions when in 1975 a 'rounded character formation' of the individual pupil is introduced as a main aim of primary and lower-secondary education in tandem with the time-honoured objective of training specific skills. Particularly subjects within liberal arts and crafts are strengthened within the curriculum as means of securing this character formation, but increasingly as optional courses with no assessment or evaluation, unlike core skills such as science and Danish language and literature. The young people I met at the youth club in the late 1980s were educated within this framework and personalised, as it were, the conditional success of Ellen Key and the movements of educational reform set in motion nearly a hundred years previously. Imagination and creative processes explored through arts and crafts were no longer oppositional signs of societal critique but had become incorporated into the very fabric of education.

Developing digital creativities

In 2005 I co-conducted an ethnographic study in a provincial town of Denmark where students, aged 12–13 and 15–16, from two school classes and over a period of three weeks, produced their own narratives by means of computer animation, the software programme Photoshop or stop-motion animation. The digital animation project formed part of a larger cultural venture, incorporating also professional drama, oral storytelling and museology. As a partnership across education and various cultural sectors, the project was funded by the Ministry of Culture and aimed to empower young people in all parts of the country through exploratory cultural practices. Two key conditions made this project different from the one I had conducted nearly 20 years previously. It was positioned as part of an explicit cultural strategy, and it was defined as a school project while being facilitated by professional animators and storytellers and with students working both on the school premises and in out-of-school workshops. In scholarly terms, the research design of the two studies was very similar. We observed the participants' individual behaviour and group interactions; we conducted individual interviews with teachers and professional animators after the storyboard phase and did focus-group interviews with pupils after the production phase. In our analysis of the narratives, we focused on material properties, thematic elements and formal aspects such as multimodal re-combinations, editing and the use of sound (Nyboe and Drotner, 2008).

Our results confirmed other studies, including the one I conducted on video-making in the late 1980s, in documenting the various phases of creative media production, its basic dimensions in terms of technical affordances, skills constraints and importance for identity work (Sefton-Green, 1999; Kearney, 2006; Goldmann, *et al.*, 2008). Unlike my video project, the animation study illuminated ways in which digitisation and the technical convergence of all sign codes into one platform serve to foreground post-production in the overall process, and make mashups, or cut-and-paste practices, key aesthetic dimensions (Gilje, 2008; Perkel, 2008). Moreover, the two studies are set within different institutional contexts. In the youth club, the video course was led by a young film professional, and the participants defined their activities as leisure-time pursuits. The animation project was led by a joint team of animation professionals and the students' ordinary teachers. Also, the young participants defined the project as school-based while its subject and the work processes involved clearly challenged their received notions of schooling, as is indicated by their extensions of their spatial and temporal routines.

Indicative of this dual positioning were the teachers' choices of roles. From early on, they disengaged themselves from the actual work processes and only stepped in at moments when they saw student discussions and conflicts in need of pedagogical intervention. Unlike the students, they did not challenge their professional self-perceptions or modes of work during the project. When interviewed they were nearly all at pains to define the importance of the exploratory and creative processes involved in the project, while at the same time signalling an inability, or unwillingness, to facilitate such processes as part of their professional tasks. To be a maths or mother-tongue teacher seemed incompatible with undertaking digital experiments.

Harnessing creativity for knowledge economies

Without making too easy comparisons, it seems evident that the differences encountered in the two studies are to do with technological changes, with different relational compositions and institutional positioning. Moreover, the wider policy circumstances are different. While my video project was framed by a widely accepted discourse on cultural democratisation, the animation study was carried out at a time when Danish education and cultural discourses were deeply influenced by two conflicted discourses. One the one hand, the 1990s saw an intense preoccupation with defining core skills and subjects and with quantitative indicators of student performance at all educational levels. On the other hand were heated debates on national identity formation and the perceived risks to cultural, not social, coherence. The indicator discourse was spurred by international comparative surveys, such as PISA and ROSE, in which Danish students fared rather poorly in terms of spelling and maths, for example. That they did very well in terms of collaboration and problem-solving went almost unnoticed in public debate. Conversely, the national identity discourse served to reinvigorate normative perceptions of culture, culminating in a major initiative taken by the Ministry of Culture in 1995 to define seven cultural canons that should operate as educational guides of cultural coherence.

The teachers in the animation project were positioned at the intersection of these dominant discourses that directly cut across the domains of education and culture and indirectly high-lighted tensions within the social domain. When mapped onto this discursive framework, the teachers' ambivalence may be seen as attempts at manoeuvre within these tensions. The indicator discourse foregrounds the importance of defining core subjects, and hence a core professional identity, that downplays explorative learning processes and new (digital) means of expression. The national identity discourse, however, makes much of narrative, of identity work and of the key importance played by culture in promoting civic engagement and social coherence, all of which the teachers recognised as positive elements in the students' practices.

On a grander canvas, the animation project bears witness to current dilemmas in defining a position for creative practices in education in general and for digital production practices in particular. The EU trends towards harnessing creativity as a lever of innovation and competi-tiveness for European knowledge economies at one and the same time serve to expand the remit of creativity and narrow its perspective. If knowledge is an engine of societal survival, obviously new knowledge is its fuel. This makes creativity and innovation critical competences in virtually all areas, as we have seen, but competences that sit ill with established traditions of evidence-based learning and assessment, and hence are notoriously difficult to implement in a systematic fashion. One answer to this dilemma is to define creativity as a means to specific ends which are more easily defined. Economic expansion and competition are such ends. The link made between creativity and knowledge economies serves to narrow the range of creativity while at the same time making claims to its wide range of applications.

Digital creativities as transformative learning

The harnessing of creativity for knowledge economies is part of a neoliberal paradigm that takes many forms and inflections. Questions have been asked about the empirical validity of know-ledge economies, the conceptual vacillation between knowledge societies and knowledge economies, and the epistemological relations between knowledge societies, learning societies and information societies (Garnham, 1998; Sales and Fournier, 2007; Hearn and Rooney, 2008). In more concrete terms, the contested nature of priorities, policies and practices has usefully been outlined and reviewed in terms of its implications for creativity and learning (e.g. Loveless, 2002, 2007; Banaji et al., 2006). However, we still need more systematic and empirically grounded analyses of the ways in which digital means of expression may facilitate future developments and organisations of creativity. So far, some headway has been made along two lines of enquiry. The first, and in policy terms most influential, defines digital means as ICT technologies, and it is often situated within a socio-cognitive tradition of thought. However, no clear correlation can be found between ICT use and educational attainment, including creative outcomes (CERI, 2007: 15). The second line of enquiry defines digital means as media for meaning-making and tends to follow constructivist traditions of learning. While no large-scale review of this tradition exists, major case studies indicate that digital media can play a formative role in creative development (Reid et al., 2002), but authors caution against simplified equations between intense activity and creativity (Buckingham, 2007; Drotner and Schrøder, 2010).

In some sense, the latter approach is more in line with recent EU claims to an inclusive educational application of creativity in order to enhance civic engagement and social coherence. Here, the storage, shaping and sharing of knowledge are increasingly implicated with digital processes. While these processes enhance distributed forms of knowledge generation and challenge the sites and settings of learning (Drotner, 2008: Drotner *et al.*, 2008), they equally serve to highlight basic issues to do with the aims, means and outcomes of learning: is education a resource for all or a few dimensions of life? Can creativity be dissociated from its applications and contexts of use? Should creative learning facilitate personal or social forms of development? The interweaving of digital media and forms of communication into everyday life in many parts of the world merits revisiting old questions in the hope that we may come up with new answers.

References

Arnold, Matthew (1869) *Culture and Anarchy: An Essay in Social and Political Criticism*, London: Smith, Elder & Co.

Banaji, Shakuntula, Burn, Andrew and Buckingham, David (2006) *The Rhetorics of Creativity: A Review of the Literature*, London: Centre for the Study of Children, Youth and Media, Institute of Education, University of London; available at http://www.creative-partnerships.com/data/files/rhetorics-of-creativity-12.pdf (accessed 20 November 2009).

Bryce, Jennifer W. (1980) Television and the family: an ethnographic approach, dissertation, Columbia University, Teachers College.

Buckingham, David (2007) *Beyond Technology: Children's Learning in the Age of Digital Culture*, Cambridge: Polity Press.

CERI (2007) *New Millennium Learners: Initial Findings on the Effects of Digital Technologies on School-Age Learners*; available at http://www.oecd.org/dataoecd/39/51/40554230.pdf (accessed 20 November 2009).

Craft, Anna (2000) *Teaching Creativity: Philosophy and Practice*, London: Routledge.

Drotner, Kirsten (1989) Girl meets boy: aesthetic production, reception, and gender identity, *Cultural Studies* 3(2): 208–25.

—— (1991/1995) *At skabe sig – selv: ungdom, æstetik, pædagogik* [Self creation: youth, aesthetics, pedagogy], Copenhagen: Gyldendal.

—— (2008) Leisure is hard work: digital practices and future competencies, in David Buckingham (ed.) *Youth, Identity, and Digital Media*, the John D. and Catherine T. MacArthur Foundation Series on Digital Media and Learning, Cambridge, MA: The MIT Press; available at http://www.mitpressjournals.org/doi/pdf/10.1162/dmal.9780262524834.167 (accessed 20 November 2009).

Drotner, Kirsten and Schrøder, Kim C. (eds) (2010) *Digital Content Creation: Creativity, Competence, Critique*, New York: Peter Lang.

Drotner, Kirsten, Jensen, Hans S. and Schrøder, Kim C. (eds) (2008) *Informal Learning and Digital Media*, Cambridge: Cambridge Scholars Publishing.

European Commission (2007) *Communication from the Commission to the European Parliament, the Council, the European Economic and Social Committee and the Committee of the Regions on a European Agenda for Culture in a Globalizing World*; available at http://eur-lex.europa.eu/LexUriServ/LexUriServ.do?uri=COM:2007:0242:FIN:EN:PDF (accessed 20 November 2009).

—— (2008) *Communication from the Commission to the European Parliament, the Council, the European Economic and Social Committee and the Committee of the Regions Improving Competences for the 21st Century: An Agenda for European Cooperation on Schools*; available at http://www.lex.unict.it/eurolabor/en/documentation/com/2008/com(2008)-425en.pdf (accessed 20 November 2009).

Garnham, Nicholas (1998) Information society theory as ideology, *Loisir et société* 21(1): 97–120.

Gilje, Øystein (2008) Googling movies: digital media production and the 'culture of apropriation', in Kirsten Drotner, Hans S. Jensen and Kim S. Schrøder (eds) *Informal Learning and Digital Media*, Cambridge: Cambridge Scholars Publishing.

Goldman, Shelley, Booker, Angela and McDermott, Meghan (2008) Mixing the digital, social, and cultural: learning, identity, and agency in youth participation, in David Buckingham (ed.) *Youth, Identity, and Digital Media*, the John D. and Catherine T. MacArthur Foundation Series on Digital Media and Learning, Cambridge, MA: The MIT Press; available at http://www.mitpressjournals.org/doi/pdf/10.1162/dmal.9780262524834.185 (accessed 20 November 2009).

Hall, Stuart (1997) The work of representation, in Stuart Hall (ed.) *Representation: Cultural Representations and Signifying Practices*, London: Sage in association with the Open University.

Hearn, Greg and Rooney, David (eds) (2008) *Knowledge Policy: Challenges for the 21st Century*, Cheltenham: Edward Elgar.

KEA (2006) *Economy of Culture in Europe*; available at http://ec.europa.eu/culture/eac/sources_info/studies/studies_en.html (accessed 20 November 2009).

—— (2009) *The Impact of Culture on Creativity*; available at http://ec.europa.eu/culture/key-documents/doc/study_impact_cult_creativity_06_09.pdf (accessed 20 November 2009).

Kearney, M. C. (2006) *Girls Make Media*, London: Routledge.

Lave, Jean and Wenger, Etienne (1991) *Situated Learning: Legitimate Peripheral Participation*, Cambridge: Cambridge University Press.

Loveless, Avril M. (2002) *Literature Review in Creativity, New Technologies and Learning*, Report 4: Futurelab series; available at http://www.futurelab.org.uk/resources/documents/lit_reviews/Creativity_Review.pdf (accessed 20 November 2009).

—— (2007) *Creativity, Technology and Learning: A Review of Recent Literature*, Report 4 update: Futurelab series; available at http://www.futurelab.org.uk/resources/documents/lit_reviews/Creativity_Review_update.pdf (accessed 20 November 2009).

Lull, James (1978) Choosing television programs by family vote, *Communication Quarterly* 26(1): 53–7.

Lund, Jørn, Albæk, Ole, Fonsmark, Anne Birgitte and Riis, Povl (1988) *Prospects and Perspectives: A Report from the Committee on Universal Values and Basic Skills* [Pejling og perspektiv: perspektivudvalgets rapport om almene værdier og grundlæggende kundskaber], Copenhagen: Ministry of Education.

Nyboe, Lotte and Drotner, Kirsten (2008) Identity, aesthetics and digital narration, in Knut Lundby (ed.) *Digital Storytelling, Mediatized Stories: Self-Representations in New Media*, New York: Peter Lang.

Perkel, Dan (2008) Copy and paste literacy? Literacy practices in the production of a Myspace profile, in Kirsten Drotner, Hans S. Jensen and Kim S. Schrøder (eds) *Informal Learning and Digital Media*, Cambridge: Cambridge Scholars Publishing.

Reid, Mark, Burn, Andrew and Parker, David (2002) *Evaluation Report of the Becta Digital Video Pilot Project*, London: Becta/British Film Institute; available at http://partners.becta.org.uk/page_documents/research/dvreport_241002.pdf (accessed 20 November 2009).

Röhrs, Hermann (1991) *Die Reformpädagogik: Ursprung und Verlauf unter internationalem Aspekt*, Weinheim: Deutscher Studien Verlag.

Sales, Arnaud and Fournier, Michel (eds) (2007) *Knowledge, Communication and Creativity*, London: Sage.

Schrøder, Kim C., Drotner, Kirsten, Murray, Catherine and Kline, Stephen (2003) *Researching Audiences*, London: Arnold.

Sefton-Green, Julian (ed.) (1999) *Young People, Creativity and New Technologies: The Challenge of Digital Arts*, London: Routledge.

Williams, Raymond (1958/1975) *Culture and Society, 1780–1950*, Harmondsworth: Penguin.

9

Democratic creativity

Ken Jones

Accounts of neo-liberal change in education often stress that the orthodoxies associated with neo-liberalism do not so much eradicate the practices they seek to replace, as incorporate them, selectively, in a new framework (Bernstein, 1990; Apple, 1995). It could be added, however, that such incorporation is rarely complete. The practices targeted for recuperation are not always and entirely amenable to it, and however persuasively dominant new discourses seek to make use of the resources of previous educational cultures, there remain residual elements that resist incorporation, often to the extent that they provide material for a practical critique of the new.

The combination of recuperation and antagonism is highlighted in the relationship between the recent creative turn in English education policy-making and the resources developed, in the name of creativity, in an earlier educational period – that of the 'post-war settlement', in which institutional reform in the name of social democratic principles combined with professional influence on curriculum and pedagogy to allow an opening for new practice. The New Labour government of 1997–2010 began its period in office with a strong emphasis on 'standards' and a top-down, target-focused agenda for ensuring their rise. After early successes, however, the rate of improvement slowed, and New Labour turned to other resources that might supplement, without replacing, its standards agenda. Creativity, in this situation, experienced a revival, and echoes of an earlier period began to resound in the present.

The encouragement given to cross-curricular work in the primary school (DfES, 2003) returned in some respects to the integrated day that was favoured in the 1970s. The emphasis of the Children's Act (2005) on links between schooling and other children's services recalled the tenor of the Plowden Report (DES, 1967). Likewise, the attempts to re-enchant the school through art and creative practice had clear progressive antecedents in the educational movements of the three decades that followed 1945 (Cunningham, 1988). At school level, too, it was not uncommon to hear teachers talking about 'the wheel turning', 'going back' to previous teaching methods and approaches which required professional autonomy and know-how (Vulliamy and Webb, 2006). Yet these recursive moves were never unequivocal, and were accompanied by a disavowal of much of the achievement of the earlier period. When the writer and teacher Harold Rosen died in 2009, his son Michael (Mike) pondered the meaning of his work and the fate it had encountered. Harold had spent a lifetime arguing that culture, language and education were inseparable: 'whatever language the pupils possess, it is this which must be built on rather than driven underground'. Yet these years of 'thought, theory and practice' had been forgotten – or, more precisely, 'wiped out' – by the governments of the 1980s and 1990s (Rosen, 2009). This was the climate in which the government-commissioned authors of the path-breaking report which re-recognised creativity felt compelled to insist that the reforms they suggested did not mean a return to the 'progressive teaching ideas of the 1960s' (NACCCE, 1999: 14); not all aspects of the past could be readmitted to the policy field. If the 'wheel' of policy did revolve, the point at which it stopped marked only a selective version of earlier work, baulking – as Michael Rosen suggests – at any rendering of 'creativity' that might link it strongly to what policy might see as cultures of dissonance.

It is at this point in the relationship between past and present that this chapter seeks to make an entrance. It aims to revisit the resources of 'thought, theory and practice' that Michael Rosen alludes to. It does so not so much as an effort at historical reconstruction, as one of intervention. It suggests that such resources can supply current projects of 'creative' teaching and learning with means to think more deeply and productively about connections between classroom processes and wider cultural practices. The chapter's material is largely drawn from a literature review, *Culture and Creative Learning*, on which I worked for Creative Partnerships in 2009. Like the review, it seeks to track 'a sequence of intense and continuing arguments about the proper meanings of "culture" and "creativity", about their salience to education, and, through education, to wider issues of equality, democracy, economics and emancipation' (Jones, 2009: 7). These arguments have involved many participants, from conservatives to 'progressive' educators, but the main focus of this chapter is on one strand of thinking – that associated with the notion that 'everyday', 'ordinary' or 'popular' culture presents both a set of unresolved issues for mass education and a means of educational renewal and innovation.

Creativity and mass culture

We can begin by sketching an educational and cultural context. Across most of Western Europe, the post-war period had seen the introduction of secondary schooling and the raising, in stages, of the school-leaving age. These changes brought into the school what the historian of the OECD, George Papadopoulos, calls 'a vastly expanded and variegated clientele'. 'Educational offerings', he adds, had to be 'made relevant' to such groups (Papadopoulos, 1994: 59). In this way, the 'problem' of working-class culture and what the school should do about it, became an important and contentious issue, fought over by contrasting intellectual tendencies.

The opinion-forming weekly, the *Times Educational Supplement* (TES), deemed, symptomatically, that 'the idea that the modern masses possess a culture worth anything, or are likely to create one, is delusory' (Whannel, 1958: 34); 'culture' in any productive sense was the work of an elite group. According to T. S. Eliot, whose ideas underpinned the disdainful judgement of the TES, it was 'an essential condition' for the 'quality' of a culture 'that it should continue to be a minority culture' (Eliot, 1948: 184). Attempting to unfix this rule, through some kind of cultural egalitarianism, would have dire political consequences. Culture, thus, was less an open field for the play of meaning than an embattled fortress, in which standards were protected and criteria of discrimination fostered. Mass education was an economic necessity, perhaps, but it was nonetheless a cultural threat.

Against this interpretation was arrayed a range of work informed, to a greater or lesser extent, by the idea that what happened in education should be aligned with a more general process of social and political change. In other European countries, such as Italy and France, the experience of anti-fascist struggle and post-war reconstruction had created conditions in which socialist politics had become an important point of reference in national life. The language of educational change was there coloured by aspirations for 'popular' and 'democratic' transformation, which were seen as credible and relatively close at hand objectives. (It was in such a situation that the work of Freinet and Malaguzzi could develop.) In Britain, too, though the idiom was different, educational possibilities were presented in terms of a wider process of cultural and political change. Education, wrote the cultural theorist Raymond Williams, was a means of 'releasing and enriching the life experience which the rising class brings with it' (Williams, quoted in Smith, 2008: 380). 'Culture is Ordinary', the title of an essay published by Williams in 1958, encapsulated an approach to education and to popular creativity that was at odds with conservatism. With other work of Williams (*Culture and Society*, 1958 and 1963; *The Long Revolution*, 1961) it contributed to the self-understanding of cultural and educational practices that from the late 1950s onwards tried to embody 'new meanings and values, new significances and experiences' (Williams, 1973: 11).

Eliot had privileged the achievements of high culture, seeing nothing of equivalent value in the popular domain. Williams by contrast aimed to ratify, alongside what he called the 'intellectual and imaginative work' embodied in high culture (Williams, 1963: 311), another kind of cultural achievement, which for him had intellectual substance as well as social weight – working-class culture, repository of 'the basic collective idea and the institutions, manners, habits of thought and intentions which proceed from this' (ibid.: 311). This 'lived culture' was understood in terms of a theory of creativity. Creativity, Williams argued in the first chapter of *The Long Revolution*, was as ordinary as culture. He sought justification for his claim in biological theory (the work of J. Z. Young) and in literary tradition, quoting Coleridge's understanding of 'imagination' as 'the living power and prime Agent of *all* human perception' (Williams, 1961: 21). Current social arrangements neglected this kind of universalist insight; they had erected 'a real barrier in our mind … a refusal to accept the creative capacities of life, a determination to limit and restrict the channels of growth' (Williams, 1963: 320). Yet in reality 'there are no ordinary activities, if by "ordinary" we mean the absence of creative interpretation and effort. We create our human world as we have thought of art as being created' (Williams, 1961: 27). Education, from this viewpoint, was one sector of a more general project to democratise creativity. It did not require a rejection of 'the culture of the selective tradition' (ibid.: 49), but it did entail bringing it into a relationship with 'the lived culture of a particular time and place', a move that was meant to enable both a revaluation of established high culture, and the release and enrichment of the 'life experience' of a class that was, in terms of its social and cultural influence, emergent.

According to Tom Steele (1997), educational institutions were an important site for elaborating this rapprochement of culture with democracy. He singles out the adult education organisations of the 1950s, in which Williams, along with other new left radicals, was involved. Others have taken the point further: it was not just the adult education class but the school that provided a site and stimulus for a cultural rethinking that aimed at the recognition of working-class culture, as well as an understanding of the impact upon it of wider social and cultural change. John Hardcastle (2008) has identified in the London of the 1950s a network of secondary teachers keen to utilise the thinking of the new left, involving themselves in a cultural exploration for which existing approaches were inadequate. One such teacher, John Dixon, wrote of the need 'to value working-class experience, and, slowly, to find ways of encouraging kids from city or country to discuss, probe and write from experience (in poetry, prose and dramatic scripts)'. There existed, he maintained, 'not merely this sort of élite culture, but some different kind of culture which it is necessary to seek out by going into other people's experience' (Dixon, 1991, quoted in Hardcastle, 2008: 17; Dixon, 1961, quoted in Jones, 2003: 144).

Others offered a different stress: the gap between school and popular culture needed closing, certainly, but the nature of popular culture itself needed to be rethought. To this extent, the definitional certainties offered by Williams needed modifying, and the notion that education could release and enrich the culture of a 'rising class' became problematic. Contrasting the new cultural forms created by a 'revolution in communications' with the very different 'norms and expectations of formal education' (Hall and Whannel, 1964: 13), Paddy Whannel stressed the tensions of their relationship. The school was not 'alert and alive to contemporary experience':

> By and large, the kind of education the teacher receives in school and training college posits an established body of cultural products to which there are certain definable attitudes. ... His pupils, however, will belong to a different world. The world of Tommy Steele and Elvis Presley.
>
> *(Whannel, 1958: 33–4)*

Social movements, culture and creativity

Thus we can see developing not just an insistence that ordinary lived culture could not be understood from the position afforded educators by the selective tradition, but also a suggestion that educators, even in their more radical projects, lacked the resources to do so; some new effort of enquiry and learning was required. The ethnographic turn made by the sociology of education in the 1970s supplied some of these resources, and initiated a tradition of enquiry that has been able to track changes in youth subcultures, and in the relation of these subcultures to formal education. Other means of understanding were supplied by social movements outside the school: Bernstein (1975) pointed out the role of black social movements in this respect. Publications like the Race Today Collective's *The Black Explosion in British Schools* (Dhondy et al., 1982) and Bernard Coard's *How the West Indian Child Is Made Educationally Sub-Normal by the British School System* (1971) made issues of 'race' and racism an important, and contested, part of the urban educational agenda. Their influence meant that 'culture' was often understood through the prism of oppression and resistance; and 'identity' or 'self-image' was seen in terms of power and empowerment. In local educational contexts, 'creativity' and 'culture' tended to be defined combatively, as qualities that needed to be asserted in the teeth of indifference or hostility. 'Do kids have culture?' asked Mike Rosen, in an account of his work at Vauxhall Manor School, in South London, 'Does the working class have culture?' The answer was 'yes', but schools often worked 'against' not 'with' it (Rosen, 1982). The making visible of this culture depended partly on students' struggles against the dominant culture of the school, and partly too on the commitment and ingenuity of teachers.

These acts of cultural assertion and recognition were linked to an attempt to remake the knowledge produced by schools – a remaking that drew on the creative energies released in a wider struggle for social change. 'Creativity', wrote Gabriel Chanan and Linda Gilchrist, 'is about the conscious, collective creation of new values by which we must live', including 'self-determination' and 'communal fulfilment' (Chanan and Gilchrist, 1974: 122). In this, schools had 'a vital part' to play, but they would not be aided by a 'traditional culture' that 'carried no conviction with many of today's teachers and pupils' (ibid.: 129).

Others argued in similar ways. The London teacher Chris Searle, who published several collections of children's writing linked by his own commentaries, wrote of 're-establishing culture in its organic, democratic sense, linking it to the real world of people who are working and struggling for control over the conditions of their lives' (Searle, 1973: 8). Publishing projects, such as that of the Hackney-based Centerprise worked along similar lines, 'presenting the idea that literacy could be a process of liberation and a weapon for social change' (Raleigh and Simons, 1996: 14). Some of this work, as Nigel Wright (1989) has pointed out, was based on an understanding, which he finds problematic, of 'working-class culture' as something both unified and in possession of an immanent potential for transformative social change. Thus, while its enquiries into contemporary culture might have gone deeper than those of Williams, it tended like him to see creativity as a securely embedded within a social force capable of achieving radical change. Other projects, however, confronted more directly the ambivalences of creativity in mid-twentieth century culture.

Youth, Culture and Photography

As Whannel had suggested, any open-ended process of cultural enquiry would discover 'ordinary' cultural forms unfamiliar to Williams, shaped not only by the experience of social class, but by the effects of mass, commodified popular culture – a culture whose relationship to a project of social transformation was, to say the least, an awkward one. Youth, Culture and Photography, a project based at the Cockpit Arts Workshop of the Inner London Education Authority between 1979 and 1985, pursued exactly those difficulties, registering the need for cultural exploration (through 'a long apprenticeship to the worlds, values and subcultures of youth' [Dewdney and Lister, 1988: 4]), and also the tensions of the encounter between an eye-opening commitment to 'ordinary culture' and a realisation that it was a site already well colonised by commodified practices.

In the book they published about the project, Andrew Dewdney and Martin Lister argued that in arts education, recognition of the cultural productivity of young people should be central. They criticised the role of the school, drawing attention to the gulf between 'what was claimed as being art in schools and the lived realities of many pupils' (ibid.: 5). Traditions of fine art were equally lacking – they 'relied on and perpetuated a mystifying view of the creative imagination' (ibid.: 2). The alternative to these moribund traditions lay in the adoption of new technical means and a new cultural stance. 'Mechanical media' – especially the still camera, chosen for its cheapness, simplicity and centrality to everyday cultural practice – provided the means. The cultural stance addressed the double role of young people, as both producers and consumers of culture. In terms of production, a word preferred to 'creativity', the project was based on young people making photographic meaning through 'encoding the meanings that they chose' from among their 'immediate topical and cultural interests' (ibid.: 7). In terms of consumption, the project aimed to explore with learners the ways in which the dominant culture 'worked through the currencies and meanings of everyday life' (ibid.: 20).

The learning at which the project aimed was presented in terms of empowerment and semiotic subversion (ibid.: 17). The former involved 'changing your own life, the life of the people you lived with on the estate' (Dewdney, 2000). The latter was more fully described:

> As they [young people] adopt new forms of expression, create new images for themselves, often contradicting or ironically commenting upon the real conditions of their lives, they *repeatedly outstrip* the current definitions and representations of its dominant culture. This may provide the generalising and incorporating dominant culture with endless opportunities for new commodities and markets, but it also provides an arena for struggles over meanings and definitions between cultures.
>
> *(Dewdney and Lister, 1988: 17)*

These were difficult struggles. The resources of commercial culture, Dewdney accepted, were 'exceptionally powerful', not just because of their reach, but because of the pleasures they offered. 'The capitalists', he commented, retrospectively, 'had all the toys … the money, the budgets, the technology' (Dewdney, 2000). This concern with the inequalities of cultural power marked a different understanding of the field from that current a couple of decades earlier, with its confident expectation that the 'rising class' had already begun a process of cultural transformation. The problems that Dewdney registered have not become, since the early 1990s, less severe.

A great divide

The long decade 1976–90 saw a succession of 'breaks', in economic, occupational, technological, social, cultural and educational fields. Patterns established earlier in the century were disrupted and remade, in ways that have been variously charted. Harvey (2005) has charted the destructive–creative processes of deindustrialisation, financial deregulation and privatisation. Hardt and Negri have identified the rise of an informational capitalism, claiming (contestedly) that symbolic or immaterial work has overtaken manufacturing as the defining economic activity of our time (Hardt and Negri, 2001). Castells has sketched the occupational structure of this post-industrial society, suggesting that it is polarised between symbolic workers, high paid and relatively secure, and generic, 'reprogrammable' labour (Castells, 1998). Correspondingly, reflecting on the consequences of the deindustrialisation of the 1980s, Mike Savage argued that the 'working class has been largely eviscerated as a visible social presence' and 'is no longer a central reference point in British culture' (Savage, 2003: 536) – a proposition that threatened the cultural project imagined by Williams and his co-thinkers.

Tracking these social changes, and much affected by what they regard as the definitive political victories of neo-liberalism in the Reagan and Thatcher years, some theorists argue that culture, too, has experienced an evisceration. It no longer provides a space in which critical practice might be developed and new political horizons opened. Instead, according to Perry Anderson, culture has been 'saturated … in the serum of capital', rendered commodified and unchallenging (Anderson, 1998: 55). This is an effect not only of a shift in ideas, but of changes in the material conditions for practice. Frederic Jameson wrote of an attempt to 'proletarianise' – that is, to subject to capitalist discipline – what he called 'all those unbound social forces [like those of the Cockpit perhaps] that gave the sixties their energy' (Jameson, 1988: 268).

A new creativity

The combined effect of the 'breaks' of the 1980s has deeply affected the tenor, source, focus, content and purpose of educational work on culture and creativity. Most striking, perhaps, has been the harnessing of 'creativity' to discourses of enterprise, severing it both from conservative definitions of the Eliot kind and from some of its links to radical critique. Partly responsible for such shifts is the discursive (and practical) dominance of neo-liberalism. Based on the supposition that 'human well-being can best be advanced by liberating individual entrepreneurial freedom' (Harvey, 2005: 2), it is a discourse well positioned both to recognise and to reshape creativity. Like that of Williams, the neo-liberal understanding of creativity goes beyond an arts-based model. Unlike his, it is firmly focused on the needs of the prevailing order: adaptation to new social and economic complexities depends less upon the capacity for expressiveness nurtured by earlier models of creativity, and more on a person's ability to draw from the entire range of their experience so as to respond productively – creatively – to new challenges. The criticism levelled from this viewpoint at the existing national curriculum is that it has no innovative element; it 'focuses on what students know rather than how they use that knowledge' (Bentley and Seltzer, 1999: 9) and so cannot rise to the challenge of adaptability. This is more than a workplace issue. Creativity is not only a set of skills, but a modality of life:

> It is about equipping people with the skills they need to live full lives; the ability to respond creatively and confidently to changing situations and unfamiliar demands, to solve the problems and challenges they face at home, in education, at work, to make a positive contribution to the life of their communities.
>
> *(Bentley and Selzer, 1999: 9)*

On this basis, the Qualifications and Curriculum Authority extended the reach of creativity across the curriculum. Its 2003 document *Creativity – Find It ...* (QCA, 2003) presented creativity as a set of mental and attitudinal qualities, discoverable in any kind of learning activity: 'questioning and challenging conventions and assumptions ... making inventive connections and associating things that are not usually related'; 'envisaging what might be'; trying alternatives and fresh approaches ... reflecting critically on ideas, actions and outcomes' (QCA, 2003).

The new stress places creativity, potentially, at the centre of learning. But it should be evident that in the process some important shifts of meaning have occurred. The stress now is on a different sort of creativity – born in different circumstances, harnessed to different purposes – from that of previous discourses. For Raymond Williams creativity was more a species-enhancing capacity than a source of economic value, but this is a meaning that has been lost in current emphases, whose ultimate grounding is in a particular set of economic requirements, and whose links to an idea of cultural democracy are imperceptible.

Resources of hope

It seems undeniable that 'creativity' has been to an extent recuperated – not simply at the level of policy, but also at that of the school. A recent report on creative school change in England found that for some schools it had become synonymous with 'enterprise', and for others a 'bolt-on' to a curriculum conceived in terms of the standards agenda (Thomson *et al.*, 2009). But that is not the whole of the matter. The resources embodied in the term continue to serve for some who work in education as a means of re-engaging with issues once thought central. Much current thinking about creative learning has an impulse towards the social and the cultural. Cochrane, Craft and Jeffrey talk about 'surfacing the learner's experience' (Cochrane *et al.*, 2008). Cochrane and Cockett (2006) account for the success of some programmes for creative learning on the grounds that they stay close to young people's experiences and interests, and do not impose a prior, fixed agenda. The same research into school practice that identified an economistic recuperation of creativity also encountered schools that, rejecting discourses of cultural deficit, sought to evaluate positively the working-class communities in which they were based, and to use local knowledge and experience to construct the curriculum (Thomson *et al.*, 2009). Particularly in primary schools, the project of early years education developed by movements of the left in some of the cities of northern Italy (Pistoia, Reggio Emilia) had an appeal. To this extent, the creative turn in English education policy has opened a door to interests that for two decades have been frozen out.

How much wider the door can be opened is a difficult question. It is certainly possible to point to examples of practice that embody principles of cultural democracy. However, these efforts are in a strong sense 'lonely': they lack the access to broader cultural and educational movements that parallel experiments enjoyed, in an earlier period. Nor have they available to them a common repertoire of understandings and practices that might connect classroom-based reflection to broader imaginings and purposes. Building such a repertoire, and elaborating an approach that might link current projects to the resources that supplied by a tradition that, for all its problems, was rich in innovations and bold in its educational vision, would establish an alternative 'creativity' to those that are now hegemonic.

References

Anderson, P. (1998) *The Origins of Postmodernity*, London: Verso.

Apple, M. (1995) The politics of a national curriculum, in P. Cookson and B. Schneider (eds) *Transforming Schools*, New York: Routledge.

Bentley, T. and Selzer, K. (1999) *The Creative Age*, London: Demos.

Bernstein, B. (1975) The Sociology of Education: a brief account, in *Class, Codes and Control*, vol. 3: *Towards a Theory of Educational Transmissions*, London: Routledge & Kegan Paul.

—— (1990) *Class Codes and Control*, vol. IV: *The Structuring of Pedagogic Discourse*, London: Routledge.

Castells, Manuel (1998) *End of Millennium, the Information Age: Economy, Society and Culture*, vol. III, Oxford: Blackwell.

Chanan, G. and Gilchrist, L. (1974) *What School Is For*, London: Methuen.

Coard, B. (1971) *How the West Indian Child Is Made Educationally Sub-Normal by the British School System*, London: New Beacon Books.

Cochrane, P. and Cockett, M. (2006) *Building a Creative School: A Dynamic Approach to School Development*, Stoke-on-Trent: Trentham Books.

Cochrane, P., Craft, A. and Jeffrey, B. (2008) 'Current government policy', paper for Implementing Creative Learning? An investigative seminar for Creative Partnerships, London: Creative Partnerships.

Cunningham, P. (1988) *Curriculum Change in the Primary School since 1945: Dissemination of the Progressive Ideal*, Lewes: Falmer Press.

Department for Culture, Media and Sport/Department for Education and Skills (1999) *All Our Futures: Creativity, Culture and Education*, Report of the National Advisory Committee on Creative and Cultural Education, London: DCMS/DfES.

Department of Education and Science (DES) (1967) *Children and Their Primary Schools*, the Plowden Report, London: HMSO.

Department for Education and Skills (DfES) (2003) *Excellence and Enjoyment*, London: The Stationery Office.

Dewdney, A. (2000) Interview (interviewer Shirley Read, British Library Archival Sound Recordings, Oral History of British Photography).

Dewdney, A. and Lister, M. (1988) *Youth, Culture and Photography*, Basingstoke: Macmillan.

Dhondy, F., Beese, B. and Hassan, L. (1982) *The Black Explosion in British Schools*, London: Race Today.

Dixon, J. (1991) *A Schooling in 'English': Critical Episodes in the Struggle to Shape Literary and Cultural Studies*, Milton Keynes: Open University Press.

Eliot, T. S. (1948) *Notes towards the Definition of Culture*, London: Faber and Faber.

Hall, S. and Whannel, P. (1964) *The Popular Arts*, London: Hutchinson.

Hardcastle, J. (2008) Four photographs in an English course book: a study in the visual archaeology of urban schooling, *Changing English* 15: 1, 3–24.

Hardt, M. and Negri, A. (2001) *Multitude*, Cambridge, MA: Harvard University Press.

Harvey, D. (2005) *A Brief History of Neo-Liberalism*, Oxford: Oxford University Press.

Jameson, F. (1988) Periodising the sixties, in *The Ideologies of Theory: Essays 1971–1986*, vol. 2, London: Syntax of History Routledge.

Jones, K. (2003) *Education in Britain: From 1944 to the Present*, Cambridge: Polity Press.

—— (2009) *Culture and Creative Learning: A Literature Review*, London: Arts Council England.

National Advisory Committee on Creative and Cultural Education (NACCCE) (1999) *All Our Futures: Creativity, Culture and Education*, London: DfEE/DCMS.

Papadopoulos, G. (1994) *Education 1960–90: The OECD Perspective*, Paris: OECD.

QCA (2003) *Creativity: Find It, Promote It*, London: Qualifications and Curriculum Authority.

Raleigh, M. and Simons, M. (1996) Where we've been: a brief history of English teaching 1920–1970 (1981), in M. Simons (ed.) *Where We've Been: Articles from the English & Media Magazine*. London: The English and Media Centre.

Rosen, M. (1982) Three papers, in S. Eyers and J. Richmond (eds) *Becoming Our Own Experts: Studies of Language and Learning Made by the Talk Workshop Group at Vauxhall Manor School 1974–79*, London: ILEA English Centre.

—— (2009) The ups and downs of a story, *Guardian*, 9 June.

Savage, M. (2003) A new class paradigm?, *British Journal of Sociology of Education* 24(4): 535–41.

Searle, C. (1973) *This New Season*, London: Marion Boyars Books.

Smith, D. (2008) *Raymond Williams: A Warrior's Tale*, Cardigan: Parthian Books.

Steele, T (1997) *The Emergence of Cultural Studies 1945–65: Cultural Politics, Adult Education and the English Question*, London: Lawrence and Wishart.

Thomson, P., Jones, K. and Hall, C. (2009) *Creative School Change Project: Final Report*, Keele and Nottingham Universities.

Vulliamy, G. and Webb, R. (2006) *Coming Full Circle? The Impact of New Labour's Education Policies on Primary School Teachers' Work*, London: Association of Teachers and Lecturers.

Whannel, P. (1958) Artist, citic and teacher, *Universities and Left Review* 4 (Summer): 33–5.

Williams, R. (1958a) Culture is ordinary, in N. MacKenzie (ed.) *Conviction*, London: MacGibbon and Kee.

—— (1958b) *Culture and Society: 1780–1950*, London: Chatto and Windus.

—— (1961) *The Long Revolution*, London: Chatto and Windus.

—— (1963) *Culture and Society: 1780–1950* (2nd ed.), Harmondsworth: Penguin.

—— (1973) Base and superstructure in Marxist cultural theory, *New Left Review* 82: 3–16.

Wright, N. (1989) *Assessing Radical Education*, Milton Keynes: Open University Press.

10

Creativity, creative class, smart power, social reproduction and symbolic violence

Bernard Darras

Mary is reading and re-reading the subject given to her by her philosophy teacher: 'Discuss this statement by Paul Valéry, and then explain your own concept of creativity. "In the areas of creation, which are also areas of pride, the need to distinguish oneself is indivisible from existence itself" (Valéry, 1956: 600).'

Mary's mind is totally blank; in fact she has no idea and she does not know how to have one. Yet she works hard and all her teachers recognise this but her success is not proportional to the amount of work she constantly does. Coming from a humble background, she is one of these hard-working and deserving students who has little general knowledge, little imagination and little creativity. If she manages to enter university, her chances of success are low and she knows it. Mary dreams of being creative and hanging out with creative people, but she has given up the idea as it is only a dream.

Creativity is generally regarded as an ability to produce new and unexpected ideas which can eliminate doubt, solve a problem or cleverly untangle complicated matters. In general, the resulting creations are adapted either to reality or to the many worlds of fiction.

Mary's teachers who are interested in creativity are divided into two main trends. Those who adhere to the romantic conception (usually artistic) of creativity believe it is a kind of gift or talent which individuals possess to greater or lesser degrees. The most radical link it to genius and inspiration that come without calculation; the most moderate believe that one can cultivate creativity by stimulating it through mind games ranging from the simple capturing of ideas to the solving of complex issues, or through techniques aimed at generating ideas, artistic activities (most often pretences unrelated to the art world) and exercises to solve various problems.

In contrast to these essentialist approaches, constructivist and pragmatist educators tend to believe that creativity is a social phenomenon highly dependent on the environment. While it may be caused, nurtured and developed through appropriate practice, technique and strategy, it can also be curbed, inhibited or broken when the environment is not socially or emotionally favourable.

In the world of education, training dedicated to teaching creativity is still rare. To name one: the International Center for Studies in Creativity at Buffalo State/State University of New York (established in 1967) is probably the first and oldest degree-granting programme in creativity in the world. The influence of Alex Osborn, the developer of brainstorming and the originator of the Creative Problem Solving process (CPS), has particularly inspired this training. More generally, the development of creativity is part of the long list of goals that have driven educational curricula, including those of arts education, for nearly a century.

Outside the school, many authors suggest different solutions to boost creativity. (e.g. Gelb, 1997). In this vein, to become creative Mary should develop her curiosity by exploring the outside world as well as her inner world to always keep her mind open to newness and even search for it. She should continually refine her senses to better understand these worlds and maintain a healthy mind in a healthy body. She should also revise her beliefs and habits and learn from her mistakes. She should obviously cultivate her knowledge of science and art to exercise her rational and emotional intelligence. She should no longer be frightened by paradoxes and contradictions, but accept them positively as they are part of the richness of life that she should learn to grasp as a whole; she would then gradually be able to forge links between ideas and even to have new ones while undertaking her creative activities and her academic studies.

In this article I will develop the hypothesis that the renewed interest in creativity in education policy not only is a cultural benefit or an economic necessity, but also results from the convergence of interests between major international agencies such as UNESCO, the OECD, the EU and the lifestyles of a new privileged stratum of the population whose creativity drives both their professional activity and their free time.

From the model of social reproduction developed by Bourdieu and Passeron, I will draw attention to the symbolic violence resulting from the exploitation of this new axis of economic and social competition and I invite the policy makers to think about creativity and education in creativity as ways of structuring society as well as valorising the dispositions of the collective and individual mind.

Creativity and priorities of the education system

Let's return to the school again. For thirty years I have been interested in the situation of arts and cultural education, and I have observed a series of successive changes of direction aiming at promoting student's sensitivity and expression abilities, developing their critical thinking and autonomy, their participation in the life of their community, exploring their culture and heritage and also contemporary creation, discovering cultural diversity and multiculturalism, meeting creators, discovering peace education and environmental protection, exploring various techniques and new technologies, and, of course, creativity.

In the troubled waters of education systems, the ship of arts education regularly changes its course, and its thinkers, experts and advisors then opt for new destinations, with an urgency which is difficult to understand. Immediately, international then national and local symposia propose debates on the advantages of this change of direction and priority and spread the good word. Not long ago, distant lands were hardly informed that a new approach was proposed. Today, thanks to the internet, information travels faster and provincialisms are perhaps less marked because the whole world resonates in unison. But in reality, this synchrony concerns the experts more than local players, who must work on the front line and manage its complexity and complications, making them more resistant to change or making them wiser.[1]

Agencies

I've often wondered who was driving these changes of direction, and who were the agents most likely to initiate such changes? Three hypotheses seem probable to me, the first being the major international agencies that drive the world; the second resulting from lifestyles, the demand and the expectations of the individuals concerned by culture and creation. The third hypothesis is probably the most likely: it is the result of the collusion between the interests of these influential players and those of major national and international agencies that represent them or in which they participate.

International agencies

Since its inception in 1945, UNESCO has regularly played a leadership role in this field. In 1995, it declared: 'The challenge to humanity is to adopt new ways of thinking, new ways of acting, new ways of organising itself in society, in short, new ways of living' (UNESCO, 1995: 11). In November 1999, Federico Mayor, the UNESCO Director-General, launched an Appeal for the Promotion of Arts Education and Creativity at School as part of the construction of a Culture of Peace:

> Today we are clearly and strongly aware of the important influence of the creative spirit in shaping the human personality, bringing out the full potential of children and adolescents and maintaining their emotional balance – all factors which foster harmonious beha-viour. … I solemnly call upon the Member States of UNESCO to take appropriate administrative, financial and legal measures to ensure that the teaching of the arts – which covers disciplines such as poetry, the visual arts, music, drama, dance and film – is com-pulsory throughout the school cycle, i.e. from nursery school up until the last year of sec-ondary school. To that end, encouragement must be given to the participation of artists, musicians, poets, playwrights, producers, film directors, actors and dancers in workshops held within school establishments to stimulate creativity and creative work.
>
> *(Mayor 1999)*[2]

In response to these broad guidelines, more specialised non-governmental associations, such as the International Society for Education through Art (INSEA), the National Art Education Association (NAEA) or the Center for Creative Communities (CCC), hold regular conferences and debates on these topics.

The Organisation for Economic Co-operation and Development (OECD), established in 1961, is also one of the major agencies that establishes and disseminates economic and social expertise. Wolfgang Michalski offers a synthetic overview of our subject:

> with increasing demands for life-long learning, a rapidly changing society which no longer asks for the reproduction of knowledge but for ideas, creativity and new ways of thinking, those challenges become cultural ones … marginal improvements in education policies based on business as usual will hardly be sufficient … Adaptability, creativity and diversity are essential to fuel the knowledge economy and society.
>
> *(Michalski, 1999)*

For their part, the European Commission and the Council of Europe have developed suc-cessive programmes, all of which involve creativity. Culture, Creativity and the Young was launched by the Council's Culture Committee in 1995, providing an overview of the issues and a survey of arts education policies in most European countries (Robinson, 1996); and 2009 was declared the European Year of Creativity and Innovation:

> Under the slogan: 'Imagine, Create, Innovate', the Year aimed to promote creative and innovative approaches in different sectors of human activity, from education to enterprise,

from arts to science. While promoting the well-being of all individuals in society, the purpose of the Year was to contribute to better equipping the European Union for the challenges ahead in a globalised world.[3]

(http://create2009.europa.eu/; see Drotner, Chapter 8)

On this occasion, several events were held in different countries. The debate 'Beyond chalk and talk: creativity in the classroom'[4] had a very explicit programme:

> Europe's economies are changing. The industrial society, which shaped and modernised Europe's societies, is transforming fast into a largely services-based, knowledge-based society. Knowledge has become the core resource, well over land, labour and capital. But are Europe's education systems, from the basic to the most advanced levels of education, designed to prepare for this new society? ... How can schools and universities foster the creative and innovative capacity of pupils and students, helping them to develop and use it throughout their life and in the future labour market? New jobs that do not even exist today call for new skills. New social needs call for new solutions.[5]

During the conferences, Odile Quintin[6] clearly defined the economic challenges: 'Our university-business forum has opened a dialogue on how university education can help or hinder the flexible learning that prepares graduates for a fluid labour market: looking at curriculum development, entrepreneurship, lifelong learning, knowledge transfer and mobility'.[7]

Of all the states involved in these studies and recommendations, Great Britain is probably the most concretely committed in this direction and is a laboratory for the turn towards creativity. Since 1999, with the *Creative Economy Mapping Documents*, then in 2001 with the Green Paper *Culture and Creativity: The Next 10 Years*, the British government has resolutely engaged in an educational, economic and industrial policy focused on creativity and aiming at stimulating the creative industries and at integrating them into the general economy, hoping that in return creativity would boost the economy. Below is an extract from the statements of the Department for Culture, Media and Sport:

> The aim of this UK Government's Green Paper is to set out a framework for creativity for the next ten years, particularly in the areas of media and culture. The paper, which places creativity at the centre of the country's identity, economy and future, recognises the vital role that culture and creativity play in children's development, in providing opportunities for employment and in overcoming social exclusion.[8]

Thus, the ten-year plan looks at ways to widen participation and access to culture through the implementation of several key initiatives designed to free excellence in individuals and institutions. Some of these initiatives include placing creativity at the heart of education and training, facilitating the access to culture through the development of an online learning resource, and providing new support for individual artists and cultural institutions. The paper, which seeks to join up policies ranging across education, economic development and culture, aims to create pathways for individuals to develop their creativity.

For its part, France has not considered the situation in the same way as its British neighbours and the concept of creativity has not been specifically highlighted; it therefore remains molten or, more exactly, diluted in the overall components of education. But, in 2010, the term 'creation' makes its first appearance at the time of the high school reform. A new so-called 'exploration' teaching is entitled 'Creation and artistic activities'. It is open to all pupils in the first year of high school wishing to explore one of the four selected areas: the visual arts, the arts of sound, performing arts and heritage. In the national consultation document preceding the implementation of this teaching, the Ministry emphasises the importance of creative industries and the impact of the internet, which dramatically changes the relationship with artworks and creation.[9] In parallel, in 2009, teaching in the history of the arts was established. This programme is supposed to be taught in primary and secondary school by volunteer teachers from all disciplines in France. It will cover without exclusivity all areas of the arts and creative industries, from architecture to design, cinema and music, a teaching approach being essentially focused on heritage and history. Thus Art and creation remain closely linked and do not allow creativity to think itself independent of this area.

Creative class

In contrast to the top-down approach that we have examined so far, let's try a 'middle-up' approach in articulating Richard Florida's model of creative class with the 'middle-up-down' approach of Ikujiro Nonaka and Hirotaka Takeuchi (1995). The latter have shown the vital role played in Japan by *middle managers* in the conversion of the tacit knowledge produced by employees into the explicit knowledge produced by the organisation and its decision makers, and vice versa. It is for this reason that we refer to their model by assuming that, in some way, creative individuals are disseminating, relaying and mediating their creative lifestyle.

For his part, Florida considers that the post-industrial society has encouraged the emergence of a new social type that is endowed with both cultural and creative capital. The interests and lifestyles of these individuals, whose occupations require regular creative engagement, are sufficiently homogeneous for them to be considered what sociologists call a social class. According to Florida, creativity attracts creativity and creative people attract creative people, producing vast social networks concentrated in the major creative centres of the world. According to Florida and his colleagues, the creative class, which constitutes around 30 per cent of the population of large urban centres, comprises five sub-groups.[10] Artists, designers and the industries of entertainment, sport and media account for 5 per cent of the creative class, which also includes health workers (14 per cent), computer science and engineering professionals (14 per cent), the sector of education, training and libraries (18 per cent), and finally the creative professionals that include senior managers, lawyers, accountants, etc. (49 per cent).

According to this new sociological division, the 'creative class' would now possess the essential power, which would allow it to shape not only the lifestyles of the present but also those of the future. Through the various processes of concentration in large urban centres – notably through the process of gentrification (the demographic and urban process resulting from deindustrialisation and post-industrial reorganisation) – the elite, characterised by a high cultural and academic capital, would have established extensive networks of influence in all areas and particularly in education. These 'bobos'[11] would form the sociological core of major urban centres, in which they would occupy creative jobs and drive cultural life during their free time. Cultural facilities and their content are dedicated to them.

The paradigm of the creative class is not unanimously accepted within the academic world and Florida's personality as 'the creative evangelist' can irritate (e.g. Vivant, 2006). The criticisms addressed to him are ideological and methodological as well as ethical, but the fact remains that he has observed well and documented many issues.

Sociologists and demographers have already noted the emergence of a new social group they have named the 'new bourgeoisie', the 'new service class' or the 'new middle class'. By focusing on the creative variant, Florida made it what he calls the 'Creative Class', whose activities, both professional and extra-professional, have a more regular and intense relationship to creativity than other segments of the population. We can add that, in addition to their practices, strategies, objectives and common interests, the members of the creative class constitute a relatively homogeneous interpretative community.

In this regard, if we compare all the major successive directions taken by education, and especially those of arts education, with the aspirations of the creative class, we can see that they match each other detail by detail. From this perspective, it is easier to understand all the changes of direction made over the last thirty years. They revolve around the concepts of man and woman as seen by the humanist ideology to which this population adheres, of whom we can draw the ideal portrait: free, individualistic, democratic and peaceful individuals, liberated from the shackles of traditions and their authority, as well as their power over sensitivity and judgement. These individuals have grown up harmoniously and are able to speak and express their singularity while respecting their community and also being tolerant of the singularity of others and of the community and natural environment. They are also actors of their time, authors or consumers of the knowledge explosion and masters of technology. They are also informed citizens able to participate in the cultural turn intended to make humanity evolve from hard power to soft power, or, better still, to smart power.[12]

The participation in smart power favoured by the members of the 'creative class' requires the development of a number of skills acquired in early childhood. To this end, curiosity is strongly stimulated, multidisciplinarity is cultivated, and different and divergent thoughts are appreciated and encouraged. The informal and formal educational environment exists preferably in a rich cultural, scientific and technological context where the pedagogy of success outweighs the pedagogy of failure. This educational programme of the creative class applies not only to knowledge and the reproduction of its professional field, but also more broadly to the creative predispositions it has encouraged.

It gathers together all the 'sciences', methodologies, methods, techniques, know-how and tips related to the development of the creative spirit and creative practices that focus around seeking, solving and sharing, and whose fields of operation obviously relate to the creative industries but also to science, research, management and entrepreneurial skills which thrive in social environments that are less and less hierarchical and repetitive, but increasingly collaborative, creative, holarchical[13] and competitive, demanding more and more initiative, independent thinking and creative leadership.

Double agency and mediation

The role of mediator that Nonaka and Takeuchi attribute to *middle managers* is exactly the role we attribute to some members of the creative class. In their daily practices, they are not only players in creativity at work and outside work, but also more formal proponents of this lifestyle. They therefore have an influence on local, national and international agencies that objectively serve their interests as individuals, as a group or even as a class, if we agree with Florida's arguments. Indeed, we believe there is more than a convergence of interest between the institutions and the aspirations of the creativists. They relay the approach adopted by major agencies and their lifestyles are relayed by them. The key words of their approach are the same and they serve as a motto or a creed to each other.

Here is a summary that we developed by combining the recurring terms of the creative approach: the rapid and permanent changes of the service-based, knowledge-based, and creativity-based society produce new ways of living, thinking, acting, organising, sharing, which require more and more adaptability, flexibility, mobility, fluidity, diversity, and entrepreneurship, leadership and competitiveness, and thus invention and innovation in all fields of science and technology, and imagination and creation in all sectors of culture and media.

Everyone is creative, everyone is a leader and an entrepreneur, so everyone is in competition with everyone else. The members of the creative class and their institutions therefore make sure the contents, values, manners and tastes that characterise their lifestyle are reproduced.

To do this, creativity is presented as a natural disposition of the human mind, as an ability that one only needs to develop to enjoy it individually and collectively, but also as a panacea for current and future issues. But reality is somewhat more complex and less peaceful. First, it is important to note that all the individuals who are supposed to be part of Florida's 'creative class' do not have the same hierarchical status: some are leaders in creative industries, while others are their subordinates; some combine a material and a symbolic capital, while most others satisfy themselves with pretences, hope and often delusion. At the periphery (and sometimes the middle) of that more or less creative group, legions of wannabes struggle to make ends meet, hoping to join the centre, to which they regularly provide some good ideas. This is the creative effect from the margins and the underground. Further, symbolically, socially and even spatially, a large part of the population is only indirectly concerned.

Although in large urban centres 30 per cent of the population adhere more or less voluntarily to the cult of creativity, the vast majority of human beings remain very far from it. For them, creativity and creation mean, above all, permanent, disturbing and inaccessible changes, loss of habits, loss of traditions and benchmarks, crisis, inhibition of action; they cause symbolic violence and its share of suffering. (See, on this topic, Belkhamsa and Darras, 2009.)

One of the founding paradigms of the theory of social reproduction described by Pierre Bourdieu and Jean-Claude Passeron (1977) in their book *Reproduction in Education, Society and Culture* concerns the power struggles between social groups through forms of symbolic violence. This symbolic violence allows a group of individuals to impose their representations, beliefs and values, and behaviours on those who do not draw concrete benefits from them, while concealing power relations behind naturalist, universalist, liberating or egalitarian approaches and ideologies.

Thanks to the media and institutions specialising in the construction of beliefs, of which the school is the spearhead, the dominant agencies strive to obtain the consent of the dominated, who more or less consciously nourish the hope of one day taking advantage of their efforts, their adhesion or their submissiveness while feeling guilty for not measuring up to the feats of the dominant.[14] Besides the effects of propaganda, the policies favouring creativity are actually internalised by those who produce them. Those who manage to impose their model of creativity reap the most benefits from it, while others try to imitate them or develop a sense of inferiority when they fail to do so. This is precisely the case with Mary and those similar to her.

Indeed, when the process for the construction of the 'creativist' domination is not highlighted, the failure to meet the creative demand appears as personal incompetence or a disability. Thus, in this area, as in many others, the school 'unconsciously' keeps the powers in place in a social world where ups and downs and other forms of social inequality are here to stay, at least for a while.

Resilience?

Although I am aware of the current social processes and of the symbolic violence that results from the logic of my argument, and although I am both sceptical and critical of 'creativist' proselytising, I continue to attribute positive qualities to creativity. This is probably one of the effects of my belonging to the creative class, its lifestyle and its reproduction. (This is probably also true for most readers of this text.)

I therefore continue to believe that creativity deserves to be developed, but I dare to hope that this development will be made with an awareness of the social issues and risks associated with it, as well as of the ethical issues raised by an education for creativity for all. 'Creativity without conscience is the soul's perdition', we could say, drawing inspiration from François Rabelais.[15]

I therefore continue to believe that if today there are good reasons to develop creativity, it is precisely because of the effects of human creativity on the human and non-human environment. Indeed, the processes of change, adaptation and transformation of the environment, such as living in increasingly large groups consuming more and more, have multiplied and complexified issues that must now be addressed by trying to limit collateral damage. We now know how in many cases the genius of mankind has become its own worst enemy.

The creativity of the scientists, technological innovations, the inventiveness of marketing and the insatiable search for newness of consumers are directly responsible for the colossal environmental disturbances caused by humanity. Surprisingly, the remedy for the negative effects of creativity is still more creativity – but, hopefully, a more responsible and sustainable creativity, two qualities that should inspire all educational programmes in creativity.

The magnitude of the task ahead leads to an industrialisation of research, creativity and innovation in an environment that is competitive, assertive and global, and where innovation benefits first the most flexible and inventive social categories and economies.

Conclusion

The social, cultural and creative elite have created an environment that is beneficial for them. However, competition is often fierce. Not only do some of their members fail to win this race for competitiveness, but even the most creative know that the weight on their shoulders can quickly turn heaven into hell. In all cases, modest or oppressed populations seem far from being able to access the creative heaven. Yet history shows that individuals deemed dull or without genius can prove to have some when the relational equilibrium changes after an encounter, an internal crisis, an accident or a mutation of the environment. In this regard, the most striking case is undoubtedly that of women from all social classes, who have been reduced to a non-creative situation for millennia; although in fact, they were often creative in their sphere but ignored by a patriarchal society and depreciated through male domination. But whenever the patriarchal and 'macho' stranglehold is loosened slightly, they prove to be very inventive and creative – as in the case of micro-credit. How many theories which established male superiority in science, technology, politics and art are being shattered in the democratic post-patriarchal societies where women take part in all these areas, despite 'macho' resistance?

These apparently contradictory examples show that there is a thin line between too determinist social approaches and a universalist essentialism. They also suggest that these creative 'dispositions' are probably distributed systemically, that is to say that their expression or inhibition depends on the social organisation adopted by the local and global system. Consequently, if the conditions for expressing creativity and invention were actually implemented, everyone could access it and benefit from it, albeit to varying degrees.

In all cases, if there is no room at the top for everyone, let's be really creative; let's imagine other geographies.

Notes

1 The large TALIS study undertaken by the OECD about teachers' practices shows that: 'the hardest issues to grapple with relate to actually improving teaching practice. Teachers in most countries report

using traditional practices aimed at transmitting knowledge in structured settings much more often than they use student-oriented practices, such as adapting teaching to individual needs. And even less so do they use enhanced learning activities that require a deeper cognitive activation of students' (OECD, 2009).

2 Amongst the various results of this declaration, we can mention the World Conference on Arts Education which took place in Lisbon in March 2006, then the World Creativity Summit which was held in Taipei in 2008. The second World Summit on Arts Education was held in Seoul, Korea, in 2010.

3 European Commission, Directorate-General for Education and Culture.

4 Brussels, 30–31 March 2009.

5 http://create2009.europa.eu/fileadmin/Content/Downloads/PDF/Events/background_paper_2nd_brussels_debate.pdf.

6 From the Directorate-General for Education and Culture.

7 http://create2009.europa.eu/fileadmin/Content/Downloads/PDF/Events/Speech_Mme_Quintin_second_Brussels_Debate.pdf (accessed 9 September 2009).

8 http://www.culture.gov.uk/images/publications/Culture_creative_next10.pdf.

9 http://www.educnet.education.fr/arts/actualites/consultationprogrammeseconde1.

10 http://martinprosperity.org/media/images/sub_groups_within_creative_class_2008.png; http://www.creativeclass.com/.

11 Term invented by the American journalist David Brooks in 2000 in the book *Bobos in Paradise*.

12 'Smart power' is a term used in international affairs and relations, defined by Joseph Nye (1990) as the ability to combine hard power (brutal force) and soft power (values and culture) into a winning strategy).

13 A term coined by Arthur Koestler (1967) in his book *The Ghost in the Machine*, a holon is both a part and a whole. In a systemic sense a system is a hierarchy of holons.

14 For Bourdieu, the dominated have integrated the approach and representations of the dominant, which does not allow them to envisage their alienation through other systems of belief. Passeron tends to grant more lucidity and more capacity for resistance to the 'dominated'.

15 'Science without conscience is the soul's perdition.' François Rabelais (1572) *Pantagruel*.

References

Belkhamsa, S. and Darras, B. (2009) L'Objet et le cycle des habitudes et des changements d'habitude. Approche sémiotique, in B. Darras and S. Belkhamsa, *Objets et communication*, Paris: L'Harmattan.

Bourdieu, P. and Passeron, J.-C. (1977/1990) *Reproduction in Education, Society and Culture*, London: Sage Publications; original French edition *La Reproduction. Eléments pour une théorie du système d'enseignement*, Paris: Editions de Minuit, 1970.

Gelb, M. J. (1997) *How to Think like Leonardo da Vinci … 7 Steps to Genius Everyday*, New York: Delacorte Press.

Mayor, F. (1999) *Appeal for the Promotion of Arts Education and Creativity at School*; available at http://www.unesco.org/cpp/uk/news/peaceart.htm.

Michalski, W. (1999) Dematerialisation of economic activity, *OECD Observer* 217–18 (Summer).

Nonaka, I. and Takeuchi, H. (1995) *The Knowledge-Creating Company: How Japanese Companies Create the Dynamics of Innovation*, Oxford: Oxford University Press.

Nye, J. (1990) *Bound to Lead: The Changing Nature of American Power*, New York: Basic Books.

OECD (2009) *Creating Effective Teaching and Learning Environments: First Results from TALIS*, Paris: OECD.

Robinson, K. (1996) *Arts Education in Europe*, Strasbourg: Council of Europe; available at http://www.creativecommunities.org.uk/pdf/2_Intergovernmental_C_E8355.pdf.

UNESCO (1995) *Our Creative Diversity*, UNESCO.

Valéry, P. (1924–56) *Œuvres I*, Paris: Gallimard; collection Bibliothèque de la Pléiade.

Vivant, E. (2006) La Classe créative, existe-t-elle?, *Annales de la recherche urbaine* 101 (November): 155–61.

11

Creativity, the arts and the renewal of culture[1]

Peter Abbs

One of the terms essential to any understanding of education must be creativity. The word has come to denote a disposition of mind which is experimental, open, engaged, a particular kind of teaching and learning where the results cannot be comprehended in advance of the process, whether it be in mathematics, the sciences, the humanities or the arts. The word is indispensable in the vocabulary of all true education and, particularly, of aesthetic education. Isn't the educated mind the creative mind? I would want to answer in the affirmative, yet in the teaching of the arts there is a problem.

In the 1960s, under the broad influence of progressive educational theory and of Modernism, the word came to carry a number of associations which have made the case for an expressive and exploratory education infinitely more difficult to convincingly formulate for our own demanding time. During the 1960s the word became all but synonymous with *originality*, with the subverting of conventions, with being different, with being individual, with 'doing one's own thing'. Virtually *any* act that broke with a norm was hailed as creative. *To be creative in the arts meant to be iconoclastic.* And yet this view distorted the deeper truths about creativity, namely that it would seem to be an inherent part of our common biological nature and that its full development requires a repertoire of received expressive forms, a living inheritance of examples and procedures transmitted by the culture. As it is in mathematics, the sciences and the humanities, so it is in the arts: one can only be significantly creative on the basis of tradition. Given a dynamic Socratic mode of teaching, *the better the tradition, the better the chances of significant creativity.*

The aim of this chapter is to delineate and interpret the creative process through whatever symbolic medium it may operate. In particular, I am keen to establish the connections and reciprocal continuities between nature and culture, between biology and symbol. It is also my belief that if we can formally understand the nature of the creative process we can begin to establish what kind of teaching best fosters it, what blunts and diminishes it.

Introduction

While creativity is, in its highest reaches, quite extraordinary, it is yet a common and everyday possession. Creativity, one might say, is the condition of our existence. It is not difficult to discern a creative energy at work in innumerable conversations, in sudden puns, spontaneous jokes, in the endless recreation of our experience into narrative form. It is not difficult to see it at work in children's play, and, of course, in infants' 'cuddlies' – those early transitional objects so precisely and lovingly described by the psychoanalyst D. W. Winnicott – in which inner emotional states and needs are given intimate symbolic form. The indispensable infant's rag is not merely a comforter, but basic material for the symbolic play of mind – for in the dawning psyche of the child the object comes to represent the absent mother. In this early symbolic leap of the psyche Winnicott saw the source of all cultural creation. In *Playing and Reality* he wrote: 'I have used the term cultural experience as an extension of the idea of transitional phenomena' (Winnicott, 1971: 99) and claimed that in all acts of symbolic creativity he saw the same interplay between separateness and union.

And yet, of course, no understanding of creativity would be complete without an emphatic reference to *dreams*. And dreaming, too, is, in one sense, very ordinary. We all seem to have dreams without effort; it is a condition of our common existence. The dream involves the curious unwilled and unpredictable condensation of impulses into images, into montage, drama, story and surreal nonsense. Our liability to dream – our unconscious power to create imaginal narrative and iconic images – demonstrates a symbolic power at work in our biological nature. Indeed, the dream may offer one major clue to our more specialised notion of creativity as it manifests itself in the various artistic and scientific disciplines. The mode of the dream is imaginal and associative in structure, not discursive and rational, and it would seem that when the discursive and the rational have reached a kind of inevitable closure, the mind, if dynamic thinking is to continue, needs to step sideways and backwards into the more free, chaotic, seemingly crazy, open, suggestive modes of the dream-mentality. Most dreams offer a surreal logic – an uncanny logic of transformation through accident, suggestion and association – in which expected categories are broken down and new, often bizarre, relationships are formed. 'Dreamed of a wonderful pie made of blackberries, thrushes' eggs, honeycomb and watercress', wrote Hugh Walpole (quoted in Brook 1983: 85), and in his dream we note the subversion of time-worn categories and a further constellation of unexpected culinary relationships.

In other words, when we talk about creative activity we may be talking about *the transference of the night-time dream-mentality to the day-time work of culture-making*. We could say that highly creative people are those who have elected the dream-mode as their *modus operandi*. They reclaim, and put to further use, those primitive modes of ideation which belong to the dynamics of the dream. They open themselves to the unconscious for their primary and potential material and then, through conscious skill and labour, develop it into aesthetic and cultural form. To adapt the eloquent words of Dryden, the art-maker takes the sleeping images of things towards the light. As I shall show, such a view is very partial and incomplete – yet it does seem to carry a certain truth about much creative activity.

I have dived into creativity rather promptly, and gone deep. I want, though, in this chapter to establish the dream as one of the major clues to creativity. I want to suggest that one of the axes for understanding creativity is vertical. It concerns the continuous traffic, moving in both directions, upwards and downwards, between the conscious and the unconscious; or, more precisely, between the conscious, pre-conscious and unconscious. This would seem, at root, a primary biological dynamic: the conversion of impulse into image – and that may not be an adequate description of the process, for the image can seldom be understood solely in terms of the impulse. In the conversion a transformation takes place; and it is in that transformation that the power of cultural life lies. But, although this is one axis, there is another that is of equal importance. This is the axis that moves from innovation to tradition and from tradition back to innovation, a continuous, subtle, reciprocal movement between the received culture and the renewed culture.

The vertical axis of creativity

I turn to the first axis of creativity, the movement between the conscious and the unconscious. I claimed earlier that one major clue to creativity may lie in the transference of the night-time dream modality to the day-time work of culture-making. In this transference the powerful unconscious patterning processes of the psyche-soma are used and elaborated in the creation of art, theory and science. Einstein answering a questionnaire about creativity in 1945 claimed that 'combinatory play' was the essential feature of productive thinking. Combinatory play – allowing for a whole range of sequencing and connecting which can both use and break the established congruences, both convert and invert the settled narratives – is another way of describing the dream modality. Of its primitive nature, Einstein was aware: he called this kind of thinking 'visual' (as opposed to discursive) and 'muscular' (as opposed to intellectual). For creative thinking to happen one must constantly step *sideways* out of the track set by logic and *downwards* into the unconscious.

Einstein wrote in answer to the questionnaire:

> Conventional words or other signs have to be sought for laboriously only in a secondary stage, when the mentioned associative play is sufficiently established and can be reproduced at will.
>
> *(Einstein, quoted in Koestler 1975: 171–2)*

Here in Einstein's famous formulation it can be seen that creativity may involve a continuous movement between primary associative ideation and secondary conceptual elaboration inside a particular tradition and symbolic form. Neatly condensed, Einstein's remark reveals the dialectics of creativity, the movements between both the vertical and horizontal axes. But to understand this dialectic we need to move more carefully. We need to examine the vertical axis through the phenomenon of the dream.

We can probably all give personal examples of involuntary acts of mind in which objects in the world are recreated in new imaginal contexts in which simple events are taken from their habitual frames and placed in new frames and their content dramatically rearranged according to another set of principles. This is what the dream and dream-phenomena do. I want to take for my example a dream of a man called Herbert Silberer.

Susanne Langer, in *Mind: An Essay on Human Feeling*, records the dream of Herbert Silberer when he is riding in a European railroad coach. Silberer, describing the starting point of the dream, writes:

> With my eyes closed, I am leaning against the corner of the compartment. Time and again the setting sun shines into my face, It disturbs me but I am too tired to get up and draw the shade. So I let it shine on me and watch the visual impressions that come as the sunshine hits my eyelids. Remarkably enough, the figures are different each time, but each time uniform. I see a mosaic of triangles, then one of squares and so on. Then I have the impression that I myself am putting together the mosaic figures in rhythmical movements. Soon I find that the rhythm is that of the axles of the train … All of a sudden the following auto-symbolic phenomenon occurs: I see an old lady, to the right, setting a table with a checkered table cloth, each square of which encloses a figure resembling one of the sun-mosaics previously mentioned, the figures are all different.
>
> *(Silberer, quoted in Langer, 1972: 286)*

The account records a steady movement from the conscious to the unconscious: from being aware of the visual impressions created by the sun, from being in a semi-conscious trance state in which he feels he is creating the mosaic effects, from, finally, sinking into sleep when the unconscious begins to recreate the phenomena in terms of narrative and character. In this account the actual sense-perception provides the immediate material for the dream imagination. By some spontaneous unconscious process, the bright sunshine is being further abstracted and recast in terms of a new matrix: an old lady is laying a table with a sun-mosaic tablecloth. The conscious hypnotic sense-perception is taking on symbolic form, is forming the material of another narrative and drama. Silberer calls his dream, as opposed to his trance, an 'auto-symbolic phenomenon'. I want to suggest the sequence demonstrates the characteristic marks of the creative process: there is a playing with patterns; there is a shifting of reference from one matrix (that of ordinary perceptual experience) to another (that of symbol and narrative); there is the transformation of ordinary experience according to some inner need, categories and, possibly, archetypes. Why is the woman there? Why is she old? Why is she laying the sun-chequered tablecloth? Here is an example of creativity: *quite ordinary* and yet, on further reflection, *quite extraordinary*, performed without effort as the individual's consciousness drifted into the unconscious and its 'auto-symbolic phenomenon'.

Susanne Langer, considering Silberer's dream, claimed that:

> It is in dream that the imaginative powers are born and exercised without effort or intention, unfold, and finally possess all departments of sense, and activate another great class of largely un-comprehended phenomena, the products of memory. Remembered sights and sounds, often unrecorded in conscious experience, sometimes whole situations especially of early life, tactile and olfactory and muscular impressions come together to form the profuse unsolicited imagery our brains create in sleep.
>
> *(Langer, 1972: 288)*

Dream, she suggests, creates the imaginative powers that are then extended to other conscious activities in the course of evolutionary development. This would explain why the first great mode of cultural thinking is mythic in nature, structured, that is to say, through deep personification, through narrative sequence and metaphor.

There are many examples, in both the sciences and the arts, of such creative activity. In her introduction to *Frankenstein* Mary Shelley explained how in a dream trance, 'with shut eyes, but acute mental vision', she saw the pale student bringing 'the hideous phantasm of a man' to life and foresaw all its terrible narrative implications:

> Swift as light and as cheering was the idea that broke in upon me. 'I have found it! What terrified me will terrify others; and I need only describe the spectre which had haunted my midnight pillow.' On the morrow I announced that I had thought of a story.
>
> *(Shelley, 1968: 12–13)*

R. L. Stevenson, in a similar manner, tells us how in a dream he was given the crucial episode in *Dr Jekyll and Mr Hyde*:

> For two days I went about racking my brains for a plot of any sort; and on the second night I dreamed the scene at the window and a scene afterwards split in two, in which Hyde, pursued for some crime, took the powder and underwent the change in the presence of his pursuers.
>
> *(Stevenson, quote in Brook, 1983: 138)*

I have taken my examples from the arts but there are many examples of the same kind of creative process in the sciences. Indeed, it was an eminent scientist, Kekulé, who discovered through hallucinatory dream images the structure of benzine and concluded a famous lecture on science with the injunction: 'Let us dream, gentlemen' (quoted in Koestler 1975: 118).

Yet, as Kekulé himself knew, dreaming is not sufficient. What is necessary is *consciously* developing a dream-like disposition; a disposition which allows the mind to enter the associative labyrinth, the surreal city, the primordial underground. In order to be creative one must develop a disposition to doodle, to let the marks create the marks that the mind then dreamily follows. The following piece of free-association, automatic writing exemplifies the process. It is by Coleridge and is taken from one of his many note-books:

> I inevitably by some link or other return to you, or (say rather) bring some fuel of thought to the ceaseless Yearning for you at my Inmost, which like a steady fire attracts constantly the air which constantly feeds it. I began strictly and as matter of fact to examine that subtle Vulcanian Spider-web Net of Steel – strong as Steel yet subtle as the Ether, in which my soul flutters inclosed with the Idea of your's [sic] – to pass rapidly as in a catalogue thro' the Images only, exclusive of the thousand Thoughts that possess the same force, which never fail instantly to wake into vivider flame the for ever and ever Feeling of you/ – The fire/ – Mary, you, and I at Gallow-Hill/ or if flamy, reflected in children's round faces – ah whose children? – a dog – that dog whose restless eyes oft catching the light of the fire used to watch your face, as you leaned with your head on your hand and arm, & your feet on the fender/ the fender thence/ – Fowls at Table – the last dinner at Gallow Hill, when you drest the two fowls in that delicious white Sauce which when very ill is the only idea of food that does not make me sicker/ all natural Scenery – ten thousand links, and if it please me, the very spasm & drawing-back of a pleasure which is half-pain, you not being there – Cheese – at Middleham, too salt/ horses, my ride to Scarborough – asses, to that large living 2 or 3 miles from Middleham/ All Books – my Study at Keswick/ – the Ceiling or'Head of a Bed – the green watered Mazarine! – a Candle in its socket, with its alternate fits & dying flashes of lingering Light – O God! O God! – Books of abstruse Knowledge – the Thomas Aquinas & Suarez from the Durham Library.
>
> *(Coleridge, quoted in Whalley, 1974: 15)*

In this hyphenated stream-of-consciousness writing Coleridge passes, with dramatic rapidity, from image to image, following through memory and association and suggestion their 'ten thousand links', thereby creating a spider-web of intimate and poetic connections. This is private incantatory writing: writing for both the direct exploration and the immediate ease of a disturbed consciousness. It is not written for an audience. It is not a poem. It is not an artefact which conforms to any genre. Not yet: but, of course, it could have become so. It is the primary polymorphic material of poetry; the auto-symbolic stuff of the dream-mind tapped by the conscious mind and allowed to flow. Were it to develop further, the next stage would be for Coleridge, *the poet*, to select, to edit, to amplify, to shape into a tighter poetic form the half-random ramblings of his own mind. Indeed, a few of the lines seem already to possess the intensity and precision of poetry: 'a Candle in its socket, with its alternate fits and dying flashes of lingering light'; 'the very spasm and drawing back of a pleasure which is half-pain'; 'my soul flutters inclosed'. These are semantic gifts from the unconscious found by the writer using his pen as a kind of divining rod to locate the subterranean elements below. They reveal what Arthur Koestler (1975) in his study of creativity described as 'the momentary regressions to earlier stages in mental evolution, bringing forms of mentation into play which otherwise manifest themselves only in the dream or dream-like state'. They reveal a creative regression back into the unconscious and into the dream modality.

Essentially, what is manifest in many of Coleridge's journal entries is a creative regression; and this movement between the conscious and the unconscious which such a regression entails I have suggested forms the vertical axis of the creative act. But the creative act invariably involves, also, a creative elaboration in terms of the symbolic form within which it operates. Physics involves a knowledge of physics, music a knowledge of music, philosophy of philosophy. This brings me to the other major axis of creativity: the horizontal axis, that between tradition and innovation.

The horizontal axis of creativity

I have claimed that the unconscious is a shaping energy, helping to determine the form of creative work, but it is also true that, in a certain manner of speaking, *symbolic forms create symbolic forms*, that art creates art, that science creates science, that theory creates theory; that, in all culture, there is a constant reworking of the established conventions, notations, images, narratives; that, at nearly all times in the creation of new art, new science and new theory, there are constant acts of plagiarism and theft, acts which are redeemed by the further adaptation to which the stolen material is deftly put before it is stolen again and cast, yet again, in another shape, always in part derivative, always in part potentially new. Creativity, in brief, cannot be understood without reference to the symbolic field in which it takes place – that complex magnetic system of allusion, notation, reference, narrative, knowledge, assumption, understanding which we call culture and, in their specific contexts, the cultures of the various symbolic forms. It is precisely *this* dialectical relationship between inherited culture and symbolic transformation, between tradition and innovation, which marks the horizontal axis of creativity.

We think of Shakespeare as prodigiously inventive – a genius of originality – yet he was also the master of all plagiarists, the best of the magpies, assembling the materials for his art from wherever he could find them. There is a story called *Amleth* written by Saxo. In this story we have a wicked uncle and a threatened nephew who plays the fool while seeking revenge; we have a girl to whom the hero is attracted but whom he does not marry; we have the ruthless murder of a spy, bitter reproaches to a faithless mother, a voyage intended to end in the hero's death, his return home and the final achievement of his revenge, in which many beside his uncle die. Amleth, in narrative terms, is the prototype of Hamlet. Only the ghost and the travelling players are missing from *Amleth*, and these, too, can be found in earlier tales by Saxo. Shakespeare simply lifts the story and puts it to further aesthetic and dramatic use.

In his *Conversations with Goethe*, Eckermann wrote:

> People are always talking of originality but what does that mean? As soon as we are born the world begins to act on us and this goes on to the end, And, after all, what can we call our own, except energy, strength and will.
>
> If I could give an account of all I owe to great predecessors and contemporaries, there would be but a small balance in my favour. I, by no means, owe my works to my wisdom alone, but to a thousand things and persons around me, that provided me with material.
>
> (Eckermann, n.d.)

Originality, it would seem, can only have meaning in terms of the origin of the debt, adaptations and transformations made possible by the material of the received culture.

The horizontal axis yields a radically different perception into the creative process from that of the vertical. And yet they are not mutually exclusive but in intricate relationship, together forming the warp and the weft of active symbolic creation.

The examples I took from writing tell a similar story. Mary Shelley in her account tells her readers that before the trance-dream in which she saw Frankenstein and the monster, she had been discussing both ghost stories and recent scientific discoveries with her close friends, who were also, as a kind of literary game, set on writing some new stories. The *genre* is there ('some volumes of ghost stories translated from the German into French fell into our hands ... "We will each write a ghost story," said Lord Bryon, and his proposition was acceded to' (Shelley 1968: 8–9). The *theme* is there. (They talked of the experiments of Dr Darwin. Perhaps a corpse would be reanimated; galvanism had given to them the idea of such things; perhaps the component parts of a creation might be manufactured (ibid.). And a conducive *social context* existed ('I busied myself to think of a story – a story to rival those which had excited us to this task. ... "Have you thought of a story?" I was asked each morning and each morning I was forced to reply with a mortifying negative' (ibid.: 25)).

In the case of R. L. Stevenson's *Dr Jekyll and Mr Hyde* the author assures us that he had 'long been trying to write a story on this subject' and that 'all the rest was made awake, and consciously' (quoted in Brook, 1983: 85). In this conscious making of art (or science or theory), all that has been culturally inherited and assimilated, consciously and unconsciously, plays its part. But even more pertinent to my theme is the way in which past formulations can provide the essential elements for the creation of the new. Mary Shelley's story takes its form from existing ghost stories and half creates a new genre (science fiction) for others to emulate and further transform. R. L. Stevenson's *Dr Jekyll and Mr Hyde* belongs to the nineteenth century tradition of the novella.

It may be no accident that the term 'self-expression' (first coined in 1892) came to birth six years after the first Berne Convention providing the international terms for literary copyright. Yet *plagiarism* (with due qualifications) may well be a better guide than *self-expression* in the arts, for certainly it was an essential prerequisite of the practice of Greek dramatists, Renaissance painters and Elizabethan poets; indeed of all traditional art-making,

Our reflections on the horizontal axis of creativity, brief as they have been, lead us towards a recognition of the place of exemplars and models, to an appreciation of Winnicott's assertion that 'it is not possible to be original except on a basis of tradition' (Winnicott, 1971: 99) and to a positive view of the place of imitation, creative theft and productive plagiarism. A good tale can take a million tellings and not thereby be exhausted. Aesthetic Modernism and educational Progressivism, in denying tradition and the place of inherited symbols, over the last few decades have badly eroded the necessary conditions for high creative achievement.

The implications of the argument for the classroom

I have argued that the mind is inherently creative, inherently disposed to culture and pattern-making, and that this creativity can be understood as a kind of indivisible double engagement with the inner and the outer, with the psychosomatic and the cultural-historical. The two axes always act in some kind of conjunction, too subtle for definitive description. In the act of creation we thus see a complex interaction between a vertical and a horizontal axis; between the conscious and unconscious, between tradition and innovation. Generalising from our observations on the vertical axis we might coin the aphorism: *No progression without regression!* Generalising from the horizontal axis we might say: *No creation without tradition* or *No transformation without the continuous internalisation of conventions.* To begin to understand creativity we need to envisage a dialectical movement between these two axes in a dynamic model of the symbol-making mind. Perhaps the main value of such an analysis is that it may help us to recognise the nature of creativity and to provide the proper structural conditions for its development.

In considering the development of creativity in the arts we must then keep constantly in mind two major axes and their moments of intersection. As teachers, we have to keep in touch with the biological roots of art-making, that conversion of impulse and feeling and mood into symbolic form, that obscure, interior movement that animates, connects and spontaneously creates inner figurative and narrative patterns. We have, in other words, to keep in touch with the rhythm of the body and the unconscious. This is to follow the line of the vertical axis.

At the same time, we have to draw on and draw in the inherited culture, all the artefacts that relate to the particular art discipline, all the techniques that have been laboriously evolved, and as much of the relevant discourse as can be understood and, perhaps, even more than can be immediately understood. This is to follow the rhythm of the horizontal axis, connecting the individual to the culture and the culture to the individual.

Our understanding of creativity calls for a complex, dialectical mode of teaching in which the teacher is constantly switching from one axis to another. In the tension created between them the creative act develops and takes its symbolic shape within the culture. The teacher of the arts has to acquire an agile intuitive sense as to which movement to make along which axis. Sometimes, for example, it is necessary not to interfere, to allow the crazy dream modality its freedom and inventiveness. A kind of anarchy! Allowing, permitting; and no judgements, no censorship. 'Let us learn to dream' (Kekulé, quoted in Koestler, 1975: 118).

At other times, it is necessary for the teacher to actually teach, to positively introduce the nature of a form, its historical development and diverse usage, or to prescriptively draw attention to a particular technique or a critical concept. Here it is a matter of 'Let us learn to labour': to use materials, to test techniques, to raid the wealth of the past, to consciously make the work of art. In the first case, then, emphasis is on the inner and the unconscious. In the second, on the cultural inheritance, the critical discourse, the set task. The final aim is to let these complementary polarities create the aesthetic field in the classroom within which our own biological creativity can flourish and develop. This is to advocate neither traditional prescriptive teaching nor child-centred progressive teaching. I would argue that such a method incorporates the productive sides of both models and forms a higher synthesis.

Notes

1 This is an abridged version of Chapter 1 of Peter Abbs (1989) 'A' is for Aesthetics, Falmer Press.

References

Brook, S. (ed.) (1983) The Oxford Book of Dreams, Oxford: Oxford University Press.
Eckermann (n.d.) Conversations with Goethe (trans. R. A. Moon), Edinburgh: Morgan Laird & Co.
Koestler, A. (1975) The Art of Creation, London: Picador Press.
Langer, S. (1972) Mind: An Essay on Human Feeling, vol. 2, Baltimore, MD: Johns Hopkins University Press.
Shelley, M. (1968) Introduction, in Frankenstein, London: Minister Classics.
Whalley, G. (1974) Coleridge's poetic sensibility, in J. Beer (ed.) Coleridge's Variety, London: Macmillan.
Winnicott, D. W. (1971) Playing and Reality, London: Tavistock Press.

12

'Creativity' and its others

The ongoing project of definition, debate and demonstration

Rob Pope

At the core of this piece is a cultural history – up to the present and into the future – of the term *creativity* and other terms associated with it. But before and after that, there are a prelude and postlude. These play with what is worked at between. Such a procedure with such a topic is arguably essential for a handbook of *creative learning*. For many of the debates in and around creativity *and* learning are precisely about how far these are necessarily matters of actual experience and experiment, practice and participation – not just definition and theorising in the abstract, sheer spectacle or mere commentary. This piece is therefore, by design, as much about the business of *creating definitions* as of *defining creativity*. You can't have the one without doing the other, always afresh, sometimes for yourself (see Joas, 1996; Pope, 2005: pt 2).

Prelude: 'creativity' now, then and again

Here are three very different observations on *creativity* from the turn of the present century. For the moment they are unidentified. Read them through and then attach a brief label to each. How, in a word or phrase, would you characterise each of these views of creativity? (Do this before reading on so as to have something to compare with the responses that follow.)

A Creativity is possible in all areas of human activity, including the arts, sciences, at work, at play, and in all areas of daily life. All people have creative abilities and we all have them differently. ... Developing creativity involves, amongst other things, deepening young people's cultural knowledge and understanding. This is essential both in itself and to promote forms of education which are inclusive and sensitive to cultural diversity and change.

B 'Creative', 'creation', 'creativity' are some of the most overused and ultimately debased words in the language. Stripped of any special significance by a generation of bureaucrats, civil servants, managers and politicians, lazily used as political margarine to spread approvingly and inclusively over any activity with a non-material element, the word 'creative' has become almost unusable. Politics and the ideology of ordinariness, the wish not to put anyone down, the determination not to exalt the exceptional, the culture of over-sensitivity, of avoiding hurt feelings, have seen to that.

C Any act of artistic and scientific creation is an act of symbolic subversion, involving literal or metaphorical transgression not only of the (unwritten) rules of arts and sciences themselves but often also of the inhibiting confines of culture, gender and society. Rethinking creativity means challenging established borderlines and conceptual categories while redefining the spaces of artistic, scientific and political action.

Here are some of the ways in which the above passages were labelled by a group of UK postgraduate teachers and student teachers:

A 'Liberal', 'Progressive', 'We're all creative now' and 'Here Comes Everybody'.
B 'Reactionary', 'Elitist', 'Moaning but right!' and 'A hymn for everyone fed up with being urged to be creative'.
C 'Radical', 'Progressive' (again), 'Trendy', 'Politically correct claptrap', 'Maybe – but jargon!'

And here, also for comparison, is a paraphrase (by me) of the three passages: (A) emphasises creativity in education as the cultivation of an openness to cultural diversity and social change; (B) is a complaint about indiscriminate populist appeals to creativity as the panacea for all ills and an attack on the 'ideology of ordinariness'; (C) celebrates creativity in terms of the subversion and reconfiguration of existing categories of thought across the sciences, arts, politics, business and education. Clearly, to state the obvious, all the above phrases and sentences offer different views and valuations of creativity: more or less positive or negative; capacious or specific; formal or informal; and so forth. Some of these overlap and appear to converge (for example, both (A) and (C) are hailed as 'progressive', though perhaps for different reasons and by different people); while others diverge or conflict; and all of them are more or less singular if not unique. (Your own labels will have been more or less different, more or less similar.) Also obvious and no less important, though implicit, is the fact that each of the passages featured comes from and contributes to a different kind of discourse. To be precise, (A) is from a government report on Creative and Cultural Education (NACCCE, 1999); (B) is from a media feature on Creativity nowadays by a BBC radio journalist (Tusa, 2003); (C) is from the flier and then programme for an academic conference in Sweden on *Transgressing Culture: Rethinking Creativity* (Third Space, 2002).

There are at least three simple yet fundamental inferences we may make from this preliminary review: (1) *creativity* is subject to differing though partially overlapping valuations; (2) *creativity* is the object of differing though connected cultural-historical discourses (all those so far are products of the late twentieth/early twenty-first centuries, for example); (3) *creativity* is a term and topic in which the present reader as well as the present writer (in our different yet connected presents) each have a say and a stake. The rest of this piece is designed to keep these obvious yet important ideas in play. It includes suggestions and questions as well as information and observations about key terms. It adds a fourth, more recent passage (D) to supplement and complicate the views of those above. And it closes with a seriously playful activity that should keep issues wide open and fresh terms in play long after the present entry has made its exit. But first we need to get our cultural and historical bearings with what 'creativity' and other, more or less closely related terms have meant and, in many cases, can still mean.

Divine 'creation' into human 'creativity'

'Creativity' is relatively – remarkably – recent. The first recorded use of the abstract noun 'creativity' in *The Oxford English Dictionary* (*OED*) is 1875; it was not even noticed by the time of the first edition of 1929 and had to wait till the second edition of 1989 to get an entry at all. From the first, 'creativity' tended to refer to a general human trait or capacity, rather than the primarily divine or specifically artistic senses of its earlier counterpart, *creation*. Raymond Williams sums up the momentousness of this shift in sense thus: '*Creativity*, a general name for the faculty, followed in the early 20th century. This is clearly an important and significant history, and in its emphasis on human capacity has become steadily more important' (Williams, 1983: 82–5). The divine or artistic senses were associated with the older term 'creation'. 'Creatio(u)n' had been around in English since at least the thirteenth century and was identified initially with 'God the Creato(u)r'. Nearly all of the early uses of the verb 'create' are tinged with a sense of divinity. It is not until the late eighteenth century, and the historical moment and cultural movement broadly identified as 'Romanticism', that we begin to get references to 'creative imagination' and then, in the early nineteenth century, to 'creative art' (sometimes with a capital A) and 'creative artists' (plural). Residually, by retrospective association with creator Gods (Christian and Classical), these tend to be seen as divinely inspired; increasingly, and in anticipation of the growing secular sense of 'creative', they are identified with being naturally gifted. The phrase 'creative evolution' became widespread amongst intellectuals from the 1920s onwards, largely because of Henri Bergson's massively influential book on the topic (Bergson, 1911). The phrase 'creative writing', though around in the nineteenth century, did not become common till the 1930s and then almost wholly in educational, specifically US, contexts (in that respect 'Creative Writing' has always been a 'creature of the academy'; see Wandor, 2008). 'Creative education' is first recorded in the *OED* in 1936, a few years after 'creative salesman' (1930). Similar processes are observable in other Western European cultures (see Steiner, 2001; Enthoven, 2009).

The overall result is an array of potential meanings for the verb 'create' and the adjective 'creative' that spans the divine, the specifically artistic and the generally human. For convenience, the basic situation can be plotted between the polarities ancient 'creation' and modern 'creativity', turning on a point in the Romantic period, as shown in Figure 12.1.

What's more, since the late twentieth century, the sense of 'creativity' has been extended to apply to the capacities of machines in general and computers in particular. Thus, building on eighteenth-century mechanist traditions of both 'God as Designer' and 'Man as Machine', 'creativity' is now invoked to cover everything from the grander claims of Artificial Intelligence – and latterly Artificial Life – to the familiar and routine instruction to 'Create File' (see Boden, 2004). Robots, cyborgs, prosthetics and potentially all-knowing information systems – in science fact as well as science fiction – are often in the picture somewhere (see Braidotti, 2002; Greenfield, 2004). Properly speaking, then, the above time-line needs to be extended as shown in Figure 12.2.

Crucially, this array of meanings is not only historically traceable but simultaneously available. Hence the often vexed arguments over what 'creating' may actually mean.

'Old' creativities for 'new': originality, genius, invention ...

Current claims for and constructions of creativity predominantly in terms of the 'new', 'novel' and 'innovative' have to be seen in the context of this deeper historical perspective. For they may

<<CREATION (divine)   <<<<<< (special) artistic >>>>>>   (general) human CREATIVITY>>

Ancient (13th C on)   Romantic (late 18th C on)   Modern (early 20th C on)

Figure 12.1 The polarities of ancient 'creation' and modern notions of 'creativity'

themselves be symptomatic of values associated with Modernity in general and with Western Modernity in particular (see Jones, Chapter 2). The standard definitions of creativity by some psychologists and educationists stress that it is 'new and valuable', 'novel and original', 'innovative and adaptive', etc. (taken from Sternberg's influential *Handbook of Creativity* (1999): chs 1, 5, 7, 12 and 22). Only Lubart (ch. 13 in Sternberg, 1999) sounds a sustained note of caution about the Modern Western assumptions that such definitions express. In their place he argues for a cross-cultural and historical perspective that revisits and re-values ancient and traditional notions of making as craft and design and, indeed, shifts the emphasis to notions of creative being and becoming – not just making and doing.

At this point, therefore, we shall add a fourth passage to the three introduced so far. This markedly complicates and re-inflects the 'creativity' agenda in ways that are pre- as well as post-Modern, and points to the potential uses (and abuses) of perspectives that are other than Western:

D But maybe creativity is the problem … [T]he creativity mobilised in the new spirit of capitalism is one based on a particular modernist artistic tradition of rule-breaking innovation, of the shock of the new. Maybe creativity has stripped out certain values associated with 'artistic practice' – innovation, inspiration, intuition, rule-breaking etc. – in a way that leaves a scarred landscape of discarded artistic practices. … In particular we might look to the ecological challenge to accumulation, which sees constant innovation as a form of waste – and to what extent cultural innovation, at unprecedented and accelerating speed, is constantly searching through past, marginal, indigenous and experimental cultures alike for the next big hit (O'Connor, 2007: 53–4).

O'Connor points to a range of political as well as aesthetic alternatives to those in the mainstream of the Modern West. At the same time, he cautions against merely reactionary attempts simply to turn the clock back nostalgically or look longingly at the supposed simplicity or purity of other, non-Western cultures. For all these terms – Modern and Ancient, Western and Eastern or (Non-Western) – carry with them the appeals and perils of binaries in general (see Carter, 2004: 43–4; Pope, 2005: 60–2). Further possibilities as well as problems are revealed if we turn to the cultural history of a whole host of other terms with which the concept of creativity is often identified. These other 'others' include *inspiration*, *genius*, *originality*, *imagination*, *invention* and *discovery*, and here we shall concentrate on just three that throw particular light on the 'old–new' aspects of the creativity debate.

'*Original*', up to the mid-18th century, carried the primary sense of 'going back to the origin', 'ancient', 'primary', as distinct from its now routine yet diametrically opposed sense of 'novel', 'new', 'never been done before'. Edward Young's *Conjectures on Original Composition* (1759) is often taken as a key reference point in the tipping over from 'old' classical to 'new' modern senses of 'original' (see Williams, 1983: 230–1; Attridge, 2004: 35–40; Pope, 2005: 57–62). Both senses are still available in the notion of 'original inhabitants' on the one hand and an 'original idea' on the other – while in advertising an 'original recipe' can have it either way. In fact, the distinction between the old and new senses can be activated by something as slight yet

< CREATION (divine) < (special) artistic > (general) human CREATIVITY> artificial machinic CREATIVITY>

Ancient	Romantic	Modern	Contemporary
(13th C on)	(late 18th C on)	(early 20th C on)	(late 20th/early 21st C)

Figure 12.2 The polarities of ancient 'creation', modern and contemporary notions of 'creativity'

significant as a change of article: '*the* original painting' refers us back to the initial version (not a copy) and invokes the earlier sense; '*an* original painting' refers us to a kind of painting that has not been done before and assumes the later sense. It is therefore important to weigh whether the originality one has in mind looks back, forwards or, indeed, attempts to do both at once. Failure to do so can result in the kind of ill-informed wrangling about just what constitutes 'an original and independent contribution to knowledge' that sometimes characterises the deliberations of research boards on the award of a PhD. *So perhaps we should think of 'creativity' in terms of 'pre-' as well as 'post-', the earliest as well as the latest – not only the 'next now' but also the 'first then'.*

'Invention' went through a similar kind of volte-face to that undergone by 'original', only at a slightly earlier historical moment. In the sixteenth century it still retained its root etymological sense of 'finding out' (from Latin *invenire, inventum*, to find out, found); hence 'inventory' as an itemised list of contents, and rhetorical *inventio(n)* referring to the finding and gathering of materials. But thereafter, particularly under pressure from the seventeenth-century scientific revolution, invention tended increasingly to acquire its now-dominant, primarily technological sense of 'making up' (see Preminger and Brogan, 1993: 628–9). 'Invention', fully grasped, therefore involves both *finding out* and *making up*, discovering what already is to bring into being what is not yet. This dual sense is inflected by Derrida in terms of 'invention of the other' (Derrida, 1992: 310–43) and will be picked up again shortly in relation to 'intervention'. *So perhaps 'creativity', too, is best grasped in terms of a* finding–making, old–new *dynamic – with equal emphasis on both aspects and without undue privileging of either.*

'Genius' is another term with a remarkably wide array of historical senses, many of which survive into contemporary usage. In classical times, genius referred to the 'spirit of place' (*genius loci*) and 'spirit of a people/tribe' (*gens*). Only much later, from the eighteenth century, did it develop from the sense of 'general facility' (a genius for fencing, riding, sailing …) to 'exceptional ability' and by extension 'an exceptional person' (a genius). Thus as late as 1780 Dr Johnson could declare, 'Every man has his genius'; and it is only in the high Romantic period (in German expressly called *Genieperiod*) that the cult of 'genius' as an exceptional quality and then '*the* genius' as an exceptional individual became dominant (see Preminger and Brogan, 1993: 455–6; Howe, 1999; Pope, 2005: 99–116). Nowadays, of course, it is common to refer to such people as Albert Einstein or Stephen Hawking or Bill Gates as 'geniuses', and to apply the label retrospectively (and anachronistically) to William Shakespeare and Leonardo da Vinci. It will be observed, however, that these are all men: culturally as well as grammatically *genius* tends to be gendered as masculine (see Battersby, 1989; Ward Jouve, 1998). Perhaps, then, we still need to look for various kinds of 'genius' in all sorts of people and places and activities, not just exceptional individuals (especially men) in conventionally high-prestige areas. *By extension, what happens to creativity if it is identified with, say, whole communities and ecologies* (genius loci revisited) *– not just individual creators or specifically designated 'creative industries'?*

5 re-, 4 trans-, 3 inter-, 2 co- and an -ing!

Creativity's 'others' also include a whole host of alternative terms that are frequently invoked but rarely interrogated in contemporary debate on the subject. For convenience, and as a kind of mnemonic, these are here gathered under the head of a number of prefixes and a suffix. To be precise, as the above heading indicates, there are 5 *re-*, 4 *trans-*, 3 *inter-* and 2 *co-*, and they include terms such as *re-cognition, trans-formation, inter-action* and *co-operation* (the hyphenation draws attention to aspects of the words that might otherwise remain dormant and forgotten). The final suffix, *-ing*, looks decidedly odd on its own. It is familiarly encountered on the ends of all sorts of verbs (see*ing*, touch*ing*, do*ing*, be*ing*, becom*ing*, etc.), and indicates that the process in question is ongo*ing* (there's another) and in that sense immediately present. It is technically what is called a continuous or progressive participle, and is picked up here to highlight a simple yet crucial shift of emphasis: from *creativity* as an uncompromisingly abstract noun (implying a singular and idealised 'thing') to *creating* as a flexibly verbal process (implying an ongoing and more or less immediate action). First, however, we need to review the freight carried by each of the prefixes in turn.

'*Re-*' *is for repetition with difference.* It signals an iterative process in which things can be done *afresh* not just again (see Deleuze, 1994). The five re-words featured here are: *repetition* itself, which initially carried a core sense of re-petitioning, 'asking again', and balances *response*, which still carries the sense of 'answering back' (and in the process perhaps prompting a further response in return). *Re-cognition* and *re-vision* are another closely related pair, here hyphenated so as to highlight the possibilities of 're-thinking' and 're-seeing' what was first thought and seen otherwise. In the terms of a Russian Formalist such as Shklovsky, a German dramatist such as Brecht or a Canadian feminist such as Rich, their function is, respectively, to 'defamiliarise' and 'make strange' and 'see with fresh eyes'. *Re-creating* is the fifth and here fundamental term: it underpins and informs all the others. We shall treat it at length at the close of this section.

'*Trans-*' *means getting across.* 'Across' is what the Latin prefix means; its Greek equivalent is *dia-*, another crucial prefix, as in *dialogue* and *dialectic* (both meaning 'across-word', the latter with a more narrowly 'logical' sense). The first three of the four trans-words featured here are: *transition*, which focuses on the point of movement or development from one state or stage to another; *transformation*, which emphasises change of form and, by extension, substance, metamorphosis (linguistically, it is associated with transformational-generative grammar and the name of Chomsky); and *transaction*, which draws attention to the exchange, usually entailing some kind of change, involved in any sustained process of action and reaction (in conversation analysis it refers to what gets 'done' through a series of exchanges). The final and, again, foundational term in the present context is *translation*. This refers not only to movement across notionally, sometimes nationally, distinct language barriers (e.g. from Chinese to English and vice versa, *inter*lingual translation) but also shifts and switches between different historical stages and different stylistic varieties of notionally 'the same language' (*intra*lingual translation): from Early to Modern English, for example, or across the discourses of contemporary government report, media journalism, academic conference and research review (as in passages A–D above). Translation is such a key concept here because it is never simply a matter of transferring or transporting items (see Bassnett 2005). What is involved is rather, to recall the other trans-terms already featured, a process of change (transformation) requiring a kind of exchange (transaction) involving various points, levels and stages of cross-over (transition). This closely corresponds to the richly powerful concept of 'dialogism' developed by Bakhtin and his circle (see Holquist 1990; Bakhtin *et al.*, 2003). Either way – whether the emphasis is on *trans-* or *dia-* – the effect is to read *across* conventional conceptions of creativity in all sorts of illuminating ways.

'*Inter-*' *operates in the spaces between.* Whereas trans- emphasises 'acrossness', inter- emphasises 'betweenness' or 'amongness'. There is a subtle and significant difference (see Bennington, 1999). Of the many inter-words that might be usefully featured (*interaction*, with its more open, less instrumental sense of relation than transaction, is one; *intertextuality*, the realisation of one text through its dynamic relation with other texts, is another). Here, I shall concentrate on just three: interplay, interdependence and intervention. *Interplay* draws attention to the spaces for play between and among elements (words, people, objects, events): the 'room for manoeuvre' in flexing, stretching, bending – even breaking and re-making – the rules of whatever 'game' is perceived to be in play. *In/ter/dependence* is here presented like that so as to draw attention to meanings that are themselves reciprocally defining and mutually dependent. In fact many a debate about how far someone or something (a person or a piece of research, say) is 'independent' or 'dependent' can be better framed by recognising varying degrees and kinds of *inter*dependence. *Intervention* is the term I offer here (and elsewhere) to open up and explore another gap between previous and currently existing binaries. It asserts a supplementary space between the two historical senses of *invention* already observed: the earlier sense of 'finding out'; and the later sense of 'making up'. *In(ter)vention* – a word which, again, is itself re-cast to help make the point – designates precisely the kind of deliberate invention that 'comes between' something as initially 'found' (a word, text or other object) so as to make it into something similar yet different: to see and say it 'otherwise'. In specifically verbal terms, as *textual intervention*, it is where active reading may turn into actual re-writing (see Pope, 1995; Knights and Thurgar-Dawson, 2006). More generally, intervention is what might be called 'interplay with attitude' or 'seriously playful transformation'.

'2 *co-*'. The latter, I must admit, is a frankly opportunist attempt to mention some of the many relevant words beginning with co- while observing a descending order from 5 to 1. For there are numerous terms sporting the prefix co- that might be featured here. *Co-operation* is at the core of all of them. The hyphen again is there by design: it emphasises 'operating *with*' and may or may not involve cooperation (usually without a hyphen) in the general sense of 'getting on with', 'agreeing to do'. Co-operation in the present sense recognises both positive and negative dimensions of 'operating with': *con*flict as well as *con*sensus; *com*petition and even *coer*cion. Co-operation thus conceived is vexatious as well as capacious. It entails 'being there with others': argument as well as agreement, power as well as pleasure, expressions of being 'with' and 'together' that may still carry traces of repression and oppression, that may still beg the question of who or what is still being excluded. All these richly many-faceted and sharply double-edged qualities of the co-words must be acknowledged if we are not to view creativity as some kind of cosily inclusive hold-all, all sweetness and light with not a trace of bitterness or shadow. For the fact is that creating something invariably involves un- and re-creating something else, and if not destroying it entirely ('The urge to destroy is also a creative urge', proclaimed the anarchist Bakunin (quoted in Pope, 2005: 155)), then at least de- and re-constructing it otherwise.

'*-ing!*' As already observed, this quite routine suffix is remarkably productive when attached to all manner of verb stems. When it comes to reconceptualising and reconfiguring notions of creativity the -ing is crucial. Creat*ing* emphasises the sense of ongoing and open-ended process, of being in on the activity as it unfolds. And yet, like creativity, it can be used as a noun too (e.g. 'Creating is difficult'). These grammatically versatile and conceptually volatile qualities of 'creating' are very handy when it comes to countering widespread assumptions about the reified and often rarefied nature of 'creativity', its idealised 'thingness'. In fact, a marked preference for words ending in *-ing* is a feature of many approaches to language and culture that are materially pragmatic and process-based rather ideally abstract and essentialist (see Braidotti, 2002; Hills, 2005). That said, as promised, there remains just one more twist in this verbal tail to ensure that casually modern assumptions about the essential 'newness' and 'nowness' of creativity do not go unchallenged.

'*Re … creating*' is here offered as the fundamental term that underpins all the others; it also itself re-combines that last suffix with the first prefix. The suspension dots *within* the word (…) are a graphic device designed to draw attention to the crucial gap that must be bridged, filled or fallen into when seeking to move from the already created to what must be created afresh: between old and new, between the usual, the familiar and the known and their respective un-s; between what was, is and becomes otherwise (see Pope, 2005: 84–90, 191–2 for an earlier iteration of this as 're … creation'; and Pope, 2008, 2009, for applications to 'National Curricula' and 'English'). *Re … creating* is a potentially empowering concept in the present context

Table 12.1 Answers given to two questions about being creative at the Open University (UK) in September 2007

Being creative means ...	Not being creative means ...
Avoiding regimes but knowing their procedures	Loving epaulettes
Taking risks	Being too busy
Believing in omelettes	Believing in unbroken eggs
Questioning and challenging what is assumed	Uncritically following rules and roles
Keeping your senses open at all times	Relying on your rationality
Spending considerable portions of the night awake – having first fallen sound asleep	Getting a job you dislike but which pays a persuasive amount of money
Doing it!	Not doing it!

because it offers a frame for constantly thinking creativity afresh, as a multiplicity: as ongoing 'creatings from some things else and other people'; not 'creation from nothing' (*ex nihilo*), as a supposedly divine or singularly mystifying one-off act.

By design, then, room must always be left for individual thinkers or different cultures to fill the idea of 'creativity' in (or out) as they see fit. This applies especially when offering to substitute another term or concept entirely. Indeed, on the principle that a definition should carry no trace of the thing to be defined, 'creativity', like any other key term, can ultimately *only* be known through its 'others'. It is the dynamic distances and differences 'across', 'between' and 'among' (*trans-*, *dia-*, *inter-*) that count, not the points of arrival or departure as such.

Postlude: on (not) being creative

Being creative means ... ?

Not being creative means ... ?

These two questions, slightly adapted, were put to around forty people, including academics, teachers, educationists, writers, artists and film makers, with a particular interest in creativity at the Open University (UK) in September 2007.[1] Here, one last time, the present reader is asked to respond before reading on. What do *you* think 'being creative' and 'not being creative' might mean? Come up with an example or an image instead of an abstract definition if you like. And feel free to respond playfully as well as seriously. The main thing is to have some words of your own before encountering those of others.

In Table 12.1 are given some responses from the above workshop to compare with yours. They can be read down or across for a variety of effects.

Finally, to close on an openly theoretical note, if you are not altogether happy with the definitions of and alternatives to 'creativity' explored earlier, you are of course free to find out or make up some more of your own. *Re ... creating* is my best shot to date. By definition, it may not be yours. Writing only appears to have the last word. Reading always has the next.

Notes

1 Part of a series of workshops funded by the Arts & Humanities Research Council on 'Creativities, Language and Literature' (subsequently the basis for Swann *et al.*, in press).

References

Attridge, Derek (2004) *The Singularity of Literature*, London: Routledge.

Bakhtin, Mikhail, *et al.* (2003) *The Bakhtin Reader: Selected Writings of Bakhtin, Medvedev and Voloshinov* (ed. Pam Morris), London: Arnold.

Bassnett, Susan (2005) *Translation Studies* (3rd ed.), London: Routledge.

Battersby, Christine (1989) *Gender and Genius*, London: The Women's Press.

Bennington, Geoff (1999) Inter, in Martin McQuillan, Graeme MacDonald, Robin Purves and Stephen Thomson (eds) *Post-Theory: New Directions in Criticism*, Edinburgh: Edinburgh University Press.

Bergson, Henri ([1911] 1964) *Creative Evolution* (trans. Arthur Mitchell), London: Macmillan.

Boden, Margaret (2004) *The Creative Mind: Myths and Mechanisms* (2nd ed.), London: Routledge.

Braidotti, Rosi (2002) *Metamorphoses: Towards a Materialist Theory of Becoming*, Oxford: Blackwell.

Carter, Ronald (2004) *Language and Creativity: The Art of Common Talk*, London: Routledge.

Deleuze, Gilles ([1968] 1994) *Difference and Repetition* (trans. Paul Patton), New York: Columbia University Press.

Derrida, J. (1992) *Acts of Literature* (ed. and trans. D. Attridge), London and New York: Routledge.

Enthoven, Raphaël (ed.) (2009) *La Création*, Paris: Perrin.

Greenfield, Susan (2004) *Tomorrow's People: How 21st-century Technology Is Changing the Way We Think*, London: Allen Lane.

Hills, Matt (2005) *How to Do Things with Cultural Theory*, London: Hodder.

Holquist, Michael (1990) *Dialogism: Bakhtin and His World*, London: Routledge.

Howe, Michael (1999) *Genius Explained*, Cambridge: Cambridge University Press.

Joas, Hans (1996) *The Creativity of Action* (trans. D. Gaines and P. Keast), Cambridge: Polity Press.

Knights, Ben and Thurgar-Dawson, Chris (2006) *Active Reading: Transformative Writing in Literary Studies*, London: Continuum.

National Advisory Committee on Creative and Cultural Education (NACCCE) (1999) *All Our Futures: Creativity, Culture and Education*, London: Department for Education and Employment.

O'Connor, Justin (2007) *The Cultural and Creative Industries: A Review of the Literature*, London; Arts Council England and Creative Partnerships.

Oxford English Dictionary (*OED*) (1929) ed. Robert Burchfield, John Simpson, *et al.*, Oxford: Oxford University Press; 2nd ed. 1989.

Pope, Rob (1995) *Textual Intervention: Critical and Creative Strategies for Literary Studies*, London: Routledge.

—— (2005) *Creativity: Theory, History, Practice*, London: Routledge.

—— (2008) 'Curriculum', 'National', 'English' – a creative critique of key terms, *English in Australia* 43.3: 29–35.

—— (2009) 'Creativity and English', in Janet Maybin and Joan Swann (eds), *A Companion to English Language Studies*, London and New York: Routledge.

Preminger, Alex and Brogan, T. P. (eds) (1993) *The New Princeton Encyclopaedia of Poetry and Poetics*, Princeton, NJ: Princeton University Press.

Steiner, George (2001) *Grammars of Creation*, London: Faber and Faber.

Sternberg, Robert (ed.) (1999) *Handbook of Creativity*, Cambridge: Cambridge University Press.

Swann, Joan, Pope, Rob and Carter, Ronald (eds) (in press) *Creativity, Language, Literature: The State of the Art*, London and New York: Palgrave Macmillan.

Third Space (2002) *Transgressing Culture: Rethinking Creativty in Arts, Science and Politics*; available at www.thirdspaceseminar.org (accessed 9 September 2002).

Tusa, John (ed.) (2003) *On Creativity: Interviews Exploring the Process*, London: Methuen.

Wandor, Michelene (2008) *The Author Is Not Dead, Merely Somewhere Else: Creative Writing Reconceived*, Basingstoke: Palgrave.

Ward Jouve, Nicole (1998) *Female Genesis: Creativity, Self and Gender*, Oxford and Cambridge: Polity Press.

Williams, Raymond (1983) *Key Words: A Vocabulary of Culture and Society* (2nd ed.), London: Fontana.

Part II
Creativity, the arts and schools

Julian Sefton-Green and Pat Thomson

Part II offers a more concrete investigation of the principles explored in Part I. Here the focus moves more explicitly to questions about schools and learning. Whilst the abstract philosophical issues about the meaning and interpretation of creativity remain, contributors here analyse how discrete Arts subjects, notions of the arts in general, norms in early childhood education and policy frameworks implement and operationalise forms of creative learning in current school arrangements. Whilst Part III offers more 'case study' or exemplary accounts of creative pedagogy and curriculum, here chapters offer more general and wider accounts of how school subjects, policies and assessment regimes determine creativity. Whilst Part I recognised that the arts have in some sense enjoyed a privileged position in relation to creativity, as many contributors note, the creativity field and the arts are not one and the same thing. However, historically Arts subjects and the arts in education have traditionally been the site of most creativity work offered in schools. It is this work which the authors in this part address.

The arts and creativity

In Part I we saw authors addressing the question of the place and nature of the arts in conceptualising creativity. In this part, Tobin, Hayashi and Zhang (Chapter 16) develop the arguments raised by Matsunobu (Chapter 5) and Leong (Chapter 6) in Part I, exploring how some norms of creativity in Chinese and Japanese cultures are translated into expectations for children in pre-schools. This chapter raises a number of challenging questions for Western and European readers, especially, for instance, in relation to ideas about creativity in Mathematics as opposed to the arts – which, as Leong and Matsunobu note, are in some ways more formal and disciplined domains than free or individualistic arenas. It additionally brings into focus expectations about childhood, play and creativity. Whilst many readers might be familiar with the norms of play in early childhood, this chapter also develops the ideas described by Jones (Chapter 2), Belfiore (Chapter 3) and Banaji (Chapter 4) from Part I that the notion of creativity as an innate property of children is as much a cultural construct as it is a description of biological development.

By contrast, Kerlan (Chapter 13) offers an analysis of the features of Arts and the Aesthetic experience that can be used to underpin curriculum and learning in schools. Building on aspects of Abbs' (Chapter 11) arguments from Part I, Kerlan identifies elements from the Arts relating to perception, the place and meaning of 'symbolisation' as well as the power of evaluation. He extrapolates a number of features from the aesthetic experience, such as attention, symbolic experience and an understanding of time, all of which he suggests provide an important mode of creative learning. These arguments open this Part II as they set the scene for a number of the chapters which follow not only here but throughout this book. Part II is concluded by Fleming's distinction between Art-based disciplinary approaches and a more generic arts-based educational approach (Chapter 19). Fleming offers this analysis as a corrective lens through which we might approach the various ways that Art and the arts have been used in educational discourse. Fleming also attempts to disentangle a key theme for this book, namely the differences between learning 'in', 'through' or 'about' the arts, by examining different pedagogic traditions, some of which use arts education as a medium for learning, as opposed to others where the Arts are the object of education.

Disciplinary knowledge, practice and policy

This volume is not a compendium of the uses of various Art educational approaches. Neither does it offer a comprehensive study of different Art disciplines: see Bresler (2007) for such a volume. We recognise Fleming's challenge about the risk of treating all Art forms as if they were interchangeable and as if different disciplinary traditions have not emerged from a diverse set of practices. Costantino and Neelands help us compare and contrast this range of intra-subject variation. Besides questions about dominant practices within each subject (of which more can be found in Hetland and Winner (Chapter 24) and Pringle (Chapter 25) in Part III), Costantino (Chapter 17) alerts us to how, even within a domain like the visual arts, creativity is a contested and an historicised attribute. It has occupied different roles within the priorities of visual art education over the last hundred years and this is reflected in differing pedagogies and assessment criteria. Neelands (Chapter 18) is interested in some of the ways that drama processes inhabit deep ways of 'being in' social relationships and how various kinds of drama education can support and develop different kinds of civic, social and inter-personal ways of being. His focus on the qualities of negotiating social life is different from the focus in Costantino on intra-personal attitudes and reflects a wider interest in the social dimensions to creative learning rather than simply an attention to the actions of and benefits to an individual.

Craft's (Chapter 14) study of competing and complementary uses of creativity in education polices across the four nations of the UK provides a comparative perspective to tease out risks, benefits, advantages and challenges in taking up creativity – despite the presumption that it represents a natural common good. Like Neelands she is interested in exploring questions of value and social purpose but finds in her policy analyses a concern with the economistic – a perspective that further develops the critiques proffered by Drotner (Chapter 8), Jones (Chapter 9) and Darras (Chapter 10) in Part I. Burnard's analysis of attempts to find ways to evaluate creative learning (Chapter 15) not only builds on Runco and Pagnani's challenges to the problem of defining and measuring creativity in Part I (Chapter 7) but shows the difficulties of the challenges of education policy, identified by Craft, for practical implementation. Burnard focuses on issues involved in evaluating creative practice across arts education – a theme taken up in Part III by Fuchs and Witte (Chapter 32) and Sefton-Green (Chapter 33).

References

Bresler, L. (ed.) (2007) *International Handbook of Research in Arts Education*, Dordrecht, the Netherlands: Springer.

13

Arts in schools as a change model

Education for the arts and aesthetic experience

Alain Kerlan[1]

There now seems to be a broad consensus on the importance of arts in academic and extra-academic education and, more largely, on the legitimacy of education for the arts for all. The educational virtues of art are recognised at global level as testified by UNESCO's symposia in Hong Kong in 2004, in Lisbon in 2006, then in South Korea in 2010, or the European and international symposium at the Paris-located Georges Pompidou Centre in January 2007. An artistic and aesthetic principle is gaining ground in the definition of the educational good. In France it emerged slowly in the 1970s and expanded in the 1990s when arts education policies were implemented. Although the place of art and artistic practices in the educational field remain insufficient, they have undeniably kept growing for the past thirty years. It is not only within school systems that art seems to be a solution, even an educational model, but also within the whole society – hospitals, firms, prisons, welfare centres, etc. – and it is expected to contribute to fostering social cohesion and balancing social and individual interests.

The powers of art: evaluation and justification

The idea of basing general education on an aesthetic foundation is not new. Schiller, the German poet and philosopher, put forward his philosophical doctrine of art in his famous *Letters upon the Aesthetic Education of Man* in the late eighteenth century. His arguments are strikingly echoed in contemporary education but also in social policies. On a regular basis, art is expected to provide support or compensate for troubles in prisons, firms, hospitals and underprivileged neighbour-hoods. Therefore social expectations come on top of educational expectations. For example, writing workshops are opened to try to stop isolation due to illness or social and economic exclusion. Or committed dance or drama artists help the inhabitants of troubled neighbourhoods voice their pain. Or visual artists work with children with learning difficulties, autistic children, hospitalised patients by opening their workshops and providing support because they are convinced of the social and human effectiveness of artistic practice.

The school in crisis now turns to the arts and artists. Educational policies in many countries regard the arts in schools as a new opportunity for educational reform. In addition, it is argued that the academic sphere is increasingly sensitive to aesthetic values and that art is part and parcel of academic education to the point that only art can change the school system and bring the right answers to the challenges faced by education in the modern world.

Should art and artists be in the service of equality, the true mission of education? Yes, of course. During the press conference for 'the plan towards the development of arts and culture at school' on December 2000, Jack Lang, the French former Minister of Education, argued that 'social inequality is above all the result of cultural inequality. It is up to education to close the gap with knowledge and culture'. He added: 'It is clear that if school cannot guarantee democratic access to art, social determinants will prevail and increase inequalities'. Should art be mobilised to fight against academic failure, loss of motivation, lack of interest in studies? Yes, probably. Valuing sensitivity and balancing school culture thanks to art and artists might contribute to some degree. Should art be used to learn better and differently? Indeed, why couldn't art be in the service of a 'method of knowledge appropriation relying on sensitive and affective intelligence, emotion'? Should art contribute to restoring self-esteem and self-confidence, fostering individual harmony, the conditions for true learning? Probably, yes, although the cathartic capacity of art to solve these problems is questionable. Should art and artists contribute to fighting violence at school, pacifying school and society? Should art be used to fight against indifference and insignificance, these evils that undermine the modern world and its education? Should art and culture help people make sense of the world? Last but not least, should art and artists be at the forefront of the opposition to the sweeping media culture?

The arguments above are all borrowed from texts and speeches related to art and culture policies in education. As can be easily imagined, the difficulty of evaluating and measuring the real effects of artistic practice is proportional to the educational and social expectations to do so. Let us confess that we sometimes convincingly defended one or several of these arguments. However, this conviction mixes a romantic vision with school consumerism. How coherent and united are these arguments? What can be the converging point other than the *instrumentalisation* of art and artistic practice to the point that art would not be valued for its own sake but only in proportion to supposed and matched effects? We are here at the heart of a paradox central to any enterprise of justification – the excess of justification casts doubts on what is allegedly justified. The concern for the justification of art is harmful to the concern for art *per se*, first because the values and *raison d'être* of art are sought elsewhere and second because any enterprise of evaluation only considers the supposed and matched effects to the detriment of the sophisticated quest for *specific effects*. The analysis of the social and educational effectiveness of art, and as a result its evaluation, is accordingly unclear, as it is the victim of both rhetorical inflation and political overdetermination. Policymaking brings the confusion between *justification* and *evaluation* to a climax. As for scientific expertise, the essential points are missed – it is necessary to be equipped with a theory on the effectiveness of art prior to any evaluation of its effects.

'Art needs no justification in terms of anything else'

When Project Zero was founded in 1964, Nelson Goodman warned that the main obstacle to a fair recognition of the educational effects of art and to the right defence of education for the arts lay in mistaken ideas concerning the effectiveness of art.

Many of these obstacles have long been identified: they are related to the inferior status of art and aesthetics in culture and education, and more generally to popular prejudices and philosophical fallacies concerning the arts. Paradoxically other obstacles arise from *the very interest in education for the arts* and, in turn, from the considerable if not excessive expectations attached to it. Nelson Goodman's analysis paved the way for a lucid recognition of the educational impact of art.

One of the main arguments – the training of citizens, the cognitive and social aims – is at the very heart of the expectations that educational policies seek to fulfil in education for the arts:

> Reaction against both these extremes has inspired elaborate arguments emphasizing extraneous psychological and practical virtues of training in the arts. It is held to soothe the spirit, sharpen the mind, increase effectiveness in daily pursuits, resolve social tensions, and so on. Whatever merit these arguments may have, they succeed mainly – by their very existence – in fostering the suspicion that the arts are worthless by themselves.
>
> *(Goodman, 1984: 154)*

Let us not misconceive the meaning of this warning. Nelson Goodman certainly does not deny that training in the arts may sharpen the mind or contribute to our happiness. He rather invites all the 'friends of art', all those convinced of the eminently educational impact of arts, to think of the performative paradoxes of the rhetoric to which we probably too often yield. By emphasising the psychological and social benefits of training in the arts, do we not make the mistake of seeking elsewhere than in the arts themselves the value that we allegedly grant them?

What is to be retained from this analysis? Nelson Goodman provides the ultimate answer: 'Art needs no justification in terms of anything else' (1984: 157). The worth of art is *intrinsic* to art itself. If art practices can change school, the key to this power lies in the very nature of art and art practices.

Aesthetic experience

I have argued that we should stop looking outside art for the effects that would justify its educational validity. We should simply and resolutely reconsider the very foundation of art and artistic activities – *aesthetic experience and behaviour*. It is in aesthetic experience and behaviour as specific human behaviour and as a relation to the world irreducible to any other relation that the intrinsic worth of art rests. And if art delivers expected extrinsic effects and educational benefits, these effects necessarily take root in this very aesthetic experience. As we have already argued, the effects of art cannot be evaluated unless a theory of the effectiveness of art is designed. Yet the prerequisite is the consideration of aesthetic experience as a singular and specific experience.

What is aesthetic experience? The anecdote of a Chinese emperor as reported by Régis Debray in *Vie et mort de l'image* (Life and death of image) is a case in point. It is said that one day a Chinese emperor asked the chief painter of his court to erase the cascade he had painted on the wall of the palace because the noise of water kept him awake. A girl who had a passion for Chinese art and culture told me of a similar experience once back from China. While she was staying and studying in Taipei, she had the great opportunity to meet an old painting master who agreed to guide her in her regular visits to the museum. It was each time a wonderful lesson in painting. The master once stopped in front of a hanging scroll and was silent. It was up to her then to talk of the work of art. She did her best to explain how she had become familiar with the work of art, the experience she gained, what she saw and felt, but to the growing dissatisfaction of her master, who was losing patience and stamping his feet. He then pointed to a lyre in the landscape and asked her: 'You speak well of what you are seeing but don't you hear anything?'

The privileged education of the girl who had a passion for China reminds me of those classes who file past in museums and exhibitions in ever greater numbers. I must admit I have mixed feelings about them: I am delighted with the democratisation of cultural artefacts once reserved for an elite and I wonder at the same time if we really offer these children and teenagers the chance of true aesthetic experience.

It also reminds me of what Maria Montessori, the great Italian pedagogue and founder of the *Casa dei Bambini*, was practising in her classroom: the *lesson of silence*. It consisted first in listening to the loudest close sounds, then paying attention to the more distant and forgotten ones, the murmur of the class next door, trees rustling in the playground, the train rushing past – living nature in the surrounding forest – that is, simply learning to listen and feel – taking children to the clearing, listening, touching, looking, smelling trees, bark and foliage, birds twittering and insects buzzing. In a word, what is the point of going to the museum if the painting is not expected to be and captured as the crystallisation of an experience of the world which is relevant to me and my world? What is the point of dance and choreography if the motion of dancers on the stage does not somehow extend the movement of my own body in ordinary experience? Whatever the work of art, there is a binding relation to the world that should be educated in the first place. This education combines culture and sensitivity; it makes aesthetic experience the foundation of education for the arts and even one of the bases of education.

We must grasp what *aesthetic experience* and *behaviour* are and what they consist of. But first, what is an *aesthetic fact*? We cannot answer this question if we do not first consider the great cultural and natural variety of objects and situations to which the qualifier 'aesthetic' refers. Jean-Marie Schaeffer notes that

> trying to understand aesthetic facts comes down to looking for what is common between a child who has a passion for a TV cartoon, an insomniac who finds rest when he listens to the twittering of birds in the early morning, an art amateur who is delighted with or disappointed about an exhibition devoted to Beuys, a reader buried in a novel, a courtier at the time of the Sun King attending a performance of Phaedra, a 19th-century Japanese lady moved by the contemplation of a garden covered with dew, villagers sitting in a circle around a Greek bard, an amateur of music attending a performance of the Ensemble intercontemporain or a concert by Led Zeppelin, tourists admiring the Grand Canyon, a tea master weighing and examining a tea bowl after drinking out of it, and so on.
>
> (Schaeffer, 2000: 13)

We would thus seek in vain the properly 'aesthetic' quality of objects and facts were they major artistic objects and facts. The 'aesthetic' nature of a scene, an object, natural sight, even an art work depends on the attitude, attention and behaviour adopted towards them. In a sense, the *Mona Lisa* itself is a mere plank. By contrast, a mere pebble or a stick picked up on the beach may gain aesthetic dignity according to the type of attention I pay them.

John Dewey too pushed for the necessary and salutary desacralisation of aesthetic experience when he invited us to find it first in 'crude experience'. He illustrated his advice with examples ostensibly borrowed from 'the sights that hold the crowd – the fire-engine rushing by, the machines excavating enormous holes in the earth; the human-fly climbing the steeple-side; the men perched high in air on girders, throwing and catching red-hot bolts'. I remember the answer of a farmer who was interviewed for a TV show on art and culture: 'When I am in my fields ploughing, my attention is sometimes drawn by a stone and it stops me because of its singular shape. Was it made by nature or by man's hand? It looks like a heart. I wonder ... It's magnificent, it's moving ... ' The moment before, there was only a stone and now, after a change in behaviour, there is a sort of aesthetic meditation and emotion – the stone in the way recalls a story common to the whole humanity, an experience of the world shared since the dawn of time. The account of this 'common man' refers in its own way to John Dewey's analyses and assumptions as part of his pragmatist aesthetics: not only is aesthetic experience not limited to the experience of art works, not only do art works have no monopoly on aesthetic experience, but it takes root in ordinary experience. According to Dewey, 'even a crude experience, if authentically an experience, is more fit to give a clue to the intrinsic nature of esthetic experience than is an object already set apart from any other mode of experience' (Dewey, 1934: 9).

There is, however, something common to the great variety of aesthetic experience – a specific form of attention and, more particularly, as Jean-Marie Schaeffer wrote, 'an intentional structure that is the same in all situations' (2000: 14). In other words, aesthetic behaviour should be considered core anthropological data and aesthetic attention a 'core component of human mental profile' (ibid.: 15). The notion of *pleasure* inherent in this specific attention to the world should also be emphasised. Aesthetic experience combines concentration and pleasure, attention and pleasure. As a result, aesthetic experience, like any authentic experience, is similar to the child's playful experience. Stendhal, who had a passion for music, is a case in point when he recalls the origin of his passion and his initial musical pleasures:

> 1/ The bells of Saint-André ringing on election day the year when my cousin Abraham Mallein was president or simply elector; 2/ the sound of the pump in Square Grenette when servants would pump water with a large iron bar; 3/ finally, the melody of a flute played by a trade clerk on the fifth floor of square Grenette.
>
> *(Stendhal; cited in Schaeffer, 2000: 14; trans. Thiery Bessy)*

The similarity between aesthetic and playful behaviour is also obvious when many artists mention their training path. One might object that these experiences only concern future great artists. But the role of childhood is no less obvious in John Dewey's most ordinary examples above. They are all part of those sights that have a great impact on childhood and are a source of delight.

I draw two conclusions that I think are of considerable importance: (1) it is in the child's aesthetic experience that one can best appreciate what aesthetic experience is; (2) education for the arts as core education and a means of change in education should be based on aesthetic experience and the human aptitude for aesthetic behaviour inherent in each child. Nurturing the time of aesthetic experience in childhood to the benefit first of childhood and then of our adult aesthetic life may be the real ambition of the educational mission in this field. Aesthetic education first presupposes the recognition of aesthetic behaviour in its anthropological foundations.

The anthropological foundations of aesthetic behaviour

Let us start from this philosophical and pedagogical principle: aesthetic behaviour is one of the very first human behaviours. Pedagogy has to do with anthropology. I'll draw on Hans-Georg Gadamer's thoughts on contemporary art to go further into the knowledge of aesthetic experience. In *The Relevance of the Beautiful and Other Essays*, Hans-Georg Gadamer argues for a return to the *anthropological foundations of art and aesthetic* experience in *play*, *symbols* and *celebration*. Gadamer's reflection has no explicitly pedagogical purpose. Its educational impact is all the more impressive: aren't *play*, *symbols* and *celebration* also proper to childhood?

Art and play

To what extent can play be regarded as one of the prime anthropological foundations of aesthetic behaviour? In keeping with Gadamer's play theory, we argue that play is the very movement of life. More exactly, play implies basic excess, a self-representation of the human being that s/he grants her/himself when there is an excess of life. Excess of life implies representation and vice versa –

123

representation is, as such, an excess of being. It is the very miracle of the work of art. It is what we learn from the observation of children playing. There is such entertainment in any game that the observer is a *potential participant*. I become a spectator of myself when I play. Gadamer adds that play is *communicative action*. Even the 'play of waves' already teaches this lesson. Thus play shares two common features – a form of fulfilment (excess of life) as well as a sharing and communication perspective. If you observe a child painting, you will almost always find these two features.

Art and symbol

Accomplished art is the field of symbolic forms, whether they are made of words or stones, colours or sounds. Aesthetic behaviour is quite familiar with form and symbol. What is a symbol? Originally, it was a means of *recognition*, the broken shard of Greek hospitality that committed each partner to reciprocate the laws of hospitality. Each part of the shard depends on the other to piece together the initial whole. Gadamer explains that aesthetic experience is the experience of a symbolism of that nature. In other words, any man is the fragment of a whole. The worth of an art work is determined by what it arouses, as experience of a whole that is never tangible but felt thanks to the art work. Even before the work of art, there is in any aesthetic experience the feeling of unity of that nature. Even 'the delight of the housewife in tending her plants' (Dewey, 1934: 3), like all the ordinary aesthetic experiences that Dewey recalled, refers to totality and accomplishment. Childhood, far from being extraneous to this sense of the symbolic, is on the contrary one of its Meccas.

Art and celebration: the experience of time

To what extent can festive celebration be regarded as an anthropological invariant of aesthetic experience? To understand what Gadamer means here, we can think of silence and the kind of distance that the museum implies, of the properly invisible frontier marked by a ring of light, the track circle and the stage curtain. The young child can soon feel that there is another world, another experience beyond, as though s/he perceived an invisible frontier, a here and there, something that is definitely demanding and in the best of cases results in a different attitude and attention to the world. *The experience of art is a specific time* experience. Gadamer, in a reflection useful to help understand one of the essential dimensions of the educational effectiveness of art, wrote: 'The essence of the time experience of art is that we learn to suspend time' (Gadamer, 1986). Learning to suspend time is exactly the power that Hannah Arendt ascribed to cultural objects. Isn't it more than ever an essential and founding learning?

From anthropology to pedagogy: the conditions of aesthetic education

Can this anthropological conception of aesthetic experience pave the way for art instruction as educational basis or as core education or even as a change model? I do think so. Observing children when they are engaged in true aesthetic experience confirms this conviction on many counts. The experience of artists in residence at nursery schools in Lyon will illustrate the pedagogical benefit of the play/symbol/celebration trilogy.

Attention and concentration

I'll first mention a few photographs of children shown in March 2005 in Lyon during an exhibition on this experience of artists in residence. What strikes the observer is the seriousness of children engaged in work with the artist. These pictures are in clear contrast with the somewhat conventional image of child joy and radiance. They show attentive faces, happy concentration and quiet penetration – a very particular form of child play when play absorbs children wholly. This is one of the fine surprises of this exhibition: *art can be a powerful lever to educate attention.* Aesthetic experience is another experience of time, not the time of bustling activity but that of celebration. Learning to suspend time comes down to learning to focus the attention of the body and senses as well as that of thought. If culture, art and artists can contribute to education, there is no need to instrumentalise them. They just need to provide access to this alternative time and experience.

Interactivity and educational relationship

The work of the artist with children – the specificity and singular effectiveness of this work – is most often based on the interactivity common to art and play. It is also part of what Gadamer calls communicative action. For example, when Vincent Prud'homme, a plastician artist, works with children of a nursery class, he sits among them and lets them work on their own or in small groups on their clay, wood and paper sculptures. Of course, he supports them in their initiatives but still remains in the background. Sometimes, when a plastic idea or solution dawns on him, it also develops communicative action. When he happens to take action in children's play-work, it is mostly on a 'technical' basis: 'It won't work this way; you might try that.' The top-down teacher–student relationship disappears and the artist speaks to the child as though he is talking to a fellow artist. Within the artist's studio, children start and perform tasks which educational psychologists would normally consider 'beyond their scope'. Education for the arts also contributes to changing what we know – what *we believe we know* – about children's and students' abilities. The work of the artist *as an artist* with children seems to open a space for new actions and abilities, and to create a specific and singular 'zone of proximal development'. At least, art education affects the educational relationship itself. A new figure of adulthood and teaching authority is emerging. Here art education is a sort of testing ground for educational relationships.

Symbolic experience and creativity

Observing children, their approaches and work in interaction with artists teaches us that *aesthetic behaviour is based in symbolic experience.* Children around Vincent Prud'homme revive the original meaning of the symbolic (see Figures 13.1, 13.2 and 13.3). Several children work on their own. For example, a girl shapes her clay and wood sculpture at the bottom of an open cardboard box. Or two girls have spontaneously set up a group. They soon seek to make connections between their constructions. A boy who was working on his own gradually built a material link between his own work (a paper 'bridge') and the common work of the two girls.

To go further into aesthetic experience, it is necessary to rediscover symbolic experience as sense-filled and founding human experience. The example of the child then becomes a lesson and a reminder for adults.

It is in this experience that the child follows in the artist's footsteps. Isn't the time of childhood, as Winnicott's works have revealed, the very time of access to the symbolic? The term 'creativity' has been so abused that we barely dare use it. Yet, if 'the reader will accept a general reference to creativity, not letting the word get lost in the successful or acclaimed creation', s/he will capture the educational benefit of the experience to which the artist has given children access. Winnicott invites us to consider creativity 'as a colouring of the whole attitude to external reality. It is creative apperception more than anything else that makes the individual

Figure 13.1 Children, art and play

Figure 13.2 Children, art and play

Figure 13.3 Children, art and play

feel that life is worth living. Contrasted with this is a relationship to external reality which is one of compliance, the world and its details being recognized but only as something to be fitted in with or demanding adaptation' (Winnicott, 1971: 87). Aesthetic experience as symbolic experience is closely related to this power.

Conclusion

Can arts in school provide a model for change? Surely art and artistic practices are, *by their very nature,* a potential tool for change in schools. When art enters a school, it is accompanied by a world and values which had previously been excluded. So artistic practices can transform the most characteristic elements of 'school structure': the organisation of time and space, the domination of written forms of knowledge, a certain concept of discipline which eliminates affectivity and emotion, the rejection or mistrust of the imagination … At least art education can affect the educational relationship itself and even children's abilities. But there is a prerequisite: a true art education must enable all children to access aesthetic behaviour, live genuine aesthetic experience and integrate child aesthetic behaviour into the artist's approach and work. The effectiveness of art is at that price. If art effects can and should be evaluated, it is within this very aesthetic behaviour that they are to be sought. While aesthetic experience is expected to serve learning and can pave the way for reading and instruction, it is primarily by making the world accessible and clear.

Still these practices, discourses and policies about art as a change model also have to be examined from a philosophical perspective, and their meaning and most significant implications should be considered the main part of the process of change in contemporary education. We first have to bear in mind that in education, as in other walks of life, things go together. Aesthetic behaviours and values enter the school environment and are disseminated within schools as well as within society and culture. Aesthetics then becomes a daily pattern of common life, and schooling is surely an important part of life. Second, art education can pave the way for a reframed school curriculum, culture and their foundations. Change here involves the whole educational paradigm itself. Instead of a purely rational, scientific educational paradigm, an aesthetic, cultural educational paradigm should be promoted. Finally, only art can bring the ideal of education – unity and harmony – to its full achievement.

Note

1 Translation from French into English by Thierry Bessy.

References

Chappuis, V., Kerlan, A. and Lemonchois, M. (2007) Arts in middle school: monographic inquiry into effects of cultural and artistic practices, papers presented to Evaluating the Impact of Arts and Cultural Education: A European and International Research Symposium, Centre Pompidou, Paris: La Documentation Française.

Dewey, J. (1934) *Art as Experience*, New York: Milton Balch.

Eisner, E. (2002) *The Arts and the Creation of Mind*, New Haven, CT: Yale University Press.

Gadamer, H.-G. (1986) *The Relevance of the Beautiful and Other Essays*, Cambridge: Cambridge University Press.

Goodman, N. (1984) *Of Mind and Other Matters*, Cambridge, MA: Harvard University Press.

Kerlan, A. (2004) *L'Art pour éduquer? La Tentation esthétique*, Quebec: Presses de l'Université Laval.

—— (2005) *Des Artistes à la maternelle*, Lyon: Scérén/CRPD.

Kerlan, A. and Erutti, R. (2007) Artists at school. The aesthetic experience at the heart of learning: evaluation of a scheme of artists in residence, papers presented to Evaluating the Impact of Arts and Cultural Education: A European and International Research Symposium, Centre Pompidou, Paris: La Documentation Française.

Schaeffer, J.-M. (2000) *Adieu à l'esthétique*, Paris: PUF.

Schiller, F. V. (1794/2008) *Letters upon the Aesthetic Education of Man*, Hayes Barton Press.

Winnicott, D. W. (1971) *Playing and Reality*, London: Routledge Classics.

14

Approaches to creativity in education in the United Kingdom

Anna Craft

Creativity as a goal of learning?

The early years of the twenty-first century brought significant attempts across the United Kingdom (and elsewhere, for example Australia, Canada, Europe and the Nordic countries, Singapore, Taiwan and more recently the USA) to highlight the creativity in education by codifying it in the curriculum and emphasising the role of partnership work to inspire and nurture creativity in young people. Creativity and learning have increasingly been seen as intertwined, and with policy change has emerged a vocabulary around learning (and pedagogy) which frames ways in which educators and researchers understand how to develop both. Woods and Jeffrey (1996), Craft (1997) and Harland *et al.* (1998) during the 1990s had distinguished between creative teaching and teaching for creativity. Creative teaching has come to be understood as focused on exciting, innovative, engaging and often memorable pedagogy, whereas teaching for creativity was more overtly focused on the creativity of the learner. Creative learning, a term which emerged more through policy than research during the first decade of the twenty-first century, remains to great degree a term in search of meaning (Sefton-Green, 2008), though it has been described by Jeffrey and Craft (2006) as a 'middle ground' between creative teaching and teaching for creativity.

What is clear is that the notion of creativity as a learning goal, as well as a desirable process through which learning may be conducted, became increasingly central to education throughout the United Kingdom over the course of the first decade of the twenty-first century, albeit perhaps rather unevenly across the four nations. This chapter focuses on what has happened in the United Kingdom in the last ten years, discusses some of the key challenges apparent in policy and practice and projects forward to some of the challenges which face educators in the UK in the next decade.

Evolving policy for creativity and learning

In England, the significance of creativity in education was highlighted in 1999 with the publication *All Our Futures*, the report of the National Advisory Committee on Creative and Cultural Education (NACCCE, 1999), chaired by the (then) Professor Ken Robinson, now Sir Ken

Robinson. This report linked creativity with culture and argued vociferously for the establishment of a clear curriculum framework for creative and cultural education, together with much more widespread practices of creative partnership in learning, enabling those with creative experience and skills working outside schools to work with those within them to nurture creativity. The NACCCE Report unleashed a range of policy activity in England, including work to codify creativity in the curriculum, and also the large-scale project Creative Partnerships, established in 2002 to support partnerships between schools and those working in the creative and cultural sectors.

In school-based education in England, two clear narratives had emerged by the end of the decade; as Cochrane *et al.* put it:

> the first of 'nurturing talent' to enable young people to progress into careers and further education in the arts, cultural and creative industries; the second to do with broader support for the notion of 'cultural learning' enshrined in the pilot 'cultural offer' of five hours a week in 10 areas around England.
>
> *(Cochrane et al., 2008: 31–2)*

Reviews of policy in England

The policy framework in England has been subject to a number of reviews. The Roberts Review (Roberts, 2006) was established in 2005 under the auspices of the Department for Culture, Media and Sport (DCMS) and the Department for Education and Skills (DfES). A review of creative and cultural development of young people and creativity in schools, as well as creativity as a set of skills to feed the creative and cultural industries, it contributed to an emerging narrative developing at the DCMS about 'Making Britain the World's Creative Hub' (Purnell, 2005). Focused on assessing progress since the 1999 NACCCE Report, Roberts mapped out a framework for creativity with a very wide remit from the early years through to early adulthood, encompassing extended schools, building schools for the future, leadership issues, including initial teacher education and professional development, creative partnership and frameworks for regulation and support.

The review's influence was extensive (Cochrane *et al.*, 2008), leading to the establishment of the Cultural and Creative Education Advisory Board (CCEAB) in late 2006. It also influenced the House of Commons Education and Skills Committee (2007), which focused on the analysis of Creative Partnerships and its achievements in its first five years. Reinforcing the view of creativity as ubiquitous, it identified a range of new priorities, including the need to find ways of assessing incremental progress in creativity, and to acknowledge the wide range of professions in which creativity is inherent.

The Government response to the Select Committee report recognised that 'creativity is not just about the arts ... it applies across all subjects' (House of Commons Children, Schools and Families Committee, 2008, App. 1: 1). Yet, it also stated that 'while there will always be scope for collaboration with other sectors, both Departments consider that Creative Partnerships' principal focus should remain on arts and culture' (ibid.: 3).

The Government's commitment to a 'cultural offer' for all young people was reflected in a range of initiatives (DCMS, 2008) and was reinforced by the government White Paper calling for greater innovation (DIUS, 2008).

The language of creativity in education by the end of 2009 was drifting, as Cochrane *et al.* (2008) predicted, toward 'cultural learning', with the McMaster Report (McMaster, 2008) on excellence in the arts describing the Creative Partnerships programme as a 'cultural' rather than a 'creative' learning programme, complemented by Find Your Talent, a cultural learning initiative for 0–19-year-olds. In mid-2010, however, following the General Election and formation of a coalition government, Find Your Talent was abolished by a government wishing to place 'a relentless focus on the basics' (Department for Education, 2010). And in 2011, Creative Partnerships, too, was axed as part of comprehensive public spending cuts.

In Northern Ireland the story of growth was similar, triggered by the NACCCE Report (NACCCE, 1999) in England. From November 2000, the publication of the strategy document *Unlocking Creativity* by the Department of Culture, Arts and Leisure (DCAL), Department for Enterprise, Trade and Investment (DETI), Department of Higher and Further Education, Training and Employment (DHFETE) and Department for Education (DE), set out an agenda for creativity in education in Northern Ireland. Its aims were to increase creativity and innovation in the workforce within a globalised and globalising economy. The strategy document launched a consultation on its proposals, which were followed by the establishment of the Creativity Seed Fund (CSF) in 2001, supported by a further document by the same four departments, called *Unlocking Creativity: Making It Happen*, with funding to help implement the aims of *Unlocking Creativity*. With a foreword by Ken Robinson, Chair of the NACCCE Report in England, *Unlocking Creativity* took its definition of creativity to be exactly the same: creativity as 'imaginative activity with outcomes that are both original and of value' (DCAL *et al.*, 2000: 24).

Seeking to turn this into reality, Creativity Seed Fund distributed support from 2001 to 2004, to projects nurturing creativity in education. It was accompanied by an evaluation programme making a series of further recommendations.

Reviews of policy in Northern Ireland

The year 2003 brought a review of the Unlocking Creativity strategy activity (DCAL *et al.*, 2003). The proposals confirmed the earlier strategy and recommended that Government departments continue to work closely with business, non-governmental organisations and individual artists in partnership across the range of educational, social and economic activity in Northern Ireland.

A plethora of activity followed in the second half of the first decade of the twenty-first century, with increasing numbers of children in Northern Ireland gaining access to creative and cultural activity through such collaborations. With an increasing emphasis on the role of the creative and cultural industries in the economy across the UK, the Northern Ireland Assembly set a target of growing the creative industries by 15 per cent by 2014. This was supported by a Creative Industries Innovation fund launched in 2008 to support the development of creative businesses.

As in England, then, creativity was seen as generally relevant and important across the curriculum, and also as a process through which education could be conducted. Opportunities to participate in creative and cultural activity through collaborations between schools and the creative and cultural sector increased. The 'cultural learning' narrative can in this way be seen to be developing in Northern Ireland as well as in England.

Reviews of policy in Scotland

In Scotland, a similar picture emerged. An Advisory Group tasked with exploring how creativity could become a more significant element of education, published its discussion paper *Creativity in Education* in 2001 (IDES, 2001), accompanied by a range of case studies. Again adopting the NACCCE definition of creativity as imagination pursued with purpose, making outcomes judged to be both original and of value, the Scottish report emphasised the need for schools to encourage experimentation and problem-solving alongside critical, reflective appraisal. It emphasised the nurturing of dispositions such as curiosity, flexibility, confidence, self-motivation, collaboration. It also recognised the need for both creative teaching and teaching for creativity, and the delicate balance between the need for structure and for freedom.

This initial discussion paper was followed by multiple initiatives across the early years of the twenty-first century in education with the close involvement of teachers. By the latter end of the first decade of the twenty-first century, a review of curriculum for learners aged 3–18, *A Curriculum for Excellence* – a rolling construction and review of the curriculum – had suggested that two key purposes of education should be to enable all children and young people to become successful learners and effective contributors. Amongst skills required for being a successful learner was the capacity to think both independently and creatively. Among the skills required for being an effective contributor was the ability to develop and to create. The review, undertaken over a period of years, led to detailed proposals for a 3–18 Curriculum for Excellence (Scottish Executive, 2010) for implementation in 2010, in which creativity (together with enterprise, citizenship, health and wellbeing) is developed across the curriculum both in relation to the generativity of young people and also in relation to pedagogy. However, despite a long period of review and development, in mid-2010, only months from the planned implementation, controversy was reported in the media as to whether Scotland's educators are ready for the greater professional flexibility and freedoms afforded by this curriculum, allegedly based on a confidential report by the education inspectorate.

The long-term review of the 3–18 curriculum, begun in 2004, was pre-dated by the Scottish Executive's strategy for enterprise in education, *Determined to Succeed*, published in 2003 and recommending better preparation for the world of work, including a greater emphasis on enterprise. The Determined to Succeed strategy launched a close collaboration between the education and business policy (Scottish Executive, 2009) encouraging education, business and parents/carers to work more closely in encouraging enterprise, creativity and exciting activities in the classroom with closer reference to the world beyond school.

Alongside this closer alliance of the wider economy with education with a focus on creativity/enterprise, in June 2005 an independent Cultural Commission for Scotland reported on the role that the arts and culture could play in developing *A Curriculum for Excellence* in practice (Scottish Government, 2005), both in relation to what young people experience in and beyond schools and in relation to teacher training and lifelong learning. The Scottish Executive's response to this in January 2006 committed to making links to culture and creativity throughout *A Curriculum for Excellence*.

To support professional innovation needed by those working in and beyond schools, the Scottish Executive introduced the Future Learning and Teaching Programme (FLaT), later succeeded by the Schools of Ambition programme, with full teacher and pupil engagement, to nurture flexible, creative learners.

As with England and Northern Ireland, then, we see in Scotland an increased commitment to cross-curricular creativity as both desired outcome and process in education, and also to the role of the creative and cultural sector in helping to develop this (and so developing to a degree the 'cultural learning' narrative). As in the policy initiatives of the other two nations, there is a direct acknowledgement of the role of creativity in the development of a vibrant economy, recognising the potential for equal partnership between those within and outside schools in doing so. Scotland was perhaps the first of the four nations to identify assessment of creativity in education as a challenge. And, rather intriguingly, with a carefully thought through, consulted-upon and evolved twenty-first century curriculum for 3–19-year-olds, it was also the first of the four nations to voice doubts from teachers and schools about their willingness and/or capability to implement it, as indicated above.

Reviews of policy in Wales

In Wales, which like England and Northern Ireland, has a statutory National Curriculum, creativity has featured but to much lesser degree than in the other three nations. Nevertheless, creativity does feature in the revised curriculum, implemented from September 2008. The Foundation Phase curriculum (for 3–7-year-olds) identifies 'Creative Development' as one of seven statutory areas of learning.

The National Curriculum for 7–19-year-olds, however, does not specify creativity as a key aspect of learning. Nevertheless, guidance for all practitioners implementing the curriculum does emphasise the importance of children and young people 'developing thinking, especially questioning, planning, problem-solving, creative and critical thinking skills' (DCELLS, 2008a: 14). Accordingly, non-statutory guidance has been developed (DCELLS, 2008b) which emphasises the role of imagination, experimentation, risk-taking, working unconventionally in the development of 'developing thinking'. The same non-statutory guidance emphasises opportunities for working creatively in the area of 'developing communication' also, in relation to evoking ideas and effects through crafting words (writing), digital space (virtual design), materials (art and craft, design and technology), movement (dance and drama) and sound (music and voice).

Like England, Northern Ireland and Scotland, in Wales, Creative and Cultural Skills, as one of twenty-five Sector Skills Councils (and representing people working in Wales in advertising, craft, cultural heritage, design, literature, music, performing arts and visual arts), developed a strategy for enriching the sector by publishing a Creative Blueprint (Creative and Cultural Skills, 2008) seeking to address technical and specialist skills gaps, higher skills needed in business and enterprise, improve awareness of training available and qualifications needed, open diversity of opportunity and develop employer and practitioner commitment to training and development. It recommended ten programmes of action, from creative apprenticeships to the development of business knowledge in creative courses, to developing a research programme to build and maintain current information about progress and impact of the Creative Blueprint.

In Wales, then, we see, later than within the other three nations, and (given its non-statutory status) with less emphasis, the recognition of creativity as a desired outcome and process in the curriculum for 3–19-year-olds as part of developing thinking. It appears, in curriculum policy statements, more tied in to the arts than the more cross-curricular picture across the other three nations. The relationships between creativity, culture and education are drawn rather vaguely for younger students, but the Creative Blueprint published in 2008 seeks to improve the creative economy through better pathways and relationships between the creative and cultural sector and education. The cultural learning narrative is much less evident in Wales than in the other three nations, except in this rather narrow sense.

Discussion: a neoliberal economic foundation

As this review reveals, it was the economy which drove each of the initiative pathways in each of the four nations of the United Kingdom. As the Ministerial Foreword to *Unlocking Creativity: A Creative Region* put it, 'the whole concept of creativity being central to Northern Ireland's ability to respond to the challenges of the global economy has been at the heart of the strategy' (DCAL *et al.*, 2003: 1). It is explicit in each of the other nations, and this story is one which is told the world over.

And yet, this neoliberal argument for creativity in the economy is not the only discourse offering a rationale for creative and cultural education, as Banaji, Burn and Buckingham (2006) acknowledge. They identify nine distinct though overlapping rhetorics of creativity evident in the policy and practice discourses of creativity in education in the first part of the first decade of the twenty-first century, drawing primarily on England but occasionally from further afield. Their argument is that only one of these nine rhetorics actually is explicitly driven by the neoliberal economic argument, where the free market and economic growth are an unquestioned 'Social Good' and where State intervention privileges the emphasis of social and economic practices that encourage private ownership and accumulation through entrepreneurial activity. The neoliberal social and economic policies adopted by the majority of the world from the late 1970s (Harvey, 2005), both reflecting and contributing to globalisation of the world's economies, set a coherent context for the educational system to nurture a version of 'universalised' creativity in generating innovation and thus economic buoyancy (Jeffrey and Craft, 2001).

This pure neoliberal argument for creativity, however, whilst coherent, is also problematic, and also may turn out to have been short-lived, as discussed next. And the problem of harnessing creativity to economic growth is just one of a number of challenges facing creativity and learning that became increasingly evident during the first decade of the twenty-first century.

Challenges evident in the first decade of the twenty-first century

Developing creativity in learning raises at least five sets of issues, discussed briefly here. The first three involve questioning implied accepted values.

Reach of the economic?

The neoliberal economic rationale for nurturing creativity in learning raises questions about the nature and purpose of both. To what extent the cult of the new, and of personal acquisition, is inherent in creativity, or economically, socially and environmentally sustainable, raises serious questions about how appropriate it is to inflate its value in learning. Arguing against this 'marketisation' of creativity (Craft, 2005), the need for wisdom in what creativity is used for, or harnessed to in learning, is urgent (Craft et al., 2008). Creativity, as value-free, can and is used to ends which may be destructive, exclusive and diminishing just as it may be used for ends that are inspirational, far-sighted and ethical. Attending to the impact of ideas (Claxton, 2008) on the immediate and wider context opens up other discourses than the purely economic. Banaji et al. (2006) note that creativity is, simultaneously with the economic agenda, valued in learning for its contribution to:

- personal and structural empowerment, social regeneration and inclusion – a 'social good' discourse;
- aesthetic cultural development at a level of field-recognition, through nurturing extraordinary talent – a 'creative genius' discourse;
- everyday symbolic and cultural practices which may critique dominant cultural values and which value the voices of the young in particular – a 'democratic and political' discourse;
- surviving and thriving in an uncertain world – a 'ubiquitous creativity' discourse;
- encouraging play and playfulness not only in the early years but throughout life – a 'play and creativity' discourse;

- both enhancing technological capability and being developed further through it – a 'creative affordances of creativity' discourse.

Clearly these discourses each engage with the economic rationale to some degree, some (for example 'creative genius' and 'ubiqitous creativity') potentially supporting it and others (for example 'social good' and 'democratic and political') potentially challenging it. Other discourses – for example 'play' and 'technology' – can both support and challenge the economic rationale depending on context.

The point, however, is that developing creativity in learning requires clarity about the role of the neoliberal rationale in conceiving of the nature of creativity and its contribution to learning. At a time when the environmental signals suggest that the timeline toward irreversible global self-destruction through climate change triggered by neoliberal policies toward the free market may now be very short, the need to generate and develop alternative ends and means could be seen as a high priority for those involved in learning, developing creativity with wisdom.

Creative and cultural elision?

As noted above, in England, Northern Ireland and Scotland, and to some degree in Wales, there is some elision of creativity and culture. With their roots in the neoliberal economic rationale discussed above, rationales for engaging the creative and cultural sector with learning include both creativity and culture. Arguments range from passing on authentic practices through apprenticeship learning, igniting interest and developing creative talent among learners, to engaging young people directly with their cultural heritage, exploring personal and collective identity and citizenship. Thus, the purposes of creative and cultural education may overlap, as argued in the NACCCE Report (1999), in that development of creativity in young people by engaging with both creativity and culture ultimately nurtures cultural development. Yet the nature of creative and cultural education is quite distinct. Very crudely put, whereas creative education focuses on the generation of novelty and change, cultural education explores continuities. Yet policies in all four nations of the United Kingdom appear to some degree to elide the two.

For those concerned with developing creativity in education, clarity is necessary about the nature of and reasons for the balance between creativity and culture in learning. This, combined with the questions raised above about the economic rationale for creativity in learning, poses potential dilemmas for educators in the United Kingdom and elsewhere seeking to develop creativity in learning.

A conservative U-turn in policy?

Although the last years of the twentieth century and the early days of the twenty-first century, as discussed earlier in the chapter, brought a massive expansion in creativity in education, the introduction of a coalition government with conservative policies in England in May 2010 appears to have brought with it high level questioning of this. Every major curriculum revision brought in by New Labour between 1998 and 2010 has been paused or cancelled. The intention to focus on curriculum 'basics' has been emphasised (Department for Education, 2010). Those involved in researching and developing creativity in education are faced with the challenge of how to respond appropriately to what appears to be a significant change in direction at a political level.

A further two sets of issues which have emerged in the United Kingdom in the first decade of the twenty-first century, however, are more practical.

The role of creative partnership

As is particularly obvious in the case of policy development in England and Northern Ireland, and perhaps to a lesser degree in Scotland and Wales, a key element in the relationship between the economy and creativity policy in education has been the development of partnerships between teachers and the visiting 'creative professionals' or artists. This has been seen as a significant model for creative work enabling young people to emulate collaborative social practices often modelled on team-working and shared problem-solving (Jeffery, 2005). Whilst claims have been made as to what creative partnership, the development of cultural and creative opportunities and a focus on creativity in education may offer young people, schools and society as a whole (e.g. Fiske, 1999; Eames et al., 2006; Thomson et al., 2009), there is little predictive evidence as yet about the contribution made solely by creative partnership to the development of creativity in young people. It is a great shame that just as such predictive research, which depends on longitudinal data, is emerging from Creative Partnerships in England (e.g. Durban et al., 2010), the programme – and its research activity – has been closed by the 'basics-focused' government.

Assessment

Of the four nations of the United Kingdom it is the Scottish teachers who have most volubly highlighted a need for clarity around what and how creativity may be assessed. In England, substantial guidance which, at the time of initial writing of this chapter, in early 2010, was in press, had by July 2010 been cancelled, in light of a 'relentless focus on the basics' (Department for Education, 2010); however, there is certainly a need for greater understanding and expertise in this area across the United Kingdom. A contentious area, in which approaches to assessment vary from those which seek to measure creativity using standardised tests, primarily used in the United States and Far East, to those which see creativity as contextualised and requiring a more complex, context-sensitive set of instruments, there is no doubt that if creativity is relevant to the heart of learning we need clarity on how to help learners move from novice to expert, from initiation to mastery. Implicit in these questions are models of 'creative cognition' (Banaji et al., 2006) which range from perspectives which view creativity as produced internally by the individual mind, to those which see creativity as produced by external contexts and cultures, as well as perspectives on knowledge itself as either objectifiable or inherently situated.

The very question of assessing creativity is for some antithetical to the whole concept. Educators involved in nurturing creativity and learning have to ask themselves what purpose or role assessment could play (for example formative, summative), what and who it might be focused on (process, product; individual, collaborative effort), who might be involved in or own the assessment (students, peers, teachers, others). It remains an underdeveloped area, and approaches to assessment will reflect perceptions of the nature and purpose of creativity in learning.

Creativity and learning: issues for the next ten years?

These five challenges named above are likely to occupy those involved in creativity and learning at the levels of both principle and practice over the coming decade. Given global economic, political and environmental change, we may also see questions emerging around at least two further issues cutting across those five challenges: *ownership* (whose hands is the future in and what role does learner participation and voice play in nurturing creativity in learning?) and *efficacy* (how do we know that what we are developing is having the impact intended, without longitudinal and large-scale controlled studies being undertaken?).

These are live issues as the coalition government in mid-2010 rushes through new education policies which seek to reduce the content of school curricula and perhaps to move away from creativity, at least in England. This retrenchment push brings with it the challenge of how educators respond, as we consider the *kinds of futures* (possible, probable and preferable) that may emerge for education. Those involved in and committed to education can be seen as 'trustees' or guardians of this aspect of our society (Gardner, 2008).

The role of the trustee is to nurture debate on values, intentions and impact – and especially at times of possible change in policy direction. At the time of completing this chapter (February 2011), the policy reversal away from the overlapping agendas for developing creativity and cultural education was revving up in England. This was seen in the omission of creativity and cultural education from the White Paper published in November 2010 (DfE, 2010b), the announcement of the English Baccalaureate (DfE, 2010c), which omits the arts, in December 2010 and the remit of the review of the National Curriculum launched January 2011, which sought to focus on a narrow core National Curriculum, leaving breadth for schools to define (and provide). All three signalled in different ways the government's intended departure from the notion of a broad and balanced entitlement curriculum for all children and young people, and the shift toward a much narrower defined core curriculum which, whilst offering practitioners and schools more freedom and flexibility, nevertheless also means detachment from core twenty-first century values and skills in relation to the State's responsibilities.

This direction being pursued in England represented a move in the opposite direction from policy in North America, Australia, South-East Asia and, apparently, the other three nations of the United Kingdom. Educators, learners, researchers, parents and others who see themselves as trustees of educational futures in England now have a highly challenging task ahead. Yet the multiple challenges we face as a globe in relation to the environment, the economy, politics and so on demand creative engagement, but in ways that do not replicate and intensify the problems we already have.

We need to develop wise creative educational futures, and with some urgency. But this challenge, with its short time-horizons, arises in apparently hostile territory (at least in England), raising questions regarding the extent to which a 'relentless focus on the basics' can stretch to encompass creative imagination toward what might be.

References

Banaji, S., Burn, A. with Buckingham, D. (2006) *The Rhetorics of Creativity: A Review of the Literature*, London: Arts Council England.

Claxton, G. (2008) Wisdom: advanced creativity?, in A. Craft, H. Gardner, G. Claxton *et al. Creativity, Wisdom and Trusteeship: Exploring the Role of Education*, Thousand Oaks, CA: Corwin Press.

Cochrane, P., Craft, A. and Jeffery, G. (2008) Mixed messages or permissions and opportunities? Reflections on current policy perspectives on creativity in education, in J. Sefton-Green (ed.) *Creative Learning*, London: Creative Partnerships.

Craft, A. (1997) *Can You Teach Creativity?* Nottingham: Education Now.

—— (2005) *Creativity in Schools: Tensions and Dilemmas*, London: Routledge.

Craft, A., Gardner, H., Claxton, G. *et al.* (2008) *Creativity, Wisdom and Trusteeship: Exploring the Role of Education*, Thousand Oaks, CA: Corwin Press.

Creative and Cultural Skills (Wales) (2008) *Creative Blueprint Summary Wales: The Sector Skills Agreement for the Creative and Cultural Industries*, June, Cardiff: Creative and Cultural Skills; available at http://www.ccskills.org.uk/LinkClick.aspx?fileticket=XJsUk5rVRrM%3D&tabid=81 (accessed 31 December 2009).

Department for Children, Education, Lifelong Learning and Skills (DCELLS) (2008a) *Making the Most of Learning: Implementing the Revised Curriculum*, Cardiff: Welsh Assembly Government.

—— (2008b) *Skills Framework for 3–19 Year Olds in Wales*, Cardiff: Welsh Assembly Government.

Department of Culture, Arts and Leisure (DCAL), Department for Enterprise, Trade and Investment (DETI), Department of Higher and Further Education, Training and Employment (DHFETE) and Department for Education (DE) (2000) *Unlocking Creativity: A Strategy for Development*, Belfast: Department of Culture, Arts and Leisure.

Department of Culture Arts and Leisure (DCAL), Department of Education (DE), Department for Employment and Learning (DEL), Department of Enterprise, Trade and Investment (DETI) and Invest Northern Ireland (Invest NI) (2003) *Unlocking Creativity: A Creative Region*, Belfast: Department of Culture, Arts and Leisure.

Department for Culture, Media and Sport (DCMS) (2009) *Taking Part: The National Survey of Culture, Leisure and Sport: Headline Findings from the 2008/09 Taking Part Child Survey. Statistical Release: 29 October 2009*, London: DCMS; available at http://www.culture.gov.uk/images/publications/08-09_Child_Baseline_report.pdf (accessed 31 December 2009).

Department for Culture, Media and Sport (DCMS) and Department for Education and Skills (DfES) (2006) *Government Response to Nurturing Creativity and Young People*, London: HMSO.

Department for Culture, Media and Sport (DCMS), Department for Business, Enterprise and Regulatory Reform (BERR) and Department for Innovation, Universities and Skills (DIUS) (2008) *Creative Britain: New Talents for the Creative Economy*, London: DCMS.

Department for Education (2010) *National Curriculum*; available at http://www.education.gov.uk/curriculum.

—— (2010b) *The Importance of Teaching*, London: The Stationery Office.

—— (2010c) *Addendum (The English Baccalaureate)*; available at http://www.education.gov.uk/performancetables/Statement-of-Intent-2010-Addendum.pdf (accessed 21 January 2011).

—— (2010d) *Review of the National Curriculum for England: Remit*; available at http://www.education.gov.uk/b0073043/remit-for-review-of-the-national-curriculum-in-england/ (11 February 2011).

Department of Education (DE), Department of Enterprise, Trade and Investment (DETI), Department of Higher and Further Education, Training and Employment (DHFETE), Department of Culture, Arts and Leisure (DCAL) (2001) *Unlocking Creativity: Making It Happen*, Belfast: Department of Culture, Arts and Leisure.

Durbin, B., Rutt, S., Saltini, F., Sharp, C., Teeman, D., White, K. (2010) *The Impact of Creative Partnerships on School Attainment and Attendance*, Slough: NFER.

DIUS (2008) *Innovation Nation*, London: The Stationery Office.

Fiske, E. B. (ed.) (1999) *Champions of Change: The Impact of the Arts on Learning*; available at http://artsedge.kennedy-center.org/champions/pdfs/ChampsReport.pdf (accessed 1 January 2010).

Gardner, H. (2008) Creativity, wisdom and trusteeship, in A. Craft, H. Gardner, G. Claxton *et al. Creativity, Wisdom and Trusteeship: Exploring the Role of Education*, Thousand Oaks, CA: Corwin Press.

Harland, J., Kinder, K., Haynes, J. and Schagen, I. (1998) *The Effects and Effectiveness of Arts Education in Schools: Interim Report 1*, Slough: NFER.

Harvey, D. (2005) *A Brief History of Neoliberalism*, Oxford: Oxford University Press.

House of Commons Children, Schools and Families Committee (2008) *Creative Partnerships and the Curriculum: Government Response to the Eleventh Report from the Education and Skills Committee, Session 2006–07*, London: The Stationery Office Limited.

House of Commons Education and Skills Committee (2007) *Creative Partnerships and the Curriculum. Eleventh Report of Session 2006–07. Report, together with formal minutes, oral and written evidence*, London: The Stationery Office Limited.

IDES (2001) *Creativity in Education: Discussion Paper*, Scotland: IDES Network.

Eames, A., Benton, T., Sharp, C., Kendall, L. (2006) *The Longer Term Impact of Creative Partnerships on the Attainment of Young People*. Final report. Slough: NFER.

Jeffrey, B. and Craft, A. (2001) The universalization of creativity, in A. Craft, B. Jeffrey and M. Leibling, *Creativity in Education*, London: Continuum.

—— (2006) Creative learning and possibility thinking, B. Jeffrey (ed.) *Creative Learning Practices: European Experiences*, London: The Tufnell Press.

Jeffery, G. (ed.) (2005) *The Creative College: Building a Successful Learning Culture in the Arts*, Stoke on Trent: Trentham Books.

Learning and Teaching Scotland (2004a) *Learning, Thinking and Creativity: A Staff Development Handbook*, Dundee and Glasgow: LTS and IDEAS Network; available at http://www.ltscotland.org.uk/creativity/index.asp (accessed 31 December 2009).

—— (2004b) *Creativity Counts: Portraits of Practice*, Dundee and Glasgow: LTS and IDES Network; available at http://www.ltscotland.org.uk/creativity/index.asp (accessed 31 December 2009).

McMaster, Sir B. (2008) *Supporting Excellence in the Arts: From Measurement to Judgement*, London: DCMS.

National Advisory Committee on Creative and Cultural Education (NACCCE) (1999) *All Our Futures*, London: DfEE and DCMS.

National College for School Leadership (NCSL) (2003a) *Leading the Creative School: A Leading Edge Seminar – November 2002*, Nottingham: NCSL.

—— (2003b) *Primary Curriculum and Creativity*, Nottingham: NCSL.

—— (2007) *Lifting the Lid on the Creative Curriculum: A Research Associate Report by Tim Burgess*, Spring, Nottingham: NCSL.

Purnell, J. (2005) *Seven Steps to Boost the Creative Economy*, press release 147/05, November; available at http://www.culture.gov.uk/reference_library/media_releases/3044.aspx (accessed 9 February 2011).

Roberts, P. (2006) *Nurturing Creativity in Young People: A Report to Government to Inform Future Policy*, London: HMSO.

Scottish Executive (2009) Determined to Succeed; available at http://www.determinedtosucceed.co.uk/dts/CCC_FirstPage.jsp (accessed 31 December 2009).

—— (2010) *A Curriculum for Excellence*; available at http://www.curriculumforexcellencescotland.gov.uk/ (accessed 1 January 2010).

Scottish Government (2005) *Final Report of the Cultural Commission, 2005*; available at http://www.scotland.gov.uk/Publications/2005/09/0191729/17347 (accessed 31 December 2009).

Sefton-Green, J. (2008) From learning to creative learning, in J. Sefton-Green (ed.) *Creative Learning*, London: Creative Partnerships.

Thomson, P., Jones, K., and Hall, C. (2009) *Final Report: Creative School Change Project*. Creative Partnerships: London. http://www.creativitycultureeducation.org/research-impact/thematic-research/ (8 May 2011).

Woods, P. and Jeffrey, B. (1996) *Teachable Moments: The Art of Creative Teaching in Primary Schools*, Buckingham: Open University Press.

15

Constructing assessment for creative learning

Pamela Burnard

Introduction

Compared with numerous other topics relating to 'creative learning', research on the assessment of creative learning is still in its infancy. One reason is that the concept of 'creative learning', lacking firm definition and development in theory, remains elusive. Another reason is that, globally, in both dominant and emerging educational discourses, public policies that mandate performance criteria, tests, targets and tables of achievement often conflict with creativity policies in education rather than co-existing with them (Burnard and White, 2008).

It is fitting, therefore, to start this chapter on creative learning assessment with an exploration of what counts as creative learning and end it with a discussion of why the alignment between assessment practice and theory is something to strive for. These two topics are at the heart of our efforts to understand and improve the relationship between teaching, educational research and educational change (Hargreaves, 1996).

This chapter considers a range of perspectives on creative learning and goes on to examine examples of the methodologies used in researching its assessment. I discuss current research which brings together the latest practices and understandings pertaining to assessment *of* and *for* creative learning and attempt to show the potential for developing consistency between assessment practices and theories about creative learning: a change in one requires a change in the other. The chapter ends with an argument drawn from research on formative assessment (Stiggins, 2002). I make a plea for assessment practices that preserve student motivation, recognising that the realities of students are independent of those of teachers or researchers (Black and Wiliam, 1998).

What counts as creative learning?

Different views have emerged on what counts as creative learning, and how *creative* learning might be distinguished from other modes of learning; amongst these are behaviourist, cognitive, constructivist and situated theories of learning (Craft *et al.*, 2007; Craft *et al.*, 2008; Jeffrey and Craft, 2006). Especially important is the notion that creative learning is a mediated activity in which imaginative achievement and the development of knowledge have a crucial role. Creative learning involves participation and is developed in relationships between people engaged in collaborative activities in which they develop their thoughts together. Craft, Cremin and Burnard (2008) regard creative learning as something which is 'situated' in the social environment; thus it is difficult to judge that an individual has acquired knowledge in general terms because achievement is not abstracted from context but seen in relation to it. In relation to what counts as creative learning, they comment:

> Creative learning is significant imaginative achievement as evidenced in the creation of new knowledge as determined by the imaginative insight of the person or persons responsible and judged by appropriate observers to be both original and of value as situated in different domain contexts.
>
> *(Craft, Cremin and Burnard, 2008: 77)*

Thus, the development of creative learning involves the learner shaping and being shaped by, as well as judging and being judged by 'appropriate observers' within the community. The presumption here is that what counts as creative learning needs to be evaluated within the classroom and its social and cultural context.

Another attempt to reach a consensus on the term 'creative learning' came from the National College for School Leadership (NCSL), with discussions circling around 'the unfettered freedom of personal expression, a natural impulse to be celebrated, developed or often subdued by education' and, by contrast, 'the discipline, practice and craft of creativity progressively developed through learning' (NCSL, 2003: 2). The point here is that what counts as 'creative learning' can entail a dialect that generates a *multiplicity* of meanings. The evident value of 'creative learning', and the principles that underpin teachers' and students' knowledge, beliefs and practices, are themes neither clarified nor acknowledged in government policy frameworks and initiatives (QCA, 2005a). In England, in 2005, six years after the justification for creativity posed in the 1999 NACCCE report,[1] within a culture of accountability and performativity, the government released a policy framework called *Creativity: Find It, Promote It!*, which proposed identifying and promoting creativity within the Early Learning Goals and in the National Curriculum (QCA, 2005b); that is, within the statutory curriculum for children from preschool age through to the age of 16. However, issues that are key to gathering reliable evidence for summative or formative assessment were not addressed. It is hardly surprising, therefore, that the message sent was essentially about value implications rather than how creative learning development might be monitored.

In 2006, a review was commissioned jointly by James Purnell, then Minister for the Creative Industries at the DCMS, and Andrew Adonis, Parliamentary Undersecretary of State for Education and Skills. This formed part of an initiative at the DCMS aimed at 'Making Britain the World's Creative Hub' (Purnell, 2005). The purpose of the review was to assess progress since the 1999 NACCCE Report and work within the existing 'direction of travel' – not to make recommendations but to provide a 'set of assumptions' upon which future policy in relation to creativity could be based. The outcome of the review was the Roberts Report on *Nurturing Creativity in Young People* (Roberts, 2006). This report set out a framework for creativity starting with the early years, and covering issues such as leadership, professional development and initial teacher education, curriculum, school design, extended services and the framework of regulations and support, as well as introducing the concept of a creative portfolio. It made a 'moral' case for advancing creativity as part of the development of young people as citizens and learners, but then went further, to emphasise 'creativity' as a preparation for work within the creative industries.

In 2006, the government's response to the Roberts' Report (DCMS and DfES, 2006) reinforced and demonstrated the importance of 'creative skills' and 'creative practice' in education and the workplace. It linked creativity to other key agendas and highlighted the main actions that should be taken to ensure that creativity could flourish. The Creative Economy Programme was launched in November 2005 to support innovation, growth and productivity in both the creative industries and education. It stressed the importance of building 'strong and sustainable' links between creativity and other agendas. Here we see the creative and cultural education agendas heavily aligned with the potential for the 'creative student', the 'creative work' of students and a 'creative workforce' to advance the economy.

More recently, the secondary curriculum for 11–14-year-olds has been radically reconceived, with personal, learning and thinking skills at its core. One of the six strands of this framework focuses on developing young people as *creative thinkers* (QCA, 2008). The Rose Review of the Primary Curriculum (Rose, 2009) also affirms the need to develop children as 'creative thinkers' across the curriculum. However, in many ways these initiatives are under-conceptualised, especially in relation to assessment. Terms like 'creativity' or 'creative learning', 'creative thinking', 'creative work' or 'creative workforce' are not thought through in terms of how teachers should devise assessments which might be *summative*: indicating where the child is now in terms of creative learning development; or *formative*: where the teacher assesses what the child or children need on the basis of what has been achieved. Nor is there discussion of how teachers might set learning outcomes or make consistent judgements about the quality of the work, in relation to either previous work or the work of a particular group, all of which are issues which should be embedded in practice and aligned, or congruent, with the curriculum (Daugherty *et al.*, 2008). Moreover, if a key goal of creative learning is to build learning identities as 'creative thinkers' and foster the development of significant imaginative achievement, then students' own self-assessments must be central. This, too, is an issue that is absent from policy documents (Burnard and Wyse, 2009).

What counts as assessment of creative learning?

The general view that one can use tests of various sorts to measure people's capacity to think creatively has resulted in a very large body of literature on general creativity (see Sternberg, 1999; Feldman *et al.*, 1994). From the first systematic empirical study of 'genius' undertaken by Galton in 1869, a mass of literature has emerged on creativity arising from the traditions of psychology, philosophy, sociology and anthropology. The 1950s witnessed a focus on psychological determinants of individual genius and giftedness. Dominating the field from 1950 to 1970, psychometric approaches relied on paper and pencil assessments that tested divergent thinking, cognitive fluency, flexibility, and the originality of a subject's responses. For example, the Torrance Tests of Creative Thinking (Torrance, 1974) were widely used to identify individuals, including children, who were 'creative'. This focus on genius and giftedness continued throughout the 1960s. After the mid-1970s, the field of creativity studies moved away from testing and toward the study of cognitive, emotional, personal and cultural aspects of creativity, primarily in adults. It also embraced the case study method, with several important studies of exceptionally creative individuals (for example Darwin, Gandhi) revealing valuable information about their childhoods. Since then we have witnessed the emergence of social psychology (Amabile, 1982) and systems theory, which have emphasised the role of environmental conditions (Csikszentmihalyi, 1994), multiple intelligences and the analysis of the lives of indisputably creative individuals (Gardner, 1993).

More recently, there has been an explosion of creativity research in education, drawing on the insights of creativity theory and rich in implications for the rethinking of assessment practice. In a study of progression in creative learning, Craft, Cremin, Burnard and Chappell (2007) worked with seven teachers and collected a range of data, including video and audio recordings, observations with field notes, informal interviews, school documentation, and digital photographs, which they used as a focus for exploration with both pupils and teachers. The aim was to explore how creative learning developed pupils' capacity for imaginative activity and led to original and valuable musical and written compositions. A key finding of the study was that creative learning was evidenced in the act of producing knowledge. Creative learning was apparent at every key stage in the ways pupils asked questions, made connections, generated ideas, explored options and evaluated their work.

The emphasis on the process by which a piece of work was created, as well as the resulting product, was also a key feature of the Arts-PROPEL project – a collaboration between the *Project Zero* research group at Harvard University and the *Project Spectrum* group at the Educational Testing Service. The idea was that students would 'write poems, compose their songs, paint portraits and tackle other "real-life" projects as the starting points for exploring the works of practising artists' (Project Zero, 2005). The projects worked from the three basic premises that assessments should take qualitative issues into account; that they should examine process as well as product; and that pupils' opinions of their own art works should be taken into account. These studies have strong implications for assessment practice and demonstrate the potential of pragmatic approaches to creative learning assessment in which students can be stimulated to think and act collaboratively and be involved both in the generation of authentic tasks and in peer assessment of the learning outcomes. Consistent with a constructivist or socio-cultural approach in both theory and practice, a key goal of creative learning is to invoke students' own self-assessments and to permit a range of assessment practices to fit different contexts and purposes whilst still maintaining internal consistency and coherence. However, this raises questions about the nature of the subject domain and whether priority should be given to one assessment approach in preference to another. For example, subject disciplines such as science and mathematics, with hierarchically ordered and generally accepted conceptual structures, may lend themselves more readily to constructivist approaches that maintain criteria that encourage and enhance rather than hinder creative learning (Burnard and Lavicza, 2010; Burnard et al., 2010).

The key themes that run through the literature concern what counts as creative learning and how assessment for different purposes can affect how the term 'creative learning' is interpreted, used and practised by different individuals and groups of people, in different communities, institutions and societies, historically and culturally. However, even if 'creative learning' is conceptualised as the grounded activity that provides a basis for significant imaginative achievement and for developing creative thinkers, formulating the practice of constructing assessments that maintain criteria that encourage and enhance creative learning and its development remains a problem.

The challenge that emerges from the literature about creative learning is the need to make explicit how learning outcomes can be captured and reported in situations where teachers and students are jointly engaged with questions about which assessment practices are most appropriate (for different subject disciplines). Another imperative is the need to examine how a student's progress can be measured and recorded to demonstrate understanding of a particular field of knowledge. Here, consideration of the different ways used in different subjects to record, evaluate and assess understanding and progress in creative learning is important (Sefton-Green and Sinker, 2000).

Researching assessment of creative (arts) learning

We can learn much from detailed, practice-based work on creativity assessment. There are accumulating reports of successful models, based on consensual assessment technique (CAT), for rating the creative quality of art products. CAT is based on Amabile's (1982) consensual theory of creativity, suggesting that creative ability is best measured by assessing the creative quality of the products that are a result of creative endeavours. CAT has been used in visual art, in poetry and in story writing. It has been widely and successfully used in, for example, Hong Kong studies of assessing creativity in products (Cheng, 2008); in assessing creativity with open tasks with many possible solutions (Hennessy and Amabile, 1999); and in cases where artists are asked to judge the drawings of primary school children (Hennessy and Amabile, 1999).

We know, from research of teacher practices incorporating CAT, that teachers do have the ability to correctly identify varying levels of creativity as evidenced in the creative products of children. One study found that, while both pupils and teachers recognised creativity as an intended outcome of arts education, students, in particular, used the term so widely (variously meaning freedom, experimentation, imagination, new thoughts, self-expression) that any measure of it is in danger of becoming meaningless. In addition, their descriptions rarely suggested any sequential or progressive improvement in 'creativity', either as a competency or as a cognitive process (Harland et al., 2000). It is interesting, therefore, to note that Boud has pointed out that 'assessment methods and requirements probably have a greater influence on how and what students learn than any other single factor. This influence may well be of greater importance than the impact of teachers or teaching materials' (Boud, 1988: 35).

At the Centre for Literacy in Primary Education (CLPE), Ellis, Barrs and Bunting (2007) have developed an assessment tool that focuses on learning in the creative arts – the Creative Learning Assessment (CLA). One of their key findings has been that teachers are looking for practical tools that are useful in assessing children's creativity. The construct 'creativity' that is used is developed from the QCA documents (making connections, imagining, possibility thinking). But the crucial issue pertaining to construct validity that remains unresolved concerns the nature and consistency of what teachers understand by the construct of 'creativity'.

Ellis and Barrs (2008) developed a model of creative learning assessment comprising six strands. These strands include confidence, independence and enjoyment, collaboration and communication, creativity, strategies and skills, knowledge and understanding, and reflection and evaluation. Each strand forms a key heading for the CLA Observation Framework, which provides guidance for teacher observations. Teachers contributed to revisions along the way and helped to shape the final instrument. The modes of assessment indicated in the guide include: classroom performance; reflective commentaries on individual, group and class portfolios; and self- and peer assessment. Teachers' records included the CLA Observation Framework, with related examples of children's work and Creative Learning Scale levels for the whole class. This framework for assessment highlights the importance of assessment for learning and encourages teachers to select a variety of materials when developing a school-based curriculum so as to provide students with holistic learning experiences.

In the current political context, with creativity policies being promoted at government and national educational levels, *the existence of 'construct definitions' of creative learning for teachers is* crucial, and it is necessary to know how, and by whom, the constructs involved are defined, interpreted and made real in relation to curriculum, pedagogy and assessment practices. We know how creative learning is perceived and expressed in curriculum documents (Burnard and Wyse, 2009). We know much less about teacher and pupil perceptions of creative learning in an inner-city school and out of school. This was the focus of a recent study which examined the nature of creative learning as experienced by children in one school. In this study, Biddulph (2009) explored an assumed gap between the actual experiences of children and teachers' perceptions of creative learning to locate a context-specific understanding. Teachers tended to focus on fostering and facilitating creative learning despite the lack of flexible school structures. While artists approach themes with open-minded imagination, teachers tend to be 'constrained to orient themselves towards the predictable, the familiar, normative standards and public accountability' (Biddulph, 2009: 51).

In the study the strongly differentiated views between children and adults about what constitutes creative learning were of particular importance. The children seemed to value imaginative activity more than their teachers. Teachers often worried about the unmotivated behaviours of children who were 'off in their own worlds', as well as about the expectations of creative learning tasks as set by learning objectives from schemes of work. Imaginative behaviour was less valued by teachers because of the ambiguous expectations of such learning outcomes. This results in an adverse relationship between individual perceptions of tasks (enjoyment, purpose, skills involved) and efficacy in the achievement of creative learning (Webster, 1992). How can creative learning (e.g. imaginative activity) be encouraged within the fixed structures, boundaries and expectations of learning and teaching as described by official guidelines?

What is the implication and impact of the teachers' construct of 'creativity' which is embodied in assessment practice? The picture that emerged from the study was that assessment practices did not enhance creative learning. Teachers used tests which encouraged rote and superficial learning, whereas the concept of 'creative learning' is both slippery and complex. The roles and responsibilities assigned to teachers and learners in both learning and assessment need to be radically transformed.

In a recent and still ongoing study (Daugherty et al., 2008) of creativity assessment the foundations of a valid assessment (that is, one which aligns curriculum and pedagogy in a symbiotic relationship that is not a line or cycle but a moving mosaic, shifting and overlapping, moving and responding to pupil perceptions, needs and circumstances) are explored. The notion of 'construct validity' is central to how the construct of 'creativity' is both perceived and applied in the curriculum/assessment relationship and in the day-to-day practice of teachers and pupils (Daugherty et al., 2008). So, where does creativity reside in assessment for different arts disciplines? What is it teachers are assessing (i.e. the construct)? How do arts teachers of different arts disciplines consistently judge something to be creative? What are the constructs used?

The seminal study of the DELTA (Development of Learning and Teaching in the Arts) project by Hargreaves, Galton and Robinson (1996), which investigated how primary school teachers assess children's work in the creative arts on an everyday basis, reported substantial agreement about the quality of different pieces of work across all scales and between the different rating scales employed in each of the art forms in the creative arts in British primary schools. Whilst all of the teachers acknowledged that they continually assess children's progress so as to enable them to guide the next stage of learning, it remains unclear what the criteria are on which teachers base their qualitative evaluations and how criteria are applied and agreed upon across primary and secondary school age groups and between secondary students and their teachers. How are creativity constructs evidenced in curriculum documents and embodied in assessment practices?

Another challenging issue for arts educators is the extent to which there are differences between teachers of different creative subjects and different age groups, and between students and their teachers.

In a recent and timely study of Creativity Assessment Practice in the Arts (CAPA), researchers sought to clarify the construct of 'creativity' as perceived and practised by teachers and students

(Burnard and Lavicza, 2010). Informed by the framework of Johnson and Onwuegbuzie (2004), the CAPA study employed a combination of qualitative data collected by *interviews* (and *contextual observations*) and an on-line *survey*, distributed via e-mail to key music and visual arts personnel across a range of primary and secondary schools in five local education authorities.

The study focused on the following research questions: (1) What is the construct 'creativity' and how is it expressed in music and visual arts curriculum documents and assessment practices across primary and secondary sectors? (2) How do teachers and students perceive the construct of 'creativity' to be manifested in music and visual arts curriculum documents and assessment practices?

Interview data from four schools (two primary and two secondary) in East Anglia informed the construction and piloting of a questionnaire which was e-mailed to 300 schools (accessing 120 music/visual arts teachers) recruited to the project from five southeastern English counties (Cambridgeshire, Essex, Hertfordshire, Norfolk and Suffolk). Instruments used in obtaining data from the schools included *observations* (each class was observed, with, where possible, some presentation of pupils' work); *interviews* (these included individual face-to-face interviews with the teachers and group interviews with the students); and *work samples/artefacts* (the collection of documentation of teachers' practices and the inclusion of assessment tasks and work samples). The *survey* included background variables as well as statements (between three and five items per concept for the development of latent variables based on the results of the qualitative study and the literature).

We received 303 responses to the survey that we were able to include in the analysis process. The initial analysis suggests that the majority of teachers (85 per cent) agreed (agreed or strongly agreed on a five-point Likert-Scale) that creativity involves taking risks and developing new/ unconventional ideas; 65 per cent of participants implied that creativity can be judged by the value invested in the art process, but at the same time many teachers (40 per cent) believed that creativity is independent of skills. In spite of this, creativity can be assessed in the school setting (75 per cent), but this judgement is often subjective (51 per cent). Participants emphasised that assessing creativity is quite difficult and adequate training would be beneficial for their work (74 per cent). However, only 42 per cent reported receiving adequate training and they said that they gained experience through their work, but only 55 per cent declared that they this experience qualified them well for assessing creativity.

Conclusions from and implications of the analysis include a consideration of the differentiated nature of *what* creative learning might mean in relation to classroom-based assessment; *where* assessment of creative learning can be practised; and *how* creative learning assessment can be operationalised in primary and secondary schools.

The role of assessment *for* developing creative learning

Since the early 1990s formative assessment has generally been used synonymously alongside the term 'assessment for learning'. The term 'assessment for learning' appears in many publications by the Assessment Reform Group (ARG) in the UK in the follow-up to the work of Black and Wiliam, in which they called for a 'clear distinction between assessment of learning for the purposes of grading and reporting and assessment for learning which calls for different priorities, new procedures and a new commitment' (Black and Wiliam, 1998: 4).

What might the characteristics of assessment for creative learning be:

- if creative learning embeds assessment as an essential part of it?
- if creative learning involves sharing learning goals with pupils?
- if creative learning aims to help pupils to know and to recognise the standards they are aiming for?

- if creative learning involves pupils in self-assessment?
- if creative learning provides feedback which leads to pupils recognising their next steps and how to take them?
- if creative learning is underpinned by confidence that every student can improve?
- if creative learning involves both teacher and pupils reviewing and reflecting on assessment data?

Popham (2008) stated that for formative assessment to exist as a distinct form of assessment, it must lead to instructional adjustments by teachers or tactical learning adjustments by students; these adjustments will affect activities or efforts already in progress. He referred to formative assessment as a planned process that involves a series of carefully considered and distinguishable acts on the part of teacher and student. Formative assessment needs to draw on formal and informal assessment methods to provide evidence of the students' current level of mastery of certain skills and bodies of knowledge. Based on this evidence teachers and students can then adjust teaching and learning strategies in an effort to ensure mastery of the necessary skills and knowledge. Several educators and researchers have identified the planned process or specific formative assessment strategies that could be fully integrated within the teaching of creative learning (Ellis and Barrs, 2008). The strategies include: clarifying and sharing learning goals and expectations with students; engineering effective discussions, questions, activities and tasks that elicit evidence of students' learning; providing feedback that informs students how to achieve subsequent learning goals; and activating students as learning resources for one another.

Next steps

Despite the championing of assessment reform by assessment specialists and governmental bodies, the assessment of students' creative learning in classrooms seems resistant to change (Torrance and Pryor, 1998). Research has cited issues such as a lack of agreement and understanding of formative assessment and the dominance of the summative assessment regime in schools. Harlen (2007) has argued against the validity of favouring one form of assessment over others, when, in fact, the whole range of assessment practices can be directed towards some aspects of learning within a specific socio-cultural setting. It follows also that without understanding the context or socio-cultural conditions of creative learning, an emphasis on any particular type of assessment may be counterproductive.

Given that the development of formative assessment has the potential to catalyse radical change, a theory that helps design and track such change would be an important resource. Research into the meeting of the worlds of theory and practice could result in a framework that will facilitate the fundamental changes required in the development of assessment practices for creative learning. Clearly, also, more work needs to be done on assessment for creative learning with a socio-cultural perspective.

We need innovative practitioner research within the field of curriculum and assessment studies – research that will change assessment policy and creative learning practices within the classroom in different socio-cultural contexts. As researchers and practitioners we need open minds and a willingness to take risks with ideas about creative learning and its assessment.

Note

1 The report *All Our Futures: Creativity, Culture and Education* puts forward a definition of creativity as an 'imaginative activity fashioned so as to produce outcomes that are both original and of value' (NACCCE, 1999: 30). The report suggested that the curriculum needed rebalancing; one of the key

recommendations was for creativity to be recognised, fostered and promoted as a teaching and learning practice.

References

Amabile, T. (1982) Social psychology of creativity: a consensual assessment technique, *Journal of Personality and Social Psychology* 43: 997–1013.

Biddulph, J. (2009) Exploring creative learning in school and out of school contexts: a phenomenological cast study, thesis submitted for the degree of Master of Education at the University of Cambridge, Faculty of Education.

Black, P. and Wiliam, D. (1998) Assessment and classroom learning, *Assessment in Education* 5(1): 7–71.

Boud, D. (1988) *Developing Student Autonomy in Learning* (2nd ed.), London: Kogan Page.

Burnard, P. and Lavicza, Z. (2010) Primary and secondary teachers' conceptions and practices of assessing creativity in the arts, *International Research Commission Conference Proceedings*, Changchun, China: International Society of Music Education.

Burnard, P. and White, J. (2008) Rebalancing pedagogy: performativity, creativity and professionalism in British and Australian education, *British Educational Research Journal* 34(5): 667–82.

—— (2009) Creativity in the primary curriculum: reconciling disconnections between policy, theory, research and practice, paper presented at the British Education Research Association (BERA) Conference, Manchester, September.

Burnard, P., Fautley, M. and Savage, J. (2010) Assessing creativity in the secondary school classroom: exploring variations in teachers' conceptions and practices, *International Society of Music Education World Conference Proceedings*, Beijing: International Society of Music Education.

Cheng, V. M. Y. (2008) Consensual assessment in creative learning, in A. Craft., T. Cremin and P. Burnard (eds) *Creative Learning 3–11 and How We Document It: What, How and Why?*, London: Trentham Books.

Craft, A., Cremin, T. and Burnard, P. (2008) (eds) *Creative Learning 3–11 and How We Document It: What, How and Why?* London: Trentham Books.

Craft, A., Cremin, T., Burnard, P. and Chappell, K. (2007) Teacher stance in creative learning: a study of progression, Thinking Skills and Creativity 2(1): 136–47.

Csikszentmihalyi, M. (1994) The domain of creativity, in D. H. Feldman, M. Csikszentmihalyi and H. Gardner (eds) *Changing the World: A Framework for the Study of Creativity*, London: Praeger.

Daugherty, R., Black, B., Ecclestone, K., James, M. and Newton, P. (2008) Alternative perspectives on learning outcomes: challenges for assessment, *Curriculum Journal* 19(4): 243–54.

DCMS and DfES (2006) *Government Response to 'Nurturing Creativity and Young People'*, London: HMSO.

Ellis, S. and Barrs, J. (2008) The assessment of creative learning, in J. Sefton-Green (ed.) *Creative Learning*, London: Creative Partnerships, Arts Council England.

Ellis, S., Barrs, M. and Bunting, J. (2007) *Animating Literacy: Inspiring Children's Learning through Teacher and Artist Partnerships*, London: Centre for Literacy in Primary Education.

Feldman, D. H., Csikszentmihalyi, M. and Gardner, H. (1994) *Changing the World: A Framework for the Study of Creativity*, Westport, CT: Praeger.

Gardner, H. (1993) Frames of Mind, London: Fontana Press.

Hargreaves, A. (1996) Transforming knowledge: blurring the boundaries between research, policy and practice, *Educational Evaluation and Policy Analysis* 18(2): 105–22.

Hargreaves, D. J., Galton, M. J. and Robinson, S. (1996) Teachers' assessments of children's classroom work in the creative arts, *Education Research* 38(2): 199–211.

Harland, J., Kinder, K., Lord, P., Stott, A., Schagen, I. and Haynes, J. (2000) *Arts Education in Secondary Schools: Effects and Effectiveness*, Slough: NFER.

Harlen, W. (2007) *Assessment of Learning*, London: Sage.

Hennessey, B. A. and Amabile, T. M. (1999) Consensual assessment, in M. A. Runco and S. R. Pritzker (eds) *Encyclopedia of Creativity*, vol. 1, San Diego, CA: Academic Press.

Jeffrey, B. and Craft, A. (2006) Teaching creatively and teaching for creativity: distinctions and relationships, *Educational Studies* 30(1): 77–87.

Johnson, B. R. and Onwuegbuzie, A. J. (2004) Mixed methods research: a research paradigm whose time has come, *Educational Researcher* 33(7): 14–26.

National Advisory Committee on Creative and Cultural Education (NACCCE) (1999) *All Our Futures: Creativity, Culture and Education. Report to the Secretary of State for Education and Employment [and] the*

Secretary of State for Culture, Media and Sport/National Advisory Committee on Creative and Cultural Education, Sudbury, Suffolk: Department of Education and Employment (DfEE) Publications.

National College of School Leadership (NCSL) (2003) *Leading the Creative School: A Leading Edge Seminar – November 2002*, Nottingham: NCSL.

Popham, W. J. (2008) *Transformative Assessment*, Alexandria, VA: ASCD.

Project Zero (2005) *History of Project Zero*; available at http://www.pz.harvard.edu/History/History.htm (accessed 30 March 2005).

Purnell, J. (2005) *Seven Steps to Boost the Creative Economy*, Ipress Release 147/05, November; available at http://www.culture.gov.uk/reference_library/media_releases/3044.aspx (accessed December 2008).

Qualifications and Curriculum Authority (QCA) (2005a) *The National Curriculum in Action: Creativity*; available at www.ncaction.org.uk/creativity/about.htm (accessed 12 December 2008).

—— (2005b) *Creativity: Find It, Promote It. Promoting Pupils' Creative Thinking and Behaviour across the Curriculum at Key Stages 1, 2 and 3*, London: QCA.

—— (2008) *Personal Learning and Thinking Skills: The New Secondary Curriculum*, London: QCA.

Roberts, P. (2006) *Nurturing Creativity in Young People: A Report to Government to Inform Future Policy*, London: HMSO.

Rose, J. (2009) *The Final Report on the Review of the Primary Curriculum*, London: DCSF.

Sefton-Green, J. and Sinker, R. (eds) (2000) *Evaluating Creativity: Making and Learning by Young People*, London: Routledge.

Sternberg, R. J. (1999) (ed.) *Handbook of Creativity*, New York: Cambridge University Press.

Stiggins, R. J. (2002) Assessment crisis: the absence of assessment for learning, *Phi Delta Kappan* 83(1): 758–65.

Torrance, E. P. (1974) *Torrance Tests of Creative Thinking*, Bensenville, IL: Scholastic Testing Service, Inc.

Torrance, H. and Pryor, J. (1998) *Investigating Formative Assessment: Teaching, Learning and Assessment in the Classroom*, Buckingham: Open University Press.

Webster, P. (1992) Research on creative thinking in music, in R. Colwell (ed.) *Handbook of Research on Music Teaching and Learning*, New York: Schirmer Books.

16

Approaches to promoting creativity in Chinese, Japanese and US preschools

Joseph Tobin, Akiko Hayashi and Jie Zhang

Introduction

In this chapter we present examples of how contemporary preschools in China and Japan are approaching the task of promoting young children's creativity.

Our topic is not to provide an overview of Japanese and Chinese approaches to arts education for young children, but instead creativity education. Arts is of course part of this story, but in China and Japan thinking about promoting creativity in young children does not center on the arts, as it does, for example, in the US, but instead is more broadly focused on education across the content areas and even beyond the content areas to the domain of interpersonal relations.

Our aim is not to present an encyclopedic description of how Japanese and Chinese preschools support the development of children's creativity but rather to provide some examples of Japanese and Chinese practices that challenge some central assumptions and in this way to introduce a critique of the ethnocentrism that characterizes much of the Western discourse about creativity, especially as applied to education and specifically to early childhood education. China and Japan are interesting contrastive cases because while they share some cultural antecedents and have had some mutual influence on each other, they have also had different histories and different contemporary socio-political-economic contexts and pressures that lead to different approaches to promoting creativity in young children.

The examples we draw on in this paper come from the study *Preschool in Three Cultures Revisited* (Tobin, 2009), a sequel to Tobin, Wu, and Davidson's 1989 *Preschool in Three Cultures: China, Japan, and the United States*. While the examples come from the new study, the analyses we present in this chapter extend the arguments in the book. Because much has already been published in English about creativity in US preschools, we focus in this chapter on China and Japan.

In the *Preschool in Three Cultures* studies we employed a research method we formally call "video-cued multivocal ethnography," but that others most often refer to as "the Preschool in Three Cultures method." In this method we make a twenty-minute video of a day in a preschool in each culture, and then use this video as a cue for interviewing teachers about their notions of best practice.

We show teachers the videotape we made of a typical day in their classrooms and ask them to explain the thinking behind the practices seen in the video. We also show these videos to other teachers and directors in each country, to get a sense of variations within each nation in how educators think and talk about their notions of best practice. In this chapter we present three examples each from the Japanese and Chinese videos, examples that show teachers engaging in practices they identified as promoting creativity.

Japan

Mastering forms

In one of the scenes in the video we shot in 2002 at Komatsudani Hoikuen in Kyoto, the teacher, Morita-sensei, leads the children in an activity of making fish out of origami paper. Throughout the activity Morita-sensei stands in front of the class demonstrating how to fold the paper and giving the children detailed instruction:

> [Folding two opposite corners of her square piece of paper in half] First we make a triangle. That's right. Our fish are now triangles. And then, fold in both sides, right. Like that, just like when you make a tulip. Then fold the two end points in, like this. And one more fold, like this. Got it? Good. No? Here, I'll help you.

To many early childhood educators in the US, this scene may seem to have little to do with creativity. All of the children in the class are instructed to make the same fish following the teacher's instruction and modeling. The children's only opportunities to make choices were in the color of paper they selected at the start and the location of the eyes they drew on the fish at the finish. The lesson contradicts several of the central Western notions of creative art activities for young children (McArdle and Piscitelli, 2002): it is teacher initiated and directed, non-individualized, and product driven.

Japanese educators who watched the origami scene found it to be such a routine classroom activity as to merit little explanation. All Japanese children are taught origami, both at home and in preschool, and the learning generally follows this pedagogical structure of the adult modeling and the child following, first learning the standard folds, then learning to make basic structures, and then combining these basic structures into increasingly complex ones. Japanese teachers often refer to these pedagogical steps using the terms *dō* ("way" or "path") and *kata* (form). To become a creative artist you have to first master the various *kata* (forms) of a *dō* (way or school). As discussed by Matsunobu in Chapter 5, creativity requires first mastering forms and rules, then extending them, and finally breaking rules and playing with established forms. There is therefore no contradiction in Japan, as there is many Western cultural notions, between creativity and direct instruction, repetition, and following models. These assumptions of Japanese art and aesthetics are mirrored in the pedagogy of the origami lesson.

Children's fighting and interpersonal creativity

The development of creativity in young children at Komatsudani is promoted not only or primarily in structured activities, such as the origami lesson, but also in activities that are purposely unstructured. As a contrast to the teacher-imposed structure of the origami lesson, we present as a second example from Komatsudani a scene in our video that shows Nao-chan, the youngest girl in the class, fighting over a teddy bear with four other girls during a free play period, as described in *Preschool in Three Cultures Revisited*:

> Yoko and the twins Reiko and Seiko are pulling and tugging on the teddy bear as Maki attempts to mediate. With help from Yoko and Seiko, Reiko eventually comes away with the bear. Nao tries to grab it away from Reiko, and Seiko intervenes, pulling on the back of Nao's dress. The three girls fall to the floor into a pile of twisting, pushing and pulling bodies. From across the room, we hear Morita-sensei call out "*Kora kora, kora kora*" (which has a meaning somewhere between "Hey!" and "Stop"), but she doesn't come over to break up the fight. Eventually, Reiko emerges from the pile with the bear, which she puts under her dress (making her appear pregnant) and then crawls under the table, where it will be harder for Nao to get at her. Reiko tells Nao, "Stop it. It's not yours, it's Reiko's." Maki suggests that Reiko should give the bear to Nao. Reiko pokes her head out from under the table and Nao says to her, "Give it to me." Seiko, Reiko, and Maki discuss what to do. Reiko says to Seiko, "You should scold her!" Seiko admonishes Nao, "That's bad! You can't just grab the bear away like that!" Nao responds, "But I had it first." Seiko replies, "But then you put it down, so your turn was over." Nao is led away to the other side of the room by Reiko, who says to her, "You can't do that. Do you understand? Promise?" Linking little fingers with Nao, the two girls swing their arms back and forth as they sing, "Keep this promise, or swallow a thousand needles." Reiko then puts her arm around Nao's shoulders and says to Nao, "Understand? Good."

When we sat down with Morita-sensei and showed her this scene from the video and asked for her reflections, she connected her non-intervention with the development of creativity:

> It is important for children to think by themselves. Children create their own rules during interactions in fights. For example, one girl says, "OK, I'll let you have this today, and you let me have it tomorrow." The important thing here is how to solve the problem on their own.

Morita-sensei emphasized that even if the children's solution to such an interpersonal problem does not seem just or logical to adults, it is important that she does not intervene, because to do so would be to undermine the children's collaborative engagement in creative problem solving. This pedagogical approach suggests that creativity is best taught indirectly. Supporting creativity requires restraint from teachers. As Morita explained: "If I intervene and tell the children to do this or that, it would be easy and quick. But it is important for children to think by themselves."

Another key point we take from this example is that creativity in Japanese early childhood is associated as much or more with the domain of social and interpersonal relations as with art. The Japanese national guidelines for early childhood education emphasize the importance of developing children's critical thinking skills, creativity, "education of the heart," social mind-edness (*shūdan shugi*), group-living skills (*shakai seikatsu*) and social relations (*shūdan seikatsu*). The guidelines state that children should have opportunities to "experience enjoyment and sadness together through establishing active relationships with friends" and to progress in their under-standing of the need for society to have rules, in this case, rules for sharing and turn-taking (Oda and Mori, 2006). An implication of the guidelines is that creativity and social relations are not separate domains but instead integrally connected. No problem a teacher could construct for her class could be as cognitively challenging and compelling or as demanding of creative problem solving as the interpersonal problems among classmates that arise spontaneously in the course of a preschool class day. These problems can become opportunities for creative problem solving only if and when teachers restrain themselves from intervening too quickly or aggressively.

Another point this example suggests is that creativity in Japanese early childhood education is seen as an activity and attribute of a group of children rather than of an individual. Morita-sensei says not that a particular child came up with a creative solution to the teddy bear dispute but instead that the group of children involved in the dispute collaboratively came up with a solution—the verb she used was *dekite kuru*—the solution "came out." This emphasis on creativity as a function of groups rather than individuals can also be seen in the popularity of whole class art projects in Japanese preschools, where groups of children will spend from several hours to several weeks constructing art works of a size and level of ambition too large for any single child to attempt on his/her own.

Free play in and with nature

As at Komatsudani Hoikuen, much of the day at both Madoka Yōchien (Kindergarten) in Tokyo is spent in unstructured play in the playground. When we asked Madoka's Director Machiyama to explain his school's curricular approach, he replied:

> The building and grounds are the curriculum. I worked for several years with an architect to design the building and grounds so that the whole school would be the children's play thing. The central idea is that the school is the children's toy. It was designed to be played with in various ways.

This concept is explained in more detail in the school's brochure for parents, which emphasizes that Madoka's physical layout offers children the chance to experience *anākī* (anarchy/spontaneity) and *ajito* by being organized with attention to *dō sen* ("lines of flow"), which the director explained means organizing the curriculum according to the anticipated routes children will take through the school. In our interviews at Madoka, Director Machiyama and the teachers frequently used the word *asobi* (play) to explain the preschool's pedagogy and curriculum. Director Machiyama described Madoka's curricular approach as *nobi nobi kyōiku* ("room to stretch" or "feel at ease"), with an emphasis on *jiyu asobi* (free play).

Free play can be enjoyed inside the classrooms. But Director Machiyama emphasized the special value of providing children with opportunities to engage freely with nature and the outdoors. Machiyama told us that because Madoka is situated in an urban neighborhood of Tokyo, he gave special attention to constructing the building and grounds so as to encourage the children to interact with the natural world. It might sound paradoxical to design and construct school grounds that provide children with contact with nature, but this paradox has a long tradition in Japanese aesthetics, which emphasize the poignancy of recreating and representing nature in human-built, miniature versions, such as the Zen garden. The fact that nature at Madoka is constructed does not mean that children have less contact with nature, but rather that nature is more compactly and concisely available to them. Within the enclosed acre of Madoka's playground there is an area of mountains (a two-meter high dirt hill), a river (a winding 50-centimeter wide stream), and a secret wood (a narrow pathway behind the administrative office planted with bushes and small trees).

The link between nature and creativity in Japan is complex: because (actual) nature is not human made, (re)creating nature requires creativity. Art in a sense is nature's opposite. The challenge of art is artificially and artfully (and therefore creatively) to represent nature. In the

Japanese aesthetic tradition such representations of nature therefore are less often realistic than highly stylized. The outdoor space at Madoka is such a stylized version of nature, providing a binary contrast to the school building, which is itself a stylized, playful version of the surrounding urban built environment. Madoka's pedagogical guiding assumption is that providing children with ample opportunities to experience the binary of the building and grounds and to explore simulations of the natural world on the hills, streams, and woods of the school grounds will allow children to both develop an aesthetic sensibility and to creatively interact with nature. Children at Madoka are encouraged not just to see and be in nature but to engage with their bodies, climbing, picking up leaves and insects, and getting dirty. In highly urbanized and increasingly urbanizing settings in Japan, as in other countries, in addition to taking urban children on occasional field trips out of the city to experience nature, efforts must also be made to bring nature inside the perimeter of the school and to thereby make it accessible on a daily basis.

China

Our Chinese examples come from two preschools. One, Daguan Kindergarten, where we videotaped both in 1984 and twenty years later, is in Kunming, the capital city of Yunnan Province in the Southwest of China. The other is Sinanlu, a well-known, progressive kindergarten in Shanghai, which is widely considered to be China's most economically advanced and international city.

Block play and creativity

The description of block play at Daguan 1989 in *Preschool in Three Cultures* is characteristic of Chinese pedagogy of that era:

> The children are told to sit at their desks. Once they are seated, the teachers distribute wooden parquetry blocks to each child. The blocks come in a small box, which also contains pictures of several structures that can be made with them. Ms. Xiang says to the students: "We all know how to build with blocks, right? Just pay attention to the picture of the building and build it. When we play games like this, we must use our minds, right? Once you are done, raise your hand and one of us will come by and check to make sure you've done it correctly. Begin. Do your best. Build according to order.
>
> (Tobin et al., 1989: 77–8)

The contrast with block play at Daguan a generation later is dramatic. In the video shot in 2002 we hear the teacher tell the children: "In a moment, I will take you downstairs to play in the block room. What will you build with the blocks? Build whatever you like. Let's see which of you builds the best things." The mood in the block room throughout this period was loud and exuberant, with children running, laughing, and screaming and the teachers joining them in their play.

The change in mood and tone between block play at Daguan circa 1984 and 2002 reflects the impact of the paradigm shift announced in the 2001 *Guidelines for Kindergarten*, which called for the introduction of a curriculum featuring "play-based teaching and learning," "active learning," and "respecting children," all of which are seen as components of promoting creativity, as the classroom teacher Dong-laoshi's reflections on the activity suggest:

> Each child used to get a small box of blocks, a practice that we can see now limited their creativity and imagination. Children who worked with the small blocks individually missed

out on the pleasure of sharing and cooperating with others. Now we have introduced the large blocks, which afford an opportunity for children to play together, providing a much larger space for them to build, exchange, and cooperate. This activity is conducive to the development of children's creativity and imagination.

These two block scenes nearly twenty years apart are a good example of a change both in material conditions and in educational philosophy that reflects Daguan's (and China's) dramatic economic rise and social transformation. In 1984 children at Daguan played with blocks sitting at desks in a gray cement room, following the explicit directions of their teachers. In 2002 the children play in a brightly colored room, dedicated to block play, with their teachers following the children's lead.

Why this change in pedagogy and the new emphasis on promoting the development of creativity? Between the periods of the old and new *Preschool in Three Cultures* studies China has become an enthusiastic and strikingly successful player in the global capitalist economy. The economic and social reforms put forward in the 1980s by Deng Xiaoping, who is widely credited as "the architect of China's economic reforms and China's socialist modernization," featured a strategy of unequal development, encouraging the growth of an entrepreneurial class in the largest cities who would create wealth and jobs that would eventually trickle down to benefit the rest of the society. The logic that ties these economic changes in China to changes in the early childhood education curriculum is explicit: To become a modern nation China must participate successfully in the global economy. To succeed in the global economy, China needs a new kind of citizen, who is more creative, risk taking, and adaptive, as well as bright and well educated. To produce this new citizen, China needs a new educational approach that begins with preschools, which need to shift their curriculum and pedagogy, becoming less didactic and controlling, and more child centered and personalized.

Most of the Chinese early childhood educators we interviewed, though well aware of this reasoning, said that their embrace of the new educational paradigm was based less on the desire to produce little venture capitalists than on their belief in the wisdom and correctness of the new ideas. Therefore, instead of viewing a shift in economic strategy as preceding and causing the changes in Chinese early childhood education philosophy, it is more useful to conceptualize the educational changes as a shift of values, beliefs, and strategies that has occurred simultaneously across multiple social domains, from economics, to politics, to child rearing. The causality goes both ways: a change in economic philosophy and material well-being in the larger society impacts what goes on in preschool classrooms, and what goes on in preschool classrooms exerts an impact, down the road, on the larger society.

Mathematics as a domain of creativity

In contemporary China, the national goal of promoting creativity is more closely tied to the domains of science, mathematics, and with business than with the arts, an emphasis which is mirrored in contemporary early childhood education. An example of this emphasis can be seen in the Sinanlu Kindergarten video pattern activity at Sinanlu. In the video we see Zouzou, a five-year-old boy, sitting on the floor during a free play period, organizing red and yellow plastic chips on a grid. Zouzou then shows his teacher the new pattern he has arranged. During the class gathering that follows, Cheng-laoshi reports, approvingly, to the class that Zouzou's newest arrangement is the fifth type of pattern created since the class began this pattern activity. Zouzou then uses red and blue markers to record his pattern on a piece of paper for the class's future reference.

In a study of mathematics teaching in preschools in China, Japan, and the US, Prentice Starkey and Alice Klein (2007) found China ahead of Japan, and both countries far ahead of the US, in the systematic support of the development of mathematical thinking in young children. In contrast to preschools in the US, where mathematics, when practiced at all in preschools, was limited to the subdomains of numbers (counting) and geometry (shapes), Chinese preschools routinely also support the practice of non-standard measurement and algebraic relations, which for young children usually takes the form of pattern activities. American preschool children routinely are encouraged to make patterned strings of different shapes and colors, as in activities stringing beads or making fruit kebabs (grape, cherry, banana slice, grape, cherry, banana slice), but teachers in the US are rarely aware of the connection of such activities to the development of mathematical reasoning, unlike a teacher such as Cheng-laoshi, who in several ways scaffolds her students experiments in pattern creation and recognition. The task Zouzou engaged in was not simply to make a pattern but to identify the number of unique patterns that could be made with three objects of the same size and shape but of three different colors.

Why this emphasis on creativity in math and science? One answer is that this reflects a traditional value China places on inventiveness and on the domains of excellence in mathematics and science. But there is a new significance and urgency to the effort to make young children creative in mathematics and science. It is tied, explicitly, to the need for China to successfully compete in global capitalism by producing a new generation of creative citizens, creative business, as well as in science, math, and engineering. To produce these new creative citizens who can lead the new economy, there needs to be a new curriculum, starting with the preschool curriculum, a curriculum that supports the development of creative thinkers, not so much in the arts as in the hard sciences and entrepreneurship.

Performance, critique, and creativity

The pattern activity at Sinanlu Kindergarten speaks not only to the new emphasis in China on mathematics as a domain of creative thinking, but also to an older Chinese emphasis on mastery, performance, and competition. Cheng-laoshi urged Zouzou to go beyond his fellow class members in the number of solutions he could devise to this particular pattern problem. When he succeeded she asked him to present his solutions to the class, and encouraged his classmates to applaud his effort.

We can see a more dramatic example of such an emphasis on mastery, performing, and competition in the Sinanlu video in a segment we call "The Storytelling King." In the Sinanlu video we see the whole class gathered on the rug and one boy, Ziyu, standing in front of them to tell a story. Ziyu announces that his story is called "Goodong," an onomatopoeic word for something heavy that drops in a pond. Here's the gist of Ziyu's story: In a forest lived many animals. One day an owl heard a strange noise in the pond, "Goodong," that scared him. He went to tell others. Those who went to check thought that there was a monster in the pond. In the end, a lion went to the pond to check only to find a ripe papaya falling from the tree to make the noise. Everyone was relieved.

Ziyu finished his story, said "Thank you," and took a seat on the floor with his classmates. Ms. Wang, one of the two teachers, asked the children what they had heard in the story. Some children said that there was an owl and the teacher asked what the owl was doing before it heard the noise. This exchange went on for a few turns before Ms. Wang asked the group whether Ziyu could be named Storytelling King. Some said "Yes" and some said "No." The children then voted. Ziyu was invited to count the votes. He won the honor by a majority, with 18 of 24 children voting "Yes." He then wrote his name on the red Storytelling King poster.

Then Ms. Wang said, "Some children didn't raise their hands. Shall we listen to their arguments? Children commented: "That story was like one we heard before." "He was not loud enough." "He did not say things clearly sometimes." Ms. Wang turned to Ziyu and asked if he agreed. He thanked his classmates for their comments and selected a storyteller for the next day.

Teacher Cheng explained how the Storytelling King activity got started:

> In the beginning, children just wanted to listen to a story that the teacher would tell. Later, a couple of children who were interested in telling stories asked if they could come to the front to tell a story. We encouraged them to give it a try. Soon, many children began to prepare their own stories and asked for their turns.

What does this activity have to tell us about creativity in contemporary Chinese early childhood education? We see in the Storytelling King activity an example of the emergence in China of a hybrid pedagogy that combines Chinese and Western pedagogical notions. The Storytelling King activity combines progressive beliefs in child-initiated curricula, a Deweyian notion of the democratic classroom, self-expression, and an emphasis on creativity with Chinese traditions of verbal performance and virtuosity (Paine, 1990), of learning as a process of "self-perfection" (Li, 2003), and a belief that is both traditional and Chinese socialist in the pedagogical value of constructive criticism.

This notion of cultural hybridity complicates the linear story we told in the previous section of China moving inexorably as a nation down a path from more didactic, teacher-directed, knowledge transmission pedagogy towards constructivist, child-initiated, and child-directed pedagogy. A final round of interviews the *Preschool in Three Cultures* research team conducted in 2007 with Chinese early childhood educators suggests that the aggressive push toward progressivism and child-centeredness that characterized Chinese early childhood education from about 1990 to 2006 has begun to be counterbalanced by an acknowledgment of the value of traditional Chinese pedagogical practices, including the value of direct instruction and the mastery of skills. The period of intense borrowing is being replaced by a period of consolidation and hybridization of foreign and domestic educational ideas.

Implicit cultural practices and the global circulation of ideas

Some policy makers in Japan and many in China, perceiving their countries to have a creativity deficit and anxious to implement reforms of education that will redress this perceived deficit, have recently been importing solutions from abroad. China has been doing so enthusiastically for the past twenty years or so, in an attempt to close its perceived creativity gap with its economic competitors. Nations of course should engage in the global exchange of educational ideas. But there can be a cost to doing so. Universalizing approaches to promoting creativity in children, including early childhood curricular approaches imported from abroad, can contribute to an unfortunate undermining of indigenous, culturally constructed approaches, and a homogenization and loss of diversity of ideas and practices, akin to the loss of biodiversity that accompanies the introduction of monoculture agriculture.

In this chapter we have introduced examples of practices in Japanese and Chinese preschools that promote creativity in ways that challenge core assumptions of Western notions of creativity and of Western early childhood educational curriculum and pedagogy. We call these approaches to promoting creativity "implicit cultural practices," by which we mean practices that though not taught explicitly in schools of education or written down in textbooks reflect an implicit cultural logic. This concept is akin to Jerome Bruner's concept of teachers' "folk pedagogy" (Bruner, 1996: 46) and to what Kathryn Anderson-Levitt (2002) calls teachers' "knowledge in practice."

The examples we have presented here are of practices found in Japanese and Chinese pre-schools that for the most part are not explained in textbooks and not taught systematically in pre-service teacher education programs. Instead they are passed on from one generation to the next via an apprenticeship model, in which new teachers learn what to do from more experienced teachers. Because these practices are implicit, they do not have much explicit support, but neither do they have much opposition. They are for the most part unmarked and, from the Japanese and Chinese perspective, unremarkable, not needing explanation, justification, or codification. Therefore, even during periods of reform, when other aspects of curriculum and pedagogy change, sometimes dramatically, these culturally implicit beliefs and practices endure.

The Japanese and Chinese cultural implicit practices we have presented here challenge some core Western notions of what creativity is and how it should be produced in young children. These include challenges to the idea that creativity is an individual rather than a collective endeavor; that creativity works in opposition to the mastery and repetition of already existing forms; that, especially in young children, critical feedback quashes creativity; and that the primary domain of creativity is in the arts.

If we had the opportunity to advise policy makers and educators in China and Japan, we would urge them, as they engage with globally circulating ideas, to value more highly their own indigenous ideas and practices, and not be in a rush to replace them. Our advice for policy makers and educators in the West would be to become more aware of the implicit cultural values in ideas about creativity that we tend to think of as universal and to be open to exposure to unfamiliar ideas from abroad. A bringing together of external and indigenous ideas can lead to the formation of new exciting approaches, such as the hybrid approach we see in the Storytelling King activity. Approaches to creativity themselves need to be creative, building on a mastery of pre-existing forms to develop new approaches suited to changing local conditions.

References

Anderson-Levitt, M. K. (2002) *Teaching Cultures: Knowledge for Teaching First Grade in France and the United States (Language & Social Processes)*, Creskill, NJ: Hampton Press.

Bruner, J. (1996) *The Culture of Education*, Cambridge, MA: Harvard University Press.

Li, J. (2003) The core of Confucian learning, *American Psychologist* 58: 146–7.

McArdle, F. and Piscitelli, B. (2002) Early childhood art education: a palimpsest, *Australian Art Education* 25 (1): 11–15.

Oda, Y. and Mori, M. (2006) Current Challenges of kindergarten (Yochien) education in Japan: toward balancing children's autonomy and teachers' intention, *Childhood Education* 82(6): 369–73.

Paine, L. (1990) The teachers as virtuoso: a Chinese model for teaching, *Teachers College Record* 92(1): 49–81.

Starkey, P. and Klein, A. (2007) Sociocultural influences on young children's mathematical knowledge, *Contemporary Perspectives on Mathematics in Early Childhood Education*, Charlotte, NC: Information Age Publishing Inc.

Tobin, J., Hsueh, Y., and Karasawa, M. (2009) *Preschool in Three Cultures Revisited: China, Japan, and the United States*, Chicago: University of Chicago Press.

Tobin, J., Wu, D., and Davidson, D. (1989) *Preschool in Three Cultures: Japan, China, and the United States*, New Haven, CT: Yale University Press.

17

Contemporary aesthetic theory and models of creativity in visual arts education in the United States

Tracie E. Costantino

Models of creativity in contemporary visual arts education reflect changes in modern and contemporary aesthetic theory, while at the same time remaining consistent with the tradition in the United States, at least, of an economic justification for art education dating back to the nineteenth century Massachusetts Drawing Act (Efland, 1990), and manifested currently in the call for twenty-first century learning skills to prepare workers for today's "creative industries" (Matheson, 2006; Pink, 2006). To put contemporary models into historical perspective, and to emphasize the relationship between contemporary art practice and aesthetics and art education curriculum in the United States, this chapter will begin with a brief overview of trends in twentieth century conceptions of creativity in visual arts education, starting with a discussion of Viktor Lowenfeld. Lowenfeld's (1947) conception of creativity as focused on the individual's self-expression and reflecting modernist art and aesthetic theories had a powerful influence on K-12 art education for over 40 years in the United States. I will then address postmodern aesthetic theories, such as Dickie's (1974) institutional theory of contemporary art, the social activist trend in contemporary art reflected in Suzi Gablik's (1991) call for a reenchantment of art, embodiment theory (e.g. Haworth, 1997), and Nicolas Bourriaud's (2002) relational aesthetics, and how they relate to a systems model of creativity, as in Csikszentmihalyi's (1988, 1999) domain theory. I will discuss how these contemporary models of creativity are reflected in K-12 art education in the United States through a selected review of literature since 1990, focusing on social reconstructionist curricular approaches, including Visual Culture Art Education (Freedman, 2003; Freedman and Stuhr, 2004), *art for life* (Anderson and Milbrandt, 2005), and ecological art education (Gradle, 2007; Graham, 2007), as well as embodiment and art education (e.g. Bresler, 2004), and creativity through interdisciplinary curriculum (e.g. Parsons, 2004). I will conclude the chapter by noting the tension between a market-driven valuing of creativity in some national educational policy with the contemporary social reconstructionist aims of art education curriculum theory.

Historical trends in conceptualizing creativity in art education

The relative emphasis on creativity in art education theory and curriculum practice reflects trends in the artworld as well as societal values manifested in education policies. Both influence art education practice at the classroom level. How creativity has been defined and recognized throughout the twentieth and into the twenty-first century reflects modernist and postmodernist values developed in the twentieth century. I use the term postmodernism to reflect a paradigm that critiques the emphasis on progress, the individual, and art-for-art's sake hailed by modernism, and instead values pluralism and the relativity of knowledge, and emphasizes the situated experience of individuals in relation to their sociocultural context. The definition and recognition of creativity also reflect the academic disciplines and standards movements of the mid- to late twentieth century, and the pressures of globalization in the twenty-first century.

Viktor Lowenfeld

Viktor Lowenfeld's profound influence on art education in the twentieth century has been extensively explored. Nonetheless, for this chapter, it is important to start the discussion with Lowenfeld as he is typically represented as the exemplar for a modernist art education theorist. Lowenfeld's views of creativity are articulated in his textbook *Creative and Mental Growth*, which was published in numerous editions, the later editions with W. Lambert Brittain. Lowenfeld's emphasis on children's creativity as intrinsically motivated and encouraged through an environment that supports exploration reflects a modernist emphasis on the individual, freedom of ideas, and manipulation of media for expressive potential. The relationship between identification of creativity in children's art at this time and modern artists such as Paul Klee, Picasso, and Jean Arp has been addressed elsewhere (e.g. Fineberg, 1997) and critiqued for its limiting view of artistic development (e.g. Pariser, 1997). However, it is important to note that Lowenfeld did not specifically advocate a complete hands-off approach by the teacher, but was more concerned with an overemphasis by art teachers on a rapid sequence of finished products in a variety of media:

> The danger is that students may begin to feel that art is nothing more than a series of little projects or a series of experimentations with materials, bearing little relationship to expression or creativity ... Fluency of ideas, flexibility of approaches, originality of responses, and seeing new relationships are apparently not nurtured by a smorgasbord of art projects.
>
> *(Lowenfeld and Brittain, 1982: 88–9)*

Lowenfeld's ideas were applied to the extreme in many art classrooms in the United States, so that art education was perceived as a loosely structured, anything-goes time of free exploration by the later twentieth century. This was, of course, misaligned with an increasingly standardized view of curriculum and schooling.

Discipline-based art education

The onset of the disciplinary movement spurred by the launch of Sputnik by the Soviet Union called for a different application of creativity from Lowenfeld's emphasis on individual self-expression to one working in the service of American global economic and political power. Discipline-based art education (DBAE) grew out of the disciplinary movement of the 1950s and 1960s influenced by the writings of Jerome Bruner (1960) to become codified as the dominant approach to art education curriculum throughout the 1980s and 1990s. While the overt aim of DBAE was not in the service of American economic dominance, it was influenced by the focus on the development of students' academic knowledge in specific subject matter. The DBAE approach can be distinguished by its subject-centered focus that brought the content of art to the fore as represented through art history, aesthetics, art criticism, and artmaking, raising the profile of art as an intellectual discipline with distinct knowledge, skills, and modes of inquiry. Unlike Lowenfeld's focus on the child, DBAE emphasized the value of the work of adult artists on artmaking within a cultural context. Indeed, in a retrospective discussion of DBAE by Stephen Dobbs (2004), creativity is hardly mentioned, except in relation to how DBAE is different from Lowenfeld's creative self-expression paradigm. Instead, Dobbs values the DBAE approach for building minds, creating problem solvers, and transmitting cultural heritage, which he sees as more in line with the general mission of schooling (ibid.: 701–2). While building minds and creating problem solvers are desired outcomes often associated with developing creativity, this was not the association intended by advocates of DBAE. Related to the emphasis on academic development at this time, identifying gifted art students was more of a focus than the notion of fostering the creativity of all students through art (see Clark and Zimmerman, 2001).

Contemporary viewpoints

Perhaps as a reaction to the dominance of the DBAE paradigm, with its emphasis on studying the work of adult artists, a more recent book by George Szekely (2006) implicitly recalls Lowenfeld by again focusing on the child's perspective about artmaking, asking art teachers to bring the practices of children's play and artmaking in the home to the art classroom. Szekely sees great creativity in children's home art studios, and advises art teachers to use children's art, not adult art, as exemplars for their lessons.

Szekely's voice is in the minority in contemporary discussions of creativity in art education as Lowenfeld's ideas are frequently critiqued in contemporary art education. In a reconsideration of Lowenfeld's contribution to art education, Judith Burton reflects that "Lowenfeld was less interested in what one might call the social purposes or *pragmatic* outcomes of creativity than he was in its quieter workings in how individuals functioned within, and made sense of, their worlds" (Burton, 2009: 323). The valuing of pragmatic outcomes for creativity, where creativity should be applied to economic competitiveness in a global marketplace as well as addressing pressing social issues, is reflected in the innovation agenda of the United States Department of Education, as well as the inclusion of creativity in the National Curriculum of Great Britain.

Contemporary art education theory, however, is more interested in the social purposes of creativity, reflecting a postmodern paradigm that puts creativity and artmaking in cultural context and values a plurality of perspectives. Kerry Freedman, an influential voice in contemporary postmodern art education discourse, sees the aim of art education as "help[ing] students understand the visual arts as *creative, social action*" (Freedman, 2007: 205). Enid Zimmerman, a longstanding scholar of creativity in art education, calls for acknowledgment of diverse cultural perspectives that define creativity:

> In respect to intercultural and global perspectives, contemporary notions about creativity and art talent development in a variety of contexts needs [sic] to be reconsidered to acknowledge a more inclusive paradigm than the pervasive notion of creative acts only as generation of original ideas and products made by a few individuals who change cultural domains.
>
> (Zimmerman, 2009: 391)

These ideas will also be evident in current models of creativity in art education practice. Like Lowenfeld's conception of creativity in art, these ideas are influenced by contemporary aesthetics and contemporary definitions of creativity.

Contemporary theories of aesthetics, creativity, and art education curriculum

Postmodern theories of art are characterized in part by the assertion that the artwork (whether permanent, impermanent, performative, digital, virtual, etc.) is situated in a particular context and is defined and evaluated by that context. The theories to be discussed here, Dickie's (1974) institutional theory, Gablik's (1991) reenchantment of art, an interest in embodiment (e.g. Haworth, 1997), and Bourriaud's (2002) relational theory, are influential in contemporary art education and have a relationship to a systems theory of creativity (Csikszentmihalyi, 1988, 1999).

The institutional theory and contemporary art education curriculum

Dickie's institutional theory was a paradigm shift in aesthetics that drew from changes in contemporary art since the mid-twentieth century, such as Pop Art, conceptual art, and performance art, which explicitly reflected and critiqued contemporary society and were often content dependent on the physical and cultural context of the artwork's exhibition. Institutional theory also explicitly acknowledges the role art critics, patrons, gallery dealers, and curators play in determining what is accepted as art. As Dickie explains, "The institutional theory of art concentrates attention on the *nonexhibited* characteristics that works of art have in virtue of being embedded in an institutional matrix which may be called 'the artworld' and argues that these characteristics are essential and defining" (Dickie, 1974: 12). Dickie's emphasis on "nonexhibited characteristics" signals a break from the modernist formalist aesthetic theory, which gave primary attention to what was within the physical boundary of the artwork—the elements and principles of design of the composition, as well as Clive Bell's intangible concept of significant form. In this way, the valuing of a creative use of media for individual expression gave way, in the institutional theory, to a valuing of creative conceptualizations. Creativity was seen less in the craft of an object than in the originality of its conception. Dickie's institutional theory of art may be considered a precedent for the expansion of artworks and artmaking considered appropriate for K–12 art education as seen in curricular approaches such as Visual Culture Art Education (VCAE) (Freedman, 2003; Freedman and Stuhr, 2004) and *art for life* (Anderson and Milbrandt, 2005), in which visual and material culture, especially from popular media, are given priority in the curriculum for inquiry and critique.

This creates some tensions: one may ask how artistic creativity (typically conceived of as making something) fits into a curricular approach that emphasizes youth empowerment through the tools of postmodern critique—usually in verbal form. VCAE does allow for visual critique through such postmodern strategies as appropriation, although some might question how creative visual critique is when creativity is defined by originality. Freedman and Stuhr address this from a postmodern paradigm:

> Conceptually grounded production processes cross over traditional boundaries of form, breaking down old borders of media-driven curriculum, and turning curriculum upside-down, so that the development of ideas are [sic] given attention first and the techniques and processes emerge as the expression of those ideas. In this way, technique and media are related to and enhance the making of meaning in creative/critical inquiry. Visual culture is an expression of ideas through the use of technical and formal processes, but these processes are not the main purpose of artistic production. ... Creative production is inherently critical, and critical reflection is inherently creative.
>
> *(Freedman and Stuhr, 2004: 825)*

This reflects a different conception of artistic creativity in which critical insights and under-standings about a social issue, typically represented by or through visual culture, are valued as creative, and not the formal visual expression itself. Criticality is valued as creativity.

The *art for life* (Anderson and Milbrandt, 2005) art education curriculum model for the sec-ondary level is also postmodern. Its comprehensive approach enlarges the four disciplines of DBAE by including visual culture, new technologies, and an emphasis on creativity within a social context. *Art for life* tries to bridge the content and skill development focus of discipline-based art education with the postmodern emphasis on the contemporary and critique of visual culture so that students may develop their creativity with a foundation of skills applied to authentic concerns that are personally and socially relevant. I include *art for life* here especially for its prioritization of creativity as one of its curricular foci. It is influenced by Dickie's insti-tutional theory of art as it sees creativity as defined within a sociocultural context. It is also important to include here as it presents a different justification for creativity in the art education curriculum from the criticality emphasized in VCAE. Anderson and Milbrandt recognize the value of authentic creative expression for cognitive development, especially for the role meta-phor plays in creativity and imagination:[1] "Art education should center creativity and meta-cognition so that students will develop higher-level thinking and the deeper learning that result from authentic instruction" (ibid.: 68). In describing creativity within the *art for life* model, Anderson and Milbrandt cite Csikszentmihalyi's systems theory of creativity as a primary resource in their conceptual framework.

The systems theory and contemporary art education curriculum

Anderson and Milbrandt (2005) highlight Csikszentmihalyi's idea that creativity is not solely a mental process but defined and valued according to the social and historical context in which a creative idea is made manifest: thus their emphasis on creativity within a social context for art education, not solely for individual self-expression.

Csikszentmihalyi defines creativity, within a systems framework, as "a phenomenon that is constructed through an *interaction between producer and audience*. Creativity is not the product of single individuals, but of social systems making judgments about individuals' products" (Csiks-zentmihalyi, 1999: 314). His systems model consists of three areas that intersect: the individual, the "domain" of the cultural or symbolic, and the social, which he calls the field. This defini-tion is consonant with Dickie's institutional theory of art, especially when the audience may be considered as the artworld with the power to decide which artists are exhibited. However, Csikszentmihalyi's model can also be applied to a less elite field, such as when art educator Ralph Smith (2006) includes students and art teachers as a part of the artworld in which his percipience curriculum is training students to sojourn (although Smith has been critiqued for being too elitist in his emphasis on Western traditions of fine art for the curriculum).[2] The systems theory of creativity also applies to a visual culture approach to art education (VCAE) as the domain and field sectors recognize the creativity in products and ideas presented by indivi-duals in popular, digital, and social media, for example. These are key areas for visual and verbal inquiry in VCAE because they have such an influence on youth. The systems theory of crea-tivity also applies to discipline-based art education, with curriculum centered on exemplar works of art by adult artists that have been recognized by Dickie's artworld institutions.

Within postmodern approaches to art education like VCAE and *art for life*, there is a promi-nent social reconstructionist aim for education that is not necessarily the case in Dickie's insti-tutional theory of art, where ethical concerns are not among the primary criteria for determining the value of an object as a successful work of art worthy of exhibit. Suzi Gablik

(1991), however, writes about the ethical engagement of artists with the world, especially concerning ecological issues, and her work has been influential on another trend in art education theory, ecological art education. Gablik rejects the aloofness of modernism and the emphasis on the individual's isolation for creating works of artistic genius (a conceptualization articulated by the Renaissance biographer Vasari in the sixteenth century in reference to Michelangelo that has had lasting influence on how artists are viewed), and seeks a reenchantment of art that emphasizes interconnectedness and social responsibility:

> I believe there is a new, evolving relationship between personal creativity and social responsibility, as old modernist patterns of alienation and confrontation give way to new ones of mutualism and the development of an active and practical dialogue with the environment.
>
> *(Gablik, 1991: 6)*

In 2007, the art education journal *Studies in Art Education* devoted a whole issue to ecological art education (vol. 48, no. 4), with Suzi Gablik contributing an article. In this issue, and elsewhere, art educators Mark Graham and Sally Gradle, for example, discuss curricular projects with high school students (Graham, 2007) (see also Spickard Prettyman and Gargarella, 2006) and preservice art teachers (Gradle, 2007) that invoke artmaking for a valuing of place. These authors also aim to raise awareness about the interconnectedness of humans with the natural and built environment.

Gradle (2007) employs a phenomenological approach to both research and curriculum development that emphasizes students' interactions with their environment as a way of knowing. Intellectually this work builds on both John Dewey's pragmatist aesthetics of art as experience, and also on Merleau-Ponty's phenomenology of the 1940s, which he applied to aesthetics in his *Phenomenology of Perception* and essays such as "Eye and Mind," exploring the role of seeing—perception—in knowing through the body's interaction with the world. He writes:

> The eye is an instrument that moves itself, a means which invents its own ends; it is *that which* has been moved by some impact of the world, which it then restores to the visible through the traces of the hand.
>
> *(Merleau-Ponty, 1993: 127)*

In his writings Merleau-Ponty applied his embodiment theory of art to the work of modern artists such as Cézanne and Matisse. John Haworth sees relevance in Merleau-Ponty's embodiment theory for contemporary art, applying it to two international artists (Michael Rothenstein and Alan Green) that exemplify "Merleau-Ponty's emphasis on the reciprocal influence of consciousness, the body, technique and materials and the importance of matrices of ideas" (Haworth, 1997: 138), as well as conceptual artists such as Sol Lewitt.

In addition to Sally Gradle's embodiment theory of ecological art education, there is a growing international trend in arts education curriculum theory relating to the role of the body in cognition as manifested through arts practice (see Bresler, 2004 and the section on the body in Bresler, 2007). Interest in the body in arts education rejects the debunked Cartesian separation of mind and body in favor of the current definition of cognition that recognizes the inseparableness of mind–body. This is reflected in the term embodied cognition. Specifically in relation to creativity, neuroscientists Helen Immordino-Yang and Antonio Damasio (2007) have developed the term emotional thought to further explicate the mind–body interrelationship and consider the role of feelings and emotion, arising in body–mind, fundamental to the creative process. Embodiment theory is perhaps more developed in dance, drama, and music education, although it is gaining interest in art education, especially from a postmodern, visual culture perspective as the popular media projects body images and ways of being that are highly influential on youth (see Duncum and Springgay in Bresler, 2007).

Although not framed literally in terms of embodiment, Bourriaud's (2002) relational theory of art is relevant for this wider discussion as it engages with notions of the institution of the artworld, especially in looking at art from the 1990s, in order to consider how contemporary art reflects and engages with contemporary society. He writes:

> The possibility of a *relational* art (an art taking as its theoretical horizon the realm of human interaction and its social context, rather than the assertion of an independent and *private* symbolic space), points to a radical upheaval of the aesthetic, cultural and political goals introduced by modern art.
>
> *(Bourriaud, 2002: 14)*

Similar to Gablik's reenchantment of art, Bourriaud sees numerous contemporary artists striving to engage the viewer physically in discussions about the "communication superhighway" (ibid.: 8) in the spaces of art that can create a "hands-on civilization" (ibid.: 15), "which takes being-together as a central theme and focuses on the 'encounter' between beholder and picture, and the collective elaboration of meaning" (ibid.: 15). Calling art a "social interstice," (ibid.: 16) Bourriaud recognizes some contemporary artists suggest a different way of relating, one that is not dependent on commerce. While Bourriaud is not prominent as a theoretical influence on art education conceptions of creativity, he seems particularly relevant for museum education and the aesthetics and art criticism components of K-12 art curriculum, such as in VCAE and *art for life*. For example, Helene Illeris (2010) has used Bourriaud as a theoretical framework in a study investigating the relevance of contemporary art for adolescents visiting a contemporary art museum. Bourriaud's relational theory of art also relates strongly to Csikszentmihalyi's systems theory of creativity, as Bourriaud judges the value of a work of art on both aesthetic criteria (which he defines as the "coherence of its form"; Bourriaud, 2002: 18) and the insight it provokes about its sociohistorical context, or, as Bourriaud explains, "the symbolic value of the 'world' it suggests to us, and of the image of human relations reflected by it" (ibid.: 18). This relational theory sets up a dialogical relationship between the individual, domain (symbolic) and field (social) within Csikszentmihalyi's systems theory as the artist comments on society and society determines the insightfulness of the artist's representation. Bourriaud's relational theory could also provide an alternative inspiration for creative art production in K-12 art curriculum, with its emphasis on human interactions in a physical space that brings people together, instead of the "communication superhighway" under critical analysis from the VCAE curriculum approach.

A final art education model to discuss which draws from the postmodern interest in contemporary art, the social reconstructionist concern for the environment and other pressing issues, and the interest in the role of metaphor in creativity and developing students' higher order thinking is Michael Parsons' conception of interdisciplinary or integrated curriculum that is focused around social problems (Parsons, 2004). As an example of this approach, Leslie Cunliffe (2008) has looked specifically at the use of interdisciplinary curriculum to foster creativity. Julia Marshall (2005) proposes an interdisciplinary curriculum approach that profiles contemporary artists employing metaphor and collage, and Costantino, Kellam, Cramond, and Crowder (2010) describe an interdisciplinary pilot project integrating art and engineering for developing creativity at the undergraduate level, which also has relevance for K-12 art education.

Conclusion

This review of the relationship between contemporary aesthetic theory and conceptions of creativity in art education in the United States reflects a belief that creativity is not something select people are born with, but that it can be nurtured and developed through education (Nickerson, 1999; Root-Bernstein and Root-Bernstein, 1999). Although political agendas in the United States and Great Britain, for example, hail creativity and innovation in their educational policy rhetoric, while at the same time advocating more standardization and accountability in practice, conceptualizations of creativity in visual arts education reflect social reconstructionist aims that seek to nurture the social purposes of creativity for the betterment of students and the world they will inherit. Bourriaud's relational theory of aesthetics also offers us a theoretical framework for fostering creativity as a major goal for K-12 art education curriculum. Art teachers, then, have varied perspectives to consult for inspiration, whether social reconstructionist or pragmatic. While an overtly social reconstructionist visual critique of contemporary society as advocated by VCAE may not always be viewed as an appropriate example of creativity by some schools and their communities, the emphasis on human relations, aesthetic embodiment, and ecological inter-relationships explored above may provide less politically charged avenues for fostering creativity in a contemporary context. Indeed, the pragmatic educational policy climate advocating for creativity and innovation may at least provide an administrative acceptance at the school level for a greater attention to different manifestations of creativity in the art room, not only exploring how creative products exhibit a care for craft and technique, but also offering creative conceptualizations that reflect students' meaning making about their contemporary experience.

Notes

1 There is a growing interest in applying findings from the cognitive sciences, such as the role of metaphor in cognition, to art education. There is not adequate space in this chapter to address this emerging literature, but the reader may wish to consult Efland (2004) and Costantino (2010), and Heid (2008) for a classroom application.
2 Smith's percipience curriculum deemphasizes art making for creative expression in favor of developing students' perceptual sensitivity to a range of artworks throughout history through art making in the early grades and an emphasis on art history and critical analysis in the later grades.

References

Anderson, T. and Milbrandt, M. (2005) *Art for Life: Authentic Instruction in Art*, New York: McGraw-Hill.
Bourriaud, N. (2002) *Relational Aesthetics* [Esthetique relationnelle] (trans. S. Pleasance, F. Woods and M. Copeland), Paris: Les Presses du Réel.
Bresler, L. (ed.) (2004) *Knowing Bodies, Moving Minds: Towards Embodied Teaching and Learning*, Dordrecht: Kluwer.
—— (2007) *International Handbook of Research in Arts Education*, Dordrecht: Springer.
Bruner, J. (1960). *The process of education*. Cambridge, MA: Harvard University Press.
Burton, J. M. (2009) Creative intelligence, creative practice: Lowenfeld redux, *Studies in Art Education* 50 (4): 323–37.
Clark, G. and Zimmerman, E. (2001) Art talent development, creativity, and enrichment programs for artistically talented students in grades K-8, in M. L. Lynch and C. R. Harris (eds.) *Teaching the Creative Child K-8*, Needham Heights, MA: Allyn and Bacon.
Costantino, T. (2010) The critical relevance of aesthetic experience for twenty-first century art education: the role of wonder, in T. Costantino and B. White (eds.) *Essays on Aesthetic Education for the 21st Century*, Rotterdam: Sense.
Costantino, T., Kellam, N., Cramond, B., and Crowder, I. (2010) An interdisciplinary design studio: how can art and engineering collaborate to increase students' creativity?, *Art Education* 63(3): 49–53.

Csikszentmihalyi, M. (1988) Society, culture, and person: a systems view of creativity, in R. J. Sternberg (ed.) *The Nature of Creativity: Contemporary Psychological Perspectives*, Cambridge: Cambridge University Press.

—— (1999) Implications of a systems perspective for the study of creativity, in R. J. Sternberg (ed.) *Handbook of Creativity*, New York: Cambridge University Press.

Cunliffe, L. (2008) A case study of an extra-curricular school activity designed to promote creativity, *International Journal of Education through Art* 4(1): 91–105.

Dickie, G. (1974) *Art and the Aesthetic: An Institutional Analysis*, Ithaca, NY, and London: Cornell University Press.

Dobbs, S. M. (2004) Discipline-based art education, in E. Eisner and M. Day (eds.) *Handbook of Research and Policy in Art Education*, Reston, VA: National Art Education Association.

Efland, A. (1990) *A History of Art Education: Intellectual and Social Currents in Teaching the Visual Arts*, New York: Teachers College Press.

—— (2004) Art education as imaginative cognition, in E. Eisner and M. Day (eds.) *Handbook of Research and Policy in Art Education*, Reston, VA: National Art Education Association.

Fineberg, J. (1997) *The Innocent Eye: Children's Art and the Modern Artist*, Princeton, NJ: Princeton University Press.

Freedman, K. (2003) *Teaching Visual Culture: Curriculum, Aesthetics, and the Social Life of Art*, New York: London: Teachers College Press.

—— (2007) Artmaking/troubling: creativity, policy, and leadership in art education, *Studies in Art Education* 48(2): 204–17.

Freedman, K. and Stuhr, P. (2004) Curriculum change for the 21st century: visual culture in art education, in E. Eisner and M. Day (eds.) *Handbook of Research and Policy in Art Education*, Reston, VA: National Art Education Association.

Gablik, S. (1991) *The Reenchantment of Art*, New York: Thames and Hudson.

Gradle, S. (2007) Ecology of place: art education in a relational world, *Studies in Art Education* 48(4): 392–411.

Graham, M. (2007) Art, ecology and art education: locating art education in a critical place-based pedagogy, *Studies in Art Education* 48(4): 375–91.

Haworth, J. (1997) Beyond reason: pre-reflexive thought and creativity in art, *Leonardo* 30(2): 137–45.

Heid, K. (2008) Creativity and imagination: tools for teaching artistic inquiry, *Art Education* 61(4): 40–6.

Illeris, H. (2010) Young people and aesthetic experiences: learning with contemporary art, in T. Costantino and B. White (eds.) *Essays on Aesthetic Education for the 21st Century*, Rotterdam: Sense.

Immordino-Yang, H. and Damasio, A. (2007) We feel, therefore we learn: the relevance of affective and social neuroscience to education, *Mind, Brain, and Education* 1(1): 3–10.

Lowenfeld, V. (1947) *Creative and Mental Growth: A Textbook on Art Education*, New York: Macmillan.

Lowenfeld, V. and Brittain, W. L. (1982 [1947]) *Creative and Mental Growth* (7th ed.), New York: Macmillan.

Marshall, J. (2005) Connecting art, learning, and creativity: a case for curriculum integration, *Studies in Art Education* 46(3): 227–41.

Matheson, B. (2006) A culture of creativity: design education and the creative industries, *Journal of Management Development* 25(1): 55–64.

Merleau-Ponty, M. (1993) Eye and mind, in G. A. Johnson and M. B. Smith (eds.) *The Merleau-Ponty Aesthetics Reader: Philosophy and Painting*, Evanston, IL: Northwestern University Press.

Nickerson, R. S. (1999) Enhancing creativity, in R. J. Sternberg (ed.) *Handbook of Creativity*, New York: Cambridge University Press.

Pariser, D. (1997) Conceptions of children's artistic giftedness from modern and postmodern perspectives, *Journal of Aesthetic Education* 31(4): 35–47.

Parsons, M. (2004) Art and integrated curriculum, in E. Eisner and M. Day (eds.) *Handbook of Research and Policy in Art Education*, Reston, VA: National Art Education Association.

Pink, D. (2006) *A Whole New Mind: Why Right-Brainers Will Rule the Future*, New York: Riverhead Books.

Root-Bernstein, R. and Root-Bernstein, M. (1999) *Sparks of Genius: The Thirteen Thinking Tools of the World's Most Creative People*, Boston: Houghton-Mifflin.

Smith, R. (2006) *Culture and the Arts in Education: Critical Essays on Shaping Human Experience*, Reston, VA: National Art Education Association.

Spickard Prettyman, S. and Gargarella, E. B. (2006) Community, collaboration, and creativity: the potential of art education to create change, *Mid-Western Educational Researcher* 19(4): 12–19.

Szekely, G. (2006) *How Children Make Art: Lessons in Creativity from Home to School*, New York and London: Teachers College Press.

Zimmerman, E. (2009) Reconceptualizing the role of creativity in art education theory and practice, *Studies in Art Education* 50(4): 382–99.

18

Drama as creative learning

Jonothon Neelands

We shall make lively use of all means, old and new, tried and untried, deriving from art and deriving from other sources, in order to put living reality in the hands of living people in such a way that it can be mastered.

(Brecht, 1995 [1938]: 189)

Drama education has the potential to be both a discipline in its own right and also a concrete and creative process for learning in other disciplinary or curricular settings. Different modalities of function and purpose may encourage different kinds of creative learning in drama, or at least what is most likely to be valued in a particular context as creative learning. This chapter considers drama both as a site and as a process for creative learning and teaching, and seeks to define some of its specific creative characteristics. The argument is that all forms of drama and theatre have acting at their heart and that learning to act in both the artistic and social sense increases young people's capacity to be socially creative.

Public acts of social and artistic creativity

Drama is considered as site and process because the culture of the drama space itself often has particular physical and psychic qualities which encourage creative processes and interactions. This is most likely to be the case in rehearsal rooms, studios and other places, which become 'open' spaces both in terms of how the space itself is used and constantly re-imagined and in terms of knowledge and the outcomes of the creative work that goes on in that space. In open space learning there are flexible and less hierarchical uses of space: and knowledge is considered provisional, problematic and unfinished. There is often a 'dethroning' of the power of the teacher, leader or director, and an expectation that learning, or rehearsal, will be negotiated and co-constructed. Open space learning requires trust and mutuality amongst participants; the circle is its essential shape. Crucially the space is open to others; it is a shared public space constituted in order to negotiate meanings socially and artistically because, as Dewey (2007: 20) put it, 'things gain meaning by being used in a shared experience or joint action'.

Drama may manifest in different ways for young people; as a curriculum subject in the arts; as an arts process used in other areas of the curriculum; as extra-curricular or community based youth theatre; as rehearsals leading to performance; as entertainment in theatre settings and as vocational training in the skills of acting and directing. It belongs to a group of creative curricular areas young people will encounter over a lifetime, rather than a lesson, in and beyond school and with life-wide impacts.

These different experiences of drama for young people may be more differentiated by pedagogic variables than by modality and function. In other words, the kinds of drama experiences that are available to young people may or may not become 'creative learning' dependent on the pedagogic approach and its effects on the quality of relationships as much as on the quality of learning. Drama is not naturally creative; it has to be processed creatively by teachers and learners.

Because of the dominant tradition of 'realism' that runs through the Euro-American models of drama on stage, screen, radio and in classrooms, there are strong potential links between drama as a creative process with learning in the humanities and Language Arts. Young people can, with relative ease, create naturalistic and lived representations of familiar places, settings and characters which can humanise and personalise their understandings of history, cultural learning, literature and poetry by returning curriculum content to authentic contexts.

At the heart of all forms of drama is the behaviour of the actor – one who acts. The centrality of human action to drama is what defines its claim to be a creative art. Ideas that form in the imagination are only given substance when they become material actions. Aristotle defined an action as an intentional behaviour guided by *phronein* (practical wisdom) which affects the world around us. Mirroring this Aristotelian sense of informed and intentional action, Mason (2003: 232) defines creativity as 'acting in or on the world in new and significant ways'. This definition foregrounds the capacity for human agency to change the world, by working in and on it; acting to make a difference. It is a reminder that the world is brought into being and shaped by human acts. In this sense, the idea of creativity is released from its sometimes vacuous policy rhetoric (Banaji *et al.*, 2006: 5) and rendered as material actions performed by actors for purposes that are new and significant.

Totus Mundus Agit Histrionem was the motto Shakespeare and his partners chose, in 1599, for the entrance to their new theatre – the Globe. The motto is often casually translated as 'All the world's a stage/And all the men and women merely players', but this is a very free translation of the Latin. Perhaps Shakespeare was aware of the subtle ambiguities of language that make a direct translation very difficult. It is also translatable as *a whole world of players; the world makes players of us all; the world provokes us to be players; our plays are driven by the world; the whole world is a playhouse; everyone is an actor.*

There is an important distinction to be made between these translations. In the alternative set we are not 'merely players', we are all social and/or artistic actors driven by events in the world to shape new social and artistic ideas and responses. No one is personal, we are all social and sociable, acting together in and on the world as well as on the stage.

Castoriadis (1997) argues that the germ of democracy that was fermented in fifth century BCE Athens was based in the ideal that a society could continually re-invent itself and the ways in which people lived together through engaging the public imagination, leading to public action based on the principles of equity, fairness and necessary participation. For Castoriadis, the theatre of Athens was a reminder of the imaginary nature of social life and the possibility of social transformations on the scale of the artistic transformations of the stage. This connection between drama and authentic democracy is critical, of course, in any discussion of its creative potential for young people facing an uncertain future.

In the *Fall of Public Man*, Sennett (1993) charts the demise of the idea and expectation that we are all social actors, performing within the polity of the public sphere. He argues that during the nineteenth century, and particularly after the failed European revolutions of 1848, public man withdrew from public life into the intimacies of the private and personal. This turning away from public action and life was mirrored in a growing fear and awe for 'performers' and performing artists and those who dared to act in public. The idea of the actor and acting came to be reserved for the 'unreal' world of the stage, becoming associated with artificial and fake responses, in comparison with the authenticity of an interior life of reaction, contemplation and thought.

Many of us are still wary of doing 'drama' or being made to 'act' because of self-consciousness and a sense that 'acting' is at best foolish and at worst deceptive. And yet, as professionals we consider 'performance data' and expect the minutes of our meetings to include 'action points' which will require social actors to act. In the smallness of these worlds we are still able to recognise the need and responsibility for us to act in new and significant ways in order to create new ways of doing things or to make what we do more ethical, efficient and effective. It is only when we turn to the wider public sphere that we seem to lose confidence in the idea of ourselves as actors whose actions can make a difference to the world we share.

Sennett and Castoriadis describe a historical trajectory away from *participation* to *representation* in the life of the society – a loss of faith in the creative potential of society to act together in order to change the ways in which we live together and with the natural world we depend on.

Participation and improvisation: playing the public

However, in many places there is a tradition of drama education, which stresses active participation and the vitality of human action as a means of transforming both imagined and real worlds. This tradition has its roots in the imaginative and role-taking play of young children and the artistic and educational developments of play into drama which find practical and theoretical expression in the work of the English drama educator Dorothy Heathcote, in particular.

In this form of drama the emphasis is on the orchestration of the 'human voices and movements' (Williams, 1954: 183) within the study-space to co-create an imagined world or context that determines the language and actions of the drama. All present are assumed to be 'players' as well as spectators of their own and others' acting in response to the demands of the imagined world. It is not a form of drama in which it is assumed that only some of us can act whilst the rest can only watch and react. It is a direct rather than directed form of drama that requires social and artistic acting together in order to create imagined worlds and events. Without the social and artistic actions of those present, nothing happens and nothing is made.

The emphasis is on 'acting' to make a difference within the dramatised context in order to illuminate how and why we 'act' in the real world now, historically and in other places different from our own. Young people take on the responsibility of role and respond to the given and virtual circumstances of the drama as-if they were actually inhabiting the situation. The defining, or unique, characteristic of drama as creative learning is that we imagine ourselves differently.

In process drama (O'Neill, 1995), young people are often asked to take on roles in order to solve problems or dilemmas; they are being asked to imagine themselves differently, to re-frame or to re-create themselves as 'others'.

Imagining oneself as the other, trying to find oneself in the other and in so doing to recognise the other in oneself is the crucial and irreducible bridge between all forms of drama and theatre work. Through role-taking young people develop their empathetic imagination and are invited to imagine themselves in new ways: as being confident; assertive; in charge; public; important.

The opportunity to improvise in role in order to bring an imagined world or context into dramatised action and discover what social actions might shape and change whatever problems and dilemmas are presented is inherently creative in a number of ways.

At a personal level, young people are invited to participate in the acts of creation required to construct an imagined world or context. The space and time of the classroom may be transformed through acts of social imagination into other places and times. Through taking on and participating in role, young people are encouraged to look at the world from other perspectives and to consider new alternatives and interpretive choices. Through this activity they may come to be creative in terms of their own personal and social identities – to begin to imagine themselves differently and to find the confidence and imaginative potential to change themselves and the world in actuality, not just in the artistic zone.

Improvisation is itself a generic creative activity that in drama requires young people to imagine and respond to the immediate in ways that are authentic and existential. It is a crucible for the creative exploration of the centrality of social context in determining human agency and capacity. To be authentic, young people must bring what they collectively know about human behaviour (*phronein*) to a newly created situation which requires their verbal and physical responses. These responses, shaped by prior experience, must be 'truthful' to the situation – to the social and cultural conventions and codes that determine the context. Improvisation flexes the muscles of young people's potential to act on and within the constraints or structure of the imagined situation. It provides the direct lived experience of the tension between social and cultural structures and the capacity for human action. The given circumstances of the improvisation determine the authenticity of what can be said and done. Given these circumstances, what can I do and say? How creative can I be within the constraints of the social, cultural and historical protocols associated with the imagined event? Moffett has described improvised drama in classrooms in this way:

> No other activity – except game playing perhaps – puts such constant pressure on the participants to think on their feet, make spontaneous decisions, exercise independence, and respond to the unexpected in a flexible, creative way as dramatic invention does. Drama integrates physical, social, and intellectual forces and undergirds the language arts curriculum because drama is life made conscious.
>
> *(Moffett, 1994: 60)*

Thinking on one's feet, making spontaneous decisions and responding to the unexpected might be considered generic creative behaviours, essential to a wide variety of creative processes in the arts, sciences and, most importantly, in life. Moffett also draws a parallel with games and playing more generally. There would, I'm sure, be a general agreement amongst other contributors to this *Handbook* that 'play' and 'playfulness' are essential to creativity.

The conditions of play

However, in some institutional contexts, play as one of the concepts associated with creativity is considered problematic. Along with the ideas of 'flow' (Cziksentmihalyi, 1990), risk, celebration of failure and discipline-specific creative acts, play challenges the normalities of schooling. How are young people to become absorbed and 'lost' in creative work in a system of short time intervals, changes of space and a prescribed outcomes based valuation system? How can 'risk' be afforded in a hyper-accountable system? How can failure be rewarded in a system that only seeks and rewards moderate(d) success? How can 'fooling around', however purposeful, be seen as legitimate classroom activity?

In his classic analysis of *Homo Ludens*, Huizinga described the conditions of play as:

> An activity, which proceeds within certain limits of time and space, in a visible order, according to rules freely accepted, and outside the sphere of necessity or material utility. The play mood is one of rapture and enthusiasm, and is sacred or festive in accordance with the occasion. A feeling of exaltation and tension accompanies the action, mirth and relaxation follow.
>
> *(Huizinga, 1978: 26)*

The first condition refers to the 'bracketing off' of play episodes from other everyday experiences. Play which is freely and knowingly entered into is time and space limited or at least requires, as in drama and theatre, that for a determined period in a determined space there will be the experiencing of reality as play(ed) rather than as continuous everyday experience. The distinction here is to do with the ontological and epistemological shift that occurs in play episodes where meanings, relationships of power and symbolic systems are disrupted and re-created. We imagine ourselves differently, we ascribe new and sometimes radical meanings to signs and objects, and we alter normative ways of seeing and experiencing. We transform time and place into other times and places. Our relationships become 'playful' rather than determined and fixed. A 'visible order' refers to the 'turn-taking' of participation associated with many playful activities as well as to the agreed structure of play episodes.

In pro-social genres of play, as Huizinga suggests, rules must be freely accepted by those taking part. Drama in schools in particular often requires the taking of extraordinary risks for all involved. The teacher is taking risks in seeking a shift in the normative power relations within the class and between the class and the teacher and even by moving back the desks in some cases. Young people must make themselves vulnerable and visible in order to participate and must know that there is protection and mutual respect for difference from within the group to match the personal and social challenges of taking a part in the action.

In every drama class students have to make a positive choice to join in or not: without this willingness bred of interest and engagement there can be no active drama. Classroom drama has to be by choice. For this reason, drama has often been associated with a rich and engaging pedagogy, based on the open negotiation or contracting of 'rules' which are freely accepted and maintained as a prerequisite for artistic work. These subtle negotiations are in themselves a modelling of direct democracy in which the class as a potential *polis* imagine and create the conditions needed for their full and meaningful participation in the social as well as artistic life of the class as community.

But the other conditions of play, which are also closely associated with process drama, may explain why drama often finds itself outside the formal curriculum. It is outside the 'sphere of necessity or material utility' – it is not necessary work with hard outcomes. Nothing is made or produced that could be of material value. But humans seek the play experience because it produces desirable states of rapture (creative flow) and enthusiasm, as well as feelings of exaltation and tension, mirth and relaxation. How many classrooms are ready to embrace this range of emotions as legitimate to the processes of schooling?

Drama as authentic learning

However, there are at least two main pathways to articulating drama and dramatic play as legitimate and necessary creative learning activities: as a means of humanising and connecting curriculum and as the practice of and for life. The first relates to the highly contextual nature of process drama, which we have discussed. Learning in drama is situational and experienced. In *Children's Minds*, Margaret Donaldson claims:

> Here is the heart of the matter. By the time they come to school, all normal children can show skill as thinkers and language users to a degree which must compel our respect, so long as they are dealing with real life meaningful situations in which they have purposes and intentions and in which they can recognise and respond to similar purposes and intentions in others.
>
> *(Donaldson, 1987: 121)*

Drama makes the abstract concrete and the unfamiliar familiar by embedding the facts and figures of the curriculum into 'real life meaningful situations'. Living and lived human experiences require these facts and figures for human purposes and motives. Slavery is existentially and experientially known and felt to be a dehumanising and degrading experience for its human cargo. Shopkeepers need maths in order to do business.

Donaldson acknowledges that all of our pre-school and much other human learning is embedded in the situation of use. But of course the range of real-life meaningful situations that can be created in school by teachers and children is limited. Unless these situations are imagined, of course. Learning through co-created imagined experience allows teachers and learners to negotiate any context of their choosing and to take on roles and exercise power relationships that are outside their normative range.

This idea that 'real life meaningful situations' help young people to think and act beyond their level is at the core of Heathcote's *Mantle of the Expert* model of drama education, in which young people imagine themselves in expert roles in order to deal with real-world and adult tasks and dilemmas (Heathcote and Bolton, 1996). For instance, a class of urban eight-year-olds in role as 'landscape gardeners' are asked by the teacher in role as the head teacher of a special school to create a garden for her pupils, some of whom are visually impaired and some of whom use wheelchairs. The pupils are asked to use their 'expert' knowledge to negotiate and design together a suitable landscape for the garden and suggest appropriate planting so that all of the pupils can get enjoyment and access the garden. The head teacher also wants her pupils to be involved in looking after the garden.

In order for the landscape gardeners to present their plan to the head teacher, they research: the needs of visually impaired and wheelchair-bound children; which flowers and plants might offer textures and smells for visually impaired people; how to design the garden so that it is interesting and accessible for wheelchair users; how sounds and textures might be used; and how to design and build paths and beds so that wheelchair users can do some gardening themselves. This is authentic creative work task-led by the demands of the situation but also motivated by compassion and a willingness by non-disabled young people to imagine the world from the perspective of those with disabilities. They are becoming 'intellectually responsible' in John Dewey's sense (Dewey, 1938).

The *Mantle of the Expert* approach is resonant with other creative pedagogical positions. In the introduction to *Authentic Achievement*, Newmann *et al.* preface the findings of large scale empirical research into effective pedagogy with these words:

> the absence of meaning breeds low student engagement in school work. Meaningless schoolwork is a consequence of a number of factors but especially curriculum that emphasises superficial exposure to hundreds of isolated pieces of knowledge. The term authentic achievement thus stands for intellectual accomplishments that are worthwhile, significant and

meaningful, such as those undertaken by successful adults: scientists, musicians, entrepreneurs, politicians.

(Newmann et al., 1995: 26)

Role-taking allows young people to work as, rather than learn about. To work as scientists rather than learn about science. To act in and on the world in new and significant ways as creative scientists do, as creative mathematicians do, as creative artists do. The work is creative because it becomes an authentic response to real-world tasks. It requires young people to act on the world informed by their curriculum experiences and active inquiry, rather than passively to receive and repeat inert slabs of knowledge.

This participatory, agentive and situated model of drama in education contains within it a strong model of 'co-constructed' teaching and learning that characterises other genres and modes of drama work with young people. For instance, Joe Arkley, an actor in the RSC ensemble, who is training for a Postgraduate Award in Teaching Shakespeare for Actors, is in role as Antigonus from *The Winter's Tale*, cruelly and wrongly ordered by King Leontes to abandon the baby Perdita to the wolves. A class of ten- and eleven-year-olds are in role as fellow courtiers and advisors on board the ship that carries them to Bohemia. In role, they discuss his options; publicly questioning and challenging Antigonus and each other; imagining what the outcomes for Perdita and Antigonus will be; exploring and critically reflecting on the shared ideas, proposed actions and their outcomes. The class move around creatively within the given circumstances of the script, struggling purposefully to find the rightness of actions for Antigonus to take that will shape Perdita's future in different ways from her father's intentions.

But Joe also recognises that every drama 'lesson' should be an artistic as well as an educational journey – his playing of Antigonus in a darkened candle lit studio, clutching a baby in a basket, is intended to create an authentic and felt theatre experience for the students. They are motivated to engage with Shakespeare's language through their existential engagement with the dilemma of the cruelly abandoned child. Joe's work is influenced by the RSC Education Department's ensemble and rehearsal room based approach to teaching Shakespeare, summarised on the RSC website as:

> Young people are up on their feet, moving around, saying the text aloud, exploring the feelings and ideas that emerge. There is a focus on physical and emotional responses, as well as intellectual, responses to the text. Active approaches are used to inform and test critical analysis. Pupils investigate a range of interpretive choices in the text and negotiate these with their teacher. Drama techniques are used to explore language, meaning, character and motivation.[1]

This is a very different approach to teaching Shakespeare from sitting at desks reading painfully round the class and being told what the language means and how it is to be understood. The stress on 'active, exploratory and problem solving methods' suggests that young people are being encouraged and given the open space to make their own connections, discoveries and journeys. The plays become scripts for action rather than texts for contemplation.

In the RSC approach, the focus is on young people making and negotiating 'interpretive choices' – will these words be spoken softly? Shouted? Shall we move or stand still? Where is this scene taking place and how does that affect our playing of it? Shakespeare does not provide these answers – there are so many possibles for young people to explore and re-invent. In making these choices creatively, they come to 'own' their own versions of the plays and to realise that they are changeable. Perhaps in doing this they might also come closer to realising that their own lives and destinies are not fixed. Interpretative choices can be made in life as well as in drama. The structures within which we live and learn are not immoveable and inert obstacles, they are open to personal and social re-imagining and re-creation.

Drama and the development of necessary social intelligence

What is critical and essential to all forms of drama as creative learning is that it occurs socially. Much of the literature on creative learning identifies and assesses personalised and individualised characteristics of creativity – asking questions, making connections, for instance (Jeffrey and Woods, 2009, Lloyd and Smith, 2004).[2] Having the confidence to ask questions in public and negotiating connections in social learning contexts can be another matter. In drama, the emphasis is on the creative potential of the group, the sharing of experiences, the co-construction of journeys into meaning. All actions have to be negotiated and will have social as well as artistic consequences.

In facing our social, economic and educational priorities we now recognise that the future will require these forms of socially negotiated action rather than individual responses and creative actions. The global problems of societies split by irreconcilable differences of belief and ideology, environmental collapse and the increasing gulf between those who have and those who have not cannot be resolved at an individual level, or by superheroes. They require new and re-invented forms of social creativity – critical hope based in collective action. The greatest challenge that young people face in drama is learning to work cooperatively with a shared purpose and learning to be mindful of self and others in the social as well as artistic dimensions of the drama work. For this reason, drama can be the site where young people discover their creative power of collective action as well as how to rise to the challenges of working with multiple interests, perspectives and other differences.

Ensemble as a bridging metaphor between the social and the artistic

Michael Boyd, Artistic Director of the RSC, captures this duality in his support for ensemble-based theatre:

> We've never had more cause to realise the grave importance of our interdependence as humans and yet we seem ever more incapable of acting on that realisation with the same urgency that we all still give to the pursuit of self interest. Theatre does have a very important role because it is such a quintessentially collaborative art form.
>
> *(Michael Boyd, quoted in Neelands, 2009: 173)*

The ensemble provides the basis for young people to develop the complex levels of social intelligence (Gardner, 1983) needed to embrace the challenges of the future, whilst also developing the social imagination required to produce collaborative social art which reflects, energises and focuses the world for young people. The social knowing which comes from acting together in an ensemble mirrors Freire's concept of 'indispensable' knowledge:

> The kind of knowledge that becomes solidarity, becomes a 'being with'. In that context, the future is seen, not as inexorable but as something that is constructed by people engaged together in life, in history. It's the knowledge that sees history as possibility and not as already determined – the world is not finished. It is always in the process of becoming.
>
> *(Freire, 1998: 72)*

Working together in the social and egalitarian conditions of the ensemble, young people have the opportunity to struggle with the demands of becoming, like the Athenian *polis*, a self-managing, self-governing, self-regulating social group who co-create artistically and socially. The social experience of acting as an ensemble, making drama and theatre that reflects and suggests how the world might become in the hope that it is not finished, is, of course, of paramount importance to our young. We pass them the burden of the world that we have made in the hope that they will in turn have a world to pass on to their children.

Notes

1 http://www.rsc.org.uk/standupforshakespeare/content/manifesto_online.aspx.
2 In terms of policy, see, for instance, Qualifications and Curriculum Authority (QCA) (1999) *National Curriculum Creativity*; available at http://curriculum.qcda.gov.uk/key-stages-1-and-2/learning-across-the-curriculum/creativity/index.aspx.

References

Brecht, B. (1995 [1938]) The popular and the realistic, in R. Drain (ed.) *Twentieth Century Theatre: A Sourcebook*, London and New York: Routledge.

Banaji, S., Burn, A. and Buckingham, D. (2006) *The Rhetorics of Creativity: A Review of Literature*, London: Arts Council of England.

Castoriadis, C. (1997) The Greek polis and the creation of democracy, in *The Castoriadis Reader*, Oxford: Blackwell.

Cziksentmihalyi, M. (1990) *Flow: The Psychology of Optimal Experience*, New York: Harper and Row.

Dewey, J. (1910) *How We Think*, New York: D. C. Heath & Co.

—— (1938) *Experience and Education*, New York: Macmillan.

—— (2007) *Democracy and Education*, Teddington: Echo Library.

Donaldson, M. (1987) *Children's Minds*, Harmondsworth: Penguin.

Freire, P. (1998) *The Pedagogy of Hope*, New York: Rowman and Littlefield.

Gardner, H. (1983) *Frames of Mind*, New York: Basic Books.

Heathcote, D. and Bolton, G. (1996) *Drama as Learning: Dorothy Heathcote's Mantle of the Expert Approach to Education*, London: Greenwood Press.

Huizinga, J. (1978) *Homo Ludens*, London: Palladin.

Jeffrey, B. and Woods, P. (2009) *Creative Learning in the Primary School*, Abingdon: Routledge.

Lloyd, K. and Smith, P. (2004) *Developing Creativity in the Primary School: A Practical Guide for School Leaders*, Nottingham: National College for School Leadership.

Mason, J. H. (2003) *The Value of Creativity: The Origins and Emergence of a Modern Belief*, Aldershot: Ashgate.

Moffett, J. (1994) Informal classroom drama, in *English in Australia* 108 (June): 64–7.

Neelands, J. (2009) Acting together: ensemble as a democratic process in art and life, *Research in Drama Education: The Journal of Applied Theatre and Performance* 14(2): 173–89.

Newman, F. *et al.* (1995) *Authentic Achievement*, New York: Jossey-Bass.

O'Neill, C. (1995) *Drama Worlds*, Portsmouth, MA: Heinemann.

Sennett, R. (1993) *The Fall of Public Man*, London: Faber and Faber.

Willett, J. (1990) (ed.) *Brecht on Theatre*, London: Methuen.

Williams, R. (1954) Argument, text and performance, in *Drama in Performance*, Harmondsworth: Penguin.

19

Learning *in* and *through* the arts

Mike Fleming

Introduction

This chapter will explore the broad conceptual distinction between *learning in* and *learning through* the arts. These constructs provide valuable theoretical perspectives on the teaching of the arts as well as useful tools for evaluating practice when the arts are used in an applied way to further creative learning. Although the two constructs overlap to some degree, they provide an indication of potential pitfalls when the elements associated with one approach dominate at the expense of the other. At its simplest, *learning in* the arts is learning within the discipline itself, learning that pertains to the particular art form. *Learning through*, as the preposition suggests, looks beyond the art form itself to outcomes that are extrinsic. For example, some writers argue that drama teaching should be more focused on learning about theatre, acting and dramatic structure, whereas others place more emphasis on the explicit development of personal, social and moral attributes and the use of the art form to advance understanding of subjects like history and RE. From this example, it may be tempting, in the context of the school curriculum, to see *learning in* as that which happens within the specialist art subjects and *learning through* occurring when the arts are employed across the curriculum to further creative learning in other subjects. However, the distinction is more far-reaching than simply being a matter of curriculum organisation because it embodies fundamental differences based on theoretical perspectives and historical traditions.

The two categories of *learning in* and *learning through* embody different approaches to aims (whether these are seen as related specifically to the arts discipline itself or are of a more general kind), content (the skills and discipline of the art form as opposed to content derived from non-art subjects) as well as curriculum organisation. They also represent different traditions in the ways the arts have been defined and justified. That is not to say that the categories are straightforward and easily distinguished; in practice there is considerable overlap between them. One of the purposes of this chapter therefore will be to explore the complexity of the categories, the degree to which they overlap and how far they can be seen as dichotomous. A second and closely related aim is to determine whether these categories or theoretical constructs have a useful purpose. It will be argued that they do have value not only in providing insights into the history of arts education but also in helping determine how a balanced and integrated approach to creative learning might be conceived.

The chapter will begin, then, by discussing the *learning in* construct. The aim will be to examine how far a coherent case can be made for associating this approach with a traditional, separatist account of aesthetics and the arts. This is a view which, taken to an extreme, could be said to foster an elitist and rarefied view of the arts. It would clearly be a mistake to attribute this belief to all advocates of a *learning in* approach. Nevertheless, by highlighting possible, if not necessary, consequences of subscribing to this view, the discussion will provide a focus for linking issues related to the teaching of the arts with wider theoretical perspectives drawn from art theory. This will be followed by a discussion of the *learning through* construct, emphasising its more democratic and inclusive nature and its closer association with contemporary practice. The final section of the chapter will provide a more balanced and nuanced examination of these polarities, asking whether anything is in danger of being lost in the dichotomous formulation if conceived too simply.

Learning in the arts

The *learning in* the arts concept focuses on the intrinsic rather than extrinsic benefits of engaging with the arts. It is less interested, for example, in whether the learning of music can improve performance in mathematics or general cognitive development (the Mozart effect), but is more focused on the value of music for its own sake. Similarly, there is less emphasis on whether the visual arts develop citizenship or make students better people, but more focus on the appreciation of art itself. It is thus associated with traditionalist aesthetics, with a conception of the arts that emerged in the eighteenth century that sought to disassociate art from utilitarian purposes. It found its strongest expression in the nineteenth century with the art for art's sake movement but has also informed more contemporary writing on the place of the arts in education (Gingell, 2000; Gingell and Brandon, 2000; Eisner, 2002; and Belfiore, Chapter 3). The more extreme versions of the intrinsic view sought to remove art from any didactic or moral purpose, making it particularly relevant to a discussion of the place of the arts in education.

As various commentators have pointed out, the term 'aesthetic' and the conception of art that it most often embodies are a 'recent arrival in the history of human thought' (Osborne, 1968: 1). Through much of human history art objects and activities such as dance were designed to serve some sort of purpose, for example as utensils, to encourage rain or to affect a cure for ill health. Osborne (1968: 13) refers to various uses of art objects, including 'a magical fetish, a temple to honour the gods and glorify the community, a statue to perpetuate a man's memory (Greece) or to insure his immortality (Egypt)'. In earlier societies art was not produced by a specialist group of people, but was 'spread through the whole community' Carey (2005: 7). As Dewey observed:

> Even in the caves, human habitations were adorned with colored pictures that kept alive to the senses experiences with the animals that were so closely bound with the lives of humans. Structures that housed their gods and the instrumentalities that facilitated commerce with the higher powers were wrought with special fineness. But the arts of the drama, music, painting, and architecture thus exemplified had no peculiar connection with theaters, galleries, museums. They were part of the significant life of an organized community.
>
> *(Dewey, 2005: 5)*

Although activities of painting, sculpture, poetry, music and drama thrived in ancient Greece and Rome, the concept of 'fine art' as a specialised, separate autonomous cultural field is 'in fact only a modern product' (Shusterman, 2000a: 3).

The term 'aesthetic' was first coined by Alexander Baumgarten in the mid-eighteenth century and the concept was refined through the theorising of Kant. There is a danger of oversimplifying Kant's views on aesthetics when summarising them because they are so closely integrated with his wider theories of metaphysics and ethics (Crawford, 2001; Wicks, 2007). However, the key element that is relevant to the *learning in* concept is the focus on the *disinterested appreciation of form* in the judgement of pure beauty which became a defining criterion for responding to art.

To be 'disinterested' is not to be 'uninterested' but it is to approach art without the kind of vested or personal interest that would detract from appreciation of the art form. Lyas (1997: 28) gives the telling example of a person who comes out from a play smiling because he invested in it, another because her daughter wrote it and another because he was seen there by his boss. The one who comes out smiling because she simply enjoyed the play represents a more disinterested approach. Similarly, someone who is going to see *Othello* may be distracted from a truly aesthetic response by the recent knowledge that his wife has been unfaithful. This last example is particularly interesting because it is precisely the ability to link art with personal experience that is arguably characteristic of the *learning through* approach. In contrast, the theory associated with *learning in* sees aesthetic pleasure as being derived from the joy of deploying imagination in free play towards the art object. According to Bourdieu (1984: 3) this notion of 'pure' gaze is 'a historical invention' and in Carey's view (2005: 10) 'the separation of art from life' was a crucial consequence of Kant's doctrine.

Perhaps the most extreme formulation of this 'intrinsic view' came from Clive Bell's formalist theory of art:

> to appreciate a work of art we need bring with us nothing from life, no knowledge of its ideas and affairs, no familiarity with its emotions. Art transports us from the world of man's activity to a world of aesthetic exaltation. For a moment we are shut off from human interests; our anticipations and memories are arrested; we are lifted above the stream of life.
>
> *(Bell, quoted in Hospers, 1969: 91)*

To the modern reader this account of the appreciation of art which seeks to detach it from ordinary living seems strange. It is a theory, as Warburton (2003: 16) has pointed out, that 'puts art beyond the contingencies of time and place'. It makes rather more sense, however, when seen in its historical context because part of Bell's intention was to defend the post-impressionists, whose work was easily misunderstood if examined for content rather than for significant form. It is therefore more plausible if the view is applied to certain forms of visual arts and perhaps to music rather than to 'art' as a general concept. Even so, Bell's view can be applied to literature, with the result that the teaching of the subject focuses on formal features such as rhyme, rhythm and structure more than thematic content or the moral message of the text (Carroll, 2001: 88). It can thus be associated with the type of new criticism associated with Leavis, manifest in the exercise of practical criticism or close reading (Eagleton, 1983: 43).

Another aspect of Bell's view that needs to be recognised is the underlying quest for a narrow definition of art through the specification of the necessary and sufficient conditions for using the term 'art'. A considerable amount of intellectual energy in the past has been expended on trying to establish defining characteristics of art as evident in different theories of representation, form, expression and intuition. However, a seminal paper by Weitz in 1956, strongly influenced by Wittgenstein's thinking on language and meaning, marked a significant change from a search for essentialist definitions of 'art' and instead recognised that the concept of art was fluid and changing. With this more open account of art there is more readiness to embrace new approaches, including popular arts forms and new technologies. The *learning in* conception, with its association with traditional aesthetics, is more at home with a separatist concept of high art or fine art.

Despite the impact of modernism and alternative approaches to the arts since the turn of the twentieth century, the intrinsic or separatist view is arguably still the conception of art that tends to dominate popular consciousness and explains a particular and widespread attitude to art. It embodies a tacit belief that the arts belong in a special sphere somehow separate from normal human activity and whose deep rewards are mysterious and confined to a privileged few. Lyas captures this separatist conception vividly:

> For many, art galleries are places where stains, largely rectangular, hang on walls. Standing before these stains, other people, often with a certain kind of accent, proclaim, often in voices meant to be overheard, that looking at these stains, has given them experiences so profound that failure to have them would have left their lives impoverished. And others look and just can't see any of this, just as others can make no sense of the noises in the sonic museum of the concert hall, or resolve the words of The Waste Land into sense.
>
> *(Lyas, 1997: 5)*

A similar view was advanced by Dewey (2005: 4) in *Arts and Experience* (first published in 1934); he referred to the 'museum conception of art' or 'compartmental conception of fine art' (ibid.: 6) that sets art on a remote pedestal. In this conception, 'art is remitted to a separate realm, where it is cut off from that association with the materials and aims of every other form of human effort' (ibid.: 2). The emphasis is on product rather than the experience of art.

Even the challenges to the traditional 'bourgeois' view of art represented by different movements such as pop, conceptual and 'found' art seem unable to escape being institutionalised and elevated to 'museum' status, with a consequent weakening of their radical intent. When found objects and whimsical pieces are treated with intense reverence or accompanied by inflated explanations about their meaning, the original purpose is lost.

To summarise: here, then, is one possible composite view of the arts embodied in the *learning in* formulation. It eschews functional and utilitarian purposes in favour of a celebration of the intrinsic rewards of engaging with arts. Its theoretical origins are derived from a search for definitions and universals that belonged to a more mono-cultural and less pluralist outlook on the world. For that reason it can lead to elitism and separatism. In contrast, the *learning through* approach can be said to be more contemporary because it is more inclined to consider the implications for education of the wider socio-cultural context. In the *learning through* approach the concept of 'art' can easily transmute into the broader notion of 'culture'.

Learning through the arts

As suggested in the introduction to this chapter, the *learning through* formulation is not confined to the specific use of the arts to enrich learning experiences in other subjects; it can also refer to the way in which the learning outcomes of specific art subjects are formulated. For example, drama may be employed to develop understanding of history (Fines and Verrier, 1974) or it may be used to further personal development (Way, 1967). In both cases, however, more emphasis tends to placed on the *experience* of the learner than on the *art product* itself (Dewey, 2005). This is a likely, though not necessary, consequence of a *learning through* approach because the learning outcomes are more likely to be of an 'ancillary' nature rather than arts based (Eisner, 1998).

Although the term *learning through* was not always used, it was arguably this conception that dominated arts education through much of the twentieth century (Abbs, 2003). The influence of progressive, child-centred approaches in education emerged in part in reaction to the authoritarian, utlilitarian and mechanical view of learning that was characteristic of the Victorian era. The influence of progressive ideas on the arts in education was the promotion of self-expression and creativity as a means of enhancing personal growth. Dance in schools was valued partly for its physical benefits but also for the way it developed social well-being. In visual art there was a movement away from systematic instruction towards more free expression and creativity as a means of developing the individual. The distinction between *learning in* and *learning through* was particularly apparent in the field of drama, which was increasingly used as a pedagogical method to bring highly imaginative teaching approaches to the classroom.

Learning through the arts takes different forms. Either it can be identified with child-centred, progressive approaches where the focus is more on the personal development of the individual, or in its more contemporary manifestation it refers to the use of the arts and creativity to promote creative learning across the curriculum. The former highlights subjectivity and feeling, while the latter is more balanced because it places just as much emphasis on cognition and objectivity. The *learning through* approach can also be associated with the individual arts subject disciplines when the justification for teaching is provided not in terms of the art subject itself but in relation to the external cognitive and social benefits. There has been much interest in recent years in the general educational benefits of engaging with the arts, although empirical research to date has not provided conclusive findings (Eisner, 1998; Harland *et al.*, 2000; Winner and Hetland, 2000; Comerford Boyes and Reid, 2005).

If the *learning in* approach is in danger of promoting a separatist, elitist, a-cultural and a-historical view of the arts, it can be argued that *learning through* represents a more inclusive, democratic and contemporary approach more suited to recognising the place of arts in education.

Further perspectives

So far this discussion has juxtaposed a negative view of *learning in* against more positive account of *learning through*, as summarised in Table 19.1. As suggested in the introduction, this dichotomous view needs some modification, with an examination of possible counter-arguments.

The danger with the *learning through* conception is that art becomes associated with narrow learning outcomes and mechanical processes, distorting its nature in the process. It is not necessary to resort to narrow definitions of 'art' to recognise that it is more inclined to the ineffable and uncertain rather than what is confined and predictable. The preposition 'through' betrays the danger of constantly passing through the work of art rather than dwelling within it (Abbs, 2003). When art is harnessed in the service of other curriculum subjects there is a danger

Table 19.1 A simple conception of learning in the arts

Learning in	*Learning* through
• art for art's sake	
• separatist	• inclusive
• traditional	• embedded
• essentialist	• purposeful
• social and cultural context neglected	• transformational
• elitist	

that the objectives of the subject become dominant at the expense of artistic form and quality. In the context of the specific teaching of arts subjects the emphasis on individual personal development through self-expression had, at its worst, a number of negative consequences. It meant a neglect of artistic tradition and any connection with the past because the primary focus was on what pupils were creating in the present. It also brought a loss of any sense of discrimination of what counts as quality because the creative experience or process took precedence over product. This in turn meant a diminution of the importance of skill development because unfettered expression was the central concern. The same dangers may be evident in more contemporary practice when the arts are employed to advance creative learning if the importance of form is neglected in the process.

However, just as the *learning in* and *learning through* concepts may be misleading if seen only as polar opposites, the critique of the self-expression paradigm of arts education can easily be exaggerated, with a consequent failure to acknowledge its pedagogic insights. It brought to the fore the importance of experience, feeling, engagement, creativity and genuine ownership. Moreover, a closer examination of some of the writers who promoted self-expression reveals their thinking to be more balanced than is often thought. Both Read (1956), in the context of the visual arts, and Slade (1954), on drama, took a strongly developmental perspective and saw the importance of an evolution from self-expression to greater emphasis on product and appreciation as pupils got older. Some of the writers on drama (e.g. Bolton, 1979; Heathcote, 1980) are often misleadingly placed in the same self-expression category as that of Slade and Way by writers such as Hornbrook (1989) and Ross (1982). However, in the drama work of Bolton and Heathcote more attention was paid to content, the nature of the experience of the pupils and the role of the teacher in elevating the quality of the drama and defining specific educational objectives. Also at the centre of their work was the importance of artistic form, woven into the fabric of the experience rather than superimposed from without. Contemporary approaches to arts education, as reflected in the UK National Curriculum and elsewhere, are not purely focused on self-expression but recommend a more inclusive view of the arts that embodies making, responding, performing and appraising. However, it is important to guard against the danger of replacing a subjectivist or romantic view of arts education with one which is objectivist but also sterile.

As demonstrated above, form was central to *learning in*, with, at its most extreme formulation, a strange disassociation of art from life. However, there is a more plausible interpretation of the intrinsic view which sees engagement with art as paradoxically a stepping out of life's mainstream for purposes of renewal in order to engage with life more productively. The Kantian notion of disinterestedness usually associated with the extreme separatist view in aesthetics has been described by Eagleton as a 'radical political concept':

> 'Disinterestedness' does not mean being magically absolved from interests, but recognising that some of your interests are doing you no good, or that it is in the interest of doing an effective job to set certain of them apart for the moment. It demands imagination, sympathy and self-discipline. You do not need to rise majestically above the fray to decide that in a specific situation, somebody else's interests should be promoted over yours.
>
> *(Eagleton, 2003: 134)*

According to Shusterman (2003), the concept of entertainment which is central to engagement with art often has superficial overtones. Arguments for teaching the arts are often conceived in terms of a contrast with 'mere' entertainment, with a consequent rejection of the notion that the arts are there to be enjoyed, which is replaced by a determination to provide specific learning outcomes and targets. This approach is sometimes driven by the pragmatics of having to struggle for recognition in an overcrowded curriculum. However, to dismiss entertainment and related concepts too readily for fear of superficiality may be to miss something important about the value of engagement with art – something the advocates of self-expression recognised. The term 'amusement' derives from the verb 'to muse', one of whose early meanings is 'to be absorbed in thought'. Shusterman (2003: 293) points out that we can associate the concept of entertainment with notions of sustaining, refreshing and deepening concentration; paradoxically to maintain the self one needs also to forget it and look elsewhere. In making space for the concept of entertainment we are not necessarily forced to elevate the superficial or embrace escapism.

A more balanced version of Table 19.1 is provided in Table 19.2, which, by paying due heed to the negatives and positives of each paradigm, erodes the distinctive nature of the categories.

How are these insights helpful to arts in education practice? In the *learning through* perspective they draw attention to the dangers of losing sight of the importance of form and quality. The word 'creativity' or the phrase 'creative learning' can easily become a blanket term that is spread unthinkingly over any form of practice to legitimise it. On the other hand, it is not necessary to subscribe to an exclusive notion of 'high art' to maintain the importance of a concept of quality established through dialogue and shared judgement. Such deliberations need to give due recognition to the ages of the pupils involved. In recent years there has been a welcome injection of funds into arts practice in schools promoting partnerships with professional arts companies. However, it is easy to become so carried away with the importance of aesthetic form and production values that the work becomes too adult-centred and insufficiently based on the experience of the pupils.

The intrinsic view, properly interpreted, is a useful reminder that the celebratory and 'entertainment' aspects of engagement with the arts need to be acknowledged and not abandoned in the search for specific learning outcomes. Despite the long historical tradition of writers proclaiming the end of art (Hegel, 2004; Danto, 1997), there may be an argument here for maintaining the concept of arts in education and resisting the implicit tendency to dissolve the concept of art into creativity and culture. On the other hand, recognition of the intrinsic value of engaging in the arts should not become an argument for closing down discussion and dialogue about purpose and value. A mutually exclusive division between intrinsic and extrinsic is hard to maintain. Any engagement with the arts is likely to bring benefits that are extrinsic and not necessarily intended. Eisner (2002: 93) has pointed out that what children learn when

Table 19.2 A more complete conception of learning in the arts

Learning in	*Learning* through
• art for art's sake	
• separatist	• inclusive
• traditional	• embedded
• essentialist	• purposeful
• social and cultural context neglected	• transformational
• elitist	
• importance of form	
• preservation of quality	• loss of identity as art
• artistic integrity	• mechanical
• skills	• instrumental
• deep concept of 'entertainment'	• reductive

working on a painting or sculpture goes beyond the learning related to dealing with the material itself. He suggests that 'Techniques represent ways of doing something but techniques also reflect ways of thinking about the thing to be done. Thus the acquisition of technique is not merely a technical achievement; it is a mode of thought' (ibid.: 146). Similarly, most examples of *learning through* are likely to have some element of learning about the form.

If the content of this chapter reads rather like an argument in favour of 'having one's cake and eating it', then that is precisely what it is. What the concepts of *learning in* and *learning through* offer is a valuable reminder of the need for balance when employing the arts to support creative learning and a tool for making judgements in this context. The process of establishing extreme positions is a useful way of informing curriculum development and teaching when the arts are used in this way, because it helps to guard against the negative consequences of sub-scribing to one approach exclusively. The appropriate balance will be found not in general conceptual discussion but in dialogue and shared judgement related to particulars, whether these be specific art lessons, cross-curricular programmes or partnership projects.

References

Abbs, P. (2003) *Against the Flow: Education, the Arts and Postmodern Culture*, London: RoutledgeFalmer.

Bolton, G. (1979) *Towards a Theory of Drama in Education*, London: Longman.

—— (1992) *New Perspectives on Classroom Drama*, Hemel Hempstead: Simon and Schuster.

—— (1998) *Acting in Classroom Drama*, Stoke on Trent: Trentham Books.

Bourdieu, P. (1984) *Distinction: A Social Critique of Taste*, London: Routledge; first published in French in 1979.

Carey, J. (2005) *What Good Are the Arts?*, London: Faber and Faber.

Carroll, N. (2001) Formalism, in B. Gaut and D. Lopes (eds) *The Routledge Companion to Aesthetics*, London: Routledge.

Comerford Boyes, L. and Reid, I. (2005) What are the benefits for pupils participating in arts activities? The view from the research literature, *Research in Education – Manchester* 73(1): 1–14.

Crawford, D. (2001) Kant in B. Gaut and D. Lopes (eds) *The Routledge Companion to Aesthetics*, London: Routledge.

Danto, A. (1997) *After The End of Art: Contemporay Art and The Pale of History*, Princeton, NJ: Princeton University Press.

Dewey, J. (2005) *Art as Experience*, New York: Penguin; first published 1934.

Eagleton, T. (1983) *Literary Theory: An Introduction*, Oxford: Basil Blackwell.

—— (2003) *After Theory*, London: Allen Lane.

Eisner, E. (1998) Does experience in the arts boost academic achievement? *Art Education* 51(1): 7–15.

—— (2002) *The Arts and the Creation of Mind*, New Haven, CT: Yale University Press.

Fines, J. and Verrier, R. (1974) *The Drama of History*, London: New University Education.

Gaut, B. and Lopes, D. *The Routledge Companion to Aesthetics*, London: Routledge.

Gingell, J. (2000) Plato's ghost: how not to justify the arts, *Westminster Studies in Education* 23: 71–9.

—— (2001) Against creativity, *Irish Educational Studies* 20: 34–44.

Gingell, J. and Brandon, E. P. (2000) Special issue: in defence of high culture, *Journal of Philosophy of Education*, 34(3).

Harland, J., Kinder, K., Lord, P., Stoot, A., Schagen, I. and Haynes, J. with Cusworth, L., White, R. and, R. (2000) *Arts Education in Secondary Schools: Effects and Effectiveness*, Slough: NFER.

Heathcote, D. (1980) *Drama as Context*, Sheffield: NATE.

Hegel, G. (2004) *Introductory Lectures on Aesthetics*, London: Penguin; first published in 1896.

Hornbrook, D. (1989) *Education and Dramatic Art*, London: Blackwell Education.

Hospers, J. (1969) *Introductory Readings in Aesthetics*, London: Macmillan.

Kant, I. (1928) *The Critique of Judgement*, Oxford: Clarendon Press.

Lyas, C. (1997) *Aesthetics*, London: University of London Press.

Osborne, H. (ed.) (1968) *Aesthetics*, Oxford: Oxford University Press.

Read, H. (1956) *Education through Art*, London: Faber and Faber.

Ross, M. (1978) *The Creative Arts*, London: Heinemann.

—— (1982) *The Development of Aesthetic Experience*, Oxford: Pergamon Press.

—— (ed.) (1989) *The Claims of Feeling: Readings in Aesthetic Education*, Lewes: Falmer.

Shusterman, R. (2000a) *Performing Live: Aesthetic Alternatives for the Ends of Art*, Ithaca, NY, and London: Cornell University Press.

—— (2000b) *Pragmatist Aesthetics: Living Beauty, Rethinking Art* (2nd ed.), Lanham, MD: Rowman & Littlefield.

—— (2002) *Surface and Depth: Dialectics of Criticism and Culture*, Ithaca, NY, and London: Cornell University Press.

—— (2003) Entertainment: a question for aesthetics, *British Journal of Aesthetics* 43(3): 289–307.

Slade, P. (1954) *Child Drama*, London: University of London Press.

Warburton, N. (2003) *The Art Question*, London: Routledge.

Way, B. (1967) *Development Through Drama*, London: Longman.

Weitz, M. (1956) The role of theory in aesthetics, *Journal of Aesthetics and Art Criticism* 15: 27–35.

Wicks, R. (2007) *Kant on Judgment*, London: Routledge.

Winner, E. and Hetland, L. (2000) The arts in education: evaluating the evidence for a causal link, *Journal of Aesthetic Education* 34(3–4): 3–10.

Wittgenstein, L. (1953) *Philosophical Investigations* (trans. G. E. M. Anscombe), Oxford: Basil Blackwell.

Part III

Creative curriculum and pedagogy

Ken Jones

Discussion of educational change – curricular, pedagogic, assessment-focused – has always been framed by wider arguments, both about the social contexts which are thought to necessitate or provide a mandate for change and about the conceptions of educational purpose which could resource and shape it. The articles collected in Part III share this intellectual lineage: from diverse positions, they are informed by an awareness of the impasses of current policies, but also by a sense of the possibilities opened up by cultural change, and by emergent classroom practice.

Some of the contributions renew a critique of educational systems that is as old as compulsory state education itself. Grant Wiggins (Chapter 34), writing of a classroom life that is 'dulled by the familiarity of typical instruction', describes an iron cage of educational practice, remote from the intellectual challenges of everyday social life, in terms as forceful as those of a Dewey or a Montessori, and locates his work explicitly in such tradition. James Beane (Chapter 20), charting the effect on school curricula of discipline-focused traditions of knowledge, returns in one sense to the themes of the Dalton Plan of the 1920s (Pankhurst, 1922). These critiques, and the alternative thinking to which they are linked, have lost none of their resonance. They are joined in Part III by other readings of the constraints of education that are shaped by the post-1990 experience of standards-driven reform, and by the mix of cultural assumptions that are encoded in it. Gunther Kress (Chapter 22) points out that such an agenda is often driven by a search for an education that 'will guarantee the requirements for authority and control'; Debra Hayes (Chapter 21) explores how teachers resolve 'the tension between creativity and control ... through the adoption of standard classroom practices'; James Beane constructs his arguments for change against those of a traditionalist right incapable of addressing the new. Helen Nixon and Barbara Comber (Chapter 27) perceive in current policy a tendency to 'contain and limit' literacy within narrow forms.

The response to these constraints is intellectually bold, but tactically pragmatic and 'responsible' – the temptations of pure critique are resisted. Kress is quite categorical in his presentation of the unsurpassable limits of existing models of education: they are geared to the reproduction of old habits, in a world of radical instability; only the normalisation of creativity can sustain a productive response to change. For Wiggins, likewise, all creative work has an element of the destructive; it undermines traditions, habitual ways of seeing, unexamined ideas. Pringle, in her focus on new kinds of art education (Chapter 25), emphasises their demanding, destabilising effects. But none of the chapters is focused simply on a denunciation of unproductive practice; all are specific in their dissections and precise in their evocation or description of alternatives. In this sense, their responses to the limits of contemporary policy are as much constructive and tactical as they are critical. Some contributions – McDougall and Trotman's (Chapter 29), for instance – derive possibilities for change from their work in the interstices of standards-driven educational systems, and are able to seize on small experiences to sketch a larger project. Similarly, Thomson (Chapter 31) and Fuchs and Witte (Chapter 32) chart how the inability of current structures to address marginal cohorts of students opens some opportunity for innovation. Other writers, Dezuanni and Jetnikoff (Chapter 28) and Hayes (Chapter 21) in Queensland, for example, are able to describe work done in the highways laid down by more generous, system-wide programmes of reform. Many are alert to the resources offered by educational and cultural practice outside the school, but all are emphatic that a formal education, albeit remade, is essential to creative learning: to borrow a formulation of Durkheim's, it can make out of the haphazard encounters of experiential something comprehensive and systematic (Durkheim, 1925).

A repertoire

In their reflections on the remaking of practice, the chapters draw from a surprisingly consistent repertoire of theories, practices and problematisations. This repertoire is internationalised; its resources are utilised in Australia as much as South Africa, Britain as well as the United States. Alongside this border-crossing commonality, there is an attention to the particularities of place: much of the work gathered here reflects on the adaptation, in local circumstances, of a powerful set of 'travelling' ideas and provocative questions.

The foremost influence is Vygotskian. Students are seen as active constructors of meaning; meaning-making is a social process. Formal education draws on the resources of student experience, but seeks to frame that experience in more systematic ways. This complex emphasis aims to understand learning in a double way – as a process rooted in questions of identity and extra-school culture, and as something negotiated, shaped and led by the school. Linked to this 'classroom Vygotskianism' is a wider but similar emphasis. Creativity in education is seen as one instance of a human capacity for social semiosis, a capacity spurned by rulers but vital as a resource for change. Gunther Kress is particularly insistent on this point; educational conflicts between traditional authority and innovative capacity correspond to political lines of divide, and attempts to develop the curriculum productively are part of a bigger project to democratise the design of social futures. This is an understanding which, in sometimes muted and sometimes more vocal forms, underpins most of the articles collected here.

The attention of some authors focuses particularly on a growing disparity between the cultures of schooling, presented as hierarchical and mono-modal, and extra-school cultures that are linked to technological affordances promoting new forms of sociality, whose democratic potential is obvious, if not strongly realised. Young people, from this perspective, have access to semiotic resources that could enable a repositioning of the learner, as a 'full' and expert member of a remade community of educational practice. The articles by Nixon and Comber (Chapter 27) and McDougall and Trotman (Chapter 29) ground their exploration of new educational potentials on such perceptions of contrast and possibility; their tendency is to 'authorise' students' perspectives on the world around them. In a different idiom, Fuchs and Witte's report on the assessment of cultural competencies in Germany (Chapter 32) suggests that the competencies developed through informal education and engagement in artistic practice often lie beyond the reach of the understandings codified in the assessment regimes of schools; and that much can be gained through an attempt to register and accredit them.

In this context, several authors have recourse to the concept of 'funds of knowledge' developed by Luis Moll and his co-researchers (Moll *et al.*, 1992). Creative practice from this point of view depends upon questions of recognition. Educators have a responsibility to understand the cultures of learners, in ways that go beyond polarities of describing deprivation or celebrating identity, in order to understand learners as people already inserted into relationships that produce reserves of knowledge at the same time as they reproduce inequalities. Ferreira and Janks' account of 'TRC pedagogy' in post-apartheid South Africa (Chapter 30) vividly suggests how such an approach can extend the customary limits of classroom knowledge, validate the experience of usually subordinate groups, and in doing so bring different kinds of knowledge and experience into productive relationship with each other. 'The pedagogy used', they comment, 'opened the curriculum to different communities' funds of knowledge' and in the process 'challenged what counts as valued knowledge'. Thomson, writing about projects of 'active citizenship' in Tasmania (Chapter 31), makes a similar point: if schools can set up an engagement between students and communities, of a kind that is attentive to the particular funds of knowledge that each side brings to the encounter, then it is possible that their role in the 'production of educational disadvantage' can be disrupted. Debra Hayes (Chapter 21), through detailed study of curriculum innovation in Queensland, Australia, suggessts how teachers can emphasise 'the contingent and contested nature of knowledge', in order to offer young people insight into how 'knowledge is produced and worked with in [diverse] disciplinary contexts'. She offers studies of classrooms where teachers do not 'just facilitate students' access to knowledge', but by working alongside them 'as they engage with knowledge' enable them to experience 'its potential and its limitations'. Creative curricula and pedagogy, understood as culturally informed attempts to organise learning socially, in ways that cross the boundaries separating the classroom from the world, offer transformational possibilities.

The resources that can be brought to such a project do not exist only among learners. The articles by Pringle and by Adams suggest that in disciplinary fields and institutions outside education and beyond the school, ideas and practices have been developed that can enrich the way that teaching and learning are organised. Pringle's account of gallery education as an encounter with the 'process of action, reflection and experimentation' that drives the making of art (Chapter 25), and Adams' discussion of the lessons of 'Room 13' (Chapter 23) are informed by the pedagogic turn in art practice, a turn that has resulted, according to Adams, in a model of pedagogy that is 'far less didactic' than most of what happens in school art rooms, and is 'driven instead by a community, collaborative production model'. Hetland and Winner (Chapter 24), likewise, report on a project that offers a systematic and progressive account of developing studio thinking across other kinds of classrooms.

Adams' chapter describes arts practice in just one primary school setting, and draws from that setting a possible model for other places. The sophistication of the practices he explores highlights a difficult problem. The demands that articles in Part III implicitly make of teachers – that they develop a knowledge of the lifeworlds of students, the modalities of contemporary arts practice, and of the value to pedagogy of ethnographic research methods – are large and complex. Teachers, it is argued, need to be a bridge between community and curriculum, and to be instigators of a practice in which pedagogy is informed by anthropology as well as art. It is difficult to avoid the conclusion, here, that new models of teacher education are needed if the agendas sketched in these chapters are to be developed – Adams' presentation of the artist/teacher as a hybrid, and essential, classroom figure is one step towards such remodelling. The attempt, current in English policy, to confine the education of teachers to the teaching of basis skills, the possession of subject knowledge, and the management of behavioural problems is far removed from the creative agenda, and it arguably lacks that agenda's capacity to engage with contemporary culture and its educational implications.

Problematisings

The purposes of schooling, of course, are economic at the same time as they are cultural, and even the most informal of learning environments is not without relevance to processes of valorisation. 'Creative digital cultures', as Sefton-Green suggests in Chapter 26, may from one point of view appear as instances of mass creativity, but from another they should be understood in terms of their structuring by commercial interests. What are presented as the requirements of the labour market dominate policy-making at a national level, and form the backdrop not only to the standards agenda, but to claims that 'creativity' can supply the needs of the cultural sector and the soft skills of service industries. At this point, the relationship between 'school' and 'world', so central to progressive educational thinking, takes on a new dimension. Questions of certification become prominent, and with them the requirement upon educators to think about their practice in ways which engage with, rather than step around, schools' economic role. Several contributors offer a basis for such an engagement, in forms that vary from Wiggins' robust denunciation of a traditional, self-enclosed education, which offers no 'external goal or destination to supply meaning and context' (Chapter 34), to Fuchs and Witte's (Chapter 32) demonstration that creative and cultural education can meet new economic needs at the same time as it can respond to the interests and capabilities of excluded groups of students. Hetland and Winner explore how what they call 'Studio Structures' – that is, habits, processes and attitudes derived from the Art Studio – 'can support the development of classroom cultures that nurture creativity', suggesting that learning in the arts, built on these disciplined and disciplinary principles, could contribute a great deal to making classrooms more creative.

Perhaps the most extended presentation of the issues that 'creative education' must negotiate, and the publics it must face, is given by Julian Sefton-Green in Chapter 33. Sefton-Green argues that assessment, far from being an afterthought to deliberations on what constitutes creative curriculum and pedagogy, is in fact a core issue. It is here the varied experiences and demands that traverse the creative agenda come together in palpably difficult ways. Creative educators, wishing to cross the borders between formal and informal learning, schooled and unschooled cultures, find themselves, so far as questions of evaluation and judgement are concerned, in territory that is less well mapped. The authority of the traditional curriculum was underpinned by the established prestige of disciplinary knowledge, and also – as Bourdieu insisted – by its cashability; cultural capital could be translated into economic capital. Creative education is less securely positioned. Its championing of unrecognised funds of knowledge and of informal learning means that it has abandoned the safety of institutional authority for an unending process of negotiation with other systems of value-making and judgement. At the same time, as McDougall and Trotman (Chapter 29) suggest, it is involved, particularly at secondary and tertiary level, with the development of certification that answers both to student interest and capability and to 'economic need'. In addition, it seeks to acquire status in a competitive and strongly hierarchical qualifications market. These pressures could be read as paradigmatic. What is visible at the level of assessment serves also to highlight the coming dilemmas of curriculum and pedagogy. Only the most careful probing of the demands and pressures that arise from the entry of creativity into mainstream education can provide a basis for its continuing success.

References

Durkheim, E. (1925) *Moral Education: A Study in the Theory and Application of the Sociology of Education* (trans. Everett K. Wilson and Hermann Schnurer), New York: The Free Press.

Moll, L., Amanti, C., Neffe, D. and Gonzalez, N. (1992) Funds of knowledge for teaching: using a qualitative approach to connect homes and classrooms, *Theory into Practice* 31(2): 132–41.

Pankhurst, H. (1922) *Education on the Dalton Plan*, New York: E. P. Dutton.

20

Curriculum integration and the disciplines of knowledge[1]

James A. Beane

At a conference on curriculum integration, a speaker who admitted that he had only recently been introduced to the concept said, 'From a quick look at various readings, it seems that the disciplines of knowledge are the enemies of curriculum integration.' Unwittingly or not, he had gone straight to the heart of perhaps the most contentious issue in current conversations about curriculum integration. Simply put, the issue is this: if we move away from the subject-centred approach to curriculum organisation, will the disciplines of knowledge be abandoned or lost in the shuffle?

As an advocate for curriculum integration, I want to set the record straight. In the thoughtful pursuit of authentic curriculum integration, the disciplines of knowledge are not the enemy. Instead they are a useful and necessary ally.

What is curriculum integration?

Curriculum integration is not simply an organisational device requiring cosmetic changes or realignments in lesson plans across various subject areas. Rather, it is a way of thinking about what schools are for, about the sources of curriculum, and about the uses of knowledge. Curriculum integration begins with the idea that the sources of the curriculum ought to be problems, issues and concerns posed by life itself (Hopkins *et al.*, 1937; Lurry and Alberty, 1957; Dressel, 1958; Noar, 1966; Beane, 1993b; Vars, 1991). I have argued elsewhere that such concerns fall into two spheres: (1) self- or personal concerns; and (2) issues and problems posed by the larger world (Beane, 1993a, 1993b). Taking this one step further, we might say that the central focus of curriculum integration is the search for self- and social meaning.

As teachers facilitate such a search within a framework of curriculum integration, two things happen. First, young people are encouraged to integrate their learning experiences into their schemes of meaning so as to broaden and deepen their understanding of themselves and their world. Second, they are engaged in seeking, acquiring and using knowledge in an organic – not an artificial – way. That is, knowledge is called forth in the context of problems, interests, issues and concerns at hand. And since life itself does not know the boundaries or compartments of what we call disciplines of knowledge, such a context uses knowledge in ways that are integrated.[2]

Notice that, in order to define curriculum integration, there must be reference to knowledge. How could there not be? If we are to broaden and deepen understandings about ourselves and our world, we must come to know 'stuff', and to do that we must be skilled in ways of knowing and understanding. As it turns out, the disciplines of knowledge include much (but not all) of what we know about ourselves and our world and about ways of making and communicating meaning. Thus authentic curriculum integration, involving as it does the search for self- and social meaning, must take the disciplines of knowledge seriously – although, again, more is involved than just the correlation of knowledge from various disciplines.

What is the problem?

Theoretically, defining the relations between curriculum integration and the disciplines of knowledge is easy. But that act does not resolve the tension over how those relations work in the practical context of curriculum integration. Part of the reason lies not with the disciplines of knowledge themselves but with their representation in the separate-subject approach to the curriculum. Put another way, the issue is not whether the disciplines of knowledge are useful, but how they might be appropriately brought into the lives of young people. And more than that, do they include all that might be of use in the search for self- and social meanings?

A discipline of knowledge is a field of inquiry about some aspect of the world – the physical world, the flow of events over time, numeric structures and so on. A discipline of knowledge offers a lens through which to view the world – a specialised set of techniques or processes by which to interpret or explain various phenomena. Beyond that, a discipline also provides a sense of community for people with a shared special interest as they seek to stretch the limits of what is already known in that field. Those on the front edges of a discipline know that disciplinary boundaries are fluid and often connect with other disciplines to create interdisciplinary fields and projects (Klein, 1990).

Though school-based subject areas, like disciplines of knowledge, partition knowledge into differentiated categories, they are not the same thing as disciplines. Some subjects, like history or mathematics, come close, but they are really institutionally based representations of disciplines, since they deal with a limited selection of what is already known within the field. That selection is based on what someone believes ought to be known (or is not worth knowing) about some discipline by people who do not work within it or are unfamiliar with its progress to date. Other subjects, like biology or algebra or home economics, are subsets of disciplines and are limited in even more specialised ways. And still other subjects, like career education or foreign languages, may lay far-reaching claims of connection to some discipline, but their presence in schools really has to do with economic, social or academic aspirations.

In this sense a discipline of knowledge and its representative school subject area are not the same things, even though they may be concerned with similar bodies of knowledge. They serve quite different purposes, offer quite different experiences to those who encounter them, and have quite different notions about the fluidity of the boundaries that presumably set one area of inquiry off from others. These differences are substantial enough that the identification of a school subject area as, for example, 'history' amounts to an appropriation of the name attached to its corresponding discipline of knowledge. Subject areas are, in the end, a more severe case of 'hardening the categories' than are the disciplines they supposedly represent.

I make this distinction not to demean the work of subject-area teachers or to relegate them to a lower status than disciplinary scholars. Rather, I wish to point out that calling for an end to the separate-subject approach to school curriculum organisation is not at all a rejection or abandonment of the disciplines of knowledge. But in saying this, I want to quickly warn that such a claim does not simply open the door to a renewal of 'essentialist' conversations about the 'structure of disciplines' or their 'teachability' that Jerome Bruner and others encouraged in the past (Bruner, 1960; Ford and Pongo, 1964; King and Brownell, 1966; Alpern, 1967) and that are now revisited in lists of national and state content standards.

It is worth noting that Bruner himself apparently recognised this risk, when, 10 years after the publication of *The Process of Education*, he considered the work's place in education policy. Having just spoken of poverty, racism, injustice and dispossession, he said this:

> I believe I would be quite satisfied to declare, if not a moratorium, then something of a de-emphasis on matters that have to do with the structure of history, the structure of physics, the nature of mathematical consistency, and deal with curriculum rather in the context of the problems that face us. We might better concern ourselves with how those problems can be solved, not just by practical action, but by putting knowledge, wherever we find it, and in whatever form we find it, to work in these massive tasks. We might put vocation and intention back into the process of education, much more firmly than we had it there before.
>
> *(Bruner, 1971: 29–30)*

It is from just this kind of thinking that the case for curriculum integration emerges. Creating a curriculum for and with young people begins with an examination of the problems, issues and concerns of life as it is being lived in a real world. Organising themes are drawn from that examination. To work through such themes, to broaden and deepen our understanding of ourselves and our world, and to communicate these meanings, we must necessarily draw on the disciplines of knowledge. Again, therein lies much of what we know about ourselves and our world, ways in which we might explore them further, and possibilities for communicating meanings. Our reach for help in this kind of curriculum is a purposeful and directed activity – we do not simply identify questions and concerns and then sit around and wait for enlightenment to come to us. Instead, we intentionally and contextually 'put knowledge to work'.

Inside the subject approach

More and more educators are coming to realise that there is a fundamental tension in schools that current restructuring proposals are simply not addressing, no matter how radical their rhetoric might otherwise be. That tension has to do with the curriculum that mediates the relationship between teachers and young people. After all, teachers and their students do not come together on a random or voluntary social basis – they do not meet casually and decide to 'do school'. Instead they are brought together to do something – namely the curriculum – and if that curriculum is fraught with fundamental problems, then the relationships between teachers and students will almost certainly be strained.

Advocates of curriculum integration, myself included, locate a large measure of that tension in the continuing organisation of the planned curriculum around separate subject areas. While more complete critiques of the separate-subject approach have been offered elsewhere (Brady, 1989; Beane, 1993b; Connell, 1993), I want to touch on the major points of contention in order to clarify the claims made earlier in this article.

First, the separate-subject approach, as a selective representation of disciplines of knowledge, has incorrectly portrayed the latter as 'ends' rather than 'means' of education (Dewey, 1915; Henry, 1956; Brady, 1989). Young people and adults have been led to believe that the purpose of education is to master or 'collect' (Bernstein, 1975) facts, principles and skills that have been selected for inclusion in one or another subject area instead of learning how those isolated elements might be used to inform larger, real-life purposes.

Second, since the Eight-Year Study of the 1930s, we have been getting signals that the separate-subject approach is an inappropriate route even for those purposes that its advocates claim for themselves (Aikin, 1942), As that study and others after it have indicated, young people tend to do at least as well, and often better, on traditional measures of school achievement when the curriculum moves further in the direction of integration.

Third, the separate subjects and the disciplines of knowledge that they are meant to represent are territories carved out by academicians for their own interests and purposes. Imposed on schools, the subject approach thus suggests that the 'good life' consists of intellectual activity within narrowly defined intellectual areas (Bloom, 1987; Hirsch, 1987; Ravitch and Finn, 1987). the notion that this is the only version of a 'good life', or the best one, or even a widely desirable one, demeans the lives of others outside the academy who have quite different views and aspirations. It is a remnant of the same 'top-down' version of the curriculum that has historically served the people in schools so poorly.

The fact that those academicians who so narrowly define the 'good life' happen to be mostly white, upper-middle class and male means that the knowledge they prize and select is of a particular kind. Such knowledge is of course the cultural capital of that limited group, and thus the cultures of 'other' people have been marginalised in the separate-subject approach. This is why the traditional question of the curriculum field, 'What knowledge is of most worth?', has been amended to 'Whose knowledge is of most worth?' As Michael Apple has pointed out, the fact that subject-centred curricula dominate most schools 'is at least partly the result of the place of the school in maximizing the production of high-status knowledge' (Apple, 1990: 38).

Pressing this point a bit further, we can see how such knowledge works in favour of the privileged young people in whose culture it is regularly found, while working harshly against those from nonprivileged homes and nondominant cultures. In this way, the separate-subject approach plays more than a small role in the 'sort and select' system that has been an unbecoming feature of our schools for so long. While curriculum integration by itself cannot resolve this issue, the use of real-life themes demands a wider range of content, while the placement of that content in thematic contexts is likely to make it more accessible for young people (Iran-Nejad et al., 1990).

For most young people, including the privileged, the separate-subject approach offers little more than a disconnected and incoherent assortment of facts and skills. There is no unity, no real sense to it at all. It is as if in real life, when faced with problems or puzzling situations, we stopped to ask which part is science, which part mathematics, which part art and so on.

We are taken aback when young people ask, 'Why are we doing this?' And our responses – 'Because it will be on the test' or 'Because you will need it next year' – are hardly sufficient to answer that question, let alone justify placing anything in the curriculum.

The deadening effect the separate-subject approach has on the lives of young people cannot be overestimated. In too many places, students are still taught how to diagram complex sentences as if that were the key to the writing process, still made to memorise the names and routes of European explorers, still taught the same arithmetic year after year, page after page, with no particular connection to their lives. I believe such irrelevance has also had a deadening effect on the lives of many teachers. Had they known that this would be their routine for 30 years or more and that high tension would result, many would probably have chosen a different line of work. And who could blame them?

The separate-subject approach is a legacy of Western-style classical humanism, which views the world in divided compartments. This view was shored up in the last century by the theories of faculty psychology and mental discipline that described the mind as a compartmentalised 'muscle' whose parts were to be exercised separately by particular disciplines (Kliebard, 1984). The reasoning faculty, for example, was supposedly exercised by the 'objective logic' of mathematics, and the assumption was that the heightened reasoning abilities could then be applied to any new situations, including social ones.

Though faculty psychology and mental discipline were discredited by the turn of the century, both live on in some interpretations of split-brain and multiple intelligence theories. And suspect as it has become, classical humanism still looms large in curriculum organisation as part of 'official knowledge' (Apple, 1993).

Knowledge in an integrated curriculum

Having exposed the shortcomings of the separate-subject approach, we may know turn back to the happier relations between curriculum integration and the disciplines of knowledge. How does knowledge look in the context of curriculum integration? What happens to the disciplines of knowledge? How are they used?

In practice, curriculum integration begins with the identification of organising themes or centres for learning experiences. As previously noted, the themes are drawn from real-life concerns, such as conflict; living in the future; cultures and identities; jobs, money and careers; or the environment. In some cases, the themes are identified by teachers; in the most sophisticated instances, they emerge from collaborative planning with young people (Zapf, 1959; Beane, 1991, 1992; Brodhagen et al., 1992; Brodhagen, 1995). Planning then proceeds directly to creating activities to address the theme and related issues. There is no intermediate step in which attempts are made to identify which subject areas might contribute to the theme.

This is a very important distinction, since curriculum integration, in theory and in practice, transcends subject-area and disciplinary identifications; the goal is integrative activities that use knowledge without regard for subject or discipline lines. Pretenders to this approach, such as 'multidisciplinary' or 'interdisciplinary' arrangements, may not follow a strict subject-centred format, but they nevertheless retain subject-area and disciplinary distinctions around some more or less unifying theme (James, 1972; Bernstein, 1975; Jacobs, 1989). (This structure is typically demonstrated by the fact that a student's schedule still involves a daily rotation through various subjects, even though the teachers may be attempting to use a common theme.) In curriculum integration, the schedule revolves around projects and activities rather than subjects. The disciplines of knowledge come into play as resources from which to draw in the context of the theme and related issues and activities.

For example, in a unit on 'living in the future', young people might survey their peers regarding their visions of the future, tabulate the results, compare them to other forecasts, and prepare research reports. Or they might look at technological, recreational, entertainment or social trends and develop forecasts or scenarios of probable futures for one or more areas. Or they might study past forecasts made for our own times to see if the predictions actually came true. Or they might develop recommendations for the future of their local communities in areas such as population, health, recreation, transportation and conservation. Or they might study the effects of ageing on facial features to imagine how they might look when they are older.

In a unit on 'the environment' they might create simulations of different biomes with real and constructed artefacts and offer guided 'tours' of their work. Or they might experiment with the effects of pollutants on plant growth. Or they might set up and manage a recycling programme in the classroom or school. Or they might identify the raw products in various clothing items and investigate where they came from, find out who makes them, and analyse the environmental and economic impacts of the entire process. Or they might identify environmental problems in their local community and seek ways to resolve them.

I have used the word 'or' between activities, since an integrative unit may involve one or any number of them. The point is this: any careful reading of the activities should reveal that, if they are done thoughtfully, they will draw heavily on a variety of disciplines of knowledge for facts, skills, concepts and understandings.

For example, in constructing surveys, tabulating data and preparing reports, one would need to draw heavily from the social sciences, language arts and mathematics. Suppose that some young people did not know how to compute percentages or make graphs. Obviously the teacher(s) would help them to learn how to do these things, or, if necessary, find someone else who knew how to do them. In experimenting with the effects of pollutants on plant life, some young people might not know how to carry out controlled tests. In that case, someone would teach them how to do that. Does this mean that schools would intentionally employ teachers who know 'stuff' from the disciplines of knowledge? Certainly! But in curriculum integration, teachers work first as generalists on integrative themes and secondarily as content specialists.

Note that, in curriculum integration, knowledge from the disciplines is repositioned into the context of the theme, questions and activities at hand. Even when teaching and learning move into what looks like discipline-based instruction, the theme continues to provide the context and the motivation, It is here that knowledge comes to life, has meaning and is more likely to be 'learned'. Particular knowledge is not abstracted or fragmented, as is the case when its identity and purpose are tied only to its place within a discipline or school subject area.

Repositioning knowledge in this way raises two issues that cannot be ignored. First, subject-area sequences that have previously defined the flow of knowledge tend to be rearranged in curriculum integration, since knowledge is called forth when it is pertinent, rather than when it is convenient. While this is upsetting to some subject-loyal teachers, we should note the irony that sequences often vary from school to school and from state to state. In other words, sequences are more arbitrary than those who construct and defend them would have us believe.[3] The fact that even some subject-area associations have moved away from traditional notions of sequencing should tell us something. In the end, though, advocates of curriculum integration are more interested in the rhythms and patterns of inquiring young minds than in the scopes and sequences of subject-area specialists. The work done within the context of curriculum integration *is* a curriculum; there is not another 'curriculum' waiting in the wings to be taught.

Second, it is entirely possible, even probable, that not all the information and skills now disseminated by separate-subject teaching will come to the surface in the context of curriculum integration. But let's face it: there is a good deal of trivia now being disseminated in schools that would be necessary and meaningful only if and when one became a specialist in one or other discipline of knowledge, and even then some of it would probably be superfluous. In some places the separate-subject curriculum looks more like preparation for doing the *New York Times* crossword puzzle than for specialising in a discipline. Besides, the very idea of knowing all that 'stuff' is a pipedream in an era when yesterday's 'truths' seem to dissolve in the high tide of today's new knowledge.

Curriculum integration, on the other hand, calls forth those ideas that are most important and powerful in the disciplines of knowledge – the ones that are most significant because they emerge in life itself. And because they are placed in the context of personally and socially significant concerns, they are more likely to have real meaning in the lives of young people, the kind of meaning they do not now have.

Notes

1 A fuller version of this chapter was originally published as: 'Curriculum integration and the disciplines of knowledge', by James Beane, *Phi Delta Kappan Journal* 78(8) (1995): 616–22.
2 Here, and throughout the article, I am using the term 'knowledge' to include knowing about, knowing why, knowing how and so on. Thus 'knowledge' would include information, skills, concepts, processes and so on.
3 It is instructive to note that alphabetical order rather than disciplinary structure created the usual biology–chemistry–physics sequence.

References

Aikin, W. (1942) *The Story of the Eight Year Study*, New York: Harper and Row.
Alpern, M. (ed.) (1967) *The Subject Curriculum: Grades K-12*, Columbus, OH: Charles E. Merrill.
Apple, M. (1990) *Ideology and Curriculum* (2nd ed.), London: Routledge and Kegan Paul.
—— (1993) *Official Knowledge: Democratic Education in a Conservative Age*, New York: Routledge.
Beane, J. (1991) The middle school: the natural home of the integrated curriculum, *Educational Leadership* 49: 9–13.
—— (1992) Turning the floor over: reflections on a middle school curriculum, *Middle School Journal* 23(3): 34–40.
—— (1993a) *A Middle School Curriculum: From Rhetoric to Reality* (rev. ed.), Columbus, OH: National Middle School Association.
—— (1993b) *Affect in the Curriculum: Towards Democracy, Dignity and Diversity*, New York: Routledge.
Bernstein, B. (1975) *Class, Codes and Control*, vol. 3: *Towards a Theory of Educational Transmissions* (2nd ed.), London: Routledge and Kegan Paul.
Bloom, A. (1987) *The Closing of the American Mind*, New York: Simon and Schuster.
Brady, M. (1989) *What's Worth Teaching?*, Albany, NY: State University of New York Press.
Brodhagen, B.. (1995) The situation made us special, in Michael Apple and James Beane (eds) *Democratic Schools*, Alexandria, VA: Association for Supervision and Curriculum Development.
Brodhagen, B., Weilbacher, G. and Beane, J. (1992) Living in the future: an experiment with an Integrative Curriculum, *Dissemination Services on the Middle Grades* 23(9): 1–7.
Bruner, J. (1960) *The Process of Education*, Cambridge, MA: Harvard University Press.
—— (1971) The process of education reconsidered, in Robert S. Leeper (ed.) *Dare to Care/Dare to Act: Racism and Education*, Washington, DC: Association for Supervision and Curriculum Development.
Connell, R. W. (1993) *Schools and Social Justice*, Philadelphia, PN: Temple University Press.
Dewey, J. (1915) *The School and Society* (rev. ed.), Chicago: University of Chicago Press.
Dressel, P. (1958) The meaning and significance of integration, in N. Henry (ed.) *The Integration of Educational Experiences: 57th NSSE Yearbook, Part III*, Chicago: National Society for the Study of Education, University of Chicago Press.
Ford, G. and Pongo, L. (1964) *The Structure of Knowledge and the Curriculum*, Chicago: Rand McNally.
Henry, G. (1956) Foundations of general education in the high school, in *What Shall the High schools Teach? 1956 ASCD Yearbook*, Washington, DC: Association for Supervision and Curriculum Development.
Hirsch, Jr, E. D. (1987) *Cultural Literacy*, Boston: Houghton Mifflin.
Hopkins, T. L. *et al.* (1937) *Integration: Its Meaning and Application*, New York: Appleton-Century.
Iran-Nejad, A.,Wilbert, J., McKeachie, W. and Berliner, D. (1990) The multi-source nature of learning: an introduction, *Review of Educational Research* 60(4): 509–15.
Jacobs, H. (ed.) (1989) *Interdisciplinary Curriculum: Design and Implementation*, Alexandria, VA: Association for Supervision and Curriculum Development.
James, C. (1972) *Young Lives at Stake*, New York: Agathon.
King, A. and Brownell, J. (1966) *The Curriculum and the Disciplines of Knowledge*, New York: Wiley.
Klein, J. T. (1990) *Interdisciplinarity: History, Theory and Practice*, Detroit, MI: Wayne State University Press.
Kliebard, H. (1984) The decline of humanistic studies in the American school curriculum, in Benjamin Ladner (ed.) *The Humanities in Pre-collegiate Education: 83rd NSSE Yearbook, Part II*, Chicago: National Society for the Study of Education, University of Chicago Press.
Lurry, L. and Alberty, E. (1957) *Developing the High School Core Programme*, New York: Macmillan.
Noar, G. (1966) *The Teacher and Integration*, Washington, DC: National Education Association.
Ravitch, D. and Finn, C. E. (1987) *What Do Our 17-Year-Olds Know?* New York: Harper and Row.
Vars, G. (1991) Integrated curriculum in historical perspective, *Educational Leadership* (October): 14–15.
Zapf. R. (1959) *Democratic Processes in the Classroom*, Englewood Cliffs, NJ: Prentice-Hall.

21

Ways of knowing and teaching

How teachers create valuable learning opportunities (pedagogical capital) by making knowledge the means and not just the ends in classrooms

Debra Hayes

Introduction

Creative teaching and learning have the potential to disrupt standard classrooms and to produce more equitable outcomes from schooling, but it is often difficult to convince teachers to let go of familiar practices. In settings where the standard classroom is successful, it appears hard to justify the need for more creative teaching and learning, and in settings where it is not successful, it is difficult for teachers to let go of the perception of control afforded by standard classroom practices. This chapter examines the tension between creativity and control in classrooms through two Australian longitudinal studies completed in the first decade of the twenty-first century. These research projects are briefly described and their contributions to understanding the nexus between creativity and control are outlined. In particular, important differences associated with how teachers position themselves in relation to their students and knowledge are discussed. The potential of even routine practices to produce more valuable effects when teachers position themselves as knowledge brokers is explored through the classroom practices of two teachers. These teachers demonstrate high levels of pedagogical capital by providing students with open access to knowledge and supporting their engagement with knowledge producing processes.

Standard classroom practices serve diverse groups of young people in differential ways, beginning with variations in the capacity of these practices to support successful transitions from home to school. Finding ways to disrupt such practices is necessary because shaky foundations amplify the likelihood of not doing well at school and are likely to weaken levels of attendance and retention, whereas good beginnings support more secure learning pathways and enhance the likelihood of completing school and moving on from it to other forms of work or learning. Differential outcomes from schooling are the predictable, albeit generally unintended, consequences of commonplace schooling. Various technologies have been deployed in the name of limiting these consequences, such as highly specific syllabus documents, frequent standardised tests and tightly framed policy, which are intended to regulate and monitor teachers. They also produce a tension in school classrooms between control and creativity. This tension arises because systematic efforts to control teachers, as well as teachers' own efforts to control students, can work against the creativity, flexibility and innovation required to engage diverse groups of young people in learning.

In an extensive review of three decades of research on classroom life, Arnetha Ball acknowledges a longstanding interest in the literature in 'the core problem of control in schooling' (2002: 78). She traces this interest back to Lortie's (1975) research, which confirmed that classrooms are complex spaces in which teachers generally work to maintain control and a sense of order while also arousing and sustaining students' interest. Ball argues that 'The most common solution applied to the problem of control is implementation of the model of the "standard classroom", that is, a teacher-centered classroom in which students sit in rows and the dominant focus next to learning is control' (Ball, 2002: 78). Apart from their uniformity, the problem with these practices is that they are largely unsuccessful in challenging contexts (e.g. Connell, 1991; Knapp *et al.*, 1995; Hayes, 2009). Access to cultural capital and other resources compensate for standard classroom practice in less challenging contexts. It is also easier to achieve and sustain learning in the absence of high teacher and student turnover, high levels of poverty and difference, large numbers of first time leaders and early career teachers, and isolation in rural and remote areas, which are features of challenging contexts in Australia. The standard classroom is not easily disrupted in ways that support conditions more conducive to creativity, flexibility and innovation. Even so, the practices of some teachers provide insight into the nature of this problem, which is explored below by drawing upon two Australian studies.

Paying attention to what happens in classrooms

The Queensland School Reform Longitudinal Study (QSRLS) is unusual because the observation schedule that formed the centrepiece of its research design is perhaps better known than its findings. This structured observation instrument detailed twenty classroom practices that became known as *productive pedagogies* (Hayes *et al.*, 2006; Lingard *et al.*, 2000, 2003). The QSRLS[1] produced an inventory of these pedagogies in twenty-four Queensland schools over three years, 1998–2000, yielding almost 1,000 classroom observations. Each of the twenty elements of productive pedagogies was defined by a 1 (low) to 5 (high) coding scheme. Table 21.1 shows the description of the average code for each element across all the classrooms included in the study. The actual numerical average for each dimension and element is also shown in parentheses.

The findings of the study illustrate the enduring reach of the standard classroom into the twenty-first century. The overall picture of this classroom is one in which the lesson proceeds with minimal interruption, social support for the students is generally positive, and students tend to remain on task doing activities predetermined by the teacher. At least one significant issue may be treated in depth, but generally the focus is not sustained and not all students demonstrate a deep understanding of this issue, which is not required of them, and conversations with the teacher tend to be brief exchanges of information. In addition, the substance of the lesson is generally not linked to past learning experiences, the world beyond the classroom or other subjects studied at school. The cultural knowledge of students is generally not recognised or valued. Since a broad range of school types and locations were included in the study, we can assume that the standard classroom is perhaps widespread and in common usage in schools that are generally considered to be performing well (a criterion for inclusion in the study).

Table 21.1 Productive Pedagogies coding sheet (showing QSRLS averages for n = 975)

Dimensions	Elements	Description of the average code for the element across the whole study
Supportiveness (3.03)	Student self regulation (4.04)	Once or twice during the lessons, teachers must correct student behaviour or movement. There is only minor interruption to the lesson.
	Academic engagement (3.73)	Engagement is widespread; most students, most of the time are on-task pursuing the substance of the lesson; most students seem to be taking the work seriously and trying hard.
	Social support for student achievement (3.66)	Social support from the teacher is clearly positive and there is some evidence of social support among students for their peers. Evidence of special efforts by the teacher take the form of direct expressions that convey high expectations for all; mutual respect; a need to try hard and risk initial failure.
	Explicit quality performance criteria (2.13)	Some procedural parameters, advanced organisers and aspects of the general direction of the lesson have been specified but students are working without explicit statement of outcomes.
	Students' direction of activities (1.60)	Teacher makes initial selection of activity, but students exercise some control, through a choice of procedure or manner in which the task is completed.
Intellectual Quality (2.27)	Depth of knowledge (2.71)	Knowledge is treated unevenly during instruction; i.e., deep knowledge of something is countered by superficial understanding of other knowledge. At least one significant idea may be presented in depth, but in general the focus is not sustained.
	Depth of students' understanding (2.60)	Students' deep understanding is uneven. Deep understanding of something, by some students, is countered by superficial understanding of other knowledge (by either the same or other students). At least one significant idea may be understood in depth, but in general the focus is not sustained.
	Higher order thinking (2.56)	Students are primarily engaged in routine lower order thinking a good share of the lesson. There is at least one significant question or activity in which some students perform some higher order thinking.
	Substantive conversation (2.27)	Features B (DIALOGUE) and/or C (LOGICAL EXTENSION & SYNTHESIS) occur briefly and involve at least ONE SUSTAINED EXCHANGE.
	Metalanguage (1.75)	Some meta-language: the teacher proceeds through the lesson, stopping to make value judgments or commentary on language, but without providing any technical terminology, or constructive assistance and clarification.
	Knowledge is presented as problematic (1.74)	Some knowledge seen as problematic – but interpretations linked/reducible to given body of facts.

Table 21.1 (continued)

Dimensions	Elements	Description of the average code for the element across the whole study
Connectedness (2.07)	Link to background knowledge (2.62)	Initial reference or solicitation is made by the teacher to background knowledge and experience. At least some connection to out-of-school background knowledge.
	Problem-based curriculum (2.02)	Some minor and small problems (no correct solution) are posed to the students but they require little knowledge construction by students.
	Connectedness to the world beyond the classroom (1.91)	Students encounter a topic, problem or issue that the teacher tries to connect to students' experiences or to contemporary public situations; i.e., the teacher informs students that there is potential value in the knowledge being studied because it relates to the world beyond the classroom. For example, students are told that understanding Middle East history is important for politicians trying to bring peace to the region; however, the connection is weak and there is no evidence that students make the connection.
	School subject knowledge is integrated (1.76)	Knowledge mostly restricted to that of a specific subject area, with minor intrusions limited to connections with one other (separate) discipline.
Recognition of difference (1.94)	Inclusivity (4.0)	Participation of non-dominant social groups for at least half of the lesson, but not all (nor nearly all) of the lesson.
	Narrative (1.95)	Narrative is present in either the processes or content of the lesson, but the use of this narrative may only be on occasion or as a minor deviation from the main portion of the lesson.
	Knowledge of the curriculum explicitly values all cultures (1.35)	No explicit recognition or valuing of other than the dominant culture in curriculum knowledge transmitted to students.
	Group identities in a Learning community (1.19)	No evidence of community within the classroom; no positive recognition of difference and group identities; and no support for the development of difference and group identities. Students are all treated as individuals.
	Active citizenship (1.19)	The citizenship rights of students and teachers are neither discussed nor practised within the classroom.

During the many hours in which I observed teachers while conducting QSRLS fieldwork, I came to recognise ways in which the relationship between teachers, students and knowledge defines the nature of learning and teaching in classrooms. I was reminded of the earlier work of Berlak and Berlak, who described 'how teachers through their schooling acts transmit knowledge and ways of knowing and learning' (1981: 144). They articulated a set of curriculum dilemmas which distinguish between personal knowledge and public knowledge; between knowledge as content and knowledge as process; and between knowledge as given and knowledge as problematical. These dilemmas illustrate some of the possible ways in which teachers position themselves in relation to students and knowledge in classrooms. The findings of the QSRLS suggest that most teachers resolve these dilemmas by emphasising the first element over the second in each pair (i.e. they emphasize personal knowledge, knowledge as content and knowledge as given). In other words, teachers tend to position themselves as experts or sources of knowledge, with responsibility for connecting young people to selected pre-existing knowledge, whereas an emphasis of the second element (i.e. public knowledge, knowledge as process and knowledge as problematical) is more likely to see teachers position themselves as brokers or facilitators of knowledge production, and they would be more likely to work alongside students as co-learners, to be curious and to engage in the kind of knowledge production that is more open ended, requiring problem solving and the manipulation of information. Teachers who emphasise this second set of elements were uncommon among the QSRLS participants. In order to capture more of these kinds of teachers, in the second year we asked principals and teachers to recommend teachers we should observe. Layne was recommended to us by her principal.

Layne

When we first met Layne, she was a PE (Physical Education) teacher at a secondary school in a large coastal town. When it was my turn to observe her class, I recall finding her on a distant playing field, whistle in hand, umpiring a ball game between two groups of students, with another group scattered around the sidelines clutching clipboards and pens, closely observing the game. It was not a game that I was familiar with, and just when I thought I was starting to get the rules, Layne would blow her whistle and shout out a change in the rules, 'Right, now you can't score a goal if it's been touched by three people on your team, you have to hand the ball over. OK?' After about twenty minutes all three teams gathered in close to Layne, and the students who had been taking notes by the sidelines explained how the player they were assigned to observe had performed the skills required of their position on the field, and how they adapted to the changing rules of the game. This was not just a game of football. All the students on the field were required to continually reconsider how to adapt to the new rules, while playing their position and working with other members of their team; and the students on the sidelines were focused on matching criteria to the performance of the player they were observing. In conversation with Layne afterwards, I realised that there were endless permutations on the rules and roles assigned to students, and she was able to articulate a well-considered purpose for each modification.

Paying close attention to how changes in the rules of the game created new conditions, challenges and response from players was a mechanism by which Layne and her students were able to explore the contingent and shifting possibilities of arrangement that are generally taken for granted, such as knowledge, identity and social arrangements. Different agreements about what was permitted and what was disallowed produced different kinds of games requiring a diverse set of skills and interactions from the players. The students were literally thinking on the run. They were required to adapt as individuals and as members of a team. Regular opportunities to discuss their experiences and observations generated rich forms of dialogue in which the students described and compared their experiences; proposed explanations for how the shifting rules changed the game, the playing conditions and the players' responses; and speculated about how they might work more effectively as individuals, and together as a team.

Within the context of the QSRLS, Layne stood out because her classroom looked quite different to the standard classroom that we generally observed. There was nothing particularly remarkable about the classroom practices she utilised. For the most part she used routine pedagogical devices – she was umpiring a game on a field and students were taking turns to watch or participate. Even so, Layne was able to establish relationships with her students that were centrally concerned with knowledge and its production. What distinguished her practice was the value and quality of its effects, particularly those related to learning. She demonstrated strong disciplinary knowledge and expressed an unwavering confidence in her ability to teach. She viewed teaching as a series of dilemmas to be solved, sometimes on a daily or minute-by-minute basis. She maintained a firm belief in the capacity of her students to learn, and she associated difficulties that she experienced in the classroom with her practice rather than problems associated with her students and their backgrounds. She created a classroom where learning matters.

Most teachers were only observed once during each week-long visit to their school, but once a member of the research team had observed Layne, all the others were lining up to see her too because very few teachers had coded so high on our observation instrument. Her reaction to our interest suggested that she was not aware that she was doing anything different to other teachers. In a subsequent conversation with her, she acknowledged: 'No one talked about it, so I didn't know what other teachers taught.'

Given the widespread uniformity of classroom contexts, which generally include one teacher positioned at the front of an enclosed room with an old or new piece of technology for writing and displaying images, twenty to thirty students seated in desks placed in rows or some other formation, and a daily schedule that is divided into blocks of time dedicated to different parts of the curriculum, it is perhaps not surprising that these spaces and relationships take on familiar and common forms. But there is great variation in what teachers can achieve in these spaces. These variations are reflected in differences between the lower and higher codes for each element in the productive pedagogies scale. For example, most teachers acknowledge the importance of building upon students' background knowledge. They usually make an initial reference to it early in the lesson. This may involve a recount of what was done in the last lesson and a link to out-of-school experiences, but few consistently incorporate students' background knowledge and experiences into the lesson, such that the lesson shunts back and forth between known material and new material. In these lessons, students are provided with opportunities to make connections between their linguistic, cultural and world knowledge and experience, and the topics, skills, competencies at hand. Background knowledge may include community knowledge, local knowledge, personal experience, media and popular culture sources.

By highlighting background knowledge here, I'm not suggesting that it or any element of productive pedagogies should be present in *every* class. However, I do want to emphasise that there are significant variations in how these practices are implemented, and I want to underscore the important differences that arise as a result of how teachers position themselves in relation to their students and the production of knowledge. Seddon's (2001) explanation of how teachers' curriculum choices regulate students' access to particular knowledge, and thereby serve particular social ends, is very helpful in understanding this relationship. More than the requirements of the syllabus, the conscious and unconscious choices of teachers determine what knowledge should be taught, and to whom. This form of local curriculum decision making includes certain forms of knowledge, skills and dispositions while excluding others. It also determines how access to forms of knowledge is distributed across society. These decisions about content and distribution '[shape] education as a social technology that serves particular social ends' (Seddon, 2001: 308–9).

A subsequent study provided the opportunity to examine how education acts as a social technology in communities with deep needs. From 2005 to 2007, *Changing Schools in Changing Times* (CSCT)[2] was conducted in four schools, one rural and three metropolitan. All were engaged in various forms of whole school reform, and were at various stages of implementation; and all were receiving additional equity-based funding through the New South Wales Department of Education and Training Priority Schools Funding Program.[3] An important aspect of this study was ongoing dialogue between researchers and participants. While we had access to the language of productive pedagogies, we wanted a framework that described the overall pattern of classrooms, rather than its constituent parts, and we wanted a language that resonated with teachers' experiences. My colleague Ken Johnston and I developed the four quadrant framework shown in Figure 21.1 for supporting these conversations (Johnston and Hayes, 2008). This 'talking point' allowed us to discuss the classroom practices visible in the school within a broader understanding of what might be possible.

In conversation with participants in the study, most teachers stated that they aspired to achieve a negotiated interactive learning environment (quadrant D), and a very small number did, but for the most part the standard script or orderly restricted environment (quadrant B) prevailed. In these spaces, teachers spent large amounts of time attempting to achieve and maintain order and control. Some were more successful than others. In the process, learning was displaced and pushed into the background by default practices that generally took the form of completing missing words on worksheets, copying notes from the board (or some other technology) and completing other prescribed tasks which made limited intellectual demands upon the students. In these classrooms, control was tenuous and fragile. Teachers generally provided a range of commonly held explanations for why these practices represented the limits of what was possible in *this* context, at *this* time, with *these* students.

The case study nature of this research allowed us to linger in places for longer periods of time than was possible in the QSRLS. We observed a small number of teachers whose classrooms could be described as orderly enabling learning environments (quadrant C). In these spaces, learning was a more central concern and the teacher only occasionally had to take explicit steps to maintain order and control. Julie illustrated this kind of teacher.

Julie

Julie came to our attention because a number of parents had noted during interviews that their children did not bring work home from school, except Japanese, which they seemed to enjoy. Julie worked in a junior secondary school (Years 7–9) in a medium sized country town. Unlike many of her peers, who were doing time while waiting to return to the city, she had put down roots and was planning to stay. She gave the impression that she liked her subject, having spent many years living in Japan and following other career paths before deciding to become a teacher. She was respected by her colleague teachers, and had very few problems managing students' challenging behaviours.

Julie's classes ran according to a very tight script framed by different coloured worksheets, some reading aloud, teacher directed questions, cutting and pasting, and other routines practices. Over this was layered constant dialogue: unscripted and student directed exchanges,

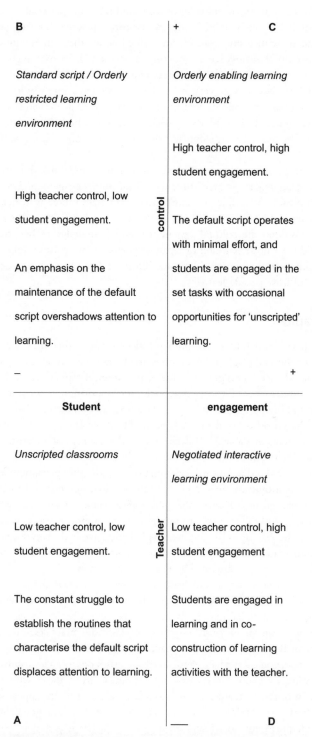

B | + | C

Standard script / Orderly restricted learning environment

Orderly enabling learning environment

High teacher control, high student engagement.

High teacher control, low student engagement.

control

An emphasis on the maintenance of the default script overshadows attention to learning.

The default script operates with minimal effort, and students are engaged in the set tasks with occasional opportunities for 'unscripted' learning.

− +

Student   **engagement**

Unscripted classrooms

Negotiated interactive learning environment

Low teacher control, low student engagement.

Teacher

Low teacher control, high student engagement

The constant struggle to establish the routines that characterise the default script displaces attention to learning.

Students are engaged in learning and in co-construction of learning activities with the teacher.

A | — | D

Figure 21.1 Four-quadrant framework
Adapted from: Johnston & Hayes, 2008, p.116.

explorations of cultural difference, mini-lessons on grammar and personal anecdotes that filled the interstices created by Julie's tightly scripted classroom practice. During an interview, she explained her concern with losing control. She talked about the settlements she reaches with students. No longer do they involve negotiating time on task in exchange for time wasted, playing games. Instead, she 'digs in' and enforces expectations and the completion of set work. When I observed her class, it was very clear that the students knew what was expected of them. When the bell rang, no one moved until she checked each individuals work. Departure from the room was gradual and orderly as each student finished. Julie achieved things with her students that other teachers with similar experience were not able to achieve in the same context.

To a casual observer, Julie's classroom might appear like any other, but in a school where teachers generally struggled to engage students in learning, engagement was widespread and sustained in Julie's classes. As well as the intellectual challenges inherent in her extended dialogue with her students, Julie's classes were places where cultural difference was a constant theme. She recognised and valued the cultural experiences and knowledge of her students, and drew upon these to build their understanding of Japanese language and culture. Julie's recollections of how she came to know and understand Japanese informed her approach to teaching and shaped her understanding of how people learn.

Pedagogical capital

Close analysis of Layne and Julie's classroom practices suggests that they were able to obtain greater value out of the pedagogical devices they used than their colleagues working in similar contexts with similar devices. This greater value or pedagogical capital[4] took the form of deeper and more sustained treatments of knowledge, including opportunities for students to engage in sustained dialogue and higher order thinking, and transparent connections between the substance of the lesson and the world beyond the classroom. These are the elements of productive pedagogies (see bold elements in Table 21.1) derived from the concept of authentic pedagogy which was developed by Newmann & Associates (1996). They asserted that when compared to conventional instruction and conventional organisations, authentic pedagogy and authentically restructured schools demonstrate overall greater rates of achievement and more equitable outcomes between equity groups. Hence, the pedagogical capital associated with the classroom practices of both Layne and Julie is likely to provide strong support for success at school, which is critically important when students lack cultural capital and have had shaky foundations at school. Layne's practice also made knowledge problematic, and Julie's was distinguished by how she worked with and incorporated cultural differences in her lesson.

The problem for teachers and school leaders is how to increase the pedagogical capital of classroom practices. The issue is not, as it is so often imagined, to implement a more diverse range of pedagogies since what matters is how pedagogies are implemented in classrooms. Hence, engagement is not an instrinsic property of classroom practices, but an effect of how teachers make use of these practices. Some teachers are able to create valuable learning effects from even routine pedagogical devices. A further issue arises because classrooms characterised by low pedagogical capital are not always easy to distinguish from those with high pedagogical capital. In other words, the standard classroom is not always as it might appear since the findings of the QSRLS show that students in both types of classrooms are generally self-regulating, engagement is widespread and social support from the teacher is generally positive. However, pedagogical capital provides a means by which these classrooms may be distinguished, and a rationale for disrupting what is commonplace.

Layne and Julie teach us that disrupting the standard classroom requires a shift in how knowledge is produced in classrooms. The pedagogical capital associated with their classroom practices may be at least partly attributed to the strength of their disciplinary knowledge, their unwavering confidence in their ability to teach, their belief in the capacity of their students to learn and their capacity to create classrooms where learning matters. It is also in large part due to how they position themselves in their classrooms in relation to their students and to knowledge. They choose to provide students with more open access to knowledge, and to engage them in knowledge producing dialogue. Their approaches are quite different: Layne emphasises the contingent and contested nature of knowledge, whereas Julie emphasises its structure and how culture produces variations in what is valued and known. Both choose to let young people in on how knowledge is produced and worked with in their disciplinary contexts. They do not just facilitate students' access to knowledge, they work alongside them as they engage with knowledge and experience its potential and its limitations.

The tension between creativity and control is a feature of classrooms that many teachers resolve through the adoption of standard classroom practices. While these practices may produce acceptable outcomes in contexts where other resources and conditions compensate for their limiting effects, in the absence of pedagogical capital they lock in differential outcomes from schooling by excluding some groups of young people from forms of knowledge and knowledge producing processes. Creative learning and teaching are more likely to happen when teachers resolve curriculum dilemmas in ways that engage students in knowledge producing processes. This requires a repositioning of teachers in the standard classroom, from standing between students and knowledge, to standing alongside them as critical collaborators in its application and production.

Notes

1 The original purpose of the research commissioned by the Queensland government was to evaluate the contribution or otherwise of school-based management to student learning outcomes. However, critical links between students, schools and extant data sets proved difficult to establish. The research did link classroom practices to student outcomes through an analysis of class sets of assessment tasks. The assumption underpinning the modified research design was that classrooms in which there were high levels of productive pedagogies were more likely to produce high quality intellectual and social outcomes for students that would be reflected in assessment practices. The tasks were chosen and supplied by teachers of English, mathematics, science or social studies in Years 6, 8 or 11 who participated in the study. Each teacher was observed at least twice during the research, and these observations were accompanied by extensive interviews about their pedagogical and assessment practices, as well as a broad range of issues related to their understanding of their schools and education in general. Extensive interviews were also conducted with principals and other key personnel in each of the research schools during each visit (Hayes *et al.*, 2006).

2 The *Changing Schools in Changing Times* research project was funded through the Australian Research Council's Linkage program in partnership with the NSW Department of Education and Training. The members of the research team included (in alphabetical order): Narelle Carey, Debra Hayes, Ken Johnston, Ann King, Rani Lewis-Jones, Kristal Morris, Chris Murray, Ishbel Murray, Kerith Power, Dianne Roberts, Kitty te Riele and Margaret Wheeler.

3 There were 2,225 state schools in NSW, but only eighty of these received this type of funding, which included an average yearly grant of Aus$200,000, as well as additional staffing and counselling support.

4 Livingston has very usefully described pedagogical capital as a subtype of cultural capital that offers an unconscious privilege to those students who possess it. In her terms, pedagogical capital 'is a quality that some students possess that enables them to arrive at the academic table better positioned to take advantage of our educational offerings' (Livingston, 2007: 1). In this paper, pedagogical capital is conceptualised as an attribute of teachers' practices.

References

Ball, A. F. (2002) Three decades of research on classroom life: illuminating the classroom communicative lives of America's at-risk students, *Review of Research in Education*, New York: AERA Publication.

Berlak, A. and Berlak, H. (1981) Dilemmas of schooling: teaching and social change, London and New York: Methuen & Co.

Connell, R. W. (1991) The workforce of reform: teachers in the disadvantaged schools program, *Australian Journal of Education* 35: 229–45.

Hayes, D. (2009) Pedagogies of place and possibility, in M. Sommerville, K. Power and P. de Carteret (eds) *Landscapes and Learning: Place Studies in a Global World*, Rotterdam: Sense Publishers.

Hayes, D., Mills, M., Christie, P. and Lingard, B. (2006) *Teachers and Schooling Making a Difference: Productive Pedagogies, Assessment and Performance*, Sydney: Allen & Unwin Publishers.

Johnston, K. and Hayes, D. (2008) 'This is as good as it gets': classroom lessons and learning in challenging circumstances, *Australian Journal of Language and Literacy* 31(2): 109–27.

Knapp, M., Shields, P. and Turnbull, B. (1995) Academic challenge in high poverty classrooms, *Phi Delta Kappan* 76: 770–6.

Lingard, B., Mills, M. and Hayes, D. (2000) Teachers school reform and social justice: challenging research and practice, *Australian Educational Researcher* 27(3): 93–109.

—— (2003) Teachers and productive pedagogies: contextualising, conceptualising, utilising, *Pedagogy, Culture and Society* 11(3): 399–424.

Lingard, B., Ladwig, J., Mills, M., Bahr, M., Chant, D., Warry, M., Ailwood, J., Capeness, R., Christie, P., Gore, J., Hayes, D. and Luke, A. (2001) *The Queensland School Reform Longitudinal Study*, Brisbane: Department of Education.

Livingston, C. V. (2007) The privilege of pedagogical capital: a framework for understanding scholastic success in mathematics, *Philosophy of Mathematics Education Journal* 20, Special Issue on Social Justice, Part 1, chapter on Social Class; available at http://people.exeter.ac.uk/PErnest/pome20/index.htm (accessed 20 June 2007).

Lortie, D. C. (1975) *Schoolteacher: A Sociological Study*, Chicago: University of Chicago Press.

Newmann, F. & Associates (1996) *Authentic Achievement: Restructuring Schools for Intellectual Quality*, San Francisco: Jossey-Bass.

Seddon, T. (2001) National curriculum in Australia? A matter of politics, powerful knowledge and the regulation of learning Pedagogy, *Culture and Society* 9(3): 307–32.

22

English for an era of instability

Aesthetics, ethics, creativity and design[1]

Gunther Kress

English cannot be thought about seriously other than as a part of the entire school curriculum and of its fullest purposes. That in turn cannot be thought about other than in the context of the widest economic, social and cultural considerations. Along with many others, I part company with current directions in asking the questions about the curriculum not from a political but from a social and cultural point of view. A political view has to take the purposes of the state into consideration; and that is where we can locate the desire for 'authority'. A state that has lost control of the national economy will need to assert control in some other domain. It can do so at the administrative and social level, as in the instance above; or it can attempt to do so at the cultural level, in determining curricula, for instance in respect to the valued texts to be taught as defining a national culture; or of the (standard form of the) language to be used or required in instruction. In a political approach, the question around curriculum and pedagogy is shaped by the needs of the state, first and foremost: 'What form of education will guarantee the requirements for authority and control?'

A social and cultural viewpoint produces different results. It does not guarantee, by any means, a consensus on these issues. However, satisfying the requirements for the exercise of state power ceases to be an issue. A social view takes the needs and problems of social organisations and those of their individual members, their structures and processes, as having prior importance. Of course, one inescapable and essential component of that environment is the economy, so that its considerations will play a significant part. Equally, the culturally distinct and differentiated groups that constitute 'the social', whatever their origins, constitutions or purposes – whether those of 'ethnic' difference, of class, gender, age, profession, regionality, taste (as 'lifestyle') or many others – become concerns in a socially oriented approach. From this perspective the question around curriculum changes: 'What is it that education should offer so that those in school might lead productive lives in their near and medium-term individual and social futures?'

This differs from a notion of education as cultural or social 'reproduction', which had focused on the requirements for the effective reproduction of social forms and processes as much as of cultural meanings and values. Crucially, the goal of 'reproduction' had assumed *stability* of social and of cultural forms, so that one of the functions of the education system had been that of guaranteeing stability in general: whether of the reliable replication of (curricular/cultural) knowledge; or the production of individual disposition oriented towards high valuations of stability. Stability and authority are soul mates, and together they had provided compatible underpinnings for state, society and culture. In educational terms they made for curricula, pedagogies and forms of administration which were in harmony with each other and with those of a society and its state. They provided a common frame, and made for smooth transitions from the social institution of education to the social and economic institutions around the school.

The goal of 'reproduction' is no longer sustainable, other than in ideologically shaped nostalgias. If the large environment in which the school exists is now one of radical *instability*, then the essential goal has to be one of *education for instability*. But *education for instability* has entirely different consequences and effects – whether for learning, for knowledge expressed in the curricula of school subjects, or for social relations expressed as pedagogies – than did *education for stability*. We can say, and readily see, that curricula currently are governed by the latter rather than the former. Yet the curriculum overall has to be able to respond robustly to the demands for an education for instability. Its first requirement is to produce an adequate response to questions about social and economic futures: 'What does the school need to offer so that those now experiencing schooling will be fully prepared for the demands they will face in their cultural, social and economic futures?'

In its outward form, this question is the same as those posed currently by policy-makers. So where is the difference? My contention is that *for policy-makers education is still conceived in terms of reproduction*, and is still seen, however implicitly, as education for stability – whether of knowledge in the shape of curriculum subjects; of practices in the shape of skills; of human dispositions in the shape of dependable performance of routine tasks; and so on. Whether in the look of current curricula or of pedagogies implemented or wished for, both speak loudly of such imaginings.

Any curriculum has to have clear answers to the question 'What is it for?' We know that curricula and pedagogies are historically shaped. The question 'What is science for?' has a different answer now from that which it would have received some 30, 40 or 50 years ago. Then it would have been answered in two ways – as preparation for a possible career in science or in areas depending on scientific knowledge, medicine for instance, and as induction into the knowledge defining the 'cultured person'. Now the answer is much more likely to focus on the ability to participate in entirely usual aspects of social life – decisions about diet, about preventative health care, sport, decisions about the environment, and so on. School science, it is assumed, provides the future citizen – or consumer – with essential means for making informed choices in such areas.

And yet there is a deeper, less historically specific level at which the answers might not differ that much between now and then. Science still provides foundational knowledge about the means by which Western cultures engage with the natural world. For Mathematics, for English, as for some other curriculum subjects, similarly 'deep' purposes might be seen: Mathematics as the subject which has its specialised means for projecting theoretically satisfactory accounts of the physical world; and English as the subject that provides means for understanding the relation of an inner world of imagination and desire with the outer world of culture and of social demands. It is at this level that I wish to discuss the question 'What is English for?' Of course, as well as the historical specificity of any form of 'English', there are cultural, regional, social, economic specificities that will make the answers seem very different in different places. I have to rely on the willingness of readers to translate my comments to the varying contexts in which they live and work. So, what is a possible justification for continuing with a subject that might be called 'English' – even though different names might begin to emerge for it in different places?

New tasks

'Is there a continuing reason for the "school" to engage with questions of imagination, creativity and innovation in their inter-relation with the cultural and social world, and if there is, then where in the curriculum is the place for this to happen?' At a second step we could ask about the specific shape of such a subject now, in the era of globalisation, of political, social and cultural fragmentation, of the new information and communication technologies. My reason for mentioning 'Science' and 'Mathematics' just above was to insist that those subjects which will remain central in the curriculum do so because they have specific, socially and culturally profound tasks. Of course, they too will need to deal with the issue of instability on their terms, from their standpoints. They are not, however, candidate subjects for fulfilling the task I have suggested for English.

I take it for granted that now, even more than before, there is an absolute need for a subject with the task of relating the world of inner work and action with the outer world of social and cultural work. In the past, that task had had the function of establishing criteria for separating a future elite from those whose future lay in supporting that elite. Now it lies at the core of all social and economic life, even if newly and differently configured. If this is so, we might as well settle for the subject that had been 'English' to remain responsible for such a task. The question of naming that subject is a separate one; it will have different answers in different places, depending largely on political and historical circumstances – in England there seems no possibility of a new name for some time to come; in a country such as South Africa the possibility of a new constellation of themes under a different name became a reality with Curriculum 2005, in which 'Communication' became the collecting label for Literature, Language, and all aspects of Communication.

The second step demands that we become specific. We can put the challenge for English starkly by pointing to the obvious. On the social side, the former articulations of its deeper purpose have lost all relevance; from that point of view, English is adrift. On the cultural, semiotic and technological side, the world of communication has undergone a revolution of the profoundest kind. On the one hand, most messages now make use of more and other modes of representation and communication than those of speech or writing – they have become multimodal. On the other hand, the dominant media are now the media of the 'screen' – whether the screen of the laptop, the mobile phone, the video or the games console – rather than the media of the page – the book, the newspaper, the magazine, the pamphlet, the newsletter. We are in the age of the new media. This is the problem for English. After all, it had been the subject that was founded on the eminence, the cultural and social dominance of the *mode of writing* (even more than that of the mode of speech) and of the *medium of the book*. For the generation now in school that is a past with little relevance. For them the *mode of image* rules representation, and the *media of the screen* dominate both production – whether as MMS or as website – and dissemination.

In this situation, there are just three options for 'English' – no doubt with many variants. It can become the 'Latin' or the 'Classics' of the present period, and await its demise into irrelevance. It can be dragged into full pragmatic relevance by becoming the subject that deals with 'Communication' both in its own right and right across the school – a new version of 'English across the curriculum' rebranded as 'Literacy across the curriculum'; and equally doomed to failure. Its existence will be relatively assured, as one of the service departments in the school. Its intellectual claims to curricular centrality, however, will have been abandoned.

But English can take up the challenge to interpret its older purposes newly. This will be both a difficult and an entirely necessary task, politically and intellectually. At the same time, it will assure its continued centrality in the curriculum, and its real significance in the lives of the young who experience that curriculum. The challenge is to develop arguments that pay the most serious attention to the real – new – tasks for English, while dismissing neither the fundamental cultural significance of certain texts nor the real claims of the economic pragmatists. English in this form will encompass its continuing underlying goals, and attend to cultural and pragmatic demands. Most importantly, for its role as a central part of the new curriculum, it needs to take the constantly present rhetoric about innovation and creativity at face value and demonstrate how it makes its essential contribution to these. The legitimate demands for relevance in the world of now are in no way incompatible with the demands for relevance in the world of tomorrow. Neither is incompatible with the profound demands for an education that places human needs for fulfilling and positive lives as non-negotiable values at the basis of educational purposes.

In an era of stability humans are seen to 'grow into' stable cultures, and into stable societies, regulated by (power expressed as) 'conventions'. Their role is to 'acquire' knowledge – often expressed as rules – of social conduct, and knowledge about the world, expressed as stable and fixed in canonical forms. Humans learn to use these rules, though they do not produce or alter them, and they learn to apply the knowledge, which, except under regulated conditions, they do not vary. Practices are fixed and stable, and achievement is judged by competent performance of existing practices. For the vast majority, creativity is neither possible nor valued; it is allowed and possible for the designated few – poets, writers and artists in various media. Hence creativity is rare, exceptional and valued only where it is socially sanctioned. Innovation is limited and usually dis-valued. Change is frowned on. Diversity is valued negatively, and discouraged; where it exists, attempts are made to integrate the diverse into the mainstream. Meaning is culturally made and expressed in socially provided forms. Meanings exist in the culture and individuals 'trade' these meanings. Meanings are produced not by individuals but by the culture and usually only the meanings of the culture can 'be meant'. The means for representing and communicating meaning are socially given, and regulated by convention, of many different kinds. Language, for instance, is seen as a set of rules that the individual 'user' of the 'language-system' understands and applies in adherence to the norms of use. The forms of communication are ranged in hierarchies of evaluation – the mode of writing is socially most highly valued, except in certain specialised communities, as in the notations of mathematics or of music. The media of communication are ranged similarly: the book is most highly valued, and it and the page are dominant.

It is clear that while these principles and assumptions may broadly be on the mark, they will have (had) distinct and variable realisations in different places at different times. It is equally clear that they have hardly any relevance to the demands of present social forms or the requirements of the present economy. Unbending adherence to norms, whatever they might be – forms of writing, modes of reading, dissemination or publication – has no utility in periods of rapid change. Doing a job in the way it was always done may have been just the thing when neither job nor practices changed. When they are likely to vary from one instance to the next, there is only dis-benefit.

Translating this to curricular and pedagogic principles, we see that in the school, too, the valued and required dispositions were those of 'competence' in the performance and application of practices and knowledge. 'Competence' and competent practice leave things as they are. It is the required disposition for periods of stability. For a while – a transitional period from the 1970s to the late 1990s – competence was superseded by 'critique'. It, too, leaves things as they are, although it does lead to investigation of the principles, interests and motives underlying uses of conventions. Critique asks, 'In whose interest?', 'With what effects for whom?' Yet however much critique expressed an unease about things as they are, it operates on the past agendas of others; it remains backward looking. Like 'competence', 'critique' is not the requisite communicational and representational orientation for the new English.

The multimodal world, as much as the wider social world, demands theories which are apt for the world as it is, rather than a world yearned for nostalgically, or wished for for reasons of power alone. So if, just above, I characterised the assumptions of that earlier world, how can we understand the new world and its demands?

Here I will look at the same factors as before, though in their new form. Again I will make no comment on curricular or pedagogic implications; readers may wish to see them in relation to a 'new English', and do so for their circumstances, their localities. In this new world, practices are not fixed or stable; achievement is judged in terms of aptness of response to changing purposes, demands and the needs of a specific task. This applies as much to contents as to shapes (genres, say) or modes (should I use image rather than writing?). Creativity is normal; individuals are not seen as *users* of norms or systems or stable practices, but as constant *transformers* of these. Creativity is not rare but is the usual condition of all social practices, representational and communicational practices no less than others. It is valued as an essential, required and usual component of all practice. Hence innovation, too, is now entirely commonplace; that is, all communicational practice is always innovatory – the resources for representing are never simply used, rather they are always transformed in their use. This applies to all instances, however banal and mundane. Change is normal. Diversity is valued, because 'difference' adds to the store of available resources, in any domain. Meaning is culturally shaped, and always and constantly individually transformed. The principles guiding the directions of this transformation are those of (socially produced) individual interest, which incorporates an understanding of all aspects of the (social) environment in which representation and communication take place. *Transformation in use* is the normal condition of meaning-making. The means for representation and communication are socially given and shaped, and constantly individually transformed. Their potentials for meaning – their affordances – are fully understood and available as a resource. Conventions are understood as past meanings made under conditions of power, and as such they too become a meaning resource to be used in the interests of the makers of messages. The forms/modes of communication still remain hierarchically ordered, though purpose overrides hierarchy. The valuations of the media have been reordered; the facilities that the different media afford are well understood, and they, in their turn, are available as a resource for meaning to the maker of messages.

It is clear that neither competence nor critique is adequate to the requirements of this world. This is a world in which the individuals – socially formed, with a full understanding of their social environment and its demands – have interests, and can act as agents in the *processes of design* which will give shape and realisation to these interests. *Design* applies to all aspects of the message: which mode shall I use for this content? What mode will most appeal to my imagined audience? What genre will best serve my purposes in relation to this audience? How shall I shape the content? Design applies to the *media of production and dissemination* as much as it does to *modes of representation*. The new screens provide the *facilities of multimodal realisation* much more than do the pages of the older media. The mobile phone now offers the possibility of texts conjointly produced in the modes of image and word. They also provide radically different *possibilities of action and of interaction*. The new screens allow me to 'write back' in ways the traditional page simply did not, and in this Roland Barthes' theoretically heralded 'Death of the author' in 1968 has resulted in an actual and radical blurring of notions of reader and author, of reading and writing.

The capacity for design is demanded by the new social conditions as much as it is by the new arrangements of the communicational world. Design places the individual's interest at the centre – not, it needs to be said, in the form of unfettered individual expressiveness, but rather in terms of the source of agency in choice and transformation. Texts as messages, and texts as sedimentations of meaning, are produced in the constant productive tension between the culturally shaped resources, with their material and historical affordances, the demands of the social environment, and the socially and effectively shaped interests of the meaning-maker. It is the maker of meaning who is central. However, meaning is no mere trade of an existing commodity. It is constantly newly made along the contours of power, interest, history and social difference. In that constant new making of meaning the resources of meaning-making are reshaped, as are the 'inner resources' of meaning-makers. But both meaning and the resources for making meaning are made by individuals in the exercise of their interests, in their transformative use of culturally made existing resources, taking account of the demands of the social environments in which this meaning-work is done. In terms of the curriculum this places the individual as learner/transformer/maker in a quite new role. At the same time, it changes the demands on forms of curriculum profoundly.

Note

1 This is a version of an article originally published as 'English for an era of instability: aesthetics, ethics, creativity and design' by Gunter Kress, *English in Australia*/AATE 44(3) (2002).

23

Room 13 and the contemporary practice of artist-learners

Jeff Adams

Introduction

This discussion of Room 13, its community of learners, contemporary art practice and colla-boration, should be seen in the context of critical writing on art education that has sought to challenge entrenched and expedient orthodoxies. As such it forms part of the wider debate in the US and the UK about transitions within art education towards the broader field of visual culture (Efland et al., 1996; Hughes, 1998). Attending to the social issues raised by engaging with contemporary art through creative and imaginative learning strategies is often problematic, and the difficulty of addressing these new modes of learning has been extensively explored in critical writing on art education in recent years (Atkinson, 2002; Addison and Burgess, 2003; Dalton, 2001; Swift and Steers, 1999; Dash, 2010; Adams et al., 2008). A common theme is the recognition of the need to encourage more extensive learning and communication methods, of the kind that are willing to embrace social and cultural dynamics as an integral, if unresolved, component of the curriculum. In this context the young school artists who comprise Room 13 represent an important development in art education, and one that has international significance. One of the key features that facilitate its distinctive pedagogy is the contemporary nature of its art practices.

I use the capacious term 'contemporary art' to refer to art exemplified in the UK by the work of the Young British Artists group (YBA) in the 1990s, and works represented in the collections of a number of high profile galleries, such as London's Tate Modern, Saatchi and Gateshead's Baltic, all of which are dedicated to displaying recent developments in the field. These developments constitute a revival in the popularity of contemporary art in Britain (Hopkins, 2000: 237–43), reflected by similar occurrences across the developed world, responding to such profound events as the cultural control of global capital (Jameson, 1998), and the expansion of urban cultural and ethnic diversity. The methods of the contemporary practices to which I refer, such as those of conceptual and performance art, with their corre-sponding concern with issues of cultural identity and the construction of subjectivity (as in the work of Sonia Boyce or Gillian Wearing, for instance), inevitably elide the boundaries between author, spectator, producer and participant, and call into question individual agency itself. This should prepare the ground for a corresponding pedagogy that is far less didactic, driven instead by a community, collaborative production model.

Yet this is usually not the case, with art education sometimes almost erased from the school curriculum or in constant status flux, having to fight frequent ideological battles against the centralised prescription of 'core' subjects. Hence the necessity to demonstrate that the practices that are found in the classroom may be seen as part of the wider contemporary art movement, and not merely an obscure adjunct operating within a proscribed institutional pedagogy that often prohibits both legitimacy and autonomy.

Of particular value to this reshaping is the artist-teacher idea, which represents a significant addition to the conceptual vocabulary of art education and the descriptive metaphors of classroom practices. As Lakoff and Johnson (1980) have demonstrated, metaphors like this are not the means merely of communicating ideas, but also of shaping the way in which the world is experienced. The effect of inscribing the title artist-teacher upon professional teacher discourse, implying that the teacher is the artist, is revealed by the increasing popularity of the term with practitioners (Hyde, 2004). Yeomans, former president of NSEAD (National Society for Education in Art and Design), established the ground for this idea when he iterated the principal of teachers retaining their own individual artistic practice (Yeomans, 1996: 244). This became one of the main principles of the UK Artist-Teacher Scheme: that teachers can improve their effectiveness as educators by maintaining and refreshing their creative activity as producers. The difficulty here is the assumption of a separation between art practice and art pedagogy: that one can still practise as an artist *despite* practising as a teacher. The idea of the artist-teacher is thus a problematic as well as an enabling concept. It presents a duality of practices: the artist repressed in the dominant discourse of pedagogy and institutional regulation, set up in opposition to the artist 'liberated' by external practices.

Nevertheless the artist-teacher idea is a powerful one in art education, since it insists upon an idea that has its foundations in a broader field, and unites teacher with artistic practitioner within a single concept.

Room 13 and the artist-learner

The complementary metaphor to artist-teacher, potentially of equal importance, is that of the artist-learner. Just as the artist-teacher idea encouraged teachers to recognise the expansiveness of their professional practice (Hyde, 2004), the renaming and classifying of the learner into the field of contemporary art encourages and supports practices that are resistant to traditional orthodoxies. This is demonstrated by the advent of the semi-autonomous, learner-managed, primary school art group Room 13, and its active engagement with contemporary practices. These artist-learners represent an important example of an emerging resistance in education to mechanistic and assessment-led curricula.

The community of art workers, teachers, resident artists and learners that constitute Room 13 has relevance in the US as well as the UK, despite its originally specific context of a remote Scottish Highlands town. This international significance lies in its responsive relationship to contemporary art discourses, and in the remarkable autonomy of its learner-managed production, both of which I wish to explore in relation to the concepts of collaboration and learning communities, within the expanded field offered by contemporary art. In their schools (Caol Primary and Lochyside Primary, Fort William) pupils have a designated space ('room 13') where they can 'drop in' during the school day and make art, in the presence of a resident artist. Art is given a high priority, and older children may leave other lessons to participate in Room 13 activities, provided that they do not fall behind with their work. Room 13's internet presence (a pupil-designed and maintained website) has helped overcome its geographical remoteness and enables it to maintain an extensive audience, and the project has been the beneficiary of substantial funding from both local government and national arts bodies (Crace, 2002), which has undoubtedly facilitated the diversity of its art production. This includes performance, installation and digital animation art, supported by seminars on theory and philosophy. Room 13 has also taken on a plurality of forms, as other schools have set up their own 'Room 13s' (Souness and Fairley, 2005: 41). The presence of artist-teachers (like long-term artist-in-residence Rob Fairley) has not prevented the learners developing a high degree of autonomy, with pupil management and administration. As pupil Danielle Souness explains:

> We take all the decisions on everything, from when we buy soap and paint, to when we pay our teachers and how much.
>
> *(Danielle Souness in Souness and Fairley, 2005: 42)*

It is not these attributes of Room 13 that are important for my argument however, key though they may be to the group's media prominence and endurance. Their innovative ideas on pedagogy and artistic practice are my prime concern. As Souness comments: 'What Room 13 does is allow us to take control of our learning' (ibid.: 42). She also offers us an account that alerts us to the centrality of identity to their practices:

> Picasso made some of the greatest works of the last century. They are beautiful and tell me a lot about what it is like to be an old man but even Picasso could never paint what it is like to be an eleven year old girl.
>
> *(Danielle Souness in Souness and Fairley, 2005: 44)*

This suggests that there is degree of awareness of the way their subjectivity as learners is constructed, and how the type of practice they are engaged in can affect this process, through a continual renegotiation of themselves as artists and learners. Important as their economic self-sufficiency and commercial activity are to the identity and character of Room 13, they are secondary to this singular feature of constantly addressing what the concepts of artist and learner mean, and what it is to occupy these subject positions. The acquisition of cultural language, and their willingness to enter into the discourse of contemporary art, is another characteristic feature of Room 13. As Hughes points out, it is often where learners accept that the material production of the work is also immersed in discourse that distinguishes their contemporary practice from more traditional models (1998: 43).

To a large extent Room 13 transcends the specificity of its origins – a remote community school experimenting with pupil authority over aspects of their learning – by its engagement with contemporary art practices. One of its more celebrated examples is *9/11*, youngster Jodie Fraser's work on the World Trade Center attacks, a canvas comprised of burned matches representing each of the victims, which was exhibited at Tate Modern in London (Room13/ ZCZ Films, 2004). Works like these clearly make a contribution to the global discourse: the issue of how to represent the attacks, the critical debate on the place of works on canvas, the value conferred on the work by its prominent media reception; all of these issues have been aired visually and in the associated debates that constitute Room 13 (Adams, 2004). The artistic discourse that pervades and encapsulates Room 13's production is characterised by an acute awareness of contextual significance of the work, in combination with its aesthetic/ perceptual aspects. This is apparent in the following description of their working practice by member Ami Cameron, where she shifts from a formalist aesthetic reading to a contextual iconography:

Sometimes a piece of work will come from just using stuff. ... Rosie's rice paintings started by using shells and food colouring because she was interested in making a painting without using paint. When she discovered using rice made a really beautiful texture she became interested in it as a common food, and all that meant; she then discovered that words like Honda and Toyota described rice fields in Japanese ... , so her paintings took on yet a new meaning.

(Cameron, 2004)

Collaboration

Room 13 participants can also be collaborators in a number of ways: first, by a cascade of learning, where members teach, share and disseminate ideas amongst the group; second, by entering a critical discourse, whereby ideas are visualised through responding, analysing and reflecting upon each other's work; and, third, by self-consciously welcoming ideas and concepts from the wider field of practice. As Cameron explained:

sometimes the best lessons are from people who come into the class or studio; we have lots of visitors and you learn from what they say and sometimes this can lead to an artwork.

(Cameron, 2004)

The collaborative artistic production of ideas in Room 13 in these senses is that of a learning community with temporary, strategic and ad hoc collaborations between teachers, artists and learners. The legitimacy of such collaborative practices has an established place within contemporary art, such as those of the Chapmans, the Singhs, the group performances of Fluxus or Hirschhorn's *Documenta* (2002).

The key relationship in the classroom collaboration is between teacher and learner, insofar as it represents a power differential greater than others likely to be encountered within the group as a whole. Ordinarily this would be viewed as merely the unequal influence of one individual (the teacher) upon another (the learners). Whilst it is difficult to argue against the privilege and inequalities that are enshrined in this teacher–learner configuration, it should be pointed out that such equalities exist in many art practices, not least those between the patron and the commissioned artist-producer. This is how artist-in-residence Rob Fairley assessed the Room 13 working associations of adults and children:

We are a group of artists working together, with the only difference being that one or two of us are technically (and arguably emotionally – although this is dangerous territory) more experienced.

(Souness and Fairley, 2005: 49)

My use of the term collaboration does not preclude individual agency; it is rather a means of describing the context within which an idea is likely to be formed, tested and materialised, whether it be through creation, reaction or critical discourse. I would also suggest that a key feature of any effective collaborative practice is that its theoretical component is displayed in the form of open discourse; it is difficult to see how collaborative practice may proceed effectively if its theoretical premises are concealed from its participants (as they may be in more didactic learning contexts). For members of Room 13, the collaborative acquisition of shared and debated knowledge is a cornerstone of their project (Cameron, 2004) and resembles a dialogical pedagogical model, whereby the power relationship is ameliorated to some extent from the traditional hierarchical model (Addison and Burgess, 2000: 28–9; adapted from Grossberg). This resembles Desai's critical stance in relation to the role and function of the art teacher, suggesting that classroom practice needs to accommodate 'a critical dialogue with learners about the role of the artist in the global economy' and question concepts such as 'artistic authority' (Desai, 2002: 319). This seems to help to open up some of the key issues that determine what the collaborative practice of artist-learners and artist-teachers might be.

To maintain the concepts of individual agency and authenticity, traditionally central to classroom art practices and assessment, one is forced to call upon dubious historical precedents, such as the professional status of the artist, the supremacy of individual agency, patronage, the requirement of a specialist audience or the validation by the expert or the 'connoisseur'. Claims that any of these are natural prerequisites to define and legitimise art practices (as opposed to being promoted by hegemonic groups) have been questioned and critiqued often (Williams, 1990; Bourdieu, 2003/1993; Dalton, 2001). Krauss (1986), to pick just one seminal example, questioned both individual agency and originality as prerequisites or conditions for an art practice. Discrediting these formerly cherished notions, her discussion of Rodin's cast sculptures, with their multiple reproduction and the collaborative nature of the casting process, demonstrates erosions of individual agency and authenticity at a time when the authority of the artist was thought to be sacrosanct (ibid.: 151–70).

Room 13's relationship to its artists in residence, teachers, guests and other contributors and their sophisticated patterns of integrated, collaborative critical production are more aligned with contemporary global art production practices than those commonly found in schools.

Communities of practice

Room 13 may be compared to the government-sponsored Nicaraguan children's mural projects during the 1980s and 1990s. In both cases the seriousness and scale of the enterprise were well understood by the children, who responded to the challenge of the projects by greatly increased production.

This was facilitated, again in both examples, by the practice of 'open enrolment' (Hopewell and Pavone, 1999: 39). This is an important pedagogical structure in the context of extreme poverty and homelessness (Nicaragua) or a compulsory timetabled schooling (Scotland). The children in both cases were allowed to conditionally 'drop in' to the art projects as it suited their desire to participate in the work. The resulting transient and temporal alliances that formed daily between the artist-learners have profound implications for pedagogy and the reproduction of knowledge within these learning communities. As Hopewell and Pavone explain,

> in any given group there will be children who may have only been coming to the workshop for a few weeks, painting alongside children who may have been coming for several years. This makes for very different levels of experience and mastery of materials and techniques within the group and therefore produces cross learning situations. The more 'advanced' children transmit their knowledge, either by their example or by directly answering other children's questions and in turn, are constantly influenced by the enthusiasm and discoveries of the new kids.
>
> *(Hopewell and Pavone, 1999: 40)*

These social learning communities have discrete epistemological structures that allow for the dissemination of knowledge and for the reproduction of the community as a learning unit over time. Structures such as these have been analysed by Lave and Wenger through their concept of communities of practice (1991: 29–43). They developed their model of 'legitimate peripheral participation' by analysing learning apprenticeships, from which they defined communities of practice as modes of learning that occur beyond formal institutions such as school and college:

> A community of practice is an intrinsic condition for the existence of knowledge, not least because it provides the interpretive support necessary for making sense of its heritage. Thus, participation in the cultural practice in which any knowledge exists is an epistemological principle of learning.
>
> *(Lave and Wenger, 1991: 98)*

The community of practice is, for Lave and Wenger, a model that enables a description of learning communities that are bound together primarily by the transference and inculcation of knowledge. A key factor in their analysis is epistemological reproduction, whereby the cycle of the learning community is completed and the novices attain competence and acquire apprentices of their own (ibid.: 98–9). The distinction that Lave and Wenger draw between learning within the school institution and the learning communities beyond it is crucial here. They argue (ibid.: 99–100) (using the case of physics) that the community of practice that is reproduced through the process of studying at school

> is not the community of physicists but the community of schooled adults. Children are introduced into the latter community (and its humble relation with the former community) during their school years. The reproduction cycles of the physicists' community start much later, possibly only in graduate school.
>
> *(Lave and Wenger, 1991: 100)*

Lave and Wenger claim that learning is so fundamentally bound up with communities of practice that schools' learning environments can only be facsimiles of learning communities and therefore, in epistemological terms, cannot reproduce themselves other than as 'schooled adults'. The learning community that is reproduced in the art classroom need not, however, be that of merely 'schooled adults'. Within Room 13's transformed pedagogical structure, it seems that there are good reasons to describe the community that is reproduced as one of art practitioners, as well as one of schooled adults. The evidence for this is to be found in both pedagogy and production – the way that the material and theoretical production of the artist-learner and teacher serves as a means of acquiring new insights and expertise – and also in the capability of the learner-producers to instruct through their acquired competence. This capacity for the learners to teach their 'apprentices' is a feature of Room 13, as Cameron explained, when questioned about the process of learning from peers:

> As I am writing this Rosie is teaching [class] P3. … the best example of one of us teaching younger ones is Danielle (who works almost totally in words and digital images) showing one of the younger ones in [class] P4 that cutting and pasting in Photoshop was just the same as making a collage.
>
> *(Cameron, 2004)*

The new critical pedagogy that occurs, through new productions and performances, means that 'instruct' need not entail the orthodox method of verbal didacticism. I am thinking here of Greenberg's (1965) idea of self-criticism, which, despite his application of the term to defend Modernist painting, is nonetheless appropriate because of his insistence on a critical discourse embedded in practice (ibid.: 9). Applied to collaborative production, this critical discourse becomes the means by which the productive activity – at once theoretical and practical – is organised and modified. As Hopewell and Pavone articulated when describing the concept of collective work:

> Real collectivity implies a qualitatively different level of consciousness in terms of a commitment to a jointly produced work.
>
> *(Hopewell and Pavone, 1999: 59)*

This is a key idea in the discourse of the collaborative art production, and a marker of actual critical/creative exchange, as opposed to the passive reception of received knowledge. A community of contemporary art practice may be said to be reproduced within the school classroom once the ownership of ideas is collaborative, and the status of new ideas is valued within the pedagogical process. If the exploration of a concept by the learners is forced into a secondary level, relative to the initiation and development of the idea by the teacher, then the community fails to reproduce as one of practitioners, and we are left with a community of schooled learners again. The Room 13 community of artist-learners and teachers is effectively reproducing itself as contemporary art practitioners, and symbolic boundaries are sufficiently weakened to allow its entry into the cultural arena of contemporary art. Events like Room 13's exhibition at London's Tate Modern (Room13/ZCZ Films, 2004) provide a means of calibrating this symbolic transgression of boundaries.

Symbolic value

The school institutional context can be a major problem for the unfettered and radical development of classroom practice of the kind proposed here. This is illustrated by Dalton in her critical analysis of art education in the UK school context:

> [Art teachers] have the executive role of carrying out and 'managing' the delivery of curricula that have been written and structured centrally, by unknown others, 'elsewhere'.
>
> *(Dalton, 2001: 123)*

The idea of fostering a learning community of artist-teachers and artist-learners in such a highly regulated environment seems slim. These critiques provide a picture of a pernicious cycle of deterioration for the status of classroom art practices, highly compromised by the imposition of the teacher in the 'service' model (Dalton, 2001). Another way of analysing value in school art is established in Bourdieu's (2003) work on the field of art production. He draws attention to the importance of belief on the value of the work (ibid.: 37), and, significantly for the artist-teacher/learner concept, he argues that one of the key questions in the designation and definition of cultural production is the struggle for

> the monopoly of the power to say with authority who are authorised to call themselves writers; or, to put it another way, it is the monopoly of the power to consecrate producers or products.
>
> *(Bourdieu, 2003: 42)*

In the case of the artist-teacher/learner the 'consecration' of practices hitherto recognised as exclusively pedagogic may be achieved by the attribution of the concept 'collaborative contemporary art', thereby increasing its symbolic value. In Bourdieu's terms the Room 13 construction of teacher and learner may be seen as fundamental to conceptions about their function and value, in that it resists classification as an interior pedagogic practice divorced from the art practices that are external to the school institution.

Bernstein's analysis of framing, classification and boundaries that govern the social relations in the school institution suggests that the more an epistemological area like school art is 'insulated' against others the more strongly classified it becomes, and the greater its integrity as a discrete entity (Bernstein, 2000: 6–9). Applying his model, the conceptual task here is to weaken the well-insulated boundary between classroom art production and the cultural field of contemporary art practice, to allow its strategic entry into this wider community, dismantling the institutional blockade that imprisons and maintains much classroom art practice in a devalued state. Room 13 represents a powerful example of this dismantling, and in this sense the learner-manager aspect of Room 13 acquires symbolic significance.

Conclusion

Admission of pedagogic art practice into the field of contemporary art has to be accomplished primarily through developing new mythologies that insist upon the validity of artist-teacher/learner production, even within the tightly regulated institutional environment, much as Room 13 has been able to transcend the ideology that renders so much classroom art anodyne. Williams rightly identified the issue of value as one of the major difficulties in this area, affecting art practices that occur outside the still powerful categories of the individual or the validating force of the art institution (1981: 318). He argues that the individual celebrated for practising the unorthodox has been highly valued in the mythology of the avant-garde (ibid.). In this same system of values teacher and learner practices are relegated to cultural categories like 'school art', in the pejorative sense (Adams, 2010). Room 13's production offers some resistance to this in that it establishes a new set of values within school art; this is achieved in part by the combination of the specific physicality of the site and space of production, the 'Room' metaphor, with the intellectual discourse of global contemporary art.

It matters that this practice is acknowledged, legitimated and valued, since it forms part of the wider debate on who has the authority to speak as 'the artist', and how this power is conferred. Taken as an example of reclamation of some of this lost authority, the collaborative practice of the artist-teacher and artist-learner does acquire additional significance. The way that collaboration, open theorising and critical discourse are features of Room 13 is one particularly significant aspect of the artist-learner formation. Strategies like these represent resistance to the imposition of the instrumentalist and formulaic pedagogic models that so effectively replicate social inequalities.

References

Adams, J. (2003) The Artist-Teacher Scheme as postgraduate professional development in higher education, *International Journal of Art and Design Education* 22(2): 183–94.

—— (2010) Risky choices: the dilemmas of introducing contemporary art practices into schools, *British Journal of Sociology of Education*, 31(6): 683–701.

Adams, J., Worwood, K., Atkinson, D., Dash, P, Herne, S. and Page, T. (2008) *Teaching through contemporary art: A report on innovative practices in the classroom.* London: Tate Publishing.

Addison, N. and Burgess, L. (2000) Contemporary art in schools: why bother?, in R. Rickman (ed.) *Art Education 11–18: Meaning Purpose and Direction,* London and New York: Continuum.

—— (eds) (2003) *Issues in Art and Design Teaching,* London and New York: RoutledgeFalmer.

Atkinson, D. (2002) *Art in Education: Identity and Practice*, Dordrecht, Boston and London: Kluwer.
—— (2003) Forming teaching identities in initial teacher education, in N. Addison and L. Burgess (eds) *Issues in Art and Design Teaching*, London and New York: RoutledgeFalmer.
Atkinson, D. and Dash, P. (eds) (2005) *Social and Critical Practices in Art Education*, Stoke-on-Trent and Sterling, VA: Trentham Books.
Bernstein, B. (2000) *Pedagogy, Symbolic Control and Identity: Theory, Research, Critique*, Lanham, MD, and Oxford: Rowman and Littlefield; originally published 1996.
Bourdieu, P. (2003/1993) *The Field of Cultural Production* (ed. and with an introduction by Randel Johnson), Oxford: Polity Press.
Cameron, A. (2004) Ami Cameron, managing director of Room 13, interview with the author 17 May, 2004 (unpublished).
Crace, J. (2002) Living colour, *Guardian*, 18 June.
Dalton, P. (2001) *The Gendering of Art Education: Modernism, Identity and Critical Feminism*, Buckingham: Open University Press.
Dash, P. (2010) *African Caribbean Pupils in Art Education*. Amsterdam: Sense.
Desai, D. (2002) The ethnographic move in contemporary art, *Studies in Art Education* 43(4): 307–23.
Efland, A., Freedman, K. and Stuhr, P. (1996) *Postmodern Art Education: An Approach to Curriculum*, Reston, VA: The National Art Education Association.
Greenberg, C. (1965/1988) Modernist painting, in F. Frascina and C. Harrison (eds) *Modern Art and Modernism: A Critical Anthology*, London: Open University Press.
Hopewell, D. and Pavone, J. (1999) *The Children's Mural Workshops*, Managua, Nicaragua: Esteli.
Hopkins, D. (2000) *After Modern Art*, Oxford: Oxford University Press.
Hughes, A. (1998) Re-conceptualising the art curriculum, *Journal of Art and Design Education* 17(1): 41–9.
Hyde, W. (2004) The impact of the Artist Teacher Scheme on the teaching of art and on the continuing professional development of art and design teachers, DES Best Practice website; available at http://www.teachernet.gov.uk/professionaldevelopment/opportunities/bprs (accessed 28 May 2004).
Jameson, F. (1998) *The Cultural Turn: Selected Writings on the Postmodern 1983–1998*, London: Verso.
Krauss, R. (1986) *The Originality of the Avant-Garde and Other Modernist Myths*, Cambridge, MA, and London: The MIT Press.
Lakoff, G. and Johnson, M. (1980) *Metaphors We Live By*, Chicago and London: University of Chicago Press.
Lave, J. and Wenger, E. (1991) *Situated Learning: Legitimate Peripheral Participation*, Cambridge: Cambridge University Press.
Room 13 (2004) Caol Primary School, Fort William, Scotland; http://room13scotland.com (accessed 23 April 2004).
Room13/ZCZ Films (2004) *What Age Can You Start Being an Artist?* Channel 4 Television, UK, January.
Souness, D. and Fairley, R. (2005/2000) Room 13, in D. Atkinson and P. Dash (eds) *Social and Critical Practices in Art Education*, Stoke on Trent and Sterling, VA: Trentham Books.
Steers, J. (2003) Art and design education in the UK: the theory gap, in N. Addison and L. Burgess (eds) *Issues in Art and Design Teaching*, London and New York: RoutledgeFalmer.
Swift, J. and Steers, J. (1999) A manifesto for art in schools, *Directions, Journal of Art and Design Education* 18 (1): 7–14.
Williams, R. (1981/1992) The Works of Art Themselves?, in F. Frascina and J. Harris (eds) *Art in Modern Culture: An Anthology of Critical Texts*, London: Open University Press and Phaidon.
—— (1990) *The Politics of Modernism: Against the New Conformists*, London: Verso.
Yeomans, M. (1996) Creativity in art and science: a personal view, *Journal of Art and Design Education* 15(3): 241–50.

24

The relationship between creativity and Studio Thinking

Lois Hetland and Ellen Winner

Does learning in the arts develop creativity in students?

The arts are often directly equated with creativity, but the connection is not self-evident. We do not draw a one-to-one correspondence between creativity and art, both because creativity exists outside the arts, and because the arts are not always creative. Derivative and routinized art (perhaps we should call it "stale" or "bad art"?) is more common than creative art that moves viewers beyond the edges of current practices, understanding, and beliefs (which we might call "fresh art," a component of "good art"). Despite these caveats, art at its best requires creativity, and serious artists must develop a creative stance toward the world and their work in it. This suggests that serious art teaching and learning also require teachers to focus on creativity and require students to develop creativity. In our own work, we have looked to the practices of such serious visual arts educators and defined eight interacting Studio Habits of Mind that visual arts educators teach (Hetland *et al.*, 2007). Could these "Studio Habits" support creativity's development if teachers used them to guide planning, teaching, and assessing? Here we explore this question.

How one conceives of creativity—that is, what creativity is—matters a great deal when considering how to develop it and how to assess the degree to which individual students exemplify creativity. Our own views about creativity grow from two nearly orthogonal positions. The first arises from Csikszentmihalyi and Csikszentmihalyi (1988), who describe creativity as having three poles—the individual, the field of expertise (that is, the people and institutions who control access to membership), and the body of work and objects created in that domain. This view has been explored by such scholars as Feldman, Csikszentmihalyi, and Gardner (1994) and Gardner (1997), and it is sometimes described as the "big C" creativity perspective—the view that cultural creatives are those who transform their domains (examples include Picasso, Freud, and Darwin).

On the surface, such a position seems to offer little to a consideration of teaching and learning that develops creativity. But this view influences thinking about teaching and learning creatively by its suggestion that creativity resides not only in individuals, but in social groups and their shared domains of expertise. Teaching for creativity, then, would involve nurturing particular patterns of behavior and thought in individuals in relationship to fields and domains of expertise, including helping them to develop capacities to notice, attend to, and appreciate work created by others in their domain, and to be aware of the field of people who construct and employ the criteria for judging how creative someone or something is. This aspect of Csikszentmihalyi's description of creativity could inform the design of curriculum, classroom cultures, and evaluation tools meant to nurture and assess creativity's development.

The second view of creativity grows out of David Perkins's work (1981). Perkins defined creativity as "adaptive novelty," which links closely to the "performance view of understanding," defined as "using what you know flexibly in response to novel circumstances" (Wiske, 1998; Blythe et al., 1998). As defined by Perkins, creativity and its near cousin, the performance view of understanding, both appear to us to be "dispositional." A disposition is a quality of a persons' character defined as being comprised not only of the skills at which a person is adept, but also of the individual's attitudes in relation to those skills—their motivations to use them and their alertness to occasions for effective use (Perkins et al., 1993; Tishman et al., 1993). Seeing creativity as a disposition offers a good deal of leverage when considering teaching and learning, because it motivates us to identify both the skill sets that make up creativity and the attitudes that support its use. Schools that aim to develop creativity in their students—such as those embracing the 21st Century Skills movement[1]—could use the dispositional concept to guide their efforts.

Studio Thinking: structures and habits of mind

The Studio Thinking Framework (Hetland et al., 2007) describes two aspects of art classrooms: (1) eight "studio habits of mind"—dispositions (that is, skills and attitudes about their uses; Perkins, Jay, and Tishman, 1993) that are taught through studio art classes; and (2) three "studio structures"—formats that art teachers use to organize time and interactions: Demonstration-Lectures, Students-at-Work, and Critiques.

We use the term Studio Habits of Mind to describe eight important kinds of general cognitive and attitudinal dispositions that are taught in serious visual arts classes.

1 Develop Craft:
   - *Technique*: learning to use tools (e.g. viewfinders, brushes), materials (e.g. charcoal, paint). Learning artistic conventions (e.g. perspective, color mixing).
   - *Studio Practice*: learning to care for tools, materials, and space.
2 Engage & Persist: learning to embrace problems of relevance within the art world and/or of personal importance, to develop focus and other mental states conducive to working and persevering at art tasks.
3 Envision: learning to picture mentally what cannot be directly observed and imagine possible next steps in making a piece.
4 Express: learning to create works that convey an idea, a feeling, or a personal meaning.
5 Observe: learning to attend to visual contexts more closely than ordinary "looking" requires, and thereby to see things that otherwise might not be seen.
6 Reflect:
   - *Question & Explain*: learning to think and talk with others about an aspect of one's work or working process.
   - *Evaluate*: learning to judge one's own work and working process and the work of others in relation to standards of the field.
7 Stretch & Explore: learning to reach beyond one's capacities, to explore playfully without a preconceived plan, and to embrace the opportunity to learn from mistakes and accidents.
8 Understand Art World:

- *Domain*: learning about art history and current practice.
- *Communities*: learning to interact as an artist with other artists (i.e. in classrooms, in local arts organizations, and across the art field) and within the broader society.

It is easy to hypothesize a relationship between art and creativity when creativity is seen as dispositional. Like creativity, the arts tie subjects together interpretively (Efland, 2004; Perkins, 1994), aim to create adaptive novelty (Perkins, 1981), and are structured so that individuals interact within a field and domain (Csikszentmihalyi and Csikszentmihalyi, 1988).

The Studio Habits of Mind emphasize interactions and synthesis among the eight dispositional categories, which explicitly represent what are often seen as core creative qualities. These qualities include risk-taking and uses of error as both diagnostic and sources of new ideas (stretch & explore), imagination and flexible planning (envision), meta-cognition and self-assessment (reflect), connecting to intuition, passion, and personal meaning (engage & persist, express), connecting to surroundings as inspiration (observe, understand art world), using materials to give thinking time (develop craft), and developing strategies of perseverance over time and through obstacles (engage & persist).

The Studio Structures offer teachers tools for developing classroom cultures that support the development of such approaches by building in extended, flexible time in which students pursue personally meaningful initiatives (Students-at-Work) with periodic introductions to relevant work by other artists and modeling of processes (demonstration-lectures) and evaluative discussion (critiques) that bring new perspectives from peers and teachers. The Studio Structures, then, support Csikszentmihalyi's poles of creative endeavor—the individual's development through work and through regular responses from the field (peers and teachers) in the context of the domain (work made by other artists).

Studio Thinking, we suggest, offers a framework to guide teachers in planning, furthering, and assessing the development of creativity in their students. And teachers of visual arts, music, dance, and drama are exploring its potential.

Studio Habits to guide curriculum design that focuses on developing creativity

Designing curriculum to support the development of creativity requires assessing the value of individual and sequenced assignments in relation to that intention and often revising. Teachers need to ask how any arts experience is related to the ways serious (that is, creative) artists work and think. What elements of artistic mind does it develop? If the answer is "skill in the techniques of [watercolor painting; linoleum block cutting; drawing the figure]" (all of which would be classified as develop craft: technique) or "recognizing artists of the twentieth century" (which would fall into the habit, understand art world: domain), then it is unlikely (though not impossible) that the lesson develops creativity. But if the lesson fosters, for example, the inclination to push beyond what a student can already do well and analyze resulting mistakes as potential ideas (stretch & explore), or if it focuses on being alert to ways the local neighborhood is a source of potential symbols for conveying meaning visually (understand art world, express), then creativity might, indeed, grow. Analyzing potential art topics, themes, lessons, and assignments through the Studio Habits makes visible to teachers the extent to which they are or are not planning instruction that nurtures students' creativity and allows teachers to hone instruction purposefully.

Analyzing resources for relevance requires teachers to ask, "How is this artist/artwork/idea connected to the ways serious artists work and think?" Beginning art teachers often show works to students to inspire them, but which works are selected in relation to what students are meant to learn is what makes or breaks the nurturing of creativity. For example, Gwendolyn Huskens's project "Medic Esthetic" uses "medical materials like synthetic plaster, bandages and stainless steel in white and skin tones" to construct designer shoes.[2] Using the Studio Habits to reflect on what considerations selecting such images might provoke can help teachers choose those that aim toward their goals—such as the development of creativity. For example, in this case, the use of novel materials (stretch & explore; develop craft: technique) to convey an opinion through the symbol system of three-dimensional objects (express) shows that the contemporary art world uses humor and juxtaposition as part of its communicative repertoire (understand art world: domain; express; envision).

Teachers also need to analyze the fit of potential assignments to the learning needs of particular students. They need to ask, "How could this experience support my students in learning dispositional elements that they most need? How does this experience align with the developmental capacities of my students?" Experienced teachers understand how to align high levels of expert concepts and processes with the nascent capacities of their students. But it is easy for less capable teachers to err either by asking too little or too much of their students, losing them in the process. If a student cannot sew an efficient running stitch, then it is folly to ask him or her to create a unique sewn "crazy quilt." Students might be able to design the object (envision) but lack the technical disposition (develop craft) needed to carry it to completion. However, recognizing students' limited craft skill and inclination, the teacher can decide: Should I dedicate time to learning technique and do this lesson later (e.g. set students up to do "stitch races" to build their speed in sewing and do the crazy quilts when they've mastered that)? Or should I adjust the craft demands of the assignment so the students can address other concerns (e.g. hot glue the crazy quilts together so the students can focus on envisioning, expressing, and stretching & exploring)? Whenever teachers are planning instruction, they need to consider the probable assumptions and limitations their students are likely to hold, and the Studio Habits can help them consider what these are and how to accommodate them.

Finally, teachers need to analyze the balance of assignments in a course or program. They need to ask, "How does this course or program address the development of the whole artistic/ creative mind?" Most teachers in the US are accountable to state or national standards, which are meant to guide the design and delivery of a balanced curriculum. However, many states implicitly privilege develop craft: technique over other Studio Habits, which can reduce the amount of time dedicated to kinds of artistic thinking that align with creative thinking. In Massachusetts, for example, two of the five main standards (Methods, Materials, and Techniques; Elements and Principles of Design) would be classified as develop craft: technique, while the remaining three (Observation, Abstraction, Invention, and Expression; Drafting, Revising, and Exhibiting; and Critical Response) would distribute among the other seven Studio Habits. Recognizing this imbalance by analyzing assignments for the Studio Habits that they emphasize, teachers can adjust assignments that develop craft by including more creativity-centered dispositions to balance the assignment's emphasis, such as express, envision, engage & persist, or reflect: evaluate (which, as Elliot Eisner [2002] says, asks artists to make critical distinctions without clear criteria—something students need to think creatively).

Studio Habits to guide classroom practice that nurtures creativity

The Studio Habits can also support students in developing creativity. At any time during classroom instruction, teachers can focus on habits emphasized in creativity, such as stretch & explore, envision, and engage & persist. By keeping such habits in mind while observing and intervening with students, teachers can bring their attention to nurturing students' creative dispositions.

Some teachers use the Studio Habits as a language to communicate disciplinary purposes to students and to other teachers. Arzu Mistry at the ASCEND School in Oakland, CA, for example, selected two habits, observe and reflect, as a focus for third grade students. She used these habits to guide her students' attention to the qualities of creative thought that she most wanted them to develop as they learned to draw portraits of family members in a unit on leadership. Arzu also used the Studio Habits as a way to explain her model of teaching to the students' classroom teacher, who learned to support her students' development in those habits when Arzu was no longer co-teaching lessons with her.

Teachers are also using Studio Habits as a language of self- and group-reflection for students. For example, Sharron Cajolet uses them with her third to eighth grade students at the Lowell Community Charter Public School in Massachusetts by asking students to reflect on various habits and then archiving sample reflections and photographs of work and students-at-work in a classroom binder that the students pour over regularly. Teachers in San Leandro, CA, are beginning to use "Thinking Walls"—informal and temporary public documentation panels that display evidence of learning and that serve as a gathering place for making connections between what students do and the kinds of learning those experiences are meant to help them develop (Hetland et al., 2010).

Todd Elkin, a teacher at Washington High School in Freemont, CA, introduces his students to the Studio Habits and asks them to paraphrase them in their own words. "Engage & persist," for example, became something like "Work as hard as you can and never stop." Elkin regularly asks students to use these "redefined" habits to guide ongoing self-assessment as students reflect on their own efforts in sketchbooks and together on blogs. Similarly, Lucinda Daily, a photography teacher at Berkeley High, CA, noted that the quality of student critiques improved dramatically after she asked students to make notes in the Studio Habit categories when they selected photos to talk about together: "I think that breaking apart the way we see in terms of the language of the Studio Habits of Mind is useful to get the kids to slow down and think about what they are looking at and take more time to really focus" (Lucinda's reflection June 10, 2005).

Studio Habits to guide assessment of creativity

Studio Habits are being used in several ways by experienced art and classroom teachers in Alameda County, CA, and by pre-service teachers at the Massachusetts College of Art and Design, to guide observations of students in the classroom and the work that they make. Three techniques each ask teachers to focus on "episodes of learning"—which might include, for example, observing students as they're working, reviewing selections from portfolios of student work, or interviewing students about their work or working behaviors.

One approach builds on simple questions teachers have written and shared with students that focus students' attention on understanding (e.g. "How can we frame the figure to improve our drawings?"). Then teachers identify and name the Studio Habits that align with and are emphasized by that goal (in this case, observe, envision, reflect: evaluate, and develop craft). When reviewing students' work, teachers consider which dispositional elements the student is demonstrating in those Studio Habits: What *skills* of observation are evident? Is there evidence that the student is developing a stronger *inclination* to observe? Or an *alertness* to when it makes sense to observe closely and give looking time? What about envisioning skills, inclination, and/ or alertness? Or skill, inclination, and/or alertness related to craft? By focusing on the attitudes, and not only the skills, of these Studio Habits, teachers can identify students' needs and promote those attitudes that enhance creative approaches while at the same time helping students develop skills that support their creative efforts.

A second technique also asks teachers to observe episodes of learning. Afterwards, they write a brief, narrative paragraph and then refine their thinking about that episode by considering their observation in relation to each Studio Habit, naming what they see through each category and then reflecting on what their observation suggests the student does or does not understand. Finally, they synthesize the data into a decision about what to do next with and for that student.

A third technique asks teachers to consider what Studio Habits students are using at phases in the process of learning. First, they describe what they've seen at a moment in time, as in the previous two approaches. They then name the focus of the students' effort by identifying the students' current phase in the process of learning. They do so by asking what the student is pursuing at the current time in the process:

- Finding the work: Is the student exploring initial ideas? Where did they come from?
- Planning and developing the work: Is the student working to get clearer about an idea before beginning to make the work?
- Making the work: Is the student beginning to make the work?
- Pushing the work: Is the student taking the work further or in new directions?
- Finishing the work: Is the student completing the piece?
- Sharing the work: Is the student sharing the piece with others?

The process, of course, is not always linear—at any given time, a student might, for example, be pushing an idea *and also* sharing it with others *and also* getting new ideas that may come into this work or be used in other projects. The purpose of identifying the phase of the process is to track patterns of focus that the student uses over the course of a project or piece, not to rigidify what must be a fluid and variable endeavor.

While these three techniques may not be feasible for assessing every student every day, teachers are gaining clarity on students whose growth puzzles them by focusing on them regularly over time. In addition, some teachers are periodically rotating all students through such focused attention to document snippets of information that can be compared over time. Teachers who use these techniques say they are building their capacities to really see learning as it is developing in the fleeting moments of the classroom experience, which improves their judgments and "just in time" interventions.

So far, we have described using the Studio Habits to identify what qualities need to be developed for creativity. But one must also look at *levels of expertise* in the Studio Habits. Low levels of each disposition equate to low levels of creative thought in those categories, so it is critical to develop indicators of higher levels in the Studio Habits. Kimberly Sheridan analyzed student-learning data during the Studio Thinking research project and identified four continua to consider when characterizing students' levels of expertise with the Studio Habits (Sheridan and Hetland, 2007). Hetland has since refined these continua into five "Dimensions of Expertise":

- complexity, which runs from (low) handling single concepts to (high) handling many, either simultaneously and/or in rapid succession;
- connections, from (low) thinking of work in isolation to (high) working with concepts in a broad range of integrated relationships of concepts and communities;
- flexibility, from (low) a rigid, rule-based approach to (high) responsive and varied approaches to thinking;
- judgments of quality, from (low) being dependent on others to interpret degree of success to (high) judging success autonomously by balancing subjective and inter-subjective criteria in relation to perceivable evidence;

- motivation, from (low) extrinsically driven to (high) intrinsically driven to achieve something of personal significance in relation to a field and domain.

The levels of these continua demonstrate lower and higher levels of creativity, with the higher levels representing a highly synthetic and creative disposition or approach. We hypothesize that developing creativity requires moving students into at least the middle zones (which requires time and effort that is often not made available because of school schedules and conflicting demands) and then providing frequent, regular experience with tasks that require practice along these dimensions.

Conclusion

While creativity extends beyond the arts, the preceding description of ways in which Studio Structures can support the development of classroom cultures that nurture creativity, and ways the Studio Habits of Mind can support the development and evaluation of creativity, suggests that learning in the arts could contribute a great deal to that endeavor. Far from a claim that "teaching arts makes people creative," this approach claims that teaching and assessing arts using the Studio Thinking framework can guide teachers to ensure that planning, instruction, and assessment all embody a balanced approach toward building a creative disposition. Such an approach requires careful attention to the three dispositional elements of each Studio Habit—skill must be developed in all habits (and not merely in developing craft), but teachers must also nurture and assess inclination/motivation and alertness/awareness (in developing craft as well as the other seven habits). While Studio Thinking was developed through research on visual arts classrooms, it is being used by teachers in all arts disciplines—dance, drama, music, and emerging art forms—as well as in other scholarly subjects (social studies, language arts, mathematics, and sciences). With support from the Studio Habits and Structures, arts teaching can become more intentional in developing the creative dispositions of the artist and, potentially, could lead educators to design, deliver, and assess school experiences that nurture creativity for students in all disciplines.

Notes

1 http://www.21stcenturyskills.org/index.php?option=com_content&task=view&id=254&Itemid=120.
2 http://www.todayandtomorrow.net/2008/10/31/medic-esthetic/.

References

Blythe, T. and the Researchers and Teachers of the Teaching for Understanding Project (1998) *The Teaching for Understanding Guide*, San Francisco: Jossey-Bass.

Csikszentmihalyi, M. and Csikszentmihalyi, I. S. (eds.) (1988) *Optimal Experience: Psychological Studies of Flow in Consciousness*, Cambridge: Cambridge University Press.

Efland, A. (2004) Emerging visions of art education, in E. Eisner and M. Day (eds.) *Handbook of Research and Policy in Art Education*, Mahwah, NJ: Lawrence Erlbaum Associates.

Eisner, E. (2002) *The Arts and the Creation of Mind*, New Haven, CT: Yale University Press.

Feldman, D. H., Csikszentmihalyi, M., and Gardner, H. (1994) *Changing the World: A Framework for the Study of Creativity*, Westport, CT: Praeger.

Gardner, H. (1997) *Extraordinary Minds: Portraits of Exceptional Individuals and an Examination of our Extraordinariness*, New York: Basic Books.

Hetland, L, Cajolet, S., and Music, L. (2010) Documentation in the visual arts: embedding a common language from research, *Theory into Practice* 49(1): 55–63.

Hetland, L., Winner, E., Veenema, S., and Sheridan, K. (2007) *Studio Thinking: The Real Benefits of Visual Arts Education*, New York: Teachers College Press.

Perkins, D. N. (1981) *The Mind's Best Work*, Cambridge, MA: Harvard University Press.

—— (1994) *The Intelligent Eye: Learning to Think by Looking at Art*, occasional paper 4. Santa Monica, CA: The Getty Center for Education in the Arts.

Perkins, D. N., Jay, E., and Tishman, S. (1993) Beyond abilities: a dispositional theory of thinking, *Merrill-Palmer Quarterly* 39(1): 1–21.

Sheridan, K. and Hetland, L. (2007) Looking for mind in student work: assessing development of the Studio Habits of Mind, presentation at NAEA Annual Convention, New York, March.

Tishman, S., Jay, E., and Perkins, D. N. (1993) Teaching thinking dispositions: from transmission to enculturation, *Theory into Practice* 32: 147–53.

Wiske, M. S. (ed.) (1998) *Teaching for Understanding: Linking Research with Practice*, San Francisco: Jossey-Bass.

25

The gallery as a site for creative learning[1]

Emily Pringle

Gallery education[2] has developed and expanded rapidly in the last ten years. This intensification is due, in part, to the perception by policy makers that galleries, through their education and outreach activities, can have beneficial impacts on social and educational scenarios. Certain galleries within the UK have facilitated learning activities for over twenty-five years and have developed various models of good practice. These are underpinned by particular theoretical understandings of:

- the nature of the art object;
- the role of the educator;
- the function of the gallery;
- the relationship of the visitor/spectator/learner to all of these.

This chapter draws on UK and international research and writing from within and beyond the sector to provide an overview of thinking relevant to gallery education. It concludes with an extended case study involving an artist educator working with adults on a vocational education course to exemplify how one form of learning and teaching within the gallery operates.

Background

This chapter looks broadly at gallery education, but is centred on a particular model that is practised most noticeably (but not exclusively) in contemporary art galleries in the UK and overseas. For clarity, it will be referred to as the 'Contemporary Gallery Education' (CGE) model. Characterised by experimental, open-ended, collaborative teaching and learning, it draws on a specific understanding of creative practice that can be identified as 'conceptual' (Godfrey, 1998). The following definition of conceptual art could also describe the CGE approach:

> Conceptual art is concerned with intellectual speculation and with the everyday. Conceptual art asks questions, not only of the art object; 'Why is this art? Who is the artist? What is the context?' – but also of the person who looks at it or reads about it: 'Who are you? What do you represent?' It draws viewers' attention to themselves.
>
> *(Godfrey, 1998: 15)*

As will emerge, scepticism and self-consciousness in relation to the negotiation of meaning are central to CGE practice.

CGE can be seen to diverge in some ways from the most traditional model that exists in certain museum education settings, not least because it tends to involve one-off, tailor-made projects involving artists, rather than standard programmes facilitated by museum educators (Stanley and Galloway, 2004). Whereas museums have been identified as 'tried-and-true sources of understandable information, places one can trust to provide reliable, authentic and comprehensible presentations of … objects and ideas' (Falk and Dierking, 2000: 2), CGE questions many of those assumptions, including 'truth', 'authenticity' and 'reliability'. This questioning stance is reflected in the form and content of gallery education sessions.

Arguably gallery education has its roots in the nineteenth century belief in the power of art and culture to improve society. In their early formulation galleries were understood to be 'educational' establishments whose function was to enable individuals to 'improve' themselves (Hooper-Greenhill, 2000). Since then gallery learning and teaching have been informed by developments in theory, policy and creative practice.

Ideas originating from the eighteenth century Enlightenment shaped the perception that art has the power to inspire and transform by enabling the viewer to transcend their everyday concerns and emotions (see Belfiore, Chapter 3). Here art is understood to be intellectually, emotionally and even ethically beneficial. This view has been challenged by critical theorists since the 1970s, who have questioned the sanctity and authority of art and the gallery, challenged cultural institutions to address cultural identity and representation (Adams *et al.*, 2003) and informed the drive to democratise gallery practice.

In the early twentieth century the concept emerged that viewing art represents a unique 'aesthetic experience' (Bell, 1993 [1914]) that is visceral and embodied rather than intellectual. Thus the appropriate response to art is predominantly emotional, and appreciation of art is a gift, rather than an acquired ability. This view has been challenged subsequently by, amongst other concepts, the identification that looking at art is essentially a cognitive activity, analogous to deciphering a text (Barthes, 1977). Furthermore, meaning in an artwork can be understood, not as an unchanging entity put there by the artist (Fry, 1993 [1909]) but as emerging through active interchange between artwork and viewer. Hence plural interpretations are equally valid and the viewer can negotiate legitimate individual meanings (Raney, 2003; Charman *et al.*, 2001: 17; Moore Tapia and Hazelroth Barrett, 2003).

Also relevant is the historic connection between gallery education and community arts practice in the UK that dates from the 1970s.[3] Community art has embraced a range of artists and activities and is characterised by:

- a belief in empowerment through participation in the creative process;
- a dislike of cultural hierarchies and commitment to the creative potential of all;
- an understanding of creative practice as a means to enter into dialogue with those outside the art professions to address issues, challenge societal structures and bring about change;
- a positioning of the artist, not as isolated and apart, but as a facilitator and collaborator.

Current practice

Gallery education is a provisional, complex and emerging profession. The scope for learning and teaching activities is broad, providing the focus is engagement with art and its contexts. CGE works with a variety of audiences, including informal visitors, community groups, and across the formal education sector. The following activities are common practice:

- informal visits to galleries by schools, families and community groups, supported by gallery learning resources (e.g. worksheets, handling objects);
- formal teaching sessions in the gallery, led by a gallery educator or artist;
- artist-led workshop sessions involving practical activities in the gallery;
- outreach projects taking place within the gallery and/or schools and community settings;
- symposia and conferences for arts professionals and aficionados;
- continuing professional development (CPD) activities for teachers and community leaders.

The majority of the CGE activities involve intense, facilitated sessions, which characteristically:

- are led by freelance creative practitioners;
- involve smaller numbers of participants, working as part of a 'learning community' (Carnell and Lodge, 2002);
- frequently involve new and challenging ideas for participants;
- can be seen to engage challenging or 'needy' participants.

These characteristics are indicative of, and contribute to, the particular CGE learning and teaching scenario. For instance, although it is difficult to define what constitutes a 'needy' participant, as suggested above, the view that art can transform people emotionally is an important, if contentious, issue. The central role of the artist as educator and the experimental nature of the teaching and learning in the gallery are also key. These are themes exemplified in the case study (pp. 237–9). The form and process of the sessions – smaller numbers discussing and working in groups, rather than lectures or guided tours – is significant, as it allows for 'co-constructivist' learning and teaching.

How artists work is particularly relevant to CGE:

- Artists can take risks, experiment and feel comfortable with ambiguity and uncertainty.
- Artists engage in 'reflective practice' (Prentice, 1995), wherein they simultaneously engage in the manipulation of materials and processes whilst critically appraising the work in order to progress it. The creative process is thus seen as a dialogue between artist and work.
- Artists are involved in 'experiential learning' (Kolb, 1984), which takes place through the connection of past experiences with new phenomena, and moves from reflection to active experimentation.

The process of action, reflection and experimentation which drives the making of art suggests that, in a CGE learning framework, the *process* of engagement must be recognised as much as any outcome; it is during this time that learning takes place.

Within CGE artists engage primarily through discussion and the exchanging of ideas and experiences. Artists are co-learners, not infallible experts, and encourage participants to experiment within the supportive environment of the learning community (Fuirer, 2005). Artists also embody the approaches they wish to develop in learners, including creative and analytical thinking, risk taking and enhancing self-knowledge (ibid.).

The pedagogy of Contemporary Gallery Education

CGE aims to facilitate engagement with original artworks and creative practice, hence a balance must be achieved between teaching interpretive skills and art historical subject knowledge and nurturing learners' personal knowledge and experience. It is important, therefore, to clarify what

Case study: An 'Art into Life' community education session at Tate Modern[4]

The artist educator has gathered together resources (a box of drawing materials, drawing paper and varied photographs) she needs for the gallery session. Today she will be working with plumbers from Lambeth College who are training for an NVQ. A gathering of approximately twenty students, almost all men, come together on the open area outside the 'Nude/Action/Body' suite of galleries.

The artist educator introduces herself. She gives her name and describes herself as an artist who makes her own work, but who also works at Tate Modern. She asks how many of them have visited this gallery before; three raise their hands. Approximately half have not been to any gallery before. However, from the short discussion it is apparent the group have a wide range of knowledge and experience of contemporary art.

The artist educator explains that they will visit one section of Tate Modern and look at some artworks in detail. Before that she would like them to do a short exercise. She hands everyone a piece of paper and pencil and asks them to draw a body. As she is handing round the paper she explains that it is up to them how they draw this body and there are no 'right' or 'wrong' ways to do this exercise. Some in the group become embarrassed at this request; some make jokes, some do not do it, but the majority complete a drawing and hand it back. The artist educator shows a selection of these drawings to the group, drawing their attention to the variations amongst the different images. She suggests different ways of approaching the subject of the body; there is the concept of the 'generic' body, for example, represented by a stick figure in one drawing. When someone says he has drawn a picture of himself she talks about the idea of the 'specific' body – someone known. The tone is good humoured and participants make jokes and tease each other. Apart from breaking the ice, there is a pedagogic element and the artist educator explains the purposes of the drawing exercise. She identifies that the variety of the drawings they have produced demonstrates that people perceive the body in many ways. Using the students' drawings to make the point, she describes how artists can interpret the body very differently.

The group moves into the 'Nude/Action/Body' suite of galleries. The artist educator has already determined the overall structure of the session and she explains how she would like them to walk fairly quickly round the whole suite and try and sum up their experience in two words. The group move off; some chat amongst themselves and only seem to glance at works, whilst others appear deeply engaged in particular paintings. Individuals begin to voice thoughts and opinions on the art; for instance, they identify shapes and colours in a painting. They begin to discuss works amongst themselves, at times disagreeing good-naturedly about what they can see and why artists might be attempting to represent particular ideas in a certain way. They articulate what they think the work is about and what they like or dislike. One woman speaks about not wanting to see naked bodies and describes the paintings as pornography. The artist educator affirms that this is a valid opinion and asks others what they feel about this issue. A short discussion amongst a small group takes place.

After approximately fifteen minutes the artist educator brings the whole group back together and asks people to share their two words. Participants are initially self-conscious and unwilling, but she presses them and eventually one person gives his words as 'personal' and 'expression'. The artist educator thanks him and asks him to elaborate on what he means by these words; what does 'expression' mean to him? The respondent gives a detailed answer about how people express things in different ways and we all have different ideas. At this point the rest of the group listen and do not contribute their own ideas on what expression might mean, so the artist educator asks for other word combinations. Others respond more confidently now and share thoughts, although they do not discuss the responses, but rather wait in turn to give their own.

After another fifteen minutes she suggests the group look at one painting in particular. The group move towards Euan Uglow's painting, *Standing Nude*, which is hanging at one end of the room. The artist educator asks the group to study the painting closely and whilst they look she voices a number of questions: 'Is this the kind of image you would have expected to see?' and 'Why might the artist have chosen to do a painting?' She discourages them from reading the wall text alongside the image, saying that these sessions are in the first instance about what they as individuals think about these works.

The group become very engaged; they voice opinions unprompted and discuss the work in some detail as a group. Some articulate what the painting reminds them of and draw on their experiences in relation to it. One woman says it reminds her of how she felt after childbirth; how tired and uncomfortable she was. Another participant observes that the woman looks 'disjointed' and her bowed head suggests she is ashamed. This provokes a discussion about the relationship between artist and model. Participants ask lots of questions: 'Why would the artist get her to stay in that position?' 'Is the artist trying to dominate or control her?' The artist educator does not provide answers to these questions, but encourages participants to articulate individual responses and discuss amongst themselves. She nurtures and facilitates the dialogue by picking up on certain comments, urging people to clarify their thoughts and allowing different speakers to voice their views.

Discussion amongst group members moves on to the relationship between artist and viewer. One man asks, 'Is the artist trying to make us feel uncomfortable or is he showing her looking uncomfortable to make us feel sorry for her?' A subsequent response by another participant that 'he [the artist] meant us to feel awkward' allows the artist educator to address the subject of artistic intention. She identifies that, as viewers, the group can only presume what the artist was intending, but they can explore what an artist tries to communicate from the clues a painting gives us. An artist makes choices regarding all aspects of the work, she says, including composition, colours and media, to communicate his or her ideas. These choices are made visible in the artwork. The participants' task is to think about their experience of the artwork in order to make sense for themselves of the choices the artist has made. She urges them to look closely at the painting once more. One man says that he can see now that the artist's positioning of the model affects how we understand the painting; if he had painted her looking relaxed we would think about it differently. The artist educator confirms the learner's observation and then goes on to suggest he remembers this issue when looking at portraits in the future.

The group gather closer in and the dialogue continues. A man asks, 'Who is the woman and why would the artist want to show her in that dislocated position? Is the artist a man?' At this point the artist educator gives some biographical detail on Euan Uglow (when he lived, where he worked and certain techniques that he used). She mentions that his paintings took a long time, which meant his models held these difficult positions, often for prolonged periods. The artist educator has begun to share her specialist knowledge of the artist, which indicates she has judged that participants are sufficiently confident with their individual interpretations that this information will enrich readings of the work, rather than narrow them.

Participants move off and exchange ideas within their groups. They no longer appear self-conscious and discuss in detail issues including who would have chosen whether the person was clothed (artist or model), as some think this differentiates 'nakedness' from 'nudity'. They touch on notions of vulnerability and strength and what it means to be exposed. The artist educator threads herself between these different dialogues. She asks and answers questions, shares her ideas, encourages participants to clarify opinions, but also listens to exchanges without speaking.

is meant by 'teaching' and 'learning' and acknowledge that the notion of 'pedagogy' adopted here is not only about the science or art of teaching, but refers to 'any conscious activity by one person designed to enhance learning in another' (Watkins and Mortimore, 1999: 3).

Recently there has been a shift from understanding teaching as the delivery of knowledge by teacher to students. Instead, learners can be seen as active constructors of meaning, with teachers as facilitators who engage students in learning processes, sparking their curiosity, improving the quality of their thinking and increasing their disposition to learn (Watkins, 2003). In particular, aspects of co-constructivist learning theory are relevant to CGE, such as:

- the importance of dialogue;
- the sharing, rather than transmission, of knowledge within a social and supportive environment – the learning community;
- the co-learning role played by the educator;
- an emphasis on experimental and open-ended learning processes.

Although activities undertaken within CGE are varied and individual projects characteristically address specific issues, this model aspires to:

- enable participants to engage with, and gain greater understanding of, original works of art and the exhibition context;
- develop participants' analytical and reflective skills;
- encourage participants to engage with art and artistic practice to develop their own creativity and creative making skills;
- develop subject-specific and cross-curricular learning.

Enabling participants to engage with, and gain greater understanding of, original works of art and the exhibition context

For individuals to engage with artworks, they need to draw on their own lives and experiences (Burnham and Kai-Kee, 2005). CGE foregrounds the individual knowledge that learners bring, whilst also recognising that artworks may no longer be associated with stable or enduring meanings. This multiplicity and instability of meaning precludes the possibility of didactic teaching, encouraging modes of interpretation that are more questioning, collaborative and provisional.

However, although CGE does not endorse one 'right' interpretation of an artwork, neither does it support the validation of every response. This would appear to contradict the notion that viewers must connect personally with the work. However, during the learning process connections are made with cultural discourses and ideas are continuously tested against the work itself. As is shown in the case study on pp. 237–9, meaning is negotiated over time, rather than being given or immediately endorsed, and although multiple interpretations are possible, the validity of these must be justified in terms of evidence visible in the artwork (Borzello, 1995; Jackson and Meacham, 1999). Thus learners are encouraged to:

- look hard;
- form initial ideas;
- question their initial responses;
- take on board contextual, art historical and other relevant concepts;
- combine personal and external knowledge to develop their interpretations;
- reflect on their experiences and recall key points of learning.

(Lachapelle *et al.*, 2003; Fuirer, 2005)

This is an ongoing, dialogic process, which deepens the experience of the work, but does not provide definitive answers. Also the dialogic nature of the learning is twofold – between viewer and artwork (as per the construction model) and between all those involved in developing shared and individual interpretations (as per the co-construction model). The learning environment and the social/cultural role that the gallery plays are equally significant, since for gallery visits to avoid being purely celebratory 'the exploration of the politics of site and curatorial practice' must be interrogated (Jackson and Meacham, 1999).

Developing participants' analytical and reflective skills

CGE recognises that any encounter with artworks is not purely intellectual; learning is motivated and enhanced by emotion as well as intellect (Taylor, 1987; Burnham and Kai-Kee, 2005). Intense experiences and emotional responses to art can lead to greater commitment and encourage participants to embark on further personal, intellectual and aesthetic investigations (Burnham and Kai-Kee, 2005; Xanthoudaki *et al.*, 2003). Equally, engaging with art can generate pleasure, happiness or satisfaction (Harland *et al.*, 2005). However, alongside these visceral and non-cognitive responses, much contemporary art has a strong conceptual basis.

Therefore participants are encouraged to think, analyse and reflect whilst exploring works of art. This process mirrors a specific understanding of the creative process.

CGE recognises that artists can have a particular relationship to subject knowledge and the artistic process that might differ from that of, for example, an art historian. Subject knowledge about contemporary art has been identified as being 'as much to do with an attitude of questioning and focused looking, as it is concerned with the detail of individual artists, movements and tendencies or with the art object itself' (Charman and Ross, 2005). Also, although CGE recognises that artists possess craft and technical skills, to varying degrees artists approach these more as methods to articulate their ideas, rather than as ends in themselves, since their mode of operation is, to a greater or lesser extent, conceptual (Raney, 2003).

Encouraging participants to engage with art and artistic practice to develop their own creativity and creative making skills

Within CGE, making and doing activities are understood predominantly as ways to develop analytical thinking and meaning – making in relation to artworks, rather than part of practical art classes. Working with techniques and materials is one way that learners can interrogate how artists use visual language to convey meaning. In this way participants learn about contemporary art practice through making, but a conceptual discourse is implicit throughout (Nicol, 2000; Pringle,

2002). This position echoes the model of creative practice outlined above. It also draws on the philosophical and ideological concepts adopted by the community art movement, wherein the desired outcomes from participation in creative activities are as much to do with personal and social learning and empowerment as aesthetic or technical prowess (Dickson, 1995).

Some tensions exist between the CGE approach, with its focus on experimentation and discursive practices, and the pedagogy of the education sector, where the emphasis can be more on practical 'doing' activities, to develop pupils' making skills, and clear objectives and definable outcomes (Sekules, 2003). Hence it cannot be assumed that teachers and pupils will automatically feel comfortable with more conceptual, open-ended learning scenarios in the gallery.

Developing subject-specific and cross-curricular learning

Within CGE, art historical and other cultural discourses surrounding works of art are interrogated and contextualised. The gallery educator's role is not to teach facts, but rather start with a work and articulate concerns that surround it, so as to reveal its complexity and enable learners to have a richer experience. Thus interpretation can be undertaken from several theoretical positions rather than being determined by the art historical canon (examples being feminism, post-colonialism, formalism, the political and social, semiotics and iconography) (Charman et al., 2001).

The potential for cross-curricular learning in galleries derives from the nature of creative practice. 'Contemporary art is inherently cross-curricular. Artists do not work in a vacuum. Their work reflects their passions and preoccupations, whether that is science, the environment, architecture and space, people and relationships, autobiography, etc.' (Orbach, 2004: 6). Contemporary art addresses social and cultural issues and can be used as a springboard for exploring worldviews as well as concerns in individuals' lives. Echoing the concerns of community art practice, within CGE the focus is on enabling participants to gain analytical and reflective skills that can make a difference to their lives, whilst raising their awareness and empowering them to engage with issues.

However, despite the opportunities for contemporary art to facilitate these forms of cross-curricular learning schools do not appear to have fully exploited its potential. This is perhaps due to schools' framing of art as essentially a practical rather than a conceptual discipline (Downing and Watson, 2004; Harland et al., 2005).

Notes

1 A version of this chapter previously appeared as: *Learning in the Gallery: Context, Process, Outcomes*. by Emily Pringle, London: Arts Council England and *engage* (2006).
2 Texts that originate outside the UK tend to use the term 'art museum', or simply 'museum', to describe what is commonly understood in this country to be an art gallery. In this chapter the word 'gallery' relates to art exhibition spaces within galleries, museums, arts centres and artists' studios.
3 Community art has embraced a range of artists and activities and the term itself is problematic to some, making absolute definitions difficult (Dickson, 1995).
4 This is a descriptive interpretation of a particular 'Art into Life' (AiL) education session at Tate Modern. This narrative is constructed from notes taken during observation of this session and informed by observations of five other sessions (both AiL and others) at Tate Modern.

References

Adams, M., Falk, J. and Dierking, L. (2003) Things change: museums, learning and research, in M. Xanthoudaki, L. Tickle and V. Sekules (eds) *Researching Visual Arts Education in Museums and Galleries*, London: Kluwer Academic Publishers.

Barthes, R. (1977) *Image, Music, Text*, London: Fontana Press.

Bell, C. (1993 [1914]) The aesthetic hypothesis, in C. Harrison and P. Wood (eds) *Art in Theory 1900–1990: An Anthology of Changing Ideas*, Oxford: Blackwell.

Borzello, F. (1995) Art gallery education: have we progressed?, *Journal of Education in Museums* 16: 6–7.

Burnham, R. and Kai-Kee, E. (2005) The art of teaching in the museum, *Journal of Aesthetic Education* 39 (1): 65–76.

Carnell, E. and Lodge, C. (2002) *Supporting Effective Learning*, London: Paul Chapman Publishing.

Charman, H. and Ross, M. (2005) *Contemporary Art and the Role of Interpretation: Reflections on Tate Modern's Summer Institute for Teachers*; available at www.tate.org.uk/research/tateresearch/tatepapers/04autumn/charman.htm (accessed 14 March 2005).

Charman, H., Meecham, P., Orbach, C. and Wilson, G. (2001) *Tate Modern Teachers' Kit: Action: Planning Your Visit*, London: Tate Gallery.

Dickson, M. (ed.) (1995) *Art with People*, Sunderland: AN Publications.

Downing, D. and Watson, R. (2004) *School Art: What's in It? Exploring Visual Arts in Secondary Schools*, Slough: National Foundation for Educational Research.

Falk, J. and Dierking, L. (2000) *Learning from Museums: Visitor Experiences and the Making of Meaning*, Oxford: Altamira Press.

Fry, R. (1993 [1909]) An essay in aesthetics, in C. Harrison and P. Wood (eds) *Art in Theory 1900–1990: An Anthology of Changing Ideas*, Oxford: Blackwell.

Fuirer, M. (2005) *Jolt, Catalyst, Spark! Encounters with Artworks in the Schools Programme at Tate Modern*; available at www.tate.org.uk/research/tateresearch/tatepapers/05autumn/fuirer.htm (accessed 10 November 2005).

Godfrey, F. (1996) Critical encounters: opt for art at the Oriel Mostyn Gallery – 1, in *Hands-on Participation and Interaction = Education? The Importance of the Artist as Educator*, engage National Conference Papers, Newcastle.

—— (1998) *Conceptual Art*, London: Phaidon Press.

Harland, J., Lord, P., Stott, A., Kinder, K., Lamont, E. and Ashworth, M. (2005) *The arts–Education Interface: A Mutual Learning Triangle?* Slough: National Foundation for Educational Research.

Hooper-Greenhill, E. (2000) *Museum and Gallery Education*, London: Leicester University Press.

Jackson, T. and Meecham, P. (1999) The culture of the art museum, *Journal of Art and Design Education* 9: 89–98.

Jantjes, G. (2001) 'Good practice' and creativity, *engage Review* 8 (Summer): 20–4.

Kolb, D. (1984) *Experiential Learning: Experience as the Source of Learning and Development*, San Francisco: Harper.

Lachapelle, R., Murray, D. and Neim, S. (2003) Aesthetic understanding as informed experience: the role of knowledge in our art viewing experiences, *Journal of Aesthetic Education* 37(3): 78–99.

Moore Tapia, J. and Hazelroth Barrett, S. (2003) Postmodernism and art museum education: the case for a new paradigm, in M. Xanthoudaki, L. Tickle and V. Sekules (eds) *Researching Visual Arts Education in Museums and Galleries*, London: Kluwer Academic Publishers.

Morgan, S. (1995) Looking back over 25 years, in M. Dickson (ed.) *Art with People*, Sunderland: AN Publications.

Nicol, G. (2000) Collaboration, communication, contemporary art, in G. Nicol and A. Plant (eds) *Collaboration: Communication: Contemporary Art*, London: engage.

Orbach, C. (2004) The ArtFULL programme: issues and opportunities, in L. Anson and H. Garrett (eds) *Encounters with Contemporary Art – Schools, Galleries and the Curriculum: The ArtFULL Programme*, London: engage.

Prentice, R. (1995) Learning to teach: a conversational exchange, in R. Prentice (ed.) *Teaching Art and Design: Addressing Issues, Identifying Directions*, London: Cassell Education.

—— (2000) The place of practical knowledge in research in art and design education, *Teaching in Higher Education* 5(4): 521–34.

Pringle, E. (2002) *We Did Stir Things Up: The Role of Artists in Sites for Learning*, London: Arts Council of England.

Raney, K. (2003) *Art in Question*, London: Continuum Press.

Sekules, V. (2003) The celebrity performer and the creative facilitator: the artist, the school and the art museum, in M. Xanthoudaki, L. Tickle and V. Sekules (eds) *Researching Visual Arts Education in Museums and Galleries*, London: Kluwer Academic Publishers.

Stanley, J. and Galloway, S. (2004) ArtFULL – gallery education as part of a national educational programme, in L. Anson and H. Garrett (eds) *Encounters with Contemporary Art – Schools, Galleries and the Curriculum: The ArtFULL Programme*, London: engage.

Taylor, R. (1987) *Educating for Art: Critical Response and Development*, Harlow: Longman.

Watkins, C. (2003) *Learning: A Sense-Maker's Guide*, London: Association of Teachers and Lecturers and the Institute of Education.

Watkins, C. and Mortimore, P. (1999) Pedagogy: what do we know?, in P. Mortimore (ed.) *Understanding Pedagogy*, London: Paul Chapman Publishing.

Xanthoudaki, M. (2003) Museums, galleries and art education in primary schools: researching experiences in England and Greece, in M. Xanthoudaki, L. Tickle and V. Sekules (eds) *Researching Visual Arts Education in Museums and Galleries*, London: Kluwer Academic Publishers.

Xanthoudaki, M., Tickle, L. and Sekules, V. (eds) (2003) *Researching Visual Arts Education in Museums and Galleries*, London: Kluwer Academic Publishers.

26

Creative digital cultures

Informal learning beyond the school

Julian Sefton-Green

No self-respecting book about Creativity can do without a section on the impact of digital technologies on the products, processes and outcomes of all kinds of creative endeavour. This chapter will focus on a particular subset of these issues as it explores the series of research projects, writings, argument and public advocacy produced over the last twenty years, all suggesting that the spread of digital technologies among young people has brought down barriers to access; and that many young people in affluent societies now have opportunities to participate in forms of creative and cultural expression and communication. The evidence supporting this hypothesis is by no means universally accepted and a series of counter-arguments essentially focusing on the role of commercial interests has been offered as contrary interpretation of these changing trends in leisure use.

This chapter will report on, describe and analyse these sets of arguments. The key theme in this account will be how participation in digital culture sets up a series of tensions with traditions of schooling, reframing the nature of learning itself. One interpretation of these tensions is that young people now have more autonomy and agency to learn and act outside of the 'gate-keeping' mechanisms of school. Alternative arguments suggest that such opportunities have been consistently hyped by neo-liberal interests and that the threats to curriculum and pedagogy are only another way of validating the privileges of social elites. Of course formal education institutions have also developed procedures to incorporate and 're-contextualise' such forms of independence and differentiation.

The chapter will conclude by suggesting that changes in learning and growth in creative opportunities may well be modifying what it now means to be a young learner today, and that although the more extreme claims for these changes cannot be sustained, curriculum develop-ment and forms of pedagogy will continually need to measure themselves against developing competences in the digital domain.

The structure of the chapter is almost a fractal for the whole book and this is no accident given how the twin discourses of creativity and new technologies have dominated narratives about education in recent years. It will begin by exploring the 'Net Generation' hypothesis, examining the core structural relationships between opportunities for creatively making and consuming digital products, and then explore how digital culture may offer creative processes for learning, leading to a review of how the digital era may or may not offer a lens for constructing broader education reform.

It is worthwhile noting that this chapter does not deal with the creative implications of educational technology – that is, how uses of digital technologies in schools and colleges, as well as in the home, in curriculum and as changing pedagogies, may or may not be offering creative learning. Here, the focus is on the broader impact of digital culture – at home and with peers.

The 'Net Generation' hypothesis

A series of writings have in effect postulated a Net Gen hypothesis, that young people born in the digital era have access to a series of experiences and have thus developed competencies which mean that learning, work, access to knowledge, creativity and indeed economic productivity have been fundamentally transformed. The dimensions of this are explored below, but it worth noting that key assumptions are deeply problematic on two levels.

The first of these relates to any notion of 'change', let alone transformation. Scholars who offer models of impact or effects in this area find it difficult to be exact about what they mean by claiming observable changes. This is partly an issue of scientific knowledge and partly a question of scholarly rigour. As there can be no experimental control groups against which we can set new kinds of exposure to digital culture, and anyway since we are talking about social phenomena, and variables relating to the specifics of the people involved will inevitably impact on outcomes, it is difficult to be precise about claims. For example, scholars of literacy have tried to compare non-print culture literacies with print cultures to explore the precise impact of the development of literacy on language, but of course such examples are exceptional and rare (see Scribner and Cole, 1981). And to escape the problem of complicating social variables scholars of the impact of the mass media have resorted to arcane research sites (Charlton et al., 2001).

There are good questions to be asked about what timescale is needed to ascertain properly long-term impacts from changes in behaviour, ability or even physiology (there has been spec-ulation about the effect on adolescent thumbs as a consequence of repeated game playing).[1] At the heart of these problems, some of which are admittedly abstruse and methodological, is a deep question about what kinds of model of effect are at work. Are we talking about changes in behaviour or changes in capacity or capability, deep rooted cognitive shifts (as in the effects of literacy) or notions of affordances – that is, how the use of tools change one's ability to imagine or carry out particular tasks? Or are these not even 'changes' so much as a new set of 'tricks'? What kind of time period is needed to observe deep changes?

Notions of effect over time are entwined with our second concern: the casual generalisations about generational change popularised by the idea of digital natives and immigrants (Prensky, 2006). Don Tapscott, an influential populariser of Net Generation impacts, has produced two books (Tapscott, 1999, 2008) whose titles (growing up and grown up) neatly express this alleged generational shift.

Rigorous studies of impact and effect in the social sciences are usually based on quantitative and comparative data. Whilst these sorts of studies exist showing changing access to the Net, for example, and changing patterns of leisure use,[2] there are (to date) no ways of evaluating the impact of changing social uses across population cohorts. Most research exploring new ways of learning is small scale and qualitative, so we have little sense of how large swathes of the population might be affected by changes in behaviour, or patterns of take up and use – and, of course, whether the impact of the use of digital technologies is equal and equivalent for all people (although there are many approaches exploring key social differentials, like gender). These questions are important and pose uncomfortable and difficult challenges.

Digital culture and the Net Generation

Some of the earliest speculation about the effects of online and contemporary computer inter-actions is some of the most ambitious in conceptual terms and most difficult to prove empirically. Sherry Turkle led the way here by exploring how the use of virtual avatars and a corresponding capacity to 'play' with identities led to a change in the formation of subjectivities – how immersion in forms of digital culture affects how we imagine our selves and who we might be and become (Turkle, 1985, 1997). Issues relating to the presentation of an anonymous self, and indeed wider ideas about how we might play with and perform aspects of our identity online – derived partly from Performance theory (McKenzie, 2001) and partly from notions about the dramaturgical nature of social life based on the work of Erving Goffman, 1990 – have flooded the literature.

It is of course the idea that persistent interaction with digital technologies has changed fun-damental aspects of how young people create and are created by themselves which lies at the heart of the Net Generation hypothesis. It is the perceived nature of the *differences* between this model of self-formation and traditional ones which, as we shall see, has led to the current dilemma as schools, teachers and parents seem to struggle to come to terms with a gap between what is expected and what they are presented with day to day.

A key area for research into changing identities has been the social arena. First we have the idea that digital technology facilitates access to a wide range of public, civic, community, interest and friendship groupings. Young people, it is argued, can interact online and can act in any of these fora with independence and authority. There have been a series of studies exploring all of these discrete areas and examining the extent to which the online life does or does not afford these new opportunities and how (and by whom) they are taken up. Of parti-cular interest seems to be the question of civics (Loader, 2007; Bennett, 2008). However eth-nographers of childhood and observers of changing forms of culture have also noted the changing role of online life for all kinds of social activity as summed up in a title of a recent book *Hanging Out, Messing Around, and Geeking Out: Kids Living and Learning with New Media* (Ito *et al.*, 2010).

Second, there is the idea that such processes support qualitatively different notions of col-lective and collaborative activity, especially those that relate to learning. Scholars of computer gaming as well as online life have noted that inhabiting rule-bound virtual worlds encourages discrete kinds of social behaviour, which has ramifications for education. Working in teams, on focused and dedicated tasks, being able to work at one's own pace and within one's own time-frames, knowing how and who to ask for support, parcelling out parts of a task, working with international and non-place-based colleagues, developing appropriate and distinct ways of talk-ing and communicating have all been investigated by various scholars as posing serious qualita-tive differences to forms of inquisitive behaviour (see, for example, Palfrey and Gasser, 2008). Again, a number of scholars have noted how such behaviours are quite specifically at odds with dominant forms of teaching and learning within the curriculum, with its individualised modes of study and assessment (see, for example, Shaffer, 2008).

Both of these foci contribute to a key issue in the literature, how being able to act with others in virtual and virtual-real worlds (that is, those online fora where there is clear reference to offline issues, whether political, civic or even just an interest grouping) changes the agency or power of the young person as a social actor. In more extreme cases young people take up roles of authority as, for example, where game players 'know' more and are expert within their own communities and knowledge domains (see, for example, Gee, 2004). Scholars have debated the precise nature of this empowerment. Crudely speaking, there is a boosters position (e.g.

Tapscott, 2008) suggesting that there has been a fundamental reconfiguration of power, agency and authority, offset by more sceptical analysis suggesting that the limits of authority are circumscribed (Willett, 2008).

The question of authority or agency is often described in terms of skills or changing skillsets – although this term is also more complex than it seems. In general the range of new skills learned in this way break down into *user* and *producer* types – both existing on a sliding scale as well as in relation to each other. User skills can be both mental and physical, covering, for example, information retrieval and manipulation or indeed increased hand–eye co-ordination as an example of the second type. Producer skills range from the ability to customise to making expressive media (O'Hear and Sefton-Green, 2004). The spread of these abilities and the different ways young people learn them though various forms of self- or peer teaching (Willett and Sefton-Green, 2002) are contested and unequal, with scant sociological evidence about reach and penetration and with case study examples often used to stand in for more general habits. Attention to the power of auto-didacticism and its various trial-and-error methods has important implications for formal education (Sefton-Green, 2004a) but this must not stand in way of a level-headed evaluation of what David Buckingham (2008) has called the 'banality' of much new media use.

The discussion, then, of the range of skills and competences demonstrated in new media use range from the capacity to manipulate computers, programmes, icons and other formal features of digital technologies to learning the rules, conventions, genres of chat rooms, games and so on – the more cultural side to these activities. Much attention has been paid to the mastery of text and its seemingly organic transmutations through different language shapes and forms in chat and other online interactions (see, for example, Pahl and Rowsell, 2006; or Snyder, 1998, 2002). The producer skillset has ranged from study of adaptation and customisation to more complex cultural activities like digital story telling,[3] film and audio, and of course websites or blogs (Stern, 2004).

The question of skills is of course related to questions of cognition. Early scholars of computers and learning have always been interested in ways that technology may or may not transform cognitive processes (Greenfield, 1984; Papert, 1993). Whilst the section above enumerated skills that might be described as discrete and were those demonstrated though action, here the argument is that different ways of thinking are at stake. There are several key domains. One is the effect on *modelling* – that is, how computer interactions support ways of imagining or conceptualising problems from ideas of space and place to mathematical relationships. Second is the issue of *meta-cognition* – that is, how we can be supported to reflect on and think between and across hitherto discrete phenomena. Third is the issue of *information processing* and the study of how changes in how knowledge is stored, accessed and retrieved affect intellectual activity (Bransford, 1998).

Finally, as has already been hinted at, one feature of Net Generation behaviours is that they support young people to emerge from more bounded social domains to act as fully empowered individuals in more public arenas. One key aspect of this is that implicit norms about barriers or boundaries to stages of the life course are crossed – for example allowing young people to act outside the home and certainly with greater independence unfettered by adult supervision. This aspect of Net Generation behaviour is the most contentious, especially, as noted, where such behaviours transgress the possibilities of regulation and threaten the protection mechanisms we are accustomed to – especially in relation to perceived 'adult' content (for extended discussion, see Zittrain, 2008). It is certainly true that a main reason why schools are shy of demonstrating interest in Net Generation behaviours is because of the (reasonable) threat of legal or moral retribution in respect of this boundary crossing.

On the other hand, it precisely this capability of young people to act in public forums, to assert their views, to express their opinions and to join in public discussion which motives our interest (Tapscott, 2008; Palfrey and Gasser, 2008). The stories of young people who have become gainfully employed through online interactions, who have become independent creators and producers and those who have managed to 'punch above their weight' are telling and contribute to the sense that the Net Generation need to be considered as possessing qualitatively different 'rights' than their chronological peers.

Although it is unclear precisely how to measure these changes, there is a generally agreed body of international research which documents a series of different behaviours and competences by some young people as a result of their use of digital technologies. We do not know how equal, far-reaching or widespread such changes are, but a series of identified behaviours which offer authentic and challenging learning experiences have been enumerated. These coalesce around a different kind of learning self – different, that is, from forms of subjectivity validated by current school arrangements – who can act with authority across a series of domains and who is accustomed to forms of collaboration, genuine challenge, experimentation, risk-taking, curiosity and expressivity: all of which converge with, contribute to and indeed are an integral part of understanding about creativity in everyday life as well as creativity at work and at play.

Different or creative?

In the context of this volume, we need to ask whether (or in what ways) these changing behaviours or competencies constitute a discrete domain for or of creativity. And second (discussed in Part IV) how they may or may not offer institutional challenges to schools if they determine changing kinds of learning.

There are a number of ways we can offer answers to the first of these questions. The first would point to an increased attention to amateur and popular forms of creative production which are a direct consequence of the everyday creativity we now associate with these shifts in digital culture (see Jones, Chapter 9). Even if we were to take a strict demarcation between the formal aspects of new media production (photography, video, websites, mash-ups, machinima) and reject an extended definition of creative consumption (posting to websites etc.), there can be no doubt that many more young people have the capability and opportunity to play with what used to be exclusive production technologies. Again, even if the numbers suggesting that young people have become producers are grossly exaggerated and even if many young people only uses the programs on their computers or phones occasionally, indisputably making and circulating media is a more common and part of everyday vocabulary. Does this feature of digital culture point to an aestheticisation of everyday life?

The languages of production are thus more widespread, even if we don't know if they are utilised. Debates about aesthetics, editing, effective communication and expression are more prevalent. This doesn't mean in and of itself, as some critics, following Willis (1990), have suggested, that we are entering a new era of popular expressiveness, but it may suggest that the artistic discourses about production values and techniques are more accessible and widespread in common discussion and debates. However, the penetration of making cultural forms through to a wider social base perhaps should be considered more an issue of the greater role of popular arts or crafts than any contribution to generic kinds of wider creativity (although in most definitions there is considerable overlap).

A key feature of debates about popular aesthetics concerns the nature of originality and the distinct contribution of forms of montage, quotation and 'mixing' (Miller, 2004). This is a distinct feature of the language of new media (Manovich, 2001). On the one hand, this has led to a discussion about the generative nature of new media production and, on the other, concerns about originality and imitation. The extent to which actual creations are generic or original, derivative and so on has ramifications for assessment of this 'turn' to the creative as a general characterisation of digital culture. Qualitative small studies of young people's creative output as well larger surveys[4] tend to characterise the inventiveness and imaginativeness of this kind of bedroom (or occasionally atelier) production space rather than making grandiose claims about creative originality.

Indeed an interest in small scale, low level but persistent creative behaviours also dominates the other side to this dimension: namely the changes in behaviour as a result of the participatory nature of forms of creative consumption. Again, definitions here have been varied but it has been strongly argued that we are now living in a era of participatory culture where playing computer games, acting on Facebook or MySpace and other online fora, posting photos to Flickr and so on all encourage not only a facility with the literacies required to 'play' in these arenas but a level of creative behaviour – and one which is the new work of consumption. This has been developed into a full blown education manifesto by Henry Jenkins and colleagues (Jenkins *et al.*, 2007) outlining programmes of reform to ameliorate the disparities in participation between social groups and arguing that such kinds of literate and creative behaviour will provide core skills for the knowledge economy.

Thus, in common with other chapters in this book, the meaning of creative behaviour associated with digital culture depends on definitions of creativity in the first place. Whilst extreme claims about actual creative behaviours need to be distinguished from estimations about how possible they may now be, there is a sense of a benevolent cultural orientation towards creativity. However, we must not overlook a clear distinction between changes in accessibility and action just as, however blurred the boundaries may be between consumption and production, distinctive kinds of 'high' and 'low' creative activities are part and parcel of youth cultures in the modern era. In some respects, however, it hasn't been so much what young people actually make that has been the focus on attention, as the changes in a sense of self and control over such technologies which has interested educationalists: and here it is the ways in which the creativity of the culture (however defined) has affected other dimensions to learning, and in particular the authority and power of the school. This is why digital culture is so crucial to the creative learning debate and it is to this that we now turn.

Creative learning/schools in crisis

A key theme underpinning the analysis of the features of contemporary digital culture is the changing autonomy of the young person, as citizen, social actor and, of course, as learner. A number of studies have both advanced and critiqued the idea that young people are positioned in a different kind of power relationship with traditional notions of authority. And the key definition of this is as student and learner.

The broadest and most challenging arguments suggest that the nature of knowledge itself has shifted. We no longer can expect to 'know' everything, even as experts (Poster, 1990); and learning by rote has become less important than knowing how to find things. Terminal examination has become tendentious in the face of changing employment as global and national economies need the work of 'symbolic analysts' (to use Robert Reich's phrase) for growth and productivity (Peters *et al.*, 2008).

On a less grand scale, we have already seen how studies of the independence and autonomy of expert game players construct a different kind of learner identity (Wortham, 2005). These notions have been consistently explored by James Gee (2004) and developed by him and colleagues in to a fully fledged critique of current learning relationships (for an extended discussion, including a critical commentary, see Sefton-Green, 2006).

If we situate these ideas within a creative learning perspective we can see how key elements of that paradigm are fully present in studies of digital culture. In the work of Gee and others we can see very clear sets of values claimed as core features of digital culture. We have the idea of intrinsic interest, of authentic and long-lasting engagements and participation in the learning domain. The relationship between teacher and taught is reconfigured, with a greater sense of equality and a key role for peers. Genuine collaboration is rewarded and open forms of communication with an attention to the completion of tasks and clear achievements are part of this outlook. From the experiences of creative consumption we have a fluent use of sophisticated technologies (often unmatched in schools) and an active interactive relationship with others and modes of information. In other words, the creativity of digital cultures doesn't reside so much in its media – that is, its capacity to support forms of visual, audio or even text production – but in its subject positions: how it situates young people in relationship to meaning or forms of engagement.

There are two key problems with this formulation. The first relates to the question of content. In the attention to process and context, questions about *what* people are learning and its uses tend to be disregarded and treated as secondary to a focus on dispositions and process. This is one valued critique of creative learning, that in an attempt to make the experience of learning more productive and meaningful (to all concerned) it downgrades the significance of disciplinary knowledge and also has no place for learning for non-immediate ends. In other words, key questions about progression, and the construction of larger understanding than that available in the experience are difficult to factor into this paradigm. A related and secondary part of this problem is that as the drivers of digital culture are commercial interests it has been argued that what young people are really learning from these experiences is no more than how to act within the all-encompassing marketplace (Rifkin, 2001).

The second issue with the positioning of digital culture as an 'organic' site of creative learning is that such arguments have been shown to play a part in larger debates about the values of public schooling and especially the unequal and problematic relationship of the market (Buckingham, 2007). Building on ideas about a 'manufactured crisis' in public education (Berliner and Biddle, 1999), it has been suggested that discourse about the educational nature of digital culture, and especially paying attention to those aspects which stress a more creative and dynamic experience, has been mobilised as part of neo-liberal attacks on public education in general as well as advancing the interests of the various manufacturers which have dominated the new economy in recent years.

Here it may be useful to consider how creative learning itself, as a discourse, has emerged out of the same set of debates: namely as a positive way of critiquing the failing and normative model of schooling. Like young people's pleasure and interest in forms of digital culture, creative learning has been defined as much by what it is not as by what it does. In other words, it is very difficult to disassociate these discussions from their immediate social context. There is no idea of a disinterested, abstract notion of creative learning, just as digital culture cannot be explored freely except from an implied opposite – in this case a generalised and heavily beleaguered notion of a common school. And of course an idea of school is no more capable of being described in common than digital culture or creative learning.

Notes

1 Or see, for example: http://www.reghardware.co.uk/2009/03/30/videogame_eyesight_research/.

2 The range of research projects led by Sonia Livingstone are good examples of this: http://www.eukidsonline.Net/.

3 For example http://www.intermedia.uio.no/mediatized/.

4 http://digitalyouth.ischool.berkeley.edu/report.

References

Bennett, L. (2008) *Civic Life Online: Learning How Digital Media Can Engage Youth*, John D. and Catherine T. MacArthur Foundation Series on Digital Media and Learning, Cambridge, MA: The MIT Press.

Berliner, D. C. and Biddle, B. J. (1999) *The Manufactured Crisis: Myths, Fraud, and the Attack on America's Public Schools*, Cambridge, MA: Perseus Books.

Bransford, J. D. (1998) *How People Learn: Brain, Mind, Experience and School*, Washington, DC: National Academies Press.

Buckingham, D. (2007) *Beyond Technology: Children's Learning in the Age of Digital Culture*, Cambridge: Polity Press.

—— (2008) *Youth, Identity, and Digital Media*, John D. and Catherine T. MacArthur Foundation Series on Digital Media and Learning, Boston, MA: The MIT Press.

Burke, A. and Hammett, R. (2009) *Assessing New Literacies: Perspectives from the Classroom*, New York: Peter Lang.

Charlton, T., Gunter, B. and Hannan, A. (2001) *Broadcast Television Effects in a Remote Community (Communication S.)*, Mahwah, NJ: Lawrence Erlbaum Associates.

Gee, J. P. (2004) *What Video Games Have to Teach Us about Learning and Literacy*, New York: Palgrave Macmillan.

Goffman, E. (1990) *The Presentation of Self in Everyday Life*, Harmondsworth: Penguin Books Ltd.

Greenfield, P. M. (1984) *Mind and Media: The Effects of Television, Computers and Video Games*, Cambridge, MA: Harvard University Press.

Ito, M., Baumer, S., Bittanti, M., boyd, d., Cody, R., Herr-Stephenson, B. *et al.* (2010) *Hanging Out, Messing Around, and Geeking Out: Kids Living and Learning with New Media*, John D. and Catherine T. MacArthur Foundation Series on Digital Media and Learning, Cambridge, MA: The MIT Press.

Jenkins, H., Clinton, K., Purushotma, R., Robinson, A. and Weigel, M. (2007) Confronting the Challenges of Participatory Culture: Media Education for the 21st Century; available at http://digitallearning.macfound.org/atf/cf/%7B7E45C7E0-A3E0-4B89-AC9C-E807E1B0AE4E%7D/JENKINS_WHITE_PAPER.PDF.

Loader, B. D. (2007) *Young Citizens in the Digital Age: Political Engagement, Young People and New Media*, London: Routledge.

McKenzie, J. (2001) *Perform or Else: From Discipline to Performance*, London: Routledge.

Manovich, L. (2001) *The Language of New Media*, Leonardo Book, Cambridge, MA: The MIT Press.

Miller, P. D., a.k.a. DJ Spooky that subliminal kid (2004) *Rhythm Science*, Mediawork, Cambridge, MA: The MIT Press.

O'Hear, S. and Sefton-Green, J. (2004) Creative 'communities': how technology mediates social worlds, in D. Miell and K. Littleton (eds) *Collaborative Creativity: Contemporary Perspectives*, London: Free Association Press.

Pahl, K. and Rowsell, J. (2006) *Travel Notes from the New Literacy Studies: Instances of Practice*, New Perspectives on Language and Education, Clevedon: Multilingual Matters Ltd.

Palfrey, J. and Gasser, U. (2008) *Born Digital: Understanding the First Generation of Digital Natives*, New York: Basic Books.

Papert, S. A. (1993) *Mindstorms: Children, Computers, and Powerful Ideas*, Cambridge, MA: Perseus Books.

Peters, M. A., Marginson, S. and Murphy, P. (2008) *Creativity and the Global Knowledge Economy*, New York: Peter Lang.

Poster, M. (1990) *The Mode of Information: Post-Structuralism and Social Contexts*. Cambridge: Polity Press.

Prensky, M. (2006) *Don't Bother Me Mom – I'm Learning!*, St Paul, MN: Paragon House Publishers.

Rifkin, J. (2001) *Age of Access: The New Culture of Hypercapitalism, Where All of Life Is a Paid-For Experience*, New York: Jeremy P. Tarcher.

Scribner, S. and Cole, M. (1981) *The Psychology of Literacy*, Cambridge, MA: Harvard University Press.

Sefton-Green, J. (2004a) Initiation rites: a small boy in a Poke-world, in J. Tobin (ed.) *Pikachu's Global Adventure: The Rise and Fall of Pokemon*, Durham, NC: Duke University Press.

—— (2004b) Literature Review in Informal Learning with Technology Outside School, Bristol: Futurelab; available at http://www.futurelab.org.uk/download/pdfs/research/lit_reviews/Outside_Learning_Review.pdf.

—— (2006) Youth, technology and media cultures, in J. Green and A. Luke (eds) *Review of Research in Education 30*, Washington, DC: AERA.

Shaffer, D. (2008) *How Computer Games Help Children Learn*, New York: Palgrave Macmillan.

Snyder, I. (1998) *Page to Screen: Taking Literacy into the Electronic Era*, London: Routledge.

—— (2002) *Silicon Literacies: Communication, Innovation and Education in the Electronic Age*, London: Routledge.

Stern, S. (2004) Expression of identity online: prominent features and gender differences in adolescents' WWW home pages, *Journal of Broadcasting and Electronic Media* 48(2): 218–43.

Tapscott, D. (1999) *Growing Up Digital: Rise of the Net Generation*, Oracle Press series, New York: McGraw-Hill Education.

—— (2008) *Grown Up Digital: How the Net Generation Is Changing Your World*, New York: McGraw-Hill Professional.

Turkle, S. (1985) *Second Self: Computers and the Human Spirit*, New York: Pocket Books.

—— (1997) *Life on the Screen: Identity in the Age of the Internet*, New York: Simon & Schuster Inc.

Willett, R. (2008) Consumer citizens online: structure, agency, and gender in online participation, in D. Buckingham (ed.) *Youth, Identity, and Digital Media*, Cambridge MA: The MIT Press.

Willett, R. and Sefton-Green, J. (2002) Living and learning in chatrooms (or does informal learning have anything to teach us?), *Education et Sociétés* 2: 57–77.

Willis, P. E. (1990) *Common Culture: Symbolic Work at Play in the Everyday Cultures of the Young*, Milton Keynes: Open University Press.

Wortham, S. (2005) *Learning Identity: The Joint Emergence of Social Identification and Academic Learning*, Cambridge: Cambridge University Press.

Zittrain, J. (2008) *The Future of the Internet: And How to Stop It*, London: Allen Lane.

27

Redesigning school spaces

Creating possibilities for learning

Helen Nixon and Barbara Comber

Introduction

The New London Group's conceptual blueprint for a pedagogy of multiliteracies has highlighted the importance of incorporating design and multiple modes of meaning-making and representation into contemporary understandings of literacy, and has emphasised the increasing importance of screen-based and digital practices (Cope and Kalantzis, 2000; Kress, 2003; New London Group, 1996). Yet other literacy researchers have noticed the increasing differences between in- and out-of-school literacies (e.g. Hull and Schultz, 2001; Lankshear and Knobel, 2003) and have argued that students' investment in new and popular literacies highlights the lack of relevance of what is typically on offer at school. Nevertheless, we believe that it is possible for literacy educators to work towards building a curriculum that is engaging for students and authorises their perspectives on the world around them. Such a curriculum might very well grow out of the arts or technology and design, with their emphases on visual and spatial modes of representation. But equally such a curriculum might incorporate critical approaches to the study of space and place. In this chapter we describe the possibilities afforded by collaborative cross-curriculum planning, in conjunction with place-based pedagogy, for the student production of imaginative, expansive and socially significant texts.

With respect to critical pedagogy, place-based educators (Gruenewald, 2003) and environmental educators (Martusewicz and Edmundson, 2005) have argued that it has often ignored the *spatial* dimensions of social practice. Yet there are potential synergies between the work of place-based educators and those concerned with critical pedagogy (Gruenewald, 2003), and also between the work of spatial theorists and those of us concerned specifically with critical literacy. Focussing on the spatial and the socially produced nature of space (and place) is very much in alignment with critical literacy's insistence on the constructedness of texts. Indeed recognition of the politics of space – how space is constitutive – is akin to the discursive construction of subjectivity. Clearly, in pedagogical terms, focussing on space allows for analysis of the constructedness of the way things are and the possibility that things might be otherwise (Freire, 1985; Greene, 1988, 1995).

A key move for us has been to work with young people and their teachers to develop place-based pedagogies where teaching and learning are designed to explore the affordances of particular places and spaces (Comber *et al.*, 2007; Comber *et al.*, 2006). A related move is working to 'open up' what constitutes literacy at a time when increasingly governments attempt to contain and limit it. This has meant searching for ways of thinking about students' and teachers' work that allow for *creativity* and *imagination* as part of a critical literacy project (Comber and Nixon, 2005; Janks, 2006). Critical literacy needs to be as much about positive representations of identity and knowledge through textual production as it is about deconstruction (Comber, 2001; Janks and Comber, 2006; Nixon and Comber, 2005). In this regard we believe Kress and van Leeuwen's application of 'design' to curriculum holds much promise:

> Teachers, for instance, may either design their own lessons or merely 'execute' a detailed syllabus designed by expert educators ... when design and production separate, design becomes a means for controlling the actions of others, the potential for a unity between discourse, design and production diminishes, and there is no longer room for the 'producers' to make the design 'their own', to add their own accent.
>
> *(Kress and van Leeuwen, 2001: 7)*

Janks (2000, 2006) has explored how 'design' – a 'catch-all word for imagining and producing texts' (Janks, 2006: 3) – is crucial in the theory and practice of critical literacy because it has the potential to move people 'beyond critique to action' (ibid.: 4). Janks demonstrates how young South Africans have worked with different media, modes and languages to collaboratively design texts that represent themselves and their worlds for young people in other places. Similarly, as we will show, in our study a critical multiliteracies approach positioned young people as agents using various existing semiotic resources for the redesign of material spaces that mattered to them.

In neo-conservative times when literacy curriculum has in many places been colonised by clocks and blocks, working in other curriculum areas may hold out some promise for critical educators. In addition, as Apple (2005) has recently argued, much counter-hegemonic educational work is accomplished 'locally and regionally' and it may be that projects which attempt to make an immediate material and visible difference in their places are most appealing to today's young people.

Urban renewal from the inside out: repositioning teachers and young people as designers

In a project entitled *Urban renewal from the inside out*,[1] two teachers, university researchers and students from the fields of architecture, communications and literacy studies worked with elementary school students to negotiate the design and re-making of a desolate space in the school yard located between a pre-school and elementary school. The school used the name *Grove Gardens* as a shorthand way of describing the project and talking about it with children. In addition to the goal of making a material improvement to the school environment, an important aim of the project was to equip student participants with repertoires of powerful social practices such as negotiation, design and consultation.

Teacher Marg Wells had for some time been working on local and neighbourhood literacies around issues of 'place' (Comber *et al.*, 2001) in the context of the very large and extended programme of urban renewal which was being undertaken in the western region, involving the demolition of most of the cheap public housing erected post-World War Two. At the time of the project there was little that students could do about what was happening to houses and the built environment in their area. However, they were in a position to improve aspects of their school playground and how it looked to them, and was experienced by them, in relation to the changing local streetscapes. An earlier survey conducted by Wells had indicated that students wanted to improve an ugly and unsafe space between the school and the pre-school which consisted of a car park and narrow asphalted path through a flat grassed area. Funding for the project provided an opportunity to document the work of Wells (Grade Three/Four) and her colleague Ruth Trimboli (Grade Five/Six) as they involved children in achieving this goal.[2]

Research design

The research design was contingent upon the negotiation of the redevelopment of the garden and the associated curriculum. Using ethnographic methods we sought to document key pedagogical events and practices, to collect the literacy assignments and artefacts, and to record teachers' accounts of children's engagement in the evolving project. Hence the research necessarily followed the garden project. Our aim was to document the change as it unfolded, and people's various imaginings and investments in that change. The teachers aimed to use the project to develop children's spatial literacies and the skills and dispositions to act in and for the community.

While the project was focussed squarely on students' participation in the development of a material space within the school grounds, as literacy researchers we were particularly interested in what happened to children's repertoires of literacy practices when teachers added *space* as a focus for learning in their already rich critical literacy and place-based curriculum. Our questions included: what did teachers and children do with architects' vocabularies, concepts, and drawing and modelling techniques? What did children imagine and envisage for this space? To what extent were they able to use various linguistic and multi-modal resources to argue for their imaginings? This is where we anticipated that critical and spatial literacies might be brought together as children learned not only to represent, but also to advocate for, particular designs.

Data corpus

The entire data corpus included artefacts produced by approximately 140 children and their teachers, and architecture, education and communication university students and academics, over an 18-month period. The children's artefacts bear traces of teaching and learning activities and conversations about space and place that happened over time. They are also texts brought into existence by the nature of the project – authentic participation in the redesign and rebuilding of a material space – and therefore do not easily fit into existing school literacy genres. Texts, which were individually and collectively produced, include verbal descriptions, poems, reflections, notes, mind maps, reports and stories; visual and hybrid visual-verbal texts such as pencil drawings and plans of bedrooms, homes, the classroom, the school and the site for redevelopment; artistic works such as paintings, collages and 3D models of ideas, imaginings and actual spaces made out of paper, card and other materials (see Figure 27.1); computer-generated 2D and 3D representations of children's designs for the site; and collective texts such as class books.

Inventing spatial pedagogies and texts for consultation

The collaborative development of the design of *Grove Gardens* required all concerned to open our minds to the pedagogical potential of the project. To some extent pedagogical approaches needed to be invented and adapted. There were no predetermined ways to move forward. The pedagogies were developed collaboratively through discussion and debriefing between the teachers and the university team. The question was how to move from our vision and intentions to a

Figure 27.1 Imagined garden spaces made of card and paper laid out to scale

realisable yet evolving curriculum. What might transfer from a university architecture or communication workshop to a primary school classroom was not self-evident. And how our critical literacy framing for the project might guide everyday classroom practice was also a matter for investigation. We cannot address all of these questions here; however, we hope to illustrate how the emergent spatial pedagogies offered particular opportunities for young people to represent their imaginings and their desires for changed spaces.

Initially architect Stephen Loo used workshop methods to introduce children to key concepts and terms related to social space, design elements and built environments. An important objective was to assist students to imagine new social spaces and built environments, and to 'translate' their imaginings and ideas into a range of media, and into forms that could be communicated to others using the children's vernacular, the language of school-curriculum learning areas (e.g. art, literacy, technology and design), and the language of architecture and design. Here we do not describe the full range of work that was undertaken (see Comber *et al.*, 2006). Rather, we focus on texts produced by Grade Three/Four students during the 'consultation' phase of the project because they represented the culmination of many iterations of curriculum work and exemplify the emergent pedagogical approach adopted by one teacher as she grappled with how to bring together critical approaches to literacy education and a focus on the spatial dimensions of meaning-making.

During this phase pairs of children were responsible for producing two texts which were later made into pages in what we called 'consultation books'. The books were a purpose-made genre that fulfilled at least two purposes. First, they allowed children to represent on paper their preferred ideas about the garden by drawing from a range of possibilities that had been developed over time, and as a result of working with various vocabularies, concepts and media. Second, they constituted artefacts that documented the children's ideas in a form that could easily be shared with and commented on by others. The first text produced was a written text that addressed questions about what students would like to see in the redesigned area and what it would look like. The second text was a visual text produced using their choice of medium, and representing their favoured plan for the design. Each visual text was produced on tabloid-size paper using a choice of paint, black ink pens, coloured markers, collage and so on. When assembling the books some blank space was left to allow children, teachers and parents to provide feedback.

In Wells' classroom, students' collective representational resources were pooled and meaning-making was a collaborative and collective enterprise, with interested audiences in sight and their comments invited. Tasks were structured and clearly framed. The children had already built up considerable knowledge of the field (garden design), and had rehearsed their preferences and arguments in numerous forums. Pedagogically, then, Wells guaranteed that student-produced texts would be expansive (through the peer collaborations) as well as socially significant (through their collective input and audience and connection to real outcomes).

We turn now to examine Grade Three/Four consultation books in which the impact of spatial thinking in children's developing literacy repertoires is made visible. We suggest that the project generated new relationships between the spatial, imaginary and material worlds children envisaged and represented.

Re-imagining space: playworlds and lifeworlds

In this section we first consider in some detail two texts produced by two boys for the consultation books and then consider what was accomplished in relation to spatial literacies in the complete corpus of book pages.

First, here is the written text produced for their first page by Adrian and Tan, aged 8–9 years:

What would I like to see in the area?
A big maze with some switches.

Why?
So kids who are waiting can play in it while they are waiting for their mum and dad to pick them up and kids can get tricked because they won't know which is the beginning and which is the end.

What would it look like? Describe.
The walls around the maze are made of cement and are painted in gold. It will be 10 metres high and it will have traps inside it. You have to find a key to get out and you have to take a friend with you.

The boys summarise what they would like to see in the area using only six words: 'A big maze with some switches'. Here they imagine the desolate school yard space transformed into a material representation of something that they are fascinated by in their leisure pursuits – 'a maze of switches'. Explaining *why* they would like to see the space designed like this, they write:

So kids who are waiting can play in it while they are waiting for their mum and dad to pick them up and kids can get tricked because they won't know which is the beginning and which is the end.

They therefore imagine the redesigned material space performing a dual social function: providing both a designated place for children to wait to be collected by their parents, and a place for pleasurable play that involves the complex and hidden spaces of a maze as well as other tricks and puzzles. When they describe how they would like the maze to *look*, we can see how they draw on their developing architectural design vocabulary and spatial literacies as they note specific details about the *height* of the walls (10 metres), the *material* used to make them (cement) and how they would be *decorated* (painted in gold). Two particular features they would like to see in the maze are that 'it will have traps inside it' and 'You have to find a key to get out'. They also stipulate that children would not enter the maze alone, but rather, 'you have to take a friend with you'.

The boys' written text therefore combines an awareness of the *social function* that the space will fulfil in the redesigned area (kids can play in it while they wait for their parents; friends will enter the maze together) with aspects of their own specific and gendered interests in mazes and other games that include puzzles and quests ('You have to find a key to get out'). In other words, their writing moves between what Lefebvre (1991) conceptualises as *perceived space* – an acknowledgement of what the space is *actually* used for (waiting for parents, playing with friends) – and *lived* space; space that is lived or experienced but which the *imagination* also seeks to change. The boys' writing shows that they are able to imagine how this newly designed space in the school yard could become a 'space of belonging' for members of the school community by improving the ways in which social relations are conducted within it. At the same time, they are beginning to imagine how, in design terms, the redesigned space could also replicate some of the features of popular culture games that they enjoy: entering a maze; confronting switches, tricks and other obstacles; and searching for ways to successfully end adventures and quests. The fact that the boys want the high cement walls of the maze to be 'painted in gold' suggests that they are well aware that their design, which is intended to change the material and 'real' lifeworld that they inhabit is, in fact, being overlaid in their plan with elements of *imagination and desire* associated with fantasy fiction and electronic game-playing. This is a mix of serious and playful writing and imagining.

As in their written text, the boys' *visual* representation (see Figure 27.2) of what they would like to see in the area also combines elements of realism (grass, pathway, toilet blocks) and elements of fantasy (winged dragon, two kinds of maze). In relation to their developing spatial literacies, we can see that aspects of the image resemble an architect's plan, with its aerial view, a sense of scale, lines that depict a pathway linking one side of the area to the other, written labels indicating whether a structure is a toilet block or gate, and icons that represent design elements such as seating structures and shelters. Architectural vocabularies, as well as design and drawing conventions, have entered their semiotic repertoires. But, as in the writing, there are also other kinds of visual elements foregrounded in this image, elements not so obviously connected with the spatial. Most noticeably different from an architect's plan is the vibrant red dragon with yellow wings that seems to be devouring one end of the pathway that links the school and pre-school. As in many fantasy genres, the dragon is comparatively over-sized in terms of scale, and its presence is further highlighted by that fact that, unlike other objects, it is depicted not from an aerial view but from a lateral view. Thus texts suggest the boys' desire for their playground space to be redesigned as a *social* place for play and adventure, but also as a space that specifically includes elements of popular culture familiar from their lifeworlds. This desire to include in the playground aspects of play that are promoted by the leisure industries was common among Wells' students and consistent with findings of the UK project *The School that I'd Like* (Burke and Grosvenor, 2003).

The book pages illustrate what was made possible by Wells' emergent pedagogical approach, which brought together a focus on developing in children the capacity to take action about things that mattered to them with a focus on spatial literacies. Of particular interest is how this

Figure 27.2 Adrian and Tan's visual text in the consultation book

pedagogy allowed diverse children to draw on the range of cultural resources they had at their disposal, and to use these resources in order to connect not only with new concepts of spatial literacy, but also with more traditional school curriculum requirements.

This creative curriculum and pedagogy also allowed Adrian and Tan to do significant identity work around masculinity, and being a pre-teen boy with an interest in computer game culture. For example, the image of the red dragon has its origins in Yugioh cards and online games, and it recurs throughout Tan's work over time. In several of his texts the red dragon is depicted in conjunction with other images and motifs familiar from quest adventure games: mazes, mediaeval weapons and keys. For example, in earlier work focussed on the architectural concept 'spaces of belonging', Wells had invited students to draw, talk and write about spaces and places in their lives in which they felt that they belonged. In response, students often created drawings of bedrooms or houses. However, an early illustration by Tan of his poem 'In My Belonging Space' depicted a bedroom–living room which contained not only the items that one might expect to find in such a space (bed, armchair, table), but also sculptures of dragons hanging from the ceiling by chains as in a dungeon (Figure 27.3, top left). Other sections of the room contained a table dedicated to weapons used in quest adventures (mediaeval weapons, shield, large dungeon key) and a large media centre containing several games consoles (labelled Game Boy, PlayStation and PlayStation 2) accurately drawn, with details of accessories, wire connections and electricity plugs (Figure 27.3, top right).

In our view this text illustrates the productive potential – for this child at least – of a pedagogical approach that encourages children to produce visual texts alongside verbal texts and allows them to draw on their popular cultural resources. When this approach was combined with a focus on developing understandings of space, children were able to work with and develop a range of spatial literacy concepts. These included abstract understandings about design and social space such as 'spaces of belonging', and more technical skills such as how to represent ratio and scale, and how to represent the relationships between objects in space.

Figure 27.3 Tan's illustration of his 'belonging space'

These achievements were not confined to one or two children in the class. On the contrary, evidence from the data corpus indicates that many children had developed significant capacities for spatial literacies (see Table 27.1). Their texts suggest that these accomplishments drew on the resources introduced by the architects and the complementary affordances of visual and verbal modes of meaning-making.

The politics of imagination: pedagogical productions of spatial and social worlds

Exploring the spatial dimensions of lived experience can provide important inroads for young people into critical literacies that are material, imaginative and creative. Working with the discourses and practices of architecture to redesign part of the school grounds opened up opportunities for children and teachers alike to think in new ways. In the process children and teachers expanded their semiotic repertoires as children engaged in imagining, negotiating and representing themselves in the spatialised world of the school and beyond.

Using space as a focus for learning and frame for curriculum design is both generative and productive; it allows all children to contribute what they know about perceived and lived space. Further, it allows them to imagine how different people might populate different spaces, and how spaces might be reconfigured and why. In their artefacts we can see traces of their class-room pedagogical history: an architect's presentation about buildings and the stories that might surround them; neighbourhood walks; discussions about local housing development issues; visits to an architecture studio and newly developed local parks.

The project illustrated very clearly Nespor's (1997: 12) argument that pedagogy is 'an ongoing collective accomplishment'; it involves 'real practices slowly accomplished over time and space, continuously modified to deal with change and contingency' (quoted in McGregor, 2004: 366). Teachers involved in the project have been willing to expand the boundaries of what sometimes seems a shrinking normative space for literacy work and at other times an overloaded curriculum. The layered nature of the curriculum and pedagogical work they carried out with the children, and the ways that it drew on multiple traditions, allowed for and encouraged a simultaneous consideration of the aesthetic, the literary and studies of society, as well as the productive effects of working across multiple media of representation and communication. Their classes were sites of a rich and recursive pedagogy that was accomplished collectively over time and space.

One of the joys of this project was the opportunity to work with teachers who were themselves creative and open to expanding repertoires of pedagogical and literacy practices. Both teachers took hold of the project with great enthusiasm and proceeded to invent possibilities for tasks, activities and genres that were responsive to what their students could already do, what they needed to work on further, and the open-ended possibilities generated by the project itself. This is not always the case in schools. Even when new initiatives and innovations claim to be new or promise opportunities for change, schools by their very nature sometimes limit what is possible, stripping the practices to simulations and reducing meaningful tasks to skeletal approximations of what they might have been. The force of school time and space, as business-as-usual, can make routine and constrain even the potentially exciting. However, in this case, the opposite occurred. The *Grove Gardens* project appeared to release the energies and imaginations of the teachers along with their students.

Maxine Greene has long written about how and why the imagination is politically significant. She has argued that 'human freedom' involves 'the capacity to surpass the given and look at things as if they could be otherwise' (Greene, 1988: 3). Being able to imagine alternatives and to imagine a better state of things is crucial. She emphasises the importance of 'the ability to make present what is absent, to summon up a condition that is not yet' (ibid.: 16). From our perspective the project allowed this kind of imagining. We see this creative design work and the associated visible material action over time as crucial to sustaining critical multiliteracies in schools.

Table 27.1 Children's accomplishments in visual and verbal modes illustrated in consultation books

Spatial literacies in verbal mode	Spatial literacies in visual mode
Make a comprehensive case about the design	Provide an overview of the space using aerial and other perspectives (e.g. elevations)
Make a persuasive rationale for the use of the space	Make an architectural plan; indicate emergent understanding of scale and ratio
Incorporate architectural vocabulary including design elements (e.g. platform, wall, pathway)	Use solid lines to demarcate edges of spaces and division of objects in space
Include significant detail and specificity (shape, size, colour, material)	Show the relationships of places and objects within a space; convey functions and relative size and shape of objects in space
Draw on appropriate discourses (e.g. aesthetic, health and safety, promotional)	Communicate the social nature of space; indicate awareness of the aesthetic dimensions of design
Transfer conceptual and representational resources (e.g. from game-playing)	Transfer conceptual and representational resources (e.g. from game-playing)

Notes

1 The project Urban Renewal from the Inside Out: Students and Community Involvement in Re-Designing and Re-Constructing School Spaces in a Poor Neighbourhood was conducted in 2004–5 by Barbara Comber, Helen Nixon and Louise Ashmore from the School of Education, Stephen Loo, Louis Laybourne School of Architecture and Design, and Jackie Cook, School of Information, Communication and New Media, University of South Australia, with teachers Marg Wells and Ruth Trimboli and students from Ridley Grove Primary School, Woodville Gardens, South Australia. The project was funded by the Myer Foundation.

2 See the Myer Foundation website at http://www.myerfoundation.org.au/main.asp. The views expressed in this paper are those of the authors and do not necessarily represent those of the Myer Foundation.

References

Apple, M. (2005) Doing things the 'right' way: legitimating educational inequalities in conservative times, *Educational Review* 57(3): 271–93.

Burke, C. and Grosvenor, I. (2003) *The School I'd Like: Children and Young People's Reflections on an Education for the 21st Century*, London: RoutledgeFalmer.

Comber, B. (2001) Critical literacies and local action: teacher knowledge and a 'new' research agenda, in B. Comber and A. Simpson (eds) *Negotiating Critical Literacies in Classrooms*, Mahwah, NJ: Lawrence Erlbaum.

Comber, B. and Nixon, H. (2005) Children re-read and re-write their neighbourhoods: critical literacies and identity work, in J. Evans (ed.) *Literacy Moves On: Using Popular Culture, New Technologies and Critical Literacy in the Primary Classroom*, Portsmouth, NH: Heinemann.

Comber, B., Nixon, H. and Reid, J. (eds) (2007) *Literacies in Place: Teaching Environmental Communication*, Newtown: Primary English Teaching Association.

Comber, B., Nixon, H., Ashmore, L., Loo, S. and Cook, J. (2006) Urban renewal from the inside out: spatial and critical literacies in a low socioeconomic school community, *Mind, Culture & Activity* 13(3): 228–46.

Comber, B., Thomson, P. with Wells, M. (2001) Critical literacy finds a 'place': writing and social action in a neighborhood school, *Elementary School Journal* 101(4): 451–64.

Cope, B. and Kalantzis, M. (eds) (2000) *Multiliteracies: Literacy Learning and the Design of Social Futures*, Melbourne: Macmillan.

Freire, P. (1985) *The Politics of Education: Culture, Power and Liberties* (trans. D. Macedo), South Hadley, MA: Bergin & Garvey.

Greene, M. (1988) *The Dialectic of Freedom*, New York and London: Teachers College Press.

—— (1995) *Releasing the Imagination*, San Francisco: Jossey-Bass.

Gruenewald, D. (2003) The best of both worlds: a critical pedagogy of place, *Educational Researcher* 32(4): 3–12.

Hull, G. and Schultz, K. (2001) Literacy and learning out of school: a review of theory and research, *Review of Educational Research* 71(4): 575–611.

Janks, H. (2000) Domination, access, diversity and design: a synthesis for critical literacy education, *Educational Review* 52(2): 175–86.

—— (2006) The place of design in a theory of critical literacy, keynote address presented at the Australian Association of Teachers of English and Australian Literacy Educators' Association Annual Conference, Darwin High School, 11 July.

Janks, H. and Comber, B. (2006) Critical literacy across continents, in K. Pahl and J. Rowsell (eds) *Travel Notes from the New Literacy Studies: Instances of Practice*, Clevedon: Multilingual Matters.

Kress, G. (2003) *Literacy in the New Media Aage*, London: RoutledgeFalmer.

Kress, G. and van Leeuwen, T. (2001) *Multimodal Discourse: The Modes and Media of Contemporary Communication*, London: Arnold.

Lankshear, C. and Knobel, M. (2003) *New Literacies: Changing Knowledge and Classroom Learning*, Buckingham: Open University Press.

Lefebvre, H. (1991) *The Production of Space*, Oxford: Basil Blackwell.

McGregor, J. (2004) Spatiality and the place of the material in schools, *Pedagogy, Culture and Society* 12(3): 347–72.

Martusewicz, R. A. and Edmundson, J. (2005) Social foundations as pedagogies of responsibility and eco-ethical commitment, in D. W. Butin (ed.) *Teaching Social Foundations of Education: Contexts, Theories and Issues*, Mahwah, NJ: Lawrence Erlbaum.

Nespor, J. (1997) *Tangled up in School: Politics, Space, Bodies, and Signs in the Educational Process*, London: Falmer.

New London Group (1996) A pedagogy of multiliteracies: designing social futures, *Harvard Educational Review* 66(1): 60–92.

Nixon, H. and Comber, B. (2005) Behind the scenes: making movies in early years classrooms, in J. Marsh (ed.) *Popular Culture, Media and Digital Literacies in Early Childhood*, London: RoutledgeFalmer.

28

Creative pedagogies and the contemporary school classroom

Michael Dezuanni and Anita Jetnikoff

> The goal of creativity in and of itself is a beautiful thing … I don't want to worry about the market place. I don't want to worry about commerce … The goal should be trying to express myself, trying to make something beautiful; trying to make something that someone can find a place for in their life.
>
> (Moby, 2009)

Moby is one of the world's most successful musicians, commercially and critically, in spite of dropping out of university to pursue a music career. Of course, there are many stories like Moby's, about 'genius' artists and innovators who have become successful with little formal education. The 'genius' narrative is powerful in contemporary Western societies and we are enamoured of the 'beautiful' things created by talented individuals who bring meaning to our lives. However, creativity surely has a role to play in school curricula. Teachers and students pursue unique and innovative ways to build new knowledge through teaching and learning processes. This chapter explores the 'creative pedagogies' of imaginative teaching and learning and the development of creative capacities in formal schooling. The chapter presents two case studies involving the creative application of new media technologies in Australian classrooms. The first involves recreating video game narratives, in a media and technology classroom; the second focuses on 'play'-based technology use in the early childhood curriculum.

We see 'creative pedagogies' as both the imaginative and innovative arrangement of curricula and teaching strategies in school classrooms and the development of students' creative capacities. The chapter begins with a brief outline of the theories and definitions of creativity that we find useful for understanding the possibilities for 'creative pedagogies'. We are particularly interested in the tension that exists between notions of creativity and innovation associated with 'productivity' and more 'open' constructs of creativity that encompass imagination, experimentation and the idea of 'possibility thinking' (Loveless 2002: 3). Our two examples are partly framed by a consideration of how formal schooling enables and constrains 'creative pedagogies'. This includes a consideration of government requirements for curriculum development, the issue of high stakes testing and the role school structures and policies play. It also considers the impact of the knowledge and skills teachers and students bring with them to the classroom. The discussion also focuses on elements of creativity and the extent to which they are identifiable in our examples.

Theorising and defining creative pedagogies

Our framework for understanding how creativity operates in classrooms places emphasis on the social production of meaning. This framework broadly draws on the work of Lev Vygotsky, who argued that creativity, fantasy and imagination are goal-directed and socially mediated (Vygotsky, 1987/1930: 347; 1998/1931: 165). Vygotsky suggests that creativity is a key aspect of learning: 'wherever in the process of understanding or in the process of practical activity, the creation of some kind of new concrete structure, new image of activity is necessary, a creative embodiment of some idea, there fantasy comes forward as a basic function' (Vygotsky, 1998/1931: 165). As past practising secondary school teachers, this formulation of creativity 'rings true' to us. To be 'productive' in classrooms often requires a creative application of new knowledge. 'Fantasising' about possible outcomes, possible reactions, possible futures and possible solutions is a crucial aspect of the experimentation that is central to learning.

Of course, in Vygotsky's approach to theorising learning, this means a socially mediated application of 'experimentation'. Willis (1990) picks up on this when he argues that creativity is an inherent aspect of young people's use of symbolic resources in both their work and leisure activities and for the formation of identities. Buckingham and Sefton-Green (1994) have explored Vygotskyan concepts to discuss the relationship between learning about media and popular culture through creative processes of identity formation. Burn (2009: 14) draws on Vygotsky to argue that creative work with new media technologies draws on 'children's cultural resources and depends on social forms of learning', including play. Sefton-Green (2000: 224–5) explicitly argues that creativity occurs in 'shared' relations between individuals. We see great potential for taking up and extending the work of these scholars to gain a better understanding of how creativity operates in digital media classrooms.

A definition of creativity in education that we find productive, as a starting point for considering our own case studies, is the United Kingdom's National Advisory Committee on Creative and Cultural Education (NACCCE). They state that creativity is 'imaginative activity fashioned so as to produce outcomes that are both original and of value' (NACCCE, 1999: 29). The five characteristics of creativity identified in the report include: using imagination, fashioning process, pursuing purpose, being original and judging value. Loveless (2002) suggests that 'creative work' in education must have originality and value to individuals, peers and society. Learning to be creative means allowing 'possibility thinking', for making choices in everyday life. Key terms of this concept of creativity that we wish to interrogate are 'purpose' and 'value' and what these mean for pedagogy.

The idea of creative pedagogies produces a tension for literacy and arts educators. This is a tension between utility and experimentation which becomes obvious when considering 'purpose' and 'value' when assessing students' 'products'. On one hand there is a focus on intangible elements of creativity like 'spark', 'insight', 'imagination', 'mystery' and learner as 'artist'. On the other hand, some teachers aim to fulfil the rhetoric of educational policy documents which prepare students for the workforce. Internationally, high stakes testing is becoming a norm in educational contexts. We believe that not everything we do in education has to do with producing future working citizens, particularly in the areas of literacy and Arts education. There is still room for Loveless' idea of 'possibility thinking', which suggests the idea of experimentation and 'fantasy', in Vygotky's sense, perhaps through more 'open' constructs of creativity. We think that formal education has a valuable role to play in the continual process of young people's identity formation (Robinson, 2009). There is room for Moby's suggestion that the creative process is valuable in and of itself. Within this frame we investigate the extent to which our local educational context enables and constrains creativity in schools.

Queensland's 'open' system of curriculum development

In Queensland we have an arguably more 'open' system than other Australian states, since we have developed a strong foundation of school-based planning and assessment. This unique system gives teachers and learners significant scope for creativity across the curriculum. The New Basics project (Education Queensland, 2010), which was implemented in selected Queensland schools between 2003 and 2008, was underpinned by the concept of transdisciplinary 'rich tasks' designed to extend students' creative and critical problem solving abilities. Beyond the New Basics project, Queensland has had a longstanding history of locally designed work programmes and units which respond to the needs and interests of their particular school communities. In spite of the national testing regime for literacy and numeracy introduced by the Federal Government in 2008 (NAPLAN), which imposes benchmark testing twice yearly (Curriculum Corporation, 2008), Queensland assessment is still largely school-based. This recent change in assessment was driven by the National Curriculum agenda, which claims to improve transparency and accountability in student achievement across the states. In its extreme form, benchmark testing, as has been seen in the UK and USA, could shut down creative opportunities (Robinson, 2009). In spite of this move, the Queensland context is still influenced by the creativity agenda and its cross-curricular applications.

Queensland's teacher-developed curriculum affords teacher autonomy, collaboration and creative pedagogy. English and the Arts (encompassing media studies) and ICT literacy are emphasised across the curriculum, so the potential to develop a multidisciplinary curriculum driven by the principles of creative pedagogies is limited only by the imagination of the individual teachers. Our case studies provide examples of some of these creative processes and products: such as video game narratives in middle school Media and Technology Studies and new media texts designed around the use of digital storytelling in lower primary (where ICTs bridge literacy/science/drama classes). The case studies presented here explain how a relatively 'open system' can provide opportunities for creative teaching and learning to take place. The first case study, about video games in secondary education (pp. 262–64), provides a macro view of these opportunities, while the second case study (pp. 264–67) provides closer analysis of classroom pedagogy and student learning.

Case study 1: the Video Games Immersion Unit project

The Video Games Immersion Unit project involved 17 fourteen- to sixteen-year-old boys learning about video games in a combined media and technology education classroom. This unit was made available as an aspect of the school's middle schooling and boys' education initiatives that aimed to engage students in ways that the standard school curriculum did not. This was a specialised three-week immersion programme, existing in parallel with the school's usual curriculum offerings. The school was a traditional inner city private boys' school with a segmented timetable aligned to subject specialisations and assessment focused on in-school testing and assignment work. The Video Games Immersion Unit provided the teachers, a media education specialist (one of the authors) and a technology educator, with an opportunity to be more creative with both content and pedagogies in the classroom. Education Queensland's New Basics project (Education Queensland, 2010) informed the development of the unit. The teachers aimed to emulate the transdisciplinary 'rich task' approach of New Basics, and to draw on that project's 'Multiliteracies and Communications Media' curriculum organiser. The unit offered the students an opportunity to experience a more 'open' curriculum that allowed many opportunities for creativity.

The unit was also organised drawing on the Queensland Studies Authority's Years 1–10 syllabus documents for Technology and the Arts, which used an outcomes-based education (OBE)[1] approach to the organisation of learning. For example, the unit aimed to meet the Year 10 (level 6) outcome for Media in the Arts: 'Students apply an understanding of media languages and technologies to design and create media texts in a range of production contexts' (Queensland Studies Authority, 2002); and the Information and Communication Technology level 6 outcome: 'Students produce an interactive media product utilising multiple media languages and technologies' (Queensland School Curriculum Council, 2002). The teachers and students were provided with opportunities for creativity via this combination of 'rich task' and 'outcomes' approaches, which arguably provided an 'open' curriculum framework. By 'open', we mean the following. For the teachers, it allowed the flexibility and autonomy to introduce a new media form to the classroom, video games, and to draw on learning outcomes from across the curriculum to construct a learning pathway. It also enabled the employment of a broad range of pedagogic techniques, including traditional instruction, project-based design work, small group discussion, both online and face to face, and multimedia production work. For the students, OBE allowed the students to focus less on specific assessment instruments and more on the learning experiences, particularly project-based team work.

As outlined earlier in the chapter, NACCCE's (1999) definition of creativity is useful to consider when thinking about creativity in curriculum. The Video Games Immersion Unit might also be thought about using these categories. Imaginative activity took place while the students were designing video games and self-representing in online spaces. Students undertook fashioning processes whilst working with digital materials to make new digital artefacts and through designing while writing, drawing and sampling. The students worked purposefully and productively in teams to design and make aspects of a video game. Emphasis was placed on students being original in their use of video game codes and conventions. Finally, the students were encouraged to judge the value of their own work and that of others according to a range of criteria. Each of these concepts is problematic, however, and in the rest of this section we will discuss how the students' work illustrates the difficulty of neat definitions of creativity and the importance of curriculum that allows a degree of teacher and student autonomy.

Students were encouraged to be 'imaginative' and 'original' in the design and production of their own video game concepts. However, there are constraints to 'imagination', particularly in relation to established games codes and conventions. The students played several games and investigated the applied games design principles before undertaking planning. Of course, the students also played games for fun in leisure time and were allowed to play games in between formal learning episodes throughout the unit. In this context, it is legitimate to ask what it means to be 'imaginative' or 'original' beyond the repetition of established norms of game design and play. We are reminded of Derrida's (1990/1978) conception of the bricoleur who draws on language to creatively produce meaning. Derrida's bricoleur, who takes part in 'free-play' to continually add something to established meanings, helps to explain the ways in which students were creative with their game designs. For example, while they designed characters that were clearly based on characters from existing games, they also brought in elements of their own, or mixed attributes of several characters to create new conceptions, all of which was part of the process of using symbolic resources for productive identity formation in an education context (Willis, 1990).

The students were creative with digital materials and technologies as they undertook 'fashioning processes' through writing, drawing, sampling and compiling. From a curriculum framework perspective, the combination of Technology and Media outcomes allowed a focus on the creative use of technologies. There were two fundamentally different ways the unit developed skills: one was more conducive to creative practice, experimentation and learning through trial and error than the other. The first pedagogic technique was a 'lock-step' approach to skills development in which an instructor used a digital projector to demonstrate a technique and this was emulated by the students. Once the majority of students had completed the task, the instructor moved on to the next skill. In the second, more 'creative' process, the students were shown the skill and given several opportunities to use it in different scenarios. In this process, the students tended to help each other and scaffold each other's learning. Furthermore, because there was no specific assessment outcome, the students were able to respond more creatively.

The students were expected to be creatively productive throughout the unit, to work as a team to create a design concept. This involved processes of evaluation, of self and others. On one level there is a kind of 'commonsense' understanding of what is 'productive' in this learning context. If the students can work together to design a game and make aspects of the game, then they might be said to have been productive. However, 'productivity' is problematic in this context, particularly when it is attached to 'creativity'. Some students in the Immersion Unit produced concepts for games that were inappropriate for the given target audience. Others purposely aimed to undermine games genres by subverting their codes and conventions. However, we would not suggest that either of these groups was 'unproductive', in the broadest sense. In this context questions must be asked about the notion of 'productivity' and how it potentially stifled creativity.

An example of the stifling of creativity emerged in the unit in relation to peer evaluation. The students were required to undertake a SWOT analysis (strengths, weaknesses, opportunities, threats), reflecting on the game designs produced by each team. Some valuable feedback was provided to most of the teams through this process. However, it was clear to the teachers that competition between the teams led to some unfair criticism. This type of criticism resulted from competition between the students, which reflected hierarchies related to perceived expertise about video games and technology. In terms of identity, this involved gendered performativity (Butler, 1990, 2004) at play amongst the students that helped to establish the masculine norms of the unit. When the students pitched their ideas to other students, they were less likely to risk their social viability by presenting ideas that failed to meet identity-related norms. This may have stifled the production of genuinely creative, imaginative or original work in the Immersion Unit space. The key point is that even in contexts where there is teacher and student flexibility, creativity might be constrained by socio-cultural factors.

Case study 2: Digital storytelling: creating multimodal texts in an early years cross-curricular classroom

One of the authors worked with two teachers, Annie and Shane, on an 'early years' digital storytelling project in a government-run primary school just outside an Australian capital city. This case study shows how creative teachers using available technologies can tap into the imagination of students, using a whole community approach to literacy across the curriculum. The Early Years Queensland Curriculum Guide recognises the importance of play as part of socialisation and identity formation. Vygotsky's (1978) work on constructivism underpins the Curriculum Guidelines. Children construct knowledge through active participation in social and cultural experiences, including play (QSA, 2006). The guide also suggests 'planning collaboratively with children as part of curriculum decision making' (ibid.: 11). With this in mind, Annie planned a Year 1 digital storytelling unit for her class. She 'modelled' the digital story of a 'litterless lunch' project, in Photo Story 3 for her students, who then 'could each negotiate their own topic, and interpret it in as many different ways as possible', as a digital story.

Using the 'zone of proximal development' (ZPD) (Vygotsky, 1978), which fills the gap between the 'actual and the possible', Annie built on the students' knowledge of their world and community. She 'scaffolded' and extended their knowledge and linguistic development through 'research'. Computer use followed intensive reading and writing and spoken exploration of the children's negotiated topics. Annie explained, 'the digital storytelling is a whole literacy event, because before they could type it, they had to read and research it, and so we had junior books brought in by the children on the particular topics'. The teacher took photographs of the children working and helped them download relevant copyright free images. Although the teacher intervened in some of the processes, each child mastered basic storytelling steps; importing and assembling the pictures, typing and narrating their own digital 'story'. This reflects media education research that children learn valuable skills in manipulating new media authoring tools (Buckingham and Sefton-Green, 1994; Burn, 2009: 14; Sefton-Green and Parker, 2000).

Drawing on the NACCCE (1999) definition of creativity, these children were using imagination to 'fashion a process'; their individual stories using technologies. Their 'purpose' was to document their stories, although to what extent they were being original, or 'judging value', is not so clear. Because Year 1 children are still learning the laborious process of handwriting, using a computer authoring programme both enabled and constrained the storytelling process. Typed letters always look perfect, which enabled the children to express what they wanted to say relatively quickly. Annie said, 'handwriting needs to be correct ... with typing they could still have a go, sounding it out ... even the special needs kids ... can say [audio record] it even if they can't write it well'. When they discovered they could audio record narration without having to type it, however, creative possibilities opened up.

One of the claims made for creativity is that it works best across disciplines (Robinson, 2009). Even though Queensland schools are no longer identified as New Basics schools, the digital storytelling activity fulfils the transdisciplinary brief of a 'rich task'. The Year 1 students were taught by four teachers across the curriculum. The school has a whole community approach to learning: parents, teacher aides and 'buddy classes' all assist the teacher and students in the learning process. Each teacher took their own class for 'literacy', which incorporates ICTs. The topic of 'space' was covered across maths, literacy, ICTs and drama. After five lessons Annie's class had developed enough techno-literacy skills to 'teach' the drama teacher (Shane) what they knew about the programme. In drama, after modelling and painting clay aliens, the students 'embodied' their 'aliens' by dressing up while the teacher photographed their individual performances. These images were imported into the Photo Story 3 programme and each child orally described their alien's characteristics, without a transcript. Speaking without typing enabled more linguistically elaborate descriptions than in the first round of 'informational' digital stories.

The drama application of the digital storytelling software was more 'playful', and allowed for 'possibility thinking' to emerge. Vygotsky's version of play relates to creativity; whereby playful activity is a means of learning 'symbolic substitution' (Burn, 2009: 14). A cloth hat pulled down over a child's eyes in a digital story symbolically became an alien 'brain' in imaginative, social play. Linguistic processes were generated creatively through storytelling based on the 'dressing up' in drama. Annie explained:

> As one followed the other the children would tell their story and the ones to follow would say, 'Ooowh I'm gonna make my story a bit bigger or better, or I'm going to be brighter than life and more heads or more brains.'

This activity fulfilled the curriculum guideline of using play to develop students' language and identity, which was part of the teachers' central purpose in the unit. The approach was original, but some students were also mimetic in drawing on and embellishing one another's narration of their aliens in their digital stories. Viewing the DVD they created, these five- and six-year-old children displayed interesting gendered 'performativity' (Butler, 2004). One pupil describing her 'alien' character wore enormous 'flying' goggles. Her arms were tucked beneath an old leather jacket, its sleeves hanging oddly. She growled, 'I have six brains. I have no arms and thousands of teeth ... And I eat boys.' Another girl was clearly playing a more stereotypical gender role. 'I have no brains,' she suggested, and her pictured alien wore a bright pink 'nightie' and sported a black patent handbag. She was posing like a magazine model. These examples illustrate the children's deployment of socialised symbolic resources (Willis, 1990) such as their knowledge of fashion, science fiction, fantasy and gender norms and relationships, which impact on their identity formation.

In this multidisciplinary approach we might think about 'value' for these early years students. There is value in the students learning linguistic and identity concepts through imaginative activity; through social forms of learning and 'play'. Each of them was trying to outdo the previous student's description. The imaginative possibilities grew as the activity continued, and this was clearly pleasurable and playful learning. One of the Year 1 'Listening and Speaking' Essential Learnings is for students to 'reflect on how or why people, characters, places, events and things have been represented in particular ways in texts and generate possible alternatives' (QSA, 2009: 4). Some of these alternatives, such as the 'brainless supermodel', were clearly gendered stereotypes. It was not apparent whether the teacher deconstructed these 'stereotypes' with these young children. Had the teacher done this perhaps the 'playfulness' of the literacy event may have been constrained; however, the learning around stereotypical identity construction may have been challenged and extended. Annie suggested the next step will

> build further on the children's technical knowledge. Now I'm planning to get the year ones to show the year fives [buddy class] just what they know and they will be able to help the students and take pictures and do more complex things with editing. It'll be a sharing of work ... it's exciting, it's fun.

The digital story project was a valuable exercise in applying playful activity with technological skills development in a multidisciplinary approach across the curriculum. Annie's thoughts on the 'open curriculum', creativity and testing certainly show her commitment to 'possibility thinking' (Loveless, 2002). In Annie's opinion,

> Without imagination and creativity we'd become very staid. So I'm always looking for ways to develop that creativity in any way possible, whether we stimulate it through images or whatever ... we want them to come up with their own ideas and to build things from that. I mean we're building minds for the future ... I want them to try as many things as possible and to come up with as many ideas as possible ... to see them blossom.

Annie's explication of the early years 'open' curriculum suggests that creative potential exercised through play is enabled due to less rigorous testing. The new NAPLAN (Curriculum Corporation, 2008) testing regime in Australia increases in complexity to Year 3. Annie expressed doubts about the ability to sustain this creative approach across the early years:

> As a year 1 teacher I don't have a lot to do with NAPLAN, but it would be very worrying if we become a school where we just teach to the testing. Because if that's what happens then our creativity becomes totally squashed ... When we do two or three weeks of

testing, the little ones are exhausted ... and if they are exhausted by constant testing ... what kind of learning is that?

Conclusion

Our case studies tell us that creativity is socially mediated and is both enabled and constrained by the kind of curriculum on offer. We deployed the NACCCE (1999) definition of creativity as productive for thinking about creativity in classrooms, but questioned the inclusion of 'purpose' and 'value'. Our key point is that even in contexts where there is teacher and student flexibility, creativity is intrinsically shaped by socio-cultural factors such as social constructions of gender stereotypes in identity. The curricular requirement for the video game designers to conform to stock 'gaming' codes and conventions perhaps mitigated the creative possibilities for that activity. The 'openness' of early childhood education tells us something about the possibilities for creativity beyond utility; that play can develop creative potential through linguistic and symbolic developmental processes using technologies. These social factors can constrain 'creative pedagogies', even as the 'open' curriculum enables creative, cross-disciplinary learning. In the wider social context government requirements such as the introduction of mandatory 'high stakes testing' foreground 'purpose' and 'value' over imagination, experimentation and 'possibility thinking' (Loveless, 2002). This potentially presents the very scenario that Sir Ken Robinson suggests can 'kill creativity in schools' (Robinson, 2009). This is a genuine threat to creativity in schools. The open curriculum, however, still enables much of the learning outside the testing situation to be playful and creative. Although government policies and school structures can steal time and space for creative 'possibility thinking', what cannot be undermined is the vital roles and resources that creative teachers and students bring with them to the classroom.

Note

1 The Queensland Studies Authority has since moved back to a standards-based approach called 'Essential Learnings', which assesses students on an A–E scale according to criteria. This was due to parental confusion over the outcomes-focused assessment and reporting system and difficulties with implementation in Queensland schools.

References

Buckingham, D. and Sefton-Green, J. (1994) *Cultural Studies Goes to School: Reading and Teaching Popular Media*, London and Bristol, PA: Taylor & Francis.

Burn, A. (2009) *Making New Media: Creative Production and Digital Literacies*, New York: Peter Lang.

Butler, J. (1990) *Gender Trouble: Feminism and the Subversion of Identity*, New York: Routledge.

—— (2004) *Undoing Gender*, New York: Routledge.

Curriculum Corporation (2008) *National Assessment Program – Literacy and Numeracy (NAPLAN)*; available at http://www.naplan.edu.au/about/national_assessment_program-literacy_and_numeracy.html (accessed 10 September 2009).

Derrida, J. (1990/1978) *Writing and Difference*, London: Routledge.

Education Queensland (2010) *The New Basics*; available at http://education.qld.gov.au/corporate/newbasics/html (accessed 9 June 2010).

Loveless, A. (2002) *Literature Review in Creativity, New Technologies and Learning*, Brighton: School of Education.

Moby (2009) The goal of creativity is beauty, Uncensored interviews.com.

National Advisory Committee on Creative and Cultural Education (NACCCE) (1999) *All Our Futures: Creativity, Culture and Education*, Sudbury: NACCCE, DfEE and DCMS.

Queensland School Curriculum Council (2002) *Information and Communication Technology Education Syllabus*, Queensland: Queensland School Curriculum Council.

Queensland Studies Authority (2002) *Years 1–10 Arts Syllabus*, Spring Hill: Queensland Studies Authority.

—— (2006) *Early Years Curriculum Guidelines*, Spring Hill: Queensland Studies Authority.

—— (2009) *Year 1 Learning Statements*, Spring Hill: Queensland Studies Authority.

Robinson, K. (2009) Ken Robinson says that schools can kill creativity, in TED.com, Creative Commons (ed.) *TED talks*.

Sefton-Green, J. (2000) From creativity to cultural production, in J. Sefton-Green (ed.) *Evaluating Creativity: Making and Learning by Young People*, Routledge: London.

Sefton-Green, J. and Parker, D. (2000) *Edit-Play: How Children Use Edutainment Software to Tell Stories*, London: British Film Institute.

Vygotsky, L. S. (1978) *Mind in Society*, Cambridge, MA: Harvard University Press.

—— (1987/1930) Imagination and its development in childhood (trans. S. Sochinenii), in R. W. Rieber and A. S. Carton (eds) *The Collected Works of L.S. Vygotsky*, vol. 1, New York: Plenum Press.

—— (1998/1931) Imagination and creativity in the adolescent (trans. S. Sochinenii), in R. W. Rieber (ed.) *The Collected Works of L.S. Vygotsky*, vol. 5, New York: Plenum.

Willis, P. (1990) *Common Culture: Symbolic Work at Play in the Everday Cultures of the Young*, London: Open University Press.

29

'Real audience pedagogy'

Creative learning and digital space

Julian McDougall and Dave Trotman

How can educators and students make sense of the plethora of creative tools afforded by broadband internet communication? Is it a 'given' that web 2.0 fosters a 'participation culture' whereby the dynamics of expert and apprentice are deconstructed as an epistemic turn reconfigures the roles of student and teacher – towards a 'pedagogy of the inexpert'? Or should we tread more carefully, bearing witness to the distinction between the democratising impulse of prosumer activity and the conditions of possibility for meaningful creativity in these new techno-social contexts.

In this chapter, three case study examples are explored to challenge assumptions and identify practical strategies in this arena: a web drama project with primary school children preparing for transition to 'big school', a university module hosted in 'Second Life' and an AS coursework unit using social networking for planning and evaluation.

Through a comparison of the three interventions, the chapter will offer some answers to questions about form, content, processes and outcome, towards a more informed approach to the realisation of creativity in new digital spaces. We are particularly interested in digital affordances in relation to the opportunities they present for students to engage with real audiences beyond the classroom walls and the school/college hall or theatre. Such opportunities exist every day, but they present real challenges to the teacher, possibly insurmountable in the orthodox construction of the curriculum and the phenomenology of the educational institution, bound as it is in time and space by the timetable, the curriculum and the authority of the teacher as 'gatekeeper'. Working carefully with these new dynamics is what we mean by 'real audience pedagogy'.

In this modest undertaking, our lines of enquiry owe a small debt of gratitude to those scholars who have contributed to shaping the insights now emerging in the field of creativity and which have informed our thinking in this chapter. Our analysis is further sharpened by a number of studies of creativity which, although significant, originate from different disciplines and from within different traditions of social science research (e.g. Willis, 1990; Fryer, 1996; Csikszentmihalyi, 1997; Sternberg, 1999). In the UK, a number of government-sponsored reports have also offered their particular 'take' on the definitions and purposes of creativity. A dominant theme in much of this work has been a compulsion to establish creativity as a 'democratic' practice framed neither by 'sectoral' interests, e.g. the creative arts, nor as the exclusive province of a gifted elite (NACCCE, 1999). Despite a paucity of research evidence to corroborate the existence of a curriculum-wide practice of creativity in UK schools, an alignment of creativity for entrepreneurial purposes, such as those expressed in the Roberts report, has become a significant aspect of ministerial interest in the field (Hartley, 2003).

Our direction in this chapter is both experimental and exploratory, and it will be useful therefore if we sketch some of the contexts of our work. For those readers who are familiar with Arts Based Educational Research (ABER), the parallels are deliberate. For those for whom this is new, the approach has gathered increasing interest among researchers whose enquiries are less amenable to conventional representation. Typically, ABER research 'texts' are designed to temporarily take the 'reader' to new psychological landscapes where new and empathic understandings can be assimilated and familiar realities recast. This, in the literature of ABER, is what Susanne Langer calls 'composed apparition' (Langer, 1957; quoted in Barone and Eisner, 2006: 98). With this aim in mind, researchers are actively encouraged to experiment with their text and representational formats. ABER then offers a means of enhancing the perspective of researcher and audience while simultaneously generating further questions for the 'reader'. Useful examples of the approach can be found in the work of Barone and Eisner (2006), Bagley and Cancienne (2001) and Richardson (1992).

A second context is provided by media education. Gauntlett (2007) provides a helpful visual metaphor for web 2.0 in which he presents the world of collaborative 'we media' creativity as a shared allotment, replacing or at least adding to the hitherto separate arrangement of individual gardens. Wesch (2009) offers a genealogy of the expression 'whatever' and suggests that while in the era of web 2.0 young people may be 'switched off' from orthodox public sphere discourses and democratic processes, they are nonetheless connected to a range of micropolitical and creative activities online. Meanwhile Buckingham (2007) and Marsh (2007) draw our attention to the 'disconnect' between the schooled curriculum and the various and increasing forms of digital learning practice in which children participate.

Advocates of a subsequent 'Media 2.0' (Merrin, 2008) claim that the notion of 'the media' as an object of study or a coherent set of power structures is outdated in the age of this 'always-already connected' world of more democratic creativity – a 'remix' culture in which any media text is likely to be amended, 'mashed up' and made subject to a range of parodic shifts by its audience, who in turn become producers; prosumer activity then becomes standard and it is no longer tenable to talk of 'new media' as separate and bracketed from traditional media.

A further context is provided by policy. Policy agents such as Ofcom, a UK regulatory body, situate 'media literacy' as key to a healthy democracy – particularly with regard to the safety and well being of children. This legitimising gesture is awkward for media educators since it at the same time provides credibility for the production of media material within the formal educational system and obliges a more or less protectionist agenda, as 'being media literate' is offered as a safeguard for children in the online age.

All of these emerging discourses are situated in close proximity to a loosely defined discourse of 'creativity' as part of media literacy and of 'media 2.0'. This discourse is connected to economic categories in the UK – 'Creative Britain', 'Creative Industries' and the introduction of a new qualification for 14–19-year-olds – the Creative and Media Diploma.

Case study 1: web drama

Web drama is a medium gaining increasing momentum in education, given its affordance of a 'real audience'. Through the use of a simple blog with embedded video and a polling facility, a more or less 'walled' audience can shape the development of the drama. *Moving On, Moving Up* is the outcome of an after-school 'film club' run at a primary school for Year 5 and 6 students, during which the students created a five-episode narrative through which they were able to dramatise (and thus externalise) a set of anxieties about moving on to secondary school. For the participants, this was a pressing issue and the expectation was that the students would 'project' their own anxieties onto the characters and that this 'distancing' through representation and narrative would be richer than a purely personal sharing of worries. The innovation, in terms of pedagogy, lies in the voting feature, through which the audience (the rest of the school, staff and students at two partner institutions – a secondary media arts college and a university college specialising in teacher training – as well as parents and friends) chose the focus for the next episode, constructed as a series of dilemmas presented to the characters and a 'What should they do now?' question on the blog.[1] The characters' talking heads introductions were uploaded to a blog, which was accessed by parents, fellow students, friends, relatives and, potentially, strangers. Interviewed about the process at the end point, the students offered a range of responses but all agreed about three things:

- The web drama had been a suitable vehicle for the discussion of anxieties about 'big school'.
- The creative (and imaginative) process of characterisation and fictional scenario-building had been essential to this.
- Most clearly, there was consensus that the 'real audience pedagogy' could not have been replaced by a more orthodox approach. Had the audience only been able to vote as a response to seeing the episodes in school assemblies or on DVD, something significant would have been lost. It was the extended, real, online audience (and the removal of time as a constraint) that made the difference. As one participant has it, 'Anyone could see it – your mums, your dads, your aunties, your grandads.'

In terms of their 'creative learning', some of the participants expressed frustration at the relatively small degree of 'hands-on' filming and editing they had experienced, in keeping with Reid, Parker and Burns' findings from a project commissioned by BECTA (Reid et al., 2002). Due to the context of a time-pressured after-school club and the necessity of filming and editing in response to the online voting so that the next episode could be uploaded on time to keep the momentum, the participants' creativity was restricted often to scripting, filming and acting and rarely post-production. Subsequently, they felt that a more substantial role in decision-making about editing, music and structure would have enhanced their creative development.

The creative dimensions of this case study are at first relatively easy to locate, e.g. in the literature on creativity Wallas's (1926) four-stage process is frequently reprised:

- preparation: identifying problems and setting goals;
- incubation: making associations and reflecting;
- illumination: seeing new configurations;
- verification and validation: balancing outcome against public judgement.

Here, within their given terms of reference, young people have been encouraged to construct their own characters, explore their identities and generate these in fictionalised 'realised form'. The projection of anxiety, however, is critical to the creative impulse of this work, and here three pivotal concepts were germane to the project: *imagination*, *empathy* and correspondent troubles and issues.

The first of these concerns the centrality of imagination to creativity. Indeed, studies of creativity have typically located imaginative work as an important precursor to creative endeavour (Eisner, 2005; Fisher and Williams, 2004; Cropley, 2001). Fisher and Williams, for example, regard creativity as 'embodied imagination':

> What imagination does is to enable the mind to represent images and ideas of what is not actually present to the senses. It can refer to the capacity to predict, plan and foresee possible future consequences. In short, imagination is the capacity to conceive possible (or impossible) worlds that lie beyond this time and place.
>
> *(Fisher and Williams, 2004: 9)*

This has an obvious and particular resonance with the creative challenges confronting the participants in this case study. However, as authorities in the field of imagination have continued to point out, imaginative work involves more than just the capacity to *image* in a detached, dispassionate or abstracted sense, but involves us in thinking, feeling and perceiving as a single and unified experience (Egan, 2008: 46). For the young people in this study, the creation of characters, events and scenarios has meant that the dimensions of their work, whilst embracing possibility thinking, have generated a more meaningful engagement in *empathic* work. The tasks involved in this first case study required young participants to adopt a form of empathic agency in their creative work. Without this requirement the tasks would have been rendered both meaningless and uncreative in the terms we have previously taken care to describe. Moreover, contrary to the 'moral panics' concerning the dehumanising effects of contemporary media technologies, we see this imaginative-empathic work as entirely in concert with the conceptions of empathy described in the discourses of care theory (Noddings, 2005) and which enrich the sorts of creative practice undertaken in this case study. Typically, the defining features of this work necessitate a 'cognitive understanding of the other's situation and emotional resonance with the other. ... Not only must the one caring emotionally resonate with the other, she must *move* to do so. She must shift herself into the other's perspective and affective life' (Noddings, 1984, 16; quoted in Verducci, 2000: 89).

We are careful to acknowledge here that it was entirely feasible, as similar transition projects have successfully managed to do, for this work to reside simply in the domain of the private imaginative-empathic. However, in embodying private troubles in imaginary characters made public, we pay intentional homage to C. Wright Mills' (1959) coupling of '*private troubles*' with '*public issues*' as a means of participants locating personal biography and historicity in the social mix.

Public voting on pupil-generated story-lines through digital means may reflect attributes commonly associated with creative practice; such as innovation, ingenuity, originality and tolerance of ambiguity (Dacey, 1989; Cropley, 2001). Indeed, we would argue that this case study meets many, if not all, of these criteria. Moreover, in facilitating a real audience pedagogy, we argue its potency in enabling young people to develop a creative 'space' in which authentic private troubles can be realised, positioned and valued as a corresponding 'public issue': a meta-narrative of the possibilities of school-to-school transition, if you will. The empowerment of personal agency is clearly a desirable thing for young people, but we are also reminded that ownership of creative outcome is of corresponding importance (Hargreaves, 1989).

Case study 2: Second Life

This second example is different in context but similar in that novelty and defamiliarisation are key to understanding the outcomes. A second year undergraduate module on 'Media Futures' was hosted in the virtual world Second Life, requiring students to teleport their avatars to a virtual lecture theatre once a week rather than to physically attend a 'real' lecture. What is important here is that the subject matter of the module is partly the experience itself – a self-reflexive set of learning outcomes. In other words, the students were engaging with a series of ontological questions about the nature of reality in relation to experience, and so to do this in a virtual space like Second Life (where the residue of the 'real' remains – through the lecturer's spoken voice and PowerPoint slides) had a learning benefit in addition to the novelty. (This might not be the same for a set of History or Maths lectures, of course.)

The striking outcome for students was that the level of response to material was much higher than for 'normal' seminars. And, most intriguingly, even very sceptical students discussed the retrospective feeling that they had 'been to' the lectures – the memory of the events was in most cases described in terms of the lecture theatre in Second Life (SL) rather than their bed-rooms or wherever they were with their laptops at the time of 'being' in the module. Some responses follow:

> The obvious pro was that I didn't have to leave the house.

> I'm not very talkative in the real world but I felt comfortable and talkative in SL.

> We should have had more lectures in SL as we were just getting into it and it was becoming more 'real'.

> Students feel more free to type their responses rather than being in a lecture and not wanting to feel stupid.

> 'Attendance' would go up in SL.

These responses are mundane on one level – they describe basic issues of access and comfort. But they set up some interesting questions about engagement and it was clear that the 'creative' (and imaginative) practice of making choices about how to represent oneself – how to 'be with others' in this virtual domain – were beneficially distracting from the practice of being a student in a set of lectures. Rich discussions took place within the module about the nature of identity in a post-modern, partly virtual society (in relation to theories and research from Baudrillard [2002], Frasca [2003], Žižek [2002] and others) and almost always these debates were enhanced by the experience of students realising their identities and reflecting on their own 'hyper-reality'. Further development of this module will feature students making films in the virtual world – setting up possibilities for setting, character, action and mise en scene that are prevented in the physical universe. The case study raises intriguing questions. To what extent is the technology available merely liberating an imaginative potential in students that was always-already waiting to be harnessed? And do videogames and virtual worlds, then, offer something beyond the classroom that connects to Egan's desire for 'imaginative education'? On the other hand, it was clear that the degrees of cultural capital required to 'self-present' and to theorise on this practice were in keeping with those required for more traditional forms of academic practice – to articulate, to reflect, to be 'self-knowing'. Research into videogames and learning that 'gives time' for respondents to go beyond a surface level tends to reveal the same unfortunate truth.

In this case study, we have, once again, experienced a powerful resonance between the 'opening out' of creative spaces and possibilities for imaginative empathic work. The reciprocity between the composed apparitions of ABER and the virtual environments of Second Life is a difficult one to resist. There is also an equally emphatic correspondence between com-mon creative traits and the desirable conditions for creativity. In particular, we have noted the following:

- functional freedom: involving the *visualisation* of different outcomes to given situations and imagining different uses of objects (Dacey *et al.*, 1998: 231);
- tolerance of ambiguity (Cropley, 2001);
- receptiveness to stimuli;
- androgyny: involving the presence of 'so-called' 'masculine' traits of autonomy and self-confidence aligned with 'feminine' traits of sensitivity, intuitiveness (we would add that in Second Life the possibility of the representation of androgynous identity is, for some participants, also one of its attractors);
- informed risk.

As the informants in this case study continued to reiterate, Second Life provides an environment in which forms of intellectual risk are enabled through the adoption of alternative persona and a different kinaesthetic dynamic of space and time. Second Life, whilst providing new possibilities for a particular form of liberation of the learner, crucially provides a palpable virtual world in which risk, ambiguity and possibility coalesce to creatively shape intersubjectivity and personal meaning.

Case study 3: evaluative blogging

This third example is very different in its institutional nature – an awarding body 'prescribing' an approach for teachers and students to follow, as opposed to a more organic pilot project like the two above, which have arguably lower stakes in terms of outcome. AS Level Media Studies is an examination usually taken at 17+.[2] The OCR examination board, which devises one such course, requires students submitting coursework for moderation (video, print, web design or audio) to use digital contexts for their work in progress and evaluations of their work. Previously marks awarded for research, planning and evaluation had been in response to either paper-based material or teacher testimony. The model offered as a template here was a blog, on which students would upload material in progress for peer evaluation, embed 'real media' with which to compare their developing work and store archives of planning and process – design drafts, research outcomes, animatics. The other difference to the previous examples is in scale – this new approach was expected of hundreds of schools and colleges and for this reason the outcomes were far more varied. Partly the experience was divided by access and surveillance – students in one institution were able to use web 2.0 platforms in school and at home, whereas others were restricted by local education authority 'firewall' blocks on social networks; thus an unintended 'digital divide' was constructed. And partly the distinction was a factor of teacher ease or unease with social networking in the lifeworld – what kind of pedagogy is required for an extended educational encounter where students take control of the majority of their learning in distributed spaces that may exclude their teacher. In this case a 'pedagogy of the inexpert' is required and it is inevitable that teacher identity, constructed for decades around a discourse of mastery and control, will be threatened.

Prima facie, this case study appears to be predicated on a fairly rudimentary framework for creativity: students fashioning their work through a mix of drafting, selection, problem-solving, sequencing, etc. – practices that may align better with some of the more routine principles of design than those we might associate with a rich creative dynamic. However, a number of the unanticipated consequences of this work have allowed us to glimpse ways in which creative spaces and digital networks might be further shaped *with* young people and the subsequent demands that this places on the would-be creative pedagogue. In adopting a post-modern reading of this case study, multiple versions of an intended curriculum innovation become mediated and inscribed through varying technological frameworks; frameworks that enable differentiated forms of agency for the informants. In some instances the existence of electronic 'safeguards' has, quite literally, framed and insulated the scope of innovation and possibility for individual creative agency. In other examples, where it has become possible to transgress such boundaries, or where such parameters do not exist, curricula become indeterminate, fluid, provocative, ambiguous and complex (Pinar, 1998: 84). The 'conditions of possibility' that are generated or impeded either by intention or accident in this case study have, then, important connections with the qualities of the creative field which we have previously highlighted: experimentation, risk, knowledge of the medium, challenge, functional freedom, etc. The creation of these conditions is a *leitmotif* that connects each of these case studies and, once again, invites us to re-examine the relationship between creative practice, creative environments, curriculum, participation and pedagogy.

Beyond the pilot project

How, then, to 'roll out', at institutional levels, creativity of this nature? How to distinguish between 'out of school' creativity – a video achieving significant 'playback' on YouTube – and formal coursework? How to deal with 'digital plagiarism' and how to construct a consensus of what counts as knowledge and of 'craft' in these contexts? And how to move beyond the constraints of the 'perennial pilot project' – drawing down small pots of funding to work on innovative experiments in temporary creative spaces while the rest of the approved educational enterprise carries on as before? If students are both a self-realising audience and 'creative natives', then the educational job of work, as we are proposing here, has to do with reflection on creative activity. Teachers of a wide range of subjects might usefully adopt approaches that arts educators use to negotiate the 'creative act' with their students. In a subject like Media, the word 'creative' appears in assessment criteria but is rarely defined or exemplified. As such it is only applied in a proximal relation to other criteria – thus as a discourse it remains both empty (in and for itself) and full (when adding weight to another unit of measurement). For this reason, wherever educators wish to develop and, usually, assess the kinds of creativity 'affordances' which new digital media seem to provide – what we are calling 'real audience pedagogy' – dynamics of parody, reimagining, imitation set against discourses of 'origination' must be more explicitly worked out in relation to what we think we want to 'measure' from learning. This is pressing. Teachers are obliged to enable critical reflection on 'being in culture' through digital participation. But the present state of play in media education, to continue with this example, seems to be that 'being creative' is measured but isn't taught – assumed either to be some kind of innate quality or somehow always-already arising from the act of 'making and doing' with new media. As Buckingham warns:

> Despite the claims of some media evangelists, digital media are not likely to result in a society of creative media producers, any more than the printing press resulted in a society of published authors. While there is certainly a democratic promise here, the realisation of that promise will require more than technology alone.
>
> *(Buckingham, 2010: 7)*

We are, then, tackling two related discourses in this analysis: on the one hand, what Buckingham calls an 'evangelical' set of precepts regarding the apparently inevitable fostering of digital creativity in the arena of 'Media 2.0' and, on the other, the institutional discourse of creativity in the English education systemworld, which is equally fraught with tensions and contradictions. The English school inspectorate, although not the most likely body to cite in relation to the promotion of creativity, reports a number of pedagogic and curriculum features that equally enable and impede creativity in schools. Amongst the barriers to creativity, *Expecting the Unexpected* (Ofsted, 2003) identifies the inability amongst teachers both to 'let go' and to recognise the creative moment. They highlight the tensions between an agenda of national testing and creativity and note the limited scope of extra-curricular opportunities for enabling pupil creativity. Many readers will no doubt see these inspection findings as indicative of a need for a more coherent analysis of the relationship between 'school', curriculum, participants, educators and researchers. It is our view that each of these case studies reiterates the connectivity of these constituent elements. Slattery, for example, argues that in the post-modern milieu, curriculum development will be the concern of a 'community of interpreters working together in mutually corrective and mutually collaborative efforts' (Slattery, 1995: 118). Drawing on the principles of the 'hermeneutic circle', Slattery's thinking reciprocates with our own analysis of real audience pedagogy, where, through the interplay of language and the creativity of interpretation, we engage in the process of understanding text, the lived experience, and the self in relation to the other (ibid.: 119). As we have previously indicated, this necessitates a significant shift in (re)cognising the spaces where creative learning can be sited. It also demands, if we are to make any legitimate claim to authentic creative endeavour, that we diffuse the power structures that permeate both the stratification of curricula and the construction of teacher, pupil, researcher roles.

Creative space, creative curricula and creative learning have all been afforded necessary attention in the mainstream educational literature. Curiously, the *evaluation* of creative educational work appears, by comparison, to have been eclipsed (see Chapters 14, 15, 32, 33). Following our observations in these case studies, we regard evaluation as a central feature of a creative pedagogy. A corollary of this is that approaches to creative evaluation mirror many of the principles of ABER outlined earlier, and, moreover, echo the words of Herbert Blumer's well-known axiom that the research must be faithful to the phenomena under investigation (Blumer, 1954; cited in Atkinson and Delamont, 2008).

Here we have offered a tentative theorisation of creative learning in digital space. Through discussion and observation with and of our participants we have attempted to 'map' some of the conditions of possibility for real audience pedagogy. Degrees of cultural capital, aptitude for risk and for identity-play, and a willingness to take part in a set of 'distancing' operations are required not only to participate but to 'achieve' in the idioms of these language games. Whether or not these types of acumen are sufficiently different to those required to succeed in the orthodox curriculum might be the focus of further enquiry. Here we merely skim the surface.

The growth of interest in creativity as a school-wide phenomenon in education in England is to be welcomed. As we have attempted to illustrate in these case studies, creativity, in the terms we have defined it, has a valuable role in the practice of 'real audience pedagogy'. As we have also argued, the conditions of possibility generated through digital space are not restricted to any particular domain of the educational lifecourse. Our enthusiasm is, though, tempered by our observations of those initiatives that have sought to cherry-pick or sponsor particular aspects of creativity. This is best exemplified in the Roberts report (2006), where creativity is framed through a language of 'the creative offer', 'commissioning', 'creative protocols and creative industries', which both reconfigures and impoverishes creativity in the interests of narrow economic imperatives (see Chapters 9, 10, 12 and 14). In advancing the possibilities of real audience pedagogy, we premise our work on the full variety and richness of the creative endeavour. As we have argued, this necessarily involves creating space and stimuli for the development of imaginative powers, embodying the sensuous, feelingfulness and empathy. In these conditions of possibility, we contend that new digital spaces enable the creation of previously unexplored landscapes for the exercise of functional freedom, ambiguity and informed risk. In our analysis, we not only retrace earlier studies of creativity but also align our interests with a number of related developments in the field of ABER research. In particular, Willis's (1990) work on symbolic creativity in the lives of young people provides a study that is situated beyond the bastions of formal education, illuminating a powerful dynamic of creative work in young people unfettered by institutional restraint and approved pedagogy. This, we argue, corresponds well with the practices revealed in the first two case studies. The encounters in Second Life, for instance, reveal something of the 'grounded aesthetic' which Willis describes as a creative process in which meanings are attributed to symbols and practices. These symbols and practices are then selected and reselected, highlighted and recomposed to offer further resonance with appropriated and particularised meanings (ibid.: 21). The power of 'new' technologies in liberating this is also not lost on Willis (ibid.: 20) (in a study of creativity that is now 20 years old). Similarly, in reporting our first case study, we have seen young people imaginatively address the conditions of possibility in primary–secondary school transition (and we bear witness to the importance of the online distribution of such imaginative work in this) to generate what Willis describes as a personalised cultural map (ibid.: 53). In light of our own work and the studies that have foreshadowed this, the ramifications for educational practice in creativity are stark. Real audience pedagogy and the corresponding characteristics of creativity necessitate approaches to educational practice which in one sphere celebrate a 'pedagogy of the inexpert' and in others require us to reconsider in much greater detail our approach to the research, evaluation and representation of creative practice in ways that we have begun to outline.

Notes

1 http://cvtvspielbergclub.blogspot.com/.
2 See http://www.ocr.org.uk/qualifications/type/gce/amlw/media_studies/index.aspx.

References

Atkinson, P. and Delamont, S. (2008) Analytic perspectives, in N. K. Denzin and Y. S. Lincoln (eds) *Collecting and Interpreting Qualitative Materials* (3rd ed.), London: Sage.

Bagley, C. and Cancienne, M. B. (2001) Educational research and intertextual forms of (re)presentation: the case for dancing the data, *Qualitative Inquiry* 7(2): 221–37.

Barone, T. and Eisner, E. W. (2006) Arts-based educational research, in J. L. Green, G. Camilli and P. B. Elmore (eds) *Handbook of Complementary Methods in Education Research*, Mahwah NJ: American Educational Research Association.

Baudrillard, J. (2002/2005) [Extract from] The spirit of terrorism, in A. Easthope and K. McGowan (eds) *A Critical and Cultural Theory Reader*, Maidenhead: Open University Press.

Blumer, H. (1954) What is wrong with Social Theory?, *American Sociological Review* 19: 3–10.

Buckingham, D. (2007) *Beyond Technology*, London: Polity Press.

—— (2010) Do we really need media education 2.0? Teaching media in the age of participatory culture, in K. Drotner and K. Schroder (eds) *Digital Content Creation*, London: Peter Lang.

Cropley, A. (2001) *Creativity in Education and Learning: A Guide for Teachers and Educators*, London: Kogan Page.

Csikszentmihalyi, M. (1997) *Creativity: Flow and the Psychology of Discovery and Invention*, New York: Harper Perennial.

Dacey, J. S. (1989) *Fundamentals of Creative Thinking*, Lexington: Lexington Press.

Dacey, J., Lennon, K. and Fiore, L. B. (1998) *Understanding Creativity: The Interplay of Biological, Psychological and Social Factors*, San Francisco: Jossey-Bass.

Egan, K. (2008) *The Future of Education: Reimagining Our Schools from the Ground Up*, New Haven, CT: Yale University Press.

Eisner, E. W. (2005) *Reimagining Schools: The Selected Works of Elliot W. Eisner*, London: Routledge.

Fisher, R. and Williams, M. (2004) *Unlocking Creativity*, London: David Fulton.

Frasca, G. (2003) Ludologists love stories, too: notes from a debate that never took place, Digital Games Research Association; available at http://www.digra.org/dl/db/05163.01125.

Fryer, M. (1996) *Creative Teaching and Learning*, London: Paul Chapman.

Gauntlett, D. (2007) *Media Studies 2.0*; available at www.theory.org.uk.

Hargreaves, D. J. (1989) *Children and the Arts*, Milton Keynes: Open University Press.

Hartley, D. (2003) The instrumentalisation of the expressive in education, *British Journal of Educational Studies* 51(1): 6–19.

Langer, S. (1957) *Problems of Art*, New York: Scribner's.

Marsh, J. (2007) New literacies and old pedagogies: recontextualising rules and practices, *International Journal of Inclusive Education* 11(3): 267–81.

Merrin, W. (2008) *Media Studies 2.0*; available at http://twopointzeroforum.blogspot.com/.

National Advisory Committee on Creativity, Culture and Education (NACCCE) (1999) *All Our Futures: Creativity, Culture and Education*, London: DfEE/DCMS.

Noddings, N. (1984) *Caring: A Feminine Approach to Ethics and Moral Education*, Berkeley: University of California Press.

—— (2005) *The Challenge to Care in Schools: An Alternative Approach to Education* (2nd ed.), New York: Teachers College Press.

Ofsted (2003) *Expecting the Unexpected: Developing Creativity in Primary and Secondary Schools*, HMI 1612, London: HMI.

Pinar, W. F. (1998) *Curriculum: Towards New Identities*, New York: Garland.

QCA (2005) *Creativity: Find It, Promote It*; available at http://www.ncaction.org.uk/creativity/about.htm (accessed 23 November 2005).

Reid, M., Burn, A. and Parker, D. (2002) *Digital Video Pilot Project*, London: BECTA.

Richardson, L. (1992) The consequences of poetic representation: writing the other, writing the self, in C. Ellis and M. G. Flaherty (eds) *Investigating Subjectivity: Research on Lived Experience*, Los Angeles: Sage.

Roberts, P. (2006) *Nurturing Creativity in Young People: A Report to Government to Inform Future Policy*, London: DCMS/DfES.

Sansom, P. (2009) *Moving On, Moving Up*, Web Drama project and research interviews; available at http://cvtvspielbergclub.blogspot.com/.

Slattery, P. (1995) *Curriculum Development in the Post-Modern Era*, London: Garland.

Sternberg, R. J. (ed.) (1999) *Handbook of Creativity*, Cambridge: Cambridge University Press.

Verducci, S. (2000) A moral method? Thoughts on cultivating empathy through method acting, *Journal of Moral Education* 29(1): 87–99.

Wallas, G. (1926) *The Art of Thought*, London: Jonathan Cape.

Wesch, M, (2009) Digital ethnography of YouTube, presentation to the Media Education Summit, Liverpool John Moores University; available at http://mediatedcultures.net/ksudigg/?p=179.

Willis, P. (1990) *Moving Culture*, Milton Keynes: Open University Press.

Wright Mills, C. (1959) *The Sociological Imagination*, London: Oxford University Press.

Žižek, S. (2002) Welcome to the desert of the real, in A. Easthope and K. McGowan (eds) *A Critical and Cultural Theory Reader*, Maidenhead: Open University Press.

30

Reconciliation pedagogy, identity and community funds of knowledge

Borderwork in South African classrooms[1]

Ana Ferreira and Hilary Janks[2]

Introduction

For Anzaldúa,

> The Borderlands are present wherever two or more cultures edge each other, where people of different races occupy the same territory, where under, lower, middle and upper classes touch, where the space between two individuals shrinks with intimacy.
>
> *(Anzaldúa, 1999, preface: n.p.)*

Classrooms in South Africa are ideal spaces in which to do borderwork. According to Ndebele, it is here that

> you have the interface of our individual histories which are seldom acknowledged in the learning environment. [The classroom] is the heart of transformation because living in South Africa today is about sharing identities and cultural experiences.
>
> *(Njabulo Ndebele, 2005)[3]*

In this chapter we explore the importance of helping students to access the knowledge and experiences of their own families and communities, and of using these resources in the classroom. In particular we wanted students to re-imagine their current identities as a result of their own explorations of South Africa's Truth and Reconciliation Commission (TRC). Our approach is informed by the work of Luis Moll and his associates on 'community funds of knowledge' (Moll *et al.*, 1992; González *et al.*, 2005). In critical multicultural approaches to education, there is a recognition that students from different communities bring different knowledges, cultural and intellectual resources, 'ways with words' (Heath, 1983), skills and social networks to school, and, moreover, that these knowledges are not equally valued. Moll and his associates' research recognises that it is hard for teachers to draw on the lifeworlds of their students if they have no knowledge of them. In their research project, teachers undertook household interviews to understand their students' lifeworlds. Moll *et al.* claim that 'by capitalizing on household and other community resources, we can organize classroom instruction that far exceeds in quality the rote-like instruction that these children [from working class Mexican communities in Tucson, Arizona] commonly encounter in schools' (Moll *et al.*, 1992: 132).

Moll *et al.* understand funds of knowledge as 'historically accumulated and culturally developed bodies of knowledge and skills essential for household or individual functioning and well-being' (ibid.: 133). For them, the *teachers* become a bridge between community and curriculum in order to develop 'ethnographically informed' (ibid.: 132) classroom practices.

In their research project on cross-generational teacher development, Comber and Kamler (2005), influenced by Moll *et al.*, used visits by teachers to their students' homes as a means of transforming classroom practices. They were able to show how to include and build on their students' funds of knowledge. They named these changes 'turn-around pedagogies' (ibid.).

In both of these projects, teachers are the catalyst for change and act as the 'bridge' between community and classroom knowledge. In our project, by making the *students* the bridge, and by incorporating Anzaldúa's (1999) conception of borderwork, we re-articulate the work of Moll and his fellow researchers in significantly different ways.

The South African research project

Our research has its origins in an invitation to participate in an international project on Reconciliation Pedagogies.[4] We wondered what such a pedagogy might look like in South Africa, where reconciliation is both over and has not yet begun.[5] What does it mean to work with South African high school students on reconciliation, seven years after the TRC completed its work? The TRC hearings were a particularly important time in our post-1994 history because of the public nature of the hearings and the role played by the media, particularly radio and television, in bringing the TRC into the homes of ordinary South Africans. In a sense, we were all asked to bear witness to the 'gross violations of human rights' (TRC, 1998: 5,1,1) that maintained the system of apartheid. With the aim of exploring the pedagogic possibilities of reconciliation, we established a South African Research Circle made up of classroom teachers and educational researchers.[6] In our initial discussions, we spent time grappling with the notion of 'reconciliation' and how to draw it into the classroom space in ways that would engage students' identities.

The TRC report asks us to think of the Truth and Reconciliation process as the foundation on which we can build our future: 'Reconciliation does not wipe away the memories of the past. ... It understands the vital importance of learning from and redressing past violations for the sake of our shared present and our children's future' (TRC, 1998: 9,149,434).

While from the outside, because of the work of the TRC, South Africa may appear to have done the work of reconciliation, we were not convinced that as ordinary citizens we, or our students, had done any reconciliation work or knew how to do it. We also had a sense that in South Africa, our apartheid history compels us to place issues of race and identity at the heart of reconciliation in the minutiae of daily life. Yet, from experience, the teachers knew that students resisted talking about apartheid, the struggle, poverty and continuing structural inequalities. The teachers' experience of high school students accords with that of McKinney with undergraduate students. According to her,

> The extent to which critique as a process is predominantly backward rather than forward looking, taking students into a past that they are frequently desperate to escape and leaving them feeling stranded in the past, is problematic in post-apartheid South Africa.
>
> *(McKinney, 2004: 71)*

High school students often express this resistance as 'boredom'. The teachers believed that apartheid history is not sexy for teenagers, that the 'bornfree' generation of black youth do not want to go on hearing about the struggle, they want to live in the now and to enjoy their freedom. In addition, white youth often feel blamed for the 'sins of the fathers' and are equally resistant. For McKinney,

> We ... need to take seriously the difficulties of young South Africans of living with the legacy of an oppressive past that was not of their making. ... We cannot ignore students' feelings of entrapment, accusation and despair and in doing so we need to find ways of tapping the optimism about being South African that many of these young people express.
>
> (McKinney, 2004: 71–2)

In the aftermath of apartheid, students' identities are profoundly bound up with questions of race, and classroom discussions about the past are often tense. We recognised that getting high school students to engage with South Africa's history would be a challenge. Dolby's research on South African youth found that Nelson Mandela's calls for a 'new patriotism' do not resonate with the youth (Dolby, 2001: 13) and that 'the nation state is not a primary point of identification and belonging' (ibid.: 12). For these reasons, we were concerned to find ways of dealing with the TRC that would intersect with students' current realities and that would not be so threatening to their identity investments that they would 'refuse' to participate. We hoped that what their communities could teach them about the TRC would hook them and that the diverse funds of knowledge from their different communities might enable them to see one another in a new light in relation to their separate histories.

The school-based teachers that we worked with talked about what they perceived to be their students' resistance to dealing with apartheid and struggle history. They believed that this meant that in their schools many of the thornier issues relating to race, history, culture and difference are swept under the carpet. The result is that it is not in the formal curriculum but in the 'kid's curriculum' that issues seem to erupt. The teachers compared stories of racial conflict around issues such as different school rules for black and white hair, and what counts as 'formal wear' and suitable music for the matriculation dance in their different schools. What is key is that all these conflicts became heated because of students' investments in their different youth identities, and the politics of hair, clothing and music. With a history of conflict in South Africa based on race and ethnicity, it seemed important to work in racially heterogeneous, desegregated classrooms. This limited our research to schools which have continued to attract a racial mix of students; these schools tend to be less mixed in terms of class, catering largely to the middle class families who can afford the school fees. We located the research with three teachers, Ingrid Barnsley, Charles Marriott and Monique Rudman, in three different secondary schools in Johannesburg. (See Table 30.1.)

As English teacher educators and researchers, our focus was on English classrooms. We chose to include Art because of the new emphasis on the relationship between the visual and the verbal in multimodal approaches to the teaching of English (New London Group, 1996; Kress et al., 2004). Critical approaches to language teaching have implications for other subjects in the curriculum, and the History researchers who are part of the project are exploring the implications for the teaching of History. A more extended account of this work has been recorded by Ferreira et al. (in press). For the purposes of this article, we focus on the second phase of this project, which deals with students as researchers of the TRC.

While in the early phase of classroom work on this project[7] some of the students were able to link their own feelings, situations or identities with the need for remorse and forgiveness,

Table 30.1 Information provided by the teachers on their professional experience, their students and their schools

	Ingrid Barnsley	Charles Marriott	Monique Rudman
Teaching subject	English	English	Art
Years of experience	18 years	15 years	10 years
Research participants[1]	Grade 11, 49 students	Grade 11, 23 students	Grade 10 , 10 students
Type of school	Model C co-educational secondary school	Independent, co-educational, Catholic, primary and secondary school	Model C co-educational secondary school
Year of desegregation	1990	1979	1990
Race scape[2] in 2005	1200 students	1000 students	1100 students
	White 40%	White 31%	White 79%
	African ⎫	African 38%	African ⎫
	Indian ⎬ 60%	Indian 18%	Indian ⎬ 21%
	Coloured ⎭	Coloured 13%	Coloured ⎭
Class scape	Suburban school: students drawn from a range of areas from high income areas to mid-to-lower income areas.	Suburban school: students mainly drawn from middle income areas.	Suburban school situated in an affluent neighbourhood. Students drawn from a range of areas from high to middle income areas.

Notes:
1 Student numbers fluctuated during the year. These numbers reflect the full complement of students who participated in this research. Because some students were absent at times, the data does not always include work from all the students.
2 We use Soudien's term 'scapes' to enable us both to deal with the dominant factors in a social analysis of South African schooling and to simultaneously call attention to the constructedness of these ways of seeing. He identifies race, class and gender as the most obvious of these scapes (2004, 93).

their work remained largely centred on the self and based on personal introspection. There was little that was located in the socio-political life of South Africa a decade after the end of apartheid. Given that reconciliation is also a national project of building the future in relation to history and memory, it was important for students to understand the social and historical situatedness of their identities in relation to those of others. We selected desegregated schools and the focus on students' community-based funds of knowledge in order to create spaces for differences to rub up against one another. These in-between spaces, where individuals confront their differences, enable what Anzaldúa (1999) calls 'borderwork'. In her research, Dolby found that as students 'collide and connect they remap identities within these spaces' (2001: 79). This use of diversity as a productive resource lies at the centre of our project.

Reconciliation pedagogy and community funds of knowledge

Within the international Reconciliation Pedagogies project, South Africa is constructed as 'a post settler society' that is addressing the 'effects of colonisation' and the TRC is given as an example of a 'national reconciliation' project that has enabled South Africa to confront its past (Hattam, in press). We decided that students needed to engage with the TRC process in order to judge its effects for themselves. Despite many criticisms of the TRC (Mamdani, 1998; Derrida, 2001; Nethersole, 2002; Posel and Simpson, 2002), as well as our own reservations, we agreed that this engagement was necessary if we were to move our students to a socially and historically grounded approach to reconciliation. Our research group collaborated in designing a unit of work on the TRC to be used in the three classrooms. It was late in the school year so this unit of work had to be short and focused. We chose four pedagogical moves:

1 *Introducing students to the TRC*: we designed a one-page handout to provide the same basic information on the TRC to students across all three sites so that they did not go into their communities as uninformed researchers. The handout had a multimodal, non-linear visual design that invited interaction and avoided privileging any particular point of view on the work of the TRC.
2 *Positioning students as researchers*: students were then required to extend their understanding by accessing their communities' experiences of the TRC process. The students were briefed on the ethics of interviews, and were given the questions which appear in Table 30.2 to use in their semi-structured interviews. In finding adults to interview, students had to draw on their different social networks to gather 'lived narratives' that would enable them to gauge the impact of the TRC on people they know. Having completed their interviews, the students shared their varied experiences in class.
3 *Written and visual representations of the TRC in the form of postcards*: students were asked to design a postcard that encapsulated in word and image what stood out for them from the TRC project.
4 *Reflection*: students were asked to produce a final, written reflection in answer to the question 'What has this project on the TRC meant to you?'

We deliberately built our understanding of the importance of students' identity locations and their access to different communities into our design of their research project. Because the TRC hearings were broadcast on public television and radio, the TRC process was a national event to which all communities had access. However, there were different levels of engagement and investment by different communities. Because the second and fourth pedagogical moves are central to our understanding of the relationship between reconciliation pedagogy, identity and

Table 30.2 Interview questions

---

1 What do you think the TRC was about? (What do you think it was for? What do you think it was trying to achieve?)

2 How did you find out about the TRC? (How did you get to know about it? How did you become aware that it was in progress?)

3.1 What can you tell me about what it was like? What stands out for you from that time? What images or stories do you remember? What stories stayed with you?

3.2 Why does this stand out? Why do you remember those particular images or stories? Why do you think you reacted/responded in the way that you did?

4 Do you think the TRC was a good thing or not? Do you think it achieved anything?

---

borderwork, the rest of the paper focuses on the students' sharing of their narratives and their reflections on the overall TRC project.

Sharing their communities' narratives: borderwork

The session in which Barnsley's students reported back on their interviews was extraordinarily powerful. It gives important insights as to the potential of reconciliation pedagogies to transform social relations. There is evidence that some shifts in identity were produced by different knowledges rubbing up against each other in the classroom space.

The students brought the stories they heard back to the classroom and it was clear that many of them had been deeply affected by what they had learnt. In a research circle meeting, Barnsley spoke from the notes she had made during class. In the following extracts taken from a transcript of a research circle meeting, Barnsley's voice is interwoven with those of her students as what was said in her class pours out of her:

> I just said today, how did you find the interviews? and these were some of their responses: many people knew what the TRC was but didn't really care ... some felt that the TRC was an example for the world to follow ... some didn't think the TRC was of any use. It just made people sad, it didn't help, it achieved nothing – there's still no similarity in black and white vision ... some say it didn't bring closure, just more attention.
>
> ... 'My mom's cousin was chopped up. The day he went out, he didn't tell his parents. Everything was always a secret. [His mother] was offered money by the TRC but she would not take it. She said it wouldn't bring back the dead.'
>
> ... Then one girl said that her, I think it was her uncle – a white girl – was an anti-apartheid activist and he went to all the hearings that were in Cape Town and what touched him was that during all the hearings there were always boxes of tissues, it was like something that stuck in his head.
>
> ... One boy's father was an anti-[apartheid] activist in the townships at the time and they went to one of the hearings, there was an apartheid policeman who specialised in torture and when it came to the trials he wanted to come forward and give his confession and no other policeman would sit next to him, so the man he tortured, who never broke, who never submitted to all his torturing techniques, eventually went and sat next to him.
>
> *(Transcript of research circle meeting, October 2005)*

For many of these students, it was their own family members who had been involved in the TRC. Suddenly the relationship between South Africa's history and their own identities was glaring. One of them reported that what he learnt was so disturbing, [because] 'it happened to us, our family – I can't believe it was my family and they didn't tell me, this is my history, it happened to us, my family. They did things that if people could confess, it would help' (Transcript of research circle meeting, October 2005).

Barnsley reports that 'When they were giving some examples of apartheid atrocities, they were the quietest class I've ever had … Everyone was listening, even the total skater boy hooligans … everyone was listening, listening, listening. So, if nothing else happens that was phenomenal' (Transcript of research circle meeting, October 2005).

But this is not the only 'turn-around' (Comber and Kamler, 2005). Two other important transformations happened. Suddenly it is the black students who have more interesting stories to tell, whose 'funds of knowledge' (Moll *et al.*, 1992; González *et al.*, 2005) are valued by the curriculum task, shifts, and white students, who are used to having their knowledge privileged by the curriculum, feel displaced. According to Barnsley,

> The white privileged ones were so pissed off, they didn't have juicy stories. They were so frustrated – I wish my mom had told me something interesting. She just doesn't know much about it, and she says, 'Oh it's in the past, let it be', and 'that's not right, how could she?' … And then there's this thug who did learn like life-changing stuff and was really saying deep things. … I think that some of those more privileged children, sort of white suburban group, were really disappointed in their parents. They were upset that this thing, that they were hearing was so momentous, had been ignored.
>
> *(Transcript of research circle meeting, October 2005)*

All students were given direct access to funds of knowledge beyond their own social networks when one of Barnsley's students invited her interviewee, Steven Kwapeng, a former freedom fighter detained on Robben Island, to speak at the school. In this way, students were exposed to the experience and knowledge of a person deeply invested in the TRC, which he nevertheless described as a 'toothless dog'.

In addition, the teacher is able to see the class 'thug' in a new light. Her previous knowledge of her students, based on 'their performance within rather limited classroom contexts' (Moll *et al.*, 1992: 134), becomes more 'multi-stranded' and effects a change in her attitude. She says:

> Thus I learned a great deal about my learners and how they can tangibly contribute to the wealth of classroom experience. I learned that I had undervalued what they had to offer. They taught me a lot – not just about the past, and by sharing the results of their interviews, but also about how classroom dynamics can shift, depending on the nature of shared experience.
>
> *(Barnsley, Teacher's journal, November 2005)*

The effects were not as dramatic in either Rudman's or Marriott's classes. Despite the students' initial hesitation in Rudman's class, she reported that 'the more they found out about the TRC, the more curious they became' (Transcript of research circle, 17 October 2005). With only nine students, Rudman's class was too small to generate a critical mass of interviews and, in addition, her students did not have access to the same range of community 'funds of knowledge' (Moll *et al.*, 1992; González *et al.*, 2005) as Barnsley's class. Nevertheless, there was one student 'who had interviewed her cousin and she didn't realise her cousin was part of the struggle … so here she was seeing this person every single day, and interacting with her and she was completely unaware of her cousin's own background in it' (Transcript of research circle meeting, October 2005).

Marriott's students had mixed experiences with their interviews: 'There were quite a few of them that seemed to have hit at least one good interview ... One guy avoided interviewing people he knew ... His family knew David Webster's[8] family ... because he didn't know if that was sensitive or not (Transcript of research circle meeting, October 2005). Overall he felt that students 'needed more time to explore the value of this experience' but that they had nevertheless 'learnt a great deal about the recent past, as well as how they felt about this past and their distance from it' (Marriott, Teacher's journal, 22 February 2006). Like Barnsley, he learnt more about many of his students and their differential access to community knowledges.[9]

Students' reflections: history and identity

In the students' reflections on the overall project, their response to the experience of interviewing and to the sharing of these experiences in class emerges as key to the success of this pedagogy for engaging with the past. Although teachers' length requirements for the written reflection task varied considerably, most students articulated their attitudes towards the TRC project without difficulty. Table 30.3 provides a quantitative analysis of the students' positions on the TRC project.

The students' responses to the TRC project were overwhelmingly positive, the majority describing it as a stimulating learning experience. We were interested to note that of the sixty-five students who reflected on the TRC project, only two students, in Rudman's class, provided the anticipated 'bored-with-the-past' response, saying that they had found the work 'boring', 'repetitive' and 'uninspiring' – the kind of response that we had initially feared. Overall, the students engaged with the past, some even demonstrating a 'turn-around' (Comber and Kamler, 2005) in their attitudes towards their own histories or History as a subject:

> I was very young at the time of the hearings. So doing research and finding out about the TRC, interviewing people made me discover interesting things about the past and why some people feel the way they do towards other races, traditions, etc.
>
> *(Barnsley's student)*

> [The project] made me appreciate South African history more than before. ... I had always [hated] history as a subject, mainly because there was too much information to be learnt and too many dates to be remembered. This project on the TRC was an informal and fun way to learn about the past. ... The project made me realise, history is not only a subject but also determines my future.
>
> *(Marriott's student)*

In Barnsley's class, many of the students spoke of having been deeply moved or otherwise affected by the stories they came across:

Table 30.3 Student positions on the TRC project

Students	Positive response to TRC project	Negative response to TRC project	Mixed response	No opinion on TRC project expressed
Rudman's	2	2	–	2
Barnsley's	37	–	–	3
Marriott's	15	1	2	2
TOTALS	54	3	2	7

It was heart-wrenching to hear real-life stories told by the person involved!

I found it very informative, I learnt something I did not know, I now have more respect for the victims of Apartheid.

I feel this project was incredibly insightful! As a young South African, I'm proud to have been informed of such thought-provoking, historical times by someone who was actually involved.

Marriott's students, having been required to respond in more detail, provided more carefully considered opinions on their experience of the project. Their responses demonstrate a considerable degree of reflectivity, both intellectual and emotional, and by and large they are characterised by students' explanations of having shifted, in various ways. Some students commented explicitly on the pedagogy of the interviews:

> After having conducted my interviews, I was amazed to such an extent about how much we can learn from others' personal experiences. ... [C]onducting these interviews was an interesting way to ... learn about the TRC through others. ... The interview process for me allowed me to learn about the TRC on a personal level and therefore it was exciting. Because of the enthusiasm of my interviewees they were more than willing to share their experiences and opinions with me; therefore it was a pleasurable learning experience.
>
> 'TRC? Truth and Reconciliation Commission? I think I've heard of it. Oh well, who cares, it's just another English piece,' those were the first words that came to my mind as this project on the TRC was being presented to us. In the beginning I felt as though I was being 'forced' to learn about South Africa's history but what I didn't bargain for was that at the end of the assignment, I wasn't bored, but rather intrigued and more interested in our past than ever.

In reporting on their interviews in class, students moved from their initial positions as listeners of narratives in their communities to tellers of stories in the classroom space. In some instances, students uncovered stories about their own relatives that enabled them to understand for the first time how their own identities are inflected by the past. In the borderlands, where different funds of knowledge enter into the same space, the students assigned different values to their respective knowledges and were able to recognise whose stories mattered:

> The people that I interviewed did not really have a big effect on me because they did not have something real to tell me. For example I heard some of my class mates report backs and they had people who were really involved in the TRC like the one was a freedom fighter. Now if I interviewed a freedom fighter I'm sure I would feel a lot different about it.
> *(Marriott's student)*

It was the students themselves who privileged previously marginalised knowledges, even as they recognised that their own knowledges were being decentred. While we would not want to claim that all students re-evaluated their own contributions in this way, there is evidence in the changed classroom dynamics and in students' increased levels of receptiveness to infer that, at least in some cases, students' senses of themselves shifted in relation to one another. This suggests the potential of this pedagogy to develop a 'heightened historical consciousness' (González, 2005: 42) that enables students to recognise how history constitutes identity, their own identity and the identity of others.

Conclusion

There can be no doubt that the pedagogy used for the TRC project opened the curriculum to different communities' funds of knowledge. Like the work of Moll and his associates (Moll *et al.*, 1992; González *et al.*, 2005), this project challenged what counts as valued knowledge: students usually disempowered by the school curriculum now had greater access to privileged knowledge which they could use to write themselves into the classroom. There are nevertheless important differences in our iteration of the work of Moll and his associates.

First, we construct *students* rather than teachers as the researchers of community funds of knowledge. By capitalising on community resources, we were able to move away from text-book history to real engagement with people's lived narratives. In this way, it was students who produced the curriculum content.

Second, although Moll's project understands funds of knowledge as both historically and culturally developed bodies of knowledge as well as the skills essential for household and individual functioning, much of the work that is translated into curriculum focuses on skills and 'labour history' (Moll *et al.*, 1992: 133). We shift the emphasis to a focus on historically developed bodies of knowledge and experience. We are less interested in how skills are acquired historically than in who people are as a result of their histories. Our work emerges from our interest in the relationship between accumulated funds of knowledge and identity.

Third, while Moll and his associates' research works towards the inclusion of marginalised community funds of knowledge into the school curriculum, we wanted to work in the borderlands by bringing multiple funds of knowledge into contact with one another in the shared classroom space. Both approaches challenge the hegemony of traditional curriculum content and disrupt power/knowledge relations. Our approach works with diversity as a productive resource for transforming the power/knowledge (Foucault, 1980) configuration in the curriculum.

That community funds of knowledge are racialised in desegregated South African schools is unsurprising. What is significant is that everyone was moved by what the students with direct access to personal experiences of the TRC had to say. Barnsley describes the listening silence in her class, and Marriott the 'reverent' atmosphere' in his. Moreover, where the pedagogy was effective, the teachers saw their students through transformed lenses, the power dynamics in the classroom shifted and students related to each other differently. Perhaps most important is that some students were able to connect with their own family and community histories in new and profound ways.

Meeting in the spaces between their differences gave students and teachers an opportunity to see one another in new ways. Desegregated classrooms enabled the teachers to do important border work. Where teachers were able to reconsider their students' worth in the light of new knowledge about them; where displaced white students became interested in what their black peers could offer from the life experiences of their communities; and where individual students reconnected with their community and family histories, the learning experience proved to be more moving than threatening. While all we can claim thus far is some powerful moments of reconciliation in 'the borderland where the space [people] shrinks … with intimacy' (Anzaldúa, 1999, preface: n.p.), it is a hopeful pedagogic beginning.

Notes

1 This chapter was originally published as: 'Reconciliation pedagogy, identity and community funds of knowledge: borderwork in South African classrooms' by Ana Ferreira and Hilary Janks, *English Academy Review* 24(2) (2007): 71–84.

2 Ferreira and Janks are equal, joint authors of this article. We would like to acknowledge the central involvement of Ingrid Barnsley, Charles Marriot and Monique Rudman, the school-based teachers, without whose commitment and teaching expertise this work would not have been possible. We are also grateful to our colleagues, Helen Ludlow and Reville Nussey, who provided valuable insights on History and pedagogy.

3 Njabulo Ndebele is quoted by M. Merten in 'In 20 years we'll wonder what the fuss what about', *Mail & Guardian* newspaper, 26 August–1 September 2005.

4 The international Reconciliation Pedagogies project, entitled Rethinking Reconciliation and Pedagogy in Unsettling Times, is led by Professor Robert Hattam of the University of South Australia. It aims to research the pedagogical nature of reconciliation processes by bringing two discourses – 'reconciliation' and 'pedagogy' – into conversation. It also includes research sites in Israel, Cyprus, New Zealand and the USA.

5 While the official TRC process has been completed, many South Africans have not yet begun to do the kind of daily work that is necessary to effect healing.

6 The core members of the Research Circle are Ana Ferreira, Hilary Janks, Helen Ludlow and Reville Nussey, all educational researchers from the University of the Witwatersrand; and Ingrid Barnsley, Charles Marriott and Monique Rudman, school-based classroom teachers.

7 The early phase of the project comprised several months of work in which teachers explored the meaning of the word 'sorry' with students, using a range of different approaches and stimulus material. Students produced lively and engaged work that dealt with socio-politically decontextualised individual experiences of apologising and feelings of remorse.

8 David Webster was a political activist who was assassinated by the State in the 1980s.

9 He discovered, for example, that one of his students was the step-grandchild of George Bizos, a pre-eminent human rights lawyer who was part of the defence team in the Rivonia treason trial.

References

Anzaldúa, G. (1999) *Borderlands/La Frontera: The New Mestiza* (2nd ed.), San Francisco: Aunt Lute Books.

Comber, B. and Kamler, B. (eds) (2005) *Turn-Around Pedagogies: Literacy Interventions for At Risk Students*, Newtown: PETA Press.

Dolby, N. E. (2001) *Constructing Race: Youth, Identity and Popular Culture in South Africa*, Albany, NY: State University of New York Press.

Derrida, J. (2001) *On Cosmopolitanism and Forgiveness*, London: Routledge.

Ferreira, A., Janks, H., Barnsley, I., Marriott, C., Rudman, M., Ludlow, H. and Nussey, R. (in press) Reconciliation pedagogy in South African classrooms: from the personal to the political, in R. Hattam, P. Christie, P. Bishop, J. Matthews, P. Ahluwalia and S. Atkinson (eds) *Pedagogies for Reconciliation*, London: Routledge.

Foucault, M. (1980) *Power/Knowledge: Selected Interviews and Other Writings 1972–1977*, New York: Pantheon Books.

González, N. (2005) Beyond culture: the hybridity of funds of knowledge, in N. González, L. Moll and C. Amanti (eds) *Funds of Knowledge: Theorising Practices in Households and Classrooms*, Mahwah, NJ: Lawrence Erlbaum and Associates.

González, N., Moll, L. and Amanti, C. (eds) (2005) *Funds of Knowledge: Theorising Practices in Households and Classrooms*, Mahwah, NJ: Lawrence Erlbaum and Associates.

Hattam, R. (in press) Reconciliation/pedagogy: a provocation, in R. Hattam, P. Christie, P. Bishop, J. Matthews, P. Ahluwalia and S. Atkinson (eds) *Pedagogies for Reconciliation*, London: Routledge.

Heath, S. (1983) *Ways with Words*, Cambridge: Cambridge University Press.

Kress, G., Jewitt, C., Bourne, J., Franks, A., Hardcastle, J., Jones, K. and Reid, E. (2004) *English in Urban Classrooms: A Multimodal Perspective on Teaching and Learning*, London: RoutledgeFalmer.

McKinney, C. (2004) 'A little hard piece of grass in your shoe': understanding student resistance to critical literacy in post-apartheid South Africa, *Southern African Linguistics and Applied Language Studies* 22(1&2): 63–73.

Mamdani, M. (1998) The TRC and justice, in R. Dorsman, H. Hartman and L. Noteboom-Kronemeijer (eds) *Truth and Reconciliation in South Africa and the Netherlands*, SIM Special, No. 23, Utrecht: Studie-en Informatiecentrum.

Moll, L., Amanti, C., Neffe, D. and González, N. (1992) Funds of knowledge for teaching: using a qualitative approach to connect homes and classrooms, *Theory into Practice* 31(2): 132–41.

Nethersole, R. (2002) Reclaiming identity as truth: on the politics of the African renaissance, *Quest: An African Journal of Philosophy* XVI(1–2): 143–50.

New London Group (1996) A pedagogy of multiliteracies: designing social futures, *Harvard Educational Review* 66(1): 60–90.

Posel, D. and Simpson, G. (2002) *Commissioning the Past: Understanding South Africa's Truth and Reconciliation Commission*, Johannesburg: Witwatersrand University Press.

Soudien, C. (2004) 'Constituting the class': an analysis of the process of 'integration' in South African schools, in L. Chisholm (ed.) *Changing Class: Education and social change in post-apartheid South Africa*, Cape Town: HSRC Publishers.

Truth and Reconciliation Commission (TRC) (1998) *Truth and Reconciliation Commission of South Africa Report*, Cape Town: Juta & Co.

31

Miners, diggers, ferals and show-men

Creative school–community projects

Pat Thomson

The notion of 'active citizenship' has a long history. Underpinning active citizenship approaches in the formal curriculum are a variety of views about the necessity for young people to take more active, creative, 'real' roles in schools. Arguments that are offered include:

- young people can learn *about* democracy and citizenship through a formal course of study, but will learn to *be* constructive members of a democracy if they have *experience* and *practice* in citizenship;
- the learnings in civics become more relevant when they are connected to actual 'real-life' democratic participation in activities – this means giving students 'real things to do' (Holdsworth, 2000) rather than having them as token participants;
- the school is a social microcosm and it is therefore important that it function in ways that are congruent with what students are being taught in the formal curriculum – this means 'good governance' (Pearl and Knight, 1999);
- many young people are alienated both from society at large and from schools (Mellor, 1998); in order to re-engage students in schools, and therefore in wider society, schools must work on ways in which young people can be reconnected with the curriculum and involved in wider school and community activities (Semmens and Stokes, 1997);
- young people are in fact already citizens (Wyn, 1995) whose rights to participate in decisions that affect them are daily violated in schools; according students more active roles is therefore to allow them to be functioning members of society.

Active citizenship projects thus typically engage young people in a range of activities which involve them contributing their skills, time and labour in activities which make a difference to somebody else (usually an identifiable 'community'). These are not the same as community service projects, where students typically do volunteer work on a regular basis in a project or service that already exists, e.g. reading to elderly people, doing gardening in a community park, running activities for small children – though active citizenship approaches share with community service projects a commitment to an ethic of care and to the practice of collective, civic responsibility. Nor are they the same as vocationally and/or entrepreneurially oriented projects in which students conceive of a project, initiate, manage and implement it, e.g. making T-shirts for sale at a local market – though active citizenship approaches share with vocational and entrepreneurial projects the practices of student led and managed activities which rely on creativity, team work and persistence.

Active citizenship approaches combine the values and ethics of service learning with the agency and practices of enterprise education in projects which may variously do any of the following:

- *Design and create a service for a community*: students might, for example, be engaged in cross-age or peer tutoring activities within their own or other schools. They might initiate and run film programmes for neighbourhood children. They might plan and run an adventure activity programme in a local child-care centre.
- *Design and create a resource for a community*: students might, for example, produce a community newspaper, website, directory or resource guide. They might collect and publish a collection of oral histories. They could build a playground for local children, paint murals on buildings, or design and print posters advertising local events.
- *Investigate and act on an issue facing a community*: students might, for example, research a social issue such as youth homelessness or school truancy, write a report of their findings and present it to the relevant authority. They could investigate an aspect of the local environment and restore a wild habitat, initiate a programme of water monitoring, or build an interpretative trail or wetland. They could become evaluators of local youth services and make recommendations for improvement.

Each of these activities involves young people in working as a group and engaging with people of different ages, interests and views. It involves them putting their own immediate self-interests aside, and working for a common good. It requires them to be organised, persistent, reliable, and trustworthy; to acquire or practice skills such as negotiation, information collection, analysis and synthesis, and oral and written communication; and to learn whatever is particularly needed to complete their project. In completing these kinds of projects students find that they are 'seen' differently by the wider community (i.e. as citizens), and they also 'see' themselves as citizens. Active citizenship projects are thus important for constructing a sense of social efficacy and a positive identity within the school and wider community (Thomson, 2007; Thomson *et al.*, 2005a, 2005b).

Active citizenship in Tasmanian schools: four cases

In 2002, the Tasmanian Department of Education, as part of its commitment to this agenda, funded twenty schools to undertake innovative action research projects to build partnerships between schools and communities. I was employed as a consultant to the programme and I ran two full-day action research workshops with funded teachers, and a day for reporting work-in-progress. Another of my tasks was to produce a final report which 'read across' the projects and the change strategy. This chapter relies heavily on field notes made during the one-day work-in-progress conference at which teachers presented their work, and during which I was able to ask questions of them. Unlike their written reports, their verbal presentations were lively, complex, often funny and, equally frequently, moving.

In order to tell this story, it is necessary to talk about the particular state in which this project occurred. I begin with some pointers to Tasmania, Australia's island state, and then go on to discuss four of the projects.

Tasmania: struggles to be different

Although Tasmania was invaded first by British whalers it was primarily colonised as a prison. The Indigenous population endured mass slaughter, European disease and the enslavement of women to single white male colonists. During the long Victorian era, accessible fertile areas were turned over to farming, and homesick immigrants planted large amounts of English vegetation and introduced animals and birds from 'home'. The vast stands of tall native timbers supported a profitable logging industry.

Tasmania is now characterised as a state of regional towns, rather than a state dominated by one large capital city, as in the rest of Australia. Also, unlike the remainder of the country, post-war Tasmania received only a few immigrants. However, Tasmania's relative racial and ethnic homogeneity has not prevented it from experiencing debates and battles over identities and politics.

Tasmania's Aboriginal peoples have asserted loudly their existence, and made public their struggles for survival and their rights to recognition and traditional lands. The Tasmanian government was the very last to decriminalise homosexuality, after a long series of highly public 'pink' protests. These identity issues are still far from settled, and this is indicative of a state with deeply conservative narratives, mores and politics. Tasmania has also been the site of environmental struggles of international significance. There were successful blockades to save wild rivers from destruction by hydroelectric power dams and protest camps remain to protect old-growth wilderness. Conservation politics have produced deep divisions in communities, a World Heritage listing for a sizeable chunk of the island and a robust Green Party which has now gained significant electoral sway not only in Tasmania, but also in the federal Parliament. Away from major population centres, scuffles over logging still continue, and it is not unusual to drive through small towns next to cars carrying anti-green stickers and pass by large signs declaring the rights of logging families to employment. Alternative lifestyle settlers and artists also live in these same communities and there is considerable local hostility between the two groups. Green and lifestyle politics are now integral to everyday life all over Tasmania.

Regional Tasmania has recently suffered considerable economic duress. As mines and forests closed, and as the market for wool and wool products declined in the face of synthetics and cheap imports, unemployment skyrocketed to become the highest in Australia. New industries based around clean and green gourmet food and eco-tourism have provided a viable living for some, but most regional towns experience their young people, saturated with globalised consumer youth cultures, leaving home as soon as they are able. Many leave the state altogether and go to the mainland to study and work. Tasmania's system of middle schools and senior colleges has been a structural disincentive for disengaged students to complete secondary schooling, and for many years the state had the lowest school graduation rates in the nation, although some schools were remarkably successful in working against the odds.

In Tasmania, divisions over differences run deep and each local 'place' in the island is uniquely inflected by locality, history, populations, networks and politics (Massey, 1995). Thinking of the 'places' within the island does not produce a unitary story. In the twenty school–community projects I supported there were twenty unique instances of sites in which these politics, events and issues were differently made material.

I now describe, albeit briefly, four of these projects. They were selected not simply because they were success stories, or because they were the only success stories from the programme: indeed, one of the funded projects intervened in the death trajectory of an endangered bird species, but it is not featured here. Rather, these stories are those that might resonate with an international audience and have some 'take' elsewhere. I have semi-anonymised each location as per conventions of ethical scholarly practice, although, as Nespor (2000) points out, the notion of anonymisation when describing the particularity of place is highly contradictory. I present these stories as factual narratives and move to discussion afterwards.

The projects

Case study 1: Show-men

Papermill is a regional city whose major industry is the subject of sporadic state and national protest. Trucks laden with old-forest logs wheel into town and container loads of paper products for domestic use and export wheel out. Most days Papermill is a sleepy place with an aging population, many of whose male members enjoy social time together in the colonial pubs in the main street. Papermill is also an important regional centre for outlying farms that rely on the sales of dairy products and wool. Papermill district high school struggles to cater for its diverse range of students, some of whom intend to study at mainland universities, while others simply see that there is no work for them and no point to school.

In 2002, local media carried the story that Papermill's annual agricultural show was dying. The show committee, made up of the town's senior men, were convinced that 2002 would be its last year. But one of the teachers at the local high school had other ideas. She applied for 'community' funds to allow her class – the school's most unsuccessful and 'difficult' students, the 'veges' as they were disparagingly called by many of the staff – to repair the fencing and animal pens at the show ground. She equipped a trailer as a mobile workshop. She contacted the local committee and the aged show-men agreed, somewhat reluctantly, to work with her boys. They were far from convinced that the town's young troublemakers – interested, as far as they could see, only in loud music, fast cars and late night drinking – were up to the task.

Because the show-men were too infirm to tackle hard physical work, and because they came from the 'old school', their mode of working with the boys was far from gentle. Yet the boys not only accepted having orders barked at them, they also worked hard and established friendly and respectful relationships with men who they previously would have dismissed with a string of four-letter epithets. The show-men, for their part, rapidly grew to like and respect the boys. The show ground was repaired.

After further discussion about the gloomy prospects for the show, the boys developed a publicity strategy which involved designing, printing and distributing leaflets far and wide. They worked with their peers at school on a school display and stalls, and they were the backbone of a team of school volunteers who worked before, during and after the actual show. Headlines in the local paper the day after the show directly attributed the first profitable event for many years to the efforts of the class.

The class did not stop there. They began work with the local police, previously their sworn enemy, to repair and repaint public toilets and the local youth club.

Case study 2: Diggers

Barracks Street, in suburban Hobart, is one of the oldest primary schools in Australia. Built in the early 1800s, it is situated in a now gentrifying lower middle-class neighbourhood of weatherboard and redbrick Victorian cottages and bungalows. It is a quiet, largely monocultural area. The once stable population has become more mobile but there are still many children whose parents and grandparents attended the school. Barracks Street counts several notable Tasmanians amongst its ex-pupils.

Two upper primary teachers decided to apply for 'community' funds to build a school history website. They wanted to bring the study of history literally to life by researching local knowledges. They believed that through using the school and the neighbourhood as the focus for inquiry they would have one lens on colonial Tasmania. They began with their classes designing and distributing leaflets for two community meetings. These meetings were very well attended and were addressed by a nationally recognised artist – a former scholar of the school. The students had developed questionnaires for all those present. They requested photographs and other artefacts and received quite a few.

The class then did library work using histories of Tasmania as well as the school's own archives to develop a social-school timeline into which they slotted the photographs, questionnaire data and interviews. With the help of their teachers, they designed a website, and the quest for further information from ex-students went digital. Over time, large numbers of former Barracks Street students responded to their online presence and they became part of the cyber-archive.

For the next phase, the teachers decided to work with a school Honour Board hung in the main foyer: this listed former students who died in the First World War. Grandparents were invited in to talk about their childhood memories of wartime, when they were at school, and these presentations were digitally recorded and added to the archive. The teachers contacted the historian at the state war memorial and the students went on an excursion to the official archives, where they were helped by the historian and library staff to research one soldier each. Every student was able to see the records of 'their' soldier, and to investigate the particular circumstances of his death. They had access to a range of documents, including those which constructed the national mythologies of the Anzac, noble diggers and Gallipoli. They were encouraged to look at the differences between documentary photos taken at the time and artistic post-hoc representations.

On Remembrance Day in 2002, the students attended the annual Dawn Service and placed flowers at the foot of their soldier's tree.[1]

Case study 3: Miners

Rocktown is located in a relatively remote part of Tasmania adjacent to a significant wilderness area and is the site of a major internationally owned mine. The mine has been the subject of state and national protest and scrutiny. It is surrounded by high mesh fences and heavy security procedures. Most of the children in the local primary school are from families whose livelihood is based in local small businesses, tourism and farming. Like many of their parents, the bulk of the students are interested in environmental issues and are overtly committed to a 'clean, green Tasmania'.

A primary teacher decided to apply for 'community' funds so that her class could restore a patch of native bush which was badly degraded by introduced plants. The plan was to build an interpretive area, which the children named, in anticipation of its outcome, Wallaby Wander. The children researched the local vegetation and worked with the local council and Parks and Wildlife officers to plot what to plant and what to remove. They designed a snaking pathway and grew tiny seedlings from seed collected from their patch of scrub. They did not, however, have enough money in the grant, or enough labour to do what they wanted. So, together with their teacher, they began to contact local businesses. A local earthmover donated his services. Another loaned bins for the collection of rubbish. Many school parents and community members volunteered time for working bees. A local landscaper offered substantial discount on gravel and sand for the path.

But the teacher was determined to get something from the biggest employer in town – the mine. She talked her way into the office of the director, who like many of the mine's workers, was from out of town. The director was shocked that the teacher had not been sent to the public relations manager, who usually dealt with requests for donations, but was convinced as she listened to the teacher explain the Wallaby Wander project that there were things that the mine could do. She organised for the children to meet employees responsible for land restoration, now a legislative requirement on all mining ventures in Tasmania. The children were then invited behind the security fences to join environmental staff replanting an area of land with endangered plants – known as RATS – rare and threatened species. They were also given a quantity of RATS for Wallaby Wander.

The class managed a mass tree planting day, involving 300 children and adults, to coincide with a national conservation day. This event garnered considerable publicity for Wallaby Wander. The students' class record of this part of the project comprised diaries, stories, student-produced newsletters and press articles, and it was awarded a state literacy prize.

Finally, one weekend in late 2002, and with the participation of large numbers of helpers, the pathway was finally laid. Wallaby Wander was officially launched in early 2003.

Case study 4: Ferals

Gumville is an old logging and forestry community. Since the protests of the 1980s it has also been home to a substantial alternative lifestyle community, known locally as the ferals. The local primary and high school cater largely for the children of timber and farming families, who vote overwhelmingly conservative in state and national elections. There is also a significant arts community in the area and some commercial art and craft outlets catering for the passing tourist trade.

An upper primary teacher applied for 'community' funds to mount a class art exhibition which would involve local artists presenting their work alongside that of students. The class wrote to all of the local artists inviting them to participate, and a handful responded. Other staff and their classes in the school were excited by the project and they asked if they could join in. Before they knew what was happening the class was organising a whole school art exhibition. But, disappointed with the response from local artists, most of whom had not bothered to answer the children's letters, the teacher decided that she would begin to solicit assistance from local businesses. Many responded in the affirmative, offering assistance with catering and display supplies.

As the time for the exhibition drew nearer, the teacher decided that she would approach the local environment centre to see what they could do to help because it seemed foolish to keep ignoring them just because they were 'ferals'. About the same time, she discovered that the local high school was organising an exhibition of its own, just one week before the primary school, despite being invited to join together. The high school did, however, provide some student art work to display at the primary event. While this lack of coordination/cooperation with the high school was very disappointing, the connection with the 'ferals' was surprisingly positive. The young people from the environment centre offered workshops on paper-making and other art and craft practices. They also provided some of their own art and craft for the exhibition. The children were able to mount an exhibition of some 700 artefacts, of which 500 were from children in the school and 200 from the community. The exhibition was opened by the mayor and relatively well attended.

In 2003, the teacher established an ongoing series of activities with the environmental centre and initiated a transition programme with the high school.

I now consider questions of place, identity and difference raised by these four projects. As noted earlier, the evidence I am using here is not based on direct interviews with the students involved, but on reports from their teachers. As such, this analysis must be somewhat speculative, and in the form of issues raised for further exploration.

Unsettling encounters?

In each of the projects students were brought together with people, living, dead and fictional, in extraordinary circumstances. Gumville students were brought face to face with the dreadlocked ferals, who did not turn out to be the lunatic fringe they had expected. As their teacher wrote in her final report:

> The coming together of a left and right organization has been interesting as students have been given opportunity to voice their attitudes and beliefs. Such a union will, I believe, allow for acceptance of diversity as well as environmental appreciation.
>
> *(Teacher, Gumville)*

Barracks Street students encountered contradictory representations of the diggers. While the daily newspaper reported only a nationalist perspective, noting that one girl had fainted during the Anzac ceremony and that many had cried, teachers reported that 'many children had become much more knowledgeable about the myth of the Anzac'. Rocktown students met the miners and discovered they were not quite the faceless environmental vandals they had imagined. As one of the students wrote in the class newspaper:

> Mineco is not a very nice environment because it is a pretty dirty industrial site and there's not much vegetation. They are working hard to make it better by restoring the native vegetation and making wetlands all over the place.
>
> *(Class newspaper, Rocktown)*

They also worked differently with adults. One parent wrote in her child's diary: 'The idea of adults working with kids is great – not adults just telling kids what to do – that is, adults also getting their hands dirty'. Papermill students worked willingly for the old showmen, shifting their relationships from mutual dislike and mistrust to respect and good will, affirming a rough-and-ready rural masculinity at the same time. Their teacher could not understand this, she told me, but she assumed it was something to do with this being 'real work' and the showmen being 'real workers'.

Some students in these projects became very different people in their local place. According to their teachers, they experienced through their projects some disruption to their customary ways of being and doing. Papermill boys were designated as 'at risk', exhibiting a range of what might be called in the UK 'emotional and behavioural disorders' at school, or 'criminal beha-viours' by police everywhere. Through their activities with the show-men, they literally chan-ged their social position in the town. From being part of the youth problem, they came to be seen, justifiably, as the youth solution. From seeing the town as an old-fashioned out of touch place only good enough to leave, the boys shifted position, to value and work for the pre-servation of its agricultural heritage. Whether this is a life-altering intervention remains to be seen. What can be a fairly claimed is that this project was a very significant disruption to the production of educational disadvantage and these students as 'other'. Sadly for the teacher, some of her colleagues told her at the end of the project that the best thing had been that it had removed the 'veges' from their classes.

Students in these projects were also brought together with significant cultural institutions and cultural capital in ways which allowed them to critically encounter local/national narratives. Barracks Street students live in a nation in which 'the digger' is iconic. Most children know about diggers through family connections, television and radio, the ritual memorial ceremonies and monuments, and the circulating representations of fallen heroes. In the year and the city in which the last Australian Gallipoli veteran died, Barracks Street children were brought face to face with the gritty pictures of incompetent military strategy and the mass slaughter of a generation of ordinary men. They were encouraged not simply to respect, but also to question. The Barracks Street teachers reported that the children were engaged in history in ways they had not seen before. They asserted that through such encounters students had had an opportunity both to re-read important local/global debates and also to work in and with tensions integral to contemporary Tasmania; however, they were not asked to produce evidence about this, since that was not the focus of the funding.

Place-based curriculum

The projects described in this chapter are also illustrative of a place-based curriculum which takes students out of the classroom to engage in the local community (Brooke, 2003). Place-based curriculum has different inflections. The US Rural School and Community Trust, for example, defines place-based education as

> rooted in the unique history, culture, environment and economy of a particular place. The community provides a context for learning. Students' work focuses on community needs and interests, and community members serve as resources and partners in every aspect of teaching and learning. The local focus has the power to engage students academically, pairing relevance with rigour, while opening windows to the world and promoting genuine citizenship.[2]

The value of place-based curriculum is often attributed to pedagogy. It is said to enhance engagement because students are learning through action and experience (Dewey, 1938). Place-based curriculum is also related to the development of relevance and meaningful purpose derived from working to produce tangible results that matter (Cumming, 1997). In the projects described here, students can be seen as community activists. In both place-based active citizenship projects students are encouraged to research their local communities to document local customs, and to design strategies for community improvement (Romano and Glascock, 2002; Wigginton, 1986). Through such students-as local-researchers projects, young people are encouraged to take up local causes, work in and on the natural or built environment, and/or contribute to urban regeneration and wilderness protection projects (Comber et al., 2001, 2002; Janks, 2002). Much of this place-based activity is trans-disciplinary, stitching together citizenship education, literacy, social science and ecological studies, for example, in ways that could be described as being 'authentic' (Anderson, 1998) creative learning.

A place-based active citizenship curriculum offers opportunities for schools to explicitly and critically foster identity work through events and tasks that allow students to encounter embedded social practices and agents that they would normally avoid. By connecting students with different peoples in their local neighbourhoods, teachers are imbricating students in the trajectories of everyday lives which are not simply local, but are also 'stretched-out' relations, practices and narratives (Childress, 2000; Massey, 1994). Projects such as those described provide opportunities not only for active citizenship but also for situated identity work, as students engage with difference(s) and are encouraged to produce texts in which they describe/inscribe themselves, those with whom they are in dialogue and their mutual place in the world.

Given current concerns about the fragmentation of communities, there is much to be gained from thinking how it is that creative learning approaches which work with place, identity/ies and difference(s) can both produce active and engaged citizens and genuinely enhance school–community partnerships and communities themselves.

Notes

1 There is a Remembrance Park in Hobart where each Tasmanian soldier killed in the First World War has a memorial tree with a plaque.
2 See http://www.ruraledu.org/rtportfolio/index/htm.

References

Anderson, G. (1998) Towards authentic participation: deconstructing the discourses of participatory reforms in education, *American Educational Research Journal* 35(4): 571–603.

Brooke, R. (ed.) (2003) *Rural Voices: Place-Conscious Education and the Teaching of Writing*, New York: National Writing Project & Teachers College Press.

Childress, H. (2000) *Landscapes of Betrayal, Landscapes of Joy: Curtisville in the Lives of its Teenagers*, New York: State University of New York Press.

Comber, B., Thomson, P. and Wells, M. (2001) Critical literacy finds a 'place': writing and social action in a low income Australian grade 2/3 classroom, *Elementary School Journal* 101(4): 451–64.

—— (2002) Critical literacy, social action and children's representations of 'place', paper presented at the American Educational Research Association, New Orleans, 1–5 April.

Cumming, J. (1997) *Community Based Learning: Adding Value to Programs Involving Service Agencies and Schools*, Sydney: Dusseldorp Skills Forum.

Dewey, J. (1938) *Experience and Education* (1963 ed.), New York: Collier Books.

Holdsworth, R. (2000) Schools that create real roles of value for young people, *Prospects* 115(3): 349–62.

Janks, H. (2002) The politics and history of the places children inhabit, paper presented at the American Educational Research Association, New Orleans, 1–5 April.

Massey, D. (1994) *Space, Place and Gender*, Minneapolis: University of Minnesota Press.

—— (1995) The conceptualisation of place, in D. Massey and P. Jess (eds) *A Place in the World? Places, Cultures and Globalisation*, Milton Keynes: Open University Press.

Mellor, S. (1998) *What's the Point? Political Attitudes of Victorian Year 11 Students*, Research Monograph No. 53, Melbourne: ACER Press.

Nespor, J. (2000) Anonymity and place in qualitative inquiry, *Qualitative Inquiry* 6(4): 546–69.

Pearl, A. and Knight, T. (1999) *The Democratic Classroom: Theory to Inform Practice*, Cresskill, NJ: Hampton Press.

Romano, R. and Glascock, C. (2002) *Hungry Minds in Hard Times: Educating for Complexity for Students of Poverty*, New York: Peter Lang.

Semmens, R. and Stokes, H. (1997) Full service schooling for full citizenship: from theory to practice, *Melbourne Studies in Education* 38(2): 115–29.

Thomson, P. (2007) Making it real: engaging students in active citizenship projects, in D. Thiessen and A. Cook-Sather (eds) *International Handbook of Student Experience in Elementary and Secondary School*, Dordrecht: Springer.

Thomson, P., McQuade, V. and Rochford, K. (2005a) 'My little special house': re-forming the risky geographies of middle school girls at Clifftop College, in G. Lloyd (ed.) *Problem Girls: Understanding and Supporting Troubled and Troublesome Girls and Young Women*, London: RoutledgeFalmer.

—— (2005b) 'No-one's a good or bad student here': an active citizenship project as 'doing justice', *International Journal of Learning*; available at http://ijl.cgpublisher.com/.

Wigginton, E. (1986) *Sometimes a Shining Moment: The Foxfire Experience. Twenty Years Teaching in a High School Classroom*, New York: Anchor Press/Doubleday.

Wyn, J. (1995) 'Youth' and citizenship, *Melbourne Studies in Education* 36(2): 45–63.

32

Alternatives in student assessment

The Cultural Competency Record (CCR)[1]

Max Fuchs and Rolf Witte

The political background

In Germany, cultural education is covered by different political fields: youth, cultural and educational policies. Each of these policy fields has its own logic, its own rules and types of professionalism. In order to understand the relevance of youth and cultural policy for cultural education one should know that Germany traditionally has a half-day school system. This is changing just now because of the poor German results in the Programme for International Student Assessment of OECD (PISA). Against this background, it is understandable that extra-curricular programmes are more important in Germany than in countries with boarding school programmes. Youth and cultural policies have the lead responsibility for such programmes. In order to offer a multitude of such extracurricular programmes and projects there is a well-organised infrastructure for cultural education outside school.

The Cultural Competency Record (CCR) was created as a means of assessing cultural competencies in out-of-school projects. The main political problem was that these programmes were labouring under a misapprehension, namely that school-specific ways of assessment, that is, giving marks, should be transferred to out-of-school education. And this could be considered as a fundamental violation of the most important educational principles in this field because the 'philosophy' of out-of-school education in Germany is to form a kind of opposition or contrast to school education. These educational principles focus on the voluntary nature of extra-curricular activities, involvement and tolerance for the mistakes of the young participants.

On the other hand, 'evaluation' in all dimensions has become relevant since the 1990s. In youth and cultural policy, the paradigm of New Public Management was implemented in all public fields, with evaluation as an important part. The question about the effects and outcomes of arts and cultural education for the individual, for groups and for society at large has mean-while become very intensive. But there were no answers because there was virtually no research in this field.

The problem of evaluation and assessment has different dimensions. First is the dimension of legitimisation: governments need to have good reasons for subsidising cultural projects with public funds. The second has to do with educational responsibility, since everybody who wants to be involved in developing the personality of others – and this is the main goal of (cultural) education – should be very careful and be accountable. And the third dimension of this question has to do with educational professionalism. Aside from a change of mentality about the idea of evaluation and assessment in the cultural field, there were some international movements that were helpful for the development of an appropriate assessment instrument.

The first movement discovered the relevance of non-formal education. This concept was used very early in the UN World Report for Education and the context of the European Union. The main goal was to find appropriate ways of recognising non-formal education. Cedefop, the European Institute for vocational training, with its programmatic slogan 'making learning visible', played an important role. A lot of different instruments were developed in different countries in order to give young people a kind of record of their competencies which could be relevant for finding a job (e.g. the '*bilan des compétences*' in France). Another interesting idea was developed by the British Council: the Personal Record of Achievement (PRA), which documents competencies and skills, like social competencies and communicational skills, that are achieved in international youth exchange programmes. A third interesting and helpful project was run by the OECD around the topic of key-competencies (DeSeCo). Through ambitious consultations with educationalists, philosophers, psychologists and others, it was possible to develop an internationally accepted concept and definition of 'key-competencies'.

And of course there was PISA, which provided a strong stimulus for the development of new instruments of assessment in cultural education. In addition to the positive effects of PISA in terms of pushing national educational policies forward to gain new momentum, PISA put cultural education inside and outside school under pressure. First of all, public debates considered the selection of particular subjects (science, mathematics and language) as a kind of hierarchy of the different school subjects: PISA subjects are the most important fields of school education; all others are less important. This possible view was supported by the fact that the PISA methodology of evaluation was not considered acceptable for arts subjects. But there were no alternative evaluation methods for these subjects. As a result, the need for legitimisation of cultural education in terms of serious methods of assessment increased.

In this situation, BKJ (which is the federal umbrella organisation of 54 national und regional arts and cultural education organisations in Germany) came up with an internal plan for creating an appropriate assessment instrument for cultural education.

The philosophy

Cultural education is a combination of arts and education which can be recognised from the background of its providers. On the one hand, there are artists, or at least people whose identification and orientation belongs to the arts. On the other hand, there are professionals with a more educational profile. When developing an assessment instrument, both sides, artistic and educational, need to be taken into account.

The teachings of the Italian educational reformer Maria Montessori were important for the educational approach. When asked about the main professional skill of educationalists, she answered: observation, observation, observation. Consequently, we developed an elaborated way of observing young people in cultural projects, especially with a view to their progress in developing competencies. As mentioned above, the concept of competencies like social and self-competence was compatible with the German concept of *kulturelle Bildung* (cultural education). So we decided that key-competencies rather than specific artistic competencies should be at the centre of our assessment process. A certain deficit by professionals in the field of educational observation constituted the background of and motivation for our activities in finding professional methods for it. We were surprised to find that even very experienced professionals were not able to give a precise description of the development of young people due to a lack of an appropriate terminology.

The second approach took into account that the subject and content of cultural projects are arts. There is an intensive debate in arts theory as to whether there is a special 'logic' of art work. For instance, what is the difference between a general movement on a stage and dance? What kind of challenges and tasks must be solved to transform a general movement into an art form, dance that is? The idea is that when somebody produces something that can be considered 'art', he or she must have solved the immanent problems of this art work. In other words, he or she has developed the necessary competencies.

The successful artistic performance of young people can be considered as proof of their educational development: the task of performing art is solved. In practice, this means that there is a strong correlation between the logic of art work and the system of competencies. Both ideas, together with the special principles of out-of-school education, were put into clear methodological system.

The Cultural Competency Record

Imparting competencies is an essential goal of cultural education. Creativity, social interest, self-confidence, the willingness to assume responsibility and successful artistic performance are enhanced by actively engaging in arts or other forms of cultural education. Theatre, dance, circus, music, literature, the media and the visual arts all support children and young people in their efforts to make sense of the world.

For Sadaf Y (17 years old) the work in the after-school theatre project became an important part of her life:

> Playing theatre allows me not to be scared of people when I have to act or speak in public. I don't need to bring myself to do it and I'm not scared any more, I can concentrate on my tasks. I have learned to keep cool and to be productive even when I'm stressed.
>
> *(Sadaf Y, 17)*

Like Sadaf, many young people spend their leisure time in institutions for cultural education, such as art and music schools for youth, theatre and dance workshops, literature clubs or media centres, children's museums, youth circuses. All those involved in these projects realise that young people learn a lot while pursuing these activities, beyond the subject matter of the project as such. Cultural education work promotes the acquisition of a host of competencies: creativity, team spirit and self-confidence, perseverance and flexibility, organisational and improvisation skills, to mention just a few.

A set of tools for documenting the effects of cultural education work on the individual youth was developed in cooperation with practitioners of cultural education, social scientists from the field of competency research and representatives from the business community. The result of this work is the Cultural Competency Record (Kompetenznachweis Kultur), an educational passport. This record clearly spells out what young people have learned on top of the artistic skills involved.

The CCR is an educational passport which succinctly describes the artistic activities pursued by the young person and the individual strengths he or she has demonstrated in the course of such a project. A procedure was developed for the documentation of competencies. Special training seminars are organised for professional full-time, part-time and voluntary staff in the field of cultural education in which they can learn how to use this procedure and become a CCR expert.

It is up to each young person to decide whether he or she wants his or her activities in cultural education to be documented in a CCR or not. Part of the concept is also to actively involve young people in producing their CCR. This raises their awareness of their own strengths. While the Cultural Competency Record provides an explicit appreciation for a young person of what he or she has accomplished in the context of a cultural education or artistic project, the young person recognises his or her own achievements through the input he or she has provided during the process. This is an essential difference to conventional report cards or attendance certificates.

The entire process leading up to the finished CCR is based on participation and reflection, including – by all means – critical reflection. For the young person, participating in this process is a challenge that both requires and promotes competencies.

In job interviews, the CCR can be the trigger for a conversation on special skills. In this conversation, the young person credibly reflects what the CCR describes and is able, because of his or her own personal input, to provide information on the cultural artistic work pursued and on the process leading to issuing of the Cultural Competency Record.

In order to be able to apply the CCR in practice, CCR experts need to develop, in a joint process involving the young people, a clear definition of what can be learned in an artistic course or a cultural, creative project, and what effect the participation in the programme has on the individual. To achieve this objective, BKJ has developed four steps that reflect the day-to-day and project work done by professionals in the field of cultural education:

- *Step 1: Project analysis*: the competencies that can be acquired during a specific cultural or artistic activity are systematically listed. They are also defined by the tasks and challenges inherent in the planned project.
- *Step 2: Observation*: the cultural education professional observes which skills and abilities the young person is showing during his or her active participation in the project or in the course. The young person trains his or her self-awareness by watching him- or herself and his or her own actions and by making notes or collecting material during the project.
- *Step 3: Dialogue*: the cultural education professional and the young person talk to each other about their experiences. This dialogue can involve a larger group. It may also include role playing and other forms of artistic expression. There are many options.
- *Step 4: Description*: the CCR expert and the young person agree on the content of the description, which focuses on the individual strengths and skills of the respective young person. Finally the CCR is issued.

In order to put the CCR into practice, BKJ offers a training course in cooperation with its member associations for those artists and cultural education professionals willing to become CCR experts. In this training course, participants acquire the necessary knowledge and learn about implementation methods. The course raises their awareness of the effects of their own day-to-day and project work, and teaches them how to use the tools of observation and dialogue, which helps participants to draw up a CCR in cooperation with the young person concerned.

The training course is divided into two stages (2 × two days) that provide general information on how to handle the CCR and on the underlying competency documentation procedure. Between the two stages, there is a period of practical implementation during which the methods are used in a real-life scenario. In order to be admitted onto the training course, participants must have a professional background in the practical field of cultural education, and they must have the possibility of implementing the entire process covered by the Cultural Competency Record.

After completion of the training, participants receive a certificate as CCR experts that qualifies them to fill in and issue the CCR to the participants in their cultural education projects.

Practical application

The CCR is primarily designed to meet the needs of the young people themselves. It raises their awareness of their own strengths and capabilities. Thus, it makes a contribution to their personality development and helps them to get started in a professional career. The CCR can be used when applying for an internship programme, job training or a job. Personnel managers will get a good impression of the strengths and knowledge of an applicant, without having to rely on the school certificate only. Because of this, the Cultural Competency Record gives a chance to young people with lower levels of academic achievement.

The CCR is exclusively issued by CCR experts, who must have completed the necessary training course; in addition, the CCR is issued by institutions and centres of cultural youth work where young people have participated in the process of a dialogue. Participation in this process is always voluntary. The CCR is then drawn up in a joint process involving the young people (their own perception and that of others). BKJ and the institution at which the CCR was acquired stamp and sign the document, giving it official recognition. The folder that is part of the record is handed over to the young person. He or she may use it for his or her own purposes and according to his or her interests.

At present, there is a network of 11 CCR service centres as member organisations of BKJ all over Germany; 2,500 CCRs have meanwhile been awarded to young participants, and every month about 50 new CCRs are being issued; 800 CCR experts have attended further training courses since the beginning of the implementation of the CCR, and 40 CCR trainers offer further training courses on a regular basis in different regions of the country.

The University of Hildesheim and Alanus University of Arts and Social Sciences at Alfter near Bonn have integrated the curriculum of the CCR training course into the curriculum for students of cultural sciences, and other universities are actually interested in doing the same.

Awarding the CCR in cultural education cooperation projects with schools is becoming more and more common, and many teachers and headteachers are very interested in the CCR. For the first time, professionals in extracurricular artistic programmes are offering an educational tool for student assessment which is really taken seriously by the formal school system in Germany.

Frequently asked questions

Does one need to be in a certain age bracket to qualify for the CCR?
It is up to each young person to decide whether he or she wants his or her activities in cultural youth work to be documented in a CCR or not. The CCR is issued for young persons between 12 (recommended minimum age) and 27 years.

For how long do young people need to have participated in artistic courses or cultural projects in order to receive a CCR?
It must be guaranteed that all four steps of the competency documentation procedure are fully implemented. The CCR expert then decides whether that is the case for his or her project. A minimum period of 50 hours for the project/course is recommended. For example, it is also possible for young people to qualify for the record when they have participated in a number of shorter separate events over a long period of time.

Is an institution entitled to issue the CCR?

No, it is not the institution but the CCR experts who are authorised to issue a CCR. Therefore, they can use this additional qualification in various different professional settings. An institution where most of the employees are qualified to issue the CCR may advertise this fact as an additional offer.

Does the CCR document the development of competencies?

The CCR provides a snapshot of the competency profile of a young person in relation to the project, course, etc. in which he or she has participated. The record therefore does not measure a development in the sense of progress or regression, but the existence of individual competencies at a certain point in time.

Does the CCR evaluate competencies?

It evaluates them by describing them in detail. It does not evaluate them in the sense of defining different levels of achievement or applying grades. It highlights the strengths of the individual!

Is it difficult to award the CCR?

No, the procedure is modelled on the day-to-day work of cultural educators. In the required training course, special attention is paid to working methods, which cultural education professionals are usually familiar with anyway. Some aspects, however, require an additional effort because the entire process calls for an intense and systematic commitment to young people.

How can the institutions benefit from the CCR?

Institutions will be able to answer the following question: 'Are we doing a good job?' The individual CCRs clearly document the work done by an institution to outside observers. They also document the educational effect achieved, in the form of competencies that are acquired in the institution. So they can be seen as evidence for the quality of the work done in the institution.

The results of two evaluations and conclusions

Some results of the two scientific evaluations of the CCR (Timmerberg and Schorn, 2009) show the strengths of the concept of the CCR. The two evaluators were the German Youth Institute (DJI) in Munich and the University of Eichstätt, Bavaria. Two hundred young people responded by questionnaire and 20 young people took part in in-depth interviews on the phone. Also, 30 CCR experts, 10 CCR trainers and 20 parents took part in phone interviews. Finally, 63 companies also responded by questionnaire.

What we wanted to find out was: 'What benefit do the different groups see in the Cultural Competency Record?'

The results showed that 50 per cent of the young participants with a CCR believe it is beneficial for their future career; 35 per cent of them were just curious to learn more about themselves. For 85 per cent of them the dialogue with the CCR expert was interesting and 80 per cent learned something new about themselves.

The most important aspect of the CCR for the participants is the process rather than the result, the CCR itself. The youngest participants (from 12 to 15 years) in lower segments of the school system got the most out of the CCR process.

CCR experts and trainers state:

- that the CCR process can be well integrated in cultural education projects;
- that their personal work became more professional by integrating the CCR process;
- that the further training course has lead to more self-reflection and a different understanding of their work;
- that the CCR process is time-consuming, but from their perspective this was time well spent;
- that the lack of time is the only reason for their colleagues not to use the CCR in their work.

Parents basically view the CCR very positively. They are informed about the CCR but not involved in the process of issuing it. Sometimes they are invited to public events where CCRs are handed out to their children, the participants of cultural education projects.

Of the companies, 98 per cent see the benefit of the CCR in the fact that participants can learn more about their strengths and weaknesses. Smaller companies in retail and services react more positively to the CCR than bigger companies in the industrial sector, because most of them don't have professional assessment systems of their own and welcome the CCR's additional information about a young candidate. Companies which have their own assessment systems do not see much added value in the CCR for their recruitment, because they are convinced that they have enough information about their candidates.

Practice, experience and evaluation clearly show that the CCR is definitely a way to make competencies visible, it supports the personal development of participants and it raises the awareness of cultural education providers. The CCR can be useful for the young people's next steps on the labour market, and the CCR improves the quality of arts and cultural education. In Germany CCR is used more and more often as an assessment tool in cooperative projects and the cultural education processes of schools, artists, arts institutions and arts education institutions. With the CCR, for the first time the non-formal cultural education sector offers to the formal school system an appropriate tool for the documentation of learning outcomes of cultural education projects, a system that goes far beyond the well-known national systems of school marks, with their equally well-known restrictions and disadvantages. It's true that the CCR process is time-consuming, but shouldn't we invest more time in promoting awareness-raising processes and in the assessment of learning outcomes?

Note

1 See www.kompetenznachweiskultur.de.

References

Timmerberg, V. and Schorn, B. (eds) (2009) *Neue Wege der Anerkennung von Kompetenzen in der kulturellen Bildung: Der Kompetenznachweis Kultur in Theorie und Praxis*, Munich: Kopäd-Verlag.

33

Judgement, authority and legitimacy

Evaluating creative learning[1]

Julian Sefton-Green

Some scholars think the idea of evaluating creativity is a contradiction in terms[2]; others think the idea of measuring creativity is a proper academic ambition (Runco, 2007; Runco *et al.*, 2010). To some extent this range of opinion is a question of definition and context. Developing skills for the creative workforce (McWilliam and Haukka, 2008) is not exactly the same thing as working with primary school teachers to enhance practice in assessing arts activities (Ellis and Barrs, 2008), or even developing play within a structured curriculum (Wassermann, 1992). Questions about the ages of the young people under discussion, assumptions and aspirations for progression, the role of adult or peer intervention, the institutional framework, the needs of external assessment, even theories of learning all impact in varying ways on this very broad field of interest.

This chapter thus has quite a narrow focus. It is not concerned with questions of standards or standardisation – nor, like Pam Burnard's chapter in Part II (Chapter 15), is it concerned with the relationships between a performativity or standards agenda and creativity. Unlike Anna Craft's chapter in the same part (Chapter 14), it is not primarily concerned with questions about policy and national curriculum reform and the role of assessment within such frameworks. This is despite the contemporary policy interest in questions about measurement and outcomes. The current era is vexed with the meaning of cross-national comparative forms of testing, often leading to intra-national school reform (Dumont *et al.*, 2010) – the European Union recently held a conference exploring how it might be possible to measure creativity and thus improve economic performance.[3]

Although the chapter will touch on questions of classroom practice and thus engage with developing and improving learning and teaching (Gardner, 2006), again this is not its main object of interest. Paul Black has written about how assessment plays a key role within learning, not just within the mechanics of formative assessment but in a range of classroom processes that enhance skills and develop learners (Black *et al.*, 2003). His concern has been to open up what he called the 'black box' of assessment, that is, the closed technocratic set of relationships between prescription and assessment, the performance of demonstrable skills and their relationship to concerns about 'deep' or 'authentic' learning. Although much of this chapter is based upon these insights and the kind of practices which they support, it is my intention to move beyond this debate.

The focus of this chapter, then, is to explore new and emerging debates about evaluation, many of which are located in value systems outside the classroom (or the black box) and which seek to instil other, different kinds of assessment within current pedagogic arrangements and classroom practice. It should be stressed that many of these accounts of innovative practice are emergent. However, within a section devoted to creative pedagogy and curriculum, it is important that we discuss forms of assessment and evaluation in order provide a secure foundation to justify the sorts of change that are explored in Part IV. Within the wider discussion about assessment and evaluation one key point of agreement is that any and all kinds of assessment and evaluation only achieve authority if there are common shared objectives and stakeholder interests between a range of parties: the learner, the teacher, the school, parents, community, employers and the wider society (Broadfoot, 1996). Although it is difficult to separate the introspective concerns of evaluation (looking inwards at teaching and learning) from its more extrinsic or contingent functions (the wider social purposes served by grades, examinations, testing and sorting), the field requires that the two foci are held in the same perspective. Whilst interpretation of the meaning of assessment and of course the purpose of qualifications and any kind of sorting by teachers and/or schools is varied, this same principle holds true for creative learning: developing evaluation is not just about procedural reform, it is about revisiting core ideas about judgement, authority and legitimacy.

The first part of the chapter outlines issues relating to evaluation in and across the Arts; it focuses especially on the development and practice of judgements as a particular feature of arts practice, before considering how changing economies of value – especially those associated with Web 2.0 and new kinds of connected learning – offer other kinds of authority and legitimacy to young people and schools. It then explores ideas about informal learning in and about music as another perspective that can show how innovative modes of evaluation strive to ensure legitimacy and authority in a more transparent and open era. In the final section, however, I suggest that these approaches need to be set against what is often regarded as a key virtue of creative learning – namely the production of certain kinds of sensibility or subjectivity – and that this later focus does not sit easily with the logic of the earlier parts of the chapter.

Judgement and the Arts

Ten years ago I was involved in a project that explored how – in what was mainly an English context – the different disciplines within the Arts approached issues of evaluation and assessment (Sefton-Green and Sinker, 2000). It examined common and different forms of evaluation that were mobilised across the Arts, from Drama, Visual Art, Design, Media Studies, Music and Creative Writing, in order to clear the ground for understanding how digital art and new and emerging forms of media might develop as a hybrid subject building on foundations supplied by discrete disciplines. Although, as we will see below, this ambition developed in unpredictable ways, and perhaps did not depend so much on arts disciplines as other commercial logics, the project raised a number of principles about evaluation within arts disciplines which I shall reprise here.

The first point derives from the work of Elliot Eisner (e.g. Eisner, 2004), who drew attention to how the processes of making judgements is central both to arts practice and art education. In a number of essays about arts and education, Eisner explicates how art education depends on various kinds of teaching about the judgement-making, both of students about themselves, and of teachers about students. He also argues that pedagogy and curriculum content depend on what he termed 'educational connoisseurship' (Eisner, 2004: 187). He is especially interested in developing theories of perception derived from practice in visual art interpretation (see Pringle, Chapter 25) to generate a deeper understanding of how judgements are made, sustained and applied in art and education contexts. Practising the making of judgements within the discipline leads to the acquisition of experience, expertise and ultimately authority, which then become a shared and wider social process.

Of course, this kind of disciplinary epistemology is practised in the Sciences and Humanities as well, albeit with different kinds of criteria about 'proof' and other forms of sceptical questioning about what constitutes evidence or facts. Eisner, however, makes a persuasive case that drawing attention to how judgements are constructed, interpreted and maintained through debate and consensus is peculiar to the Arts and thus, in essays like 'What education can learn from the arts' (Eisner, 2004: 187–208), argues that mainstream educational transactions, curriculum frameworks, school organisation and of course assessment procedures can learn from the Arts in terms of both content and underlying orientation. Key to this is the positioning of teachers as a professional community that make judgements possessing a wider social authority.

Eisner's attention to the processes of making judgements is important because he is seeking to find a different way of credentialising teacher-authority (in this case through the reference to the discipline of aesthetic scepticism) rather than simply to reify the authority of professionals. As Lucy Green argues, with reference to the work of Simon Frith on postmodernism, since we are living through an era where traditional authority is constantly under scrutiny and where commonly held values are continually questioned and contested, by definition the process of evaluation will need to become more transparent and to draw on a wider range of criteria than in the past (Green, 2000). We will see below how Green herself has taken up this challenge with reference to informal music-making.

Eisner himself is clear about his formation as a painter – hence perhaps the concern with perception; other disciplines bring other features of arts practice to the fore. Drama, Dance and Music, for example, focus on performance and on kinds of social or communal sharing. Understanding forms of making as embedded within different traditions of cultural production also draws attention to artisanal and generic features (Sefton-Green, 2000), which suggest a fairly consistent set of evaluation criteria that relate to the formal properties of a work. Yet, affect, emotion and mood are also key intra- and inter-personal criteria for evaluation in these contexts. In school an elaborate evaluation apparatus to distinguish process from product has been developed in these subjects, in order to draw attention towards these more subjective questions of learning. This often means finding ways to account for individual activity within a group setting (a vexed and problematic issue for assessment: see Neelands, Chapter 18). Despite such well-grounded counter-emphases, evaluation often seeks to account for itself as objective and disinterested. As I have described elsewhere, this sort of tension places stress on how the language of evaluation, with its rational, distanced repertoires, can achieve legitimacy in contexts from which it is often alien (Sefton-Green, 2000). An emphasis on talk, dialogue and the language of evaluation may often do no more than draw attention to the limits of evaluation rather than develop new practices; and in a social world where economies of value can be circulated with ease, this can lead to breakdown in the validity of evaluation procedures.

Web 2.0 and changing economies of value

Much of the social life lived by children and young people today does of course employ various kinds of evaluative procedures that have developed within what is known as Web 2.0 (that is, social networking and user-generated and community based participatory networks) and other dimensions of digital culture – especially those associated with gaming. Building on ideas developed further by Dezuanni and Jetnikoff (Chapter 28) and McDougall and Trotman (Chapter 29), this part of the chapter explores how these new economies of value impact on young people's understanding of meaning and authority and how they thus contribute to changing the debate about evaluation. The section also includes a consideration of how forms of multimodality – using video, text, audio and web based formats – may be expanding our ability to engage with young people in assessment contexts.

Much of the commentary about the take-up and diffusion of a range of Web 2.0 technologies has paid attention to how unmediated communication structured through open networks has allowed different and more 'democratic' forms of evaluation to circulate (Benkler, 2007; Zittrain, 2008). From studies about management of reputation systems (like Amazon ratings) to the negotiation of public opinion by citizen journalists (see Gillmor, 2006), the argument is that life online is constantly inflected by decision-making about value judgements. This principle has been expanded in a wide range of ways to include studies about the changing nature of knowledge itself (Poster, 1990); the structuring of peer review as a consequence of these changing relationships (Willinsky, 2006); and issues about the question of authority and verification in the Google era (Brabazon, 2008). In studies of gaming cultures scholars have examined the development of trust, opinion, friendship groups and authority (Gee, 2004; Shaffer, 2008; Ito *et al.*, 2010).

On this basis, which is further strengthened by the many interesting contributions to Burke and Hammett's (2009) collection, I am suggesting that these reconfigurations of authority, value systems and trust ask fundamental questions about the kind of evaluation paradigms we have encountered so far. They suggest that in their social lives, in leisure and in serious play, young people are encountering a different process of making judgements, one which is verified online, entails peer review, is open to scrutiny and is transparent. This, it is suggested, is or can be in conflict with the modality of judgement-making by an adult or teacher hierarchy – a conflict which and at times may lead to a breakdown in trust or a crisis of authority. Of course, however equal or seemingly 'just' such web-inspired mechanisms may be, it is not at all clear how they might relate to forms of assessment that facilitate transition into the labour market or to higher levels of education. Experimentations with portfolios and the use of peer reviews in higher education may suggest a way forward at school level.

Lissa Soep has written about a number of cases where she has been challenged as an educator and as a researcher by this slippage in value systems (Soep, 2010; Soep and Chavez, 2010). She describes, for instance, what happens when students she has written about as a researcher continue her discussion (unbeknown to her) through online engagements. As a teacher, albeit working in the non-formal education sector supporting young people making media, she describes how her 'authority' as an educator has be to set against other forms of approval and critique as her students and their work live on in what she describes as a digital afterlife. These dilemmas, she suggests, are emblematic of a reconfiguration of authority and of the process of judgement-making that young people now engage with, as well as their access to changing economies of value. Unless the curriculum offers ways of engaging with these new forms of meaning, schooling itself may undergo a crisis of authority.

As already noted, some interesting examples of these tensions are provided by Burke and Hammett (2009). Their book also raises a second, related question about assessment, namely how creative work produced in diverse media and in many variable formats may need responses in media that utilise other and possibly more appropriate forms of expression, beyond the written word. This raises complex challenges: responses to work may need to be 'multimodal', offered in aural, oral, visual and hyper-textual forms. Research may be in its infancy in this area but, as with the larger philosophical question about the challenges to authority systems and the need to preserve and develop trust, how we as classroom teachers develop appropriate forms of response will be a creative challenge.

Informal teaching and learning: making music

In recent years this interest in out-of-school judgements, authority crises and youth cultures has led to a more systematic theorisation of 'informal learning' (Sefton-Green, 2004). Although a difficult concept to pin down (Bekerman *et al.*, 2005; Drotner *et al.*, 2009), it offers a way of studying learning that happens out of school as a pedagogic process which can include forms of assessment and evaluation – albeit applied with different degrees of compliance than in formal schooled environments.

One of the most systematic enquires in this area can be found in Lucy Green's work for Musical Futures[4] (Green, 2008). Green aims to relate informal and out-of-school value systems to formal learning that incorporates a curriculum structured to enhance progression). At the same time, she seeks to integrate informal and formal languages of value and learning. In earlier work Green used ethnographic research to explore the distinctive ways in which popular musicians learn to play and perform (Green, 2002). She argues that the dimensions of musicality, listening, appreciating, performing, as well the informal ways in which we learn to understand more formal concepts like pitch or tone, all depend on processes of judgement-making, reflection and evaluation by ourselves with peers and in wider musical communities.

In the Musical Futures work, Green considers how:

> pedagogy in the music classroom could draw upon the world of informal music learning practices outside the school, in order to recognise, foster and reward a range of musical skills and knowledge that have not previously been emphasised in music education.
>
> *(Green, 2008: 1)*

We will look at a few such practices below, especially as where they draw on the uses of informal, peer and self-evaluation. It is worthwhile emphasising before that, in line with the arguments advanced by Soep and others above, and also with reference to comments about authority crises, how Green situates her argument. The key aim of Musical Futures is to demonstrate, by using other and different evaluative criteria, how pedagogy and curriculum can be more productively reframed in schools. For Green and others this is especially acute in relation to Music – possibly the affective domain most enjoyed and valued by students and yet one of the least successful of school subjects.

In Chapter 4 of her book *Music, Informal Learning and the School: A New Classroom Pedagogy* (Green, 2008), Green explores the processes of listening and appreciating. She examines the relationship between musical vocabulary and listening, showing how it is difficult to make sense of pupil's listening without using the formal evaluative language of Music, yet in applying such judgements we run the risk of 'missing' other ways in which understanding is manifested and made meaningful to listeners. Green writes:

> Ideally, the acquisition of technical terms through informal learning would develop over years within the school environment. On one hand, it would replicate the ways that young popular musicians outside schools gradually pick up conventional terms and technical knowledge through use and experience.
>
> *(Green, 2008: 70)*

Green then seeks to develop through an action research project a curriculum and a pedagogy that build on these insights, suggesting that 'it would also develop through integration and cross-fertilisation with more formal approaches' (ibid.: 70).

She then applies this principle to the challenge of defining appreciation – a part of formal Music education that is often bound up in judgements about class, elite status and exclusivity. She argues that if we change the kind of values and judgement we impose on students, so as to support an emergent dialogue between in- and out-of-school tastes, musical forms, genres and the wider musical culture, then music education itself will be vastly improved:

> Through informal, aural learning involving their own choice of music, pupils seem to be in a better position to make more informed judgements about the quality of performances, of compositional input and of musical products themselves. ... They are, by the same token, a little better placed to discriminate and recognise those musicians whose performance, improvisational or compositional skills are justifiably held to be above the norm as a result of technical and/or musicianly qualities. Rather than 'dumbing down' or pandering to pupils' existing levels of knowledge by allowing them to bring their own music into the classroom, I would suggest, informal learning practices that require them to listen purposively to the music and copy it as music-makers, are more likely to raise their heads, and help them to develop a more critically aware musicality.
>
> (Green, 2008: 84)

It may be that Music comprises a peculiar case study: no other discipline has such elaborated and complex social practices existing in young peoples' lives and yet such a 'problematic' academic apparatus in schools. More systematic comparison of curriculum subjects and investigation of informal learning domains need to be conducted to explore this. Nevertheless, Green's work points productively to a series of challenges: of redefining who evaluates what kind of knowledge; of problematising how language is used in evaluation; of challenging whose language of taste and understanding is being legitimated in the evaluation process, and whose judgements are presumed to carry more weight than others; and of integrating the results of such explorations into a project of re-creating curriculum and pedagogy.

Creative people

Whilst all three sections so far offer positive and sensible ways of reconciling tensions arising out of lived experiences and current practices, such approaches avoid a critical engagement with the broader social and ideological implications of creative learning, and in particular with the possibility that creative learning offers a quality of education designed to promote and even construct a certain type of person or a certain kind of subjectivity, so that its focus is less on the intrinsic value of developing certain kinds of ability than on the production of normative (employable) behaviours.[5]

Nowhere is this more evident than in discussion about the place of evaluation in developing forms of behaviour, sensibility, attitude and other notions of intra-personal attributes. Although there is no doubt that 'hard' outcomes from education – that is to say, qualifications – are 'necessary' criteria for entry into work and act as a key sorting mechanism, allocating roles to young people as they enter the labour force, they are in and of themselves not always deemed sufficient as a way of judging employability. Indeed, from the middle of the 1990s there have been attempts by employers' pressure groups and educational policy-makers to recognise that 'soft skills' are crucial and play a complementary role to qualifications in determining success at interview and at work. There is a case to answer here: while there are important differences between discussions of soft skills and creative learning, there are key overlaps, especially around a shared emphasis on collaboration and teamwork, negotiation skills, problem solving and communicating and making presentations.

Many arts education practices offer ways of developing the presentation of the self as part of their subject-discipline, and espouse presentational and performance skills. However, the current policy trend towards making a certain kind of behaviour the desired outcome of education and towards relating such behaviour quite specifically to employability and contemporary trends in labour force needs is something new, as is the suggestion that the Arts contribute to the evolution of a distinct and valuable identity. A recent OECD study (Dumont *et al.*, 2010) has elaborated on this suggestion, describing what are ultimately the intra-personal qualities of the new learner. This includes the capacity to self-regulate, to work in teams, to negotiate, to work co-operatively and within communities, and finally to be able to present oneself confidently. These are all attributes associated with the production of certain kinds of subjectivity (Rose, 1999), which in turn require new kinds of schooling.

Being creative is integral to this approach: indeed, these kinds of behaviours are seen as part and parcel of what it means to be a creative person. Recent surveys of the UK labour force show that arts graduates do in fact appear to utilise these kinds of skill across a wide gamut of employment opportunities, as can be seen from the UK graduate careers website.[6] In England again, adaptability and creativity have come to be highly valued[7]: these abilities lie at the heart of a modern or contemporary skillset. Indeed, it is clear that many descriptions of the outputs of education now attribute value to such behaviours and personality attributes – and have been forcefully criticised for doing so (Ecclestone and Hayes, 2008). The Qualifications and Curriculum Authority's (QCA) 2008 review of curriculum models talked of 'successful learners who (amongst others things) are creative, resourceful and able to identify and solve problems'.[8] Overall, attention is focused on producing a certain type of person, who possesses personal 'attitudes and attributes', who is 'confident' and 'successful'.[9] This is one of the most explicit attempts to reshape curriculum and assessment around the making of a certain kind of creative self, which highlights what has always tended to be regarded as part of the 'hidden curriculum' (Walkerdine and Lucey, 1989), and which raises ethical questions about identity, socialisation and how our subjectivities are formed. We should also note how these forms of creative behaviour are bound up with certain class-bound ways of behaving: maybe talking about creative behaviour is no more than a cipher for talking about certain kinds of middle-class attributes.

Conclusion

This chapter has attempted to explore forms of evaluation that are being developed at the edges of current practice. It has tried to show how key principles about judgement and authority that arise from the practices of arts education are developed and modulated in out-of-school cultures and in informal learning. The key argument is that forms of 'creative evaluation' and 'evaluation or assessment for creativity' need to be situated in a different set of power relations than those that traditionally pertain in relation to the curriculum. I suggest that conflicts over authority in relation to access to knowledge and its meaning are only going to become more likely as the boundaries around curriculum become less insulated from contamination and challenge. I go on to argue that these arguments overlap with others, in which creative learning is understood as part of a new regime of subjectivity, where schooling is more concerned with the production of certain types of 'person-hood' than simply the transmission of knowledge, and where thinking about the complexities of assessment takes another form.

The European Union project mentioned in the opening paragraphs of this chapter[10] encapsulates these tensions, and in some sense resolves them. It was interested in the idea of developing a way of measuring and evaluating creativity as part of a wider project to capacity build for economic competitiveness. Many of the contributors to that project were sceptical both about the ability to develop meaningful metrics and, secondly, about the value of any such comparative international process. In some ways, these criticisms were underpinned by Eisner's exploration of judgement and the same mindset about how arts practices develop qualities of scepticism and interpretation. This logic supports the principle that developing creative learning will emerge through trust, from an informed understanding of the kinds of innovative practices that are transforming young people's lives. And that only by being transparent about the question of authority can we really develop challenging, new and credible way to use evaluation to support learning in proper, valid and legitimate ways.

Notes

1 In the US, assessment tends to be used as the preferred term to describe the processes of critiquing and commenting on young people's work, whilst evaluation is used to describe the process of grading. In contrast, evaluation tends to be used in the UK to describe the range of 'softer' processes relating to opinion or improvement. In the UK, assessment is often uses to describe terminal examinations and sometimes is akin to grading. These are not hard and fast definitions and often are used loosely and informally in a range of contexts. For the purpose of this chapter I will be mainly using the term evaluation.
2 See the contributions to http://ec.europa.eu/education/lifelong-learning-policy/doc2082_en.htm (accessed November 2010).
3 http://ec.europa.eu/education/lifelong-learning-policy/doc2082_en.htm (accessed November 2010).
4 http://www.musicalfutures.org/.
5 For an extended discussion about the creative labour force, see Oakley, 2009.
6 http://www.prospects.ac.uk/cms/ShowPage/Home_page/What_do_graduates_do–2005/Arts–creative_arts–humanities_editorial/p!ecdXejg.
7 http://www.nesta.org.uk/the-hard-sell-for-soft-skills/ (accessed January 2010).
8 http://www.qca.org.uk/libraryAssets/media/Big_Picture_2008.pdf (accessed January 2010).
9 http://www.qca.org.uk/libraryAssets/media/Big_Picture_2008.pdf (accessed January 2010).
10 http://ec.europa.eu/education/lifelong-learning-policy/doc2082_en.htm (accessed November 2010).

References

Bekerman, Z., Burbules, N. C., Keller, D. S. and Silberman-Keller, D. (2005) *Learning in Places: The Informal Education Reader*, Counterpoints: Studies in the Postmodern Theory of Education, New York: Peter Lang.
Benkler, Y. (2007) *The Wealth of Networks: How Social Production Transforms Markets and Freedom*, New Haven, CT: Yale University Press.
Black, P., Harrison, C., Lee, C., Marshall, B. and Wiliam, D. (2003) *Assessment for Learning: Putting It into Practice*, Milton Keynes: Open University Press.
Brabazon, T. (2008) *The Revolution Will Not Be Downloaded*, Oxford: Chandos Publishing.
Broadfoot, P. (1996) *Education, Assessment and Society: A Sociological Analysis*, Assessing Assessment, Milton Keynes: Open University Press.
Burke, A. and Hammett, R. (2009) *Assessing New Literacies: Perspectives from the Classroom*, New York: Peter Lang.
Drotner, K., Jensen, H. S. and Schroder, K. C. (eds) (2009) *Informal Learning and Digital Media*, Cambridge: Cambridge Scholars Press.
Dumont, H., Istance, D. and Benavides, F. (eds) (2010) *The Nature of Learning: Using Research to Inspire Practice*, Paris: OECD.
Ecclestone, K. and Hayes, D. (2008) *The Dangerous Rise of Therapeutic Education*, London: Routledge.
Eisner, E. W. (2004) *The Arts and the Creation of Mind*, New Haven, CT: Yale University Press.

Ellis, S. and Barrs, M. (2008) The assessment of creative learning, in J. Sefton-Green (ed.) *Creative Learning*, London: Arts Council of England.

Gardner, J. R. (2006) *Assessment and Learning: Theory, Policy and Practice*, London: Sage.

Gee, J. P. (2004) *What Video Games Have to Teach Us about Learning and Literacy*, New York: Palgrave Macmillan.

Gillmor, D. (2006) *We the Media: Grassroots Journalism by the People, for the People*, Sebastopol, CA: O'Reilly Media, Inc.

Green, L. (2000) Music as a media art: evaluation and assessment in the contemporary classroom, in J. Sefton-Green and R. Sinker (eds) *Evaluating Creativity Making and Learning by Young People*, London: Routledge.

—— (2002) *How Popular Musicians Learn: A Way Ahead for Music Education*, Ashgate Popular & Folk Music, Aldershot: Ashgate.

—— (2008) *Music, Informal Learning and the School: A New Classroom Pedagogy*, Aldershot: Ashgate.

Ito, M., Baumer, S., Bittanti, M., boyd, d., Cody, R., Herr-Stephenson, B. *et al.* (2010) *Hanging Out, Messing Around, and Geeking Out: Kids Living and Learning with New Media*, John D. and Catherine T. MacArthur Foundation Series on Digital Media and Learning, Cambridge, MA: The MIT Press.

McWilliam, E. and Haukka, S. (2008) Educating the creative workforce: new directions for twenty-first century schooling, *British Educational Research Journal* 34(5): 651–66.

Oakley, K. (2009) *'Art Works' – Cultural Labour Markets: A Literature Review*, London: Creativity, Culture and Education; available at http://www.creativitycultureeducation.org/data/files/cce-lit-review-8-a5-web-130.pdf (accessed November 2010).

Poster, M. (1990) *The Mode of Information: Post-Structuralism and Social Contexts*, Cambridge: Polity Press.

Rose, N. (1999) *Governing the Soul: Shaping of the Private Self*, Sidmouth: Free Association Books.

Runco, M. A. (2007) *Creativity: Theories and Themes: Research, Development, and Practice*, San Diego, CA: Academic Press.

Runco, M. A., Cayirdag, N. and Acar, S. (2010) Quantitative research on creativity, in P. Thomson and J. Sefton-Green (eds) *Researching Creative Learning: Methods and Issues*, London: Routledge.

Sefton-Green, J. (2000) From creativity to cultural production; shared perspectives, in J. Sefton-Green and R. Sinker (eds) *Evaluating Creativity Making and Learning by Young People*, London: Routledge.

—— (2004) *Literature Review in Informal Learning with Technology Outside School*, Bristol: Futurelab; available at http://www.futurelab.org.uk/download/pdfs/research/lit_reviews/Outside_Learning_Review.pdf.

Sefton-Green, J. and Sinker, R. (2000) *Evaluating Creativity Making and Learning by Young People*, London: Routledge.

Shaffer, D. (2008) *How Computer Games Help Children Learn*, New York: Palgrave Macmillan.

Soep, E. (2010) Research methods for web two dot whoah, in P. Thomson and J. Sefton-Green (eds) *Researching Creative Learning: Methods and Issues*, London: Routledge.

Soep, E. and Chavez, V. (2010) *Drop that Knowledge: Youth Radio Stories*, Berkeley: University of California Press.

Walkerdine, V. and Lucey, H. (1989) *Democracy in the Kitchen: Regulating Mothers and Socializing Daughters*, London: Virago Press Ltd.

Wassermann, S. (1992) Serious play in the classroom: how messing around can win you the Nobel Prize, *Childhood Education* 68: 133–9.

Willinsky, J. (2006) *The Access Principle: The Case for Open Access to Research & Scholarship*, Cambridge, MA: The MIT Press.

Zittrain, J. (2008) *The Future of the Internet: And How to Stop It*. London: Allen Lane.

34

Creative learning

Grant Wiggins

Creative Learning is not simply about Arts-based learning or even the development of individual creativity but describes a range of processes and practices aiming to make learning at individual, classroom and whole school levels more creative in an effort to fully realise young people's potential.

(from the prospectus for this volume)

The best writing is vigorous, committed, honest, and interesting.

(*English for ages 5 to 16*, National Curriculum, United Kingdom)

What is know-how in mathematics? The ability to solve problems—not merely routine problems but problems requiring some degree of independence, judgment, originality, creativity.

(Polya, 1957: xi)

A key goal of Coach Wooden was the development of players who were creative, confident problem-solvers. He taught that it is the opponents that determine a team's responses ... Coach Wooden wanted "to be as surprised as our opponent at what my team came up with when confronted with an unexpected challenge."

(Sven Nater, a former player for Coach Wooden; quoted in Nater and Gallimore, 2005: 90)

As the editors of this volume note, it is all too easy in a discussion of creative learning to put the accent on only the first word—creative—in the phrase at the heart of this book. So, countless reformers have written about how to make students more creative and why it matters. But I propose here that we will not be much closer to better schooling until we focus on the phrase in its entirety, with each term accented equally. Until and unless the student is provided with an education in *every* subject that demands *creative learning*, school will continue to be uninteresting and ineffective for the majority of students.

My thesis presumes a rude fact: education as it is typically framed and experienced by students worldwide rarely demands much "creative learning" at all. On the contrary, success in school requires neither a *creative* response from students nor genuine *learning*—if by "genuine learning" we mean thoughtful understanding and effective transfer, as I have proposed we should define it (see http://www.grantwiggins.org/ubd/ubd.lasso; Wiggins and McTighe,

2008). From the distant past until the present, students have needed only to attend to their lessons. And as long as lessons merely require dutiful acquisition of isolated content given back on exams, instead of creative (and critical) thought, then the work of school reformers is in vain.

Nor is dreary conventional schooling solved by courses in the arts or by the infusion of various projects. Because even such additions remain add-ons with little effect on how the core curriculum is taught and learned. As long as teaching amounts to professing, and learning amounts to studying for recall, then creative learning is moot or a frill.

As I see it, then, *creative learning* is thus opposed to "boring learning" and "unfruitful learning." As the opening quotations suggest, whether the subject is geometry or basketball, creative thought is only awakened (and true engagement engendered) when student thought is constantly demanded by the work, i.e. when we are faced by genuine problems (as opposed to simplistic exercises). Penetrating another team's good defense requires creative and effective thought; so, too, with genuine mathematical problem-solving; so, too with addressing complex scenarios in history or foreign culture.

Though we often puzzle and argue over the psychology and sociology of creativity, the goal itself seems reasonably clear to me. A "creative" result is by definition a novel, fresh, and atypically helpful way of looking at things and addressing challenges. The creative is contrasted with the unimaginative, the routine, the clichéd, the boring, the ineffective. In a summary of the literature on creative thinking, Todd Lubart (1994: 290) reminds us that various researchers on creativity have defined it as "the ability to produce work that is novel and appropriate." That gets it just right, I think: being *merely* imaginative, offbeat, or inquisitive may be delightful but as educators we should not regard it as sufficient for us to say that creative *learning* has occurred. We mustn't conflate "creative learning" with mere "creativity" or creative potential, then. Based on instruction a learner may offer wonderfully interesting ideas, but that doesn't mean she has really learned anything that can be transferred to future endeavors. There has to be an "appropriate" *impact*—whether in joke telling, fine art, philosophy, engineering, or athletics. Creative learning manifests itself only in creative effects. I have learned something when I can offer something to others; when I see it and use it to make a difference. I have only had a creative learning experience when I later use my repertoire to become more clever and effective (think of the best football players on the soccer pitch, the best architects, the best legislators, the best musical conductors, etc.).

There is a vital educational implication of this view of creative learning. It is pointless to talk about genius. Only rarely in history has profound impact come on the first try. All great work involves getting and using feedback, many times, to achieve creative work: talent is *overrated*, in the words of a recent summary of the literature (Colvin, 2008). Mozart and the Beatles put in their 10,000 hours. Attention to what works and what doesn't work, and deliberate and persistent action based on those observations ultimately determines whether we are creative learners— whether in refining jokes so that everyone laughs or in solving abstruse scientific problems.

This is not as far-fetched as it may initially sound. The research on the power of formative assessment makes this very point: More feedback (and thus less teaching) yields optimal results (Hattie, 2008). In fact, as video games so clearly illustrate, creative learning demands very little "teaching" as long as there are clear challenges, good feedback, and choices for the learner to make. (Most games provide no direct instruction; people still learn and act creatively.)

But how will *anyone* learn creatively, then, if the typical teacher talks too much and the typical curriculum just marches on and on, covering each topic only once and without providing choice or challenge requiring judgment? In short, the word "learning" may ironically need *more* unpacking than the word "creative" since we have become dulled by the familiarity of typical instruction which stifles creative work.

The point of school is not to acquire stuff or get good at school. The aim, broadly speaking, is to help students make sense of experience and transfer their understandings, knowledge and skill in *future* settings. Creative learning is only elicited and developed when the learner is confronted with one novel challenge after another, interspersed with feedback and focused direct instruction. We thus aren't (yet) "really learning" when in the phase of direct instruction we merely take in what teachers and texts say and plug back into an exercise what they just taught us. We are only truly "learning" when we try to apply (and make sense of that using) what was taught. In this way, academic work is really no different from guitar or hockey: We haven't begun learning unless we *play*. We haven't truly been effective at our learning until we have *worked* at the playing so that we have become highly skilled and highly creative in using our skill.

The need for a modern approach to curriculum

A curriculum in the root sense of the word is a "course to be run." But is this a course with a destination or just an endless march to nowhere? We have up until now unfortunately defined curriculum as a slog through discrete topics followed by quizzes and exams on that content. Such a curriculum is literally pointless. There can never be creative learning in such a system. Why? Because all one is required to do as a learner is "learn" what was "taught," where what is taught is content out of context. With no external goal or destination to supply meaning and context, there is no purpose. This is hardly a new idea: Tyler said it clearly and plainly over 70 years ago (Tyler 1949: 45–60). Whitehead decried the resultant inertness of learning 100 years ago. We keep losing sight of this basic principle: that a curriculum requires a purpose external to the content by which the content is selected, prioritized, sequenced, and evaluated. It is that external performance-based purpose that gives rise to the need for creative learning.

An appropriate and modern education, for example, would focus on the goal of transfer in an ever-changing world. Creativity is required in all acts of transfer since we must always adapt or innovate in some fashion to apply prior learning to new circumstances. Such an education is modern because it honors the fact that we need to be ready for an ever-changing world. Pre-modern learning, by contrast, assumes that successful learning need only be about recall of lessons in a fixed world of verities.

Creative learning thus requires the right kind of curriculum. It depends upon establishing the tasks, conditions, and sequence necessary for students to learn to use content creatively. This is a curricular problem, not a "teaching" problem per se. For, unless the curriculum and assessments first make utterly clear to students and teachers alike that merely learning stuff is not the point, there is little hope of teaching and learning being infused with creative work. Rather, curriculum must be designed to ensure that content is treated as a means, where students have ample opportunity to use it creatively, reflect on their attempts to do so, and have opportunities to make adjustments based on such feedback.

Note that my critique of curriculum has less to do with what content we choose to teach and more with how we frame the learning of content in instructional activities and assessments aiming at transfer. Curriculum writers have to be more like video game designers than textbook writers. Yes, of course, there are lessons to be learned. But those lessons are necessary yet not sufficient—just as soccer drills are necessary but not sufficient to cause excellent play in the game. The question is: What are the best ways to learn them so that creative (and critical) thinking are elicited and required, not peripheral or optional, in instruction and assessment?

Thus, proper curricula develop learning environments and instruction that demand clever use of content by students as an outcome.

By extension, it won't do for teachers to say (as they now routinely say), "Oh, but there is no time to dwell on this recent attempt at transfer and improve it based on feedback; we must move on; there is so much ground to cover." In a modern education we do not say such a silly thing. That's like saying that there is no time to play more football games because there is so much content still to learn. Learning for transfer means that success *only* comes from refining the key performances (i.e. the use of key content) based on feedback and guidance. To press on before learners have learned from feedback is to bypass learning in the name of "coverage." And then creative learning is made impossible.

Secondary math as a painful example of the problem

I will remind readers of arguably the most dreadfully taught subjects in the curriculum to make the point more concrete: secondary-level mathematics. Algebra, geometry, and calculus as currently taught are surely among the most poorly learned subjects in the K–12 curricular pantheon—*despite* their importance. My view is not overstated: Trends in International Mathematics and Science Study (TIMSS) and Programme for International Student Assessment (PISA) results, state assessments in the United States for many years, studies of student engagement, inspection of any high school math class, and surveys of the average high school student make clear that math is boring or at least irrelevant for the great majority of adolescents in the world. By any fair, reasonable, and dispassionate measure, math teachers are simply failing at their job of getting a critical mass of students competent in mathematics beyond those already good at and interested in it.

But why would anyone be surprised by this if they were to closely examine typical curriculum, instruction, and assessments? The day-in and day-out work fails to meet the most basic conditions of intellectual engagement. Little or no creative learning is required by the way math is taught and assessed in secondary schools. Students confront isolated and artificial topics and exercises, and the larger meaning remains an eternal mystery as the coverage unfolds bit by isolated bit with no larger picture or purpose in view.

It need not be so, of course. Mathematics is neither inherently boring nor pointless. Nor must one sacrifice core content in mathematics to make the learning creative. How, then, is curricular transformation made in which content is *not* sacrificed and yet creative learning *is* required, elicited, and yielded? That is the design challenge in curriculum and assessment.

The Polya quotation at the head of this chapter (p. 316) provides the clue. Until and unless the curriculum is framed around genuine *problems* demanding creative response there is obviously no need for creative learning on the part of students (or creative teaching on the part of teachers).

Polya's work is surprisingly little known by mathematics teachers in schools now, though his message is at the heart of all math reform agendas. His aim was to assist high school and college teachers in coaching problem-solving—the aim of mathematics as stated in all standards documents:

> What is know-how in mathematics? The ability to solve problems—not merely *routine* problems but *problems requiring some degree of independence, judgment, originality, creativity*.

Seems obvious—but, alas, herein lies a key long-time oversight. Most teachers do not carefully distinguish a problem from an exercise:

An exercise is a question that tests the student's mastery of a narrowly focused technique, usually one that was recently "covered". Exercises may be hard or easy but they are never puzzling ... the path toward the solution is always apparent. A problem, is a question that cannot be answered immediately. Problems are often open-ended, paradoxical and require investigation before one can come to a solution. Problems and problem solving are at the heart of mathematics. Research mathematicians do nothing but open-ended problem solving.

(Zeitz, 1999: ix)

Yet, though countless books have been devoted to mathematical problem-solving, in them we often get no clear definition of what a real problem is and isn't.[1] Authors presumably assume that it is obvious what a "problem" is.

Alas, as any thorough inspection of secondary school mathematics classes and tests shows, that presumption is problematic. Most math assessments and assignments involve relatively simple exercises and always have (see, for example, Archbald and Grant, 2000).

The point is generalizable. Socratic Seminar, working with primary source texts and artifacts in history, playing football well as a team or developing a jazz guitar solo elicits creative learning because thoughtfulness is demanded by the task. And that is of course why law, medicine, engineering, and business have moved to problem-based learning as a key design approach. Yet it is still rare to find such pedagogies in school.

I know from painful experience that this reasoning often falls on deaf ears. As noted above, we can expect to hear: "Grant, this is all well and good, but the state/provincial/national tests demand that we focus on low-level algorithms and facts. There is no time for real problem-solving and it won't pay off on test day." Most teachers I have interviewed think this is the source of our problem: They think they know what real problems or creative learning experiences are but they cannot focus on them for test-related reasons.

This plausible claim turns out to be incorrect, despite conventional wisdom. A close look at the released items from states that release their entire tests and provide item analysis for each question suggests that conventional wisdom is mistaken, as I have elsewhere argued (Wiggins, 2010). There are numerous higher-order questions on all tests; disappointingly low performance results on such inferential questions are the norm.

So, what must we see more of in school? Real problems, of course. Let me share some. The first three problems sketched below involve applied mathematics and the remainder involve pure or mixed mathematics:

- What's the price point for maximal sales and profit of homemade sugar cookies at a Varsity basketball game?
- How much available landfill volume is needed to handle the waste generated each year by our school? How much needlessly clean water is used for flushing toilets in our school—and what might be other viable solutions for using "gray" water?
- What's the fairest way to rank-order teams where many don't directly play one other (e.g. national college basketball during the season)?
- Among grandfather's papers a bill was found: 72 turkeys $_67.9_ The first and last digit of the number that obviously represented the total price of those fowls are replaced here by blanks, for they are faded and are now illegible. What are the two faded digits and what was the price of one turkey?
- The length of the perimeter of a right triangle is 60 inches and the length of the altitude perpendicular to the hypotenuse is 12 inches. Find the sides of the triangle.

- A train is leaving in 11 minutes and you are one mile from the station. Assuming you can walk at 4 mph and run at 8 mph, how much time can you afford to walk before you must begin to run in order to catch the train?
- Pick any number. Add 4 to it and then double your answer. Now subtract 6 from that result and divide your new answer by 2. Write down your answer. Repeat these steps with another number. Continue with a few more numbers, comparing your final answer with your original number. Is there a pattern to your answers? Can you prove it?

You might not love all seven of these, but they surely fit the criteria of real problems reasonably well. The solution path is neither stated nor painfully obvious; there is a bit of a puzzle in each one (usually in terms of implicit assumptions and unobvious solution paths); some seem unsolvable at first glance; and the solution will depend upon some mucking around as well as the development of and careful testing of a strategy. Most importantly for our discussion, creative learning is needed in all real problem-solving.

Where are these problems from? The middle two examples come from the famous Stanford University Competitive Mathematics Examination for high school students, developed by our heuristics mentor, the author of *How to Solve It*—Georg Polya (Polya and Kilpatrick, 1974).

The last two problems are noteworthy for a different reason. They are excerpted from the published problem sets given to all 9th grade math students at Phillips Exeter Academy, one of the top private schools in the United States. Math class at Exeter is entirely problem based. Students are given these problem sets each week, and homework consists in being prepared to offer your approach and solutions (or difficulties) in class the next day. In short, Exeter takes it as a given that the point of math class is to learn to solve problems. Content lessons often follow upon the attempts to solve them rather than always preceding them.

Their detailed departmental mission statement makes their aim and methods clear:

The goal of the Mathematics Department is that all of our students understand and appreciate the mathematics they are studying; that they can read it, write it, explore it, and communicate it with confidence; and that they will be able to use mathematics as they need to in their lives.

We believe that problem solving (investigating, conjecturing, predicting, analyzing, and verifying), followed by a well-reasoned presentation of results, is central to the process of learning mathematics, and that this learning happens most effectively in a cooperative, student-centered classroom ...

To implement this educational philosophy, members of the PEA Mathematics Department have composed problems for nearly every course that we offer. The problems require that students read carefully, as all pertinent information is contained within the text of the problems themselves—there is no external annotation. The resulting curriculum is problem-centered rather than topic-centered. The purpose of this format is to have students continually encounter mathematics set in meaningful contexts, enabling them to draw, and then verify, their own conclusions ...

The goal is that the students, not the teacher or a textbook, be the source of mathematical knowledge.[2]

Once you see what Exeter is doing, you cannot help but wonder about the problem of non-problems in math class—especially since this is what a student can expect in all serious college math (and science) courses.

Until and unless all mathematics courses and (especially) assessments are built backwards from problems, and until such problems are constructed *before* the lessons are planned, we should not be surprised by frustratingly inadequate student achievement on challenging tests.[3]

The drill vs. the game: the problem of transfer

Transfer does not occur by mere practice and recall of discrete techniques. It requires judgment in context—hence, adaptation that requires "novel and appropriate" responses. Consider "playing the game" of math. The typical math experience is more like sideline drill work than the game of endless strategizing and problem-solving. Students are learning content but not learning how to transfer content to new, unfamiliar and unending problems that happen in real play.[4]

A true story from my soccer coaching days illustrates the problem of transfer nicely. We had been working hard in practice on drills related to creating space to make ball advancement and scoring threats more likely. But in the next game, none of what we had worked on was being transferred. I grew frustrated, especially at my captain, and yelled: "Liz!! All the things we worked on all week!" She yelled back, in the middle of the game: "I would, Mr. Wiggins, but the other team isn't lining up the way we did the drills!" As we know from the research, and as I saw painfully on the soccer field, transfer is unlikely through just a steady dose of repetitive drills.[5]

That's arguably the problem of secondary math education in a nutshell.[6] If teachers were to more fully grasp that the goal of "problem-solving" is really a sub-set of the goal of transfer, they would more likely see that their creativity-deadening regimen of only discrete exercises is inherently incapable of causing transfer of learning. Anecdotally, I can report that this is highly useful construct in changing teacher beliefs. Once we ask them to frame teaching as the challenge of teaching for transfer, most teachers instantly see that many of their most frustrating experiences involve students' failure to transfer their learning. And they more easily see that typical instructional and assessment approaches will not yield such transfer.

Transfer is of course notoriously difficult to achieve, as researchers from 100 years ago to the present have reminded us (for a summary of the research on transfer, see Committee on Developments ... , 2001: ch. 3). What we *do* know is that transfer requires ideas to facilitate pattern recognition, and varied contexts (all of which demands creative learning):

> Students develop flexible understanding of when, where, why, and how to use their knowledge to solve new problems if they [are instructed in] how to extract underlying themes and principles from their learning exercises. ... Research has indicated that transfer across contexts is especially difficult when a subject is taught only in a single context rather than in multiple contexts. ... When a subject is taught in multiple contexts, and includes examples that demonstrate wide application of what is being taught, people are more likely to abstract the relevant features of concepts and to develop a flexible representation of knowledge.
>
> *(Committee on Developments ... , 2001: 236, 62)*

The Exeter approach in mathematics can thus be understood as the transfer of the idea of games and scrimmages to mathematics: each of the many problem sets (and which notably have recurring types of problems in different guises over time) is just practice in transfer and on-field problem-solving in which players not only use a repertoire but develop the needed self-assessment skills for later tests of problem-solving.

Curricular sequence

In creative learning, important and complex tasks recur: that is another curricular lesson from sports and athletics. It follows that the sequence of learning must change from what has been done for centuries in writing and implementing curricula. The direction of traditional courses unfolds in the same unfortunate way: *first* you acquire all the knowledge and skill in the subject, and only *then* do you get to make personal sense of it and transfer it. This makes no pedagogical sense *if* the long-term goal is creative and effective transfer of learning. Rather, we must from the start practice "playing the game" while *simultaneously* acquiring basic knowledge and skill. Think about how musicians, artists, athletes, lawyers, and teachers actually learn their craft from the very beginning: a constant movement back and forth between learning content and applying it; between the drill and the game; between exercises and performance challenges and problems; between theory and practice; etc.

As Dewey noted long ago, the typical curricular sequence confuses the logic of the *content* with the natural flow for the learner of mastering new learning—what Dewey called a confusion between the "logical" and "psychological" approach to design. This "logical" march through topics inhibits understanding as well as creative work. One need only do as one is told: "Yours is not to reason why, yours is but to cross multiply." The derisive term in both math and science for the learning is "plug and chug"—just follow the rules. It is uncreative, undemocratic, and pedagogically ineffective.

What follows, then, generally for reform of curriculum frameworks and sequence—in math and elsewhere? The answer should be clearer: the curriculum should be framed and organized by recurring and increasingly demanding questions and problems, not topics and exercises; by real-world performance demands, not discrete skills; around the game, not the drills; around transfer, not inert abstractions. You must therefore practice and improve at solving problems—in the broadest sense—from the start and throughout your education—if you are to be prepared to use your education creatively and effectively in the future.

In the current era we also now better understand scientifically what heretofore has been stated just through allegory and metaphor. *Only* the learner can cause this learning; the teacher can only design a learning environment, facilitate meaning-making, and offer some lessons. The learner must construct, test, and often rethink all their learning in order to *really* learn it. Teaching does not cause genuine understanding, as Socrates pointedly notes in his summary of the Allegory of the Cave; the goal is to turn the mind, to awaken thought.

Here's the rub, also clear from Plato's Allegory onward: the learner typically resists creative learning. We all too easily remain content with our current meanings and abilities. (This is perhaps more true of teachers than students, an irony also addressed in Plato's Dialogues.) *All* creative work is destructive work, to put it in terms of our topic. We destroy traditions, habitual ways of seeing, icons, and unexamined ideas of others and in ourselves when we create something new. Genuine art, thought, actions are threatening. We destroy one world view to make another enticing or at least interesting. We eradicate old and trusted habits of performance to advance to higher levels of performance—in science as well as soccer.

Furthermore, we now also know from research just how little learners are blank slates. They bring important preconceptions (and misconceptions) to their work—habits of mind that are not changed by new knowledge alone and that impede transfer. We know, too, that learning to overcome dead-ends in our attempts to learn and understand requires skilled metacognition: recognizing what "moves" are and aren't called for here, in this context; knowing what to try when you get stuck; knowing how to self-monitor our ongoing learning and performance, and adjusting, as needed, on the basis of self-assessment and feedback. (Note Sven

Nater's description at the outset (p. 320) of Coach John Wooden's approach to the challenge of handling opponents.)

Feedback and its use

Great creative works, in other words, be they practical, aesthetic, or conceptual, are only achieved through *significant* amounts of assessments and adjustments en route on recurring challenges, in the face of obstacles, counter-arguments, counter-evidence, hostile reactions, etc. Yet, what curriculum today is adequately planned to leave room for such iteration of trials, errors, and insights in trying to use core content?

Consider the implications of looking primarily at the impact of learning rather than just the accuracy of recall on discrete knowledge and skill questions in student assessment: Did the performance *work*? Was the purpose *achieved*—even if in an unorthodox or unexpected manner? Creativity can only be evoked and developed if we assess for such impact. "We care less about how you get there, but get there—*wow us* with your results!" is the spirit of creative learning for "novel and appropriate" impact. Scoring criteria and rubrics must hammer the aim home. The point of performance assessment is not to have students merely emulate the form and content of past performances and performers, but to emulate the best *effects*, e.g. the ability to persuade an audience, satisfy a client request, or solve a problem. Otherwise we *do* stifle performance crea-tivity. Alas, too many current writing rubrics, for example, *do* run the risk of undercutting good writing when they score only for focus, organization, style, and mechanics—without once asking judges to consider whether the writing is powerful, memorable, provocative or moving—all impact-related criteria.

When "impact" criteria are highlighted in assessment; when "form" and "process" criteria are downplayed, we in fact open the door to greater creativity, not less. Because now a learner might and likely will find a *new* way to achieve a more significant impact. Unless we highlight "impact" criteria the student in fact has no genuine performance goal other than to please the teacher or mimic orthodox approaches. "Is this what you want, Mr. Smith?" is a vital sign of the failure to teach students that performance criteria are not about custom or teacher preferences but about what actually tends to be novel and appropriate—i.e. what really works.

What is an implication for curriculum? The content must include study of many *diverse* models of excellence and non-excellence at meeting performance goals creatively if they are to ever succeed at meeting such goals themselves. And as the system of karate belts, rankings in chess, cross-country racing times, computer game scoring, or weight reduction systems reveal, such models also improve the *incentive* that comes from seeing ourselves get progressively better and better over time against such models.

What is feedback?

But creative learning will only occur if teachers provide genuinely helpful and appropriate feedback. In part because teacher feedback is often so inappropriately judgmental, many well-intentioned teachers wrongly come to believe that feedback stifles creative work. While it is true that *bad* feedback does so, good feedback is about ensuring improved impact. What is good feedback? Truly helpful feedback attends to the end, the ultimate desired outcome, and gives you information about how you did against that bottom-line goal. We hit the tennis ball and see where it lands, we give a speech and hear (as well as witness) audience reaction as we speak, we design an experiment and check the results for error, we use the word processor and the spell checker underlines misspellings, we sound out a word and realize in context that it must be dessert and not desert—feedback. Though we use the word *feedback* more loosely in day-to-day talk to encompass many kinds of effects or reactions, here I narrow the meaning of feedback to its more technical meaning: information about what and was not accomplished, in terms of a specific and intended goal. It has nothing to do with evaluation or guidance. Feedback is merely the answer to the question: What happened?

Consider: People laughed at the first joke but not at the second and third joke. Why? What can I learn from the feedback about how to make them laugh at all three? The peer reviewers all say that my scene at the old mill in my short story is vividly portrayed but the scene in the hero's kitchen was opaque and unclear—not my aim. "You said, 'Uh' in your talk fourteen times, and you mostly looked down at your notes and not at the audience"—feedback in terms of engagement, from someone in the audience. Feedback is thus not merely a factual account of what happened or vague responses, but what specifically happened in terms of a specific aim I sought to achieve. Note that the language of feedback is thus descriptive, not evaluative. It is information about what we did or did not do in light of a purpose. Note, too, that my creativity is not stifled by such feedback. Indeed creative work depends upon attending only to the desired result.

This definition and the examples enable us to see what feedback *isn't*. Feedback is not praise or blame. Nor is it guidance (i.e. advice based upon prior results and feedback) or evaluation (a value judgment about the worth of the results). "Good job!" and "Try harder!" are *not* feedback, therefore—though people loosely describe both as such. Praise and advice can certainly be useful; but valid descriptive feedback is *always* useful, empowering—the source of all creative learning. It is actionable information that I may not have noticed but can profit from attending to. A grade or score is rarely adequate feedback, therefore: it is not truly formative assessment if all we do is conduct a typical test midway and give back scores. How would the tennis player improve if all the coach did was shout out marks (while the player did not see where the ball went)? How would the public speaker become skilled and poised if there were never a real audience and experts merely wrote back with letter grades a few weeks later?

When we ponder the (over)reliance on formal graded or scored tests we also can see how far we are from making feedback central to learning and learning creative. A one-shot "secure" exam at the end of the semester or year is as little likely to improve student performance as merely being given a single letter grade at season's end (and no other information) by a tennis or voice coach, after being tested on some drills that you weren't told were going to be tested. One of our aims in school reform must therefore be to create assessments that provide far better usable information—feedback—and many built-in opportunities to use it. Indeed, without better feedback (and guidance based on the feedback) in student assessment, there is little point to precise scores or firm value judgments. We need less evaluation and more feedback in short. The mixing up of the two ideas, as noted teacher of writing Peter Elbow (1986: 231–2) says, "tends to keep people from noticing that they could get by with far less measurement."

What, then, must assessment be to be highly educative (see Wiggins and McTighe, 1998)? What are the elements of an effective feedback and learning system? As the above comments suggest, helpful assessment requires:

- known complex performance goals;
- known complex tasks reflective of the goals;
- known standards and criteria by which work is judged;
- ongoing feedback in light of goals, tasks, and criteria;
- honest yet tactful framing of the feedback;
- constructive advice for making improvements immediately.

329

As this analysis also suggests, performance improvement is a well-designed series of continuous and iterative steps—the so-called feedback *loop*. A deliberate system of feedback "loops," in which I constantly confirm or disconfirm the results of my actions (by attending to the visible effects of *prior* feedback acting on that information), is how all successful performance develops and eventually occurs to high standards. As Peter Senge put it in his well-known book on management, to get feedback is not to "gather opinions about an act we have undertaken. ... [Rather] in systems thinking, feedback is a broader concept. It means any reciprocal flow of influence" (Senge, 1990: 79). In education, that means that a "learning system" is one in which I receive not only enough data until I get the task done properly, but opportunities to reveal my learning via self-adjustment in later and deliberately repeated assessments.

Conclusion

Most of this essay does not entail highly creative thinking on my part. I am channeling arguments made by Socrates, Comenius, Kant, and Hegel; and brought to fruition by Herbart, Dewey, Maria Montessori, Pestalozzi, and others. (Though, sometimes, creative work reminds us shockingly of how we have lost our way.) Genuine learning is *always* creative learning: to understand is to invent, Piaget famously said. What will it take for we educators to be more creative learners, and finally make schooling suit the modern age?

Notes

1 See, for example, http://www.nctm.org/Catalog/product.aspx?id=12577.
2 http://www.exeter.edu/academics/84_801.aspx.
3 See Chapters 3–5 in Wiggins and McTighe (2008) for more on designing curricula backward from 'cornerstone' tasks and related rubrics.
4 See Wiggins on *Quantitative Literacy* at http://www.maa.org/SAUM/articles/wigginsbiotwocol.htm.
5 We should note that this unending regimen of mere sideline practice of exercises not only fails to prepare students for real problem-solving and higher-level courses, it greatly reduces the likelihood of engagement. How many soccer or basketball players would do years of exercises without being allowed to play the game until some arbitrary standard of ability were established? Is it any wonder, then, that so many students dislike mathematics? (See 'Lockhart's Lament' and 'Why Is Mathematics So Boring?'; available at http://www.maa.org/devlin/LockhartsLament.pdf).
6 Note that the TIMSS surveys of American teachers highlighted the striking difference between US and Japanese teachers: we say the aim is "skill," where the Japanese say the aim is "to think" (Hiebert and Stigler, 1999: 71).

References

Archbald, D. A. and Grant, T. J. (2000) What's on the test? An analytical framework and findings from an examination of teachers' math tests, *Educational Assessment* 6(4): 221–56.

Colvin, G. (2008) *Talent Is Overrated: What Really Separates World-Class Performers from Everybody Else*, New York: Portfolio/Penguin Press.

Committee on Developments in the Science of Learning with additional material from the Committee on Learning Research and Educational Practice, National Research Council (2001) *How People Learn: Brain, Mind, Experience, and School: Expanded Edition*, Washington, DC: National Academies Press.

Elbow, Peter (1986) *Embracing Contraries & Explorations in Learning and Teaching*, New York: Oxford University Press.

Hattie, J. (2008) *Visible Learning: A Synthesis of Over 800 Meta-Analyses Relating to Achievement*, New York: Routledge.

Hiebert, J. and Stigler, J. (1999) *The Teaching Gap: Best Ideas from the World's Teachers for Improving Education in the Classroom*, New York: The Free Press.

Lubart, T. (1994) Creativity, in R. Sternberg (ed.) *Thinking and Problem Solving*, San Diego: Academic Press.

Nater, S. and Gallimore, R. (2005) *You Haven't Taught until They Have Learned: John Wooden's Teaching Principles and Practice*, Morganstown, WV: Fitness International Technology, Inc.

Polya, G. (1945) *How to Solve It*, New Haven, CT: University of Princetown Press.

—— (1957) *Mathematical Discovery*, vol. 1, New York: Wiley.

Polya, G. and Kirkpatrick, J. (1974) *The Stanford Mathematics Problem Book*, New York: Dover.

Senge, P. (1990) *The Fifth Discipline: The Art & Practice of the Learning Organization*, New York: Doubleday Currency.

Tyler, R. (1949) *Basic Principles of Curriculum and Instruction*, Chicago: University of Chicago Press.

Wiggins, G. (2010) Why we should stop bashing state tests, *Educational Leadership* 67(6): 48–52.

Wiggins, G. and McTighe, J. (1998) *Understanding by Design*, Alexandria, VA: Association for Supervision and Curriculum Development (ASCD).

—— (2008) Put understanding first, *Educational Leadership (Reshaping High Schools)* 65(8): 36–41.

Zeitz, P. (1999) *The Art and Craft of Problem Solving*, New York: Wiley.

Part IV

Creative school and system change

Pat Thomson

Creative learning can – and of course does – exist in just one classroom in a school. However, when we begin to think how it is that creative learning approaches might spread from one classroom to another, we are thinking about institutional change. And if we have in mind an entire school working with creative approaches to learning/teaching, then we are inevitably talking about whole school change.

While there is a growing body of literature that talks about school change, there is very little which connects this with creative learning. Indeed one of the critiques one might make of the change literatures is that so much of it is silent on the question of what kind of learning is important. There are of course exceptions and some of the major contributors to Part IV are those people who work on school change for specific learning outcomes. The goal of this section of the *Handbook* is to gather together research on programmes, strategies and issues that are likely to be the most helpful to understanding and doing school change that has creative learning at its heart. This part of the *Handbook* is therefore organized differently from the other three. There is linking editorial comment throughout Part IV, which places chapters in the context of the broader change literatures.

We begin with a discussion of some of the key issues in school change and then introduce the question of purposes. A chapter from Andy Hargreaves (Chapter 35) elaborates on what it might mean to educate for a twenty-first century knowledge society. We then go on to discuss what the change literatures often call 'capacity building'. There are several chapters which show how it is that schools and school systems can support creative learning, and significant shifts in teachers' classroom practices and routines. Nick Owen (Chapter 36) reports on an artist-in-schools programme from the point of view of the school, while Arnold Aprill (CAPE US), Gail E. Burnaford (Florida Atlantic University) and Pat Cochrane (CAPE UK) (Chapter 37), and Jorunn Spord Borgen (the Cultural Rucksack, Norway) (Chapter 38) show how such arts and artist–teacher partnership programmes operate more broadly. These chapters, together with the next three, highlight the importance of support external to the school. Ann Lieberman and Diane R. Wood (Chapter 39) report on the longstanding National Writing Programme (US) and the ways in which it supports and sustains a network of teachers. David Holland (Chapter 40) discusses research into different forms of networking that occurred in the English Creative Partnerships programme, and the findings of his empirical research are expanded by complementary research conducted by Richard Hatcher (Chapter 41). The final chapters focus on systemic whole school change programmes. Catherine Burke (Chapter 42) discusses attempts to change pedagogies concurrently with changes in the material environments of schooling, Michael G. Gunzenhauser and George W. Noblit (Chapter 43) examine the A+ school reform programme in the US, and Moira Hulme, Ian Menter and James Conroy (Chapter 44) analyse the ways in which creativity has been operationalised in the Scottish education system. In conclusion, David Parker and Naranee Ruthra-Rajan (Chapter 45) report on the learnings about school change gained from Creative Partnerships, which does have as its aim the generation of creative learning approaches across schools and the wider school system.

Purposes for change

There are generally two major reasons for suggesting that schools need to change. They are (1) that schools fail too many children and (2) that schools do not fit children for life in the twenty-first century.

Making schools fairer

Statistics gathered in individual schools, in school systems and in various nations confirm that success in schooling is largely determined by parental income and levels of education. Despite the level of mass schooling rising over time, poverty is overwhelmingly a determinant of life chances. While schools cannot create an equal society, they can and do make a demonstrable difference against these odds. In order to redress the failure of schools to educate all pupils, change must focus on:

- pedagogies, resources and tasks that assist students, or a greater range of students, to meet requirements;
- activities that promote social learning, motivation, and improve school ethos;
- support for teachers to invent, use and sustain a wider range of pedagogical strategies;
- activities that support respectful and reciprocal relations with pupils, families and the wider community.

These strategies often cut across longstanding school conventions of grouping, testing, setting and promoting students. They question the 'standards' approach. Followed through, this analysis logically leads to a transformative approach to whole school change.

Schooling for the future

There are an interrelated set of arguments about why schools do not equip students for the future.

Schools are based on out of date thinking

Mass schooling developed in the Industrial Age to serve the needs of an industrial society. Tyack and Cuban (1995: ch. 4) note that schools emerged in the nineteenth and twentieth centuries in a remarkably common form across the world. They call this organisational form a *grammar*, whose elements include: one teacher, one class; age-grade promotion; and a curriculum divided into subjects through which students progress in a linear fashion. This 'grammar' treats pupils as cohorts, and assumes they will learn at much the same rate, in the same order and in the same way. Pedagogy treats children and young people predominantly as a whole class with some additional small group work. In contrast, students' work is assessed and judged as if it was an individual accomplishment. We now understand that children are not all the same and they learn in different ways and at different rates. They also have different interests, strengths and weaknesses, which schools must recognise and cater for.

Schools are not educating children and young people for the new economy

Globalisation has brought sweeping changes to national economies. The semiskilled and unskilled employment that was dubbed 'working class labour' – and seen as a lesser opportunity in life – has all but disappeared from many parts of the country. In its place are a new range of jobs, all of which demand much higher levels of education (Aronowitz and Cutler, 1998; Reich, 1991; Rifkin, 1996). Those who work in manufacturing are now expected to manage high-tech machines which require both literacy and numeracy beyond 'basic skills' (Gee *et al.*, 1996; Kincheloe, 1999). Accompanying this slimmed-down, more skilled manufacturing sector is a burgeoning service sector where, at the bottom, work is tenuous and poorly remunerated. But even here, workers are expected to demonstrate high levels of team work, initiative and 'customer service' behaviours (Du Gay, 1996). There is thus a new onus on schools to ensure that children are equipped to enter this changed labour landscape. Young people face a future in which they must continually make risky decisions about which work and training options best position them to avoid long and debilitating periods of under- or unemployment (Dwyer and Wynn, 2001).

We live in high-tech times and this creates new opportunities for schools

Since the early 1990s there has been a rapid growth of information and communication technologies (ICTs). These have not only changed the way in which work is accomplished, but also dramatically altered communication between people and nations (Castells, 1996, 1997, 1998) and transformed youth and popular cultures (Buckingham, 2000; Kenway and Bullen, 2001; Sefton-Green, 1998). It is not simply that schools must educate children and young people for a vastly changed labour market and a different world. Education itself can benefit from ICTs, which offer new possibilities for the storage, archiving, representation, sharing and processing of information. The challenge for schools, then, is not only to educate children for the knowledge society but also to educate in, through, with and about this new interconnected world. The 'networked society' also offers a new organisational form for schools. Through the development of new strategic alliances which are local and global, staff and pupils can exchange ideas, undertake projects, develop joint programmes and add significantly to the learning available to all in the extended community. ICTs underpin this new form of communication and learning.

We live in a society which is fragmenting

A knowledge society is also one in which social ties and communities are weakened (Etzioni, 1993; Putnam, 1995). As the privileged become global knowledge workers, and seek to isolate themselves in gated communities, cities polarise and the poor are increasingly isolated in specific neighbourhoods (Davis, 1992; Pacione, 1997). In these circumstances marginalised populations need access to a range of 'full service' social services. These must not duplicate the bureaucratic and uncoordinated approaches of the past, but be sensitive to local and individual needs and differences. But there must also be social healing, and work to create linkages between different communities and neighbourhoods, so that population diversity does not become the cause of deep antagonistic social divisions and exclusion.

There is no blueprint for redesigning schools for the future. Directions for change usually involve some of the following:

- breaking away from the notion that learning only occurs in classrooms with teachers at set times;
- abandoning the notion that learning occurs in a linear fashion through age-grades and rigid subject boundaries;
- catering for individual and group interests, concerns, experiences, cultures, knowledges and languages;
- learning in and through a wide range of media, activities, experiences and texts;
- focusing strongly on critical, higher-order thinking using self-regulated and meta-learning strategies;
- promoting a range of ways for children and young people to work together as well as separately, face to face and through various mediated forms;
- creating partnerships with a range of organisatons and institutions, including other schools, in order to provide integrated and rich learning opportunities.

The argument for a futures oriented schooling is elaborated by Andy Hargreaves in Chapter 35.

References

Aronowitz, S. and Cutler, J. (eds) (1998) *Post-Work: The Wages of Cybernation*, New York and London: Routledge.

Buckingham, D. (2000) *After the Death of Childhood: Growing Up in the Age of Electronic Media*, Cambridge, Oxford and Malden, MA: Polity Press.

Castells, M. (1996) *The Information Age: Economy, Society and Culture. The Rise of the Network Society*, Oxford: Blackwell.

—— (1997) *The Information Age: Economy, Society and Culture. The Power of Identity*, Oxford: Blackwell.

—— (1998) *The Information Age: Economy, Society and Culture. End of the Millennium*, Oxford: Blackwell.

Davis, M. (1992) *City of quartz: Excavating the Future in Los Angeles*, London: Vintage.

Du Gay, P. (1996) *Consumption and Identity at Work*, London: Sage.

Dwyer, P. and Wynn, J. (2001) *Youth, Education and Risk: Facing the Future*, London: Routledge Falmer.

Etzioni, A. (1993) *The Spirit of Community: The Reinvention of American Society*, New York: Touchstone.

Gee, J., Hull, G. and Lankshear, C. (1996) *The New Work Order: Behind the Language of the New Capitalism*, Australia: Allen and Unwin.

Kenway, J. and Bullen, E. (2001) *Consuming Children: Entertainment, Advertising and Education*, Buckingham: Open University Press.

Kincheloe, J. (1999) *How Do We Tell the Workers? The Socioeconomic Foundations of Work and Vocational Education*, Boulder, CO: Westview Press.

Pacione, M. (ed.) (1997) *Britain's Cities: Geographies of Division in Urban Britain*, London: Routledge.

Putnam, R. (1995) Bowling alone: America's declining social capital. *Journal of Democracy* 6(1): 65–78.

Reich, R. (1991) *The Work of Nations: A Blueprint for the Future*, New York: Simon and Schuster.

Rifkin, J. (1996) *The End of Work: The Decline of the Global Labour Force and the Dawn of the Post Market Era*, New York: Putnam.

Sefton-Green, J. (ed.) (1998) *Digital Diversions: Youth Culture in the Age of Multimedia*, London: UCL Press.

Tyack, D. and Cuban, L. (1995) *Tinkering toward Utopia: A Century of Public School Reform*, San Francisco: Jossey Bass.

35

Twenty-first century skills are on Mercury

Learning, life and school reform

Andy Hargreaves

Four change imperatives

More than ten years ago, generational researchers William Strauss and Neil Howe (1997) anticipated a great disruption when our world would take a great Turning. After three earlier turnings that defined a time of prosperity, optimism, security, pragmatism and social conservatism in the 1950s; a period of cultural and spiritual awakening in the 1960s and 1970s; and an era of individualism, self-centredness and general unravelling in the 1980s and 1990s; Strauss and Howe predicted a Fourth Turning, which, they claimed, would be as dramatic as the last Fourth Turning in the Great Depression of the 1930s. This turning, they argue, brings economic collapse and financial ruin, insecurity and conflict, and a shaking of society to its very foundations, with the emergence on the other side of structures, cultures and politics, as well as value and belief systems, that are profoundly different. At the Fourth Turning, people can start to turn outward again, beyond themselves, in search of the spirituality, sustenance and support that can connect them once more to their fellow women and men. But this is not guaranteed.

Although the Fourth Turning is born of crisis, it beckons with the prospect of great trans-formations and opportunities. Yet it does not show what these are. This is a defining moment for us all. In the Fourth Turning, we face three immense challenges and one ambiguous opportunity of worldwide and earth-shattering proportions:

- the aftermath of global economic collapse;
- the spread of excessive affluence that has reduced the quality of most people's lives;
- the imminent impact of climate change that threatens the very survival of our species;
- the generational renewal of the workforce, heralding a new generation that will soon assume the leadership of the future.

First, as international financial guru Mohammed El-Erian (2008) argues, in the midst of a great global disruption when economies are collapsing, it is a time in economic and educational life either to pare down our budgets, reduce our ambitions and turn in on ourselves, or to embark on a new course that can lead us towards a better place, a new high point of innovation, creativity and prosperity. Education is an essential part of this better economic path. So are twenty-first century knowledge and skill.

Second, beyond a minimum level of comfort and adequacy, increased wealth and affluence do not lead to an improved quality of life. In *The Spirit Level: Why More Equal Societies Almost Always Do Better*, Richard Wilkinson and Kate Pickett (2009) bring together compelling data accumulated by a range of international organisations that show disturbing inverse relationships between economic and consumer affluence on the one hand and quality of life on the other. Beyond a basic level that removes people from poverty, they show, affluence combined with high economic inequality does not improve people's quality of life, and often actually worsens it.

Looking at international comparisons on the highly influential PISA tests (Programme for International Students Assessment), Wilkinson and Pickett find that 'more unequal countries ... have worse educational attainment' (2009: 105). They also discover that 'more children drop out of high school in more unequal US states' (ibid.: 107). They reach the inexorable though politically unpopular conclusion that schools cannot turn everything around by themselves: 'If ... a country wants higher average levels of educational achievement ... it must address the underlying inequality which creates a steeper social gradient in educational underachievement' (ibid.: 30).

In *Collateral Damage*, Nichols and Berliner (2007), painstakingly show how white US students from the dominant culture perform just as well as dominant cultural groups overseas. It is poor and minority students who perform as dismally as international peers in under-developed nations. The reasons, they also show, have to do with poverty – with children from poor families lacking effective prenatal care, screening for health and sight problems, adequate and nutritious diet, or protection from lead poisoning and from toxic waste dumped in close proximity to lower class communities. Poor children also tend to be surrounded by other children and families who have multiple problems arising from lack of local services, poor transportation, absence of available employment, residential segregation and so forth.

The third challenge is an ecological one. In her brilliantly tragic novel *The Stone Gods*, Jeanette Winterson (2008) portrays end-of-the-world scenarios, from Easter Island to the near future, as cataclysmic events that are repeated time and again. All of these societies and ecologies are destroyed when prosperity turns into greed and conflict that despoils the environment on which the prosperity itself was founded. In his discussion of the challenge of climate change, Anthony Giddens describes this phenomenon as over-development, where 'affluence itself produces a range of ... profound social problems' (Giddens, 2009: 72). As long ago as 1972, the Club of Rome controversially foresaw the time when there would have to be limits to growth because civilisation would exhaust the resources on which its continued development depends (Meadows *et al.*, 1972). Much more recently, ardent environmentalists like Bill McKibben (2003) have urged us to acknowledge when we have achieved or acquired 'enough' information, choices, work, possessions or growth. The insatiable demand for never-ending increases in test scores and rising standards, everywhere, could be added to his list.

The much-used phrase of sustainable development or growth is clearly no longer achievable or desirable in the developed nations. It is a contradiction in terms. Pure sustainability, or sustainable living, must now be the goal instead. The challenge is so massive that education for sustainable living (not for sustainable development) is an indispensable imperative for twenty-first century learning and change. It is a matter of life and death.

Finally, the early years of the twenty-first century also hold out an immense but ambiguous opportunity. As the Boomer generation retires and moves on from teaching and other leadership positions in society (OECD, 2005), it will be replaced by the more direct and demanding generational successors of Generation X and even more of Generation Y – sometimes called the Millennial Generation (Howe and Strauss, 2000). This generation, now entering its early thirties, is one that is already introducing ideas and incorporating technologies that are closer to the cultures of today's children and youth. When this generation moves into leadership in great numbers towards the end of this next decade, it will bring approaches to life and leadership that are swift, assertive, direct, team-based, task-centred and technologically savvy. At last, almost effortlessly, this will herald in many of the classroom and organisational transformations that have been advocated, dreamed about and merely experimented with for decades. But will these transformations be deep, critical and sustainable – bringing lives and communities together to solve common problems in the public interest? Or, will their activities be technologically slick and superficial – a metaphorically self-centred world of MySpace and iPhones – promoted by a generation of ADHD, narcissistic 'followers' or 'stalkers'? Will social networking sites strengthen communities or, as Pope Benedict has worried aloud, will they destroy the more substantial ties that bind us together? Responding to these issues is a generational challenge of twenty-first century learning and leadership regarding how to live our lives.

There are, then, four imperatives of change in living and learning for the twenty-first century:

- the economic imperative of developing twenty-first century learning for an innovative and creative economy;
- the social justice imperative of developing better lives for all in a world that reduces inequalities;
- the ecological imperative of education for sustainable living;
- the generational imperative of developing dynamic and responsible citizens and leaders for the future who can properly address the other three imperatives.

The Way of Mercury

Although 2009 was the European Commission's Year of Innovation and Creativity, the supposedly twenty-first century skills agenda of innovation, creativity and flexibility has its origins stretching back more than thirty years. As long ago as 1976, Daniel Bell invented the term *knowledge society* to describe a post-industrial world beyond large-scale factory production that would require an educated workforce capable of working in services, ideas and communication. By the early 1990s, management guru Peter Drucker (1993) was anticipating a post-capitalist society where the basic economic resource of society would no longer be capital or labour but knowledge, and where the leading groups of this society would be 'knowledge workers'. In education, Phillip Schlechty (1990) was among the first to proclaim that the business of public education should shift to developing knowledge workers who would perform knowledge work. Meanwhile, former US Secretary of Labor, Robert Reich (2001), argued that in a world of spiralling consumer choice, competitive companies needed the skills that could advance speed, novelty, cleverness, creation, invention, communication and empathy with customer desires. Those who possessed these skills were what Reich called symbolic analysts. The direction of public education, he argued, needed to move towards producing more of these people.

In the early years of the twenty-first century, as the way of standardisation, memorisable content and tested basics was ironically entrenching itself more and more deeply into many public education systems, leading international organisations like the Organisation for Economic Cooperation and Development (OECD) began to take up the knowledge economy cause. Their report on *Knowledge Management in the Learning Society* (OECD, 2000) linked knowledge management to the challenges created by acceleration of change, which, they argued elsewhere,

339

raised 'profound questions for the knowledge students are being equipped with and ought to be equipped with' in the schools of tomorrow (OECD, 2001: 29). A world of fast capitalism characterised by just-in-time production and instant, widespread global communication (Harvey, 1989) required people with individual and collective ingenuity who could innovate and solve unanticipated problems swiftly and efficiently together (Homer-Dixon, 2000).

By 2003, I had discovered the pervasive negative effects of excessive competition and stan-dardisation in US and Canadian schools (Hargreaves, 2003), and was comparing these to a vision of knowledge society schools that gave priority to the following:

- deep cognitive learning, creativity and ingenuity among students;
- research, inquiry, working in networks and teams and pursuing continuous professional learning as teachers;
- problem-solving, risk-taking, trust in fellow professionals, ability to cope with change and commitment to continuous improvement as organisations.

Teaching for the knowledge society, in other words, would promote creativity, flexibility, problem-solving, ingenuity, collective (shared) intelligence, professional trust, risk-taking and continuous improvement.

As well as strong skills in literacy and mathematics and core subjects, twenty-first century students must be comfortable with ideas and abstractions, good at both analysis and synthesis, creative and innovative, self-disciplined and well organised, able to learn very quickly and work well as a member of a team, and have the flexibility to adapt quickly to frequent changes in the labour market (ibid. xviii–xix).

Tony Wagner (2008) identifies seven essential skills for adolescents and the modern economy that are rather reminiscent of the knowledge economy skills listed before: critical thinking and problem-solving; collaboration and leadership across networks; agility and adaptability; initiative and entrepreneurialism; effective communication; accessing and analysing information; and curiosity and imagination. Yong Zhao (2009) points out that many Asian competitors are already moving far faster in these directions than the US.

The strategically influential US Partnership for 21st Century Skills (2009: website), involving twelve states working in harness with large foundations and corporate leaders from the tech-nology sector, amplifies many of these preceding emphases in listing the essential skills that should permeate throughout the twenty-first curriculum – creativity and innovation; critical thinking and problem-solving; communication and collaboration; information, media and technological literacy; flexibility and adaptability; initiative and self-direction; social and cross-cultural skills; productivity and accountability; and leadership and responsibility.

These twenty-first century skills are neither Venus-like, child-centred and permissive, nor Mars-like top-down and standardised. Instead they are like the winged messenger of Mercury – characterised by speed and communication in the pursuit of profit, trade and commerce. This mercurial way promotes economically useful cross-curricular skills in learning; new patterns of professionalism as well as professional interaction and networking among teachers; and more rapid and flexible ways of managing change in organisations.

This Way of Mercury seemingly addresses three of the four twenty-first century imperatives outlined at the beginning of the chapter (pp. 337–339). Its emphasis on developing the skills and processes that accelerate innovation and knowledge circulation are presented as being instrumental to regenerating a floundering economy. This culture of innovation and ingenuity can also address the environmental challenges of climate change. Engaging with the digital and attitudinal realities of twenty-first century learners also promises to creates harmony rather than discord between the educational system and its new schools of the future, on the one hand, and the students along with their younger teachers who have been born digital, on the other. Economically, environmentally and demographically, the twenty-first century skills agenda and its implications seem to make sense in all these three respects!

However, the twenty-first century knowledge and skills agenda and the version of change it represents fall short in four respects:

- it overstates the advanced nature of the creative skills required in the new economy;
- it does not address the missing imperative of social justice and increased equality;
- it corrupts and compromises twenty-first century ideals by clinging on to time-pressured performance goals related to standardised testing;
- its addiction to speed leads to superficiality and mercurial unpredictability.

First, not all or even most of the work skills of the twenty-first century are twenty-first century skills. Matthew Crawford (2009) argues that many of today's middle class are not dealing at work with complex problems using judgement and discretion together. Instead, a great deal of white-collar work has been reduced to standardised operations. This is routine cubicle work, not advanced knowledge work. What kinds of education do so-called knowledge workers or cubicle workers actually need? Prepare them to think critically and deal with complexity in this unchallenging world of work and we may merely be sowing the seeds of white-collar dissatisfaction and disaffection. It's not just the people and their skills that need to change in the twenty-first century economy. The meaning of work has to be transformed as well.

Second, the twenty-first century skills agenda omits the knowledge, skills and qualities that are beyond the world of business and sometimes directly opposed to it. Where in the twenty-first century skills agenda can we be sure that schools will develop future leaders who will practice corporate integrity? Who will preserve the landmark commitments established by the vast network of schools belonging to Facing History and Ourselves (www.facinghistory.org), that physical and emotional bullying are already two or three steps along the short continuum that leads to genocide? How can we be sure that our teachers will teach that torture is always wrong, even in the name of democracy?

Attending to diversity sounds fine as a twenty-first century skill, but it can mean little more than learning to get along better with a range of others in the workplace. How can we be sure that this skill will also include the necessity of understanding not only that Israel and Palestine, Hutus and Tutsis, Hindus and Muslims or even the Cripps and the Bloods each have a right to exist, but that they must learn to live together? Bland statements of skills can let too many educators off the ethical hook.

And where, anywhere in this list, is there any attention to ecological and organisational sustainability – to being prudent and thrifty in our lifestyles, buying smaller rather than bigger homes and vehicles, repairing rather than discarding broken items, sharing resources with our neighbours instead of guzzling greedily alone, avoiding working our people to death, refraining from exporting our pollution-producing factories to developing countries as a dubious method of meeting domestic environmental targets, and so on? How, in this list of skills, can we be sure we will fight for sustainability, agitate for the eradication of poverty, and increase our common commitment to quality of life and social equality? None of these things are, of course, explicitly prohibited. Any of them is possible. But unsustainability is not an option, and we cannot afford for it to be one!

Third, the twenty-first century knowledge and skills agenda is being pursued in many nations in the context of and in tension with a re-branded version of large-scale and remarkably standardised reform that we call LSR 2.0. This reform model has been even tighter in its imposition of ends than its predecessors such as the National Curriculum reforms of the UK or No Child Left Behind in the US, yet considerably more flexible in its orchestration of means (Elmore and Burney, 1997; Barber, 2007; Hopkins, 2007; Fullan, 2006; Levin, 2008; McKinsey & Company, 2007).

In LSR 2.0, government establishes a small number of specific goals, such as system-wide literacy and mathematics targets, and provides greater oversight in their prescription and pacing. Test score data are the focus of professional learning communities of inquiry in schools and districts that identify gaps and inconsistencies and design swift interventions accordingly. Collegial coaching and leadership supervision, through 'walk-throughs', 'instructional rounds' and other methods, provide technical support to teachers while also ensuring they comply with or demonstrate 'fidelity' to the reforms. League tables and school comparisons printed in newspapers and digital media inform the public about student achievement results, and parents in underperforming schools are given opportunities to transfer their children to others with better results. Educators are encouraged to build lateral learning networks to generate professional motivation and drive change, and the public has access to information about teacher quality and student achievement levels. The government sponsors semi-private alternatives such as charter schools in the US, inner-city academies in the UK or supplementary programmes for students who have been in struggling schools. Politically imposed timelines for improvement are linked to short-term election cycles, and the failure of schools to meet these leads to escalating amounts of intervention, so that, in general, intervention is inversely related to success.

Advocates of LSR 2.0 claim increased standards in measurable improvement, narrowed achievement gaps, enhanced professional quality and motivation, system-wide impact and increased confidence in public education and the capacity of political leaders to manage it. Critics are more circumspect (see Hartley, 2007; Chapman and Gunter, 2009; Hargreaves and Shirley, 2009). The continuing overemphasis on tested and targeted basics marginalises attention to arts, social studies, innovation and creativity that are essential for competitive success in twenty-first century knowledge economies. There is also an inverse relationship between narrowly tested achievement and the development of the whole child and its overall wellbeing (UNICEF, 2007; Honoré, 2008; BBC, 2009). The persistence of standardisation in order to appease short-term political contingencies both limits the creative, economically relevant skills that schools can develop and ignores all those socially beneficial outcomes that exist beyond the economy. This is double jeopardy. Indeed, the twenty-first century knowledge and skills agenda proposes to infuse new skills into what can easily remain an unchanged curriculum. LSR 2.0 wants to have its cake and eat it.

This raises the fourth issue: speed. In 2005, I led an evaluation of a large school improvement network that had been established as a response to the plateau that England's achievement results had reached under its LSR 2.0 strategy. Raising Achievement Transforming Learning (RATL) comprised over 300 secondary schools that had experienced a dip in student achievement scores over one or two years. Its approach was to promote improvement by schools, with schools and for schools in peer-driven networks of lateral pressure and support, where participating schools were connected with each other and with self-chosen mentor schools, and invited to conferences that supplied them with inspiration, technical support in analysing achievement data, as well as a menu of short-, medium- and long-term strategies for improving teaching and learning and also achievement results. The network's architecture emphasised transparency of participation as well as of results, and most of its momentum and cohesion were basically lateral rather than top-down in nature (Hargreaves et al., 2006).

The network was astonishingly innovative and, in conventional outcome terms, also highly successful. Two-thirds of the schools improved at double the rate of the national secondary school average in just two years. Pushing beyond and against the surrounding context of England's Third Way, RATL elicited immense enthusiasm from educators. They were grateful for assistance in converting mountains of data into practical knowledge that could be acted upon to improve student achievement, and they were appreciative of the concrete strategies they had gathered through conferences, visits with mentor schools and ideas exchanged on the online web portal. Here was a change network that recognised how, with a little external organisation and support, energised educators could find and apply solutions in their own settings that produced demonstrable success!

Yet RATL still had to accommodate the pressing accountability processes of Third Way England, with their relentless and politically driven pressure for ever-increasing and publicly displayed scores in examination results and standardised achievement tests. The consequence was what we call addictive presentism.

Teachers' effervescent interactions amounted to a kind of hyperactive professionalism where they hurriedly and excitedly rushed around swapping successful short-term strategies with their mentors and each other in order to deliver the government's narrowly defined targets and purposes. The vast majority of strategies that teachers adopted were simple and short term, or 'gimmicky and great' ones such as paying former students to mentor existing ones, having examiners share their grading schemes with students, establishing ways for students to access study strategies online from peers in other schools, and supplying bananas and water to hydrate the brain and raise potassium levels on test days. At conferences, school leaders engaged in speed-dating activities, where they rotated in brief interactions of two or so minutes, swapped a successful strategy and then exchanged business cards as they left.

What was missing was a process where educators could also develop and realise inspiring purposes of their own, or engage in deeper professional conversations about transforming teaching and learning. Schools became addictive organisations, on successions of obsessive yet evanescent highs concerned with meeting targets, raising performance standards, identifying microscopic achievement gaps and adjusting strategies right down to continuous, just-in-time interventions and miniscule managements of progress with every individual child.

The ironic result of all this is a new conservatism where collaborative interactions are pleasurable, but also hurried, technical, uncritical and narrow. Preoccupation with data-driven improvement distracts teachers from deeper engagements with teaching and learning. An overwhelmingly short-term orientation leads to opportunistic strategies to improve results that secure only temporary success.

The age of instant information conspires with the political pressures of short-term election cycles to create a mercurial system of superficiality and unpredictability.

We need an educational reform and leadership strategy that attends to the long term as well as the short term. This strategy must recognise that many business environments require not just speed and agility, but also the carefully honed craft skills of cooking, carpentry or even software development that it takes 10,000 hours or more of practice and persistence to hone to an expert level (Sennett, 2008; Gladwell, 2008). It must also recognise that children and adults should not be obsessively overscheduled; endlessly inundated by the truncated and accelerated interactions of email, texting and Twitter; or digitally immersed in the seductions of cyberspace at the cost of enjoying the outdoor challenges and renewing fulfilments of natural space (Honoré, 2008).

The Way of Mercury is driven by a fast world of rapid learning where personalisation of learning is actually consumer-like customisation of how learning is accessed (quicker, slower; online, offline; in school, at home, on multiple pathways) rather than a way of connecting learning to personal interests, family and cultural knowledge and future life projects. It is a world of inescapable and endless targets, of constant accountability, of delivering services to communities as if they were individual consumers, and of obsessions with making continuous just-in-time adjustments to never-ending flows of statistics.

The Way of Mercury witnesses greater frequencies of interaction and communication but in the hurried teams of commerce, not the enduring relationships of communities. Leaders who possess and value all these quicksilver attributes are identified and developed early and accelerated quickly as individuals who suit the new system, but collaborative work in depth with other leaders is limited. In the Way of Mercury, the nimble and the smart prevail over the steady and the just.

Down to earth

It's time to come down to earth – to think about the past and the future as well as the present, to care about our world as well as our work, to push for sustainability as well as success, and to commit ourselves to the common good of others and not just to the narcissistic pursuit of acquiring or developing things for ourselves.

This way begins with an inspiring and inclusive mission not a vague embracing of 'world class standards' or a limiting of our sights to increases in test scores. The teaching and learning of the Fourth Way is deep and mindful, and so is the learning of professionals. It addresses the deep structures of disciplines, the lasting metaphors and legacies of different cultural traditions, the compelling questions and concerns of our times, and the interests that learners pursue in their individual and community lives. This learning is often slow, not speedy; reflective and ruminative, not just fast and slick. Indeed, says psychologist Guy Claxton (1997), it is this very kind of learning that is essential for developing creative thought. Reflecting, slowing down, stopping – these are the things that foster creativity and breakthroughs (Honoré, 2004; MacDonald and Shirley, 2009).

Being down to earth doesn't merely entail delivering services to the poor and their communities as if they were low-cost consumers, but develops community with them in relationships of active and engaged trust through extended school days, paid community appointments and robust community organising.

In the way of earth, teachers' lives matter as much as their students'. Teachers and schools work together, but teachers work in thoughtful, evidence-informed communities that value both hard data and soft judgement, applied to deep and compelling questions of professional practice and innovation. They do not just hurl themselves into hurried meetings to produce just-in-time reactions to streams of test score data. And schools do not merely network with distant partners. They also collaborate rather than compete with immediate neighbours, in pursuit of a higher common good in a culture and a shared community where the strong help the weak amid lives lived together.

References

Barber, M. (2007) *Instruction to Deliver: Fighting to Transform Britain's Public Services*, London: Methuen.

BBC (2009) Primary education 'too narrow'; available from http://www.bbc.co.uk/2/hi/uk_news/education/7896751.stm (accessed 20 February 2009).

Bell, D. (1976) *The Coming of the Post-Industrial Society*, New York: Basic Books.

Blair, T. and Schröder, G. (1999) *The Third Way – die neue Mitte*, London: Labour Party and SPD.

Chapman, C. and Gunter, H. (2009) *Radical Reforms*, London and New York: Routledge.

Claxton, G. (1997) *Hare Brain, Tortoise Mind: How Intelligence Increases When You Think Less*, New York: HarperCollins.

Crawford, M. (2009) *Shop Class as Soulcraft: An Inquiry into the Value of Work*, New York: Penguin.

Cusick, P. A. (2002) *A Study of Michigan's School Principal Shortage*, East Lansing, MI: Education Policy Center, Michigan State University.

Drucker, P. (1993) *Post-Capitalist Society*, New York: HarperCollins.

El-Erian, M. (2008) *When Markets Collide: Investment Strategies for the Age of Global Economic Change*, New York: McGraw-Hill.

Elmore, R. F. and Burney, D. (1997) *Investing in Teacher Learning: Staff Development and Instructional Improvement in Community District #2, New York City*, New York: National Commission on Teaching and America's Future, Consortium for Policy Research in Education.

Facing History and Ourselves: Holocaust and Human Behavior official website, http://www.facinghistory.org/resources/hhb.

Fink, D. and Brayman, C. (2006) School leadership succession and the challenges of change, *Educational Administration Quarterly* 42(1): 62–89.

Fullan, M. (2006) *Turnaround Leadership*, San Francisco: Jossey-Bass.

Giddens, A. (1999) *The Third Way: The Renewal of Social Democracy*, Malden, MA: Polity Press.

—— (2009) *The Politics of Climate Change*, Malden, MA: Polity Press.

Gladwell, M. (2008) *Outliers: The Story of Success*, New York: Little, Brown missions, memory and meaning, *Educational Administration Quarterly* 42(1) (February): 42–61.

Gross, N., Giacquinta, J. B. and Bernstein, M. (1971) *Implementing Organizational Innovations: A Sociological Analysis of Planned Educational Change*, New York: Basic Books.

Hargreaves, A. (2003) *Teaching in the Knowledge Society: Education in the Age of Insecurity*, New York: Teachers College Press.

Hargreaves, A. and Goodson, I. (2006) Educational change over time? The sustainability and nonsustainability of three decades of secondary school change and continuity, *Educational Administration Quarterly* 42(1) (February): 3–41.

Hargreaves, A. and Shirley, D. (2009) *The Fourth Way*, Thousand Oaks, CA; Corwin Press.

Hargreaves, A., Halász, G. and Pont, B. (2008) The Finnish approach to system leadership, in B. Pont, D. Nusche and D. Hopkins (eds) *Improving School Leadership*, vol. 2: *Case Studies on System Leadership*, Paris: OECD.

Hargreaves, A., Shirley, D., Evans, M., Stone-Johnson, C. and Riseman, D. (2006). *The Long and Short of Educational Change, an Evaluation of the Raising Achievement/Transforming, Learning Project for the Specialist Schools 14.*

Harvey, D. (1989) *The Condition of Post-Modernity*, Oxford: Blackwell.

Havelock, R. and Havelock, M. (1973) *Training for Change Agent: A Guide to the Design of Training Programs in Education and Other Fields*, Ann Arbor: University of Michigan, Institute for Social Research.

Havelock, R. G. and Zlotolow, S. (1995) *The Change Agent's Guide* (2nd ed.), Englewood Cliffs, NJ: Educational Technology Publications.

Homer-Dixon, T. (2000) *The Ingenuity Gap: Facing the Economic, Environmental, and Other Challenges of an Increasingly Complex and Unpredictable Future*, New York: Knopf.

Honoré, C. (2004) *In Praise of Slowness: How a Worldwide Movement Is Challenging the Cult of Speed*, New York: HarperCollins.

—— (2008) *Under Pressure*, New York: HarperOne.

Hopkins, D. (2007) *Every School a Great School: Realising the Potential of System Leadership*, Maidenhead: Open University Press.

Howe, N. and Strauss, W. (2000) *Millennials Rising: The Next Great Generation*, New York: Vintage Books.

Levin, B. (2008) *How to Change 5000 Schools: A Practical and Positive Approach for Leading Change at Every Level*, Cambridge, MA: Harvard Education Press.

MacDonald, E. and Shirley, D. (2009) *The Mindful Teacher*, New York: Teachers College Press.

McKibben, B. (2003) *Enough: Staying Human in an Engineered Age*, New York: Henry Holt & Co.

McKinsey & Company (2007) How the world's best-performing school systems come out on top; available from http://www.mckinsey.com (accessed 25 November 2008).

Meadows, D. H. *et al.* (1972) *The Limits of Growth. A Report for the Club of Rome's Project on the Predicament of Mankind*, New York: Universe Books.

Nichols, S. and Berliner, D. (2007) *Collateral Damage: How High-Stakes Testing Corrupts America's Schools*, Cambridge, MA: Harvard Education Press.

Oakes, J. and Lipton, M (2002) Struggling for educational equity in diverse communities: school reform as social movement, *Journal of Educational Change*, 3.3–3.4: 383–406.

OECD (2000) *Knowledge Management in the Learning Society*, Paris: Organisation for Economic Cooperation and Development.

—— (2001) *Schooling for Tomorrow: What Schools for the Future?* Paris: Organisation for Economic Cooperation and Development.

—— (2005) *Attracting, Developing and Retaining Effective Teachers – Final Report: Teachers Matter*, Paris: Organisation for Economic Cooperation and Development.

Partnership for 21st century skills: The leading advocacy organization infusing 21st century skills into education official website, www.21stcenturyskills.org/index.php.

Reich, R. (2001) *The Future of Success*, New York: Alfred A. Knopf.

Schlechty, P. (1990) *Schools for the 21st Century: Leadership Imperatives for Educational Reform*, San Francisco: Jossey-Bass.

Sennett, R. (2008) *The Craftsman*, New Haven, CT: Yale University Press.

Smith, L. M. and Keith, P. (1971) *Anatomy of Educational Innovation*, New York: Wiley.

Strauss, W. and Howe, N. (1997) *The Fourth Turning*, New York, Three Meadows.

United Nations Children's Fund (2007) *Child Poverty in Perspective: An Overview of Child Well-Being in Rich Countries*, Florence: UNICEF Innocenti Research Centre.

Wagner, T. (2008) *The Global Achievement Gap*, New York: Basic.

Wilkinson, R. and Pickett, K. (2009) *The Spirit Level: Why More Equal Societies Almost Always Do Better*, London: Allen Lane.

Winterson, J. (2008) *The Stone Gods*, London: Penguin Books.

Zhao, Y. (2009) *Catching Up or Leading the Way: American Education in the Age of Globalization*, Alexandria, VA: ASCD.

Part IV Editorial comment
Capacity building
Introduction

Pat Thomson

One of the key concepts in the educational change literatures is the notion of capacity building.

This term is also often seen in the development literatures (e.g. Baser and Morgan, 2008; Cavaye, 2000; Eade, 1997; Weidner, 2002), where it refers to the process in which a group of people are supported to become self-sufficient. Those in crisis are not simply given the help that they immediately need, but are supported to build capacities to help them in the long term. Agencies work to facilitate the development of knowledge, skills and dispositions in individuals at the same time as the community develops the material and social/cultural infrastructure necessary for self-management. Thus, in the majority world, rather than simply give food, aid agencies might teach villagers to grow non-traditional cash crops, to process them and to form a cooperative to market them more widely. They might set up clinics which train local health workers and schools that raise the education levels to the point where the community is producing its own trained workforce. The goal of this kind of capacity building strategy is to produce independence and reduce or eliminate reliance on gifts and/or professional assistance. Such capacity building must connect with and value existing structures and ways of doing things in order to have 'traction', but it often also challenges and changes established patterns of belief and behaviour at the same time.

In education, much of the meaning attached to capacity building is the same as it is in development discourse. Researchers (e.g. Bascia and Hargreaves, 2000; Bullough, 2007; Datnow and Castellano, 2000; Elmore, 2004; Fullan, 1993; Hargreaves and Evans, 1997; Levin, 2008; Lieberman, 1986; Lieberman and Miller, 2001; McInerney, 2005; McLaughlin *et al.*, 2006; McLaughlin and Talbert, 2001) suggest that capacity building for change in schools entails:

- *Building new knowledge, skills and dispositions*: for individual classroom teachers for example, this may mean adding to their repertoire of practice, building new disciplinary knowledge, changing taken-for-granted ways of doing their everyday work. For teams of teachers this may mean new forms of collaborative discussion, using new but common language and adopting different standards through which to evaluate their practice. Such approaches often go under the broad umbrella of building 'professional learning communities'. However, a body of research suggests that there are sometimes difficult micropolitics in such ventures

(Datnow, 1998; Tittle, 1995) and lack of progress caused by lack of criticality in the group (Achinstein, 2002; Westheimer, 1998).

- *Developing new material and social/cultural infrastructures*: teams and schools may need to adapt or transform the management structures they use: to review, evaluate and plan; to consult; to make decisions; and to distribute and organise the resources of time, space, money and people. They may also need to intervene in the ways in which the symbolic resources of the school – the metaphor, symbols and rituals embedded in routine communications media, displays and meetings, for example – re/present and re/produce the school as an organisation and as an 'identity'.
- *Connecting with and valuing existing ways of doing things but also challenging established patterns of beliefs and behaviours*: change needs to make sense to people and thus must build on what they already know and can do, but also what they want to know how to do. At the same time, significant change often requires school staff to reject things that they hold dear or were taught were appropriate. The literature suggests that: teachers can feel deskilled during change; some wait to see whether the ends justify the means before they commit to being involved; many select and take up what does not challenge their existing practice; and others simply resist.

Capacity building requires coordinated leadership and management directed to both cultural and structural changes. School staff must be excited, challenged and engaged by the reasons for the processes of capacity building. Programmes which focus on capacity building generally have three foci – the individual and their passions, curiosities and needs; groups and their collective energies, knowledges and interests; and the whole organisation and its agreed priorities and directions for change. This requires a range of supports, including, among other things:

- for individuals: coaching, peer observation, personal growth planning, practitioner inquiry support for formal study, release time from duties;
- for groups/teams: participatory action research, timetabled team meeting time, budgetary support, critical friends;
- for the whole school: good formal and informal communication mechanisms; programmed time for sharing and discussion; participatory decision-making structures; accessible review and planning processes, external networks which critically support and add to school practices.

Reform literatures attest that the 'grammar of schooling' – that is, the ways in which schools are routinely organised – is very hard to shift (Tyack and Cuban, 1995). Furthermore, significant and sustained change takes considerable time to achieve (Hargreaves and Fink, 2006; Thomson, 2007). This is because capacity building is not a quick fix. It is also because it is more likely to succeed if there is both internal effort and positive, critical outside support. This external support needs to be in multiple forms, ranging from the provision of new intellectual and material resources and the employment of advisers engaged in ongoing dialogue with the school, to the alignment of system goals, management structures and accountability systems.

The chapters that follow collectively show these facets of capacity building. They focus by and large on building capacity in the arts and to a lesser extent in creative learning approaches.

References

Achinstein, B. (2002) *Community, Diversity and Conflict among School Teachers: The Ties that Blind*, New York: Teachers College Press.

Bascia, N. and Hargreaves, A. (eds) (2000) *The Sharp Edge of Educational Reform: Teaching, Leading and the Realities of Reform*, London: Falmer.

Baser, H. and Morgan, P. (2008) *Capacity, Change and Performance*, Brussels: European Centre for Development Policy Management.

Bullough, R. (2007) Professional learning communities and the eight year study, *Educational Horizons* (Spring): 168–80.

Cavaye, J. M. (2000) *The Role of Government in Community Capacity Building*, Brisbane: Department of Primary Industries and Fisheries, Queensland Government.

Datnow, A. (1998) *The Gender Politics of Educational Change*, Washington, DC: Falmer Press.

Datnow, A. and Castellano, M. (2000) Teachers' responses to Success for All: how beliefs, experiences, and adaptations shape implementation, *American Educational Research Journal* 37(3): 775–800.

Eade, D. (1997) *Capacity Building: An Approach to People-Centred Development*, Oxford: Oxfam.

Elmore, R. (2004) *School Reform from the Inside-Out*, Cambridge, MA: Harvard University Press.

Fullan, M. (1993) *Change Forces: Probing the Depths of Educational Reform*, London: Falmer.

Hargreaves, A. and Evans, R. (1997) Teachers and educational reform, in A. Hargreaves and R. Evans (eds) *Beyond Educational Reform: Bringing Teachers Back in*, Buckingham: Open University Press.

Hargreaves, A. and Fink, D. (2006) *Sustainable Leadership*, San Francisco: Jossey Bass.

Levin, B. (2008) *How to Change 500 Schools: A Practical and Positive Approach for Leading Change at Every Level*, Cambridge, MA: Harvard Education Press.

Lieberman, A. (ed.) (1986) *Rethinking School Improvement: Research, Craft and Concept*, New York: Teachers College Press.

Lieberman, A. and Miller, L. (2001) *Teachers Caught in the Action: Professional Development in Practice*, New York: Teachers College Press.

McInerney, P. (2005) *Making Hope Practical: School Reform for Social Justice*, Brisbane: Postpressed.

McLaughlin, C., Black-Hawkins, K., Brindley, S., McIntyre, D. and Taber, K. (2006) *Researching Schools: Stories from a Schools–University Partnership for Educational Research*, London: Routledge.

McLaughlin, M. W. and Talbert, J. E. (2001) *Professional Communities and the Work of High School Teaching*, Chicago: University of Chicago Press.

Thomson, P. (2007) Making education more equitable: what can policymakers learn from the Australian Disadvantaged Schools Programme?, in R. Teese, S. Lamb and M. Durubellat (eds) *International Studies in Educational Inequality: Theory and Policy*, vol. 3, Dordrecht: Springer.

Tittle, D. (1995) *Welcome to Heights High: The Crippling Politics of Restructuring America's Public Schools*, Columbus: Ohio State University Press.

Tyack, D. and Cuban, L. (1995) *Tinkering toward Utopia: A Century of Public School Reform*, San Francisco: Jossey Bass.

Weidner, H. (2002) Capacity building for ecological modernisation, *American Behavioural Scientist* 45(9): 1340–68.

Westheimer, J. (1998) *Among Schoolteachers: Community, Autonomy and Ideology in Teachers' Work*, New York: Teachers College Press.

36

Outsider | insiders

Becoming a creative partner with schools

Nick Owen

Introduction

Urban regeneration partnership initiatives – in which the public, private and voluntary sectors collaborate in order to bring about the management of public services within neighbourhoods – have been a feature of the UK's political landscape since the Thatcher government of the 1980s. The concept of partnership has consequently been adopted within education, although, as Diamond suggests, presenting them as 'Change agents in the way they bring together different (and sometimes competing) interest groups (means) regeneration partnerships are, therefore, often the sites of unresolved interest' (Diamond, 2002: 296).

The Aspire Trust is an independent Social Enterprise and registered charity, born from a public sector parent which itself had been infected increasingly with private sector values and practices since the early 1980s.[1] As such, it is a stark example of how the private, public and voluntary sectors can interact to generate new ways of working, encourage the emergence of new cultures of education development and produce new financial models for strategic development and operational delivery.

Collaborative working and partnership development have been essential values in establishing our work with schools and wider cultural networks. This chapter will identify, through one case study – that of the secondary school Oldershaw School in Wallasey – the keys to the success and failure of those working relationships; discuss what constitutes effective creative partnership working in schools; and suggest models of practice which are transferable to other settings and contexts in which 'outsiders' work with and as 'insiders'.

Collaborative working and partnership development: bracing oneself for the future

Whatever the funding regimes which support the business, and whatever strategic partnerships are called into play to facilitate the work, the *cultural realpolitik* of the practice Aspire aims to develop is dependent on the success (or otherwise) of the relationship building which comes into play when artists meet teachers. In order to navigate our progress through these relationships we have found it particularly beneficial to theorise our practice through the underpinning theoretical framework of Insider–Outsider Theory.

When an artist comes to a school, they are faced with a number of options as to how they engage with the cultural practices of the school and how they work with educators in that school: whether to adapt to and assimilate into the host culture, whether to resist it, challenge it, ignore it or imagine that there is no discrepancy between the two. There are a multiplicity of choices of engagement, disengagement, embedding and embodiment: or what Padilla refers to as 'assimilation, acculturation or accommodation and pluralism' (Padilla, 1980, cited in Kearney, 2003: 37). On the one hand, the artist can be viewed as 'infectious outsider', capable of providing new approaches to learning and a source of new technical skills. On the other, they can also be seen as 'outside interference', capable of disrupting school timetables and providing an irritating distraction to the core business of teaching the national curriculum. Insider–Outsider Theory helps provide a conceptual understanding of what happens in these insider–outsider interactions.

According to Lindbeck and Snower (2002), Insider–Outsider Theory is placed within the domain of economics, and specifically within the field of labour economics and macroeconomics. Dobbie elaborates upon these models by referring to the concept of hysteresis, 'the property of systems (usually physical systems) that do not instantly follow the forces applied to them, but react slowly, or do not return completely to their original state: that is, systems whose states depend on their immediate history' (Dobbie, 2004b: 3; Wikipedia, March 2007), which is of relevance to our work, as

> it is for these reasons that hysteretic systems have been variously described as 'historical systems', and as systems in which 'Where you get to is determined by how you get there'.
> *(Buiter, 1987: 24)*

Another important idea for thinking about insiders and outsiders is offered through readings of performativity, most notably by Butler (1990) in her work on identity and sexuality. As Gauntlett explains, 'gender is a performance; it's what you do at particular times, rather than a universal who you are' (Gauntlett, 2008: 150). Day *et al.* also address the question of the identities involved in change: they challenge the concept of identity as being intrinsically stable and argue instead for its intrinsic fragmentation, arguing that 'teacher identities may be more, or less, stable and more or less fragmented at different times and in different ways according to a number of life, career and situational factors' (Day *et al.*, 2006: 601).

Taken together, these concepts suggest that educators and artists roles are *what you do* as opposed to a *universal what you are*: identity is thus constructed and performed through what actions and roles one performs. But what you do as a teacher is not fixed. Teachers' identities are being refashioned continually. Ball (2004) argues that in England performativity and management have transformed teachers' identities through an increasing emphasis on efficiency over ethics and this has effected the reconfiguration of their identities into technicians. Bottery and Wright (2000) similarly make the case that the modernisation of the teaching profession has entailed teachers being both de-professionalised (through the erosion of their professional autonomy) and re-professionalised, through new regulatory structures and cultures.

The question of the identity of the 'outsider' and 'insider' is thus a more complicated issue than one interpreted solely through the framework of employment status. It is not a fixed state which an individual possesses, but involves choices being made by its protagonists; and once those choices are made, the system they inhabit may demonstrate hysteresis; that is, it may react slowly, may not return completely to its original state, prior to the introduction of the 'outsider'.

These issues of the relationship between 'insider' and 'outsider', how they communicate, what they expect of each other and what effect they have on the hysteretic system that is a school culture are the focus of this chapter.

Case study: De-schooled? Re-Engaged! (the Dere Project) at Oldershaw School

Over 2007/2008, Aspire's associate musicians – Martin Milner, Nicki Dupuy and Andy Escott – developed some exciting creative music opportunities with pupils and staff at the Oldershaw School in Wallasey, Wirral, and two partner primary schools. Funded substantially by Youth Music and a host of other charitable donations, the project De-schooled? Re-Engaged! aimed to bring about the inclusion of vulnerable and 'at risk' children aged between 5 and 14 years from the most socially deprived areas of Wallasey. The project sought to 're-attach' them to learning and routes of positive personal development through collaborative working practices between musicians and educators.

Musicians' practice: how they approached the project

The Aspire musicians described their own creative practice based upon improvisatory music-making growing out of a range of holding forms and starting points appropriate to the group. They have worked with various musical genres and approaches from formal, structured music to free improvisation. All three of the team had a strong background in both performing and education: Nicki, for example, has a strong background in jazz and other popular music as a bass player, and as a percussionist in Brazilian and Cuban forms. She also sings and plays other instruments. As a composer she has also worked with electronic and computer generated music to produce pieces for dance, film and for multi-media sound installations – also incorporating a strong element of environmental sound. Andy, on the other hand, makes music on whatever instruments/materials are to hand and can formulate songs based on improvisation and jamming.

All three saw their own creative practice very closely informing their school-based work in a variety of ways, which suggests that their approach is based partially on a modern notion of apprenticeship. Martin, for example, often improvised, sometimes freely, more often within specific genres. He also promoted composition, in the sense that he devised holding forms and starting points for the groups he played with. Nicki was able to address music in a wide sense and adapt to situations as necessary. She favoured working creatively using improvisation, improvisational structures and also learning about music using structured songs and pieces. She was interested in exploring sounds and working with found-sound sources to develop pieces. Andy brought his experience of making music into the workshop environment and encouraged the same approach as a model for the children to use when writing.

These were not solely practising musicians who knew little of educational theory or peda-gogies. Martin, for example, was a trained teacher with two years experience teaching music at secondary level and two years part time at Liverpool Institute of Performing Arts. They all drew on a wide variety of intellectual resources: the traditions of Community Music practice as developed since the 1960s; Search Pedagogy of the Oppressed (Freire, 1993); Deschooling (Illich, 1971); the Reggio Emilia approach; group dynamics theory; coaching skills, including neurolinguistic programming (NLP); and shamanic and spiritual ideas, including Buddhism. Nicki had explored aspects of learning theory, applied theatre practice and a variety of approaches within Community Music practice, as well as having worked with Reggio Emilia theories and practice. Andy related particularly to the experiential learning he had developed based on his experience of working in bands and workshopping over many years: through experimentation, learning and listening to participants, and watching and learning from other music practitioners.

The musicians' relationships with the host school and pupils

At the start of the project, the musicians' expectations were high in view of the resources and workers employed and the fact that it was planned to take place over a year. They expected to be able to develop music-making practices that engaged and inspired young people who were struggling with school; and to share and disseminate these practices with educators and musicians. They also expected to be able to show positive impact of these practices on the lives of the participants. They were all committed to the ideals of working with disengaged and vulnerable children and young people, using music as a means of engaging them in meaningful development over a relatively long period. Andy said:

> I wanted to engage the young people having difficulties in education, with the excitement that music has given me over the years, to inspire them into believing that they are capable of much more, and to prove to their peers and teachers that they possess talent and potential well beyond their perception.
>
> *(Andy)*

The relatively long-term nature of this project meant that they were able to develop ongoing relationships with pupils that were supportive, positive and predominantly informal. They were able to present themselves as adults who had something new to offer, inspiring confidence in what they were doing; in Martin's case, as a group leader who could hold the group securely whilst allowing everyone to express their ideas and emotions so that they could create and learn together in an atmosphere of enjoyment:

> The relationships formed with the participants were mutually beneficial: we saw respect and friendships being formed within groups that we're confident will be long lasting.
>
> *(Martin)*

Musicians did not just play the role of musicians during the project, however, but also found themselves adopting a number of educational roles during the project, such as teacher, instructor, mentor/role model, social activist, catalyst for inspiration and change, and even co-learner. Nicki explained it thus:

> In presenting structured material, e.g. instrumental technique, the role is teacher or instructor. When playing an instrument, singing and in my behaviour towards them (respect, listening, good communication, etc) – role model. In listening to their ideas and noticing how they create new ways of doing things and reflecting this back to them – co-learner. In responding to their questions and desires about future music-making – mentor. In introducing ideas about how to create a piece of music, how to make a solo – catalyst for inspiration.
>
> *(Nicki)*

Project aims and objectives

Within the broad strategic direction of the project, the musicians had a range of connected and integrated aims and objectives for the project. As Martin put it:

> Broadly I wanted to convince the participants that they are musical themselves, and to help them become confident in making music. I wanted to challenge ideas that music is only made by professional musicians. I wanted to show that any group can make music toge-ther. I wanted to inspire the participants to use their own imaginations to devise ways of organising sounds into patterns by thinking about how groups can and do work.
>
> I wanted to convince the educators that one doesn't have to be a professional musician to coordinate music-making in groups, especially in primary schools, where there are few specialist music or musical teachers.
>
> *(Martin)*

Nicki's emphasis was more focused towards encouraging participants' development and their self-empowerment by creating a positive environment and attitude to learning and self-direction. In some cases she also identified that it was about establishing a meaningful relationship with participants as an adult, based on development of trust, as this was an issue for some young people, particularly the older participants at the secondary school. It was also about

> enhancing their confidence with regard to music-making and to working with others ... and for them to develop a relationship to music that could be carried forward into the future that would enrich their lives and carry with it the possibility of transferring that to other meaningful and positive experiences in their lives.
>
> *(Nicki)*

Andy further articulated the link between performing musically and performing socially whilst also offering a critical view of what prevents this from occurring in many school sites:

> I wanted to enable the participants to believe that they have ability, not just musically but using music to bring out self-confidence, discipline and creativity. Music can be made by anyone and on almost anything; the sooner educators starts engaging young people and listening to them about what they actually want to learn, and allowing them to have a go, the sooner they will be empowered to produce it in a way they enjoy and is fun. Locked musical instrument cupboards and rooms increase the level of distrust that children feel; my approach of allowing the children to play any instrument and letting them explore it and ask for help when they need it instils a self-discipline and respect that can't be taught.
>
> *(Andy)*

How the musicians worked on the project

The musicians worked by introducing ideas to educators for group music-making that were easy to adapt and use with groups of children and young people and by introducing to participants the idea that their own music is just as valid as what they consume as listeners. The idea that anyone has the ability to create music, write real and well-constructed songs, and have fun playing and making music was an essential pedagogical approach. Children were introduced to a range of specialist musical technical language which was relevant to the work but care was also taken to use non-confrontational language based on respect. Some musical notational ideas were also introduced to the children, but the notion of form was the main element discussed, for example verse/bridge/chorus/middle eight.

The musicians had to adapt to a variety of working environments, sometimes at short notice, including ordinary classrooms, music classrooms, school halls, external playground spaces, school canteen and school library; and occasionally had to negotiate for appropriate spaces. Whilst there were occasions when they wanted to ignore division bells for classes if the group was in flow, they were sometimes unable to do this partly because of the children's own anxiety about not sticking to the school timetable. Their practices also had the effect of challenging the school's institutional structure, although some individuals within the school structure did find the work positive, particularly the learning mentor at the Oldershaw School. These challenges were sometimes accommodated, sometimes ignored; but the pressures of the school timetable could be circumvented by, for example, performing impromptu gigs at break time either indoors or outside. Space to play in was a consistent issue at Oldershaw, which led to the musicians feeling that they were undervalued by the school staff, although there was a recognition too that schools are very busy places during the school day and have to contend with a variety of pressures and concerns from many different quarters.

The musicians were able to bring a range of new resources to the classroom, including many new musical sound sources, a variety of electrical band instruments and hand-held percussion, and a PA system which enabled them to add vocal contributions to amplified music:

> We found in the primary schools particularly that as most of the children had never been allowed to use the school instruments anything we introduced or used from the school was new to them.

> *(Martin)*

The heart of the project was about using music to re-engage children in to the school community and this involved challenging many issues for both participants and educators. Participating young people brought issues of low self-esteem and confidence as well as personality clashes between individuals. One group of Oldershaw students mentioned that they were regarded as 'the mongs' (short for mongrels) by fellow students, for example. The team used these issues to strengthen the group dynamics and this helped form bonds within groups. They used these kinds of incidents to instigate directions for musical creativity, and instil feelings of self-belief without having to address directly the negative connotations the comments had evoked. Because of the positive nature of the sessions, and the fun that was had, most problem solving was done by the participants – they tended to self-police, with interventions from the team when conversations got too heated or safety was an issue. Where possible the team used these moments as inspiration for different kinds of music-making.

But working with colleague educators produced a different set of problems due to the different cultures of education, with our informal and personalised approach in conflict with more conventional classroom management styles. This was particularly visible in the relationship with some members of the school's senior management.

A particularly important aesthetic challenge was the idea that music is just for the *talented few* and that young people had to be technically *good* in order to start making music. We also challenged the ideas that one person has to be in control of the creative process and that there is always necessarily a right or wrong way to do something: this implicitly challenged any sense that any of the participants were not valuable in themselves and so contributed to the increasing confidence and self-esteem that was witnessed in young people as the project developed.

The project consequently offered opportunities for divergent or original ways of thinking: music-making was posed as a problem and the devising of solutions led to music. We encouraged creative thinking through focused questions, and rewarded original and even unusual solutions with praise. Participants were given opportunities to come up with their own ideas, to extend the ideas we were already working with, to try out these ideas and find out if they could make them work. The hands-off approach and the freedom participants were allowed to express themselves musically allowed for originality and 'left-field' ideas to develop naturally.

This approach meant that the project was able to offer participants the opportunity to work beyond their comfort zone. This applied not just to the young participants but also to the participating educators. As Martin explained:

> There were several moments when challenging behaviour (such as pupils standing on desks while singing) had to be balanced against the fact that the pupil was engaged with the group and contributing creatively.
>
> *(Martin)*

Pupils claimed that when they were encountering new ideas and practices, these were initially a challenge to them (playing a solo in front of others, leading a group, learning a difficult song or rhythm). For some, concentration was a challenge; for others leading a group was a new experience that they enjoyed getting to grips with. For some participants, having enough trust in an adult to create a relationship was a continual challenge that was addressed over the length of the project. Whilst many successes were encountered, relationships remained potentially fragile and difficult for the participants concerned, and considerable skill and sensitivity were required of the team in order to sustain the fragile nature of these emerging relationships. Andy pointed out that the different type of relationship that the team offered was another way in which participants were held out of their comfort zone:

> I'm not a teacher in the conventional sense of the word, therefore the standard pupil–teacher relationship that the participants were used to didn't exist ... this actually challenged many of them as the rules that they abided by were different. There was a different and more honest level of respect that developed as a result of this.
>
> *(Andy)*

Opportunities for co-learning between the team, the young people and school staff were also significantly in evidence as the project progressed – although there were times too when these opportunities were not fully exploited. As Martin explained:

> We worked alongside educators and were able to share our knowledge of music-making with their knowledge of the children. In my mind these were among the best sessions. Sadly the staff in question both left the school. In Oldershaw we sometimes worked while the learning mentors were (voluntarily) present, enabling us to have informed conversations about the group and what we were doing.
>
> *(Martin)*

We found that where members of staff were able and willing, there was an exchange of ideas between all parties. The learning mentors at Oldershaw, for example, became, voluntarily, highly involved in the project, and much knowledge and experience were shared, particularly in 'down time' after sessions. By contrast, one of the partner primary schools where we also worked ensured that several teachers and teaching assistants were involved in the project and several cross-curriculum ideas were discussed, but, as far as we know, these were rarely acted on. And even though the music specialist took a lot of the presented musical ideas, he did not apply the interpersonal approaches inherent in the pedagogical processes being used. The Oldershaw School took more from the team than this. All too frequently, though, staff were not present or involved in the work. Constraints of time and pressures on staffing contributed to this situation, but the team also felt that in some cases there were misunderstandings about the project and the approaches that were being used.

However, despite this opportunity not being fully grasped, it was clear that the work had a strong impact on participants and that many of them developed considerable skills as musicians and grew in confidence. There was extensive evidence of practising and fine-tuning in between sessions. In Oldershaw participants came to sessions having written and reworked lyrics, refined drum grooves and changed bass lines in the week preceding. At one of the partner primary schools the children came up with names for their band, practised and performed in front of audiences and came up with new ideas off their own backs; and at the other, one student was devising and experimenting with making music on whatever he could find in his spare time!

Mike Crookes, the learning mentor at Oldershaw, hoped that the children who took part would become enthused about the project. He felt he had a very positive relationship with all three musicians and found that his relationship with the children changed during the project, with him getting to know some of the children much more than he had previously. He saw the project as a means of allowing participants to have fun, to build up confidence and self-esteem, to work co-operatively; and of re-engaging pupils with school.

He heard the musicians speaking at a level that the children understood, and also liaising professionally with staff, adapting to the school environment as necessary. To him the project offered ways for the participants to explore their musicality and develop and learn new skills:

> It was a good experience for young people and adults/staff to learn from each other. especially young people teaching young people. It definitely challenged the children who took part, some of whom responded brilliantly. The project was continued during break times in school. They definitely reflected on their work with me and some wanted to continue practising. There was an increase in confidence in participants as they became more proficient, and especially after the performance.
>
> *(Mike Crookes, learning mentor, Oldershaw School)*

Reports from parents, learning mentors and other educators showed that individuals had changed significantly, becoming more confident, making friends more easily, becoming happier; in some cases there was also an increase in self-esteem accompanying that confidence.

> I think the Aspire Team are an amazing, gifted group of people. Their talents need to be recognised. They did so much for Chrissie in all areas of her development but mainly for her emotionally, inspiring her with such confidence in herself. I can't thank the team enough and both Chrissie and myself feel very sad that this cannot work in Oldershaw permanently. THANK YOU, KEEP UP THE GOOD WORK!!
>
> *(Parent of Chrissie, Year 9 pupil, Oldershaw School)*

This increase in confidence and self-esteem may well be the lasting legacy of the project. All the participants who performed live will have had a lasting experience unlike anything many of them had had before. The time and energy and dedication that they put into making music will hopefully lead them to believe that they are able to achieve far more than they may have thought possible. The feedback we received from mentors, and in particular from the head teacher and staff at Riverside, confirmed that the project had a monumental effect on behaviour, attendance and involvement in class for several 'difficult' and 'unmanageable' pupils.

Making change stick

Whilst it was satisfying to produce a body of work which was evidenced, documented and which supported the case for an approach to a different form of music-making, it was disappointing immediately after the project finished that we had not been able to disseminate our work more widely, or to develop ongoing projects for the participants who wanted to carry on making music. The project had clearly made a difference to a lot of young people previously labelled difficult or at risk. The length of the project and our ability to work with the same children for a year made them feel worthy, wanted, and helped them develop trust in adults and belief in consistency and in their own abilities.

However, we were concerned that it would only be a matter of time before the same patterns and problems that the participants experienced before the project began to rear their heads again, and the levels of confidence, trust and respect that the project started would be erased. We were concerned that the change initiated by the engagement with outsiders would not stick and that the hysteretical nature of the system would mean a return to previously tried and tested forms of attitude, behaviour and disengagement.

However, at Oldershaw this anxiety proved to be unfounded. At the final performance event of the project, the group was invited to perform their self-composed material to an audience of over 100 children and adults. The performance lasted a full hour. From being a group of disaffected young people whose main experience of being watched by a group of adults was confined to teachers in classrooms, and perhaps in some cases by social workers visiting their homes, the performance experience, as mediated by the musicians, gave them an experience of being listened to sympathetically, within a spirit of appreciation and in an atmosphere of celebration. The memory of that experience was to last with those young people for months to come.

Mike Crookes, too, noted not only the excitement the children got from performing, but also the 'buzz' he got from watching them perform. The work had led to not only increased levels of self-appreciation by the young people of themselves, but a change in attitude by their learning mentor towards them: something which has proven to be irreversible. Once different behaviours and identities had been chosen and performed, there was no undoing those choices and the consequence for others from those choices.

Concluding remarks

Whilst the musicians had to leave the building at the end of their contracts, Mike Crookes noted that for many months members of the group were coming up to him asking, 'When's Andy coming back?', 'When's Martin coming back?', 'When's Nicky coming back?' For some of those young people, their engagement with outsiders has left an indelible memory for them of achievement, success and validation. This may not have made them easier children to teach; it may not have had any long-term effect on making them any more compliant to adapting to the school's behaviour policy: but it did make them more resilient in dealing with the demands of school life; it ensured that they have stayed in school and in some instances continued to expand their interest in music and performance. In all cases, school staff were confident in ascribing those changes to the young people's participation in the programme.

For Aspire, the project also proved to be a significant influence in determining how we have continued to employ practitioners and involve them in schools projects. Rather than attempt to introduce outsider artists as surrogate teachers, we now focus on introducing practitioners who are markedly outside the common culture of the school – whether this be through their appearance, language, skill base, cultural backgrounds or other defining features which mark out their 'otherness' within the day to day realities of school life.

This state of affairs, though, is neither stable nor easy to maintain; but though the introduction of artists and their involvement in the lives and learnings of young people and teachers do mean that the changes they catalyse might be slow, they are long lasting, memorable and irreversibly life changing.

Note

1 The Aspire Trust ('Aspire') was originally set up under the auspices of the Aspire mini-Education Action Zone (mini-EAZ), which operated within Wirral's Excellence in Cities (EiC) programme from 2002 to 2004. Initially conceived as a vehicle to extend the provision of the EAZ (by fundraising or by managing Extended School provision, for example), the Trust built a reputation for developing arts programmes predominantly within the mini-EAZ school cluster. When the EAZ's funding came to an end and Wirral EiC was remodelled, this provided the ideal opportunity to build on this work by establishing the Trust as independent charity and social enterprise.

References

Ball, S. (2004) Education reform as social Barberism: economism and the end of authenticity, *Scottish Educational Review* 37(1): 4–16.

Bottery, M. and Wright, N. (2000) *Teachers and the State: Towards a Directed Profession*, London: Routledge.

Buiter, W. (1987) *The Right Combination of Demand and Supply Policies: The Case for a Two Handed Approach*, NBER working paper no. 2333, Cambridge, MA: NBER.

Butler, J. (1990) *Gender Trouble*, New York: Routledge.

David, T. G. and Wright, B. D. (eds) (1974) *Learning Environments*. Chicago and London: University of Chicago Press.

Day, C., Kington, A., Stobart, G. and Sammons, P. (2006) The personal and professional selves of teachers: stable and unstable identities, *British Educational Research Journal* 32(4): 601–16.

Department for Education and Skills (DES) (2006) Education outside the classroom manifesto; available at http://www.dfes.gov.uk/consultations/downloadableDocs/Consultation%20document%20-%20Word%20Version.doc (accessed 7 March 2006).

Diamond, J. (2002) Strategies to resolve conflict in partnerships: reflections on UK urban regeneration, *International Journal of Public Sector Management* 15(4/5): 296–306.

Dobbie, M. (2004a) The insider outsider theory: some evidence from Australia, *Australian Journal of Labour Economics* 8(2): 181–202.

—— (2004b) Macquarie University, Department of Economics Research Papers, 0407.

Freire, P. (1993) *Pedagogy of the Oppressed*, London: Penguin Books.

Gauntlett, D. (2008) *Media Gender Identity: An Introduction*, Abingdon: Routledge.

Hughes, B. (2001) *Evolutionary Playwork and Reflective Analytic Practice*, London: Routledge.

Illich, Ivan (1971) *Deschooling Society*, New York: Harrow Books.

Kearney, C. (2003) *The Monkey's Mask: Identity, Memory, Narrative and Voice*, London: Trentham Books.

Lindbeck, A. and Snower, D. (2002) *The Insider–Outsider Theory: A Survey Institute*, Bonn: Institute for the Study of Labor.

Lindon, J. (2005) *Understanding Child Development: Linking Theory to Practise*, London: Hodder Arnold.

O'Brien, L. and Murray, R. (2007) Forest School and its impacts on young children: case studies in Britain, *Urban Forestry 65*.

Palmer, J. (1998) *Environmental Education in the 21st Century: Theory, Practice, Progress, and Promise*, London and New York: RoutledgeFalmer.

Stevens, J. (1985) *Search and Reflect*, London: Community Music.

37

The grit in the oyster

Creative partners as catalysts for school reform in the UK and the US

Arnold Aprill, Gail E. Burnaford and Pat Cochrane

Long-term partnerships: CAPE and CapeUK

The Chicago Arts Partnerships in Education (CAPE) in the US and CapeUK in the UK are both dedicated to school improvement through long-term partnerships between schools and creative practitioners. CAPE was founded in 1993 and CapeUK in 1997. Although completely independent, the two organisations have a strong collegial relationship – regular transatlantic visits and dialogue enable sharing and refinement of practice and comparison of approaches emerging within different contexts.

CAPE in the US is a nongovernmental agency, initiated by a group of philanthropic foundations and corporations, that supports long-term partnerships among artists and arts organisations (representing all arts disciplines) and kindergarten through secondary educators and schools in Chicago, with a focus on schools in disenfranchised neighbourhoods. One of CAPE's primary strategies is 'arts integration' – an approach to teaching and learning in which artists and teachers co-plan curricular work that connects arts learning and learning in other academic areas.

CapeUK is a not for profit company based in the north of England. Initially inspired by the model of sustained partnerships in the US, CapeUK explores how such long-term partnerships between schools and external agencies can bring about sustainable change in schools by influencing leadership, curriculum design and pedagogy (Cochrane and Cockett, 2007). Over the past twelve years CapeUK has supported both national and regional school-based partnerships, acting as the initial model for the national Creative Partnerships programme. Between 2008 and 2010 CapeUK was commissioned to advise government in England on creativity in education.

Both organisations work to prepare children and young people for 'an unknowable future' and the challenges of the twenty-first century, forming networks of schools that nurture and support the development of creativity in young people in all areas of their learning and lives. Partnerships are encouraged to move beyond the safe space of traditional arts education partnerships, where a visiting artist 'delivers' an experience, to a more conceptual space in which innovative approaches to pedagogy can emerge, focused on the capacities of the children, and enabling them to be active agents in the process (ibid.).

By attending to creative and peer to peer learning in an era of top-down national curriculum in England and an increased focus on testing in the United States, both models were initially working against the current of their times. Both organisations experienced similar frustrations with hierarchical curricular models that constrained the development of capacities that would sustain children and young people in an increasingly complex and rapidly changing world, and both initiatives explored the links between in-school and out-of-school learning.

Creativity rhetoric in the policy environment

Over the last ten years, creativity has become increasingly prominent in policy in both countries. In the UK there has been a gradual but significant shift of policy since *All Our Futures* (DfES, 1999) argued that creativity is a core capacity for twenty-first century learning, defining creativity as: 'Imaginative activity fashioned so as to produce outcomes that are both original and of value'. Since then initiatives such as the Qualifications and Curriculum Authority Creativity (QCA) *Creativity: Find It Promote It* research project, the Creative Partnerships initiative and a new secondary curriculum in which the creative development of young people is a specified aim have supported schools in developing creative approaches to learning and teaching.

In the United States the National Center on Education and the Economy (NCEE) published a report of the New Commission on the Skills of the American Workforce, entitled *Tough Choices or Tough Times*, in 2007. The report describes a new world that depends on

> a deep vein of creativity that is constantly renewing itself, and on a myriad of people who can imagine how people can use things that have never been available before, create ingenious marketing and sales campaigns, write books, build furniture, make movies, and imagine new kinds of software that will capture people's imagination and become indispensable to millions.
>
> *(NCEE, 2007: xxiv)*

School leaders, practitioners and researchers in both the US and the UK are working to develop appropriate approaches to the observation, documentation and assessment of creativity, which has been increasingly recognised as an important dimension of developing pedagogy for creative learning (HMSO, 2007; Ofsted, 2010). This effort has become increasingly urgent in the US, where more and more school reform efforts are becoming focused on 'data driven' teaching policy and practice.

We outline here four sets of shared principles which CAPE and CapeUK have adopted to sustain creative development within shifting, at times contradictory, policy contexts.

Shared principles

Sharing creative responses to standards and policy mandates through documentation and public discourse

The launch of CapeUK in 1998 coincided with the introduction of national literacy and numeracy strategies that directed primary schools to spend an hour a day on literacy and numeracy. Many schools cut the time spent on other subjects, leading to the charge that the curriculum had become impoverished. Although schools were advised to maintain a 'broad and balanced curriculum' (DfES, 2003), inevitably there was a tendency to focus on those areas which were tested, subject to scrutiny in nationally published league tables, and supported by national guidance and waves of top–down, centrally organised and led training. A similar narrowing of the curriculum was experienced by educators in the US in response to the national *No Child Left Behind* legislation, which officially endorsed arts education but, by focusing on testing literacy and numeracy, had a chilling effect on the teaching of the arts, social studies, science and physical education (Crocco and Costigan, 2007).

Both organisations work to assist schools in responding to such policy mandates in ways that support on-going school innovation and growth. CAPE coined the term 'radical compliance' – a pedagogical stance in which externally imposed literacy and numeracy strategies become opportunities for exploration and creativity through enquiry-based investigation of content, and through the representation of student work processes and thinking in multiple media – an attitude of 'uncovering' rather than 'covering' content standards. Both organisations challenge the prejudice that 'creative learning is not rigorous' by implementing research-based approaches to teaching closely aligned with indicators of creative learning: joint productive activity, literacy across the curriculum, connecting school to students' lives, challenging activities, and teaching through conversation and dialogue (Center for Research on Education, Diversity, and Excellence website).

Both CAPE and CapeUK are committed to sharing their investigations of teaching for creative learning with multiple audiences (peers, parents, communities, policymakers, etc.) through multiple media (print media, digital media, exhibitions, reports, presentations, performances, conferences, etc.).

The emergence of new technologies has made possible online documentation for capturing both the products and processes of creative learning. This documentation can subsequently be accessed by a broad base of teachers, artists and other stakeholders to reflect upon and share effective teaching practices, and to explore rich and varied portraits of student learning in action.

'Layered research' involving practitioners in collaboration with professional researchers

Both CAPE and CapeUK support sustained partnerships among schools and creative practitioners as a mechanism for transforming schools into creative spaces for learning, and both have discovered that a key to that transformation process involves re-visioning teachers, artists and learners as co-researchers exploring, representing, and re-representing their teaching and learning. Both, independently, initiated a practice of *action research* (educators developing *enquiry* questions about their practice, and then systematically collecting data from their practice to answer their questions in order to share insights with their peers and the field). CAPE theorises that arts integration provides a wider range of languages for students and teachers to investigate and represent their thinking, thereby creating a richer and more nuanced data set for action research on creative learning, and greater engagement by teachers in rethinking how they teach.

The particular innovation that both CAPE and CapeUK had implemented was in not only conducting action research as a regular part of on-going professional development, but also creating a system of 'layered research' – in which practitioner research is informed by and informs research conducted by professional researchers studying both creative learning in students and teacher growth as educators for creativity.

Such an enquiry focus also seems to have a particular impact in arts-based partnerships, where the energy can tend to focus on the excitement of project delivery rather than interventions which have the potential to lead to long-term developments in pedagogy or practice.

To help schools and external partners think through what kind of partnership was most helpful for them at a particular stage of their development CapeUK outlined a continuum of arts partnerships practice ranging from a visiting artist running a one-off project in a school to the process of enquiry-based practice (see Table 37.1).

Analysis of the Creativity Action Research Awards (CARA) – a national CapeUK-led programme of over 300 small scale action research partnerships between a teacher, a creative practitioner and a research mentor – suggested that the enquiry process itself, when supported by an external mentor maintaining an enquiry focus, was a powerful driver of change and sustainability. The impact on professional development and shifts in organisational thinking were found to be more significant than had been originally anticipated from a relatively small investment of time and resources (Craft *et al.*, 2007). Enquiry was emerging as the 'grit in the oyster' of effective creative partnerships.

Explicit attention to what is meant by creative learning

At the heart of the enquiry was the 'grit' of being explicit about what we mean by creativity. If we want to develop the creative capacities of children and young people, then we have to be explicit about what we mean by that. In 2003 the QCA in the UK published a simple set of indicators which characterised children's behaviours when being creative. These were:

> questioning and challenging; making connections and seeing relationships; envisaging what might be; exploring ideas, keeping options open; reflecting critically on ideas, actions and outcomes.
>
> *(QCA, 2003)*

Although this didn't include some of the more challenging and uncomfortable aspects of creativity, such as risk-taking and handling uncertainty, its simplicity was helpful to many teachers and practitioners in assessing the impact of their practice. Cape UK adapted these indicators for use within the CARA programme to stimulate teachers and practitioners to focus on the developing creativity of the young person, rather than design of a creative project or

Table 37.1 From artist into schools to layered research – a continuum

Artist into schools	Presentations or performances by external partners. Artists into school to work with pupils with little or no teacher engagement. One-off projects disconnected from other work done in the school.
Teacher apprenticeship	External partners leading the work with teachers observing and working alongside to learn some of their skills – with an aim to implementing this kind of work post-project.
Joint working	Teachers and partners working closely together to 'plan, do and review' a project.
Enquiry based practice	Teachers and partners working jointly to explore and refine an enquiry, leading to a plan for working with pupils and for tracking their learning. Adult reflection informs the next stages of work with pupils and a robust joint reflection that analyses the project.
Layered research	Enquiry based practice as above but with support of researcher analysing and feeding back findings from a network of enquiry programmes or projects over an extended period of time.

Source: Adapted from guidance developed by P. McGuigan, for CapeUK.

activity, and to support the conceptual shift from 'teaching creatively' to 'teaching for creativity'. These were further adapted in the US to drive reflection in the CAPE partnerships.

Long-term analysis of children's engagement in Creative Partnerships programmes suggests that when actively engaged in creative learning (Raw, 2009) children will demonstrate a range of behaviours, including: fascination, risk-taking, confidence, divergent thinking, seeing and solving problems, co-learning, and improved language and verbal reasoning. Creating learning contexts in which these capacities are nurtured in children and young people is central to CAPE and CapeUK's practice.

Professional development incorporating enquiry

Practitioners engaging in action research is a powerful means of professional development (Cordingley *et al.*, 2003; Doherty and Harland, 2001; Furlong and Salisbury, 2005). Research into CAPE's methodology strongly suggests that the value added by integrating the arts into teacher action research rests in the capacity of creative partnerships to accelerate the effectiveness of professional development in transforming teacher practice (Burnaford, 2007).

CAPE and CapeUK both chose to provide professional development to teachers and artists *together*, seeing the discourse between teachers and artists *during* the process as perhaps the most powerful element of professional learning. Teaching for creative learning involves an element of risk, exploration and uncertainty that may lead to friction between creative and sometimes experimental approaches and the more regulated nature of education systems. However, such friction can be productive. The differences in approaches to teaching and learning between teachers and creative practitioners form a generative tension that expands the practice of both, creating a safe space in which both teachers and creative practitioners can try out new teaching strategies that challenge the habits of all partners, and make room for student initiative (Jeffery and Ledgard, 2009).

A cascade approach to professional learning, in which a strategy is presented to a selected group of practitioners who are then responsible for sharing it more widely within a school community or network, is unlikely to be effective in supporting creativity or innovation (Elmore, 1996). For teachers to be able to support children's creative development, they need to have an understanding of a creative process which can only be developed by individuals experiencing and practising being creative themselves – or exercising the 'muscles of creativity' (Claxton, 2000). Effective professional development for the teaching of creative learning tends to combine the following:

- immersion in a creative process – in which participants experience risk-taking, facing and working through challenges, working collaboratively and towards an outcome or presentation of some kind;
- analysis of this personal experience of creativity, relating this to implications for teaching and learning;
- designing, applying and reflecting upon approaches to creative learning with children and young people;
- documenting new practices and insights, and sharing those findings with audiences that matter to teachers and creative practitioners through a variety of media – what CAPE calls 'going public'.

Enquiry is an essential ingredient of this process. Teachers and partners develop their own questions about a compelling issue in their own context, but alongside this the core question in relation to creativity is: 'What is it that as a teacher leader I am doing to support the children's creative development? How do I know that *they* are becoming creative?'

Principles in practice: layered research in action

The following description of nurturing networks of enquiry is drawn from the US experience, but the approach of generating on-going discussion and exploration with practitioners is common to both organisations.

'Veteran' CAPE artists and classroom teachers have been engaged in enquiry with the CAPE staff and the CAPE research team for many years (Burnaford, 2007; Burnaford and Aprill, 2008). The partners are now being challenged to discuss how their arts integration work reflects creative thinking, and how that creativity can be documented. Partner artist and teacher teams were introduced to indicators of creative thinking based on the model developed by the QCA and adapted by CapeUK (Cochrane and Cockett, 2007).

Across the CAPE network, teachers and artists are asked to discuss and document how they, as artists and teachers, might see these indicators manifested in children and young people. They are also asked to brainstorm how they as adults in classrooms might intentionally teach to scaffold these indicators of creativity. These cross-school discussions are useful for teachers in stimulating reflection with their colleagues back in their own schools (see Box 37.1).

Teachers and artists are then asked how they might illustrate or provide evidence of creativity in one or more of these areas. Their comments contribute to CAPE's efforts to document and describe creativity in arts integration projects. Other data sources include: student interviews conducted by the research team; culminating performance and exhibit artefacts; and online documentation of student, teacher and artist work in schools. Finding patterns across classrooms and grade levels concerning student thinking and learning is one credible and rigorous response to the essential question, 'What are students learning through arts integration?' Researchers in arts education have consistently called for assessment that is authentic and responsive to the arts

---

Box 37.1 Veteran Partnerships Professional Development Discussion Questions

What does 'learning to be creative' mean in your CAPE project work?
What do students do when they are being creative?
What do you do when you are feeling or being creative?
Some questions to guide your conversation:

- When do these creative moments happen most often?
- Under what circumstances?
- How do artists and teachers actively teach for these moments to happen?
- Can you recall when those moments of creative energy have happened in your CAPE work? Were they planned?
- How can you work toward making these moments happen more often in your classes?

Because we are trying to document learning this year, how might you share these creative moments on your documentation template? What might illustrate or provide evidence of creativity in one or more of these areas for your students?

---

themselves. This investigation of creativity and creative thinking is an attempt to further define such assessment.

Engagement of the participants in the design of the research initiative is essential to the continuing enrichment of the projects and the learning of the adults and the students involved. Discussions among teachers and practitioners underscore the importance of awareness of the *creative process* in arts education, and provide essential data for the research process.

The discussions are analysed by the CAPE researchers, and then fed back to the teacher/artist partnerships, enabling them to build on their practice (see Table 37.2).[1]

Partnerships as a sustainable structure for creative school reform

The dialogue between CapeUK and CAPE in the US has validated both organisations' commitment to supporting creativity in schools by organising professional communities that build teacher, artist and student capacity to ask hard questions, and to reflect on their work in an open-ended but systematic manner. Both the supportive structures and the generative tensions between practitioners in well-facilitated partnerships stimulate the necessary risk-taking and the crucial energy needed to sustain the on-going professional development and collective action research necessary for meaningful change at scale.

A growing body of research is showing that when effectively managed and implemented, creative partnerships have a positive impact on children's learning, motivation, judgement, and ability to engage with concepts and complex reasoning. A significant contribution could be made by further comparative analysis of:

- methods for investigation and examination of student work;
- approaches to analysing progression in creativity;
- what the practice of teaching for creativity looks like and what approaches to professional development support this;
- how creativity manifests itself in different domains of learning or subject disciplines.

The challenge that both CAPE in US and CapeUK face is: 'How does one scale up an initiative based on intense inter-relationships?' Guidance documents and audit processes are unlikely to drive a process of change. The target culture has created a climate in which practitioners from all spheres become adept at satisfying audit requirements and apparently complying whilst resisting real change. Change in teaching and learning comes about when practitioners develop an integrated, profound and authentic understanding of pedagogy for creativity based on co-constructed learning. Professional learning and enquiry are key to this process.

The results of CAPE Chicago's veteran partnership creativity studies and the findings of the CapeUK Creativity Action Research Awards both speak to the power of effective partnerships to scaffold creative thinking. The on-going collaborative reflection made possible by sustained partnerships generates *collective enquiry*, resulting in *practice-based school reform* – the only form of school reform that actually makes a difference for student learning.

Shifting from an industrial economy model of education, which tended to devalue creativity, to an information economy model of education, which seeks to foreground creativity, requires scaffolds and engines to propel and assist the transformation. What are our sustainable natural resources that can serve as these scaffolds and engines for creativity? It is the belief of CAPE and CapeUK that sustained partnerships make possible continuous innovation and creative thinking through on-going *dialogue* among creative practitioners (who are eternal 'problem-seekers'), educators (who are eternal stewards of learners' development) and the learners themselves.

Table 37.2 How is creativity fostered in Veteran Partnership CAPE projects? Synthesis of results

Creativity in student thinking: Data collection and analysis categories	Veteran partnership outcomes by indicators	Future considerations
a. Questioning, challenging	Attention to compelling inquiry questions and an Action Research stance by adults increased opportunity for students to challenge and question. Teams that focused on student ownership had more student work that questioned or challenged the norm. Questioning and challenging was related to the degree of student decision making	Provide opportunities for artists and teachers to showcase where and when students make decisions. Design documentation to incorporate student questions. Attend to student inquiry questions, not just as a frame for the unit, but as entities to be answered during and at the end of the unit.
b. Connecting, seeing relationships	Connections framed in student work appeared in four categories: 1) Linking recognized extreme opposites 2) Highlighting dueling symbol systems 3) Juxtaposing unlikely/unexpected pairs 4) Introducing new symbol systems	Encourage teachers to take the lead on connecting arts and non-arts documentation of learning. Share the four categories of creative connections and ask teams how they address them in their units.
c. Envisaging what might be, Imagining, Innovating	The CAPE methodology (working with the organizing principle of Big Ideas) encouraged conceptual thinking Teachers who explicitly asked 'What if' encourage students to imagine and be innovative.	Return to the Big Idea and encourage innovative ways to deal with concepts. Use documentation of past projects as examples of innovation, engaging teachers, artists and students in discussion.
d. Coping with uncertainty	Requires process documentation in order to capture; student work may not yield evidence of how and when students deal with uncertainty during units. The more student-directed the learning, the more opportunity students had to cope with uncertainty and solve their own problems creatively.	Build documentation opportunities around in-process work, not just end-of-unit requirements. View documentation as a place for feedback, discussion and ongoing deliberation on dilemmas, rather than a static repository. Provide documentation opportunities for illustrating when students direct, make decisions, and make choices.

(continued on next page)

Table 37.2 (continued)

Creativity in student thinking: *Data collection and analysis categories*	*Veteran partnership outcomes by indicators*	*Future considerations*
e. Reflecting critically	Artist and teacher reflections were documented; student reflections were seldom documented. Student reflections tended to be unit evaluation statements rather than critique/feedback statements that indicated creative thinking about the units. Documenting class discussions was a promising tool for showing evidence of reflecting critically as well as collaboratively.	Provide professional development on critique and feedback approaches for use with students. Work on questions and possible approaches to deepen and embed processes of critique in projects.

Source: Categories adapted from Cochrane, P. and Cockett, M. (2007) by Gail Burnaford for Chicago Arts Partnerships in Education

Although external agencies with a strong commitment to enquiry, layered research and long-term sustained investment in professional development can have a significant influence on individual teacher practice and pupils' experience, sustained and systemic change is ultimately dependent on the climate of leadership within each school. The capacity of the head teacher or school leader to act as the 'lead enquirer', nurturing and enabling partnerships, supporting others to engage in reflective practice, creating space for experimentation and teacher leadership, and pursuing enquiry themselves is key to school reform.

Tables summarizing CAPEUK and CAPE principles for creative classrooms

Table 37.3 Long-term partnerships that share their creative responses to standards and policy mandates through documentation and public discourse

Aspects of Teaching and Learning	Decrease	Increase
Role of external creative partners	Short-term, one-off visits, workshops, performances	Long term collaborative relationships
Teacher role in curriculum design	Teachers as receivers of pre-designed teaching and learning strategies	Teacher as co-creators and leaders of teaching and learning strategies to scaffold creative learning
The audiences for teacher work	The classroom as sole audience for teachers' work	The school, the community, the profession as audiences for teachers' work on teaching for creativity
Audiences for student work products:	Teachers as sole audience for students' work	Peers, communities, the world of real work as audiences for students' work as creative learners
Representations of student and teacher work	Reliance on display of final products and grades as representations of learning	Documentation of both creative process and products through multiple media

Table 37.4 Layered research (involving practitioners in collaborations with professional researchers)

Aspects of Teaching and Learning	Decrease	Increase
Role of professional researchers	Research *on* teachers and creative partners	Research *with* teachers and creative partners
Role of practitioner action research	Action research limited to professional development for practitioners	Practitioner action research informing professional research, and professional research informing practitioner action research on teaching for creativity

Table 37.5 Professional development incorporating enquiry

Aspects of Teaching and Learning	Decrease	Increase
Professional development content	Predesigned teaching strategies in delivery system model	Enquiry into strategies for teaching for creativity as part of a layered research design
Receivers of professional development	'One size fits all' professional development delivered to select teachers, separate from professional development delivered to select creative practitioners	Teams of teachers and creative practitioners who enquire together to develop original approaches to creative learning for their whole school contexts
Professional development provision	Professional development to practitioners by 'experts' external to the school or partnership	Professional development between enquiring practitioners that encourages professional community and teacher and creative practitioner leadership

Table 37.6 Explicit attention to what is meant by creative learning

Aspects of teaching and learning	Decrease	Increase
Student agency in learning	Students as receivers of 'instruction'	Students investigating content as creative thinkers taking action in the world
Focus of learning and teaching process	Attention to creative teaching	Attention to teaching for creativity and students' behaviours, attitudes and habits of mind when being creative

Note

1 For a similar analysis of process in the UK, see Raw (2009) and McGuigan *et al.* (2005).

References

Burnaford, G. (2001) *Rethinking Professional Development: 'Action Research' to Build Collaborative Arts Programming*, Fowler Colloquium Proceedings, University of Maryland Press, College Park; available at http://www.lib.umd.edu/PAL/SCPA/fowlercolloq2001paper3.html.
—— (2007) Moving toward a culture of evidence: documentation and action research in the practice of arts partnerships, *Arts Education Policy Review* 108(3): 35–40.
Burnaford, G. and Aprill, A. (2008) What are students learning? Creativity and content learning in long-term arts integration partnerships. The 2007–2008 Veteran Partnerships Evaluation Report, unpublished evaluation report, Chicago: Chicago Arts Partnerships in Education.
Burnaford, G., Aprill, A. and Weiss, C. (2001) *Renaissance in the Classroom: Arts Integration and Meaningful Learning*, Mahwah, NJ: Lawrence Erlbaum Associates.

Claxton, G. (2000) *Hare Brained, Tortoise Mind: How Intelligence Increases When You Think Less*, New York: Harper Perennial.

Cochrane, P. (2008) Is professional enquiry the essential grit in the oyster of creative partnership work in schools? Presentation to the teacher research symposium Making a Difference in Music Education, Cambridge University.

Cochrane, P. and Cockett, M. (2007) *Building a Creative School: A Dynamic Approach to School Development*, London: Trentham Books.

Cordingley, P., Bell, M., Rundell, B. and Evans, D. (2003) *The Impact of Collaborative CPD on Classroom Teaching and Learning*, in Research Evidence in Education Library, London: EPPI-Centre, Social Science Research Unit, Institute of Education, University of London.

Craft, A., Chappell, K. and Best, P. (2007) *Analysis of the Creativity Action Research Awards Two (CARA2) Programme Evaluation Report*, prepared by Exeter University; available from CapeUK, Leeds.

Crocco, M. and Costigan, A. (2007) The narrowing of curriculum and pedagogy in the age of accountability: urban educators speak out, *Urban Education* 42(6): 512–35.

Department for Education and Skills (DfES) (1999) *All Our Futures: Creativity, Culture and Education*, London: DfES.

—— (2003) *Excellence and Enjoyment: A Strategy for Primary Schools*, London: DfES.

Doherty, P. and Harland, J. (2001) *Partnerships for Creativity: An Evaluation of Implementation*, Slough: National Foundation for Educational Research.

Elmore, R. (1996) Getting to scale with good educational practice, *Harvard Educational Review* 66(1): 1–26.

Facer, K. and Pykett, J. (2007) *Developing and Accrediting Personal Skills and Competencies: Report and Ways Forward*, Bristol: Futurelab.

Furlong, J. and Salisbury, J. (2005) Best practice research scholarships and evaluation, *Research Papers in Education* 20(7): 45–83.

House of Commons Education and Skills Committee (2007) *Creative Partnerships and the Curriculum. Eleventh Report of Session 2006–7. Report, together with formal minutes, oral and written evidence*, London: The Stationery Office Limited.

Jeffery, G. and Ledgard, A. (2009) *Teacher Artist Partnership Programme*, Leeds: CapeUK.

McGuigan, P., Cockett, M., Craft, A., Fisher, R., McGregor, S. and Storr, J. (2005) *Building Creative Futures: The Story of the Creativity Action Research Awards*, Leeds: CapeUK.

National Center on Education and the Economy (NCEE) (2007) *Tough Choices or Tough Times: The Report of the New Commission on the Skills of the American Workforce*, San Francisco: Jossey-Bass.

Ofsted (2010) *Learning: Creative Approaches that Raise Standards* (report number HMI: 080266), London: HMSO.

QCA (2003) *Creativity: Find It, Promote It!*, London: Qualifications and Curriculum Authority; available at http://bit.ly/fG82Hp (accessed 3 February 2011).

Raw, A. (2009) *Looking Inside Creative Learning*, Leeds: CapeUK.

Websites

CapeUK out of school hours learning programme, http://www.outofschoolhours.org.uk/

Center for Research on Education, Diversity, and Excellence, University of California, Berkeley Graduate School of Education, http://crede.berkeley.edu/research/crede/standards.html

Chicago Arts Partnerships in Education (CAPE), www.capeweb.org

Creative Partnerships, www.creative-partnerships.com

Creative Partnerships in Education (CapeUK), www.capeuk.org

38

The Cultural Rucksack in Norway

Does the national model entail a programme for educational change?

Jorunn Spord Borgen

The Nordic context and the Cultural Rucksack

Generally speaking, arts and culture programmes serve two aims. First, arts experiences and participation are expected to have an immediate impact on each individual as a person. Second, most cultural programme projects are constructed for educational purposes (Eisner and Day, 2004; Lindberg, 1991). According to Gee (2004), contradictory educational and cultural agendas seem to agree on a broad range of assertions about the capacity of the arts, which include assisting in spiritual and moral development, improving academic performance, and inducing psychological and even physiological well-being. Nevertheless, arts and cultural education is characterised by multiple voices and hopeful eclecticism and a wide variety of practices (Borgen, 2006; Stankiewicz *et al.*, 2004). The three most common models for exposing pupils to arts and culture in schools are:

- integrated: arts and culture are integrated components of general education and school subjects;
- partnerships: arts, business, philanthropic and government organisations supportive of arts education cooperate in partnerships with schools;
- external: arts and culture institutions offer programmes that schools can purchase.

What can be expected from the different models varies, according to the research literature (Eisner and Day, 2004). While the cultural agenda may dominate in the external model, a balance between educational and cultural agendas is most likely to happen in the partnership model. The integrated model seems to pave the way for several practices in schools. The Cultural Rucksack national system was introduced as a partnership model initiative, and is currently a nationwide system to *supplement* the curriculum in primary and secondary education (grades 1–13). The goal is that everyone in school should be given the opportunity to appreciate culture and the arts, and to express themselves through different forms of art and culture, irrespective of gender, place of residence and social or economic background. All pupils should have some Cultural Rucksack-related experiences during the school year. In 2010, the Cultural Rucksack offered programmes to schools in eight categories: theatre/performing arts, visual arts, film, music, literature, cultural heritage and cross-over art.

But what kind of model for arts and culture in school is the Rucksack today, ten years later? What challenges does the Rucksack model meet?

The empirical data for this article are collected from a qualitative research evaluation carried out in 2006 (Borgen and Brandt, 2006) and a survey of schools conducted in spring 2009 (Vibe et al., 2009).

The Cultural Rucksack system model

The Nordic model of education is dominated by a 'culture-in-school-discourse', a discourse characterised by intentional arts and cultural education and expectations about positive consequences for individual and society (Trondman, 1998). The roots are to be found in the progress of the public school system and the development of the 'Nordic model of education' (Aasen et al., 2006). In the Norwegian Report on Core Curriculum (R-1993), arts and culture are described as an indispensable component of a quality general education. Norwegian pupils are expected to identify themselves individually as cultural participants through education (Reid, 1998).

As part of the Nordic welfare state model, the Norwegian school system is an egalitarian, redistributive system with full public school coverage and very few private schools. The Education Act and the National Curriculum apply to the entire country, with authority delegated to county and municipal authorities.[1] The municipalities are the local administrative and governing units and, as school owners, are responsible for primary and lower secondary education, while upper secondary schools are administered by the counties.

The Cultural Rucksack was developed step by step from 2001 onwards, and in 2003 it became a national scale experimental scheme. After a research evaluation the Rucksack became a permanent feature concurrent with the Norwegian school reform in 2006, the Knowledge Promotion Curriculum Reform (K06), though it was not part of the reform itself.

The guidelines[2] and funding for the Cultural Rucksack are provided by the Ministry of Culture, while the Ministry of Education is responsible for the school, the arena where the programme is delivered. A coordinating state-level secretariat for the Cultural Rucksack is organised under the Ministry of Culture.

The system of government and the economic hierarchy in the Cultural Rucksack

The Cultural Rucksack system model is basically a top-down structure with full state funding. Guidelines, communication, and arts-related and cultural content are interdependent in the programme. The Cultural Rucksack has grown out of local and regional experiments and partnerships. Local initiatives came during the late 1990s, often initiated by passionate individuals in the arts and cultural institutions, and by public agencies. There was a prevalent 'let a hundred flowers bloom' attitude and support for bottom-up processes for the development of new programmes available to children in school. The idea was based on the idea of cultural experiences as compared to the lunch packet Norwegian children bring to school in their rucksacks.

The first time funds were allocated to the Cultural Rucksack was in the government budget for 2001. The approximately 20 million NOK (Norwegian krone) (€2.5 million) budget was a supplement to existing funding of arts and cultural public agencies and institutions. There were few guidelines for the funding, as the idea was to provide some seed capital for innovative local and regional partnerships with schools.

In 2002, a group of politicians brought arguments from the Nordic 'culture-in-school-discourse' into the governmental budgetary debate and presented a new financial model for the Cultural Rucksack. The Storting (the Norwegian Parliament) greeted these ideas with approval, deciding that the Cultural Rucksack, from 2003, was to be financed by the funds allocated to culture from the surplus income from Norsk Tipping, the state-owned gaming company. A plan for a step-by-step funding increases was made, and from 2005–6 onwards the Cultural Rucksack received approximately 160 million NOK (€20 million) annually. The Cultural Rucksack went from receiving supplementary funding and seed capital to become a fully financed programme 'overnight'. Following this decision, a mandatory guideline document was delivered by the Ministry of Culture as a White Paper to the Storting, Report No. 38 (2002–3).

The key for the distribution of funding is laid down in Report No. 38; 20 per cent of the funding is allocated to national institutions within the areas of music, film, performing arts and visual arts, and also to some regional museums, the Arts Council Norway and the Directorate for Cultural Heritage. The 19 county-based cultural offices in Norway are in charge of distributing the remaining 80 percent. These cultural offices are made up of producers, tour organisers, coordinators and so on, who make touring plans and invite the municipalities to take out a subscription to the programmes offered each year. At least one-third of this regional funding is used for coordination and arts productions and cultural events; one-third is allocated to the municipalities for local activities in accordance with a principle of local autonomy; and the last one-third of this funding is left for the counties to use as they see fit. It is a requirement that the county cultural offices contribute from their own budgets to administrative costs towards the realisation of the Cultural Rucksack.

It is recommended that each municipality has a Rucksack coordinator who is in charge of selecting concerts, theatre performances and exhibitions and so on, and keeps contact between schools and other partners of the Rucksack organisation. This coordinator can be an art teacher, a librarian or an art school teacher. Each school is also advised to have a coordinator who takes part in the municipal Rucksack organisation. Figure 38.1 illustrates the system of government and the economic hierarchy in the national model. Figure 38.1 also illustrates the two parallel administration channels for the Cultural Rucksack (Ministry of Education and Research, and Ministry of Culture and Church Affairs). Consequently, the arts and culture presented to the pupils in schools are dependent on two factors: (1) the chosen norm for the distribution of funding from each county to the municipalities; and (2) the interests, qualifications, agendas and pedagogies of the individuals in charge of the various positions in the system. The interaction between these two factors provides the foundation for the arts and culture programmes the children get access to in school.

A possible balance between educational and cultural agendas?

The Cultural Rucksack is expected to give every child in school the opportunity to appreciate cultural and artistic expressions, and also to express themselves through different forms of art and cultural activities. The word 'learning' is not mentioned once in the mandatory guidelines. Even so, appreciation of arts and culture necessarily contains a learning aspect (Freedman, 2003).

In the Cultural Rucksack programme, education and arts and culture, having two different political governmental structures and encompassing two different fields of knowledge, are intended to develop cooperative practices within the school. After an initial partnership model period, and on the ground work with the Nordic 'culture-in-school-discourse', an integrated

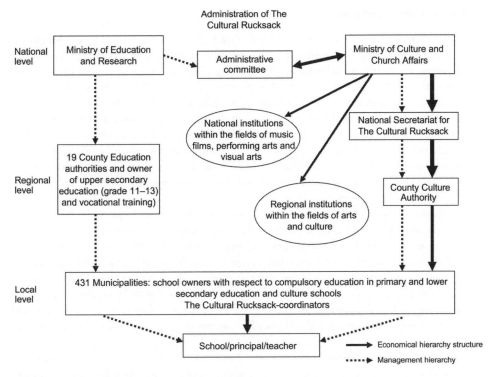

Figure 38.1 Administration of the Cultural Rucksack

model for arts and culture in school seemed to be a natural step further when the Rucksack system became a national and fully financed programme in 2003. However, since the county-based cultural offices decide the funding available for the municipalities, and since they have usually already selected the programmes the municipalities can choose from, and set the touring schedules, most schools and teachers have had little direct impact on or control over what pupils actually experience in relation to the Cultural Rucksack from 2003 onwards. There are few contact points between schools, school owners (the municipalities) and the counties except that local Rucksack coordinators can take part in annual markets and conferences. Another arena for dialogue between the counties and the municipalities is the planning and report system. The municipalities are obliged to submit a three-year plan to the county-based cultural office annually to get their part of the funding.

Nevertheless, the responsibility for the quality of education in the national school system is assigned to the municipal school owners, who are accountable for national educational policy goals; the teachers and schools are responsible for the time children spend in schools. With this imbalance between the educational and cultural agendas built in, the nationally implemented, experimental Rucksack system from 2003 onwards resembles an external model and not the integrated model the mandatory guidelines prescribe. When the Cultural Rucksack became a permanent feature concurrent with the Norwegian school reform in 2006, there existed the possibility of constructing a new balance between the educational and cultural agendas and strengthening the Cultural Rucksack as an integrated model for arts and culture in education.

Evaluation and findings

Two evaluations have been conducted over the years: in 2006, commissioned by the Ministry of Culture, and in 2009, commissioned by the Directorate for Education and Training.[3] To establish a foundation for further development, the Storting asked for a research evaluation of the experimental period from 2003 to 2006. The goal for the spring 2006 evaluation (Borgen and Brandt, 2006) was to provide an overall picture of the Cultural Rucksack. The evaluation strategy was to cover the entire effort by those involved in the Rucksack by using a vertical projection strategy. This was expected to provide a grasp of the different positions, interests and perspectives on arts and cultural education, and give an understanding of the visions and practices governing the project. Besides interviews, case studies, analyses of documents, plans and reports, among other things, a self-evaluation document produced by the 19 county-based cultural offices was an important tool in the evaluation.

Four municipalities in four counties were strategically chosen as sample cases for the study and subsequently visited by the researchers. Semi-structured interviews with 90 individuals involved in the Cultural Rucksack programme were conducted with representatives from the political decision level, national institutions, regional and local authorities, and teachers and headteachers at the school in which the arts and cultural education is carried out. The interviews had three different functions. Pilot interviews were conducted to frame problems and test relevant informants. We conducted one-hour, semi-structured face-to-face interviews with informants in important operational and coordinating positions, and telephone interviews with informants having special duties related to the programme as part of their positions.

The pupils are hardly visible in the Cultural Rucksack system (see Figure 38.1). We conducted school interviews with 38 ten-year-old pupils in four schools about their arts and culture experiences related to the Cultural Rucksack. Based on random alphabetical selection, one girl and one boy were interviewed together for about 30–45 minutes.

All interviews were transcribed and analysed thematically in order to identify, compare and contrast elements as they emerged from and recurred in several different contexts (Jensen, 2002). The evaluation is an all-level study of the national model, giving insights into the differences in perspectives and experiences among those involved.

Trends and imbalances in the 2006 evaluation

Due to the fact that the system for bottom-up feedback from schools to the counties was underdeveloped compared to the strength of the top-down structure in the model, the evaluation found imbalances between educational and cultural agendas. In 2006, scarce statistics and a lack of evaluation tools showed a Cultural Rucksack organisation with little focus on system development. However, the concept of professionalism and artistic quality were highlighted.

Pupils in a traditional audience role meeting traditional art, mediated by professional artists, seemed to be the most frequent programme element offered to the schools. The pupils would most frequently experience music (mostly concerts offered by the Norwegian Concert Institute) and cultural heritage (mostly field trips to local cultural heritage museums). The third most offered art experiences were theatre/performing arts and visual arts. New art forms such as film and cross-over arts were scarce.

The evaluation found that the county-based cultural offices were important gatekeepers for this repertoire, quality and funding systems. However the municipalities were also influenced by local individuals involved in the Rucksack organisation. A disparity between mandatory means and results in the schools was reported in the interviews. Cultural values, standards and quality criteria were competing with educational and child-centred methods and new forms of creative teaching and learning. The following cases illustrate the disparate agendas.

In one case, the municipality treated the Cultural Rucksack programme as an 'extraordinary' supplement to the ordinary school curriculum and as an external model for arts and culture in school. The pupils had classes in painting and drawing together with artists in a culture centre outside the school and without their teacher. The pupils had also been to concerts without their teacher. In the interviews these pupils had weak memories of their painting classes. They told us that 'the concert was strange', and the communication with the artists 'a bit scary'. Since she had not been with them, their teacher reported having no tools for helping the pupils develop verbalised expressions of these experiences. Overall, the pupils at this school possessed few relevant concepts when talking about their art experiences.

Another school applied a 'child-centred' model, and this municipality emphasised that the pupils should develop their understanding of arts and culture both as products and as processes. During the first years of the Cultural Rucksack period this municipality received seed capital to develop a partnership with artists and university researchers, and developed a model for 'experiencing, creating and learning' through film, theatre, music and visual art projects. This approach contains three steps; first, teachers participated in a course with artists in order to experience the processes their pupils were to be guided through during the project, and also to learn about the art form; second, the pupils were brought through the same experiences; finally, teachers, artists and pupils together produced and/or performed a relevant artistic work.

In a theatre project, artists, teachers and 50 pupils experienced a theatre performance and then worked together for one week to produce a play, which was subsequently performed for their school and families. After performing in the classical play *Peer Gynt* by Henrik Ibsen, a boy told the interviewers, 'I didn't know I was able to do things like this.' A girl said, 'I didn't know what theatre was until I did this play.' Obviously, these pupils were equipped with an advanced vocabulary for and ability to reflect on their art experiences. An important realisation for the participants was how seemingly chaotic situations are actually meaningful processes in the arts; another was that sharing experiences with friends and families provides a basis for communication and knowledge about arts and culture in the social context to which these children and teachers belong.

The school using the 'child-centred' model seemed to handle the balance between educational and cultural agendas explicitly, arguing that multiple perspectives are needed to develop an understanding of the value of arts and culture in society, and to give pupils tools to use in their everyday lives. By contrast, there was no clear view about what arts and culture were about among pupils and teachers in the school approaching the Cultural Rucksack as 'extraordinary experiences'.

Among the many informants in the evaluation, professional artists and central 'premise suppliers' in arts and culture usually supported the 'extraordinary experiences' model for the Cultural Rucksack. According to them, professional artists should manage the content and be in charge of deciding what 'to send' to the schools, which these informants characterised as 'the receiving unit'. The art activities among the pupils should also be under professional supervision and tutoring, according to this approach, and the expected positive long-term effects of the art experiences were taken for granted.

The 'child-centred' model, on the other hand, found resonance among headteachers, teachers and pupils in the schools. The headteachers and teachers interviewed argued that the Cultural Rucksack should be integrated into everyday life at school and at home. They agreed on the importance of letting the pupils participate in the arts and cultural processes to impress upon them the overall importance of arts and culture in society. Those informants from the arts and culture side who supported this model were artists who had been working with schools for several years, and artists working with traditional music and cultural heritage. Some avant-garde artists also preferred this model because, as they saw it, the role of arts in society has changed from having a charismatic, distanced role to being something more social and relational, thereby requiring new forms of child-centred pedagogy.

The 'extraordinary experiences' model seems to represent an external model and pursues an implicit cultural agenda, attempting to implement given values, standards and rules in the schools. By contrast, the 'child-centred' model attempts to balance educational and cultural agendas and seems to represent an integrated model developed from an experimental partnership model, and also to introduce new forms of pedagogy that track the changing roles of arts and culture for children, both in school and in society at large.

Verification of trends in the 2009 survey

In spring 2009, a representative national survey was conducted among Norwegian headmasters from 488 schools (48 per cent response rate) and municipal education departments in 115 municipalities (77 per cent response rate) (Vibe *et al.*, 2009). The questionnaire was developed on the basis of the evaluation findings from 2006 (Borgen and Brandt, 2006).

The survey asked the respondents to report on each of the eight art forms, and 32,883 programmes were reported to have taken place in the Cultural Rucksack during the school year 2008–9 (Vibe *et al.*, 2009). The 2006 evaluation found that traditional art forms such as music and theatre were the most commonly experienced art forms, and that the pupil was put in an audience role by the Cultural Rucksack. The picture drawn by the 2009 survey reaffirms this as a steady trend.

The 2009 survey asked headteachers and school owners how artists and cultural institutions were cooperating with schools to reach the goals concerning pupil outcomes laid down in the Cultural Rucksack. The statement that pupils learn to become an audience is supported by 92 per cent of the respondents; 91 per cent also agree with the statement that the Cultural Rucksack is most effective when pupils participate in activities and processes together with artists or teachers in school; 58 per cent of the schools reported that they have no influence on the programmes offered; and 42 per cent of the schools have undertaken programmes from the Cultural Rucksack that were not suited to the pupil group.

On the other hand, most schools (80 per cent) thought that artists understand the diversity among the pupils, and 70 per cent agreed with the statement that artists respect the school organisation. However, 47 per cent also agreed with the statement that artists need help and support from teachers to handle groups of pupils. The 2009 survey underlines the homogeneity of the national model, and that handling the balance between educational and cultural agendas in everyday life in the schools is challenging. But it also indicates that the schools have respect for the professionalism of the artists and others represented in the Rucksack system.

Further development of the Cultural Rucksack

After the 2006 evaluation, the Cultural Rucksack was given new mandatory guidelines, Report No. 8 (2007–8), from the Ministry of Culture. Until 2008, the task of the national model was to ensure that the pupils were given *professional programmes*. This made room for several forms of professionalism, including both professional artists and professional programmes. Teachers and artists could work together as equal partners in workshops, artists could visit schools with their programmes, and classes could visit museums and other institutions for education and so on. A substantial change in Report No. 8 (2007–8: 9) was that the Cultural Rucksack became a programme for 'ensuring that pupils have the opportunity to participate in artistic and cultural activities provided by *professionals in the cultural sector*'. In 2008, the Cultural Rucksack changed from an integrated model to an external model of arts and culture in school:

> The cultural sector is responsible for the artistic and other cultural activities, while the school is responsible for integrating the activities into the school day and the school curriculum and for ensuring that preparation and follow-ups are carried out in connection with the various activities under the programme.
>
> *(Report No. 8, 2007–8: 9)*

In terms of management hierarchy, the role of professional art and culture is strengthened, while the role of the school and local involvement is weakened. Despite new mandatory guidelines strongly emphasising local enthusiasm, activity and involvement, there is no prescription for school, teacher, pupil or parent involvement. Instead, the new mandatory guidelines and the solid state funding make room for a strong external, national, top-down model that operates independently of bottom-up signals concerning which approaches can actually be successfully integrated into everyday life in the schools.

From 2008 the guidelines focused largely on the development of traditional art forms 'delivered' to schools, thereby placing the pupils in traditional audience roles, rather than the development of new forms of child-centred pedagogy. The Cultural Rucksack has become an example of how artists and art organisations have succeeded in erecting an image of themselves as indispensable to arts teaching and learning, and of the increasing mistrust of schools and local initiatives and practices (Gee, 2004). The broader field of arts and culture in Norway has, in other words, been doing marketing for a national programme and for professional artists as being a guarantee for quality control with respect to the Cultural Rucksack.

The Cultural Rucksack, like most arts and cultural educational programmes (Eisner and Day, 2004), has grown out of practice, and is weakly connected to theory and research, although it is permeated by good intentions. As is well described in the literature, it takes time to change practice-based arts and cultural education. The 2006 evaluation provided insights into several successful practices agreed on by teachers and artists together in everyday schools. One could say that a hundred flowers bloomed in the shadow of the official model. An example is the 'child-centred' pedagogy developed during the early experimental period and funded by seed capital. The municipality in question is a city and can therefore more easily develop this innovative model further than a small municipality can. One of the weaknesses of the post-2008 model seems to be that there are no incentives for experimenting with and developing new arts and culture pedagogies adapted to the twenty-first century; rather we are left with a system for keeping up well-known traditional forms.

The Cultural Rucksack model therefore seems to embody a disparity between the means and the goals of being relevant and supportive to teaching and learning in primary and secondary education. The Cultural Rucksack's future development seems to be highly dependent on individual communication, flexibility and trust, and as such the current model is poorly equipped to meet the twenty-first century. The aim to give all pupils in school opportunities to appreciate culture and arts should be realised also by giving them opportunities to express themselves through different cultural and artistic means (Report No. 8 (2007–8): 9), and this goal is nowhere close to being realised.

Notes

1 Norway has 19 counties, 431 municipalities and a population of 4.7 million people (2009), of whom 8.9 per cent are immigrants. The smallest municipalities have about 1,000 inhabitants, whereas Oslo, the capital, has approximately 550,000 inhabitants.

2 From 2003 to 2006 the main mandatory guideline document was the White Paper to the Storting, Report No. 38 (2002–3) from the Ministry of Culture. The Cultural Rucksack was also discussed in the White Paper on art and culture in schools, Report No. 39 (2002–3) from the Ministry of Education and Research. From 2008, new principles were laid down in Report No. 8 (2007–8) *Cultural Rucksack for the Future* from the Ministry of Culture and Church Affairs.

3 The Norwegian Directorate for Education and Training is responsible for the development of primary and secondary education. The Directorate is the executive agency for the Ministry of Education and Research in Norway.

References

Aasen, Petter, Telhaug, Alfred Oftedahl and Mediås, Asbjørn (2006) The Nordic model in education: education as part of the political system in the last 50 years, *Scandinavian Journal of Educational Research*, 50 (3), London: Taylor & Francis Group.

Borgen, Jorunn Spord and Brandt, Synnøve S. (2006) *Ekstraordinært eller selvfølgelig? Evaluering av den kulturelle skolesekken i grunnskolen* [Extraordinary or inevitable? Evaluating the Cultural Rucksack (TCR) in compulsory education in Norway], Oslo: NIFU STEP Rapport nr. 5/2006 (Norwegian only).

Borgen, Jorunn Spord (2006) Barn og kunstformidling – tradisjoner, begrunnelser og perspektiver [Children and arts education: traditions, perspectives and educational goals], I: *Tidsskrift for Børne-og ungdomskultur*, 51 Odense Syddansk Universitetsforlag (Norwegian only).

Eisner, Elliot and Michael Day (eds) (2004) *Handbook of Research and Policy in Art Education*, Mahwah, NJ: Lawrence Erlbaum Associates.

Freedman, Kerry (2003) *Teaching Visual Culture: Curriculum, Aesthetics, and the Social Life of Art*, New York and London: Teachers College Press.

Gee, Constance Bumgarner (2004) Spirit, mind, and body: arts education the redeemer, in Elliot Eisner and Michael Day (eds) *Handbook of Research and Policy in Art Education*, Mahwah, NJ: Lawrence Erlbaum Associates.

Jensen, Klaus Brun (ed.) (2002) *A Handbook of Media and Communication Research: Qualitative and Quantitative Methodologies*, London: Routledge.

Lindberg, Anna Lena (1991) *Konstpedagogikens dilemma* [The dilemma of arts education], Lund: Studentlitteratur (Swedish with English abstract).

Ministry of Church, Education and Research (1993) *Core Curriculum for Primary, Secondary and Adult Education in Norway*, Oslo: Ministry of Church, Education and Research.

Ministry of Education and Research (2006) Knowledge promotion reform; available at http://www.regjeringen.no/en/dep/kd/Selected-topics/compulsory-education/Knowledge-Promotion.html?id=1411.

Reid, William A. (1998) Systems and structures or myths and fables? A cross-cultural perspective on curriculum content, in Bjørg B. Gundem and Stefan Hopmann (eds) *Didaktik and/or Curriculum: An International Dialogue*, New York: Peter Lang.

Report No. 38 to the Storting (2002–3) from the Ministry of Culture and Church Affairs.

Report No. 39 to the Storting (2002–3) from the Ministry of Education and Research.

Report No. 8 to the Storting (2007–8) from the Ministry of Culture and Church Affairs.

Stankiewicz, Mary Ann, Amburgy, Patricia M. and Bolin, Paul E. (2004) Questioning the past: contexts, functions, and stakeholders in 19th-century art education, in Elliot Eisner and Michael Day (eds) *Handbook of Research and Policy in Art Education*, Mahwah, NJ: Lawrence Erlbaum Associates.

Trondman, Mats (1998) Den kulturpolitiska brännpunkten – om behovet och konsten att studera kultur i skolan [The cultural policy focal spot: on the art of studying culture in school], in *Nordisk kulturpolitisk tidsskrift* [Nordic journal of cultural policy research] 3, Borås: Bibliotekshögskolan i Borås (Swedish only).

Vibe, Nils, Evensen, Miriam and Hovdhaugen, Elisabeth (2009) *Spørsmål til Skole-Norge. Tabellrapport fra Utdanningsdirektoratets spørreundersøkelser blant skoler og skoleeiere våren 2009* [Questions to Norwegian schools], Oslo: NIFU STEP Report 33/2009.

39

From network learning to classroom teaching[1]

Ann Lieberman and Diane R. Wood

In the more than one hundred years since public education began in the United States, almost every decade has seen efforts to reform schools. From the efficiency movement of the 1920s to the Great Society programs in the 1970s and from the "Reform Era" of the 1980s to the 1990s emphasis on standards and accountability, movements and policies have come and gone. Despite intensive efforts, federal and state policies have been largely unsuccessful in improving how schools are organized, how teachers teach and what content students learn.

Only since the early 1990s has attention been paid to the role of teachers as primary actors in schools and school reform. Only recent research illustrates, for instance, how teachers develop pedagogical knowledge, and the conditions and contexts that support this development (Cochran-Smith and Lytle, 1993; Fullan and Hargreaves, 1996; Lieberman and Miller, 1999; McLaughlin and Talbert, 1993; Rosenholtz, 1989), as well as how teachers control the success or failure of change efforts (Fullan with Stiegelbauer, 1991). Based on these understandings, some researchers (Darling-Hammond, 1993; Little, 1993) have suggested

> a different approach to producing, sharing and using knowledge, a different paradigm for educational policymaking, one in which policymakers shift their efforts from *designing controls* intended to direct the system to *developing capacity* that enables schools and teachers to be responsible for student learning and responsive to diverse and changing student and community needs.
>
> *(Darling-Hammond, 1993: 643)*

They have recognized that policies which enable teachers to become members of professional communities, build on local knowledge, and explore solutions to problems and practices that occur in particular contexts offer the best hope for meaningful change. In short, they urge the recognition of "inside knowledge" (created by teachers) as well as "outside knowledge" (created by reformers and researchers, etc.) as valuable and necessary for changing their practices (Putnam and Borko, 2000).

Despite these convincing calls to place the professional development of teachers at the center of school reform efforts (Cochran-Smith and Lytle, 2001; Hawley and Valli, 1999; Lieberman, 1995; Darling-Hammond and McLaughlin, 1995; Sykes, 1999), the forms and substance of professional development have remained virtually the same for decades. Typically, professional development approaches construct teachers as passive consumers of pre-packaged knowledge or, at best, compliant participants whose role is to absorb information from the research and reform communities, whether or not it is useful or appropriate (Little, 1993; Cochran-Smith and Lytle, 2001).

As technology changes the way people communicate, work, and learn, and an increasingly diverse population of students attend the nation's schools, demands on teachers become increasingly intense and complex. Teachers must learn how to incorporate technology into their practices and to reach students with widely ranging cultural and familial backgrounds. The bureaucratic structures of most schools, however, make change and adaptation difficult. The tendency is to bring in outside experts to "develop" teachers through a "one size fits all" set of solutions that often fail to distinguish between different teaching styles, school, or classroom contexts, or between the needs of novice or experienced teachers. While school bureaucracies succeed in the sense they can process large numbers of students, they have difficulty responding to changing social and economic conditions and the constantly shifting needs of schools, teachers, and students (Hargreaves, 1994).

In contrast to – or perhaps because of – this history of failure to improve teaching, a new approach, involving teachers as primary actors in their own development, has become increasingly recommended and practiced. Where traditional professional development approaches have not attended to the culture of teaching or the specific contexts of different schools, successful educational reform networks pay particular attention to the building of a professional community that supports teachers, respects their knowledge, and values contextual as well as generalized knowledge. These are precisely the principles on which the National Writing Project (NWP), arguably the most successful teacher network in the USA,[2] has constructed its organization and subsequently expanded it. Unlike most professional development efforts that take place in bureaucratic cultures marked by hierarchical relationships, the NWP builds a professional community characterized by lateral roles and relationships. The NWP, like other such networks,[3] succeeds in reversing the paralyzing effects of isolation, privatism, and conservatism that Lortie (1975) described as characteristic of teachers' work cultures over two decades ago. The NWP, again like other networks, has created the kind of collaborative culture that changes the way teachers learn and relate to one another (Sarason, 1996; Veugelers and Zijlstra, 2001). We wanted to see for ourselves how the NWP accomplished this, so we launched a two-year study of two NWP sites,[4] one centered at University of California at Los Angeles (UCLA) and the other at Oklahoma State University (OSU).

The National Writing Project: linking community, learning, and efficacy

The National Writing Project, in existence for twenty-six years, has kept its focus on writing and literacy even as it has adapted to new conditions and broader constituencies. Among its functions as the central body of a decentralized network, the national office distributes financial assistance, visits sites to support and evaluate programs, attends to questions of equity, and helps to spread program models from one site to another. The NWP also raises additional funding to provide for special projects that advance its work. And several of these projects have become networks in and of themselves (i.e. the Urban Sites Network, Rural Network).

Each of the 167 NWP sites, all housed at university campuses, runs a five-week Summer Invitational Institute, sponsors professional development opportunities both during the summer and the school year, and positions NWP teachers, called teacher consultants, to play active roles in the professional development of other teachers and in school change initiatives. We chose our two sites because of their differing contexts and histories. The UCLA site, of course, encompassed a large metropolitan area, while OSU embraced a dispersed geographical region that includes a mid-size city, small towns, and rural areas. At the time of our study, the metropolitan site was over twenty years old, while the dispersed site was only six years old.

We wanted to explore in these two sites how NWP enacted its unique approach to professional development in quite different geographical, historical, and cultural contexts. Because the summer institutes initiate new teachers into the culture, we believed that it was essential to observe them firsthand. But we also wanted to know how teachers' experiences in the institutes subsequently shaped their practices. Thus, the directors helped us choose three exemplary teachers from each site. One from each site was chosen because she distinguished herself during the immediately preceding summer institute and was, of course, brand new to the NWP. The others had been active members, or teacher consultants, of the NWP for several years. Over the course of our two-year study, we observed these six teachers in their classrooms, met their students, and interviewed them on site in order to explore what, if anything, they were using from their NWP experience.

In addition, we encouraged the teachers, already proficient writers, to narrate their experiences as classroom teachers and to re-envision these narratives as research data. Each teacher chose two to three students to closely follow over the year. We asked them to document carefully the student's academic progress by writing field notes and collecting samples of their work, and to assess their own teaching in light of the students' relative achievement. From this extensive documentation, we supported them in writing complex narratives that tracked their own learning from the Writing Project, their struggles to implement that learning in their classroom practices, and the effects these efforts had on particular students. Toward the end of the year we brought the directors and the six teachers together in Los Angeles to listen to and provide feedback to each other on the narratives that they had written.

Our study, then, had three tiers: documentation of the Invitationals, NWP influences on classroom practice, and teachers' perspectives on how their NWP involvement affected students' learning. For purposes of this article, we draw primarily on our analysis of the summer institute experiences, because these set the cultural conditions for initiating new members, and on what we learned from two of those new members as we interviewed them and observed them in their classrooms.

The core activities

In studying the institutes at both sites, we found that the core and ancillary activities, as well as the learning environments, were similar in both sites. On the first day of the institute, the directors modeled the core activities and we observed the usual fear and anxiety attendant on a new experience as the teachers participated in them. By the second day, the teachers themselves were voluntarily taking over the core activities – a remarkable transformation in only twenty-four hours. These core activities worked powerfully to build professional community, instill a sense of efficacy among participants, release teachers' collective knowledge and expertise, and create a highly participatory professional culture capable of supporting shared leadership and risk-taking.

The author's chair

To take the author's chair involves volunteers literally sitting before colleagues to share an unfinished poem, the beginning of a story, or a piece prompted by other activities in order to receive feedback from the audience. As the weeks unfold during the institute, teachers come back to the author's chair in order to read their revised drafts, which reflect deeper insights and more graceful writing – the benefits of peer critique. As teachers observe and participate in the processes surrounding the author's chair – writing, sharing, reflecting, revising – they come to realize that these stages in the writing process, when undertaken deliberately and consciously, not only strengthen writing, but also suggest a powerful paradigm for conceptualizing, approaching, and transforming teaching (Wood and Lieberman, 2000).

Writing groups

For two or more days a week, four or five teachers work with a "writing group." They share their writing, give and receive feedback, and revise and rewrite as time allows. Encouraging potential writers to write and bolstering their confidence to share their writing requires both an understanding of, and participation in, the various stages of the writing process. (During the institute teachers experience pre-writing activities such as: generating topics, brainstorming, organizing by clustering ideas, mapping or outlining, etc.) One teacher, reflecting the view of others with whom we talked, spoke of the luxury of having concentrated time to write in order to recapture the passion and subjective meaning that writing for an interested and sympathetic audience often releases:

> The best a-ha for me was being in a writing group and having a chance to write – getting good, sensitive criticism. I had forgotten what it was like to write. My life had developed so many other stresses that I realized that I had not written myself in years.

As writers and learners, teachers *get* feedback on their writing and make empathic connections to their own students' struggles with writing. As teachers, they learn how to *give* feedback so that writers can improve their work. They learn that if they are going to support a climate where meaningful feedback is possible, they have to be able to give critical feedback. They move beyond the "making nice" culture so prevalent in most school cultures, which makes even constructive criticism of colleagues taboo. As one teacher said:

> It reminds you that people's writing is personal, and that when I critiqued people's writing, student writing, that I need to be sensitive and not just tear it apart, or not just say it's good, when it isn't.

By the end of the institute, the teachers have learned that getting constructive, critical feedback actually improves what they're capable of doing. They see how their own learning flourishes in the company of people who honestly want them to do their best. They recognize, therefore, the power of learning as a social phenomenon and remember that power as they make classroom plans for fall.

The model lesson

During the institutes, each teacher teaches a lesson to the rest. These lessons include the goals they hold for their students, the materials, resources, and activities, and, if appropriate, the standard this lesson helps to reach. In the process of teaching these lessons, the teacher learns from constructive feedback – and from reflection and practice – what it means to be a "good presenter." Such characteristics as solid organization and preparation, knowledge of subject, communication of its significance, and the impact on students are considered and discussed. In going "public" with work, teachers make implicit understandings explicit, both to their audience and, most importantly, to themselves. This kind of learning goes beyond the subject of the lesson and teaches what it means to be a part of a community of colleagues who take each others' work seriously – seriously enough to give constructive criticism as well as encouragement. Teachers learn how to make good ideas even better and how it is possible to tailor powerful practices to particular contexts and learners.

Building a learning environment

While the activities described above anchor each institute day, other activities fill the hours from nine to three o'clock, such as mini-lessons on teaching vocabulary words or using similes. There are "quick writes" (five-minute thought pieces on a particular idea or reflection). Directors raise pressing issues affecting the schools for discussion, suggest books or articles to read, and make available a variety of resources. As the days go on, it is hard not to get swept up in the subtle changes of tone, format, and pacing. Participants move from sharing their often deeply held emotional experiences in writing to intellectual discussions about the role of the states in setting standards, meeting emotional, intellectual, and practical needs of the participants.

The rhythm and pace of the institutes provide participants time for reflection and dialogue, all too rare in most school cultures. Even the voluntary task of keeping the log of each day's activities plays a deceptively important role. Every morning the "logger" reports on the highlights of the previous day, providing time to revisit key ideas and insights. As teachers become more comfortable with one another, the log expands to include pictures, humorous descriptions, and more intimate details about the nature of the group and its idiosyncrasies. The logs not only document the learning experiences of the group, they help to build community by raising awareness of the growing shared experiences and the deepening relationships that enrich daily activities. One participant captures her experiences particularly well:

> The Invitational was a magical time. We did all the lessons as if we were students. It became part of the fiber of the day. We practiced. We experienced. We thought about it all. We wrote letters saying how we would use the ideas. Every time I wrote a letter, I was modifying lessons in my classroom. It was a time to be reflective on myself as a person, as a teacher.

Principles of teacher development: the Writing Project way

The philosophy, variety, and pace of the activities during the five-week institute have, teachers say, a transforming effect on their teaching. Teachers are provided with a variety of opportunities, not only to shape ideas for use in their own contexts, but to take leadership in and become members of a larger professional community. The institutes enact a set of key principles that succeed in finding teachers' strengths, building on their knowledge, and supporting their development.

Teachers learn by teaching other teachers

Teachers who come to the NWP are expected to teach other teachers. Instead of assuming that they must learn only from experts, teachers learn that they have valuable knowledge that can be shared and built upon by other teachers. The assumption here is that teachers' knowledge, rather than "outsider knowledge," is the *starting place* for learning. Because what they know and experience matters, they begin to openly and unashamedly talk about successes and failures. Increasingly secure about the value of their own knowledge, they actively expand their inquiry by seeking out articles, books, and people to help them address the complex problems that they are exploring.

Teachers learn from making their work public and having it discussed and critiqued by a group of peers

Teachers come to understand that learning from one another involves having the courage to go public with their teaching practices. They find that peers can help them to: clarify purposes of a lesson or strategy; articulate their objectives; learn how student interest and needs are linked; relate these interests to the kinds of teaching strategies they use; and discuss their means of assessing what students learn.

Learning to write and learning to teach have a great deal in common

As teachers take the author's chair, it becomes self-evident that writing as a process is implicitly and explicitly connected to the process of teaching. Writing and teaching are both social acts, although some of the work must be done alone. Both require craft and skills that have to be learned and mastered: the broader the repertoire, the more craft confidence, the greater the knowledge of subject, the better the chance of being successful in reaching one's audience – in writing and teaching (Grossman, 1990). The level of artistry will vary with the talent and insights of the practitioners, but without craft and content knowledge it will have less chance to emerge.

There are strong value commitments in the NWP but methods and means to get there are non-ideological

Although teachers come to the NWP with different views and different practices, no one is criticized for the types of viewpoints they present. Feedback is non-judgmental and non-ideological. Nevertheless, while differences are respected, the commitments and values are implicit in the forms and practices of the institute. For example, it is axiomatic that writers become more involved when they have a choice of subjects; that writing helps learners think and express themselves more clearly; and that writing as a social process benefits the individual and the community – both personally and professionally.

Teaching is accepted as messy, uncertain and unfinished: "habits of mind" include a deeper understanding of how to make sense of the environment

As teachers continue to work with each other, they make public the fact that teaching is "messy" and filled with uncertainty. While they may acknowledge this privately and learn to "make do" on their own, the context of the NWP encourages them to question their practice publicly, and to seek and share solutions with others. These "habits of mind" become part of the community's norms, turning problems into possibilities for rethinking and reworking teaching practice. And these "habits," as two teachers attest, often remain with many after they return to classrooms:

> When school started after the institute, I started thinking what can I do to solve some of these problems and to be helpful and supportive of my colleagues. It was like the institute was sitting there waiting to come out and I started looking at problems in a whole new way.

> The Writing Project is like an "angel on my shoulder."

Being part of the NWP community provides an alternative to the usual routinized practices, collegial isolation, and alienation that plague many teachers in their schools. Having affiliation with the NWP as an "angel on their shoulders," these teachers turn toward asking questions rather than passively receiving answers, they take risks and try new strategies, and they turn to colleagues seeking better ways to reach students rather than to blame students for their lack of success.

Connecting personal and professional learning, teachers learn by taking different roles and seeing the world through different perspectives

Shifting roles provide multiple opportunities to experience the "lived lives" of teachers and learners – emotionally as well as intellectually. Teachers learn objective facts and subjective truths: from specific suggestions for improving a lesson, to how it feels to have one's work critiqued, which instructs them, in turn, in how to fulfill the role of the critic. They become active and interactive, and learn to develop themselves and their colleagues rather than waiting to be "developed" by the latest experts. Passivity gives way to passion. Instead of adopting prescriptions devoid of context, NWP teachers learn to adapt new ideas to fit the particulars of their classrooms.

Teachers develop professional leadership skills for the classroom and the profession

In the process of teaching peers, some NWP teachers find that engaging adults in professional development experiences can be as stimulating and challenging as developing good strategies for use in the classroom. These teachers, then, become invaluable consultants in their schools and districts, creating "Writing Project-like" environments for their colleagues. In doing so, they adopt a professional identity that extends beyond the walls of their classrooms and promote the professionalism of other teachers. For some teacher consultants, this becomes a life changing opportunity:

> I never thought of myself as a leader. I had never had an opportunity to present. This led to my thinking differently of what I might do as a professional and expanded my thinking in many ways. The NWP is a significant part of my professional life.

The article then goes on to show the way in which this professional learning experience outside of the school was taken back into the classroom, where it became a way of teaching, rather than a project or set of lessons. Lieberman and Wood conclude by arguing that the power and sustainability of the program is due to its networked nature.

We asked the authors to reflect back on the NWP for this handbook and to write a post-script to their article which highlighted those aspects of the program which now seemed most important.

Epilogue

When Diane Wood and I first thought of doing a study of the National Writing Project in the US we talked with many teachers who said that going to the NWP's summer institute was like "magic." When we asked for an explanation, they were unable to give us any. Indeed when you observe the summer institute, which is a centerpiece of the NWP, it is not obvious why teachers find it so magical.

But as we set about finding out what made this "magic" we began to understand that there was a set of social practices that served as an *approach* to learning and community. It was these practices that motivated, encouraged, and developed in the participants a way of thinking about their own and their students' learning. These practices not only uncovered what the "magic" was, but helped create a language and a set of ideas in the NWP that has made it so successful with teachers. This integration of organization and involvement of teachers may be one of the most creative programs we have ever seen in the US.

At the heart of the experience is the idea that teachers' knowledge and the unwrapping of what they do needs to come first. When teachers go public with what they know, they join a community of practice and get engaged and excited about their own learning. When they get involved in a writing group, they realize what it takes to write well. When they read and critique research, they see the excitement of learning something new and analyzing its meaning with colleagues. This kind of organization of learning when taken together energizes and motivates teachers toward social learning. Wenger has it right. Social learning is about participation and finding meaning in one's work (Wenger, 1998). The social practices that we observed included:

- approaching each colleague as a potentially valuable contributor;
- honoring teacher knowledge;
- creating public forums for teacher sharing, dialogue, and critique;
- turning ownership of learning over to learners;
- situating human learning in practice and relationships;
- providing multiple entry points into the learning community;
- guiding reflection on teaching through reflection on learning;
- sharing leadership;
- promoting a stance of inquiry;
- encouraging a reconceptualization of professional identity and linking it to professional community.

(Lieberman and Wood, 2001: 22)

During the summer institute teachers quickly see that they are the learners and that much of what happens to them can be used in their own classroom. By the second day of the institute, teachers are teaching a favorite lesson, they are working in a writing group, and some of them have taken the author's chair to read their writing to get feedback. The first day the instructors bring food, but by the second day one or more of the participants is bringing it. Almost the whole day appears to be run by the participants. Teachers learn that they do not have to control everything in the classroom. Students can be in groups, they can give feedback to their peers, they can teach each other ... They also learn the process and content of what it means to be a writer. Rather than just assigning a topic they learn that writing is a process and there are ways to get ideas, that revision is a part of the writing process, and that their peers can help them improve their work by their feedback and critique. It is less about skills and more about an *approach* to deep learning and inquiry where teachers change their identity from being "just a teacher" to realizing that they are in a developing community. It is part of this new identity that helps teachers think in more complex and creative ways about their teaching – continually asking questions, struggling with teaching dilemmas, going public with their teaching, expanding their repertoire and, for some, learning how to teach adults as well as students. Whether they are novices or experienced teachers, they recognize that they now know why they went into teaching and that being in a professional learning community is an essential part of their growth and development.

"Magic" is providing opportunities to go public with your work; to experience what it means to be in a community; to learn from others; to develop a way of giving and getting feedback; and to accept the responsibility of becoming a professional. Deep learning and continuous struggle to know more and do more with one's teaching and learning become a part of a teaching life.

Notes

1 In 2002 Ann Lieberman and Diane Wood published an article in the *International Journal of Educational Change* about the US National Writing Project. Here we reprint the first part of their article, which describes the programme, its context, and its operation.

2 Since 1973 the Writing Project (NWP) has served more than 1.8 million participants in its five-week Summer Invitational Institutes, which initiate teachers into the writing project, and the professional development activities that it offers. Over 100,000 teachers are now involved in Writing Project activities every year. Supported primarily by federal funding, the NWP, through its national office at the University of California at Berkeley (the location of the first Writing Project site), is the hub of, at this writing, 167 sites in the United States. These data come from the Annual Report of 1997 (and personal conversations with the Executive Director) published by the National Writing Project, University of California, Berkeley.

3 We use the terms network, partnership, and collaborative interchangeably. These groups are formed as national networks, with local affiliates, regional groups, or collaborative formed across districts or among schools (e.g. the National Writing Project, the Action Research Collaborative, and the Southern Maine Partnership). All are organizations external to particular schools but create agendas based on school improvements rooted in practice.

4 A site consists of a collaboration between a university professor and a teacher, who apply for a "basic site grant" to hold a Summer Invitational Institute and to provide professional development activities in a particular place. Each initial grant is $20,000, and each site must keep records and produce an annual report of activities, as well as provide survey data for the NWP.

References

Cochran-Smith, M. and Lytle, S. (1993) *Inside/Outside: Teacher Research and Knowledge*, New York: Teachers College Press.

—— (2001) Beyond certainty: taking an inquiry stance on practice, in A. Lieberman and L. Miller (eds.) *Teachers Caught in the Action: Professional Development in Practice*, New York: Teachers College Press.

Darling-Hammond, L. (1993) Reframing the school reform agenda: developing capacity for school transformation, *Phi Delta Kappan* 74(10) (June): 753–61.

Darling-Hammond, L. and McLaughlin, M. W. (1995) Policies that support professional development in an era of reform, *Phi Delta Kappan* 76(8) (April): 597–604.

Fullan, M. and Hargreaves, A. (1996) *What's Worth Fighting for in Your School?*, New York: Teachers College Press.

Fullan, M. with Stiegelbauer, S. (1991) *The New Meaning of Educational Change*, New York: Teachers College Press.

Grossman, P. (1990) *The Making of a Teacher*, New York: Teachers College Press.

Hargreaves, A. (1994) *Changing Teachers, Changing Times: Teachers' Work and Culture in the Postmodern Age*, New York: Teachers College Press.

Hawley, W. D. and Valli, L. (1999) The essentials of effective professional development: a new consensus, in L. Darling-Hammond and G. Sykes (eds.) *Teaching as the Learning Profession: Handbook of Policy and Practice*, San Francisco: Jossey-Bass.

Lieberman, A. (1995) Practices that support teacher development: transforming conceptions of professional learning, *Phi Delta Kappan* 76(8) (April): 591–6.

Lieberman, A. and Miller, L. (1999) *Teachers: Transforming Their World and Their Work*, New York: Teachers College Press.

Lieberman, A. and Wood, D. (2001) When teachers write: of networks and learning, in A. Lieberman and L. Miller (eds.) *Teachers Caught in the Action: Professional Development in Practice*, New York: Teachers College Press.

Little, J. W. (1993) Professional development in a climate of reform, *Educational Evaluation and Police Analysis* 15(2): 129–51.

Lortie, D. (1975) *Schoolteacher*, Chicago: University of Chicago Press.

McLaughlin, M. W. and Talbert, J. (1993) *Contexts that Matter for Teaching and Learning*, Stanford, CA: Context Center for Teaching and Learning in Secondary Schools.

Putnam, R. T. and Borko, H. (2000) What do new views of knowledge and thinking have to say about research on teacher learning, *Educational Researcher* 29(1) (January/February): 4–15.

Rosenholtz, S. J. (1989) *Teachers' Workplace: A 5'0(4°1 Organization of Schools*, New York: Longman Press.

Sarason, S. (1996) *Revisiting the Culture of the School and the Problem of Change*, New York: Teachers College Press.

Sykes, G. (1999) Teacher and student learning: strengthening their connection, in L. Darling-Hammond and G. Sykes (eds.) *Teaching as the Learning Profession: Handbook of Policy and Practice*, San Francisco: Jossey-Bass.

Veugelers, W. and Zijlstra, F. L. (2001) School development and professional development in networks of schools, paper for the symposium Social Geographies of Educational Change: Contexts, Networks and Generalizability, Barcelona, March 11–14.

Wenger, E. (1998) *Communities of Practice: Learning, Meaning, and Identity*, Cambridge: Cambridge University Press.

Wood, D. R. and Lieberman, A. (2000) Teachers as authors: the National Writing Project's approach to professional development, *International Journal of Leadership in Education* 3(3): 255–73.

40

Public policy partnerships for creative learning

David Holland

Introduction

Partnership has become an increasingly ubiquitous feature of the delivery of public programmes in education, health and other areas, particularly in the UK. In recent years, partnership working has even been tested as a means of managing and delivering creative education. This chapter reports on partnerships developed by Creative Partnerships (CP).

Creative Partnerships commissioned research to develop a language and framework for understanding the different types of relationships involved and their value. This research was framed as an evaluation of partnerships, a new field of inquiry that, as some researchers have put it, is dogged by 'methodological anarchy and definitional chaos' (Ling, 2000: 82). Despite this lack of certainty, useful insights emerged from the research that may be applicable to other programmes that attempt to promote the development of creative learning. This paper outlines key aspects of the research, and highlights the structures that underpin the partnership approach of CP and the challenges that are faced in delivering a programme in this manner.

Public policy partnership in context

Creative Partnerships was developed in the context of growing support for partnership working across public services in the UK. Indeed, since the 1990s, partnership working has emerged as a cornerstone of public policy, seen to be an effective means of driving forward the modernisation of public services. It is part of a broader discourse of networked governance, characterised by the loosening of statist welfare delivery whilst simultaneously recognising the failure of markets to deliver acceptable forms of welfare provision (Le Grand and Bartlett, 1993; Glendinning *et al.*, 2002). The government has consistently emphasised this 'collaborative discourse', where partnership represents a 'third way' between centralised bureaucratic hierarchies and the market (Glendinning *et al.*, 2002).

The rise of partnership working is reflective of the perennial quest of government and policy-makers for coordination (Hudson *et al.*, 1999). Partnerships are formed with the view that no single agency has the expertise or resources to tackle multi-dimensional socio-economic problems, and that people and agencies need to have a stake in a solution in order to support it. This notion is termed 'collaborative advantage' by theorists (Huxham, 2003). Beyond collaborative advantage, partnerships are also believed to offer a number of other benefits, including economies of scale, economies of scope, learning between partners and the rationalisation of service provision.

Because of the promotion of partnership working across the public sector, partnership has become a precondition for many important sources of funding. A number of models have been developed that seek to identify and describe types of partnerships conceptually, based on an aspect of partnership working. Two of these models are drawn on in this chapter. The first is purpose based and the second is process based.

Long and Arnold (1995) developed a typology for describing partnerships based on their general purpose; this consists of four partnership types:

- pre-emptive partnerships, which are set up to defuse a situation that is currently or potentially hostile;
- coalescing partnerships, which bring together parties that depend on each other to accomplish their goals but typically compete for projects and resources;
- exploration partnerships, which research or investigate areas of joint concern, bringing together parties that have not worked together in the past;
- leverage partnerships, which allow each party to make a modest investment in return for a relatively high social, political or financial return.

This partnership typology is useful because it provides a framework for understanding the context in which partnerships are formed and the nature of the initial engagement between parties.

Frank and Smith (2000) identify four types of process-related partnerships:

- contributory partnerships, where one leading organisation retains all control and the partners just provide additional resources or funds to achieve an objective;
- consultative partnerships, where the leading organisation retains control and responsibility but is genuinely open to advice from partners on design, implementation and monitoring;
- operational partnerships, where one organisation retains most control but the partners share the work, resources and information – the objectives of co-operation reflect the different interests and needs of the organisations involved;
- collaborative partnerships, where control, ownership and risk are shared through joint decision-making which solves a problem affecting all the partners in some way.

This process-related model is useful for consideration of partnership because it identifies the 'ownership' of the partnership and the terms of engagement between partners.

Partnership working in Creative Partnerships

Creative Partnerships aimed to support thousands of 'innovative long-term partnerships' between schools and creative professionals. It developed a network of partnerships with local and regional strategic agencies, cultural organisations, schools and young people. In order to facilitate this network of partnerships, an operational structure was designed primarily for the purpose of developing and brokering relationships, with directors developing strategic relationships and advancing the wider agenda, programmers brokering relationships with schools and other stakeholders around developing programmes of creative activity, and operations managers ensuring that appropriate contractual arrangements and systems are in place to support project delivery. By spreading partnership management responsibilities between key staff, the programme has ensured that there are sufficient resources to develop and maintain partnerships and that partnership management is seen as a key aspect of day-to-day activities.

There were three broad areas or types of CP partnership working:

- strategic partnerships: partnerships with local authorities, government agencies and third sector organisations that often seek to position CP within larger local and regional agendas;
- programmatic partnerships: partnerships with schools, cultural organisations and other intermediaries on the development of a programme of activities;
- project partnerships: partnerships with schools, teachers, creative practitioners/organisations, and children and young people on the development and delivery of individual creative projects.

I will discuss each in turn.

Strategic partnerships

CP developed the creative education agenda through strategic engagement with local government (particularly education services), the cultural sector and other public and not-for-profit organisations. Beyond influencing educational and wider policy agendas, strategic partnership was also a key aspect of ensuring the legitimacy of Creative Partnerships in many local areas. A key structure that the programme instituted to facilitate partnership working was local partnership boards. These boards provided advice and support and in some cases served a governance function for the programme in local areas. Local boards were often based around exploratory and coalescing partnership – that is, they brought together organisations that would not normally interact around a new agenda or competing interests and organisations around a shared vision. One creative director described the exploratory nature of her partnership board thus:

> It's an unusual group ... those people wouldn't usually meet. Because of that ... it's an interesting configuration.

A creative director and creative programmer in one of the offices consulted suggested that the local partnership board represented a coalescing partnership as some of the members (particularly local authorities) were initially competitive. Creative Partnerships, in some cases, provided a means of (as one creative director put it) 'bring[ing] local authorities [together] around larger agendas that all can engage in'.

Where local interests (both public and community) were well organised and vocal, partnership boards played a near-governance function for CP area offices, monitoring and reviewing progress against objectives and scrutinising budgetary decision-making, but in many cases, the input of the group was largely high level. As one creative programmer comments, 'they are not massively active partners, to be honest. It's a case of running things by them'.

Some partnership board members felt that the ability of the partnership boards to take a more active role was hindered by a structure in need of further development. As one board member expressed it:

> It's really a sounding board primarily, but from what I saw from the other members it could have a wider remit. There was a lot of knowledge and talent around the table, which is always interesting. I'm sure this could be further developed.

The underpinning process of the partnership boards was characterised by those interviewed as largely consultative and, at times, collaborative. Most area offices thought the consultative process useful. As one creative programmer put it:

> It makes us reflect on our practice. The process of stepping back and telling external people what's going on is very helpful and important.

In some cases, the process is a collaborative in that partnership board members are encouraged to use the space provided to develop collaborations between themselves (that may or may not have been directly related to the Creative Partnerships programme). Many local partnership board members, representing private companies, schools and local authorities, commented that being on the board led to opportunities to collaborate with other board members on areas of work outside the Creative Partnerships programme. The exploratory nature of partnership working on the board may support such collaborative processes.

Nevertheless, few local partnership boards were operationally focused and fewer still operated as a mechanism for leveraging additional funds for projects. Overall, partnership boards provided a distinct opportunity for the programme to develop strategic partnerships but did not generally operate to their full potential.

Beyond the board structure, there were three other CP strategic partnerships that were significant – those with local government, creative and cultural sector organisations and schools.

Local government

Partnerships between CP and local authorities were largely 'networked', that is, both CP and its local authority partners looked for opportunities for collaboration around complimentary interests. One creative director commented:

> The local authority is a key partner ... The relationship is key to CP ensuring there is dialogue in developing a county-wide creativity agenda and, more generally, [in ensuring that] CP is strategically aligned to other county-wide initiatives.

For the most part, partnerships with local government are of an informal nature, relying on personal contacts between key individuals, according to one creative director:

> I would say that we work through personal relationships ... that works for us because we have strategic relationships through other projects we work on ... ones that have existed for a long time. There is a certain amount of trust that has developed.

In some cases, engagement was maintained within more formal structures, such as local authority working groups, particularly where CP tried to embed its activities within larger policy agendas.

As noted, partnerships with local authorities were often coalescing; that is, they sought to bring together local authorities or at least work across a number of local authorities, with a view to decreasing competition between the authorities and focusing on larger regional or sub-regional issues. Some were also often about leverage, encouraging the local authorities to deploy financial resources or strategic influence to support the creative learning agenda. In some cases this led to the funding of local authority posts dedicated to the promotion of creative learning.

Cultural and creative agencies and organisations

Many of Creative Partnerships' strategic relationships with cultural organisations and agencies were of an informal character. As one creative director stated:

> We've got existing relationships. We can call on people from ... different cultural organisations but it's not highly formal – it's all about relationships. It's about trust. That's how the cultural sector is.

There were cases when these strategic relationships are established on a more formal basis: 'where we feel there is a gap in terms of skills, etc, we make formal overtures to [cultural agencies] and cultural organisations'.

Some of CP's strategic partnerships with cultural agencies and organisations were operational and others were leverage partnerships. As one creative director stated:

> Very little of our work is handing over money to cultural organisations or others. We try to work with organisations to see where our objectives overlap and pool resources to strategically address common aims.

Still other partnerships with cultural organisations and agencies were exploratory, with one CP partner saying: 'It has been a catalyst for new formations'.

From interviews with relevant stakeholders, it appeared that strategic engagement of cultural agencies and organisations by CP was not as developed as its links with local government. There were a number of reasons for this, including the fact that many Creative Partnerships area offices believed the programme was primarily an educational rather than a cultural initiative. Another challenge of partnership working with cultural agencies and organisations was the difficulty of managing expectations with regards to funding. As one creative director reported:

> It is important that we develop 'friendships' with a range of organisations, but many organisations, especially initially, tend to view partnership with us in terms of money, seeing us as a funding agency.

Competition for funding and profile not only affected partner organisations and the local and regional 'markets' for cultural and educational programmes, but also made it important for Creative Partnerships to develop effective local and regional networks, particularly where influential organisations challenged CP due to competition. According to one creative director:

> [A prominent local arts organisation] was antagonistic and obstructive because they bid for the [Creative Partnerships] programme themselves and didn't get it. So over time, we have had to nurture key allies.

Creative Partnerships offices also developed partnerships with other local and regional strategic agencies, including those whose remit involves regeneration and local economic development. One such partner suggested that their relationship with Creative Partnerships was largely based on leverage, saying:

> Both organisations were very stretched, so forming a partnership was beneficial to both, as they were both able to up their game with more money, more resources and ability to cover larger geographical areas.

David Holland

Programmatic partnerships

The research found three key kinds of programmatic relationships: schools, young people and creative and cultural organisations.

Partnerships with schools

Due to the aspirations of the programme to contribute to school change and engage children and young people, schools were a primary partner at a programmatic level. From interviews with CP staff, cultural organisations, creative agents and schools, it appeared that CP partnerships with schools were largely exploratory, operational and formal. Partnerships were exploratory because CP was instrumental in exploring issues of relevance to schools and bringing schools and creative practitioners and/or cultural and creative organisations together to develop programmes of activity. Partnerships were operational in the sense that the role of CP was to develop processes and structures to support the development and delivery of activity.

The importance of the area office working directly with schools led some offices to take a key role in the formation of programmes of activity in schools. One creative director stated:

> We are quite hands on, which means that we go into the schools, meet with the head and senior management team. We help work on defining what they want and get a sense of the context and then employ the appropriate creative agent to lead the programme. Once that happens, we stand back.

As another creative director described it:

> CP in our region takes a 'school centred' approach. Schools identify need with the Programmer and then the Programmer helps them find partners and leads them through the process of developing the project.

The overriding purpose of CP partnerships with schools was exploratory. This meant that, at times, CP took a challenging stance toward schools. As a creative director commented,

> CP tries to be broker, but questions and challenges schools to help them shape effective and challenging projects that are likely to address their need.

Beyond the exploratory purpose of the partnership between CP and schools, the partnership process was largely operational, though the degree of direct operational guidance varied between regions, as did the formality of operational processes. In one region consulted, a creative programmer described a highly formalised process of exploratory partnership, stating:

> We have a clear model of working. When a school successfully becomes a CP school, they do a diagnostic about what they can achieve with CP … We then ask them do an action plan about what they want to do with CP. That comes back to [the creative programmer] so we know what they are doing. Then they get on with running the programme.

In some regions, CP coordinators (also called school coordinators) were appointed within each school to lead on the coordination of the programme of activity within the school. School coordinators were generally highly respected teachers or members of the senior management team who maintain close working relationships with creative agents and the Creative Partnerships area office. In other cases, area offices sought to avoid cultivating a direct relationship with a single individual. As one creative director put it:

> The main point of contact in school varies. We do work with teachers or heads of department as quasi-coordinators but we tried to adopt as a principle that we do not engage with one person in a school, but rather with the school at large, as we are interested in instigating whole school change.

Most offices, however, emphasised the importance of having a clear channel of communication to one designated coordinator, and all stated that developing relationships with the senior management team (particularly the head teacher) was essential to the success of partnerships with schools and thus the development and delivery of the programme.

Though they are important for the development of the programme, the multiple levels of engagement with schools around the development of a programme required a great deal of school time, which, as a school coordinator put it, 'is difficult for schools where time is short'.

Partnerships with young people

Young people were, in some settings, meaningfully involved in the development of projects within schools. Creative Partnerships area offices are generally committed to this way of working. As one creative director stated:

> I think that there are some good examples where children and young people are involved in planning projects. It is increasingly a priority for us and for schools.

In some areas, Creative Partnerships sought to support schools in developing the mechanisms already in place to give children and young people a voice in decision-making. As a creative director put it:

> In terms of how young people get involved, we use what is already working in the schools … It's about thinking about what works within the school and how they can consult meaningfully.

Some partners are highly idealistic about the nature of the relationships between teachers, creative practitioners, and children and young people. One partner said, 'Everybody is equal – children, teachers, artists; this is a unique opportunity'.

Despite such positive portrayals of the degree of partnership working with young people, there were difficulties for teachers and creative practitioners in acclimatising themselves to this way of working. A deputy head teacher cautioned that 'sometimes practitioners are neither respectful nor empathetic to the young people's voice'. Some young people did suggest that they had been able to develop better relationships with their teachers through Creative Partnerships. A statement provided by one school's students asserted:

> We have been able to develop relationships such as those in Creative Partnerships through being able to talk to teachers and being more relaxed around each other.

It seems clear from the CP experience that, in order to ensure that young people are given an appropriate voice in this or similar programmes, teachers and practitioners will have to change the ways in which they work together on the development of projects for young people. Giving children and young people greater autonomy and responsibility will likely rely, as Hall *et al.* argue, 'on teachers and artists being willing to work together as partners, to respect one another's expertise and to give time to exploring theoretical standpoints and analysing young people's work' (2007: 617).

Partnerships with cultural and creative organisations

Cultural and creative organisations were often engaged by CP area offices on the design of programmes – these relationships were often coalescing and exploratory partnerships. Partnerships were coalescing in that they often bring together a number of organisations, who may have competed with one other for funding and profile, to work collaboratively on the development of a programme of activity with CP. Partnerships were operational in that they were concerned with the development, management and delivery of activities. As a creative director stated:

> Our partnerships with cultural organisations are practical partnerships. They provide pro-gramme mentors [or creative agents] who work with schools. Sometimes cultural organi-sations are delivery partners, hiring artists to undertake activity. In other cases, they are employed directly.

As this statement suggests, in some cases cultural organisations played a key coordinating role in the development of programmes of activity, acting as creative agents. According to another creative director, 'cultural organisations work as Principal Partners … this is where a cultural organisation is partnered with one school … these organisations then broker relationships with artists'.

A representative of a cultural organisation that acted as a creative agent described the role as such:

> It's about brokering relationships to make sure that the school get what they want and what CP want and to make sure that the artists aren't exploited. Sometimes schools want to stand back; sometimes the schools don't get that it is about partnership, so my role is ensuring that [this understanding] is in place and being around to ensure a common language.

Facilitating communication and ensuring that the needs of all parties are considered is an essential part of the success of partnerships, bringing together diverse constituents. In some cases, cultural organisations were able to fulfil this key supporting function for the programme.

Building partnerships with cultural and creative organisations was essential to the programme, because of the influence they had within the local creative and cultural community. In many ways such organisations acted as gatekeepers, making them key partners for brokering relationships with individual creative practitioners. The influence of these organisations, however, proved both supportive of and challenging to Creative Partnerships activities. As a creative director stated:

> There was a bit of a cultural mafia in [our area] which had close relationships with a number of practitioners. This made it very difficult [for us to engage] new entrants to work with CP. We had to find ways to formally engage with a range of practitioners, but it was difficult.

Not only did cultural and creative organisations, in some cases, present an obstacle to Crea-tive Partnerships engaging creative practitioners, but the programme also had to support the development of partnerships between competing organisations. As one creative programmer recounted:

> Before, they never spoke to each other. [CP] has given them a way of talking to, supporting and learning from each other. They can now collaborate on projects, but they were competitive before.

The delivery of projects was closely related to the development and management of a programme of activity within schools. However, at the level of project delivery, teachers and young people took on a more significant role in partnerships. Because of the range of stakeholders (or partners) involved and the focus on delivering a desired outcome, tensions and misunderstandings often arose around conflicting and/or unclear objectives and differing languages, approaches and expectations.

Communication was cited as a major challenge facing partnership between schools and creative practitioners. As one creative agent stated:

> It is a partnership and people need to spend time investing in communicating together and bringing their learning to the programme. Regular open communication is vital.

Beyond recognising the necessity of investing the necessary time for communication, some argued that there were issues of language that make it difficult for partners to work effectively together. As a creative agent put it:

> Schools speak a very different language from artists. Even if you use that word partnership, what do you mean by it? The words mean different things to different people.

Beyond issues of language another issue cited by some interviewees was the professional inclinations of schools and creative practitioners. As one creative agent describes, the challenge is to move those involved beyond these inclinations: 'The challenge is pushing the artists and pushing the schools to work outside of their comfort zone'.

Another issue concerned ownership and responsibility within partnership working. As one creative agent argued:

> Sometimes schools want to stand back; sometimes the schools don't get that it is about partnership ... [It is important] to make sure that CP is a partnership, so that it is two way in terms of learning, so that the artist learns and informs as well as the school.

Another creative agent argued that the most successful project she worked on was one in which teachers developed an idea and selected the practitioners that would deliver the project. She argued: 'They then had ownership. Teachers sometimes feel like you're doing it to them, and they need to feel that they are doing it with them'.

While interviewees highlighted a number of difficulties in engaging schools (and teachers more specifically) in taking responsibility for the development of partnerships with creative practitioners, creative practitioners also presented a number of challenges to the process. As one head teacher commented, 'Rather than appreciating other people's point of view, sometimes you can get arrogance from the practitioners'. A creative agent suggested that practitioners sometimes felt oversensitive in a school environment, because of unfamiliar complex organisational politics and structures.

Getting not only schools but also creative practitioners (and/or cultural organisations) to work in a different way has been a challenging though fruitful part of the partnerships brokered by CP. As a creative director argues: 'The most successful projects are those in which practitioners and [cultural and creative] organisations have committed to working in a different way'.

Project partnerships were exploratory in purpose (for the most part), formal in organisation, in a market mode of governance, and operational and collaborative in process. Partnerships were exploratory in that they have brought together educational professionals, creative practitioners, and children and young people to investigate different approaches to learning. Project-related partnerships were often formal as expectations were often defined by partnership agreements between practitioners and schools, at times involving young people. Partnerships were operational due to the importance of shared ownership of organisational matters, and often collaborative in that there was joint decision-making around the development and delivery of projects.

Costs and benefits of partnership working

Increased efficiency is often regarded as the major contribution made by partnership working. For example, it brings partners and stakeholders to work together who previously would not have done so, thus building capacity. Moreover, at a strategic level, formal agreements between several partners may introduce greater consistency in activities. Partnership working also improves intelligence and helps partners to generate new ideas, and encouraging the development of cross-agency and cross-sectoral networks could have economies of scale and economies of scope.

Clearly, efficiency is a major factor for policy-makers when having to take funding decisions. In a scenario where two or more programmes may have similar outcomes, the most desirable alternative is often chosen on efficiency grounds (Rice, 1997). In the case of CP, policy-makers might choose to fund a programme specifically focusing on science skills and knowledge rather than supporting creative activities. Thus, if partnership contributes to improving efficiency in the CP programme, this may provide the decisive argument.

In the case under examination costs were incurred by CP offices and all the partners mentioned. In the case of CP the costs were relatively straightforward, mainly relating to staffing and programme costs. In terms of partners, there was primarily in-kind support – in particular the time invested by school coordinators, head teachers or members of the partnership boards, but also materials and equipment, or facilities – and sometimes substantial cash contributions.

These costs varied across the different types of partnerships. In the case of strategic partnerships, costs were particularly high in terms of the time that board members invest in the programme (e.g. during bi-monthly meetings). As compared to strategic partnerships, the most important costs at the project level can be found in the materials or equipment provided for the project (e.g. a school providing audio-visual equipment to produce a film) or in the facilities being used (e.g. a cultural organisation opening its studio for rehearsals).

In addition to the above, it is important to note that there were sometimes hidden costs, especially through displacement. For example, a teacher may spend more time on preparing lessons and developing their creative approach, but as a result would spend less time on reading subject specific journals and following recent developments, or on marking exams. The opportunity cost of giving up one alternative in favour of another needs to be taken into account.

Conclusions

Partnership was a key aspect of the day-to-day delivery of the Creative Partnerships programme. It also became a way of describing the range of aspirations and practices of the programme. The notion of partnership implicitly conveys ideas of sharing costs, brokering new kinds of learning, accessing additional resources for the education system, and generally facilitating and organising a way of bringing more people with different ideas and practices into schools. The nature of the partnerships developed by the programme, however, showed significant variation. Some partnerships were developed around resources, some around wider local or regional strategies, some around communities of interest. In some instances, CP participated within networks. In others, programme officers directed activities, taking on actual or presumed leadership.

Key observations and insights to emerge from the research on CP partnerships are:

- the programme may have an aspiration of working in partnerships, but partnerships may vary considerably in both style and substance;
- partnerships for the development of programmes and projects require significant management and the development of trust between parties – agreements and contracts alone cannot provide these;
- strategic partnerships are key for wider impact, but may not be fully utilised.

The costs associated with partnership working are not limited to the financial investment made in programmes and projects; partner costs need to be considered more explicitly in planning and delivery. Increased efficiency from coordination and alignment may compensate for some of these costs.

References

Frank, F. and Smith, A. (2000) *The Partnership Handbook*, Ottawa: Human Resources Development Canada.

Glendinning, C., Powell, M. A. and Rummery, K. (2002) *Partnerships, New Labour and the Governance of Welfare*, Bristol: Policy Press.

Hall, C., Thomson, P. and Russell, L. (2007) Teaching like an artist: the pedagogic identities and practices of artists in schools, *British Journal of Sociology of Education* 29(5): 605–19.

Hudson, B., Hardy, B., Henwood, M. and Wistow, G. (1999) In pursuit of inter-agency collaboration in the public sector: what is the contribution of theory and research?, *Public Management: An International Journal of Research and Theory* 1(2): 235–60.

Huxham, C. (2003) Theorizing collaboration practice, *Public Management Review* 5(3): 401–23.

Le Grand, J. and Bartlett, W. (eds) (1993) *Quasi-Markets and Social Policy*, London: Macmillan.

Ling, T. (2000) Unpacking partnership: the case of health care, in J. Clarke, S. Gewirtz and E. McLaughlin (eds) *New Managerialism, New Welfare*, Thousand Oaks, CA: Sage.

Long, F. and Arnold, M. (1995) *The Power of Environmental Partnerships*, Fort Worth, TX: Dryden Press.

Rice, J. (1997) Cost analysis in education: paradox and possibility, *Educational Evaluation and Policy Analysis* 19(4): 309–17.

41

Professional learning for creative teaching and learning

Richard Hatcher

How can experiences of creative learning in classrooms be most effectively shared with other teachers and other schools to inform school and system change? This chapter explores how teachers conceptualise and articulate creative teaching and learning, and the institutional and systemic structures and processes which facilitate or constrain collaborative professional learning for creativity. It situates its analysis in two overlapping policy contexts. One is the problematic juxtaposition of 'creativity' and 'performativity' in the official policy agenda. The dominance of the 'standards agenda' and its associated competency model of professional learning powerfully shape and restrict teachers' understanding of and engagement with creativity in teaching and learning. The other policy context is provided by the dominant discourse of change in and across schools through knowledge transfer and acquisition. The paper is based on two research studies (Fautley and Hatcher, 2008; Fautley *et al.*, 2011) and draws on a range of theoretical resources – the burgeoning literature on professional collaboration, work process learning, activity theory and network theory – to develop a critique of current dominant policy and practice and suggest an alternative perspective.

According to Hodkinson and Hodkinson (2005: 111), the dominant model in education policy discourse in 'a deeply technically rational audit culture' is of professional learning as acquisition. There are five interrelated reasons why this is an inappropriate model for professional learning in the school system, and particularly so for creativity in teaching and learning.

1 Professional learning for creativity is not reducible to the transfer and acquisition of pre-programmed knowledge. Engeström (2001), a leading proponent of activity theory, terms this kind of learning 'radical exploration'.
2 It is not consensual: it entails challenging the dominant logics of practice (Ball and Maroy, 2009).
3 The dominant model tends to neglect the situational specificity of school and classroom contexts (Hager and Hodkinson, 2009).
4 In order for professional learning to generate new practices by teachers, not simply the replication of imported practices, it requires not just procedural and performative knowledge – 'practical knowledge' – but also theoretical knowledge (Eraut, 2003, 2007a, 2007b; Griffiths and Guile, 2003; Hodkinson and Hodkinson, 2004, 2005).

5   Professional learning typically entails not one-way transfer but a collaborative process of mutually creating new knowledge, combining experiential and reflective learning to elicit tacit knowledge and integrate it with codified knowledge through what Fielding *et al.* (2005) call joint practice development.

The contrasting perspectives of what can be called the knowledge acquisition and knowledge generation models provide a framework for examining some empirical evidence of professional learning for creativity. The largest-scale initiative to promote creativity in schools in England is Creative Partnerships' government-funded programme of creative practitioners working in classrooms with teachers. Research by Fautley and Hatcher (2008) explored two phases of professional learning through Creative Partnerships projects: the interaction between the creative practitioner and the participating teacher; and the subsequent process of knowledge and practice sharing and development between the participating teacher and other teachers not involved in the original project, in the same school or other schools. The research took place in five local authorities in the West Midlands, and was funded by local Creative Partnerships. Interviews were carried out in 22 schools: 6 secondary schools, 2 middle schools, 11 primary or first schools, 1 nursery and 2 all age special schools. A total of 29 interviews were conducted with 36 teachers. Our focus was on the accounts of the projects offered by participating teachers and the language they employed to talk about creativity.

We asked teachers involved in Creative Partnerships projects what were the key features in terms of creativity in teaching and learning. The large majority of teachers' responses referred to aspects of creative teaching which had the potential to facilitate creative learning: new technical skills; innovative and active learning activities; pupil initiative and collaboration; cross-curricular themes; real life experiences and purposes. In this respect our findings correspond closely to what Doherty and Harland (2001: 40) call 'The conditions perceived to be conducive to developing creativity in the learner'. Some teachers described pupils' creative learning in these terms; for example:

> Creativity is strongly linked to the whole concept of independent learning because it's to do with being able to generate ideas which can help you solve problems, so we saw a real link there, creative thinking, independent, autonomous thinking, problem solving as well.

But they were the exception. The large majority of teachers did not refer to pupils' creative learning or the causal relationship between the facilitating conditions and creative learning, even when specifically asked. If teachers cannot easily articulate pupils' creative learning and how it was generated by teaching for creativity in Creative Partnerships projects it raises fundamental questions about the professional learning that projects are intended to promote: what had teachers learned from the creative practitioner to inform their own subsequent practice and to disseminate to other teachers?

First, what did they learn from the creative practitioner? The principal task for the teacher is not to attempt to emulate the specialist expertise of the external creative practitioner but to understand the underlying principles in order that the teacher can generate their own subsequent creative teaching and learning. As Thomson *et al.* (2009: 69) say, 'It is the teacher's professional capacity to translate the creative practitioners' work into pedagogical principles which counts', and that requires not just experience but 'intellectual work' (ibid.: 70). In fact it is a complex process. First, there are two elements of the creative activity: the pedagogic or teaching dimension and the creative pupil learning dimension. The creative practitioner may have a sophisticated and theoretically informed understanding of these, or it may be largely

---

Box 41.1

Some schools recognised the need to focus on making processes of creative learning explicit.

> *When you say 'that's what Creative Partnerships hoped', to what extent did they make that hope explicit? To what extent essentially did they come in, do exciting things, and rely on teachers implicitly drawing lessons from it?*

My professional view is that Creative Partnerships left that to be too implicit. Now that wasn't just Creative Partnership's fault that was just the school's perception of how it was going to work as well. So that this particular project in my view was too dependent on teachers' professionalism to see the learning for themselves.

On a fortnightly basis, my entire staff are involved in a teaching and learning programme where we are far more explicit about the quality of teaching, the quality of our own learning, and our professional development internally through a much more exciting provision of seminars and sharing best practice and teams leading teams within the school. Rather than being bogged down in old fashioned meetings with agendas. So although they still exist, there is now this teaching and learning programme in place which we have been using to unpick more general professional issues, some of which have been raised with our own involvement with Creative Partnerships.

(Head teacher)

---

undeveloped. Second, these two elements may be made explicit by the creative practitioner, or may remain tacit, embedded in her practice. The more undeveloped and unformulated they are the more work the teacher has to do to mentally reverse-engineer the activity and construct for herself the pedagogic knowledge and principles which could generate it. And then, even if the two elements have been made explicit by the practitioner, the teacher needs to rework them in order to subsequently apply them in ways appropriate to her own purposes and capacities, her understanding of children's creative learning and her teaching situation. As Eraut (2003: 72) points out, 'learning to use theory in practical situations is a major learning challenge in its own right'. Rather than the simplistic notion of knowledge transfer, this is a complex process of conceptual interpretation and knowledge-making and application.

Other research studies of professional learning in Creative Partnerships projects (Hall *et al.*, 2007; Galton, 2008) indicate how problematic this process is. Galton found that few teachers

> wished to engage in discussions concerning the rationale for the creative partner's approach to learning and creativity. Most wished for '*hands on sessions*' where they could acquire new knowledge and skills. For some, it was simply a question of applying what was offered fairly uncritically. … Such transfer of knowledge between creative practitioner and teachers, without deeper understanding of the processes involved, is therefore likely to be superficial.

> *(Galton, 2008: 78)*

Hall and her colleagues found in their study of three Creative Partnerships projects that 'There was an assumption that theoretical perspectives, the framing of activities and their purposes did not need to be shared and debated' (Hall *et al.*, 2007: 617). The impact on subsequent teaching and learning was limited to 'replicability of the project's processes, so that it can be repeated at different times with different children' (ibid.: 617).

How can this be accounted for? The explanation lies principally in the problematic – I would say contradictory – relationship between creativity and the dominant pedagogic model of the past decade embodied in the standards agenda. Although the large majority of teachers we interviewed regarded creativity as contributing to raising pupil attainment, a view receiving official endorsement from Ofsted's report *Learning: Creative Approaches that Raise Standards* (Ofsted, 2010), in practice the standards agenda has had negative consequences for creativity in schools because it has focused teachers' work on the product of children's learning, its measurable outcomes, rather than on the processes of learning. For many teachers and schools conscious of the pressures of performativity, creativity, however desirable, was perceived as a risky departure from the focus on basic skills and test and exam syllabuses. Hall *et al.* (2007), explaining the poverty of theoretically informed interactions between teachers and creative practitioners in their research, speak of a clash of pedagogic cultures. Whereas creative practitioners tend to adopt competence pedagogies, focusing on the process of developing the learner, teachers tend to adopt performance pedagogies oriented to the product in order to satisfy the outcomes-driven standards agenda.

Furthermore, the standards agenda has provided teachers with a vocabulary of measurable pupil attainment but has deprived them of a repertoire of pedagogic language and concepts with which to think and talk about pupils' learning. As Burnard *et al.* suggest,

> One of the reasons why it is so difficult to capture the complexities of children's learning is that we often do not possess a well-founded language to classify, relate, document and communicate about the different kinds of thinking we observe.
>
> *(Burnard et al., 2006: 248)*

For many teachers the issue of assessment represents the greatest tension between creative learning and the standards agenda and the most problematic issue for teachers to resolve, because it lies at the interface between imposed forms of external evaluation and the need to assess complex processes of learning. Ellis and Barrs (2008: 74) pose the question: 'if creativity involves originality and the use of the individual imagination, how can these qualities be judged against a set of predetermined criteria? The assessment of creative work will always involve interpretation and negotiation. Creative learning challenges conventional thinking about assessment and demands changes in forms of assessment'. As Thomson *et al.* (2009: 39) found, 'teachers often appeared to be held back by the lack of alternative assessment examples and a rich assessment-specific language'.

I draw here on a two-year study of two secondary schools engaged in transforming their curriculum to promote creative teaching and learning (Fautley *et al.*, 2008; Fautley *et al.*, 2011). The research was funded by Creative Partnerships, which has awarded 'Schools of Creativity' status to the two schools. According to the two head teachers,

> the biggest block to creative learning I think in the curriculum remains the assessment regime, and what we're doing with Creative Partnerships now is saying, 'Let's look afresh at what we mean by assessment.'
>
> *(Matthew Milburn, Kingstone School, Barnsley)*

Massive assessment issues. Teachers need a huge amount of quality reflective time framing quite rigorous questions and seeking insights into what's really going on for young learners in creative processes. That I think is a massive challenge for us if we're going to help teachers and children recognise what serious learning is going on in this environment.

(Tim Boyes, Queensbridge School, Birmingham)

A key concern of teachers teaching the new curriculum using innovative teaching methods was whether they were also satisfying the external assessment regime. A reliance on the use of subject-based National Curriculum assessment criteria failed to capture much of the active learning which was taking place in the new programmes. Teachers realised that new forms of assessment were needed:

the standard assessment is 'sit down in silence by yourself and answer these questions', which is I guess what schools around the country use, but if we're going to be teaching the students in groups and pairs and asking them to develop group skills and research skills then perhaps we need a different way of assessing.

(Teacher, Queensbridge School, Birmingham)

As the new pedagogies became more secure, then so too did realising the limitations of existing assessment methods based solely upon the acquisition of knowledge and skills:

In the end, the school is assessed in how it performed in high-stakes nationwide assessments. So we do have to still prepare students for that, but within the year, we have been able to be much more creative with our assessments. ... As a teacher, I feel very much empowered and freed up to be creative with my assessment, and I have been given time to do it, which has been a useful thing. If I hadn't it would have been very difficult.

(Teacher, Queensbridge School, Birmingham)

At Queensbridge another new strategy was the use of comment-only marking, where grades are not given:

I mean, is it right that we give them a level, or is it more productive that they get a comment? I think that's all starting to come into play and I think it is important. I know I respond better to praise ... I'd much prefer someone to say, 'Well done, that's really good.' So I suppose that the same would work for children, and I think sometimes comments are much more important than actually realising that they're at a level 6.

(Teacher, Queensbridge School, Birmingham)

This observation also reveals a departure from thinking that National Curriculum levels are the main modality for assessment.

In order to obtain a broader picture of the individual learning taking place, the Kingstone team began to develop e-portfolio assessments. They enabled students to keep track of their learning experiences and personal development, and later became part of a new summative assessment process which involved oral presentations, described in more detail by Matthew Milburn:

The new model of assessment that we have developed at the school is based on an hour long interview about learning. The conversation is informed by a raft of evidence that the pupil collates. The interview involves an adult significant to the child (often a parent or carer), four of their peers (selected by the teacher), the teacher and an adult who is unknown to the pupil. We've used school governors, local employers or Local Authority officers to play this role.

We are working with primary and nursery schools as well as the local college to pilot this assessment approach with children of a range of different ages. The use of the Virtual Learning Environment should mean that the evidence that the child collates is transferable across schools and throughout education.

(Head teacher, Kingstone School, Barnsley)

The dissemination of teachers professional learning for creativity within and between schools

I turn now to the second phase of professional learning through Creative Partnerships projects: the dissemination to other teachers. First, within schools. We found a wide range of responses. While some schools saw creativity as integral to mainstream teaching and deliberately used Creative Partnership projects as catalysts for whole school change, others isolated creativity from the mainstream curriculum, compartmentalising it in a separate time in the week or the term. In those schools Creative Partnership projects tended to remain locked in the classroom or classrooms where the projects took place, with little or no influence on the rest of the school. In a comparable study, based on interviews with teachers who had been involved in CP projects, Downing *et al.* (2007) found that just over half of the teachers had not been involved in sharing their learning about the project in staff meetings. Galton (2008: 79) found that 'Few headteachers saw the creative partnership initiative as a vehicle for changing the school's approach to teaching and learning'.

The explanation for the failure of many schools to share professional learning for creativity, in addition to the conflict, real and perceived, between creativity and the standards agenda, is the absence of a school culture and procedures for collaborative professional development. As Thomson and Sanders (2010: 80) found in their study of creativity and whole school change, 'only a few of the schools had the kinds of structures for professional development, governance and review/planning that allowed staff and students to take a major role in building a new "community of practice"'.

Most schools today belong to one or more local school networks (Higham *et al.*, 2009; Hargreaves, 2009). Fautley and Hatcher (2008) examined the extent to which existing networks could be utilised for promoting professional learning for creativity and new networks could be established for that purpose. Networks already in existence ranged from geographical clusters of schools to authority-wide forums. Their function as vehicles for professional learning for creativity was very limited. Their agendas tended to be dominated by the standards agenda, the pressure of which determined a narrow focus on performance which tended to marginalise creativity:

I don't think it's high on the agenda because we've got a massive agenda so in fairness it hasn't filtered back into the cluster. Everybody is so focused on writing reading, maths, behaviour, transition.

(Head teacher)

There are high schools that work in collaboration but that's usually focusing on key skills and functional skills and those kinds of things.

(Teacher)

These networks had in effect become vehicles for the transmission of a government agenda through 'action at a distance': measurable performance outcomes establishing the logic of action which governed the networks (Thompson, 2003; Hatcher, 2008). They exemplify Jessop's (2002: 237) concept of heterarchy: network forms which enable the state 'to secure political objectives by sharing power with forces beyond it and/or delegating responsibilities for specific objectives to partnerships'.

As a result of their managerial function, existing networks generally involved only head teachers, not classroom teachers directly involved in creativity teaching. We asked teachers whether there were opportunities for them to create their own collaborative links for creativity with other teachers in the network schools or to construct their own networks. There were very few examples in our research. Insofar as there was dissemination of Creative Partnerships projects to other schools it tended to be presentations at showcase events, or just the circulation of DVDs. Instances of joint practice development for creativity between schools were extremely rare because of the absence of an existing culture of teacher collaboration between schools, the pressure on time as a result of the intensification and extensification of teachers' work and the lack of resourcing for release from teaching commitments.

Professional learning for creativity and workplace learning theory

The research evidence reveals the limitations of professional learning from Creative Partnerships projects, both by participating teachers and by other teachers in the same school and in other schools. I have identified the principal reasons: the dominance of the standards agenda and the weak development of a culture of collaborative professional learning in the school system. I now want to develop a fuller analysis by situating professional learning for creativity in the wider context of workplace learning theory.

My starting point is Felstead et al.'s (2009) Working as Learning Framework. It situates specific learning situations in the holistic concept of 'productive system', which comprises the totality of social relations in a process of commodity production. A productive system comprises two axes, each consisting of a series of linked networks of social relations. The vertical axis is the 'structure of production', consisting of a hierarchy of levels of control. The horizontal axis is the 'stages of production'. At their intersection is the work situation, which, as a learning environment, can be expansive or restrictive. In terms of professional learning for creativity in schools, the vertical axis comprises the imposition of the standards agenda by government at the macro level and by school management at the meso level, and its influence over the classroom teacher at the micro level. The horizontal axis comprises the 'stages of production'. In the case of a creativity project they extend from its initiation by a creative practitioner through to its impact on mainstream provision. Within the school system the professional learning environment for creativity is restrictive rather than expansive because of the combination of the pressures of the standards agenda and the silo character of the organisation of work, in classrooms, year groups, departments and separate school workplaces.

In the context of the Working as Learning Framework, activity theory provides a toolkit of concepts which enable a closer focus on professional learning for creativity in schools. In the productive system of schooling, what is the commodity which is being produced? Warmington and Leadbetter (2010: 72) argue that 'regardless of the specified, momentary object of any particular activity ... , the object of any activity system also comprises the social production of labour power, or rather labour-power potential'. The object of professional learning for creativity, including Creative Partnerships projects, conceived of as activity systems, is to develop the labour-power potential of the participating teacher and, through her dissemination activities, that of other teachers, i.e. their enhanced capacity for future teaching for creative learning. Earlier I described the flow of knowledge and practice during and following a Creative Partnerships project. We can now place an extended version in the framework of 'stages of production', as follows:

creative practitioner → teacher → other teachers → teachers' labour-power potential → pupils' creative learning

Each of these transitions entails boundary-crossing between different professional identities (creative practitioners and teachers; teachers with different specialisms) and between different situational contexts within schools (pupil age groups; subject areas) and between schools. The boundary zones between them are the sources of professional learning through interaction as teachers' existing categories of thought and practice are called into question; a process of moving from what Engeström (2007) calls stabilisation knowledge to possibility knowledge. Middleton (2010) reveals how this learning process can be elicited through discourse analysis of participants' communicative action and subsequent reflection.

Marketised networks – a new 'structure of production'

The research on which this chapter is based took place during the period of the New Labour government. The Conservative–Liberal Democrat coalition government which replaced it in 2010 furnishes a policy context which differs in an important respect from its predecessor's: the promise of more autonomy for schools within a more marketised system. There are ambivalent implications for creativity. More autonomy and less top-down prescription may open up more space. But the pressure on performance, especially by lower-performing schools, remains. Creativity may also be constrained by the government's predilection for a return to 'traditional methods' and a subject-divided curriculum. A further constraint results from the two key policies of Academies and 'free schools'. They are likely to lead to the widespread emergence of chains of schools outside local authority networks, in many cases with commercial involvement. There are two predictable negative effects on professional learning for creativity. One is reduced opportunities for collaboration between schools outside their chain (Evans and Stone-Johnson, 2010). Hill found that leaders of chains of schools

are failing to take advantage of sharing and learning from other chains. The conviction that the particular teaching and learning model they have developed is right could inhibit their openness to learn from the experience of others, particularly since some chains are beginning to claim intellectual property rights for their teaching and learning model.

(Hill, 2010: 32)

The second consequence is that chains tend to impose a standardised model, again restricting creativity (Hill, 2010; Lubienski, 2009).

Implications for research, policy and practice

The combination of the Working as Learning Framework and activity theory provides a fruitful theoretical context for future research into professional learning for creativity in schools, in two respects. It enables it to benefit from cross-fertilisation with research beyond the school system in the whole field of workplace learning. And it provides a set of powerful forensic tools for investigating the situated interactional processes of professional learning.

The analysis in this chapter also has implications for future policy and practice. I will draw out three.

First, the struggle to integrate creativity into the mainstream discourse of teaching and learning remains to be completed. The evidence demonstrates that far from being a diversion from raising attainment, it can contribute significantly to it (Fautley *et al.*, 2011). However, there is a danger: the assimilation into and subordination to the 'performance' agenda of a domesticated creativity reduced to a procedural skill. For example, the Confederation of British Industry (CBI), in its agenda for schools, lists one of seven elements in employability as 'Problem solving – analysing facts and situations and applying creative thinking to develop appropriate solutions' (CBI, 2010: 9). *Critical* creative learning entails problem-making as well as problem-taking, and creative cognitive processes informed by conceptualised knowledge (Young, 2008).

Second, the professional learning environment in the school system needs to be transformed in order to enable distributed and generative knowledge and practice within schools and across networks of schools (Hargreaves, 2010). Simplistic notions of knowledge transfer and acquisition need to be replaced by an enriched conception of collaborative expansive professional learning. Innovation and change in the school system require systematically planned boundary-crossing within schools and between schools by teachers (with creative practitioners as well where feasible), engaged in joint practice development based on evidence of successful creative learning. The biggest challenge is to establish cross-school networks of teachers as the principal vehicles for professional learning for system change, colonising existing 'mainstream' networks and creating new ones where creativity is the principal object (as exemplified in Cochrane and Cockett, 2007).

Third, teachers (and creative practitioners) need a theoretically informed understanding of creativity in teaching and learning, the ability to disembed and construct theorised knowledge from practical experiences of 'creativity' to generate new practice, and the language to articulate it to themselves and to other teachers. In our view this entails paying close attention to the fine-grain of pupils' thinking. Some empirical research studies which make visible the processes of creative learning (for example, Burnard *et al.*'s (2006) study of 'possibility thinking' in the early years, and some of the accounts in Craft *et al.* (2008)) can alert teachers to the features of creative learning and provide a language to articulate them.

References

Ball, S. J. and Maroy, G. (2009) Schools' logics of action as mediation and compromise between internal dynamics and external constraints and pressures, *Compare* 39(1): 99–112.

Burnard, P., Craft, A., Cremin, T., with Duffy, B., Hanson, R., Keen, J., Haynes, L. and Burns, D. (2006) Documenting 'possibility thinking': a journey of collaborative enquiry, *International Journal of Early Years Education* 14(3): 243–62.

CBI (Confederation of British Industry) (2010) *Fulfilling Potential: The Business Role in Education*, London: CBI.

Cochrane, P. and Cockett, M. (2007) *Building a Creative School*, Stoke on Trent: Trentham Books.

Craft, A., Cremin, T. and Burnard, P. (2008) *Creative Learning 3–11 and How We Document It*, Stoke on Trent: Trentham Books.

Doherty, P. and Harland, J. (2001) *Partnerships for Creativity: An Evaluation of Implementation*, Slough: NFER.

Downing, D., Lord, P., Jones, M., Martin, K. and Springate, I. (2007) *Study of Creative Partnerships' Local Sharing of Practice and Learning*, Slough: NFER.

Ellis, S. and Barrs, M. (2008) The assessment of creative learning, in J. Sefton-Green (ed.) *Creative Learning*, London: Creative Partnerships.

Engeström, Y. (2001) Expansive learning at work: toward an activity theoretical reconceptualization, *Journal of Education and Work* 14(1): 133–56.

—— (2007) From stabilization knowledge to possibility knowledge in organizational learning, Management Learning 38(3): 271–5.

Eraut, M. (2003) Transfer of knowledge between education and the workplace, in H. P. A. Boshuizen (ed.) *Expertise Development: The Transition between School and Work*, Heerlen: Open Universiteit Maastricht.

—— (2007a) Theoretical and practical knowledge revisited, paper presented at the 12th Biennial EARLI Conference 2007, Budapest, Hungary, 28 August–1 September.

—— (2007b) Learning from other people in the workplace, *Oxford Review of Education* 33(4): 403–22.

Evans, M. P. and Stone-Johnson, C. (2010) Internal leadership challenges of network participation, *International Journal of Leadership in Education* 13(2): 203–20.

Fautley, M. and Hatcher, R. (2008) *Dissemination of Creative Partnerships Projects*, Birmingham: Birmingham City University.

Fautley, M., Gee, M., Hatcher, R. and Millard, E. (2008) *The Creative Partnerships Curriculum Projects at Kingstone School Barnsley and Queensbridge School Birmingham: Research Report*, Birmingham: Birmingham City University.

Fautley, M., Hatcher, R. and Millard, M. (2011) *Re-Making the Curriculum*, Stoke on Trent: Trentham Books.

Felstead, A., Fuller, A., Jewson, N. and Unwin, L. (2009) *Improving Working as Learning*, London: Routledge.

Fielding, M., Bragg, S., Craig, J., Cunningham, I., Eraut, M., Gillinson, S., Horne, M., Robinson, C. and Thorp, J. (2005) *Factors Influencing the Transfer of Good Practice*, London: DfES.

Galton, M. (2008) *Creative Practitioners in Schools and Classrooms*, Cambridge: University of Cambridge.

Griffiths, T. and Guile, D. (2003) A connective model of learning: the implications for work process knowledge, *European Educational Research Journal* 2(1): 56–73.

Hager, P. and Hodkinson, P. (2009) Moving beyond the metaphor of transfer of learning, *British Educational Research Journal* 35(4): 619–38.

Hall, C., Thomson, P. and Russell, L. (2007) Teaching like an artist: the pedagogic identities and practices of artists in schools, *British Journal of Sociology of Education* 28(5): 605–19.

Hargreaves, A. (2009) Labouring to lead, in C. Chapman and H. M. Gunter (eds) *Radical Reforms*, London: Routledge.

Hargreaves, D. H. (2010) *Creating a Self-Improving School System*, Nottingham: National College.

Hatcher, R. (2008) System leadership, networks and the question of power, *Management in Education* 22(2): 24–30.

Higham, R., Hopkins, D. and Matthews, P (2009) *System Leadership in Practice*, Maidenhead: Open University Press.

Hill, R. (2010) *Chain Reactions: A Thinkpiece on the Development of Chains of Schools in the English School System*, Nottingham: National College.

Hodkinson, H. and Hodkinson, P. (2004) Rethinking the concept of community of practice in relation to schoolteachers' workplace learning, *International Journal of Training and Development* 8(1): 21–31.

—— (2005) Improving schoolteachers' workplace learning, *Research Papers in Education* 20(2): 109–31.

Jessop, B. (2002) *The Future of the Capitalist State*, Cambridge: Polity Press.

Lubienski, C. (2009) *Do Quasi-Markets Foster Innovation in Education? A Comparative Perspective*, Education Working Paper No. 25, Paris: OECD.

Middleton, D. (2010) Identifying learning in interprofessional discourse: the development of an analytical protocol, in H. Daniels, A. Edwards, Y. Engeström, T. Gallagher and S. R. Ludvigsen (eds) *Activity Theory in Practice*, Abingdon: Routledge.

Ofsted (2010) *Learning: Creative Approaches that Raise Standards*, London: Ofsted.

Thompson, G. F. (2003) *Between Hierarchies and Markets*, Oxford: Oxford University Press.

Thomson, P. and Sanders, E. (2010) Creativity and whole school change: an investigation of English headteacher practices, *Journal of Educational Change* 11(1): 63–83.

Thomson, P., Jones, K. and Hall, C. (2009) *Creative School Change Research Project: Final Report*, London: Creative Partnerships.

Warmington, P. and Leadbetter, J. (2010) Expansive learning, expansive labour: conceptualising the social production of labour-power within multi-agency working, in H. Daniels, A. Edwards, Y. Engeström, T. Gallagher and S. R. Ludvigsen (eds) *Activity Theory in Practice*, Abingdon: Routledge.

Young, M. F. D. (2008) *Bringing Knowledge Back In*, London: Routledge.

Part IV Editorial comment
Whole school change
Introduction

Pat Thomson

Much of the change literature focuses on processes, the how of reform. We have suggested Part IV that the why is also important. In this concluding set of chapters we will show that what and where are also vital. In a nutshell, we will suggest that if reform initiatives do not start with a clear and articulated imaginary of changing learning in classrooms – and this does not mean simply doing what has always been done better than at present – then there will be little actual change in learning.

The Creative School Change Project, funded by Creative Partnerships, examined forty schools across the country over three school years (Thomson *et al.*, 2009). One of its key findings was that schools which simply focused on the processes of change – that is, they confused means and ends – were highly likely to begin and end with process – they never reached the stage where changing everyday learning became a priority (see Table 1). They did not begin with a clear view of what learning in classrooms needed to become.

The Creative School Change Project conducted intensive case studies. One of these was a secondary school which for four years focused strongly on changing the school culture, through a series of exciting extra-curricular activities. However, they could not get past pilot projects in a narrow range of curriculum areas. The senior leadership found it had to join another reform project and create the energy/focus to 'start again' in order to get a more holistic focus on what was being taught to whom, why and how. In contrast, those schools in the study which began with a creative learning focus were able to take up other aspects of school change. These were necessary supports for the new kinds of interactions between teachers, students and knowledge that were brought about through creative learning approaches.

There is, as we noted at the outset of Part IV, very little in the way of research into systemic programmes which aim to produce creative learning across entire institutions. There is, however, research into related reforms which clearly shows the importance of starting with learning, curriculum and pedagogy and maintaining the focus on learning, curriculum and pedagogy.

Pat Thomson

Table 1 Starting points

Starting point	Change consequence
Changing the way pupils learn – a focus on creativity as teaching method	Sound basis from which to consider knowledge, assessment, grouping, ethos, and management practices. Often one in conjunction with changing organisation of learning
Changing the way learning is organised – a focus on blurring disciplinary boundaries	Sound basis from which to consider knowledge further, assessment, ethos and management practices
Changing the way learning is assessed – a focus on providing more creative means through which students can represent and demonstrate learning	Only happened in a few places – but accompanied changing the ways in which pupils learn. Would be a sound basis from to consider knowledge further, assessment, grouping and ethos as well as management practices
Changing what counts as learning – a focus on expanding knowledge and skills beyond the national curriculum	Still had to consider assessment, grouping and ethos as well as management practice
Changing who teaches – a focus on changing the composition of the school workforce on a permanent basis	Only significant in schools where major change had been effected in pedagogical process
Changing the school culture – a focus on changing the symbolic systems enrichment activities of the school and/or relationships parents/community members and organisations	Often stayed at this stage or went to pockets of innovation. Mainstream curriculum was unaffected. No systems in place to initiate change in core subject pedagogies
Changing the school organisation – a focus on changing the spread of leadership, and/or the distribution of time/money/space, and/or the decision-making structures	Often accompanied pedagogical change. If this was the major strategy then it tended to promote pockets of innovation.

Source: Thomson *et al.*, 2009

Reference

Thomson, P., Jones, K. and Hall, C. (2009) *Creative Whole School Change: Final Report*, London: Creativity, Culture and Education; Arts Council England. See also www.artsandcreativityresearch.org.uk.

42

Creativity in school design

Catherine Burke

Introduction

In December 1960, following a period of intense activity in the renewal of school buildings after the Second World War, the *Times Educational Supplement* published a prediction of future educational transformation. The author of the article, K. Laybourne, at the time chief inspector of schools in Bristol, was confident that the first moves towards this transformation were already in evidence. Today, in the throes of the largest commitment to educational transformation through building renewal since that time, it is worth reflecting on his words. He confidently assured readers that

> By the year 2000 the schools themselves will move closer to the world. The school building will become a base from which children operate, rather than a place in which they are isolated for a fixed number of hours each day. Much of the teachers' work will be to plan and interpret … The interpenetration of school and neighbourhood will be promoted by buildings in which design will become ever more open … the classroom 'box' will disappear … the main spaces will be very varied so that to pass from one to another will be a pleasing experience in itself.
>
> *(Laybourne, quoted in Lowe, 2007: 46)*

Clearly buildings matter. School buildings signify many things but primarily a visible commitment by the local community and/or state to the education of its young. The planning of schools is never random and always reflects ways that relationships in education are envisaged: relationships between adults and children, children and their peers, areas of knowledge, and between school and community. When carried out by architects fully committed to and knowledgeable about education in the widest sense, and aware of the historical and international development of theories of learning as well as contemporary trends, school buildings can become a progressive force for change. Their relative 'distance' from the world, as indicated by Laybourne, is an interesting and often overlooked feature. Clearly, Laybourne's prediction was wrong except in the sense that the internet now has the potential to bring the world into the classroom. However, the 'interpenetration of school and neighbourhood' does imply a change in the basic form of school that has not yet been realised on any significant scale. The stumbling block for radical change over the past decades, and still today, is the classroom – that taken for granted, universal component of school.

A creative curriculum sits uneasily in the traditional school building, arranged as a series of more or less identical spaces. While buildings matter, the most novel designs are never as powerful as a creative teacher who has the confidence of the community and government. Past attempts by teachers to fully exploit creativity in learning have succeeded, more often than not, in spite of the building. For a time in England during the middle decades of the twentieth century, a vision of the whole curriculum rooted in the arts brought architects and educators together to learn from innovative teachers experimenting with space to support learning through doing. This knowledge then informed the design of new school buildings according to a revised view of the child as an inherently creative being alongside a clear set of principles and values that were understood and shared by architects at the heart of government and educational advisors in the regions. The common view that they shared and articulated to the international community, who were at that time also facing the challenges of educational renewal, was based on a set of principles, values and practices that are still relevant today. The notion of education through the arts is not new and in fact was of primary influence for many seeking to design and build for creativity in the past.

Challenging the 'hegemony of the classroom'

Primary schools designed in England during the period from the 1940s to the 1960s were considered to be internationally pioneering. The buildings, furnishings and fittings as well as the outdoor areas were considered in detail to promote a form of pedagogy that respected the natural growth of the child and supported inherent characteristics of curiosity, activity, interpretation and re-creation. It was suggested that the pupil be regarded more as an artist than as a technician and the school environment should be fashioned to promote this idea. This was a high moment in the perceived relationship between creativity in education and the built environment. A consensus emerged and became embedded at the highest policy levels that a new form of school should be created according to a radical change in the way that pupils and teachers were viewed as creative artists in their everyday practice.

While this was a dominant discourse in the immediate aftermath of the Second World War, the principles of designing to support creativity were already established, mainly within the independent school sector, and there was an important legacy of involvement of artists and designers in school building construction and decoration that formed a foundation for this important moment of change and challenge to the institutionalised arrangements of school.

From the time of the laboratory school of John Dewey, the 'Casa dei Bambini' or Children's House of Maria Montessori and the remodelled school, youth centre and fair-garden of Edward F. O'Neill, to name some prime examples, the pursuit of creativity in the curriculum has long been associated with the design or remodelling of spaces for teaching and learning (Burke, 2005; Burke and Grosvenor, 2008). A common factor has been the pursuit of the classroom-free school given the argument that more loose and varied arrangements of space together with mixed age groups and collaborative teaching were more likely to support opportunities for creativity in learning. Rather than open plan, such envisaged and designed environments were often an amalgam of a wide variety of spaces designed to offer opportunities for practical construction as well as for quiet contemplation; for group activities and for individual study.

Making learning 'real' and meaningful meant challenging the 'hegemony of the classroom', as David L. Medd (1917–2009) described it. Medd, who became one of the most important school architects in the twentieth century, was a pupil for four years at Oundle School, an independent progressive institution where, until 10 years before, head teacher Frederick William Sanderson (1857–1922) had shaped an educational environment that promoted learning through doing. As Medd later recalled, the school at that time was almost self-supporting. It had its own power station and produced electricity for the town; had its own forge for shoeing horses for the local farm; had a metal workshop; and cast its own frames for iron desks: 'It was all absolutely wonderful: you were creating your own surroundings'.[1]

Sanderson was clearly an educator with an acute sense of the possibilities of arranging space in new ways and encouraging his staff to be spacious in their teaching. He suggested,

> If science is spaciously taught it will impress its spirit on the whole school and will give a fresh stimulus to the older studies and will add new life to them. Such buildings should be built more after the manner of museums, with long and commodious galleries or labs with well lit bays or side chapels as they have been called and adjoining workrooms. There will be fewer classrooms for the classroom is competitive and dominant and represents the knowledge of things that are, rather than the search of things yet to come. … Schools must be equipped spaciously, spaciously, and they must have spacious staff.
>
> *(F. W. Sanderson, quoted in Wells, 1924: 146)*

There are intriguing similarities between the idea of an ideal school environment espoused by Sanderson and the plans eventually drawn up during the 1950s and 1960s by David Medd and his wife and professional partner Mary (née Crowley) Medd for new primary schools in London, such as Eveline Lowe (1967), a school that had differentiated zones for various prescribed activities, bays to support individual or group study and corridors with built-in, well lit display units and cabinets (see Figure 42.1).

The importance of display and correctly lit presentations of materials, as in a gallery or museum, was recognised at this time by educators and designers who were convinced of the power of good design on the young (Grosvenor, in Lawn and Grosvenor, 2005). Sanderson and the Medds would have agreed that school design should be 'educationally driven', meaning that the most innovative and progressive approaches to teaching and learning should be studied and carefully observed in situ in order to produce an environment that fits and, moreover, indicates to teachers where their innovations or experimentations might become more fully expressed and supported. The possibilities of school, as understood by these leading architects as they came to professional maturity in the 1940s, was partly influenced by their own experience of a rare and progressive education but also by the opportunity to travel, connect and network with educators, designers, artists and architects across Europe in their formative years (Burke, 2009, 2010; Burke and Grosvenor, 2008).

'Education through art' and the school building as teacher

A conviction in the essential relationship between the design of buildings and furnishings and the enhancement of creativity in the curriculum has its origins in the inter-war period, when many artists, architects and designers devoted their careers to school based work. British teachers and others began to publicise the work of artists in Europe, such as the dance artist and educator Rudolph Laban (1879–1958) and the children's art educator Frank Cizek (1865–1946) of the Academy of Fine Arts, Vienna. Laban, in turn, directly influenced an English dance educator and later advisor, Diana Jordon, who became a significant promoter of a new approach to movement and dance during the post-war period. In 1921, Francesca Wilson (1888–1981), a school teacher

Figure 42.1 Eveline Lowe interior

from Birmingham, organised two touring exhibitions of art made by children in the classes of Cizek (Roberts, 2009). To some, such exhibitions and associated publications were a revelation. The artist and educator Robin Tanner (1904–88), at that time a student teacher, recalled:

> It was as if the conviction we had always had of children's potentialities was suddenly presented, alive, before us.
>
> *(Tanner, quoted in Griffin-Beale, 1979: xi)*

Tanner had first taught in a south-east London elementary school during the 1920s, where he had children paint large-scale murals directly on to their classroom walls (see Figure 42.2).

Such ideas and practices encouraged an extended notion of architecture to allow for an appreciation of the school building as a sensory teacher permitting freedom of movement, first-hand experience and learning in an atmosphere of beauty.

The educational vision that was promoted before and during the war was trans-Atlantic in scope. The Bauhaus, founded in 1919 by Walter Gropius in Germany, was in essence an institution aligned to the philosophy of integrating art and architecture through an extended vision of how these forms might be defined and practised. With the rise of Fascism in Europe, and the subsequent destruction of the Bauhaus in 1933, England played host to a number of architects, artists and designers en route to the United States (Benton, 1985). Several of these individuals met with educators, artists and designers while in Britain, and some were employed to carry out commissions related to education or schooling (Lawn and Grosvenor, 2005; Burke and Grosvenor, 2008). Thus alliances of individuals were formed who were in broad agreement that the educational environment should as far as possible through its material design reflect the

Figure 42.2 Children painting a mural in a classroom, London. From Tanner (1987)

essential humanity of children and their teachers, and be planned to nurture the development of each child in a warm, comfortable and enriching setting that ensured social and cultural growth.

Several European émigré architects, Ernö Goldfinger, Carl Franck, Joseph Berger, Peter Moro and Eugene Rosenberg, became involved in English school building renewal during the 1950s. They worked with committed regional chief education officers such as Stuart Mason in Leicestershire, Henry Morris in Cambridgeshire and John Newsom in Hertfordshire.

Morris had many friends and colleagues in the world of art and design and through these contacts he was able to intercept László Moholy-Nagy (1895–1946) on his way from the Bauhaus to America in order to commission him to design the colour scheme for the walls of Linton Village College. And after much local opposition, Morris succeeded in having Impington Village College designed by the émigré architect Walter Gropius with Maxwell Fry (Ree, 1977: 73–7). Herbert Read's 1943 publication *Education Through Art* included a short section considering how the physical structure of the school might become 'an agent of aesthetic education', citing Impington Village College as the best contemporary example (Read, 1943: 297–8). The gradual recognition of Impington Village College as one of the most significant examples of modernist architecture in public buildings in Britain at the time encouraged Morris in his conviction that architecture could be a force for education (Burke and Grosvenor, 2008: 86; Ree, 1977: 75). During the post-war years, he argued publicly for an extended definition of architecture as 'part of the essence of education' (Ree, 1977: 99).

In Hertfordshire County Council, where the Medds practised from 1946 until they left to join the Ministry of Education in 1949, 100 new schools were built by 1954 and another 100 by 1961. Chief education officer John Newsom, who believed strongly in the power of the environment as an educator, persuaded the county authorities to release funds for new artworks in the schools. Some of these were secondary schools. At Barclay School in Stevenage, completed in 1949, Newsom succeeded where Morris had failed in having a Henry Moore bronze, 'the family group', set in the grounds.

Approaches to art education in this period were spurred by a belief in the universal human capacity for creative expression, with inevitable implications for teaching and schools. Education through art would be communicated through the everyday artefacts encountered in public spaces, the buildings and the furniture and fittings that they contained. It is not surprising, therefore, that school buildings, which were coming to be seen as the crucible of a more civilised and peaceful world, became subject to these notions.

In the wider political context, the role of the arts in signalling freedom of expression and the role of the state in promoting democracy through municipal and public works were an important dimension. The opportunities afforded by the destruction caused by war, technological developments in new materials and components coupled with a sense, held strongly by some educationalists, that the arts were an important platform for public nation building and the development of social and civic sensibilities, resulted in a period of innovation in school building.

A creative curriculum: Story of a School

During the war years, creative approaches to curriculum were found to be operating in the most unlikely settings where teachers, some new to the profession, were experimenting with time, space and materials towards a practice that recognised the inherent creative tendencies of children.

Classroom spaces, designed to seat between 40 and 60 children in regimented rows were found to be wholly unsuitable for creative work that was carried out at a scale larger than a pupil's desk and so teachers encouraged pupils to spill out to use every possible available space, including floors, halls and corridors (see Figure 42.3). It was such freedom of movement, evidenced in such ordinary, inner-city state schools as Steward Street School in Birmingham, England, that persuaded some architects to reconsider and reject the classroom as the principal organising block in schools.

At Steward Street, a creative curriculum was put in place whereby the whole of learning and teaching was carried out through the creative arts. Led by A. R. Stone during the war years, the school came to the attention of Alec Clegg and Louis Christian Schiller, at that time education advisors for nearby Worcestershire. Schiller was appointed first senior inspector for primary education in 1946 and Clegg became chief education officer for the West Riding of Yorkshire a year earlier, later recruiting Stone as advisor for Movement and Dance. Stone had been introduced to Rudolph Laban's philosophy and practice of movement by Diana Jordon, education advisor and inspector, for which the old school hall was utilised. Stone believed that 'all the arts have a common beginning in movement', and movement, flow and a challenge to the traditional arrangements of classroom teaching and learning characterised the innovative pedagogy practised at his school (Stone, in Ministry of Education, 1949: 10).

A short illustrated pamphlet, *Story of a School*, was one of the most widely distributed publications about post-Second World War schooling, distributed by the Ministry of Education to every English and Welsh school in 1949 (and again in 1954). It told the story of this Victorian three-storey building, surrounded by factories in a densely inhabited area of the city. In a world where pupils had little experience of beauty, Stone told the story of how a new view of the child and the role of the creative arts at the centre of education encouraged profound learning and new relationships of knowledge. The illustrations contained in the pamphlet showed creativity in action. Allowing 'Flow' from one art form to another was recognised here as good practice, as was children's own decision making within a structured setting 'from their art to their compositions; from their art to their writing; from their writing to their lettering' (Ministry of Education, 1949: 27–8). Making illustrations and creating written stories are presented in symbiotic relationship, one encouraging and relying on the other so that finally art might become an integral part of composition, not merely an illustration. Such an emphasis on 'flow' impacted on ideas about the design of new school buildings that might enhance connectivity, relationships across subject areas and activities.

Story of a School demonstrated to all its many readers that a school building, dating from the late nineteenth century, with unsuitable wooden floors, poor lighting, a lack of workshop space and heavy school furniture, could also be a 'school of tomorrow' if innovative teaching approaches and new ways of seeing children and teachers were adopted. It was to such schools, where innovation and experimentation were observable, that architects from the Ministry of Education Architects and Buildings Branch were directed by the Inspectorate (HMI). There they could study first hand important trends in the direction of a creative curriculum, which in turn would influence the design process in new school construction. Architects at the Ministry of Education Architects and Building Branch (Development Group) relied on this intelligence in order to communicate with teachers about the design of new schools.

Figure 42.3 Interior of Steward Street School, 1949

Buildings designed to fit the child and their teacher

The post-war consensus for primary education was toward the pursuit of knowledge 'in its fuller sense' and a view of the child as 'artist' rather than 'technician' – maker of meaning, inventor, experimenter and discoverer. It was believed that school buildings should support, rather than suppress, the natural energy and exuberance of children, and thus required integrated open spaces inside and out. This challenged the way that traditional classroom arrangements worked against a new emphasis on confidence and friendliness in school based relationships and the associated atmosphere of informality in lessons. Their design attempted to recognise and enhance the blurring of divisions between adult and child; age groups of learners; parts of the school day; the inside and outside; and between subjects of the curriculum. The prevailing model was a pedagogy that allowed children to take elements of their learning from start to finish without interruption, 'to seize the opportunity and catch the moment'. The idea was to see how far it was possible, through the opportunities offered by national school building renewal, to (without discouraging teachers who preferred traditional methods) encourage those teachers who were exploring approaches that more fully utilised space and equipment.

The schools designed at this time were light, airy, modern and economical, with the following design features:

- where moving from place to place was a intended to be a pleasant experience;
- where no two learning spaces looked the same and a range and variety of spaces were provided to reflect as far as possible the range and variety in children;
- permitting of deep and lasting 'first-hand' experience;
- where 'opt out' spaces were provided where children could be quiet if they chose to;
- where the views out of the school were as pleasurable as possible;
- where storage was integrated in furnishings and fittings to cater for the capacities of children and their teachers;
- uncluttered environments;
- where children were comfortable and could move easily from place to place and where there was a continual flow of bodies from one activity to another supported by a team of teachers working cooperatively;
- domestic and homely, where children had their own workspace with their materials to hand, where they had their own home bay with toilet and cloakroom close by; there were large kitchens equipped to provide midday meals, as well as special cooking bays where young children could learn the art of cooking;
- where all spaces were utilised for learning and teaching spaces, including halls, corridors and outside areas (often covered with verandas); window sills and outside walls were positioned to be at the correct height for the age group concerned to encourage socialisation and individual reading;
- where living things flourished, including school pets, plants, trees, gardens; courtyards and the spaces in-between the buildings were designed to be occupied more often than not for learning and playing.

Primary education was conceived of less as a preparation for the future and more as a fulfilment of a child's growth and stage of development. For this, a new kind of teacher was required with a new view of themselves, of education and of the child. A key element in the success of any school designed according to this conviction was teacher training and in-service professional development. Schiller and later HMI Robin Tanner developed innovative teachers' courses where teachers met with architects, artists, designers, philosophers, scientists, dancers and musicians and experimented with their own capacities in creativity.

As Christian Schiller put it, 'we have come to place fulfilment of growth as a major task in all primary schools', and this had direct implications for the education of the eye. He went on to explain this according to the impact of new ways of thinking about children's development: 'With such ideas in the air, we begin to look at children differently … our observation of young children begins to reveal not the quantity of performance, but the quality of growth' (Schiller, in Griffin-Beale, 1979: 61). In the traditional, mechanistically driven institutionalised school, which had developed over the first half-century of state education, children were, it was argued, viewed as technicians. Henceforth, they should become regarded as artists. As Schiller put it,

> we have need to use the language not of building and mechanics but of biology – roots, nourishment, growth – since we are concerned not with machines but with living growing beings. If we think in terms of how children grow roots, into what they grow roots, and how these can best be nourished, we must use words which express such ideas.
>
> *(Griffin-Beale, 1979: 64)*

Alec Clegg had worked alongside Schiller during the war years in Worcestershire developing what became known as the 'Hereford courses' for serving teachers in Hereford and Worcestershire. In-service training courses were considered by Schiller to be a vital component in building teachers' confidence around the transformation of relationships within school buildings. Although a mathematics specialist, he was convinced of the principle of first-hand experience and believed that both children and teachers could gain knowledge, skills and self-belief only from direct engagement with the arts. For ten days, teachers would paint, write poetry, perform movement and mime – 'all intended to boost their image of their own potential, so that ultimately they might heighten expectations for their children' (Griffin-Beale, 1979: xi).

Schiller became a close friend and collaborator of David and Mary Medd and was keenly interested in architecture and the design of new primary schools. Occasionally, a direct suggestion might be made whereby the design of the interior might be altered to enhance a view of the child as inherently creative in body and mind. Thus, Schiller is noted to have remarked to the Medds that the basic structures of the school hall – the pillars – might be turned over to use as a climbing frame. An adaptation of this idea was made at Finmere school, in Oxfordshire (1959), where climbing ladders were put in place in one of the larger areas (see Figure 42.4).

HMI Robin Tanner, on one formal visit to Brize Norton Primary School in Oxfordshire, recognised what he considered to be a 'growth point' in a space created by head teacher George Baines as an 'opt out' area. Baines, as head teacher of a school housed in a Victorian building, had rearranged internal spaces to enhance the domesticity of the school. From his own pocket, he had bought a second-hand sofa, a rug, a small table, and arranged a space where a child might choose to sit for a while. Tanner recognised the idea and, without comment, left the school, returning later on the same day with a piece of Welsh linen which he draped over the back of the battered and worn sofa. He placed a tasteful vase of flowers on the windowsill and then asked Baines if this was now what he had intended. The idea was that the space should speak to the child of the intended purpose and expected behaviour through the choice and arrangement of well-designed material artefacts that always celebrated human achievements.

Tanner encouraged the Medds to visit Brize Norton and to observe closely the innovations introduced in the interior arrangement of space and objects, and from these observations they went on to design school environments that emphasised comfort, domesticity and contained a variety of opportunities for different groupings. The buildings were always research in practice. At Woodside Junior School at Amersham (1957), *Building Bulletin* 16, recording in fine detail the design process and rationale, was published to coincide with the opening.

Conclusion

There are some evident consistencies over time connecting the notion of the creative child, teacher and curriculum with the design of the built environment and the internal arrangements of space in schools. This has been much easier to achieve in the past in primary schools than in schools for older children, where there has been greater resistance to the separation of age groups and subject areas. There are important principles and values that have influenced design in the past and these connect strongly with the ideas voiced by children and young people today whenever they are consulted on their preferred school environment. Comfort, 'opt out' spaces, domestic arrangements and opportunities to make learning 'real' occur regularly, and this is true across generations and cultures (Burke and Grosvenor, 2003, 2008). The story of school building for creativity in the past reminds us strongly of the importance of teacher training and continued professional development for teachers if they are ever to be 'spacious' in the sense envisaged by F. W. Sanderson at the turn of the twentieth century and E. F. O'Neill during the inter-war period (Wells, 1924; Burke, 2005).

The Cambridge Primary Review (2009: 1) has noted that in schooling today, 'memorisation and recall have come to be valued over understanding and inquiry, and transmission of information over the pursuit of knowledge in its fuller sense'. It was the pursuit of knowledge in the fuller sense that preoccupied those who took advantage of the school building programme after the war in re-imagining school drawing from the best of 'good practice' that had grown from the schools themselves. What was achieved, for some decades, was a symbiosis between teachers in schools and architects saturated in a belief in the creative capacities of humanity who were in positions of authority and able to drive educationally pioneering school building design.

Figure 42.4 Finmere primary school

Note

1 British Library sound archive, national life stories; Architects Lives. David L. Medd, interviewed by Louise Brodie, 2006.

References

Benton, C. (1985) *A Different World. Émigré Architects in Britain 1928–1958*, London: RIBA.

Burke, C. (2005) 'The school without tears': E. F. O'Neill of Prestolee School, *History of Education* 3: 263–75.

—— (2009) 'Inside out': a collaborative approach to designing schools in England, 1945–72, *Paedagogica Historica* 45(3): 421–33.

—— (2010) About looking: vision, transformation, and the education of the eye in discourses of school renewal past and present, *British Educational Research Journal* 36(1) (February): 65–82.

Burke, C. and Grosvenor, I. (2003) *The School I'd Like: Children and Young People's Reflections on an Education for the Future*, London: Routledge.

—— (2007) The progressive image in the history of education: stories of two schools, *Visual Studies* 22(2): 155–68.

—— (2008) *School*, London: Reaktion Press.

Cambridge Primary Review (2009) *Towards a New Primary Curriculum*, Interim Report published 23 February, Briefing Document, Cambridge: Unversity of Cambridge.

Griffin-Beale, C. (ed.) (1979) *Christian Schiller in his own words*, National Association of Primary Education.

Lawn, M. and Grosvenor, I. (eds) (2005) *Materialities of Schooling: Design, Technology, Objects, Routines*, Oxford: Symposium Books.

Lowe, R. (2007) *The Death of Progressive Education*, London: Routledge.

Ministry of Education (1949) *Story of a School*, Pamphlet no. 14, London: HMSO.

Ree, H. (1977) *Educator Extraordinary: The Life and Achievement of Henry Morris*, London: Longman.

Read, H. (1943) *Education Through Art*, London. Faber and Faber.

Roberts, S. (2009) Exhibiting children at risk: child art, international exhibitions and Save the Children Fund in Vienna, 1919–23, *Paedagogica Historica* 45(1–2) (February–April): 171–91.

Tanner, R. (1987) *An Autobiography of Robin Tanner*. London: Impact Books.

Wells, H. G. (1924) *The Story of a Great Schoolmaster*, London: Chatto Architects Lives. David L. Medd, interviewed by Louise Brodie, 2006.

43

What the arts can teach school reform

Michael G. Gunzenhauser and George W. Noblit

Educational reform in the US has been a decidedly dismal affair. It began as a backlash to school desegregation, calling for excellence over equity. It named educators as responsible for a mediocre system and blamed students for their supposed lack of learning. This of course was a shell game by business leaders to place the blame for a lackluster economy on someone else (Philipsen and Noblit, 1993). The problem was defined subsequently as schools not being enough like business, especially in terms of production systems. The solution according to business leaders was that schools were insufficiently instrumental in their logic. School reform then was meant to make schools more goal driven and to align standards, curriculum, instruction and student learning so that improved test scores resulted. Instrumental logic, in other words, was to produce more learning and better test scores.

School reforms were designed with this instrumentality in mind. They addressed the supposed key variables and set the conditions for the aligned systems to work efficiently (Springfield and Datnow, 1998). These designs then were implemented. The logic seemed impeccable—if you did what was instrumentally logical with high fidelity then you should get the test score results you wished (Desimone, 2002). Yet after almost 30 years of school reform in the US, no one is convinced that school reform has led to better achievement. The current stance is that this is because the standards are problematic, but we have concluded it is because instrumental logic does not work the way the policymakers and business leaders think. In this case, school reform is not something to be done *to* educators and students. Rather it needs to be something that *engages* educators and students. There are potentially many ways to engage educators and students, but we have come to the conclusion that one effective way is to use the arts as a vehicle for school reform. We base this conclusion on our studies of the A+ Schools Program in North Carolina (NC), from its expansion into other states in the US, and from its sustainability over time (now 15 years).

In this chapter, we offer the A+ Schools Program as an alternative to instrumental reasoning and especially the focus on fidelity in school reform efforts. Fidelity limits the engagement to doing what is expected. A+, in contrast, created a set of values even as it encouraged local schools to use these values and a loose set of practices to adapt A+. Schools were not expected to look alike, but they were encouraged to engage people at the local level and across the A+ Network in "building the plane while flying it." We want to be clear. There is considerable instrumentality in A+ but it is created as the schools try to figure out how to best do A+ in their situation. It is less so in the reform effort itself, which was a loose collection of practices, a commitment to more arts and arts integration, and a network organizational form. Through struggling with these, we saw the schools in the program developing a set of values that brought them together—but did not make them alike. There was not a design that the schools could implement with fidelity, but A+ Schools were able to satisfy the high-stakes accountability system of NC. While there were low-performing schools among the A+ Schools, the proportion was 5–7 percent of the A+ Schools compared to roughly 25 percent among schools as a whole for any given year. The A+ Schools Program has much to teach policymakers about school reform and about the limits of instrumental logic in school reform endeavors.

In what follows, we describe our studies of the A+ Schools Program and the A+ Program itself. Next we situate A+ as a school reform that values creativity, equity, process, and responsibility, and explore manifestations of those values in the A+ Program. These values offer us a different way to think about school reform—a view of what school reform could have been.

Studying A+

This chapter emerges from our analysis of intensive research of the A+ Schools at three stages in the program's history. We have studied the A+ Schools Program over a nine-year period, beginning in 1995 with an evaluation of the pilot phase of the North Carolina A+ Schools Program. This research, funded by the Kenan Institute for the Arts, yielded a set of seven evaluation reports, released in 2001 (Kenan Institute, 2001). In 2002, field research began on the North Carolina program, this time in the form of a sustainability study funded by the Ford Foundation.

In the study of the pilot phase, from 1995 to 2000, the research team used a mixed-methods design to interpret the meaning that participants in the project made of the A+ Program in their individual school settings as well as documenting the reform initiative as a whole. The team of principal investigators and doctoral students devoted about 180 person days to data collection each year during the pilot phase. Throughout the pilot phase, at the A+ Program level the team interviewed A+ personnel, Kenan Institute personnel, and state policymakers and observed program meetings and professional development activities.

Data collection in individual schools varied by year, but in general we surveyed and interviewed stakeholders, principals, teachers, parents, and students over time. We analyzed accountability test results. We also conducted onsite case studies of the schools over the five-year period of major data collection. These were ethnographic case studies, with an emphasis on our ongoing analysis of schools (and the overall program itself) as cultural institutions with beliefs, values, and practices that were significant to understanding the ways in which the program was being implemented. The data set was extensive and led to a large set of final reports in 2000–2001 (Kenan Institute, 2001). The Ford Foundation grant led to two more years of data collection and writing. The details of research methods are discussed in those reports and in our book (Noblit et al., 2009).

Below we will describe the history of the program by way of setting up the values which A+ developed. Valuing the arts in education led to a distinct set of values that the schools struggled to embody, and were better for it. We also wish to be clear that we understand there are many problems with such terms as values. Learning from poststructuralism, we see values not as "things" but as categories always being made and unmade. We also note that the values we offer were also in relation with each other and other discourses, including those of arts education and educational reform. Moreover, these values are also in opposition to other arts education discourses and, as we emphasize, the instrumental logic of school reform in the US. We give them here more as a heuristic rather than a finding. They are not the truth but more one way to understand.

A history of the A+ Schools Program

The North Carolina A+ Schools Program began in 1995 after an 18-month planning process that brought together a broad range of stakeholders, including state policymakers, cultural arts experts, educators, and representatives of arts and philanthropic organizations. The Thomas Kenan Institute for the Arts administered the program, raised and distributed funding, and coordinated professional development. After an initial four-year pilot phase, A+ eventually expanded to include other schools in North Carolina (45 schools to date) and led to the creation of a tri-state network of schools by 2004 (A+ was then part of the University of North Carolina at Greensboro), including the Oklahoma A+ Schools, which began in 2002, and the Arkansas A+ Schools, begun in 2003. In the envisioned A+ model, the program was to fund specialists to teach weekly classes to every student in visual art, music, dance, and drama and to collaborate with classroom teachers, so that arts instruction would be integrated in regular subjects and instruction in all areas would become more thematic and integrated. The plans were for both more arts and more arts integration. Classroom teachers would infuse the arts in their instruction, collaborate on thematic units, and focus on the higher-order concepts that make up the North Carolina Standard Course of Study. As envisioned, the Kenan Institute would provide professional development at the beginning of the program and on an ongoing basis as needed. A significant element of the A+ Program is that its implementation took an unpredictable course from its initial planning.

In North Carolina, the planning process was supported politically at the state level sufficiently enough to have been included in the proposed state budget for the 1995 fiscal year, yet early on, A+ ran headlong into the shift away from school reform and toward accountability. Despite the shift in policy and the balance of power, the A+ Program was sufficiently situated politically to remain in the state budget, cut from $1.5 million to $500,000. The leadership of the Kenan Institute and the A+ Schools Program was remarkably effective throughout the program but nowhere more so than in the political origins of the program. As a new arts foundation, the Kenan Institute linked with at least 10 other foundations, arts policy proponents, and arts educators to initiate and implement the reform effort. A+ was part of a strong social and political network from its inception, which is integral to successful reform efforts (Elmore, 1996; Lieberman and Wood, 1992). Of critical importance was the fact that these networks operated outside the educational policy framework of North Carolina, yet involved a set of school and districts leaders from the beginning.

The specific implications of the shift to accountability were twofold. First, the A+ Program had insufficient resources to provide all schools with arts teachers. While the lack of funding was (and still is) lamented by principals, teachers, and other supporters of the program, the schools in effect took ownership of the reform process. Having been introduced to A+ at the first summer institutes, the A+ Schools had to adapt what they had learned to their contexts and the limitations of the funds available from their school districts and local arts councils. Second, an early principals' meeting signaled that A+ was to be a very participative reform, with the Kenan Institute fostering the dialogue with the schools and handling the political and communicative challenges. The early instances of shared decisionmaking, both among framers of the reform at regional planning meetings and among principals at their first joint meeting, formed the basis for the A+ Schools Network, set the stage for defining the essential elements of the A+

Program, and established important ground rules for expanding the program to other states. Fundamental to the growth of the network was the creation of professional development specialists, called A+ Fellows, from among the personnel at A+ Schools. This became a "brain trust" in many ways.

The Kenan Institute and the A+ Fellows planned the summer institutes around a set of commitments about the arts, curriculum planning, and collaboration, with schools encouraged to adapt to their local contexts. Collaboration, arts integration, curriculum management, multiple intelligences, thematic unit planning, and experiential learning were the main aspects of professional development. Each summer, whole school staffs were invited to attend week-long summer institutes and during the year A+ provided staff development at the local school sites. There were also meetings of the principals and coordinators (teacher leaders from each school) of the A+ Schools at least twice a year. Philanthropic partners and arts activists also met to help support the program and to work the wider political arena.

The A+ Schools Program originated outside of government and had a powerful and adept intermediary and funder in the Kenan Institute and its allies. A+ used a multiple network mode of organization that was highly participatory in decisionmaking about both the wider reform and local school adaptation. The A+ Schools Program had both intensive and extensive professional development that was linked to state mandated curriculum but focused on how to teach this curricula in, with, and through the arts. This meant the schools had more arts offerings, more arts integration, and a better coverage of the state curriculum than in other schools we studied in NC. At the schools, there were a set of common practices that often came into play, including: hands-on instruction; two-way arts integration (arts in other courses, other courses in arts courses); addressing multiple intelligences in the design of instruction; interdisciplinary, cross-classroom thematic units; and common planning periods by discipline and/or grade and then also with arts teachers. The A+ Schools were often vibrant with informances (curricula-based, arts-integrated, low preparation performances), performances, displays of artwork, artists working with students and teachers, classrooms working together on thematic units, and so on. Schools developed identities around the arts and arts integration that made them unique in some sense but also signaled their membership in the A+ Network.

By 2005, the A+ Network matured into a loosely coupled consortium of artists, higher education faculty, and educators from 42 schools in North Carolina, 31 schools in Oklahoma, and 16 schools in Arkansas. This network focuses on an extensive and multilevel (teachers, A+ coordinators, and principals) professional development program that has enabled the schools to receive ongoing professional development, learn from each other, and collaborate over time.

Values of the A+ Schools Program

Our studies have led to the interpretation that the A+ Schools Program developed four interrelated values that helped to organize its work: creativity, equity, process, and responsibility. A+ invites schools to make arts the centerpiece through thematic instruction and curriculum integration. The standard curriculum is engaged, which in North Carolina includes comprehensive treatment at all grade levels of multiple forms of the arts. Various forms of curricular and instructional material may be incorporated, so schools are not constrained by particular products or methods. The A+ Schools came to see themselves as different from other schools and, we concluded, the differences were based in a set of values. These values were not so much embodied, accepted practices as they were problematics that engaged participants at all levels of the reform effort. Most importantly, this engagement was also set against high-stakes accountability and the instrumental logic of educational reform in the US.

Creativity

The A+ Program is not alone in its valuing of creativity, particularly among arts programs. In the United States, the arts and arts education have found themselves beleaguered and undervalued. Typically at the margins of the school curriculum and ever vulnerable to being eliminated, arts educators have for several decades sought to raise the profile of their subject matter in the curriculum. A major goal for arts educators has been to improve the quality of arts instruction nationwide, fostering greater creativity and appreciation for the arts (Eisner, 1998, 1990). There have been two major approaches in the US: one to increase the creative potential of arts instruction, and the other to demonstrate the benefits of arts in the instruction of other content. Educators, researchers, and policymakers in the US have addressed the impact of the arts on student learning and skill development (Catterall, 1998). Others have combined these notions to explore their fundamental implications for teaching and learning (i.e. NACCCE, 1999; Parsons, 1998). Yet with all this, there are a wide variety of approaches that US schools have taken to incorporate the arts into curriculum and instruction (Herbert, 1998; Hoffman-Davis, 1999).

In North Carolina, arts education has contended with the changing perceptions of the importance of creativity and instrumentality. In the 1980s, arts instruction was an integral part of the state's Basic Education Plan (BEP), when school districts hired arts specialists in large numbers. For several years, more schools had greater numbers of arts specialists than before. In nearly all cases, implementation of the BEP added courses to the existing curriculum, and the arts competed for attention along with other parts of the curriculum. In subsequent years, with growing enrollments, tightening budgets, and greater local discretion, many of these positions were lost. When the A+ Schools Program began in 1995, many elementary, middle, and high schools in the state employed visual art and music teachers only, and many of these teachers were itinerants serving two or more schools. Arts integration was rhetorically promoted but little practiced.

Placing the arts in the BEP reflected one national approach, which has been to define the arts as "basic" to the curriculum. In its most widespread incarnation, this notion took the form of Discipline-Based Art Education (DBAE). An approach to visual art education with roots in the aesthetic theories of educational philosophers in the 1960s and 1970s, notably Harry Broudy and Eliot Eisner, DBAE gained prominence in the early 1980s through adoption by the J. Paul Getty Trust. It was an effort to treat the visual arts as a discipline—similar to other academic disciplines that traditionally are more highly valued in education (Wilson, 1997).

In contrast, the A+ Schools Program does not approach the arts solely for their own sake. This distinction is evident in at least three ways.

First, the A+ Schools Program has been from the beginning an expansive approach to instructional innovation, with arts integration the focal point for delivering not only meaningful artistic experiences but innovative instruction across subject matter areas as well. The emphasis in professional development in the A+ Program is less on the development of aesthetic sensibilities and critical dispositions and more on developing arts and arts-integrated instruction. The A+ Program gives schools a greater opportunity to use the values of the program as a way to think about the entire instructional program.

Second, unlike some arts education initiatives, the program incorporates the four art forms of visual art, music, dance, and drama into instruction. The inclusion of all four art forms expands the abilities of and opportunities for children to learn. It also places within the school building up to four arts specialists who are available for collaboration with classroom teachers. In this sense, the A+ Program requires a large pool of personnel resources.

Third, the A+ Program takes a holistic approach. As a reform focused on the entire curriculum, the A+ Schools Program begins with individual schools to effect cultural changes through implementing arts integration. These schools become a network and work on collective issues. As a network, they have approached school reform as a creative endeavor. A+ recognizes the importance of district-level support for the program, and it encourages opportunities for community connections and collaboration, making them part of the creation of local adaptations of A+.

Instead of trying to resolve the dilemma often expressed as creativity versus instrumentality, the A+ Schools Program has worked to mediate the opposition of creativity and instrumentality. A+ schools foreground their value of creativity and, by integrating the arts across the curriculum, absorb the issue of instrumentality. They embrace and value the arts, but they also use the arts as the focus of school reform.

Equity

The second main value of the A+ Program is equity. The A+ Schools in North Carolina have used the slogan "Schools that work for everyone." The original A+ Schools reflected the diversity of schools in the state, and were, in the words of one proponent, "everyday schools." Some of them had histories of low student test performance and all of them were unprepared for how much testing was to come to dominate their lives. While the program did not take a stand on ability grouping or tracking, the emphasis on team planning and multiple modalities for learning challenged the notion that children were more or less intelligent than their peers.

The program acknowledges Howard Gardner's (1983) theory of multiple intelligences through professional development sessions, and schools are encouraged to engage the theory with greater complexity on their own. But in the context of the A+ Program, multiple intelligences is largely a rationale for the importance of arts instruction and the efficacy of multiple approaches to instruction in all areas of the curriculum. Unlike schools based specifically on Gardner's multiple intelligences theory, in the A+ Schools, the theory has served as a philosophical metaphor for grounding the efficacy of arts integration. Few of the A+ Schools have delved substantially into the specific instructional implications of multiple intelligences theory that groups affiliated with the Harvard Project Zero have (e.g. Krechevsky, 1991).

The program's specific, metaphorical use of multiple intelligences theory is a backbone of the A+ valuing of equity. Teachers in the few A+ Schools that had been labeled "low-performing" spoke repeatedly of the efficacy of arts-based instruction for reaching children who were performing poorly through instruction presumably geared solely toward building mathematical and verbal intelligence. Importantly, the A+ Schools were able to satisfy the state's accountability program in part by embracing the A+ approach to "enriched assessment."

With the mantra of "Schools that work for everyone," A+ Schools were challenged to be accountable for achievement of all students. The metaphor of multiple intelligences (Gardner, 1983) boosted teachers' beliefs that instruction could be altered to teach curricular concepts more broadly. Teachers believed that broader instructional strategies would reach more students. Because emphasis from the beginning was placed upon the concepts around which the state curriculum had been built, and since state testing is aligned with the state curriculum, A+ positioned schools to perform well in the state's accountability program, which they did. In any given year some schools may not have reached expected growth, but they used A+, at least in part, as a way to turn that around for the next year.

The A+ Schools' experience with arts-integrated instruction made clear the limitations of the state accountability program for their own assessment needs. As a result, the A+ Schools sought and received funding from federal Goals 2000 initiative to address assessment directly. The resulting series of conferences about assessment was an exploration of a concept of "enriched assessment." Members of the A+ Network sought and shared authentic assessment techniques and artistic demonstrations of learning that aligned the curriculum, authentic assessment, and testing. The search for enriched assessment became an ongoing process, signifying the program's continual engagement with methods for operationalizing the value of equity.

Process

In NC, the common process associated with school reform was implementation of the design with fidelity. Reforms were mandated and schools complied by doing what they were told as closely as they could. A+, though, asked the schools what they thought an A+ school should look like. Clearly there was an emphasis on more arts, arts integration, and multiple intelligences, but the educators were asked: What should these look like and what could their schools do with them? Early on, this frustrated many of the school administrators, who simply wanted A+ to tell them want to do—like other reforms. Over time, however, schools and the reformers began to appreciate the significance of process as a way to engage ideas and values. Rather than imposing a rigid model and enforcing adherence to particular methods, the Kenan Institute instead exposed school personnel to a series of philosophical and instructional ideas through week-long Summer Institutes and professional development programs offered during the school year, then encouraged interpretation and innovation to suit individual school contexts. By encouraging implementation decisions to be made at the school level, the Kenan Institute devolved control over the direction of the program to educators and their creative collaboration. When schools asked what they should be doing, the response from the Kenan Institute, and later the Network itself, was (as one principal expressed it) "What do you think?" The result was a series of creative innovations, adapted to numerous goals, contexts, and local constraints.

By valuing process, the A+ Schools Program's network structure confronts a dilemma concerning school reform initiatives—where to initiate school reform. Early in the recent school reform era, it was argued that the schools should be the locus of reform (Joyce et al., 1983). As time has passed there have been arguments that the need for consistency across the levels of schooling (school, district, state, and national) means that school reform needs to "scale up" and become more systemic (Elmore, 1996). Systemic has at least two meanings in this context: reforming school systems as wholes; and functioning more like a tightly coupled system than the "loosely coupled" organizations that Weick (1976) and Meyer and Rowan (1978) have described as characteristic of educational organizations.

As with many school improvements, there are many accounts of successful individual school efforts at incorporating the arts more fully, at least over the short term. The difficulty of incorporating the arts into education is how to sustain this in multiple school settings. Broad, sweeping changes in education rarely happen, and top-down reforms tend to stifle creativity and inhibit local control (Fullan, 1994, 1999). That is partly because schools have cultures, and these cultures are slow to change (Pink and Noblit, 2004). External policies get reinterpreted, misinterpreted, modified, mediated, and otherwise ignored within the context of school cultures.

The A+ Schools Program resolved the top-down/bottom-up dilemma (Shields and Knapp, 1997), by focusing on the importance of process at multiple levels. When schools applied, they were required to document an 85 percent vote of teachers in favor of A+, indicating "buy-in." Buy-in in this form was necessary but not sufficient, and we came to understand the significance of the concept "engagement," which, more complex than buy-in, captures the extent to which schools identified and engaged with A+ and each other (Barry et al., 2003). Engagement meant schools had to become part of the A+ Network, and define their own interpretation of the program, allowing them to weave A+ into their cultures through unique implementation strategies.

The origins of A+, traumatic given the unexpected underfunding and new accountability pressure, enabled the reform to develop in a more democratic way than most. The program relied on the schools for creative resolutions for the lack of funding. Without these new funds, schools continued the commitment to a wide set of arts offerings using local funds and grants. With fewer arts teachers than originally envisioned, A+ had to rely on the classroom teachers to succeed (i.e. dance as physical education, curriculum planning as a teacher led endeavor); and consequently ownership of the reform spread to more teachers.

The reform process had benefits. Since schools interpreted the program for their own settings, their adaptations took into account local beliefs and constraints. Change occurred at multiple levels—classroom, grade level, school, and district—but always built around instructional innovation. Because innovation was encouraged, schools felt freer to innovate, to share successes, to be candid about mistakes and limitations, and to learn from their challenges and those of others.

There are certainly drawbacks and tradeoffs associated with this emphasis on process. Some of the forms of implementation have been unpredictable, and some schools have struggled to implement an A+ Program that is appropriate for their contexts. Challenges included tightened resources, limited access to professional development, staff turnover, and conflicting state and school district priorities. These were weathered by the continued participation in the A+ Network, and this has solidified the commitment to the process as an ongoing engagement.

Responsibility

In an era of increasing public school accountability, teachers are expected to be responsible in new ways for their students' learning. In their study of high schools responding to high-stakes accountability programs in four states, Carnoy, Elmore, and Siskin (2003) focus on the importance of teachers' taking responsibility for student learning within school buildings. They argue that taking responsibility for student learning is an essential component of building capacity in schools, which is ostensibly the larger goal of accountability initiatives, rather than merely compliance with accountability mandates. These researchers make an important distinction between external accountability (the demands imposed on schools by districts and states) and internal accountability (schools' own views of student learning and how to prompt progress). Schools with strong internal accountability, they argue, are more likely to meet the demands of external accountability systems, particularly if all members of the school community maintain high standards and expectations for student success.

Other theorists and researchers seek to invoke greater responsibility into accountability systems by expanding the notion of who exactly is responsible for student learning. Contributors to Sirotnik's (2004) edited collection take issue with the extent to which accountability systems allow lawmakers and policymakers to evade responsibility for public education. When he surveys the terrain of accountability, Sirotnik argues that greater attention needs to focus on what he calls "responsible accountability." A fundamental rethinking of accountability, Sirotnik and his contributors suggest, would include historical considerations of public school accountability, particularly the responsibility that individual districts entrust to their elected school boards. At the same time, he calls for systemic supports for equitable opportunities for student learning. More specific aspects of his notion of responsible accountability include resources and opportunities for professional development and responsibility for full, expanded notions of curriculum, beyond areas mandated for testing.

A+ Schools struggled with the tension between the external demands for accountability and their own responsibility for student learning (Biesta, 2004). A+ Schools at the beginning of their second year encountered high-stakes accountability at full force, when all elementary and middle schools were categorized based upon student performance on tests in reading, writing, and math. While a lower proportion of A+ Schools were named "low-performing" than across the state as a whole, pressure mounted for schools to raise their test scores.

For its part, the A+ Schools Program offered teachers the opportunity to become more intentional about teaching the state curriculum, to teach holistically, and to collaborate across the school. The A+ Program encouraged schools and teachers to be more focused on the state curriculum, specifically on the higher-order concepts that A+ professional development staff encouraged teachers to make the centerpiece of thematic units. Because teachers in A+ Schools plan together, instructional concepts are presented in multiple forms and are reinforced. With classroom teachers and arts specialists all using artistic forms of instruction, the intention is for children's educational experience to be innovative and expansive, with greater opportunities for engagement and creativity. In such ways, A+ enhanced teacher and school-level responsibility for student learning.

Furthermore, the A+ Program encouraged parental and community involvement. Particularly significant to several of the schools, as mentioned below, was tying the mission of the school more closely to the needs of the local community. This expansion of involvement reflected a value on community responsibility for public education.

Conclusion

The A+ Schools Program is a relatively unique initiative in the arts and in school reform in the US. It values creativity, equity, process, and responsibility. These values are interrelated. The approach to the creativity and instrumentality dilemma was a direct result of the program trusting in process—creative responses emerged to the struggles to implement the A+ Program. With Network and Kenan Institute guidance and support, this reform effort responded creatively to the challenges of local schools and communities and of state policy changes. As a reform "written in pencil" (as it is commonly put by A+ participants), it rewrote itself repeatedly both collectively and in the individual schools. Of course, to those reformers who believe that fidelity to a specified process is necessary for schools to improve, A+ would be anathema. Yet this is precisely the significance of A+ to school reform. We can see a different possibility for school reform in A+—one that engages schools and the values of their communities and, by taking and expanding responsibility for student learning, can satisfy the demands of external accountability as well. We think this reform effort teaches us that a focus on the arts can create and sustain substantive school reform that outstrips the instrumental logic that has characterized recent school reform efforts (Noblit *et al.*, 2009).

Acknowledgment

This research was funded by the Thomas Kenan Institute for the Arts and the Ford Foundation. However, it does not necessarily reflect the views of these organizations.

References

Barry, N. H., Gunzenhauser, M. G., Montgomery, D. and Raiber, M. (2003) *Oklahoma A+ Schools: Research Report Year One: 2002–2003*, Edmond, OK: Oklahoma A+ Schools.
Biesta, G. J. J. (2004) Education, accountability, and the ethical demand: can the democratic potential of accountability be regained?, *Educational Theory* 54(3): 233–50.

Carnoy, M., Elmore, R. and Siskin, L. S. (eds.) (2003) *The New Accountability: High Schools and High-Stakes Testing*, New York: Routledge Falmer.

Catterall, J. S. (1998) Does experience in the arts boost academic achievement? A response to Eisner, *Art Education* 51(4): 6–11.

Desimone, L. M. (2002) How can comprehensive school reform models be successfully implemented? *Review of Educational Research* 72(3): 433–79.

Eisner, E. W. (1990) Discipline-based art education: conceptions and misconceptions, *Educational Theory* 40 (4): 423–30.

—— (1998) Does experience in the arts boost academic achievement?, *Arts Education Policy Review* 100(1): 32–8.

Elmore, R. (1996) Getting to scale with good educational practice, *Harvard Educational Review* 66(1): 1–26.

Fullan, M. G. (1994) Coordinating top-down and bottom-up strategies for educational reform, in R. F. Elmore and S. H. Fuhrman (eds.) *The Governance of Curriculum*, Alexandria, VA: Association for Supervision and Curriculum Development.

—(1999) On effecting change in arts education, *Arts Education Policy Review* 100(3): 17–18.

Gardner, H. (1983) *Frames of Mind: The Theory of Multiple Intelligences*, New York: Basic Books.

Herbert, D. (1998) Model approaches to arts education, *Principal* 77(4): 36, 38, 40–3.

Hoffman-Davis, J. (1999) Nowhere, somewhere, everywhere: the arts in education, *Arts Education Policy Review* 100(5): 23–8.

Joyce, B., Hersh, R. and McKibbin, M. (1983) *The Structure of School Improvement*, New York: Longman.

Kenan Institute (2001) *The A+ School Program: Evaluation Reports*, Winston-Salem, NC: Thomas Kenan Institute for the Arts.

Krechevsky, M. (1991) Project Spectrum: an innovative assessment alternative, *Educational Leadership* 48(5): 43–8.

Lieberman, A. and Wood, L. (1992) *Teachers—Their World and Their Work: Implications for School Improvement*, New York: Teachers College Press.

Meyer, J. W. and Rowan, B. (1978) The structure of educational organizations, in M. W. Meyer, J. H. Freeman, M.T. Hannan, J. W. Meyer, W. G. Pfeffer and W. R. Scott (eds.) *Environments and Organizations*, San Francisco: Jossey-Bass.

National Advisory Committee on Creative and Cultural Education (NACCCE) (1999) *All Our Futures: Creativity and Education*, Warwick, England: NACCCE.

Noblit, G., Corbett, H., Wilson, B. and McKinney, M. (2009). *Creating and Sustaining Arts-Based School Reform: The A+ Schools Program*, Albany, NY: SUNY Press.

Parsons, M. J. (1998) Integrated curriculum and our paradigm of cognition in the arts, *Studies in Art Education* 39(2): 103–16.

Philipsen, M. and Noblit, G. (1993) Tricky business: corporate conceptions of educational reform, *The High School Journal* 76(4): 260–72.

Pink, W. and Noblit, G. W. (2004) *Cultural Matters: Lessons from Field Studies of Several Leading Reform Strategies*, Cresskill, NJ: Hampton Press.

Shields, P. M. and Knapp, M. S. (1997) The promise and limits of school-based reform: a national snapshot, *Phi Delta Kappan* 79(4): 288–94.

Sirotnik, K. (ed.) (2004) *Holding Accountability Accountable*, New York: Teachers College Press.

Smith, M. S. and O'Day, J. A. (1991) Systemic reform, in S. H. Fuhrman and B. Malen (eds.) *The Politics of Curriculum and Testing*, Bristol, PA: Falmer Press.

Snyder, S. (2001) Connection, correlation, and integration, *Music Educators Journal* 87(5): 32–9, 70.

Springfield, S. and Datnow, A. (1998) Introduction: scaling up school restructuring designs in urban schools, *Education and Urban Society* 30: 269–76.

Weick, K. (1976) Educational organizations as loosely coupled systems, *Administrative Science Quarterly* 12: 1–19.

Wilson, B. (1997) *The Quiet Evolution: Changing the Face of Arts Education*, Los Angeles: The Getty Education Institute for the Arts.

44

Creativity in Scottish school curriculum and pedagogy

Moira Hulme, Ian Menter and James Conroy

Introduction

This chapter charts the increased promotion of creativity across the formal curriculum for maintained schools in Scotland (IDES Network and Learning and Teaching Scotland, 2001; SEED, 2006; HMIe, 2006a; LTS, 2009). Successive polices have sought to reconcile creativity, curriculum innovation and enterprise, including *Determined to Succeed*, the *Future Learning and Teaching* programme (2001–7) and the *Schools of Ambition* programme (2006–10). Creativity-oriented teaching and learning processes are increasingly deployed in a repertoire of interventions designed to tackle disaffection, promote 'better behaviour' and improve achievement among the lowest attaining 20 per cent of pupils (the so-called 'NEET group' – those deemed at risk of being Not in Education, Employment or Training). In addition to targeted interventions, new opportunities for professional creativity are extended in the relaxation of curriculum prescription.

Two significant trajectories are evident from this review of recent curriculum reform: (1) a stronger focus on individual capacities, which emphasises the development of 'creative thinking', 'creative teaching' and 'creative learning'; (2) a discernible 'affective turn' evidenced in renewed interest in the management of emotions and dispositions in the educational process. Drawing on some initial responses from the profession to the revised curriculum framework (University of Glasgow, 2009), we highlight the professional challenges of balancing freedom and responsibility and offer a vignette from the *Schools of Ambition* programme to illustrate the deployment of creativity within strategies to regenerate schools.

The erosion of the traditional view of education as transmission has opened up new spaces for deliberation over curriculum, pedagogy and assessment in Scotland. Yet, despite a changing landscape and the active promotion of creativity in education, it is not easy to shift existing paradigms and long-established practices. Within a framework of professional accountability, a hybrid creativity emerges that looks back to child-centred pedagogies and which seeks to foster teacher and learner dispositions fitted to the future challenges of a putative knowledge society. Some continuity can also be identified with the meritocratic tradition, for example through the celebration of resilience, self-efficacy and self-regulation. Somewhat contradictorily, therefore, it is suggested here that the many paradoxes within the creativity agenda reduce a concomitant commitment to risk taking and questioning that might be considered integral to the pursuit of a creative stance. This hybrid creativity is the consequence of a collision – or, less dramatically, interaction – between earlier forms of creativity and the performativity that is associated with new forms of governance (Newman, 2001; Newman and Clarke, 2009; Hartley, 2003).

Background and context

Scotland is a small country with a resident population of 5.1 million, among a UK population of 60 million. Although responsibility for education and training was formally devolved from the UK Government to the Scottish Parliament in July 1999, Scotland's education system has long enjoyed relative autonomy from England. Prior to political devolution, Scotland resisted the move to standardised tests implemented in England and Wales[1] and developed national guidelines for its own broadly based *5–14 Curriculum*. The agenda for change is influenced by enduring educational inequalities associated with socio-economic status, poverty and deprivation (OECD, 2007: 41). Although attainment has increased since 2002, the gap between pupils with the highest and lowest levels of deprivation has remained constant (Scottish Government, 2009). The number of young people aged 16–19 years not in education, employment or training, around 1 in 7, is a particular cause for concern. The school curriculum in Scotland is at a point of transition, with full implementation of a new 3–18 years curriculum, the *Curriculum for Excellence*, from August 2010 and the introduction of new national qualifications from 2012/13.

Interest in creativity in education is not new – it figured large in policy documents of the 1960s – but policy makers' interest in creativity in education has been renewed through the association of creative capacity with economic growth. Creativity is re-conceptualised as an 'employability' attribute. The resurgence of interest in creativity avoids the use of explicit child-centredness, using such business-derived terms as flexibility and personalisation. The *National Priorities in School Education* (SEED, 2004a) explicitly promote the development of creativity and ambition and there has been an increasingly close coupling of creativity and innovation through enterprise and entrepreneurial education. The schools' inspectorate portrait of effective citizenship education illustrates the re-contextualisation of creativity in the current policy framework. Creativity in the sense of originality is given value in its relation to enterprise, which is equated with 'responsible citizenship':

> The Scottish approach emphasises promoting citizenship through participation in cultural activity. Creativity, flair and enterprise are essential qualities for citizens of the 21st century.
>
> *(HMIe, 2006b: 3)*

Since devolution in 1999, the tensions around creativity in the school curriculum and school management have sometimes been very visible, at other times less so. Under the first series of Labour-led governments, school education was very clearly led by the Scottish Executive Education Department (SEED). Higher education and the enterprise agenda were the responsibilities of the Enterprise, Transport and Lifelong Learning Department (ETLLD). From 2003, several school-oriented programmes, such as *Determined to Succeed*, the Scottish Qualification for Headship, and the *Schools of Ambition* initiative (see pp. 441–42), were shaped by both government departments. By contrast, the development of a creative arts agenda in schools was less visible and relied heavily on a small number of individuals and organisations, including an Education Officer at the Scottish Arts Council.

The emphasis on entrepreneurship in education attracted the interest of wealthy business-people who sought to influence education. The Hunter Foundation, a philanthropic organisation funded by Sir Tom Hunter, a venture capitalist who models his charitable work on that of

Andrew Carnegie, has promoted entrepreneurial leadership in schools (see Deakins *et al.*, 2005) amongst strategies designed to address the needs of the lowest achieving pupils (the 'bottom 20 per cent'). The intervention of Hunter and one or two others (including Lord Irvine of Laidlaw) has been controversial in the Scottish context (especially by comparison with England (see Ball, 2007)). Increased private steering and the encouragement to adopt a strongly capitalist approach to entrepreneurship – both exemplified by the approach of the Hunter Foundation – have not been broadly popular, either within the teaching profession or within wider sections of the community.

Such tensions and ambiguities have persisted under the new administration, led by the Scottish National Party since 2007. The overall effect of these policy developments is a redefinition of creativity within education that challenges its historic links with romantic notions of individuality and artistic endeavour.

Curriculum reform, performance and professional agency

In this section, we consider the possibilities for creativity-oriented teaching and learning processes in the revision of the curriculum for Scottish schools. The new curriculum aims to achieve 'clearly defined rounded outcomes for young people, smoother transition between different stages of education, and new choice, space and time within the curriculum to teachers and schools to design learning to suit the needs of young people' (SEED, 2004b:14).[2] During 2007–8 guidelines called *Experiences and Outcomes* were published for each of fourteen 'curriculum areas'. Following publication of the draft guidelines an extensive formal consultation was undertaken to support the implementation process (University of Glasgow, 2009). A range of data was collected over twelve months by a variety of mechanisms, including online questionnaires, feedback from schools trialling draft guidelines, teacher focus groups and telephone interviews with local authority personnel.[3]

Focus group transcripts from the consultation process revealed a tension between enhanced levels of professional autonomy and the removal of secure and familiar frameworks for govern action within both primary and secondary schools. The introduction of a greater degree of flexibility entered work contexts where the parameters of professional responsibility had shifted towards the management of learning resources and environments for learning (curriculum delivery), rather than curriculum design (curriculum building). Many teachers noted a tension between the aspirations of *Curriculum for Excellence* to extend professional autonomy and create new spaces for creativity-oriented teaching and learning, and their perceptions of an outcomes-driven system of assessment. Despite a new inspection framework, that affords a 'greater role for self-evaluation' and a 'strong focus on capacity building' so that 'inspection will be done *with* the school rather than *to* the school' (HMIe, 2008a: 3), teachers remain wary of unsettling practices previously deemed 'effective'. A professional challenge articulated by teachers was how to balance calls for innovative and creativity pedagogies with continued demands to raise standards evidenced through conventional 'hard' performance indicators:

> Everything we do is measured all the time. Everything has to be measurable, so I'm wondering what the balance is between active learning, creativity and freedom and 'the measure'.
>
> *(Primary headteacher, Numeracy)*

> There seems to be almost a double vision – one in which we are empowered and we are able to develop new things and we are professional enough to do that; and then somebody else with a slightly different agenda will come along and assess and evaluate us. There will

have to be a change in the relationship between how we are assessed and evaluated by our colleagues in other professional areas.

(Principal teacher secondary, Literacy and English)

You have these two different worlds. People want results and they want the assessments done; and then you've got this other world saying we should be spontaneous, make opportunities for activities and experiences. The two things very often don't marry at all.

(Principal teacher secondary, Expressive Arts)

There is a strong association of professionalism with planning. Accounts offered by teachers in twenty focus groups (across the fourteen curriculum areas of Curriculum for Excellence) suggest that the publication of the draft sets of *Experiences and Outcomes* evoked an audit response. Schools/departments were mapping current practice against the predetermined criteria of the revised curriculum. However, whilst attending to content coverage and progression, this auditing of practice could have the effect of re-positioning the document as a new set of standards to conform to, rather than as a stimulus for more engaged critical reflection. From this perspective, the revised curriculum in certain contexts might replace one 'prescriptive' framework with another, displacing re-professionalising aspirations. Significant tensions were identified between a need for detailed 'exemplification' and a commitment to exploration and imaginative use of the draft *Experiences and Outcomes*, albeit within the constraints of available local resources.

The circulation of multiple discourses and opposing modalities present a confounding mix for many school professionals. A culture of performance, models of school leadership based on 'linearity and control' (Macdonald, 2003), teacher cultures of compliance and economistic models of education run counter to narratives of devolved leadership, personalisation, collaboration, creative and inquiry-based learning. As official pedagogic discourse becomes more weakly classified, contestation intensifies as alternatives are presented. The disturbance and high-level anxieties experienced by some among the profession reflect the insertion of progressive elements of *Curriculum for Excellence* within performance modes. The response of Education Authorities to these vocal concerns has been to frame the classification of the new discourse more strongly.

In understanding the range of teacher responses, it is useful to revisit the introduction of the previous curriculum framework. Non-statutory programmes of study were published and national monitoring of attainment developed through the introduction of national tests in reading, writing and mathematics. Although distinctive in adopting a 'lower stakes', 'test when ready' approach, the availability of national tests progressively came to 'stand in' for teachers' own interpretation and locally developed assessment. The introduction of new national qualifications in the late 1990s contributed to perceptions of an increasingly assessment-driven culture within secondary education:

National tests soon became high stakes. There was little incentive for teachers to consider a wider range of evidence, or to challenge a test result on the basis of their own judgement, especially when their perception that what mattered was test results appeared to be confirmed by their experiences. HMIe, promoting the government policy that tests should form part of the assessment arrangements in a school, pressed for test results as confirmation of teachers' judgements. In these circumstances, the perception that national test results were what mattered developed and became ingrained.

(Hutchinson and Hayward, 2005: 229)

Concern that testing was displacing teachers' professional judgements led to an increased focus on formative assessment, but this was restricted to the pre-national examination stages. The separation of curriculum, pedagogy and assessment is a recurring issue in the reform of school education in Scotland. Many participants reflected favourably on the high level of central direction given in earlier reforms, including the provision of units of work for national qualifications. Thus, even a cursory review of policy over the previous decade suggests that the professional space for pedagogic and curriculum innovation and leadership has contracted, leaving many within the profession, especially in secondary schools, ill placed to respond to the new opportunities extended through a degree of curriculum flexibility.

The 'affective turn': creativity, self-esteem and school improvement

In the previous section we identified tensions between progressive and performance elements of the standards and creativity agenda. In this section we develop our argument by suggesting that the creativity/progressive agenda is itself problematic, specifically that it is implicated in new forms of rule. This is evident in the commodification of children's well-being and in the redirection of 'the energies of schools towards ... the management of children's emotional lives', a process articulated by Furedi (2009: 167) as 'the unhappy turn to happiness'.

Recent work on emotional literacy and the development of caring thought (as exemplified, for example, within Philosophy for Children) draws attention to the affective domain in support of learning and the promotion of responsible citizenship. There has been a great deal of attention focused on children's emotional literacy, emotional well-being and emotional resilience in policy circles in recent years. Sharp (2001: 1) defines emotional literacy as 'the ability to recognise, understand, handle and appropriately express emotions'. Much of this attention has been predicated on concerns around behaviour management and inclusion and the pursuit of positive post-school destinations for young people. In Scotland, this is evident in the work of the Discipline Task Group established in 2000 and the subsequent development of a raft of initiatives, including restorative practices, staged intervention, 'being cool in school', the Solution-Oriented School (SOS) programme and the Trojan (inclusion) project.[4]

The enhancement of self-esteem or self-worth has long been a central tenet of primary education in UK schools. Self-esteem is associated with having the 'confidence to act' (Cigman, 2001), feeling competent or possessing optimistic beliefs regarding self-efficacy. Many contemporary initiatives draw on the 'positive psychology' advanced by Martin Seligman (1990, 1995) in his work on 'the optimistic child'. There has been an expansion of interest in esteem within strategies to tackle exclusion, disaffection and underachievement. Mental health professionals and psychotherapists have become the 'cultural retailers' of the self-esteem concept (Slater, 2002) and trainers have engaged in lucrative 'policy entrepreneurship' (Ball, 1994), advancing the merits of interventionist strategies to repair an 'esteem deficit'. The self-esteem movement developed from early interventions in the USA such as the California Task Force to promote self-esteem and personal and social responsibility (Cruickshank, 1999; California State Department of Education, 1990). It is championed in the UK through commercial companies such as the Pacific Institute and Learning Unlimited.

In both the USA and the UK, concerns have been voiced about these developments by commentators in higher education (Baumeister *et al.*, 2003; Emler, 2001) and in the media (Toynbee, 2001). Ecclestone and Hayes (2008), who draw on Furedi's (1997, 2004) fear thesis, have expressed disquiet over the rise of a 'therapeutic pedagogy' which aims to 'empower' less confident learners to overcome (self-imposed) barriers to the achievement of learning goals. Fineman (2000) has pointed to the commodification of 'emotional intelligence' (EI) as a newly constructed competence to be traded by trainers. Research conducted by Emler (2001) found that low self-esteem was damaging to the individual, but did not promote anti-social behaviour. He also questions the positive relationship that is often assumed between self-esteem and academic attainment; arguing that both high and low achievers mediate results according to pre-existing views of themselves. Emler concludes that therapeutic approaches to tackle the self-esteem deficit are little more than 'snake oil remedies'. Other writers have adopted a governmentality perspective and have suggested that the self-esteem movement proceeds from a deficit model in which targets of intervention need to be worked upon to encourage 'care of the self', to re-make themselves as virtuous self-regulating subjects. Helsby and Knight (1998: 6) argue that the notion of empowerment here is one that 'appears to value atomized, technique-centred empowerment of execution, rather than holistic, critically-aware empowerment of conception'.

> Self esteem ... has much more to do with self-assessment than with self-respect, as the self continuously has to be measured, judged and disciplined in order to gear personal 'empowerment' to collective yardsticks ... a forever precarious harmony ... has to be forged between the political goals of the state and a personal 'state of esteem'.
>
> *(Lemke, 2001: 202)*

The relationship of the affective with the performative is complex and ambiguous, at points complementary and seemingly contradictory (apparently opposed to performativity). The pervasive use of target setting within the school improvement cycle offers a point of complementarity. Targets for age-related performance are monitored against performance outcomes. The purpose of target setting is to encourage self-responsibility by moving from what has been achieved at a particular point in time to what *can* be achieved in the future (enhancement). There has been a discernible shift from reliance on summative assessment towards a much stronger focus on formative and ipsative assessment. This is premised on the belief that dispositions to learning are not fixed but can be altered with appropriate feedback from skilled teachers. By attending to the affective, a narrative unfolds in which it is possible to fail constructively, a process of 'failing forwards'. The skilled educator supports the learner in building emotional resilience and developing reflective self-esteem. Cigman (2001: 573) offers a composite of the 'good failure' who is 'motivated to struggle, to tolerate pain' for whom '"I can" is supplemented (not as a prediction but as an intention) by "I will"'. From this perspective, educational failure is reconfigured as a problem of 'self-care'.

In the following section, we offer an example of the alignment of creativity with interventions to scaffold the regeneration of schools. The policy document *Ambitious, Excellent Schools* (SEED, 2004a) afforded greater freedom for schools to tailor learning to the needs of their pupils. Within a framework of national guidance, schools were encouraged to explore 'flexible, creative and innovative' approaches to school improvement. The *Schools of Ambition* programme, launched in 2005 by Peter Peacock, Education Minister in the then Scottish Executive (formed by a coalition between the Labour Party and the Liberal Democrats), was at the forefront of these developments, designed 'to bring about a step change in ambition and achievement' (SEED, 2004a: 12). Local authorities responded in different ways to the opportunity to prepare submissions for schools to enter the *Schools of Ambition* programme. Applications were supported from schools deemed 'most in need of transformation' following HMIe inspections and from 'successful' schools with a track record of innovation. Fifty-two schools were admitted to the programme between 2005 and 2007. Each school received additional funding (£100,000 per annum, around 3 per cent of an average secondary school budget) over a three-year period to implement a locally negotiated plan for transformational change. All the

Schools of Ambition have a focus on the development of pupil confidence, self-esteem and ambition, and eleven schools have explicitly identified the promotion of 'creativity' within their transformational plans. We focus here on one school story, that of Braeview Academy. This vignette illustrates the way in which 'creativity' is put to work in the public performance of school improvement. It illustrates how the language of professional autonomy and personal empowerment is used within a policy frame that allows the reformulation of educational problems as issues of self-care and emotional well-being.

Braeview was among the first tranche of *Schools of Ambition* announced in June 2005 and like many of the schools faced challenging circumstances and a troubled history. Braeview Academy was the new identity given to the integrated community school[5] that emerged from the closure in 1996 of two secondary schools in a disadvantaged area of Dundee, Scotland's fourth largest city, with the highest concentration of poverty outside Glasgow and home to a cluster for biotechnology and digital media industries. Twenty-six per cent of the 663 pupils are entitled to free school meals. In 2004, HMIe rated the school one of the worst in Scotland, with an unprecedented ten unsatisfactory scores. A new headteacher was appointed in January 2005. In the summer of 2008 HMIe ended on-going engagement with the school after two follow-through visits, reporting that 'Many key aspects of the school's work had been improved and some "transformed"' (HMIe, 2008c: 1).

A range of alternative curricula complement changes to the school estate, including the creation of a multi-purpose performance and teaching space, the 'Ambition Hall'. State of the art facilities were combined with care to create a sense of history and tradition. Newly created honour rolls listing past head boys and girls, school dux[6] and headteachers line the walls to 'show that people stay' according to the headteacher (Seith, 2009). Local authority cultural coordinators organised a series of expressive arts activities for pupils identified as 'vulnerable' in collaboration with school guidance personnel. These activities were designed to offer pupils who did not identify strongly with the school the opportunity to make their mark and included: 'Take a Seat' (a project to design and personalise chairs for the drama department); a graffiti wall art project with Dundee Contemporary Arts Centre; and the design and production of stained glass windows for the entrance foyer (to reflect the school's vision). Dundee Repertory Theatre works in close partnership with vulnerable pupils in masked drama productions. The City Council has supported a Writer and Composer in Residence. New partnerships with the local further education college extend opportunities for vocational learning, including sound engineering to support the school radio station.

This range of activity and the relative stability achieved do not correlate neatly with gains in pupil attainment as measured through conventional performance indicators. The headteacher is quick to note the symbolic force of *School of Ambition* status, 'It wasn't about the money. It was about the very human emotion of feeling important and having something that other people did not have. Underpinning all this was the idea that we had been chosen, selected' (Seith, 2009). Curricular innovation at Braeview, supported by teacher development, sought to strengthen social capital and address a perceived esteem deficit. It has not closed the opportunity gap but has enabled the fabrication of a new school story.

Conclusion

Initiating change through programmes of targeted intervention such as *Schools of Ambition* or the *Future Learning and Teaching* programme, or preparing for implementation of a new curriculum such as *Curriculum for Excellence*, school professionals find themselves caught betwixt and between competing paradigms. They often contend with the double-edged sword of innovation and evaluation. The *Schools of Ambition* were at once 'empowered' and 'responsibilised' through limited devolved decision making. Whilst devolved budgets opened up spaces for local deliberation ('power to'), priorities continued to be framed by the exercise of 'power over' schools, which sought to exploit and channel creativity towards particular ends. In addition, novice project coordinators, accountable to Scottish Government Advisors and local authority Quality Improvement Officers, found themselves embroiled in positional politics influenced by notions of territoriality and subject to overtures from commercial consultants and training providers offering packages to assure, accelerate and measure their rate of 'innovation'.

Teachers' responses to the revised school curriculum reveal familiar fault lines between autonomy and prescription. The commodification of creativity as 'another good that schools can help to produce' (Bentley, 2003: 2) has the potential to take adventurous learning and risky pedagogies and render them safe within school structures and processes geared towards conformity. The pressure from sections of the profession for centrally provided exemplification may yet produce the re-establishment of new targets for authorised versions of creativity. As Brundrett (2004: 74) has argued, 'It is hard to conceive how activity can really be creative if it is formularised and bounded and inherently antithetical to the different, the new and the innovative'. Stoll and Temperley (2009: 16) give an early signal that 'creative leadership' may represent 'working with pupil performance data in new and creative ways … focusing on new ways of pupil tracking and data sharing'. In respect of the content of the revised curriculum, responses to the consultation reveal disquiet over a perceived lack of criticality. For example, the submission from the Royal Society of Edinburgh in response to the publication of the draft *Experiences and Outcomes* for Literacy and English, Expressive Arts and Social Studies notes:

> There is insufficient attention to the language of criticism, to developing the capacity to critique and interpret cultural outputs, historical movements, or social events or to judge between different levels of quality … Despite all the attention to defining the curriculum liberally, there are some rather worrying ways in which it seems to have been conceived too narrowly. One general example is in connection to the apparent prescription of ethical outcomes. For example, students will be expected to adopt 'an enterprising attitude'. The purpose of a curriculum is to stimulate informed debate and to ensure that students have the critical tools to engage with that debate, not to prescribe the conclusions.
>
> *(Royal Society of Edinburgh, 2009: 3)*

Creativity is moving from the periphery to occupy a more central position within policies informing public education in Scotland. Changes in practice will be dependent on (1) the capacity and will of the profession to 'unlearn' established practices and habitual responses and (2) the capacity of the system to adopt a stronger learner orientation over a performance orientation. One of the many paradoxes implicit in the development of a futures-oriented curriculum is the insertion of licence to think differently within systems that have often sought to be teacher- and future-proof.

Notes

1 The Scottish Survey of Achievement introduced in 2005 provides national (rather than school-level) attainment data on the standards being reached by pupils in some subject areas at Primary 3 (age 7–8), Primary 5 (age 9–10), Primary 7 (age 11–12) and Secondary 2 (age 13–14) stages.

2 SEED (2004) *Ambitious Excellent Schools*, Edinburgh: Scottish Executive.

3 More complete details of the project methodology are included in the full report from the project, available at http://www.ltscotland.org.uk/Images/GUfinalreport_tcm4-539659.pdf.

4 For further information, see *Better Behaviour Scotland*: http://www.betterbehaviourscotland.gov.uk/.
5 Integrated community schools, modelled on the North American concept of the full service school, were established in Scotland from 1999 to encourage closer joint working among education, health and social work agencies and professionals.
6 Dux of School is awarded to the student who attains the best aggregate result over all subjects in the external examinations and is similar to the North American concept of a valedictorian.

References

Ball, S. J. (1994) *Education Reform: A Critical & Post-Structural Approach*, Buckingham: Open University Press.
—— (2007) *Education plc: Understanding Private Sector Participation in Public Sector Education*, London: Routledge.
Baumeister, R. F., Campbell, J. D., Krueger, J. I. and Vohs, K. D. (2003) Does high self-esteem cause better performance, interpersonal success, happiness, or healthier lifestyles?, *Psychological Science in the Public Interest* 4: 1–44.
Bentley, T. (2003) *Distributed Intelligence: Leadership and Learning*, Nottingham: National College for School Leadership.
Brundrett, M. (2004) Leadership and creativity, *Education 3–13* 32(1): 72–6.
California State Department of Education (1990) *Toward a State of Esteem: The Final Report of the California Task Force to Promote Self-esteem and Personal and Social Responsibility*, Berkeley: California State Department of Education.
Cigman, R. (2001) Self-esteem and the confidence to fail, *Journal of Philosophy of Education* 35(4): 561–76.
Cruickshank, B. (1999) *The Will to Empower: Democratic Citizens and Other Subjects*, Ithaca, NY: Cornell University Press.
Deakins, D., Glancey, K., Menter, I. and Wyper, J. (2005) Enterprise education: the role of headteachers, *International Entrepreneurship and Management Journal* 1: 241–63.
Ecclestone, K. and Hayes, D. (2008) *The Dangerous Rise of Therapeutic Education*, London: Routledge.
Emler, N. (2001) *Self-Esteem: The Costs and Causes of Low Self-Worth*, York: Joseph Rowntree Foundation.
Fineman, S. (2000) Commodifying the emotionally intelligent, in S. Fineman (ed.) *Emotion in Organizations* (2nd ed.), London: Sage.
Furedi, F. (1997) *Culture of Fear: Risk-Taking and the Morality of Low Expectation*, London: Cassell.
—— (2004) *Therapy Culture: Cultivating Vulnerability in an Uncertain Age*, London: Routledge.
—— (2009) *Wasted: Why Education Isn't Working*, London: Continuum.
Hartley, D. (2003) The instrumentalisation of the expressive in education, *British Journal of Educational Studies* 51(1): 6–19.
Helsby, G. and Knight, P. (1998) Preparing students for the new work order: the case of Advanced General National Vocational Qualifications, *British Educational Research Journal* 24(1): 63–79.
HMIe (2006a) *Emerging Good Practice in Promoting Creativity*, Livingston: HMIe.
—— (2006b) *Education for Citizenship. A Portrait of Current Practice in Scottish Schools and Pre-school Centres*, Livingston: HMIe; available at http://www.hmie.gov.uk/documents/publication/efcpcp1.pdf (accessed 6 April 2009).
—— (2008a) *Special Edition on HMIe's New Approaches to Inspection*, Livingston: HMIe.
—— (2008b) *The Newsletter of HM Inspectorate of Education* (Autumn); available at http://www.hmie.gov.uk/documents/publication/hmiebriefau08.html (accessed 7 July 2009).
—— (2008c) *Report on Follow Through Inspection of Braeview Academy*, 29 April, Dundee Council, Dundee: HMIe; available at: http://www.hmie.gov.uk/documents/followup/5339731BraeviewAcad%202FT.pdf (accessed 10 July 2009).
Hutchinson, C. and Hayward, L. (2005) The journey so far: assessment for learning in Scotland, *Curriculum Journal* 16(2): 225–48.
IDES Network and Learning and Teaching Scotland (2001) *Creativity in Education*, Dundee: IDES Network and LT Scotland.
Learning and Teaching Scotland (LTS) (2009) *Curriculum for Excellence: Experiences and Outcomes*, Glasgow: LTS; available at http://www.ltscotland.org.uk/curriculumforexcellence/ (accessed 14 January 2010).
Lemke, T. (2001) The birth of biopolitics: Michel Foucault's lecture at the College de France on neo-liberal governmentality, *Economy and Society* 30(2): 190–207.
Macdonald, D. (2003) Curriculum change and the post-modern world: is the school curriculum-reform movement an anachronism, *Journal of Curriculum Studies* 35(2): 139–49.

Newman, J. (2001) *Modernising Governance: New Labour, Policy and Society*, London: Sage.

Newman, J. and Clarke, J. (2009) *Publics, Politics and Power*, London: Sage.

Organisation for Economic Cooperation and Development (OECD) (2007) *Reviews of National Policies for Education: Quality and Equity of Schooling in Scotland*, Paris: OECD.

Royal Society of Edinburgh (2009) *Submission to Learning and Teaching Scotland on Curriculum for Excellence Draft Experiences and Outcomes for Literacy and English, Expressive Arts and Social Studies*, 27 June, Edinburgh: Royal Society of Edinburgh.

Scottish Education Department (1965) *Primary Education in Scotland*, Edinburgh: HMSO.

Scottish Executive Education Department (SEED) (2002) *Determined to Succeed: A Review of Enterprise in Education*, Edinburgh: SEED.

—— (2004a) *Ambitious, Excellent Schools*, Edinburgh: SEED; available at http://www.scotland.gov.uk/Resource/Doc/26800/0023694.pdf (accessed 8 July 2009).

—— (2004b) *National Priorities in School Education*. Edinburgh: Scottish Executive.

—— (2006) *Promoting Creativity in Education: Overview of Key National Policy Developments across the UK*, Edinburgh, SEED; available at http://www.hmie.gov.uk/documents/publication/hmiepcie.pdf (accessed 4 July 2009).

Scottish Government (2008) Statistical report on the progress made by the Scottish Government's Closing the Opportunity Gap programme and recommendations for the future measurement of achievement of the programme's aims and objectives, January; available at http://www.scotland.gov.uk/Publications/2007/12/07105255/9 (accessed 6 July 2009).

—— (2009) *Statistics Publication Notice Education Series: SQA Attainment and School Leaver Qualifications in Scotland, 2007/08*, Edinburgh: Scottish Government; available at http://www.scotland.gov.uk/Publications/2009/03/09154229/0 (accessed 7 July 2009).

Seith, E. (2009) The arts of going from run-down to cool, *Times Educational Supplement Scotland* (TESS), 12 June; available at http://www.tes.co.uk/article.aspx?storycode=6015418.

Seligman, M. (1990) *Learned Optimism*, New York: Knopf.

—— (1995) *The Optimistic Child*, New York: HarperCollins.

Sharp, P. (2001) *Nurturing Emotional Literacy*, London: David Fulton.

Slater, L. (2002) The trouble with self-esteem, *New York Times*, 3 February, Section 6: 44–7.

Stoll, L. and Temperley, J. (2009) Creative leadership: a challenge of our times, *School Leadership and Management* 29(1): 65–78.

Toynbee, P. (2001) At last, we can abandon that tosh about low self-esteem: the psychobabblers' snake-oil remedies have been exposed as a sham, *Guardian*, 28 December; available at http://www.guardian.co.uk/education/2001/dec/28/research.highereducation.

University of Glasgow (2009) *Collection, Analysis, and Reporting of Data on Curriculum for Excellence Draft Experiences and Outcomes: Final Report*, report submitted to Learning and Teaching Scotland. Published 2 April; available at http://www.ltscotland.org.uk/Images/GUfinalreport_tcm4–539659.pdf.

45

The challenges of developing system-wide indicators of creativity reform

The case of Creative Partnerships, UK

David Parker and Naranee Ruthra-Rajan

Introduction

Creative Partnerships is a unique government funded creative learning initiative. Since April 2009 it has been managed by the charity Creativity, Culture and Education (CCE) but prior to this it was administered from within Arts Council England. While the nature and ambitions of all the projects it has run might vary from place to place, a common thread of rich partnerships, developed between schools and the creative and cultural sector, weaves its way through the whole programme. It is committed to ensuring that young people have access to a wide range of cultural and artistic experiences, believing not only that this increases enjoyment and confidence, but crucially that it unlocks their creativity. Such ambitions understandably come under considerable scrutiny from funders and all those concerned with educational provision for young people. In our capacity as the research directorate for the programme much of our time has been spent inviting the necessary scrutiny in the form of a sustained programme of research and evaluation.

Our challenge as managers of a series of large-scale research and evaluation projects was to collect evidence of impact and to develop theoretical and practical insights about this significant and sizeable programme. We knew from early national evaluations (Sharp *et al.*, 2006) and Fullan's (2002) work on long-term systemic change in education that the programme would need to bridge the divide between top-down accountability models of change and those based on the creation of professional learning communities from the bottom up. In order to ensure our research and evaluation could feed into both we sought to develop understanding about two key elements arising from the work on the ground: first, a sense of how Creative Partnerships worked effectively with schools and the creative and cultural sector, and to help spread that learning in a formative sense, essentially to critically reflect on good practice and processes with a view to ongoing improvement and the development of a shared community of practice; second, to begin to look for evidence of impacts on a number of fronts, but particularly with respect to young people, parents, teachers, schools and the creative sector itself.

In this chapter we will outline some examples of work we commissioned and managed as a means of meeting the second of these challenges and to give some sense of the ways findings were used to inform our understanding of effect and impact.

How the programme operates

First, it is necessary to briefly lay out some of the basic principles underpinning the workings of the Creative Partnerships programme so that the reader can set the descriptions of the research that follow into a broader operational context.

From the very beginning Creative Partnerships has pushed at the boundaries of operational rules. In 2002 each local area was expected to work with 15–20 schools but many quickly moved beyond these targets to work with more. By 2005/6 the research we had commissioned showed us that there was a pluralism to the work which gave a sense of different strands of activity beneath one overarching programme. Creative Partnerships formalised these strands into discrete programme 'offers' in April 2008. Since that time the programme has comprised:

- Schools of Creativity: a small cohort of 57 schools with a responsibility to develop their practice while sharing their learning with a network of other schools;
- Change Schools: around 800 schools whose development is supported by Creative Partnerships for three years to bring about significant changes in their ethos, ambition and achievement;
- Enquiry Schools: around 1,200 schools that work with Creative Partnerships for a year on resolving an identified issue within the school.

Creative Partnerships begins with the School Improvement/Development Plan, which lays out the major priorities of each school. Sometimes it will help a school develop its plan; in other cases it will take aspects of the plan and work with the school to develop projects that address the issues identified. With the issues identified the process moves forward through the relationship between creative professionals and the school. Creative professionals are key participants within the Creative Partnerships programme. They fulfil one of two roles – creative agent and creative practitioner – the former acting as an overseer of the programme in a school, helping guide and shape the planning and reflection, the latter serving as a co-deliverer of projects within the programme in a school, working directly alongside teachers with young people in the classroom and beyond.

Context and history

Recognising the value of external practitioners working in partnership with a school is not, of course, exclusive to the Creative Partnerships programme. An important precursor to the programme in England was the Arts Education Interface (AEI),[1] which was managed by Arts Council England. AEI was described then as a 'mutual learning triangle' (Harland et al., 2005), an equitable process of negotiated practice implicating teachers, pupils and artists. This strong element of partnership working, and mutual learning, was a key dimension within Creative Partnerships when it first began.

Thinking internationally, there are three useful comparisons to the work of Creative Partnerships. Learning Through the Arts (Canada)[2] and Kulturkontakt (Austria),[3] which focus on learning through the arts in partnership with an external practitioner, and the Coalition of Essential Schools (USA),[4] which focuses more generally on school change and improvement.

While each of these programmes in its own way encapsulates an element within the Creative Partnerships programme there is no single comparator that straightforwardly offers a mirror of the programme, in terms of either scale or purpose. Learning Through the Arts places an emphasis on interpreting and delivering the curriculum through artform disciplines, which itself develops out of the long history of arts in education. Kulturkontakt emphasises partnerships and long-term relationships between artists and schools, which develops out of a sustained state commitment in Austria to funding a programme of artists working in educational settings. And the Coalition of Essential Schools promotes cultures of continuous improvement and powerful professional learning communities focused on student achievement, to support and promote innovative and effective teaching.

Creative Partnerships, consciously or not, is clearly borrowing from and inheriting aspects of these varied histories, continuing with work that emerges from and links back into a number of different paradigms.[5] Creative Partnerships is particularly interesting, in that it brings together these prior histories through an implied causal hypothesis – the notion that creative skills and behaviours are essential to high quality twenty-first century learning, that schools can help develop such skills if they mobilise their capacities effectively (staff, time, learning spaces, etc.) and that creative professionals (artists, architects, scientists, designers, etc.) offer a particularly effective approach to making that process of change and development happen.

Researching impact

From the outset, even before the programme was fully operational, there was general interest from many quarters – government funders, schools, parents, local authorities – in establishing the nature and extent of Creative Partnerships' impact.

However, it is tremendously challenging to craft definitive and singular accounts of impact from the complex ecology of schools. In acknowledging these difficulties and tensions we have developed a range of research and evaluation projects, each looking at particular themes, rather than invest in a single overarching national evaluation. In doing so we have broadened the type of findings generated, extended the range of researchers we have worked with and linked outcomes back to comprehensive theories of learning and practice. Not only are the insights we will describe derived from multi-method approaches, they are also generated by a multiplicity of expertise and institutional affiliations that add a particular richness to the mix. In the following sections we will lay out a selection of studies and their main findings, focusing in turn on themes of attainment, attendance and parental involvement, and then suggest why these separate studies, and the way they were commissioned, seemed to offer us the most effective means of describing impact.

Impacts on educational attainment

During 2006 the National Foundation for Educational Research undertook a study of 13,000 young people who had participated in Creative Partnerships activities. The NFER team made use of the government's National Pupil Database (NPD) to investigate whether there was a relationship between young people's participation in Creative Partnerships activities and their academic achievement.

The attendance data on young people participating in Creative Partnerships projects was collected via 'attendance data sheets' which were distributed directly to schools taking part in the pilot stage national evaluation (Sharp et al., 2006). NFER distributed these on a termly basis over two academic years (2002/3 and 2003/4). The data sheets were sent to the teacher leading on Creative Partnerships activity in each school (known as Creative Partnerships coordinators), who was asked to provide information on young people involved in activities that were funded by Creative Partnerships.

By combining the two datasets (the NPD and the NFER evaluation data) this study was able to provide a national dataset with pupils involved in Creative Partnerships flagged for each year. Multilevel modelling was used to examine whether there was a difference between those young people involved in Creative Partnerships and those not, when all relevant background factors were taken into account.

The evaluation involved young people from a wide range of year groups (from Foundation Stage to Year 13). NFER grouped the young people in relation to the end of key stage assessments, as follows:

- for young people in Year 6, progress was compared from Key Stage 1 to Key Stage 2 for those involved in Creative Partnerships and those not;
- for young people in Year 9, progress was compared from Key Stage 2 to Key Stage 3;
- for young people in Year 11, progress was compared from Key Stage 3 to GCSE.

The findings from the analysis of Creative Partnerships data compared with the national population suggested that the initiative reached schools serving more disadvantaged communities and with a higher proportion of people from diverse minority ethnic backgrounds. Interestingly, however, the young people who attended Creative Partnerships activities tended to be less disadvantaged than those in the same schools – in terms of having a statement of special educational needs, eligibility for free school meals (at Key Stages 2 and 3) and prior attainment. This corroborated findings from Thomson *et al.* (2009) and the anecdotal evidence acquired through monitoring and school visits, where we had found Creative Partnerships sometimes being used as a reward for good behaviour rather than a proactive and targeted intervention.

When compared with national data, the analysis of young people's progress showed no evidence of any significant impact of participating in Creative Partnerships activities at Key Stage 2 or Key Stage 4 and a very small positive impact at Key Stage 3. Although this was a seemingly small impact it did suggest that we may need to continue to look at attainment data, given the long-term nature of the Creative Partnerships intervention.

More encouragingly, an analysis of within-school data revealed that young people who were known to have attended Creative Partnerships activities outperformed their peers in the same schools to a statistically significant extent at all three key stages.

Impacts on pupil attendance at school

While the multilevel modelling and analysis of pupil attainment offered some interesting but ultimately suggestive correlations between Creative Partnerships and improvements in performance there were other aspects of pupil behaviour we wanted to investigate. NFER worked on a project in 2008 exploring the possible impact on attendance. The study used school-level aggregate data to compare absence rates and exclusions in Creative Partnerships schools with those in schools not participating in Creative Partnerships. This found:

> Participation in Creative Partnerships was shown to be associated with an educationally significant reduction in total absence rates in primary schools and that this reduction increased over a period of some years as Creative Partnerships became more established in

these schools. Total absence rates in schools that had been participating in Creative Partnerships for four years were almost one percentage point lower than in otherwise comparable schools with no history of involvement with Creative Partnerships.

(Kendall et al., 2008: 8)

Establishing impacts of a magnitude deemed to be educationally significant is extremely rare, but at the same time it is important to note that while there were some big impacts they were far from evenly spread across schools of different types. There was very little to suggest an impact in secondary schools, for example, although in the case of permanent exclusions they have become such a rarity that it would be difficult to show any demonstrable improvement.

This study, especially when seen within the context of other research Creative Partnerships has commissioned where strong themes of re-engagement and motivation emerge, suggests that much of the effect of the programme may be in terms of condition-setting, principally through the establishment of a changed perception of school among those young people with the strongest anti-school dispositions. If this were the case one might not expect to see significant impacts on attainment until further into the future.

Impacts on parents

As we have already mentioned, there was a good deal of anecdotal evidence suggesting that Creative Partnerships may have been positively affecting a sense of re-engagement with schools, particularly among young people and to some extent their teachers. We were curious to discover whether this might also be true of parents. There is now strong evidence to suggest that a key predictor of the attainment and well-being of young people is the extent to which their parents are actively involved in their education (Henderson and Berla, 1994).

We were interested to find out whether Creative Partnerships might be helping to foster positive links between parents and their children's schools and commissioned the Centre for Literacy in Primary Education (CLPE) to undertake a study focusing on parental involvement. The CLPE set out with the following research question: 'If a creative approach to the curriculum is beneficial to children, what are parents' understandings of these benefits?' (Safford and O'Sullivan, 2007: 7).

The research was partly prompted by anecdotal evidence and observations in previous research projects (Safford and Barrs, 2006) suggesting that children communicate their enjoyment of school-based creative projects to their parents to a much greater extent than their work in the core literacy and numeracy curriculum.

The research began in the Spring Term of 2006 with the CLPE team trialling their school and parent questionnaires. These were subsequently refined following feedback from senior school staff at three primary schools and one secondary school, and from a number of parents. The parent questionnaire was then used as an oral prompt document to ensure consistency in taped interviews. Senior school staff (headteachers, deputy heads or Creative Partnerships coordinators) completed written questionnaires.

In the Summer Term of 2006, the questionnaire for senior school staff was sent to 200 schools which had participated in Creative Partnerships. Schools were selected to represent a wide regional distribution and a balance of rural, urban, large, small, primary and secondary schools (although there are many more primary schools than secondary schools which are involved in Creative Partnerships). From this national survey, 65 questionnaires were returned. From the returned school questionnaires, follow-up interviews with 16 senior school staff and with 34 parents in 13 schools were organised in the academic year 2006–7.

The early indications were that a great deal of rich and productive talk was generated about school through the descriptions of creative activities by young people while at home. According to parents who participated in the study, when children are engaged in short-term or long-term creative projects they:

> extensively describe these experiences at home. Furthermore, when creative projects in school are sustained, these home discussions appear to influence parents in a number of ways. Some parents feel they understand more about what their children are learning in school, and they begin to develop perspectives on their children as learners and on what constitutes learning in and out of school. Children's enthusiasm for creative projects also causes some parents to become critical of the core curriculum, and they perceive creative programmes as offering alternative long-term benefits which positively influence children's aspirations as well as their learning.
>
> *(Safford and O'Sullivan, 2007: 1)*

However, further evidence emerged to suggest deeper involvement in the school itself. Creative Partnerships appeared to offer low-risk invitations which encouraged some parents to engage with teachers and the whole school, in a few cases even taking on employment at the school as a result of involvement in creative projects. Whilst some parents may lack confidence to support their children in more formal school-based tasks, for example literacy and numeracy, they seemed to feel more able to extend creative programmes at home. The CLPE research suggested this typically occurred through parents working alongside children on extended tasks and through visiting cultural and artistic venues such as galleries and theatres.

Finally, the report suggests that children's engagement with creative programmes has a deeper effect on the individual learning of parents themselves. In some cases this led to the take-up of cultural and other learning opportunities for themselves as well as for their children.

Impacts on the creative sector

It was also important to explore the potential impacts of Creative Partnerships beyond schools. A research study undertaken by BOP Consulting in 2006 began to investigate the kinds of impact that may be felt among individual creative practitioners.

One of the objectives of Creative Partnerships is to build the capacity of the cultural and creative sectors to work effectively with schools, and provide opportunities for cultural and creative professionals to enhance the skills they need to work in educational settings. Evidence from the BOP study suggests that Creative Partnerships has achieved this objective in three ways.

In the first instance,

> [Creative Partnerships (CP)] has provided space and time for a core of practitioners to develop their disciplines in an organic, fluid way that allows experimentation. CP working is process, rather than product, led. This creates room for innovation, experimentation and development of practice, and is a unique offering to creative and cultural practitioners in the education market.
>
> *(BOP Consulting, 2006: 30)*

Second,

> [Creative Partnerships] has equipped a core pool of practitioners with a strong under-standing of the education market. Whilst many had gained experience of the education

sector under the traditional 'arts education' banner, the Creative Partnerships 'way of working' was relatively new. The collaborative, participative approach encouraged by Creative Partnerships fostered a deeper understanding of the needs of schools, and closely related creativity to whole school change. Furthermore, practitioners were equipped with the consultancy, negotiation and change management skills to develop, manage, and evaluate future education work – be this in a Creative Partnerships environment, or in an independent school programme for creativity. In this sense, Creative Partnerships has helped in developing a pool of 'market ready' practitioners.

(BOP Consulting, 2006: 30)

Third,

Creative Partnerships has succeeded in building a model for creative and cultural practitioner CPD. Each Creative Partnerships office has used a combination of formal structured training, and informal 'on the job' learning to equip creative and cultural practitioners with the skills they need for continued practice progression, collaboration, and crucial transferable skills that will prove relevant in a variety of settings, be they education, publicly funded or commercial markets.

(BOP Consulting, 2006: 30)

There were also interesting findings around the profile of creative practitioners the programme recruited. Thirty-five per cent of creative practitioners had been working in the sector for less than three years. This group of emerging professionals gained the biggest benefits from Creative Partnerships in terms of new skills, confidence and CV enhancement. This is significant because traditionally government intiatives and training programmes find it tremendously difficult to reach beyond the longest established and biggest companies.

Approximately half of creative professionals working with Creative Partnerships went on to develop other work and employed other creative professionals as a result of their involvement in the programme. BOP estimated that around 70 per cent of Creative Partnerships funding, up until 2006, went directly to creative practitioners, and went on to suggest this is a highly significant investment in the development of the creative industries in England (BOP Consulting, 2006: 28).

What were the advantages of commissioning a series of separate studies?

Going some way towards revealing an overall sense of impact for a programme like Creative Partnerships, with its complex and interwoven sets of personal and institutional interests – pupils, teachers, schools, local authorities, cultural and creative professionals, government departments – depends on a research and evaluation programme that can flex and keep pace with changes to delivery on the ground.

Our decision to invest in a range of smaller scale studies, rather than a longitudinal, overarching study allowed us to avoid the following potential pitfalls:

- *Ossification of the research design*: the risk that the original research instruments and approaches within a single study would be outmoded through developments to the delivery and focus of the programme over time
- *Generalist approach and breadth diluting accounts of the nature of impact and effect*: a large scale single study may have missed the in-depth accounts of practice offered by smaller scale

studies. For example, understanding the nature of change as it is experienced by key participants in schools can be captured more sensitively and be understood in greater detail by specialist researchers who have a background in schools or organisational change.

- *Single causal factors oversimplifying impact*: by looking at aspects of Creative Partnerships impact through separate studies we were able to move beyond simple 'sketch' accounts of impact and build a fuller, richer account of the mix of factors involved in success and failure.
- *No opportunity for additional corroboration of research findings*: by commissioning a series of separate studies we were able to indirectly test the findings of prior research, thereby strengthening the validity of some findings, but also suggesting others may require further study and additional verification.
- *Focusing on funders' needs to the exclusion of all others'*: commissioning separate studies allowed us to address needs and interests of those responsible for managing projects, those researchers working in the field, and those teachers and creative practitioners working in the classroom, as well as offering accounts that met funders' needs.

The application of one study: how has research been used?

These varied accounts represent just a few of the studies Creative Partnerships has commissioned since 2002.[6] Each investigation of impact has served a dual purpose; as well as giving an impact assessment through capturing the current state of play, they also concern themselves with detailed descriptions of Creative Partnerships processes that have helped to inform overall development of the programme. In that sense the research offers both formative and summative accounts, giving us descriptions of achievement, but always with an eye to improving further, learning key lessons and building on what has worked best.

Creative Partnerships continues to grow and adapt. As we have already mentioned, the programme was redesigned in 2008 and much of the thinking behind that process was directly informed by research findings. One of the key studies that informed these ongoing developments was the Creative School Change research project (Thomson *et al.*, 2009). The study had an ambitious scope, looking at partnership, sustainability and long-term change. It aimed to explore how schools have understood and mobilised Creative Partnerships to construct school change of different sorts through a process of active appropriation and interpretation.

Three important issues emerged from the study during the early stages and retained a primacy throughout the life of the project. They were:

- school culture and ethos;
- creating different learning opportunities for students;
- spreading and embedding change across the school.

In terms of the first of these, school culture and ethos, it became clear that Creative Partnerships had made some contribution to changing the ethos and overall feel within particular schools. Many studies have shown the importance of the intangible or invisible aspects of school life, the so-called 'hidden' curriculum which is emblematic of the schools' overall values and approach to broad educational goals. Thomson, Jones and Hall show a range of ways in which Creative Partnerships had helped make important gains in shifting ethos and culture. They highlight changes to the physical appearance of the school, the range of activities available for young people (usually involving expertise and resources from out of school), a new rhetoric in the stories schools told about themselves, a sense of seeing themselves differently and more positively – all of these aspects were evidenced from extensive field visits to school.

With regard to the second theme, the creation of different learning opportunities, there was strong evidence for markedly experiential ways of teaching and learning fostered through collaborations between teachers and creative professionals. Often this would mean restructuring the curriculum, making lesson times and topics of study more malleable, giving rise to integrated units of work in primary schools and better coordination between subject areas across single topics in secondary schools.

The final theme, spreading and embedding change, was hugely significant for Creative Partnerships because a central objective of the programme was to help foster and support long-term change. The report was able to isolate some strong examples of this kind of embeddedness, but they were the exception rather than the rule. Much more common was to find 'pockets of innovation' that required some further structural or resource shifts in order to build school-wide 'know-how'.

From all of these observations there emerged some clear challenges to the thinking underpinning the programme. Key questions posed included:

- How can we diagnose what it was about particular creative activities that allowed previously disengaged students to get involved?
- How can we recognise and make explicit the kinds of pedagogies involved in creative activities and apply those more generally to classroom practice in all subjects?
- How can we draw on existing expertise in integrating curriculum?
- How can we develop expertise and confidence in less teacher-directed modes of instruction?
- How can we lead and develop a top-down and bottom-up change process?
- How can we build a community of creative practice?

With these questions in mind, and set alongside the other interim and complete research findings, Creative Partnerships was able to complete a year-long process of programme development consultations with local and national stakeholders, reshaping the programme to directly address as many of these issues as possible. This culminated in the redesigned programme we have referred to and which has been operating since April 2008.

The development of a national application, planning and evaluation process was one of the main operational changes at the heart of this redesign. This was also a response to the 2006 Office for Standards in Education (Ofsted) report on the Creative Partnerships programme, which confirmed findings from much of the independent research we had commissioned – they too observed improvements in attainment, behaviour, motivation and attendance – but also stressed that attention should be paid to the following:

- ensuring that the reasons for a school's inclusion in the programme were clear;
- ensuring that the school's aims were precise and that the needs of pupils had been assessed and incorporated in the programme planning.

The model of planning and evaluation that has been used since 2008 forges strong links between the Creative Partnerships programme and the school's ongoing Improvement Plan, allowing external inspectors from Ofsted to see a clear connection between the creative activities and the long-term vision for change the school has set for itself.

Conclusion

Creating a robust body of evidence that is both exploratory and evaluative and which takes as its focus a complex and multifaceted government funded initiative is itself a complicated undertaking.

Our approach, as we hope to have exemplified above, is to have managed a series of separate research commissions rather than a single overarching study. This has offered a number of advantages in spite of the multiplication of the many logistical and operational complications inherent in this work.

First, we have been able to build a loose alliance of objective researchers, each with their own particular sets of expertise and experience. From time to time we bring the various research teams together to cross-refer in an informal way, and we have found this has strengthened our understanding of the thematics that run across the separate studies.

Second, the variety of methodological approaches and the distinctiveness of each enquiry has helped to test the high-level messages that seem to emerge from our findings. Our strongest intuitions as colleagues of peers interested in the ongoing management of the programme have sometimes been confounded, and fresh insights have often emerged unexpectedly but in ways that have informed our thinking.

Third, key findings have been corroborated by separate studies, often with no explicit intention or particular focus on the theme in question. For example, several studies have in their own ways contributed to the overall picture of improved teaching and learning through the Creative Partnerships programme – the British Market Research Bureau survey of headteachers (BMRB, 2006), Thomson *et al.* (2009), NFER's attainment and attendance studies (Eames *et al.*, 2006; Kendall *et al.*, 2008a, 2008b) all have in different ways built a depth of understanding and helped to enhance the validity of impact narratives.

Fourth, and perhaps most importantly, the selection of studies here and the remainder available on the CCE website have been able to inform quickly and purposefully how we refine and develop the Creative Partnerships offer, better understanding the key drivers for long-term change and success, and acknowledging that while Creative Partnerships plays a significant part it is always the schools themselves who must appropriate whatever opportunities and challenges are embodied in this national initiative.

Notes

1 Arts Education Interface: http://www.nfer.ac.uk/nfer/publications/AEI01/AEI01_home.cfm?publication ID=164&title=The%20arts-education%20interface:%20a%20mutual%20learning%20triangle?
2 Learning Through the Arts (LTTA): http://www.ltta.ca/.
3 Kulturkontakt: http://www.kulturkontakt.or.at/.
4 Coalition of Essential Schools (CES): http://www.essentialschools.org/.
5 For a fuller account of the historical and theoretical background preceding Creative Partnerships, see Fleming, M. (2010) *Arts in Education and Creativity: A Literature Review* (2nd ed.), Newcastle: CCE; and Jones, K. (2010) *Culture and Creative Learning: A Literature Review* (2nd ed.), Newcastle: CCE.
6 A comprehensive list of all published reports and summaries of works in progress can be found at http://www.creativitycultureeducation.org/.

References

BMRB (2006) *Creative Partnerships: Survey of Headteachers*, London: BMRB (British Market Research Bureau).

BOP Consulting (2006) *Study of the Impact of Creative Partnerships on the Cultural and Creative Economy*, London: BOP.

Eames, A., Benton, T., Sharp, C. and Kendall, L. (2006) *The Longer Term Impact of Creative Partnerships on the Attainment of Young People*, Slough: NFER.

Fullan, M. (2002) *The New Meaning of Educational Change* (4th ed.), New York: Teachers College Press.

Harland, J., Lord, P., Stott, A, Kinder, K., Lamont, E. and Ashworth, M. (2005) *The Arts Education Interface: A Mutual Learning Triangle?* Slough: NFER.

Henderson, A. T. and Berla, N (eds) (1994) *A New Generation of Evidence: The Family Is Critical to Student Achievement*, Columbia, MD: National Committee for Citizens in Education.

Kendall, L., Morrison, J., Sharp, C. and Yeshanew, T. (2008a) *The Impact of Creative Partnerships on Pupil Behaviour*, Slough: NFER.

—— (2008b) *The Longer Term Impact of Creative Partnerships on the Attainment of Young People: Results from 2005 and 2006*, Slough: NFER.

Office for Standards in Education (2006) *Creative Partnerships: Initiative and Impact*, Ofsted.

Safford, K. and Barrs, M. (2006) *Many Routes to Meaning: Children's Language and Literacy Learning in Creative Arts Work*, London: CLPE and Creative Partnerships, Arts Council England.

Safford, K. and O'Sullivan, O. (2007) *Their Learning Becomes Your Journey: Parents Respond to Children's Work in Creative Partnerships*, London: CLPE.

Sharp, C., Pye, D., Blackmore, J., Brown, E., Eames, A., Easton, C., Filmer-Sankey, C., Tabary, A., Whitby, K., Wilson, R. and Benton, T. (2006) *National Evaluation of Creative Partnerships*, Slough: NFER.

Thomson, P., Jones, K. and Hall, C. (2009) *Creative School Change Project*, Nottingham: University of Nottingham.

Part IV Conclusion

The importance of pedagogically focused leadership

Pat Thomson

The Creative School Change Project (Thomson *et al.*, 2009) showed that in schools that made significant changes the head teacher and other senior leaders had high levels of pedagogical expertise and were committed to learning more about pedagogies. They used pedagogical principles to guide the public narratives used about the school, underpin the decisions that were made and build the imaginaries of possible futures that were developed. Pedagogical expertise does not mean a technical knowledge of methods, but rather a deep understanding of the ways in which curriculum, assessment, grouping, pacing, tools, activities and methods come together in real classrooms with real students. This knowledge was also situated in the particular context. Pedagogical expertise was applied to think about the specific issues which arose from serving particular children and young people, for particular and clearly articulated purposes. While other school staff had detailed knowledge of syllabus and summative assessment requirements, it was in particular the head's reservoir of intellectual resources and practical know-how about pedagogies that provided the direction for and optimism about change.[1]

In the Creative Whole School Change Project it was largely, but not exclusively, early childhood and some primary schools where heads had this expertise. One school, guided by its head, had abandoned ability grouping altogether, incorporated students' perspectives into the curriculum and the school more generally, and was in the process of reviewing and changing curriculum structures. Three nurseries, where heads were inspired by the student-led, pedagogic observation-driven processes of Italian preschools (Edwards *et al.*, 1998), offered a highly experiential and exploratory play-based curriculum. Three primary schools were working on a 'funds of knowledge' (Gonzales *et al.*, 2005) approach to curriculum, one in combination with a 'concerns-based' approach (Beane, 1997) to student assignment planning. In each of these cases the head not only gave permission for experimentation and development to occur but also actively sought out new intellectual resources, worked alongside and in conversation with teachers, and changed management structures to support the new directions.

Pedagogically focused leadership required the following:

- *Serious and worthwhile purposes, understood to be so by the wider school community*: without exception, schools that made comprehensive changes towards creative learning shared a commitment to equity and inclusion and took a balanced approach to the mixed mandates

459

of schooling, working to keep in productive tension uneasy bedfellows – children and young people's entitlement to a rich education for citizenship, family life, and work; the requirement to meet the mandates of the national curriculum, and the desirability of making their schools locally accountable. Layered on top of this, some schools had also developed additional purposes – educating children and young people to live in and with communities that are ethnically, racially and culturally diverse; teaching children how to live sustainably; understanding what it means to be a 'global citizen'; and how to live and have agency as a young person designated as 'having special needs'. These purposes infused every aspect of the school and were the litmus test in decisions about whether to do something or not, or whether creative learning approaches had succeeded or failed.

- *Leadership and management working together*: leadership in the most creative schools focused not simply on leading but on the allied and aligned management tasks. Processes of review and planning were designed to support and spread the findings of smaller scale pilots and projects; budgets, staffing and timetabling were kept in tune with emerging and changed priorities; and communication channels within the school and between the school and its various communities were open and encouraged conversation. Schools did not therefore find themselves faced with 'pockets of innovation' which were unable to be scaled across the school and beyond.

- *Recognition and management of tensions*: change of course has to do more than start. It must be sustained. Schools that were able to sustain change overlaid strategies rather than run them as stop-start processes or in competition with each other. This overlaying of interventions, one after another, mobilised sequences of activities that built on shared organisational learnings, responded to changing circumstances and resources, and which were comprehensible and logical to those in the school community. The pace of change was not exhausting, and head teachers managed the flow of initiatives into the school in ways that ensured that they 'fed the bureaucracy' (Haberman, 1999) – that is, they did what was required and mandatory – while following locally agreed directions.

The Creative School Change Project was conducted in and with schools which served highly marginalised communities. While some had outstanding inspection reports and were well above the danger-line for student test and exam results, many were not. They had to work hard at the tasks of meeting system expectations and imposts while also maintaining a direction they held to be more fruitful in the longer term. In order to do more than survive and manage to get by, schools needed to draw on other forms of knowledge – pedagogical, curricular, political – than that which was provided through official channels. This was not a question of shucking off a dependent culture and releasing creativity, but rather one where the balancing of tensions embedded in priorities and practices was everyday life. What maintained their commitment, energy and inspiration was the imaginary of a school in which every child was engaged in creative learning.

Note

1 This concurs with Robinson's (2007) New Zealand study, which argues for the importance of both transformational and pedagogical leadership.

References

Beane, J. (1997) *Curriculum Integration: Designing the Core of Democratic Education*, New York: Teachers College Press.

Edwards, C., Gandini, L. and Forman, G. (eds) (1998) *The Hundred Languages of Children: The Reggio Emilia Approach. Advanced Reflections* (2nd ed.), Greenwich, CT: Ablex Publishing.

Gonzales, N., Moll, L. and Amanti, C. (2005) *Funds of Knowledge*, Mahwah, NJ: Lawrence Erlbaum.

Haberman, M. (1999) *Star Principals: Serving Children in Poverty*, Indianapolis, ID: Kappa Delta Pi.

Robinson, V. (2007) *School Leadership and Student Outcomes: Identifying What Works and Why*, Melbourne: Australian Council for Educational Leaders.

Thomson, P., Jones, K. and Hall, C. (2009) *Creative Whole School Change: Final Report*, London: Creativity, Culture and Education; Arts Council England. See also www.artsandcreativityresearch.org.uk.

Index